MAKING ACCOUNTING DECISIONS

ACCOUNTING PUBLICATIONS
OF SCHOLARS BOOK COMPANY

Editor, Robert R. Sterling

MAKING ACCOUNTING DECISIONS

George J. Staubus

Scholars Book Company
4431 Mt. Vernon
Houston, Texas 77006

Library of Congress Cataloging in Publication Data

Staubus, George J
  Making accounting decisions.

  Bibliography: p.
  Includes index.
  1. Accounting. I. Title.
HF5635.S82   657   77-71549
ISBN: 0-914348-19-1

To Sarah

CONTENTS

Contents xiii

LIST OF EXHIBITS

FOREWORD

It is a certainty that accountants and accounting theorists disagree about almost everything, including the nature of their disagreements. That certainty, however, like all certainties, is subject to the tests of experience and revision if we academics and practitioners allow ourselves to consider seriously that areas of agreement do exist, that theory is implementable, and that the boldest changes can and do find their ways into accounting practice.

One source of such change is to be found in the following pages. Making accounting decisions is an essential process to all accountants, and George Staubus has written a text that discusses that process in detail—a text that marries theory to practice, idea to implement. *Making Accounting Decisions* is the culmination of 25 years of research and experience, first to define the fundamental purpose of accounting—to provide information useful for the decision processes of those who read and are affected by financial statements—and then to offer a well-developed means of achieving that purpose. Staubus carefully builds the decision-usefulness objective into a working system. The end product is substance for a solid course for serious accounting students. Included in the text are rich source materials and stimulating study questions that ask students to examine a variety of pertinent, controversial, and fascinating issues.

Staubus is Director of Research and Technical Activities of the Financial Accounting Standards Board, on leave of absence from the University of California, Berkeley, where he is Professor of Business Administration. His articles have appeared in numerous journals throughout the world. His books include *A Theory of Accounting to Investors* (1961), *Activity Costing and Input-Output Accounting* (1971), and *Objectives and Concepts of Financial Statements* (with W. John Kenley, 1972).

These earlier publications provided firm ground for the present volume. It is solid, exciting, and important to all of us, academics and practitioners alike. *Making Accounting Decisions* is a work of maturity and strength. I commend it to you.

Robert R. Sterling

PREFACE

Accounting decisions rarely have been of momentous import to society. Accounting is for specialists—narrow-minded specialists in the view of those who fancy themselves savants. Denigration of a field of endeavor is a comfortable defense against the pain that would be caused by an admission of ignorance. But accounting *has* been of interest primarily to accountants, and a few managers and financial analysts, until recently.

An information service, such as accounting, may attract concerned attention for one of two reasons: either it provides information that is of great interest, or it fails to provide the interesting information that is expected of it. In the quarter-century immediately following World War II, economic growth in large corporate enterprises created a strong demand for information useful in the planning and control of operations. The accounting profession responded with rapid development of managerial accounting techniques. The accounting and financial side of business served satisfactorily, on the whole, and was respected by those businessmen who depended on it.

The twentieth century's second wave of interest in securities markets, which may be dated from 1954 in the U.S., also created a demand for accounting information. In the early years of this boom, accounting appeared to serve reasonably well; at least, investors complained very little, perhaps because they were satisfied with the results of their investment activities. But in the 1960s problems arose, first in particular industries where it appeared that excessive optimism on the part of investors may have been related to misleading accounting practices. By the early 1970s dissatisfaction with the performance of the accounting profession became general, even including accountants themselves (and their insurance companies). In this decade of our discontent we accountants feel a strong need for an integrating structure that can serve as a basis for developing standards and techniques that can yield more satisfactory financial information for those who must make investment decisions, and more satisfying work for those who accumulate and report much of that financial information.

The rapid development of accounting theory during the last twenty-five years, and longer, is difficult to reconcile with the stagnation in external reporting practice. Although most of us would probably hesitate to suggest that the theorists have provided the basic structure required to solve all of the problems practicing professionals now encounter, it surely would not be unreasonable to say that there have been developments in accounting theory in recent decades that have not been adopted in practice. In fact, one could argue that practice has completely ignored all of the major theoretical developments of the last half-century. (See chapter XV.) How can this be explained?

One explanation that academic accountants find easy to accept is that the institutional structure of accounting provides no incentives to change the basic principles that are now followed. As we suggest in chapter I, the present set of principles was created by managers and managers' accountants who are still relatively comfortable with it. While the auditing profession nominally has had the power to change those principles, it, too, has lacked the incentive. The best specific example of rigidity in the institutional structure is the clause in the standard form of auditor's opinion, which states that the financial statements present their information fairly "in conformity with generally accepted accounting principles applied on a consistent basis." How can accounting principles evolve in a progressive fashion if any change must be flagged as if it were a defect?

Many professors and students see these institutional features as the fundamental reason for stagnation in "generally accepted accounting principles." But members of other branches of the profession may not see the problems in the same light. The frightening specter of potential liabilities to investors, and auditors' inability to justify imposing on their own unwilling clients standards that other auditors are not following make it unreasonable to expect a particular auditor to "stick his neck out" by outlawing a conventional practice. These fears shift the burden to the legal system and to the accounting profession as a whole, which could, as a body, make significant changes in accounting principles.

Notice that the academic branch of the accounting profession has not been assessed with any share of the blame for accounting stagnation. Is this justifiable? I have mentioned that there have been significant developments in accounting theory in recent decades; surely the professors deserve some credit for those developments. But have those theoretical developments, and the substantial strides that have been made in empirical research in the last decade, paid off? As of this date, the unequivocal answer must be no! I see two reasons for this, both representing failures by academic accountants. One is our reluctance to move our theoretical developments into the basic accounting curriculum where they could be added to the tool kits that our graduates take into practice. The other is our failure to bridge the implementation gap that separates theory from practice. This book is based on the premise that progress can be made in these two directions by forging the theoretical advances into a practical framework for making accounting choices—a framework that is teachable at the advanced bachelor's degree and the master's degree levels and that embodies those practical concerns that formerly were excluded from theory and gave it an "ivory tower" image. If accountants see the adjectives "theoretical" and "practical" as contrasting terms, we have evidence of the implemention gap referred to above. That gap should be closed, and theory should be put to work in ways that will permit it to earn its keep.

The role of normative accounting theory is to provide a basis for making accounting decisions at all levels: from the International Accounting Standards Committee and such national standards-setting bodies as the Financial Accounting Standards Board, through accounting associations and institutes, accounting committees in specific industries, company accounting policy authorities, to the individual accountant who must decide how to record one event at a time.

The framework for making accounting decisions that is described in the pages that follow begins with a broad objective, then adds, in chapter III, a set of criteria for making accounting choices that can contribute to achieving that objective. The most critical criterion is relevance of the attribute being measured to the decisions of the data users; reliability, comparability, timeliness, cost, and others are also helpful. If accounting is viewed as a purposeful process of gathering useful data, accountants must identify the probable uses of the data that are gathered. Otherwise, the data would be useful only by chance. The needs of external parties for financial information about the firm are reviewed in chapter IV. Cash flow potential emerges as the focal point, and both stock and flow data are viewed as pertinent evidence of future cash flows.

Key stock concepts are discussed and defined in chapter V; their measurement, excluding consideration of the measuring unit problem (inflation), is the subject of chapters VI, VII, and VIII. The first step in those chapters is to describe the major measurement methods, each of which is used in measuring a key attribute of an asset or a liability. Then the methods are appraised and ranked on the attribute relevance criterion. Finally, the other criteria, especially reliability, are brought into the discussion.

Changing price levels are interpreted, for reasons discussed in chapter IX, as a phenomenon that changes the significance of the monetary measuring unit. Procedures for compensating for that weakness in a key accounting tool are explained in chapter IX and the arguments for, and against, "common unit accounting" are given a good deal of attention. In chapter X, the differences between earnings computed without adjusting for the change in the size of the monetary measuring unit and earnings computed under common unit accounting are analyzed in some depth.

My approach to these issues is clearly a balance sheet approach. Income and its components are given little attention in the first ten chapters, where the measurement of stocks of cash flow potential is emphasized. Chapters XI and XII, however, are devoted to flows: the former to revenues, expenses, gains, losses, and income; the latter to liquidity flows and the related topic of risk.

The first twelve chapters are written on a general level; the measurement and reporting problems typically associated with specific financial statement items are discussed only as examples are needed. Once the general framework is established, its application to common balance sheet accounts becomes interesting. In chapter XIII, the framework is applied to the types of assets and liabilities that are common in financial industries: loans, investment securities, and monetary liabilities. Depreciable plant assets are the subject of chapter XIV. Implementation issues come to the fore in these chapters, especially the tradeoff between attribute relevance, on the one hand, and reliability and cost on the other. If the more relevant measurement methods are applicable to any assets or liabilities, those items seem likely to be found in financial companies. A much weaker case for measuring the more relevant attributes is found in the area of long-term plant assets.

The final chapter offers a series of concluding comments that invite the reader to examine for himself the relationship of accounting, as it has been and can become, to the larger context of western societies.

A word about the general character of this book seems appropriate here. I have made no attempt to cover the main themes in modern accounting theory; the book is not a survey of accounting theories. Rather, it is limited to an unabashedly personal theory—mine. This is not to say that it is all original with me, but simply that it is what I believe to be the best framework for making accounting decisions that is available in 1977 and has a chance of reaching generally accepted status in the twentieth century. Some of the major building blocks of this framework were fashioned between 1951 and 1957 when I was writing my dissertation and the early drafts of *A Theory of Accounting to Investors*. Examples are the decision-usefulness objective and approach to accounting theory and the common unit-current value measurement scheme. Others, such as the criteria approach and the market value simulation view of depreciation-fixed asset accounting, evolved in more recent years. But when the fifteen chapters of text are put together, they include only one theory, not a review of contemporary accounting theories. The conscientious student deserves more.

The abundance of supplementary materials included in the book are aimed at helping the student gain a broader perspective on the fundamental issues in accounting theory. The text of most chapters is supplemented by what I consider to be the most interesting, provocative, and economical reading materials that I know. Especially represented are excerpts from documents published by the major accounting organizations in the English-speaking countries. Additional reading suggestions are listed at the ends of all chapters except the last. Those fourteen chapters

also include a list of study questions that are designed to stimulate
students to examine, apply, and question my views and to develop
their own. Full references for textual citations will be found in
the bibliography.

Acknowledgements

Portions of this book are based on previously published work.
Adaptations, clarifications, and revisions naturally followed. Chapters II through VIII include material adapted from chapters 7
through 12 of *Objectives and Concepts of Financial Statements,* which
I co-authored with W. John Kenley in 1972; my thanks to him
and to the Australian Accounting Research Foundation for permission to adapt that text. Other more specific adaptations and
reproductions of text and EXHIBIT materials and the Appendix
selections are acknowledged where they appear in the following
pages. I am grateful to the publishers and copyright holders who
have granted me permission to make use in this volume of my
own earlier published work and that of other writers whose insights
have been used in quotation: the American Accounting Association;
Mr. E. M. de Windt; Professor Melvin N. Greenball; Richard
D. Irwin, Inc.; Irving Kristol; the Oklahoma Society of CPAs;
The Ronald Press Company; Scholars Book Company; Mr. Thomas
I. Storrs; and the *Wall Street Journal,* Dow Jones & Company,
Inc.

The list of people who have made significant contributions to
the development of my ideas and to getting the current version
of them into print is long. Some of those who must not be neglected
are (1) my former students at the University of California, Berkeley,
such as Rowland Atiase, Winnie Coddington, and Shahid Waheed,
as well as Bonnie Jack at the University of Kansas; (2) my colleagues
on the 1974–76 American Accounting Association Committee on
Concepts and Standards, External Reporting: James Boatsman,
Joel Demski, John Kennelly, Kermit Larson, Lawrence Revsine,
Robert Sterling, Jerry Weygandt, and Stephen Zeff, from whom
I learned more than this book reveals; (3) Dayna, Dena, Donna,
Anita, Barbara, Gwen, Sharon and especially Pat Murphy in Kiyo
Noji's clerical pool at Cal; (4) R. Jean Eros, my editor; and (5)
Robert R. Sterling, constructive counselor, fearless publisher, and

accounting theorist *par excellence*. Any weaknesses found in this book may well be due to my stubborn refusal to take their advice.

George J. Staubus

ABBREVIATIONS

AAA	American Accounting Association
AICPA	American Institute of Certified Public Accountants
APB	Accounting Principles Board
FASB	Financial Accounting Standards Board
GAAP	generally accepted accounting principles
NRV	net realizable value
SEC	Securities and Exchange Commission

MAKING ACCOUNTING DECISIONS

CHAPTER I

THE STATE OF ACCOUNTING PRINCIPLES

This book is based on the premise that external financial reporting by business enterprises is not making its maximum potential contribution to society.[1] Putting it another way, financial accounting in Western countries can be improved by some changes that would add more to the value of accounting reports than they add to their cost. The purpose of this first chapter is to provide some support for this premise as well as justification for the writing of another book on accounting theory. If you find yourself in agreement with all of the currently accepted practices described in subsequent paragraphs, you may not like the remainder of the book. So be it. Our frame of reference will be American GAAP (generally accepted accounting principles).

SOME APPLICATIONS OF GAAP

Let's begin with a few examples of financial reporting in the U.S. in recent years. In each case, give some thought to this question: "Is this the way an intelligent layman might reasonably expect income and ownership interest to be computed?" If the answer is no, chalk it up as a questionable feature of current

---

[1] This sentence should raise in the reader's mind the first (and perhaps second and third) of many questions stimulated by the contents of this book. Many of the ideas expressed herein are the untried suggestions of one person and should not be accepted as worth any more than the reader's analysis and experience indicate is warranted. Others are more generally accepted or are supported by objective evidence. The reader should always question assertions that appear to lack support.

1. Company A was interested in acquiring Company B, which had 200,000 shares outstanding with a quoted market value of $20 each ($4 million total) and a book value totalling $1 million. The stockholders of Company B were willing to accept $5 million in cash or 100,000 shares of Company A. The management of A had the opportunity to issue 100,000 shares to a large institutional investor for $5 million cash, but decided to issue these shares directly to Company B shareholders instead, receiving all of Company B's stock in exchange. Company B was liquidated into Company A and net tangible assets of $1 million were recorded on A's books along with $1 million of stated capital, additional paid-in capital, and retained earnings.
2. In the year of acquisition, Company A sold for $800,000 net assets (which had been part of B) representing 25 percent of B's value (for which A "paid" $1,250,000), and recorded a profit of $550,000 (= $800,000 − $250,000). The assets sold were plant facilities that provided excess capacity in one product line previously manufactured by both A and B.
3. Company A operated the remaining newly acquired divisions through the following year, reporting a profit thereon of $50,000 while consuming acquired assets that had a market value when acquired of $100,000 but that were recorded at $25,000 in the pooling.
4. In the third year, Company A sold the remaining assets (including intangibles) acquired with B for $1,500,000 and reported a profit of $775,000 based on the remaining recorded value of $725,000. Company A had "paid" $3,625,000 for these assets

Query 1: Would it be unreasonable if an observer characterized this series of events as follows: Company A "paid" more than market value to acquire B; it sold off a portion of these overpriced assets at a loss and reported a profit; it operated the remainder at a loss and reported a profit, then sold them at a loss and reported a profit?

Query 2: Is it not true that a series of events similar to 2, 3, and 4 above could occur in an ongoing (unpooled) concern with similar results?

Query 3: Is it reasonable for nonaccountants to express a lack of faith in this type of accounting?

Several of the examples above have raised serious questions

about the possibility of undervaluation of assets. Examples of apparent overvaluation are also plentiful. The following case is typical:

> Boothe Computer Corp. said its 1972 year-end report will include a special charge of about $35 million to reduce the carrying value of its portfolio of IBM 360 equipment. The special charge will be based on an assessment in progress of current and projected lease rental rates and will include the $13 million reduction announced in connection with the company's third quarter earnings report. . . .
>
> The company said that because of the writedown, it doesn't expect to report either a profit or a loss from its System 360 computer leasing business until net asset value is recovered in 1978. The original cost of the equipment involved was about $215 million, Boothe said.[3]

Nor are the valuation problems limited to the left-hand side of the balance sheet. In 1970 Leasco (now Reliance Group, Inc.) showed one issue of outstanding securities (described as convertible preferred stock) at $4,390,000 (as established in a pooling of interests). However, its terms called for a cumulative dividend of $7,878,000 per annum until the company is required to redeem the issue with a payment of $197,197,000 spread over 1991–93—unless the common rises in value sufficiently to induce the holders of this preferred to convert. Considering that the common was, at the balance sheet date, selling at a price which made the conversion value of the preferred less than 43 percent of its liquidating value, counting on conversion would not seem wise. If the convertible preferred had been shown at its redemption value, the common shareholders' equity would be negative (Briloff, 1972). The $4,390,000 figure was derived from the stated value of the shares received in exchange in the pooling. Which valuation should be used in determining the common stockholders' equity?

These examples do not, of course, prove that GAAP are wrong; they were presented only to show why many people are questioning the value of GAAP. Even if these cases do illustrate weaknesses

---

[3] "Boothe Computer" (1973, p. 7). Reprinted with permission of *The Wall Street Journal,* © Dow Jones & Company, Inc. (1973). All rights reserved.

in GAAP, we cannot assume that such weaknesses can be remedied. But a substantial and influential group of people, including accountants and users of financial statements, believe that improvements can and must be made and that accounting should not be credited with doing a good job for the public under current conditions. One of Canada's best-known accountants (Ross, 1966, p. 16) expressed it this way: ". . . the best of financial statements are not only failing to do their job but are apparently not even designed to attempt to do such a job." A past president of the American Institute of Certified Public Accountants (AICPA) agrees (Stone, 1971, p. 146): "There is ample evidence that the financial statements we presently prepare are not very useful." These appraisals of the current performance of financial accounting, with which we concur, are the stimulus for the remainder of this book.

THE INSTITUTIONAL SETTING

The financial statements published in corporate annual reports are prepared by, or under the direction of, the management of the corporation. The auditors examine the financial statements, along with the underlying records and other evidence, and render an opinion as to whether they have been prepared in accordance with GAAP.

While the origins of GAAP are not entirely clear, it is fair to say that accounting practices evolved rather loosely until the mid-1930s. At that time the AICPA and the American Accounting Association (AAA) began publishing statements that had a major impact on accounting principles.[4] Until then most accounting work was performed by employees of the reporting entities, so that entity managements must have influenced the evolution of GAAP, and, it is commonly agreed, have continued to do so. As a result, accounting principles have, to some extent, been tailored to fit

---

[4]The earlier isolated thrusts in the direction of establishment of accepted principles by such bodies as the AICPA, the Federal Trade Commission, the Interstate Commerce Commission, and the National Association of Railroad and Utilities Commissioners are viewed as having a minor impact on accounting practices as a whole.

the needs of managers—as managers see them. How does this situation affect financial reporting?

Managers' Control over Financial Reporting

Managers are experts at achieving goals. They are expected to utilize whatever tools they can command in order to reach their objectives. If accounting principles can be used in a manner that will contribute to their objectives, they can be expected so to use them. At this point, a careful analysis of management objectives, supported by irrefutable evidence, would probably be welcomed by some readers, but for the sake of efficiency only two plausible examples of management goals will be considered. Suppose that managers aim to maximize the market value of the corporation. Such a goal has significant implications for management's preferences in the area of accounting principles. For one thing, costs must be minimized—including the price of all inputs acquired through negotiations with other parties, such as employees, suppliers, lenders, and underwriters of new securities issues. The success of their negotiations with these parties (and with customers) may be enhanced by controlling the information about the firm which is available to the other negotiators. Financial reports are, of course, a source of such information so managers like to exercise some control over the contents of those reports. Note that success for the manager (in these negotiations) often means less success for the other party, whether he be a prospective lender, shareholder, employee, supplier, or customer. It follows that the accounting principles that are good for managers may not be good for other parties. This raises a question about who should have the power to choose the accounting principles.

Another plausible goal of managers is to be rated as successful by those parties who have some power to grant or withhold favors that managers desire, including compensation, advancement, prestige, power, and so forth. Ratings of managerial success are typically based partly on financial statement data, especially the net income line. This is another reason why managers would want control over accounting principles, and why they might prefer either those principles that tend to yield data that indicate better performance than would be indicated via alternative principles, or those principles that, once adopted, still give managers some choice as to how given events are to be reported.

Under present GAAP, managers appear to enjoy a moderate degree of control over such reporting. The general features of GAAP that give managers partial control over the reporting of their activities include:

1. *Alternatives.* Managements may now choose from among two or more methods of accounting for the same events, in many cases. Examples are the alternative inventory cost flow assumptions, the alternative depreciation patterns (straight-line time, units-of-production, sum-of-the-years-digits, etc.), flow-through or deferral of the investment credit, and capitalizing or expensing exploration costs in hardrock mining companies. These types of choices available to managements do not depend at all on the nature of the transactions; identical events may be reported on one method by one company and on another method by another company. But there is a limit to the choices available at any one time; switching back and forth from year to year is not acceptable. For practical purposes, this limits the management's opportunities to choose a reporting method for any one category of events to the choice made when events of that category first occur and one possible change to another method, although a second change could be made after a few years.

   In other cases, managements may choose from among alternative accounting methods by making minor changes in the events being reported. For example, a company wishing to acquire plant assets for long-term use with financing being provided by a financial institution may arrange to own the assets and show a liability to the financial institution or it may lease the assets and (under 1976 rules) keep the assets and liability off the balance sheet, with related changes in the income statement. Or a business combination may be structured as a purchase or as a pooling of interest. In these cases, management may have to accept a slightly less advantageous arrangement in order to obtain the most favorable financial reporting treatment—so the shareholders may bear some cost for the sake of the company's, and managers', image.

2. *Judgment.* Managers may exercise some control over finan-

cial reporting in a number of areas in which judgment is required in determining the amounts to report. Examples include provisions for uncollectibles, inventory write-downs, salvage values and lives of depreciable assets, lives of intangibles, and provisions for pension costs.

3. *Out-of-date measurements.* Whenever a balance sheet includes an asset or liability at an old valuation that is materially different than its current value, an opportunity may exist for managers to influence the earnings reported in a specific period independently of their performance on behalf of shareholders. The general technique is to sell undervalued assets or pay off overvalued liabilities in periods when the managers wish to increase the reported earnings, and to sell overvalued assets or pay off undervalued liabilities in periods when the accompanying loss can be absorbed with little difficulty. Under the best of circumstances, a management can maintain a steady up-trend in earnings for several years in the face of unsatisfactory performance on solid economic criteria. Hartford Fire Insurance Company apparently sets an investment earnings target at the beginning of the year and then calls on a substantial reservoir of "instant earnings," or "instant losses," in the form of a portfolio of investment securities carried at cost, as needed to meet the earnings target. This is described in the *Annual Report* of Hartford's parent (International Telephone and Telegraph Corporation, 1971, p. 15) as follows: ". . . present accounting rules require the sale of securities in order to record these earnings generated by appreciation. Hartford, therefore, sells securities to realize investment gains each year which are equivalent to the appropriate historical rate of return on its portfolio of stocks." Some managements value their right to such control very highly. For example, Gordon E. Crosby, Jr., chairman of USLife Corporation, was quoted as saying, ". . . we're going to sell all of our commons" if the Accounting Principles Board (APB) requires the reporting of common stocks at market value with unrealized gains and losses included in income as they occur rather than as realized by sale (*Wall Street Journal*, 1971, p. 5). Liabilities can also provide a pool of instant earnings. In several years McGraw-Hill purchased its own outstanding bonds (selling at far below the price at which they appeared

on McGraw's balance sheet) and reported gains in operating income; in 1973 more than \$2 million was so reported.[5] In addition to companies with readily marketable securities owned or owed, natural resources companies are also in good positions to achieve instant earnings—by selling off undervalued assets in bulk transactions rather than utilizing them in their own production operations.

This basic feature of financial reporting (managers' partial control over the reporting process) may be understood better if we consider an analogy. Suppose that students at a university prepared their own grade reports based on a grading system over which they had some control. They might naturally be tempted to take options and make judgments that would lead to higher grades. Similarly, it is natural for managers to use whatever power they have to control the reporting of their own performance. Any of us would be tempted to take advantage of such opportunities. Of course, some students would see that debasing the grading standards would harm their interests, but if many students (or managements) took advantage of the options available to them, the entire grading system (financial reporting system) would become unreliable. This feature of the fundamental institutional set-up permits bias in financial reporting. We would prefer a minimum of immediate control over the measurement process by those whose performances are being measured.

Efficient (Perceptive) Markets

When we express concern with management's exercise of control over financial reporting we assume that readers of financial statements are likely to form different opinions of the firm's position and operating success if the numbers reported in financial statements are different, even though the underlying economic phenomena are the same. This assumption of *differential perception* may not be justified. According to the *efficient market hypothesis,* the aggregate effect of actions by buyers and sellers of a security

---

[5] Since 1975, the Financial Accounting Standards Board (FASB), in *Statement No. 4,* has required that most gains on extinguishment of debt be treated as extraordinary items.

will result in the same price for the security regardless of which accounting method is chosen, *if* enough information is available from any source to permit some investors to adjust reported results based on the accounting method *in use* to results based on an alternative method which the investors *prefer.* In short, it is hard to fool "the market" by choice of accounting practices. For example, if Company A uses sum-of-the-years-digits depreciation and discloses that straight-line depreciation differs by X, and if the investment analyst believes straight-line depreciation is appropriate, then the analyst can add X to the reported earnings of Company A and compare the sum with earnings of other companies that use straight-line depreciation. (See chapter IV, pp. 102–106, for more on the efficient market view.)

Alternatively, advocates of "bottom line fixation" say that investors give great attention to the key financial statement items, especially net income and earnings per share. Any effect on such items due to selection of accounting methods will lead to a different perception of the firm's success and can affect some investors' decisions and, therefore, the market price of the firm's securities. This type of investor behavior permits corporate managers to influence the market by judiciously choosing accounting methods and estimates over which they have some control.

No matter which of these views one accepts, it seems reasonable to assume that management control over the reporting of earnings can have two undesirable effects:

1. Some unsophisticated investors may be misled by the results of accounting practices chosen for purposes other than informing investors. If they are misled, they are likely to be harmed even if the market, heavily influenced by sophisticated investors, does keep securities fairly priced so that all investors have an equal chance. Two possible types of harm are:
   a. Investors may *misjudge the risk* associated with a security and purchase one that is unsuitable for their investment objective;
   b. Investors may misjudge the value of securities and attempt to switch from one they perceive as overvalued to one they believe is undervalued, thereby *incurring excessive transaction costs.*

2. The efficiency of the market as a whole in pricing securities
   fairly requires that *someone* see through any accounting
   practices that are chosen to achieve the effect desired by
   management. If the accounting methods are not disclosed
   at all, or if the quantitative effects of the difference between
   alternative accounting methods cannot be estimated by
   enough market participants to result in fair pricing of
   securities, then even sophisticated investors can make poor
   decisions if managers choose accounting methods that
   convey misleading information to readers of financial
   statements.

For these reasons, we feel that, from the standpoint of investors,
it is undesirable for managers to be able to choose from among
alternative accounting methods.

THE AUDITOR'S POSITION

How does the auditor fit into this picture? We all understand,
of course, that the auditor's role is to give an independent opinion
on the financial statements prepared by the management and
its accountants. This opinion is intended to assure readers of the
financial statements that those statements can be relied upon to
report fairly the financial position, results of operations, and
changes in financial position of the reporting company. Since
shareholders in U.S. corporations indirectly bear more than $1
billion a year in audit fees, they presumably believe that auditors'
attestations are valuable. In addition to acting as independent
auditors, CPAs have an additional opportunity to serve users of
financial statements. Committees of their associations have played
a fairly heavy role, over the last few decades, in the development
of the accounting principles that the company managements follow
in the preparation of their reports.

How does this arrangement work in practice? First, consider
the working conditions. (1) The auditor must examine reports
summarizing transactions and other economic events. These events
do not all fit neatly into preconceived categories; some are borderline cases. (2) In some judgment areas such as uncollectibles, the
possible amounts to report span a continuous range, so it is difficult
to say at what point along the continuum an amount becomes

unacceptable. In the presence of uncertainty and a naturally optimistic management, an auditor can easily be caught in an acquiescent mood. (3) Auditors spend much more time with client personnel than with users of published financial statements and, as the years go by, gain a better understanding of the problems of the business being audited. In some cases, they are more sympathetic to the management than to the unknown investors and their problems. We tend to find our acquaintances more reasonable than strangers. (4) When the accounting rule-making bodies are considering a proposed change, managers in the affected industries are motivated and organized to act more effectively in presenting their views to the rule makers than are investors.

Now, add to all of these circumstances another fact: auditors have traditionally been hired, fired, and paid directly by the managements, even though the shareholders may rubber-stamp the selection of auditors and the cost is effectively borne by the shareholders—in the short-run. One can only marvel that auditors represent the shareholders' interests at all. Clearly, the potential for a lack of independence "in mental attitude" is very great. An excellent analysis by Sterling (1973, p. 66) sums up the auditor's difficult position:

> The major problem facing public accounting today is its lack of power. First, in comparing the power of authority to the responsibility, we find that the responsibility far outweighs the authority. The public accountant must act judicially but he has not been given the power to enforce his rulings. His ultimate weapon is resignation and silence, which puts him in a conflict-of-interest position. No other profession that I know of is put in a position where it must make economic sacrifices in order to enforce the judgments for which it is responsible. The authority is lessened further by the existence of competition among accounting firms. Resignation from an engagement might be an effective means of enforcement if it were not for the fact that other firms may take the engagement and issue an opinion.
>
> Second, in comparing the power of the public accountant to that of management, we find that management's power far outweighs the accountant's. This imbalance is not undesirable per se. When one considers the fact that accountants must judge managements, however, it is not only undesirable,

it is intolerable. It would wreck the legal system if litigants were able to hire and fire judges. It would be equally damaging to the legal system if litigants were able to select from diverse or flexible laws as they saw fit. The same is true in regard to accounting: if accountants are to judge managements, then we must deny managements the power to hire and fire accountants and the power to select from diverse accounting principles as they see fit.

Failure to Establish Objectives

It should be apparent that auditors are not to blame for the unsatisfactory state of accounting practices. They know where their responsibilities lie and they want to carry out those responsibilities. Unfortunately, the circumstances of their situation have not, until very recently, motivated them to take the time from their daily work to make the investment needed to set the accounting profession on the proper course. *They have neglected to establish clear and fundamental objectives.* Without proper objectives to serve as a foundation for their work, auditors have had difficulty attempting to build and make use of a set of generally accepted accounting principles. False starts, bitter arguments, and a slow rate of progress have characterized the development of accounting principles in the last half-century. What else could be expected without clear-cut objectives?

The most fundamental literature of the American profession has paid very little attention to objectives. The American Institute's first major statement about accounting principles, published in 1938, got as close to the target as anything else it published until 1970. The most relevant passages follow (Sanders, Hatfield, and Moore, 1938, pp. 1–2):

> Making effective and effectively maintaining as near as may be the distinction between the capital and income of a particular enterprise are the ultimate objectives which determine the activities of accountants and the functions of accounting.
>
> With accounts planned with an eye to these objectives and accurately kept, and with statements made from them without misrepresentation or concealment, accounting facilitates the conduct of business, the achievement of its purposes, and the orderly division of its income among the contributors.

The accountant provides the principal business executives with statements of financial condition and results prepared objectively as to the facts reported, but subjectively as to an understanding of the needs of those who will use them. In this manner accounting performs its function of assisting even the most constructive and imaginative efforts of the executives, which efforts must be based upon a clear understanding of the financial condition, cost of operation, and resulting income of the business.

Accounting also contributes to the determination of the various equities or interests in business . . .

Furthermore, accounting facilitates compliance with the various statutory requirements. . . .

The tasks delineated in these paragraphs are important, but they do not constitute a truly fundamental objective. A statement that sets maintenance of the distinction between capital and income as an "ultimate" objective of accountants gives us a clue that the remainder of the statement will not deal with fundamentals.

Another good example of absence of objectives appeared in a critical issue of the Accounting Research Bulletin series (the AICPA's pronouncements on accounting principles from 1939 to 1959), namely *ARB No. 29,* "Inventory Pricing," issued in 1947 and still in effect as chapter 4 of *ARB No. 43* (AICPA, 1975, pp. 9342–43):

A major objective of accounting for inventories is the proper determination of income through the process of matching appropriate costs against revenues. . . .

Cost for inventory purposes may be determined under any one of several assumptions as to the flow of cost factors (such as first-in first-out, average, and last-in first-out); the major objective in selecting a method should be to choose the one which, under the circumstances, most clearly reflects periodic income.

This amounts to saying: "Our objective is to calculate income accurately; the way to do it is to choose that method which most accurately reflects income." Is this an unambiguous instruction that can lead to only one solution?

In 1953, when the Committee on Accounting Procedure made a major effort to restate all of its previous work, it touched on objectives in the introduction (AICPA, 1975, p. 7091):

> The test of the corporate system and of . . . corporate accounting ultimately lies in the results which are produced. These results must be judged from the standpoint of society as a whole—not merely from that of any one group of interested persons. . . .
>
> The fairest possible presentation of periodic net income . . . is important, since the results of operations are significant not only to prospective buyers of an interest in the enterprise but also to prospective sellers.

Unfortunately, there is no evidence in subsequent pages of the document of any effort to build on these ideas; what appeared to be an interest in fundamental objectives was not pursued.

These quotations represent the greatest attention to fundamental objectives of accounting that we have found in AICPA material published prior to 1970, the year a new era began to emerge. The significance of this background to our current situation should be apparent if we remember that nearly all of our current GAAP were solidified before the profession became interested in objectives.

Lest the reader think that the American profession deserves special attention on this point, we submit the following remarks from the British profession (Council, 1952, p. 8):

> The Council cannot emphasize too strongly that the significance of accounts prepared on the basis of historical cost is subject to limitations, not the least of which is that the monetary unit in which the accounts are prepared is not a stable unit of measurement. In consequence the results shown by accounts prepared on the basis of historical cost are not a measure of increase or decrease in wealth in terms of purchasing power; nor do the results necessarily represent the amount which can prudently be regarded as available for distribution, having regard to the financial requirements of the business. Similarly the results shown by such accounts are not necessarily suitable for purposes such as price fixing, wage negotiations and taxation, unless in using them for these purposes due regard is paid to the amount of profit which has been retained in the business for its maintenance.
> . . . the purpose for which annual accounts are normally

prepared is not to enable individual shareholders to take investment decisions. [p. 2]

The point is that the accounting profession, consisting primarily of company accountants and auditors, did not, prior to 1970, establish any clear and fundamental objectives that could serve as a basis for a useful set of accounting principles. That situation set the stage for "the new accounting," which rests squarely on a clear-cut objective as a foundation for making accounting decisions. We now turn to this objective.

ADDITIONAL READING SUGGESTIONS

Beaver, William H., "The Behavior of Security Prices and Its Implications for Accounting Research (Methods)" in "Report of the Committee on Research Methodology in Accounting," *The Accounting Review* (Supplement 1972), pp. 407–37.

——, "Implications of Security Price Research for Accounting: A Reply to Bierman," *The Accounting Review* (July 1974), pp. 563–71.

Bierman, Harold, Jr., "The Implications to Accounting of Efficient Markets and the Capital Asset Pricing Model," *The Accounting Review* (July 1974), pp. 557–62.

Boothman, Derek, et al., *The Corporate Report* (Accounting Standards Steering Committee, 1975), section 4.

Briloff, Abraham J., *Unaccountable Accounting* (Harper & Row, 1972).

Chambers, Raymond J., *Securities and Obscurities* (Gower Press, 1973).

Hatfield, Henry Rand, "What Is the Matter With Accounting?" *Journal of Accountancy* (October 1927), pp. 267–79; rpt. in Stephen A. Zeff and Thomas Keller, eds., *Financial Accounting Theory I: Issues and Controversies*, 2d ed. (McGraw-Hill, 1973), pp. 503–11.

Stamp, Edward, "The Public Accountant and the Public Interest," *Journal of Business Finance* (Spring 1969), pp. 32–42; rpt. in Stephen A. Zeff and Thomas Keller, eds., *Financial Accounting Theory I: Issues and Controversies*, 2d. ed. (McGraw-Hill, 1973), pp. 607–20.

―――― and Christopher Marley, *Accounting Principles and the City Code: The Case for Reform* (Butterworths, 1970).

Sterling, Robert R., "Accounting Power," *Journal of Accountancy* (January 1973), pp. 61–67.

STUDY QUESTIONS

1. As you read the paragraph in this chapter on the Penn Central, did you feel that its critical tone was appropriate? Is stability of reported earnings a criterion of good accounting? What circumstances may have justified the wide variations in the Penn Central's earnings?

2. Consider the Owens-Illinois case reported early in the chapter. In the light of the efficient market hypothesis, what harm is done by reporting securities investments on the cost basis in the balance sheet and income statement as long as market value is disclosed in supplementary financial information or notes accompanying the financial statements?

3. Answer the queries at the end of the business combinations example given in this chapter (p. 4).

4. Describe several additional examples of "instant earnings," preferably from published financial statements you have seen.

5. Give several examples, in addition to those mentioned in the chapter, in which corporate management and corporate accountants have the opportunity to control reported earnings. Would "manipulate" be too strong a word to substitute for "control"?

6. Do you believe that auditors can, and typically do, approach their work with a truly independent state of mind?

7. Put yourself in the position of a company president who sees, in the last quarter of the year, that he is not going to meet the earnings target that the board of directors set at the beginning of the year and announced to a meeting of security analysts early in the year. Your company is a conglomerate that holds many different types of assets and has many diversified liabilities.

    (a) List some strictly accounting techniques which you could consider to help you meet your earnings target.

(b) List some operating and financial techniques which might contribute to your earnings statement without being in the long-run interests of the stockholders.

(c) Assume the situation is reversed—that you have excess earnings this year—but you are concerned about your ability to meet the earnings target the board is discussing for the coming year. What could you do now to improve your chances of meeting next year's target?

(d) Do you believe that after several years of great pressure to meet your firm's financial objectives and after taking advantage of many opportunities to change the reported earnings by accounting, financial, and operating gimmicks, you would resist any efforts by the FASB (or other authority) to limit your opportunities to "manage earnings"?

8. What disagreements do you have with the first sentence of this chapter?

9. It can be argued that senders of information should understand the decision processes of those receivers who use the information for decisions that are important to the senders. But once the senders accept that view, they are in a position to manipulate the user-decision maker by controlling the information he gets. Can one result be that biased information goes to the user? For example, if as a manager I know that investors place a higher price/earnings multiple on the shares of firms with steadily rising earnings per share, would you expect me to attempt to report steadily rising earnings per share? Does my responsibility to shareholders require this? Permit it? How important is the right of a sender to exercise such control? From the point of view of receivers? Senders? Society? Accountants? Comment.

CHAPTER II
THE DECISION-USEFULNESS OBJECTIVE

We have seen that the public practice branch of the accounting profession had not articulated and utilized any fundamental objective of accounting prior to 1970. But the practicing group should not be singled out for criticism. The committees of the AAA that were appointed to prepare statements on fundamental aspects of accounting did little better until 1966 (except for one supplementary statement in 1955). (Nor, to our knowledge, did academic groups in other countries.) AAA committees attempted to formulate sets of basic accounting principles or standards on four occasions: in 1936, 1941, 1948, and 1957 (see AAA, 1957 for all four). In each of these statements some casual attention was given to purposes or functions of accounting or uses of financial statements, but the 1941 statement was the only one which gave any emphasis to a purpose, function, or use (pp. 52–53):

> The purpose of periodic financial statements of a corporation is to furnish information that is necessary for the formulation of dependable judgments. A knowledge of the origin and expiration of the economic resources of a company and the resultant changes in the interests of its creditors and investors is essential to this purpose, and these facts should be expressed in such a manner as to make the financial statements both intelligible and, as far as possible, comparable with statements of other periods and of other corporations. The reader of a statement should be able to assume that, in the absence of clear indications to the contrary, certain basic principles or standards have been followed. To achieve this end a unified and coordinated body of accounting theory is required.

This paragraph was headed "The Basic Assumption" and was

printed in italics. Unfortunately, there followed no evidence of a connection between this encouraging position and the principles listed in the remainder of the statement. As of mid-century, nothing in the literature suggested that accountants both recognized explicitly a user-oriented objective of accounting and looked to that objective in making their choices of accounting methods to apply in practice.[1]

ACCEPTANCE OF THE DECISION-USEFULNESS OBJECTIVE

In 1953, I submitted to the University of Chicago faculty a dissertation that explicitly adopted the decision-usefulness objective and used it as a basis for a conceptual structure (Staubus, 1954). The first chapter of the dissertation included an analysis of the information needs of various groups of users of financial statements and the possible responses of accountants to those needs. Considering the weights of the needs of the various groups and their power to enforce their desires, I concluded that "published corporate financial statements should emphasize information for short- and long-term investors" (p. 18), including creditors: "If it is agreed that information for investors' decisions is the primary goal of accounting to parties other than management (and governmental agencies), the next stage of the inquiry should be directed toward the determination of the type of information that is useful for that purpose, the possibility of providing it, and attainable substitutes" (p. 104).

Pursuing this approach I concluded that "every investor wants to forecast the firm's ability to pay (money) when payment is desired, and legitimately expected" (p. 17). Investors' interest in the firm's ability to pay requires them to be "interested in forecasting the pattern of cash inflow into the firm in excess of cash outgo for the purposes that rank higher than the payment of their

---

[1] It would not be fair, however, to claim that no authors recognized the uses of accounting data. In fact, it could be argued that the greatest individual contributors to accounting thought in the first half of the twentieth century also gave the most attention to uses of accounting data. See, for example, May (1943, especially chapter 2, "The Uses of Accounts and Their Influence on Accounting"); Paton (1922, pp. 5, 7); and Vatter (1947, pp. 8–9; and 1950, passim).

[return]" (p. 12). The analysis assumed that choices of accounting principles required awareness of who was going to use the accounting outputs for what purpose, and how. The decision-usefulness objective provided a solid foundation on which to build.

Ensuing years saw this dissertation converted to *A Theory of Accounting to Investors* (Staubus, 1961). It, too, was based squarely on the decision-usefulness objective: The "first postulate of this study" was that "accountants should explicitly and continuously recognize an objective or objectives of accounting" (p. viii). Because the book was limited to accounting to investors, it was appropriate to emphasize "that a major objective of accounting is to provide quantitative economic information that will be useful in making investment decisions" (p. viii). A few paragraphs from the first chapter, "Establishing the Objective," define accounting and summarize the approach (pp. 10–11):

> Accounting means identifying, classifying, and measuring, and then reporting, the effects of economic events upon a specific economic unit.
>
> This statement not only may make some small direct contribution to our understanding of accounting, but it also provides a basis for raising some questions that must be answered by anyone who is to construct a theory of accounting. For example: What is an economic event? Should all economic events affecting the economic unit be reported? What techniques of measurement are applicable to which types of events? How should the economic events and their effects be classified for reporting? What forms of reports are helpful, and how often should they be presented? For what purposes should the reports be presented?
>
> This last question is the most fundamental of all. In answering, we must remember that accounting is a practical activity and must meet a need if it is to continue. It is a useful activity, and its objectives must be thoroughly understood by those who are to participate in it. Accounting is an informative activity; it provides information to assist those who have to make economic decisions. These decisions may be of various types. Decisions relating to investing; decisions relating to buying and selling commodities and services; decisions to produce, to pay, to bill, or to insure; and decisions relating to tax collections—all are likely to be easier to make if

accounting reports are available. *The purpose of accounting is to provide information which will be of assistance in making economic decisions.*

The kind of economic decision that needs to be made will determine the usefulness of various items of information. For this reason, specific types of decisions must be considered by the accountant who measures and reports the economic events bearing upon the economic unit. One general class of decisions is related to granting credit to, or investing in, the economic unit. The persons making such decisions may be called "investors." Another group of decisions relate to the administration of the affairs of the unit. These decisions are made by managers. Other parties involved in types of decisions relating to an economic unit include employees, suppliers, customers, and governmental taxing and regulatory agencies; those not concerned in any special way may be considered "the general public." These persons who have to make decisions about the economic unit are possible beneficiaries of accountants' work. In order for them to enjoy those benefits, the accountant must consider their needs and wishes for information.

In January 1955, Raymond J. Chambers' classic "Blueprint for a Theory of Accounting" was published. Chambers stressed that the "basic function of accounting" was "the provision of information to be used in making rational decisions" (p. 25). In 1955, the AAA issued Supplementary Statement No. 8, "Standards of Disclosure for Published Financial Reports." It was the first group report to give explicit attention to "objectives," under which heading the following important paragraph appeared (AAA, 1957, p. 47):

> Since the ultimate test of the quality of any communication is its effectiveness in conveying pertinent information, the initial step in the development of standards of disclosure for published financial statements is the establishment of the purposes to be served. The potential users of corporate reports include governmental agencies, short- and long-term creditors, labor organizations, stockholders, and potential investors. Since in all likelihood the needs of these groups cannot be served equally well by a single set of statements, the interest of some one audience should be identified as primary. Traditionally, this has been the stockholder group.

More importantly, the committee did not forget this paragraph as it continued its deliberations on standards of disclosure: "In considering disclosure standards, therefore, the Committee has been concerned primarily with the use of financial statements (1) in making investment decisions and (2) in the exercise of investor control over management" (p. 401). It appeared that the decision-usefulness approach had been given sufficient recognition to ensure an extension of its influence in future studies on accounting principles.

When in 1957 the AAA published a fourth statement on accounting principles under the title "Accounting and Reporting Standards for Corporate Financial Statements—1957 Revision," the opportunity to draw up a set of standards based on decision usefulness seemed to present itself. The result was, however, disappointing. The introduction was weak and the sections on "Underlying Concepts," "Assets," "Income Determination," and "Equities" substantially ignored decision usefulness. Only in the last section, "Standards of Disclosure," based heavily on the 1955 Supplementary Statement No. 8, did the committee mention that "The use by investors of published financial statements in making investment decisions and in exercising control over management should be considered of primary importance" (p. 7). By passing up a major opportunity, the committee delayed for nine years the publication of an Association-backed general statement based on the decision-usefulness objective of accounting.

Other prominent examinations of accounting principles in that era also failed to adopt the decision-usefulness approach. Moonitz (1961, pp. 4–5) rejected the idea because he did not feel that accountants could answer the questions, "Useful to whom?" and, "For what purpose?" The subsequent Sprouse-Moonitz (1962) monograph also rejected the approach. The last two studies of accounting principles to avoid the decision-usefulness approach were the University of Illinois Study Group Statement in 1964 and Paul Grady's "Inventory of Generally Accepted Accounting Principles" in 1965. Because Grady's was, from the beginning, intended to be a descriptive study of accounting principles, it had no room for any new ideas about what accounting *ought* to accomplish. The Illinois group considered a broad objective statement such as "the measurement of economic events and the supplying of information for economic decision-making" to be "of limited assistance in an attempt to state the basic postulates and broad principles of accounting." Instead, they chose to emphasize a version of stewardship as "a more specific identification of the primary purpose of accounting" (pp. 2–3).

The turning point in the official and sponsored literature came in 1966. The AAA Committee to Prepare a Statement of Basic Accounting Theory bought the decision-usefulness approach lock, stock, and barrel. While it was not able to carry through as far as one might have hoped, the Committee's contribution to popularizing both the decision-usefulness objective and the standards to be used as criteria for evaluating potential accounting information (especially relevance, verifiability, and freedom from bias) was immense. One can only speculate about the extent to which the substantial dissatisfaction with accounting practices in the late 1960s and early 1970s would have been avoided if *A Statement of Basic Accounting Theory* (ASOBAT) had been produced in 1957 (as it apparently could have been). It does seem clear, however, that in the mid-1970s it is playing a big role in the deliberations of accounting policy-making bodies, such as the FASB and SEC. Every sponsored study of fundamental ideas in accounting since 1966 has emphasized the decision-usefulness objective, and several have developed substantial structures of ideas on this basis.

APB Statement No. 4 (1970) was the first AICPA document to recognize the decision-usefulness objective. It also emphasized qualitative objectives: "Certain qualities or characteristics make financial information useful. . . . Relevance . . . Understandability . . . Verifiability . . . Neutrality . . . Timeliness . . . Comparability . . . Completeness" (pp. 35–38). This statement was a great leap forward for the accounting profession in the U.S. It was followed by the strongly decision-oriented statement of the Study Group on the Objectives of Financial Statements in 1973 (see Appendix II-1). Financial executives also have recognized "that the content of corporate financial reports should primarily be established on the basis of the information requirements of their principal users: the investor-stockholder, the investor-potential stockholder, and the investor-advisor groups" (Financial Executives Institute Committee on Corporate Reporting, 1972, p. 2).

The acceptance of the decision-usefulness objective in the early

1970s has not been limited to the U.S. The accounting profession in Australia, under the leadership of its Accounting and Auditing Research Committee, gave a hospitable reception in 1972 to a development of measurement and reporting concepts based on the decision-usefulness objective (Kenley and Staubus, 1972). The Canadian Institute published Skinner's work (1972), which emphasized that "the ultimate objective of accounting" is "to convey information that is relevant to the needs of the user" (p. 304). Movement in this direction is also apparent in Britain, according to a 1974 survey of opinion: "The traditional stewardship objective of accounting is still widely acknowledged as important. There appears to be growing consensus, however, that the provision of information to assist shareholders with their investment decisions should be recognized as a second important objective of accounting statements" (Carsberg, Hope, and Scapens, 1974, p. 172). Another British view (Boothman et al., 1975, p. 28) did not emphasize decisions: "The fundamental objective of corporate reports is to communicate economic measurements of and information about the resources and performance of the reporting entity useful to those having reasonable rights to such information." In general, however, it seems safe to say that today many leaders of the accounting profession—academic, public, and industrial—in the English-speaking world have accepted the decision-usefulness objective as an approach to accounting decisions.

LIMITED, INTERMEDIATE, AND INEFFECTIVE OBJECTIVES

Despite the rapid strides made towards the clarification of the objectives of accounting in the last ten years, the idea that financial statements should serve the people to whom they are addressed is still far from universally accepted. Accountants must, in other words, recognize that the ultimate objective of accounting is to provide information that is valuable to its users in making decisions. Until they do so, their conceptions about accounting objectives will be characterized by several types of problems.

First, accountants commonly tend to limit their concern to only a part of their responsibilities. We still find accountants who precede their comments with a phrase such as "from the accounting point of view," when they should concentrate on the user's point of view instead. We must take care to avoid thinking of accounting for accountants. And in the U.S., in particular, accountants, especially auditors, find themselves constantly thinking of possible liability for losses incurred by the users of financial statements. Their apprehension forces them to emphasize their own protection rather than their service to users.[2] While the battle to establish reasonable objectives for accounting may appear to be substantially won, as measured by the statements of leaders of the profession, we still have a long way to go before the mass of working accountants will be accomplishing these objectives with their everyday work.

To the extent that accountants do recognize users of financial statements, there is still the danger that they will take too narrow a view. For example, one survey of corporate executives disclosed that "90% of companies interviewed accord the present stockholder top priority in financial reporting" (Rice et al., 1972, p. 72). If present stockholders were given excessive weight, the information needs of prospective stockholders, creditors, and others might be neglected.

A third problem is that accountants tend to weigh excessively such intermediate objectives as objectivity or conservatism at the expense of ultimate objectives. Sterling (1967) has demonstrated that conservatism has been used as the overriding criterion for choosing between alternative valuations of assets and liabilities. This amounts to setting conservatism as a major objective of valuation. Although many of us believe that conservatism has an appropriate role to play in financial reporting, it has never been demonstrated that the degree of conservatism presently encompassed in GAAP is consistent with meeting the needs of users. Similarly, objectivity has often been referred to as the primary objective of accounting rather than as one of the desirable attributes of useful information. As a result, accountants have sometimes chosen to report objective information that is not relevant to the needs of any user. But "Objectivity, in the purest sense, as an end in itself is a pointless goal for information providers" (Rosen, 1972, p. 5). We cannot implement the decision-usefulness objective

---

[2] There presumably is a difference between providing the most useful information to investors and providing information that will minimize losses that might be recoverable from accountants who provided misleading information.

without identifying some intermediate objectives, such as qualities that make information useful. However, we must take care to avoid confusing any intermediate objective with the objective of providing valuable information.

Another common defect in the thinking about the objectives of accounting has been the emphasis upon qualities such as "truth" and "fairness," which have obvious merit but are ineffective. They are not operational goals that can serve as criteria for choosing between alternative accounting methods. If we know that one of the alternatives is untrue or unfair, we can reject it immediately. But how can we choose between LIFO and FIFO, or between capitalizing and expensing research and development costs, on a criterion such as truth? You and I can argue all day about which method is more truthful without ever reaching agreement. Consider a 1972 conclusion about the Australian profession's views (Kenley and Staubus, p. 12):

> The overriding objective of financial reporting as now interpreted is to disclose all information necessary to provide a true and fair view of the state of affairs of a particular entity as at the end of the period of accounting and of the profit or loss it earned during the period of accounting.

We criticized this objective because it did not provide a good basis for building a set of practical standards, and we noted that "the computation of profit for its own sake is a poor ultimate objective of accounting because it offers no useful guidance about how to compute profit—the major area in which accountants are seeking guidance" (p. 42). Similarly, objectives such as "to provide reliable financial information about the economic resources and obligations of an enterprise and the changes therein" are ineffective because they do not provide any guidance about how to identify or measure economic resources, obligations, or changes in them.

Defining the Primary Objective

One question that could be raised about the decision-usefulness objective is whether it includes the control and accountability role of accounting (see Cyert and Ijiri, 1974). Everyone familiar with accounting recognizes that it plays a major role in managerial control in general and internal control in particular. Is this role encompassed in the decision-usefulness objective? The answer seems to be a qualified yes—the qualification being that "decisions" must be interpreted broadly. Without settling on a formal definition of control, we can suggest several views of it that include decisions based on accounting information:

1. Managerial control is aimed at ensuring adherence to plans. Accounting contributes to this managerial function through reports that compare actual financial quantities, such as costs, with standard or budgeted amounts. Actual control requires subsequent *decisions*, such as decisions to investigate variances and to change methods of operations. Accounting provides part of the information for such decisions.
2. The operation of an accounting system motivates personnel at all levels to work towards goals of the firm. In this way the accounting system affects a person's *decisions* about his own behavior.
3. The existence of an accounting system serves to deter behavior not consistent with the firm's objectives. Accounting affects employees' *decisions* about dishonest or wasteful acts by providing information for *decisions* by superiors and shareholders regarding the continued employment, or even prosecution, of the employees.

These views suggest that, although the control objective is an important part of the decision objective, it need not be stated separately. If we seem to be stretching the use of "decisions" too broadly, then a control clause should be added to the brief statement of the objective of accounting. If not, the following statement will suffice:

> THE PRIMARY OBJECTIVE OF ACCOUNTING IS TO PROVIDE FINAN-
> CIAL INFORMATION ABOUT THE ECONOMIC AFFAIRS OF AN EN-
> TITY FOR USE IN MAKING DECISIONS.

Accounting has important positive and negative effects beyond influencing decisions of users, but these effects must be considered distinctly secondary—more in the nature of by-products that occur incidentally rather than by design. They will be discussed in connection with the evaluation of alternative accounting methods in chapter III.

ADDITIONAL READING SUGGESTION

Anton, Hector R., "Objectives of Financial Accounting: Review and Analysis," *Journal of Accountancy* (January 1976), pp. 40–51.

STUDY QUESTIONS

1. Have you found any clear-cut recognition of the decision-use-fulness objective as the primary objective of accounting in literature published prior to 1960 other than those cases discussed in this chapter? If yes, did this literature include any follow-up in the sense of applying the decision-usefulness objective in solving accounting problems?

2. For readers who are not Americans: Do you have any evidence that development of clear and appropriate objectives of accounting has occurred more rapidly in your country than in the U.S.?

3. In the early 1960s, *Accounting Research Studies Nos. 1* and *3* by Moonitz and by Sprouse and Moonitz received cool receptions by the APB; the authors had not adopted the decision-usefulness approach. Do you think the studies would have enjoyed a better reception if they had explicitly adopted the decision-usefulness approach? Or was the profession simply not ready to make any significant changes in the environment of the early 1960s?

4. At what point(s) in ASOBAT did the Committee break the chain of reasoning based on the decision-usefulness objective and present unsupported recommendations or conclusions?

5. Is minimizing the firm's cost of capital an appropriate ultimate objective of accounting from the social welfare point of view? From the management's point of view?

6. Is stability of reported earnings over time an appropriate intermediate objective of accounting from the viewpoint of the SEC? From the viewpoint of shareholders?

7. How can one object to recognition of the presentation of a true and fair view of an entity's state of affairs and its periodic profit or loss as the basic objective of financial statements?

8. What is meant by the stewardship objective of accounting?

9. Does the decision-usefulness objective include the control function of accounting or should the control objective be stated separately?

10. "The objective of providing the means for establishing accountability may be considered as a fundamental objective of financial statements" (Cyert and Ijiri, 1974, p. 31). Do you agree? Is accountability included in the decision-usefulness objective?

CHAPTER III

GENERAL APPROACHES TO MAKING ACCOUNTING DECISIONS

Decision usefulness is now widely accepted as the appropriate objective of accounting. It can provide a great deal of guidance to accountants who are dedicated to serving the users of their product. It is not quite broad enough, however, to serve as a basis for all accounting decisions made by policy-making bodies representing all segments of society because users of accounting data are not the only parties who have an interest in how accounting is done. Those whose performance is being reported upon and those who pay for accounting activities should also have a voice in accounting decisions if all of society is to be considered. In this chapter we outline a broad approach to making accounting decisions, a comprehensive framework for use in evaluating competing accounting proposals and choosing among them.[1]

It is important to specify that accounting is an economic service, just as telephone service, transportation, or management consulting is an economic service. Decisions as to which activities are to be performed must be made on an economic basis. The decision-usefulness objective of accounting focuses accountants' attention on the decision models of users of accounting data. As a consequence, accountants now tend to favor logical, organized, economic approaches to all decisions—even those of accountants. At this point, we want to focus our attention on a decision model that accountants can use directly in making their own decisions. We seek to model a technique for making accounting decisions.

---

[1] Much of this chapter was published in Staubus (1976b).

THE INFORMATION EVALUATION APPROACH

Decisions pertain to future actions. When we make a decision we choose a course of action. The most general economic decision rule is:

TAKE ANY AND ALL ACTIONS (EXCEPT COMPETING ACTIONS) THAT HAVE PREDICTED INCREMENTAL BENEFITS IN EXCESS OF PREDICTED INCREMENTAL COSTS.

The most common textbook example of this decision rule is to set the firm's short-run output level at the rate at which marginal revenue equals marginal cost; that is, take all production-increasing actions that offer greater increments in total revenues than in total costs. In the case of an accounting decision that involves a proposal to add an accounting activity to existing activities, we choose to take the proposed action if it offers net incremental benefits. This approach has been mentioned frequently in the literature of accounting in recent years, usually by emphasis on the need to compare the cost and value of information; it is currently labelled "the information evaluation approach" to accounting decisions.[2]

---

[2] Most references to the cost and value of accounting data appearing in accounting literature prior to the mid-1960s were rather casual. For example, "The acceptability of the solution . . . depends upon the cost of applying the theory compared to the gains to be derived therefrom" (Staubus, 1952, p. 104). The serious consideration of cost and value of information by accountants appears to date from the Ph.D. dissertation of Gerald A. Feltham at the University of California, Berkeley in 1967: "A Theoretical Framework for Evaluating Changes in Accounting Information for Managerial Decisions." Two other Berkeley Ph.D.s of that period, John Butterworth (1967) and Theodore J. Mock (1969), also contributed to the development of the information evaluation approach. The major works available as of this writing include Joel S. Demski, *Information Analysis* (1972), and Feltham, "Information Evaluation" (1972). Two other concise descriptions of the information evaluation approach appear in chapter 1 of Demski and Feltham (1976) and in an AAA committee report (1974).

The origins of information evaluation can be traced to work in decision theory by statisticians such as Abraham Wald, *Statistical Decision Functions* (1950), and to game theory studies including John von Neumann and Oskar Morgenstern, *Theory of Games and Economic Behavior* (1944). Statisticians became interested in the cost of information in connection with "optimal stopping" rules for sequential sampling and they questioned the value of information implicit in the "squared

The breadth of the information evaluation approach depends upon the interests of the evaluator. For example, as a member of a management team, the evaluator may be concerned only with the contribution that the information system makes to firm profits. In such a case the value of information is limited to its effects on incremental profits through better management decisions, and the costs, including auditing costs, are limited to those borne by the firm. But it is more likely that the information evaluator will have additional concerns, because the manager will have goals other than profit maximization, such as greater salary, prestige, and longevity in office for himself. The effects of the alternative information systems on the achievement of all of these goals, stated in terms of utility instead of money (i.e., adjusted for the shape of the manager's utility function), should be taken into consideration. It should be clear that such an evaluation is a complicated task. The information evaluation approach could be outlined as follows (adapted from Demski, 1972):

1. Identify all alternative information systems.
2. For each system:
   a. Identify all possible signals (numerical values of output variables) which the system could give.
   b. For each of these signals:
      1) Determine the corresponding decision maker's action.
      2) Identify the events associated with this action.
      3) Attach utilities to each event.
      4) Assign probabilities to each event.
      5) Determine the expected benefit (utility) of this signal.
      6) Determine the net benefit of this signal by deducting its cost (disutility).
      7) Assign a probability to the generation of this signal.

---

loss function" of least squares computations of regression lines and correlation. Another landmark in the literature was David Blackwell and M. A. Girshick, *Theory of Games and Statistical Decisions* (1954). In the meantime, Jacob Marschak was developing a theory of teams which included an information evaluation function. In the 1960s economists began to apply the term "information economics" to the area concerned with the cost and value of information. During that decade Jacob Marschak, at UCLA, and Roy Radner, at Berkeley, wrote several journal articles (individually and jointly) and their efforts culminated in *The Economic Theory of Teams* (1972).

    c. Determine the expected net benefit of operating this system.
3. Select the information system with the largest expected net benefit.

If the information evaluator is outside the entity to which the accounting decision relates directly, he must consider the goals and needs of parties other than management in order to judge the value of information to those parties. The auditor, for example, may want to consider the information needs of investors, but he may be willing to neglect the auditing cost because it is a benefit to him. Or a systems consultant may seek to develop an information system that will serve both internal and external users who are making a variety of types of decisions on the basis of the output of the system. At a still broader level, an accounting policy-making body such as the FASB or the Accounting Standards Committee (in Britain) may consider it appropriate to take into consideration the benefits that a proposed information system (or accounting method) offers to any and all segments of society, as well as any costs borne by any segment of society. When these costs and benefits are thought of as losses or gains in utility to individuals, we have what is called a social welfare approach to the evaluation of alternative information systems.

THE SOCIAL WELFARE APPROACH

The social welfare approach to making accounting decisions can be modelled as illustrated in EXHIBIT III-1. (The EXHIBIT shows only a sample of the parties that could be affected and a sample of the potential effects on them.) The criterion of choice is aggregate utility to members of the society; the accounting method that is perceived as offering the greatest aggregate utility is the one to be selected. The decision maker must compute and compare the aggregate utility offered by each method. The aggregate utility associated with any one method is the sum of the positive utilities and negative utilities (costs) that the method yields to various members of society. The expected utility of the information system to one member of society is the algebraic sum of the incremental values of the information in whatever uses

Exhibit III-1
Social Welfare Approach to Accounting Decisions

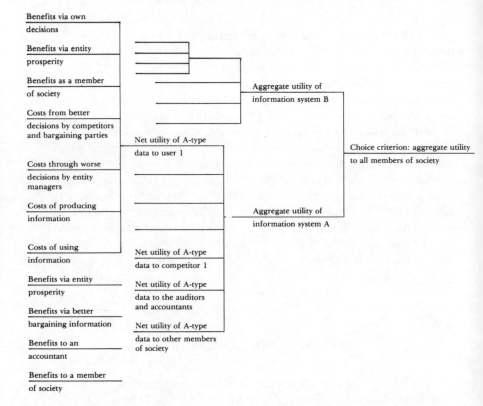

he makes of it, and the incremental costs that information system will impose on him. The incremental values may arise both from his use of the information to make decisions that yield higher payoffs than the decisions he would make without that type of information, and from higher payoffs due to the decisions of others.

We may summarize the potential positive and negative payoffs to various groups that result from producing any particular type of information under general headings, as follows:

A. Potential positive payoffs from an accounting method.

1. Direct payoffs to parties associated with the entity (present and prospective owners, creditors, suppliers, customers, employees, and government taxing and regulatory bodies) through (a) improvements in their own decisions using information supplied by the entity and produced with the accounting method or information system in question, and (b) higher direct compensation from the entity due to its more effective management and greater profitability with the aid of the information in question.
2. Payoffs to competitors through more useful information about the reporting entity's activities.
3. Diffused benefits through better functioning of the economy, such as through allocation of resources, reduction of variation in level of economic activity, and effects on the division of income between investment and consumption.

B. Potential negative payoffs from an accounting method.
   1. Reduction in profitability of competitors (and in distributions to its constituents) through better decisions by the reporting entity.
   2. Reduction in profitability of the reporting entity through better decisions by its competitors and by its creditors, suppliers, customers, and employees who bargain with the entity.
   3. Reduction in profitability of the entity due to effects upon management decisions of reporting to shareholders and others by the accounting method under evaluation.
   4. Costs of producing the information, such as accounting and auditing costs.
   5. Costs of analysis and use of accounting information.

The signs of any of these payoffs may be reversed.

Now let's consider the implementation of this approach to accounting decisions by, say, the FASB, briefly outlining the steps involved:

1. Identify the accounting problem to be solved.
2. Identify the alternative accounting methods (information systems) available to solve the problem.
3. Identify the parties who might be affected and the nature of the potential effects.

4. Determine, for each party affected, his utility function over wealth.
5. For each use of each user, and for each nonuser affected, quantify the possible positive and negative utilities emanating from an accounting method; attach probabilities to these utilities; then aggregate the utilities for each party. Repeat for each accounting method under consideration.
6. Aggregate the expected values of utility for all individuals affected.
7. Compare the aggregate utility produced by information system A with that produced by information system B; choose the system that produces the larger.

The social welfare approach could be refined further. For example, we have not discussed the time horizon over which benefits and costs are to be aggregated or the discounting of future payoffs. Nor have we discussed how to determine the shape of the utility functions of the interested individuals. But perhaps we have said enough to illustrate why the social welfare approach has not been utilized by policy-making bodies such as the APB or the FASB or by individual accountants. It simply cannot be implemented at this time, nor is it likely to be in the foreseeable future except in the simplest of cases. The measurement problems are formidable. In fact, economists do not know how to construct a social utility function even if they can determine all individual utility functions; thus we cannot aggregate the utilities of the various parties affected by an accounting choice.[3]

---

[3] "If we make the ethical judgment that individual (user) tastes are to count in comparing financial reporting alternatives, and if we require our concept of optimality to display certain almost innocuous requirements, Arrow's famous impossibility theory guarantees that no such evaluation concept exists. . . . There is no method of selecting among social alternatives that is not imposed or dictatorial, responsive to individual tastes, independent of irrelevant alternatives, and provides a complete, transitive, and reflexive ranking of the social alternatives" (Demski and Feltham, 1976, p. 8; see also Arrow, 1963).

One partial solution to this problem that is often mentioned but rarely considered adequate is adoption of the Pareto optimality criterion, viz., make any change in accounting methods which will make someone better off and no one worse off. This criterion does not require making tradeoff judgments regarding utilities of different individuals.

Nevertheless, we do believe that conceptualizing the aggregate social welfare approach yields some useful insights into the decision-making problem in accounting. If nothing else, it may help us to see how difficult it is for a policy-making body to satisfy everyone. One accounting method may have the most favorable effect on one user, while another method may have the best effect on another user (or nonuser). For example, a union that represents employees may choose the method that tends to show the higher profit in the short run in order to strengthen its claim that the company can afford to pay higher wages, but the management and shareholders may prefer the output of the more conservative method for decision-making uses. This example is only one of many that show how divergent interests and objectives complicate the choice of an accounting method. So we must find some systematic approach to evaluating the needs of users. The ensuing paragraphs outline a more practical procedure.

A Practical Approach to Accounting Decisions

The measurement problems that we have noted in the aggregate social welfare approach to accounting decisions lead us to a qualitative approach that can be more easily implemented while still working towards the social welfare objective. EXHIBIT III-2 illustrates the criteria approach. It involves the use of qualitative surrogates for the benefits derived from using particular types of information and ordinal evaluations of the extent to which each alternative accounting proposal meets each surrogate criterion. Each user can rank the alternative accounting methods on the basis of each surrogate benefit criterion and on the cost criteria, then judge the total impact of each method on him. The user can then communicate his choice to the person or body making the accounting decision. In order to arrive at a decision, the decision maker must weight the choices of the various users. Alternatively, the decision maker may himself judge the competing proposals on each criterion on behalf of each user, and aggregate all of these results.

A word about the terminology may be helpful here. We may

EXHIBIT III-2

CRITERIA APPROACH TO ACCOUNTING DECISIONS

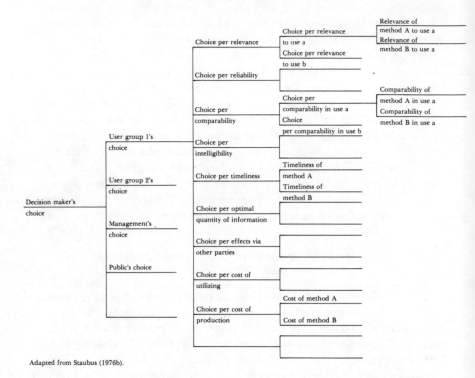

Adapted from Staubus (1976b).

call the concepts involved "criteria of valuable information."[4] Accounting decision makers must judge the extent to which each

---

[4]The genesis of the present criteria framework appeared in Staubus (1961, p. 50): "There are two criteria for appraising measurement techniques, one on the conceptual level, the other related to the application of the concept: the *relevance* of the type of evidence utilized to the problem of predicting future returns to investors; and the *accessibility* of the evidence. The latter criterion includes such variables as the difficulties in making estimates and computations, fees to independent appraisers, and the risk that bias may reduce the reliability of measurements. This criterion can be applied only on a case-by-case basis as the accountant's judgment dictates. Relevance, on the other hand, is subject to a general analysis." There followed a tabulation of measurement methods ranked on the basis of their relevance to the decisions of residual equity holders.

alternative accounting proposal meets these criteria. Alternatively, we could use the term "attributes" and speak of "attributes of valuable financial information" or "desirable attributes of financial information." Because the term "attributes" is used heavily in connection with measurable attributes of objects and events, we prefer to avoid it in this connection. We could also speak of "desirable qualities" or "desirable characteristics" of information; we might use the phrase "qualitative objectives," as the APB did in *Statement No. 4*, or "standards for accounting information," in accordance with the usage in ASOBAT. Any of these alternative terms would fit our usage. But the phrase "criteria for the evaluation of accounting methods" carries the connotation most consistent with the procedure we are describing.

Now let's outline the steps involved in the criteria approach, so that we can compare them with the steps required for the social welfare approach (see pp. 37–38 above).

1. Identify the accounting problem to be solved.
2. Identify two or more possible solutions—the alternative accounting methods (information systems) to be evaluated.
3. Identify the users and nonusers affected by the choice.
4. Identify each user's uses and methods of use, i.e., decision techniques, and the nature of the effects on nonusers. Intragroup differences must not be overlooked.
5. For one user group and one criterion, rate the alternative accounting methods for each use and then combine the ratings for all uses by that user group. Repeat for each criterion and each user group.
6. Combine the ratings on the various criteria to obtain a user group's choice. Repeat for each user group.
7. Combine the choices of the various user groups to obtain a final choice of accounting method (if the decision maker must consider the wishes of more than one user group).

Note that this process does not involve cardinal measurements at all; rankings (ordinal measurements) play the leading roles along with undefined judgment processes for weighting the various criteria, uses, and users. It is clear that the margin of a method's superiority in steps 5 and 6 is important; so are the weights given to the various criteria in step 6 and the weights assigned to the various user groups in step 7; however, no quantification scheme is recommended for these steps. This procedure is clearly less structured than the aggregate social welfare approach but it appears to be better organized than the approaches taken by accountants and accounting policy-making bodies in the past. Does it represent the most systematic technique that is feasible at the present time?

Space is not available for the completion of EXHIBIT III-2 but we have filled out enough to indicate that the choice of method on the basis of any one criterion for one user group can be subdivided to allow for several different uses by one group; it can also allow for different decision processes by different members of a user group. The methods may rank differently among these uses and users. For example, one member of the management group may rank weekly performance reports over monthly reports on the criterion of timeliness, while another manager may prefer the monthly reports because a week is not long enough to give a clear reading of the operation.

One other observation may be of interest before we turn to the specific criteria. Reading from the left in EXHIBIT III-2, we immediately encounter a primary classification on the basis of user groups. This classification suggests that the needs of the various user groups represent major segments of the accountant's concern; it also suggests that accounting might be divided on the basis of user groups for various purposes, including education. Thus, for example, we could study how to meet the information needs of investors, managers, and taxing agencies, through courses in investor accounting, management accounting, and tax accounting. Such courses would cover the decision models used (and useful) in investment, management, and taxation decisions. Classification of user groups and their needs might well lead accountants to a higher level of service to users than they could achieve otherwise. We recommend it.

CRITERIA FOR THE EVALUATION OF ACCOUNTING METHODS

The interpretation of the proposed criteria may be easier if the reader agrees with two points that have been taken into consideration in their selection. First, in each case a criterion may be partially met, that is, met to a degree. There are degrees of attribute relevance, for example; it is not a go, no-go criterion.

Rarely will a criterion be met perfectly, but complete failure on a criterion is also uncommon. As a consequence, the user must make tradeoffs, perhaps sacrificing a bit of relevance for the sake of greater reliability, or lower cost of production. Secondly, any accounting method that scores zero on any one of the seven benefit criteria would be unacceptable. A minimal passing mark on each of the criteria is a necessary but not a sufficient condition for the acceptance of an accounting proposal. That is, in each case it is possible to imagine an appraisal on one criterion that would be so poor that it could not be offset by high ratings on other criteria.

Attribute Relevance

The first criterion of a useful accounting datum is its relevance to the user's decisions.[5] More specifically, the attribute to which the datum relates must be relevant to the user's decision process. *An attribute of an object or event is relevant to a decision if knowledge of its quantity, degree, or existence will help the decision maker (a) identify promising alternative courses of action and judge their feasibility, or (b) identify and evaluate possible outcomes of available courses of action.* How knowledge of attributes assists a decision maker in *identifying* alternative courses of action and possible outcomes is difficult to specify and will not be discussed here. Chambers has described one use of attribute data in judging the *feasibility* of a course of action—use of exit prices in judging an entity's current capacity to pay cash (1966, pp. 92–93); that use does not appear to be as common, however, as use in *evaluating* outcomes of feasible course of action, so the latter will be emphasized here. The outcomes can only be in the future, so prediction is required.

Relevance does not guarantee that the particular datum (number) provided will be useful—its failure to meet one or more of the other criteria could make it useless; relevance requires only that the number pertain to an attribute in which the decision maker is interested.

An alternative view is that a relevant attribute is one called

---

for by a decision model but we are not concerned with whether the decision process has been modelled or not. We must remember that a model is an abstract representation of something; we are more concerned with the actual decision process, whether it has been or can be modelled effectively or not.[6]

Please note that we are using the word "relevant" in a specific way here. In a more general sense, everything we do in accounting should be relevant to accounting objectives. But we are limiting the relevance criterion to the relationship between an attribute being measured and a user's decision process. The emphasis this definition places on the necessity that accounting decision makers become acquainted with the decision processes of users is as obvious as it is unavoidable if accountants do not wish to depend upon serendipity to make their products useful in decision making. Users' decision processes are the subject of the next chapter.

Reliability

Users of financial data prefer that it have a high degree of reliability. *Reliability is that quality which permits users of a datum confidently to depend on it as an accurate representation of the specific phenomenon it purports to represent.* There is close correspondence between reliable information and "reality." For example, if an asset is allegedly valued at historical cost, the amount shown is reliable if it represents the sum of the sacrifices made to acquire it. We do not consider such a valuation unreliable just because it does not represent the current market value of the asset. If market value is the attribute of which the decision maker needs a measurement, historical cost is irrelevant to the decision at hand but it is not necessarily unreliable.

An acceptable level of reliability is a necessary, but not a sufficient, condition for valuable information, because reliable information is not necessarily useful. A 1935 timetable may give reliable information about the time the first train of the day stopped at the local station in 1935, but that information may not be useful to a commuter deciding when to leave his home on a 1975

---

[6]For definitions of relevance that do not agree with the above, see Feltham (1972, p. 84) and Sterling (1972, p. 199).

morning. Or we may have reliable information about the price paid by another party for an asset in which we have no interest, or about some irrelevant attribute of one of our assets.

Reliability has so many facets that a review of the underlying sources of *unreliability* may be helpful. The fundamental reason why financial statements often have unreliable components is that accountants must make many choices, estimates, and judgments in applying the various measurement and classification rules that they employ. The principal sources of unreliability may be put into these categories; there may be others:

1. *Predictions.* These include lives, salvage values, and service patterns of amortizable assets of all kinds; failure of a debtor or other contracting party; and worthlessness of assets. Different accountants will use different prediction techniques, involving different predictors and coefficients.
2. *Allocations,* i.e., splitting a sum into parts with the aid of a base that is not perfectly suited to the task. Examples are distribution of a cost among functional divisions, assignment of overhead to products, costing of joint products, and amortization of long-lived assets. Accountants make choices in connection with the selection of a base, accumulation of base data, and calculations.
3. *Predetermined overhead rates and standard costs.* The accountant's choice of using or not using such methods and the manner in which he uses them, especially the disposition of variances, can make considerable difference.
4. *Selection of evidence in other cases.* For example, when current market prices are being used there may be a choice of bid, asked, average, or last sale prices; choice of market; choice of publisher of the quotation, and so forth.

These categories should be sufficient to remind us of the many opportunities for variation in the application of GAAP or any similar set of principles and rules. The results actually reported by the accountant will be influenced by a variety of circumstances:

1. Bias such as conservatism; lack of objectivity or of independence on the part of the accountant or other party involved in these estimates and choices.
2. Habit, consistent use of established practices, and rule-of-thumb approaches. These factors may either contribute to or detract from the reliability of the results.

3. Uncertainty, and the substitution of point estimates for probability distributions of future outcomes.
4. Error in data supplied to the accountant which are used as predictors, price quotations, or base data for allocations.
5. Weak association between predictors and attribute to be predicted, or between basis of allocation and cost being allocated.
6. Prediction techniques; constants, variables, and coefficients used.

Any user of accounting data who is thoroughly familiar with the many possible sources of unreliability will take them into consideration; he will avoid relying heavily on any measurement made in circumstances that he believes may lead to bias or errors in predictors, or that require a choice from a wide range of possible outcomes. The naive user may be misled unless accountants give some clues in their reports about the degree of reliability of various financial statement items.

A negative approach to reliability focuses on the potential for manipulation, poor judgments, and errors in the application of accounting rules. The more possibilities we see for such defects, the less reliable we consider the results to be—since we usually are unable to ascertain, as the data are being used, whether such defects are, in fact, present. Many presently accepted accounting procedures permit, indeed require, choices on the part of the accountant; if they did not, accounting would hardly be a professional field. An unsympathetic critic could easily argue that most of our current practices in the areas of fixed assets, intangibles, uncollectibles, and manufacturing cost accounting are so "soft" as to yield completely unreliable results.

Before we jump to such a conclusion, however, we should consider a major safeguard against unreliability built into current GAAP: consistency and the associated requirement for reporting accounting changes. For example, when a depreciable fixed asset is acquired, the accountant must choose the cost elements to be capitalized, estimate the life and salvage value of the asset, and select the depreciation pattern (straight-line calendar, sum-of-the-years-digits, etc.) to be used. The range of choices that he can make at the time of acquisition is wide. But his choices must hold for the life of the asset, or when he makes any change, he must then disclose it. Similarly, if an accountant or management team admits a personal bias into the deliberations, both short- and long-term consequences of the initial decisions must be weighed. Once these initial choices are made, the company is "stuck" with them as long as it holds the asset, or else it must disclose any material changes that it makes. These consistency and disclosure requirements contribute significantly to the reliability of the financial statement data.

However, we should also consider a contrasting example. If a company's policy on accounting for research and development costs involves capitalizing the costs of specific projects that are judged to have a "high probability of resulting in a profitable product," the accountant not only has a great deal of freedom each year, but he can also vary his interpretation of this policy from year to year.[7] We conclude that some accounting procedures involving choice are more susceptible to manipulation than others.

Now let's look at several components of reliability that accountants have recognized. ASOBAT named verifiability and freedom from bias as two of its four accounting standards (1966). *APB Statement No. 4* identified verifiability and neutrality as qualitative objectives of accounting. Ijiri and Jaedicke (1966) expressed reliability, objectivity, and bias in mathematical terms, while McKeown's (1971) measure of accuracy encompassed verifiability and bias. What do these various terms mean and how do they relate to reliability?

Verifiability. According to *APB Statement No. 4,* "Verifiable financial accounting information provides results that would be substantially duplicated by independent measurers using the same measurement methods" (1970, p. 37). McKeown (p. 28) measures verifiability as

$$V^{-2} = \frac{1}{n} \sum_{i=1}^{n} (x_i - \bar{x})^2$$

$$\text{or} \quad V = \sqrt{\frac{n}{\sum_{i=1}^{n} (x_i - \bar{x})^2}} = \frac{1}{\sigma}$$

---

[7] The American reader should be aware that FASB *Statement No. 2* prohibits capitalizing research and development costs.

where σ is the standard deviation of x. The number arrived at by the ith measurer is x_i. It is assumed that n different measurers are measuring the same object by the same method but that they end up with different numbers. The distribution of the various measurements about their mean ($\bar{x}$) is described as *dispersion*. But note that the dispersion is not normally known in a practical setting because we normally do not have a sample of measurements of the same thing; dispersion does not exist for one observation. However, experienced accountants working with a familiar problem, such as estimating uncollectible receivables for a department store, may be able to judge the dispersion that would result if a sample of accountants were to estimate those uncollectibles. Thus, experience is a basis for judging the verifiability of a measurement made by a relatively "soft" method if the circumstances are known. Experimentation is another possible basis for judging verifiability, or dispersion. Variations in personal bias on the part of several individual measurers can contribute to dispersion, as can any of the other variations in the circumstances of measurement listed above. Finally, we must remember that a highly verifiable measurement is not necessarily "correct." All it means is that other measurers would see it the same way; they may all be in error.

One difficulty with the McKeown measure of verifiability is that it is not expressed in a form that permits comparison of the verifiability of a set of measurements of a high-value object with a set of measurements of a low-value object. For example, if the standard deviation of several measurements of an asset is \$20,000 and the mean of the measurements is \$1 million, the verifiability of the set of measurements (per McKeown) is 1/20,000, a very low figure. If, in another case, the mean is \$100 and the standard deviation is \$40, the verifiability, 1/40, is much higher. It appears that it would be helpful to express these measurements in a comparable manner.

Adapting a suggestion made by Abdel-khalik (1971),[8] we propose

---

[8] "Unlike the Ijiri-Jaedicke model, it appears that *the complement of the coefficient of variation* would be a better measure of reliability than the variance. This preference, on my part, is due to several reasons. For one thing, the coefficient of variation (and its complement, of course) is independent of the magnitude of the asset's or the transaction's value. Secondly, the complement of the coefficient

that the complement of the coefficient of variation, that is,

$$1 - \frac{\sigma_x}{\bar{x}}$$

be used as a standard measure of verifiability. On this basis, the verifiability of the measurements of the valuable asset mentioned above is $1 - (20,000/1,000,000) = .98$, while the verifiability of the measurements of the low-value asset is $1 - (40/100) = .60$; the former has the higher degree of verifiability. If $\sigma_x > \bar{x}$, verifiability is negative—not an intuitively obvious interpretation but perhaps an acceptable one.

Bias. Objectivity, neutrality, independence, and freedom from bias are terms used to signify a state of mind that permits an observer to perceive phenomena and record his perceptions without influence from his personal stake in the phenomena in question, or the uses to which his record of those phenomena may be put. An objective observer "calls them as he sees them," and he sees them as they are without considering who may benefit or suffer as a result. Because bias can only occur when choices are made, we have associated it with the opportunities for choice listed above in this subsection (p. 45). Here we are concentrating on personal bias; the term "bias" is also used in the literature to mean systematic bias that is inherent in a measurement method and can be estimated and removed by a correction technique.

Accuracy. McKeown (p. 28) defines accuracy as follows:

$$A^{-2} = \frac{1}{n} \sum_{i=1}^{n} (x_i - T)^2$$

$$A = \sqrt{\frac{n}{\sum_{i=1}^{n} (x_i - T)^2}}$$

---

of variation is more consistent with the intuitive assessment since the higher the complement of the coefficient of variation, the higher the reliability" (Abdel-khalik, 1971, pp. 468–69). That is not true of Ijiri and Jaedicke's (1966) measure although it is true of McKeown's.

where x_i is a set of n measurements of the same thing and T is the true measure. Accuracy is, then, a combination of verifiability and any difference between the mean of the sample of measurements and the true value. The latter difference is sometimes called bias. Thus, according to McKeown (p. 29),

$$A^{-2} = V^{-2} + (\bar{x} - T)^2 = V^{-2} + B^2$$

where B is bias. Accuracy, in this meaning, is only applicable to predictions—which permit a subsequent determination of T. The only reasonable meaning of T for a past event is $\bar{x}$, unless we are willing to say that one observer (say, the one who is most qualified or who is working under the most favorable conditions; see McDonald, 1967) has the truth while others do not. Consensus (lack of dispersion) is the final word on observations but not on predictions; outcomes of predictions can be observed and accepted as truth for comparison with individual predictions or the mean of a sample of predictions—providing there is no dispersion among several observations of the outcome.

Comparability

In accounting, comparability is important because accountants and others need to compare data when using them; an isolated datum is rarely of much use. The information value of the data is enhanced by the application of similar accounting practices to similar events. It is not enhanced, of course, by treating significantly different events as if they were similar. An accounting method rates low on the comparability criterion if it permits identical objects or events to be reported as if they were different or different things to be reported as if they were identical.

We can identify five different types of comparability that can be significant:

1. *Interperiod comparability* of financial information relating to one firm, including consistency of accounting method. Users expect statements to be prepared in the same way over time so that they can detect changes in the fortunes of the company. Interperiod comparability requires:
   a. Consistent use of the same broad principles, or disclosure of changes.

    b. Consistent interpretation and application of principles, e.g., minimum acquisition costs to be capitalized, or variances to be allocated.

    c. Consistent classification of items.

    d. Consistent degree of conservatism or liberalism applied by the accountant and management.

    e. Comparability of the measuring unit employed in comparative statements.

2. *Intercompany comparability,* especially among firms within one industry. This quality of financial information enhances its value to analysts who are constantly comparing firms within an industry.

3. *Interline comparability* on any one financial statement. A sum reached by adding unlike units cannot be accurately labelled. Users of data prefer that numbers of meters and numbers of yards not be added, subtracted, or used in the computation of a ratio. Similarly, the monetary units reported in any one articulated set of financial statements should be as nearly identical as is possible, although useful results may be obtained without achieving perfection. Canadian dollars and U.S. dollars should not be added; 1965 U.S. dollars and 1975 U.S. dollars should not be added because a 1965 dollar is not the same measuring unit as a 1975 dollar.

4. *Intraline comparability.* The several components that are aggregated for presentation as one amount should be comparable.

5. *Comparability of the lengths of the reporting periods.* Regular reporting periods for any one company facilitate comparisons over time; identical reporting periods for different parts of a company and different companies facilitate comparisons of the data of the reporting entities.

Careful examination of these types of comparability may reveal overlap between comparability and components of both relevance and reliability. But this overlap seems preferable to the possibility that comparability would be neglected if it were subsumed in the other criteria.

Effects via Other Parties

Any person who chooses among alternative accounting methods should consider the effects of each method on his own interests through the actions of other parties. A dramatic example was the 1971 controversy over the choice of the liberal "flow-through" method or the conservative "deferral" method of accounting for the "investment credit" permitted by the U.S. Internal Revenue Code. The APB apparently believed that the deferral method yielded data that were more *relevant* to the decisions of investors, but its view did not prevail. U.S. Treasury Department officials, who intended that the investment credit spur investment in plant and equipment, argued for the liberal flow-through method because they thought that the credit would have a more favorable impact on the economy, *via the decisions of business managers,* if its contribution to income could be reported immediately. Corporate managers, who were interested in the effects that the chosen method would have on themselves and their corporations *via the investment decisions and management appraisals of investors,* also preferred the flow-through method. Although investors, as usual, exerted little influence, they may well have been influenced by the prospective effects that the deferral method would have on the price of their securities *through the market actions of other investors.* It seems likely that the effects via other parties criterion was the key criterion in the ultimate decision, made by the U.S. Congress (and President), not to prohibit any method. Most corporations have chosen the flow-through method.

EXHIBIT III-3 illustrates the process by which an evaluator's choice of an accounting method can affect his interests via other parties. An accounting method chosen by an evaluator may influence another party either through the latter's use of accounting data yielded by the method chosen, or through his anticipation of the way the method would report his prospective actions. The Treasury officials' concern with managers' response to the method used to account for the investment credit illustrates the second type of influence; managers presumably would be more likely to purchase fixed assets if they knew that the flow-through method were being used. It was the influence of actual accounting outputs on investors, however, that managers (as evaluators) had in mind when they expressed a preference for the flow-through method.

When *company managers* evaluate alternative accounting methods for internal reporting, they give a great deal of attention to the methods' effects on their own interests via others—especially

EXHIBIT III-3

EFFECT OF AN ACCOUNTING METHOD ON AN EVALUATOR'S INTERESTS VIA OTHER
PARTIES

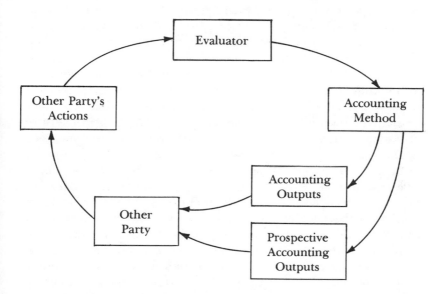

Note: The EXHIBIT indicates why Henry Cuevas has suggested
the term "boomerang effect" in conversation with the author.

subordinates. The effect of performance reports on the motivation
of subordinates is one of the prime considerations in the selection
of internal performance-reporting methods. Managers' interests
in external reporting, which is generally considered separable from
internal reporting, are also directed towards the effects the reports
will have on others. In this case, the "others" are primarily investors
(creditors and owners). Managers appear to prefer those accounting
methods which result in or permit relative stability of reported
earnings, because it is believed that investors interpret stability
as evidence of lack of risk; the lower the risk in an investment,
the lower the required rate of return. Thus, managers believe
that using accounting methods that yield stable reported earnings
lowers the firm's cost of both debt and equity capital (and raises
the price of the firm's stock). Similarly, managers appear to prefer

accounting methods that yield higher reported earnings. Their preference is based on the "bottom line fixation" view mentioned in chapter I, in which investors tend to apply the same price/earnings multiple to the reported earnings regardless of the accounting methods used, so that higher reported earnings are translated into higher stock prices. On the other hand, managers may opt for the more conservative method if they are concerned about the use of the firm's financial statements by union leaders in formulating bargaining goals. In all of these cases managers are concerned about the effects that the accounting data will have on their interests by way of the actions of others; they may give this factor great weight when they choose an accounting method.

Shareholders' evaluation of accounting methods may also be affected by their perception of the effects the methods would have on others. For example, the effects that the reported earnings may have on union negotiators, mentioned above, may be of concern to shareholders, too. Another example is owners' likely preference for financial statements that help the firm obtain credit on favorable terms.[9] But the "other" group that might well be most important in this connection is management; shareholders must be concerned about the effects that external reporting methods can have on management decisions. When managers face a difficult problem, they perceive that one solution to it will be reported in the financial statements in a manner that makes them look bad, while another possible solution will make them look good, at least in the short-run; managers' perception of this difference may well influence the decision—to the detriment of shareholders.

More simply, if good decisions will reduce the reported earnings and bad decisions will increase them, managers may be motivated to make bad decisions. In such a case, goals are not congruent; when managers meet a major goal—high short-run earnings, for

---

[9] A peculiarly American case in which investors must consider the effects on them via other parties is the choice between LIFO and another cost flow assumption in an inventory. Regardless of which method gives the most useful information for investment decisions, investors must consider that if LIFO is not used for external reporting it may not be used for computing taxable income. The effect on investors via the Internal Revenue Service may be material.

instance—then a goal of shareholders—high value of the firm, which depends upon discounted long-run earnings—may be neglected. Any accounting method that contributes to a lack of congruence (to disharmony) of managers' and shareholders' goals has a strike against it in the eyes of the shareholders. Actions that are good for the shareholders must be reported as good for the shareholders; management actions that are detrimental to shareholders' goals should be reported as detrimental. Poor measurements of income and wealth lead to poor evaluations of managers' performance which, in turn, lead to poor decisions by managers. An accounting method's contribution to the harmony of managerial and shareholder goals is oné element of "effects via other parties"—an important criterion for the evaluation of accounting methods.[10]

The basis for "disharmony" in an accounting system is failure to measure assets and liabilities at their ideal economic values to shareholders. The problem encompasses the whole area of accounting measurement; a few examples will serve to illustrate it.

1. Over- and undervaluation of any asset or liability may affect a decision regarding its retention or disposition. Undervalued assets are excellent sources of instant earnings, as are overvalued liabilities. In his desire to meet an earnings target, a manager may sell an asset or pay off a liability on terms that are actually unfavorable to the owners. Similarly, a manager may fail to dispose of an asset or a liability on favorable terms because he is unwilling to "take the loss" that would be reported on the income statement. When assets or liabilities are carried at out-of-date values, wise dispositions easily can be reported as loss transactions and unwise dispositions can be reported as successes.

2. Managerial planning and decision making frequently involve careful calculations (and use of decision models) such

---

[10] Demski and Feltham (1976) use the term "decision influencing" in connection with the effects subsequent reporting can have on the decisions of managers. Another descriptive term is "ex ante effects of accounting choices on managerial decisions." Prakash and Rappaport (1976) emphasize the "feedback effects" of accounting on management decisions and the economy.

as discounted cash flow analyses and economic order quantity calculations. It is possible, under some accepted accounting practices, that a decision-making analysis may indicate the wisdom of a particular course of action and that subsequent events may occur exactly as predicted, but that the financial statements may indicate that poor results were achieved. For example, if a discounted cash flow analysis of an investment project that yields a constant cash flow over its life indicates a rate of return of 12 percent, the financial statements based on customary straight-line depreciation will show a return on net investment that is much lower than 12 percent in the first year of the project's life and much higher than 12 percent in the last year—even if the predictions on which the discounted cash flow analysis is based were perfect. Straight-line depreciation in these circumstances scores low on the harmony criterion.

3. The use of the completed contracts method of accounting for long-term construction projects instead of the percentage-of-completion method can bias a manager in favor of short contracts if he feels the need to report more profit in the short-run; a less profitable but shorter job may be ranked over the more profitable, long-term contract.

4. Failure to capitalize costs that are expected to yield future benefits may discourage many desirable activities, e.g., research and development, training, preventive maintenance, holding of land or securities that yield little or no "income" in the short-run, and introduction of new products or development of new markets.

5. Omission from the accounts of the detrimental effects of management actions on "human assets," of public attitudes towards the firm, or of possible class action suits on behalf of customers, employees, or neighbors may cause managers to give insufficient weight to such factors in making their decisions.[11]

6. There is also the possibility of what might be called the two-cushion bank shot. Consider the issue of whether uninsured fire and casualty losses should be reported as

---

[11] Note that the inclusion in the overall evaluation framework of the views of all interested parties, including the general public, recognizes the "externalities" pertaining to entity operations.

losses on the income statement in the period in which they occur. Alternatively, "self-insurance reserves" may be established by regular periodic charges to expense in amounts similar to the insurance premiums that would have been paid if the risks had been insured against and actual losses charged to the reserve instead of against income. If investors are believed to be averse to instability in reported earnings, then managers may be reluctant to report losses as they occur (unevenly), and they may incur the cost of uneconomical insurance if self-insurance reserves are not permitted. As a result, investors may prefer that the FASB permit self-insurance reserves in order to encourage managers to economize on insurance costs.

It should be clear that these examples do not represent endorsements of any particular accounting method, because only one of the nine criteria included in our scheme for evaluating alternative accounting proposals has been considered here. Consideration of other criteria, especially reliability, may cause shareholders and others to reject the methods that contribute the most to harmony of goals.

When a broadly based *policy-making body such as the FASB* makes accounting decisions on behalf of the society as a whole, it may take into consideration the possible *economic side effects* of accounting standards, that is, the effects that accounting data might have on the economy other than those due to the data being used by decision makers in the intended ways. Examples of economic side effects are included in EXHIBIT III-4 (excluding the third and seventh cases which illustrate primary effects). Other examples are competitor's use of publicly reported data, effects on management bonuses based on reported earnings, imposition of price controls or excess profits tax based on indicated profitability of business in general or a particular industry, risks of liability on behalf of auditors and managers, and costs of producing and using accounting information.

EXHIBIT III-5 illustrates the mechanism of economic side effects as viewed from the perspective of a policy-making body. The reader is urged to give special attention to notes (D) and (F) accompanying that EXHIBIT. We suggest that the market's perceptiveness, or ability to perceive the underlying economic

EXHIBIT III-4

EXAMPLES OF ACCOUNTING DECISION SITUATIONS IN WHICH EFFECTS UPON AN INTERESTED PARTY VIA OTHER PARTIES MAY BE SIGNIFICANT

Interested Party	Accounting Choice	Other Party	Potential Effect	Probable Choice
Taxing authority	Treatment of tax incentives in accounting to investors	Managers of reporting entity	Effect on internal investment decisions	Flow-through
Shareholders	Treatment of tax incentives in accounting to investors	Managers of reporting entity	Effect on internal investment decisions	Deferral
Managers	Treatment of tax incentives in accounting to investors	Shareholders	On appraisals of managerial performance and on share investment decisions	Flow-through
Shareholders	Asset and liability measurement methods (and "instant earnings" and "instant losses")	Managers	Decision to sell or hold an asset; decision to retire debt prematurely or not	Current value methods
Managers	Asset and liability measurement methods	Shareholders	Appraisals of managerial performance; share	Historical cost

	(and "instant earnings" and "instant losses")		investment decisions	
Shareholders	Capitalizing or expensing research, development, exploration, and "human asset" costs	Managers	Expenditure decisions	Capitalization of successful investments
Shareholders and managers	Choices affecting debt/equity ratio, working capital, stability, and level of earnings	Lenders	Extension of credit and terms	"Liberal" methods
Shareholders and managers	Inventory cost flow assumption	U.S. Internal Revenue Service	Tax liability of entity	LIFO
Top managers and owners	Any choice of method of reporting results vs. plans	Any subordinate manager	Decisions by subordinates not in interests of owners	Methods providing congruence
Managers and shareholders	Any choice affecting reported earnings	Union representatives	Bargaining on labor contract	Conservative methods

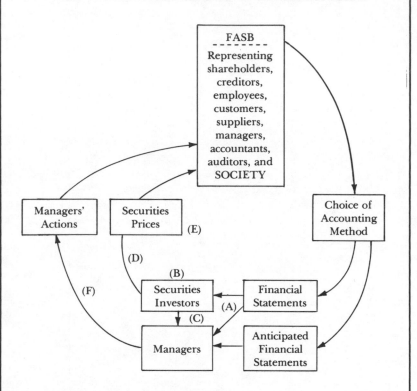

EXHIBIT III-5

EFFECTS VIA OTHER PARTIES: THE FASB AND ECONOMIC SIDE EFFECTS

(A) Computations of managers' bonuses may be based on reported earnings.

(B) More broadly, the parties whose perceptions could be of concern to managers might include depositors, union officials, legislators, and others whose use of company financial statements could affect the company or its managers.

(C) Securities investors exercise varying degrees of control over managers.

(D) This effect depends on investors being influenced by the choice of accounting method, sometimes called bottom line fixation, market inefficiency, or market misperception.

(E) If (B) is not a security investor, (E) is not a security price, but may be deposit levels, wages, legislation, or something else.

(F) This influence depends on managers believing in (A), (C), or (D).

phenomena regardless of which accounting method is used for reporting those phenomena, together with managers' belief or lack of belief in market perceptiveness, is critical to a policy-making body that is concerned with how much weight to give to potential economic side effects of a change in accounting standards.

Finally, a note about the rights of nonusers of financial reports is in order in this section. An example is the chart-oriented securities trader who does not read financial statements or data derived from financial statements. His welfare may be influenced by the effects of financial statements on the actions of others who trade in the market, and thereby affect the price of the security and the nonuser's profits. Needless to say, he is not likely to have much to say to the FASB (or a similar body), and the FASB is even less likely to give significant weight to his problem. Other nonusers (the general public) who are indirectly affected by financial statements through managers' and investors' actions that influence the general level of economic activity would appear to merit more consideration.

Intelligibility

This criterion is intended to encompass the concepts of understandability and readability. It asks that the accountant consider whether and how financial statement information is communicated effectively. Any accountant who is seriously interested in communicating with users knows that his financial reports must be intelligible in order to be useful. He must know the strengths and limitations of the readers of financial statements. He may need to prepare different sets of financial statements for different classes of readers, if their backgrounds and vocabularies in accounting and finance are different, in order to convert data into intelligible, meaningful, and useful information.

To communicate effectively, the accountant must use classifications that are meaningful to the user, not just to himself. He must supply informative headings, juxtapose related data, and present net figures that the user typically wants to know. He can also use techniques of visual presentation to attract the reader's attention to key items within a report. These and other components of statement format can be used to advantage by the accountant who wants to make his work valuable and useful.

Timeliness

There are two types of timeliness. One is *frequency* of reporting, which refers to the length of the reporting period. Should it be a month, quarter, half-year, or year? It is possible to report too frequently or too infrequently. If the period is too short, a report on operations may be too heavily influenced by random or seasonal variations in the firm's activities; as a result, the data may be misleading or not worth the user's time. But if the reporting period is too long, the user is required to wait too long before obtaining and using the information included in the reports. Such a delay is related to the other type of timeliness—*lag* between the end of the reporting period and the date when the financial statements are issued. Because information is always used for predictions, its value is always related to the lag, or delay, in reporting.[12]

EXHIBIT III-6 illustrates the relationships between the net value of information and timeliness: frequency and lag. The zero point on the time axis represents infinitely short reporting periods or immediate reporting after the end of the period. The negative segment of the frequency curve indicates costs of producing and utilizing data in excess of the benefits. The shape of the lag curve in the negative lag range indicates that predictions are more valuable than ex post reports, other things (including reliability) being equal.

Optimal Quantity

Several concepts that relate to the quantity of data supplied to users have been discussed in the literature. The APB (1970, p. 39) included *completeness* as a qualitative objective: "Complete financial accounting information includes all financial accounting data that reasonably fulfill the requirements of the other qualitative objectives." *Disclosure* is given a great deal of emphasis in the traditional literature of accounting and in recent efforts of the SEC. For example, Moonitz (1961, p. 50) postulated that "Account-

---

[12] Gregory and Van Horn (1960, p. 349) emphasize *interval* and *delay* instead of frequency and lag.

EXHIBIT III-6

RELATIONSHIP BETWEEN VALUE OF INFORMATION
AND FREQUENCY AND LAG IN REPORTING

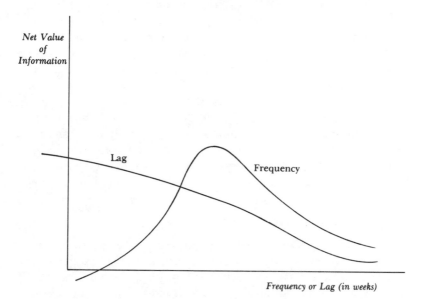

ing reports should disclose that which is necessary to make them not misleading." *Materiality* has perplexed practitioners for decades. *Significance* and *sufficiency* have also been advanced as criteria for the evaluation of information (Snavely, 1967). The literature of information economics stresses *optimal partitioning* and *optimal aggregation,* where partitioning relates to the fineness or coarseness of the classification scheme employed, and aggregation involves merging separate events for reporting. The dangers of "information overload" have also been recognized. Obviously, all of these concepts are related to the quantity of data reported.

The question is this: How far should the accountant go in providing detailed data the value of which may not exceed the cost of producing and utilizing it? Three components of the question come to mind. First, the accountant must consider the extent to which he should break down or condense general categories of double-entry accounting data, such as assets, liabilities, revenues, and expenses, for presentation to users. Or, starting with the original events that he records, the accountant asks, "How much should events be aggregated before they are reported?" Secondly, the accountant must determine how much additional descriptive material, including captions, parenthetical comments, and accompanying notes, he should include in the financial reports. Finally, he must consider how to include in financial reports things of positive or negative value that are not brought into the double-entry system, such as contingent liabilities and valuable attributes of the entity, which do not meet the criteria for inclusion as an asset. Thus the criterion of optimal quantity of data requires that the accountant find satisfactory answers to each component of the question. But the necessity for cost-benefit comparisons may cause some readers to prefer the merger of this criterion with the criteria of cost of utilization and cost of production.

Costs of Producing Accounting Data

People who emphasize the maximization of value of financial information to users often neglect the costs of performing accounting activities: salaries, depreciation, equipment rental, supplies, audit fees, and so on. But accounting costs are not negligible. American Telephone and Telegraph (1975), for example, showed accounting expenses of $786,802,000 on its 1975 income statement, an amount equal to 2.7 percent of its revenues. And the entire revenues of the auditing branch of the accounting profession—probably well over $1 billion annually in the U.S.—are accounting costs. One reason why the information evaluation approach to external financial reporting decisions has not been used effectively is that the people who have the best feel for the costs (managers and owner-managers of firms) are not the same as those who enjoy the benefits (absentee investors, government officials, and, in a sense, auditors), and most of the accounting choices have been made by the former. Such circumstances make cost-benefit-efficient decisions very difficult. As an analogy, consider how a society made up of 100 university students and 100 childless adult taxpayers—don't ask what happened to the students' parents—might decide how much money to spend on university education and what portion should be paid by the students in fees. The usual solution is to select policy makers (elected officials or members of the FASB) and empower them to decide and impose their decision on the rest of us. We should not be surprised that this policy-making process works poorly; it is surprising that it works at all.

However, we should recognize that shareholders bear the firm's accounting costs to the same extent that they bear other operating costs of the firm; managers do not pay these costs out of their own pockets. The final incidence of the cost presumably is on consumers of the firm's products. The benefits from better decisions by investors also tend to be diffused throughout the economy, in the long run. As we said early in this chapter, implementation of the aggregate social welfare criterion of accounting systems is not feasible at the present time.

Even a straight comparison of internal accounting costs is difficult enough, especially when one of the methods under consideration is unfamiliar. The typical reaction of someone who is familiar with one procedure is that a proposed alternative is more difficult. This view may reflect his vision of "first time through" performance; the "leaning curve" phenomenon is not as prominent in the first picture he sees. In addition, we must keep in mind that new services such as new price indexes or published price quotations may become available if a new method is widely adopted; they might reduce the costs of producing data. Finally, we must not forget the role that computers can play in reducing the cost of what would be tedious calculations and retrieval of data by older methods.

We must be careful to avoid allowing ignorance and a vague feeling of "difficulty" associated with a new technique to be converted into an unsupported argument that the new method is too costly. This is especially relevant to the evaluation of alternative asset measurement methods and to the general price level restatement proposal, since the costs of these aspects of accounting are relatively small compared to the costs of the routine, high-volume procedures such as those pertaining to billing and receivables, disbursements, inventory quantities, and payroll accounting. It seems quite unlikely that the total annual accounting costs of the average firm would be increased by more than 2 to 4 percent (after the first time through) by any choice from among the widely discussed measurement methods, including historical cost adjusted for changes in a general price index. The costs of accounting must be taken into consideration without using them as a club to beat down any proposal for change.

Costs of Utilizing Accounting Data

The criterion, costs of utilizing accounting data, is closely related to two of the criteria discussed above: intelligibility and optimal quantity. The costs of utilizing accounting data increase if the financial statements and accompanying material are not easily comprehended by the users; if they are poorly organized so that the user must spend time searching for data that he wants to consider together; if the user must make his own additions, subtractions, and divisions in order to obtain the sums, differences, and ratios he needs; or if he must plow through many pages of details in order to extract the data he needs. These costs take the form of consumption of the user's own time, salaries of professional analysts, and subscription fees for investment services. Although the difference between the cost of using the data produced by one accounting method and the cost of using that produced by another method may seldom be material, we should keep it in mind in the few cases where it is pertinent.

The relationship between the two cost criteria and the optimal quantity criterion is illustrated in EXHIBIT III-7. If the accountant starts with the most valuable data he can accumulate and report, then adds the next most valuable data and so on, we can draw a declining curve of incremental value as the quantity of data increases. If the combined cost of producing and utilizing data increases more than proportionately to the increase in quantity as the receiver's analysis chores multiply, we may superimpose a rising and convex cost curve on the same graph. The point on the quantity scale at which the incremental value equals the incremental cost marks, conceptually, the optimal quantity of data to accumulate and report. We conclude that the optimal quantity criterion cannot be applied independently of the cost criteria.

Predictive Power

A number of accounting writers who are deeply interested in empirical research and statistical tests believe that the usefulness

EXHIBIT III-7
VALUE AND COST OF DATA INCREMENTS

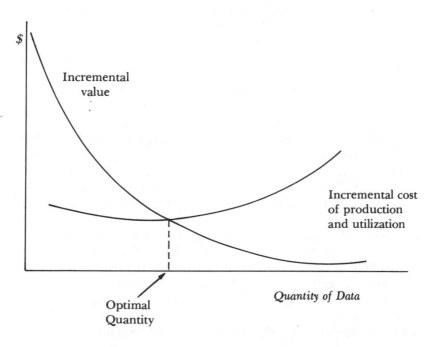

Incremental
value

Incremental cost
of production
and utilization

Optimal
Quantity

Quantity of Data

of accounting data in predicting phenomena of interest to users is a criterion that should be used in evaluating alternative accounting proposals. Thus, Beaver, Kennelly, and Voss (1968) recommended the use of *"predictive ability"* as a criterion.[13] McDonald (1967) suggested the use of *correlation* as a criterion related to predictions; a broader criterion would admit any statistical measure of *association*. Even more generally, *predictive power* could be adopted as a criterion of valuable information, because decisions almost universally involve predictions, and because the decision maker typically uses accounting data to predict outcomes of

---

[13] Greenball (1971), however, pointed out that accounting measurements do not predict or have the ability to predict; people predict, often with the aid of accounting data.

alternative strategies, or to predict state variables on which those
outcomes depend.[14]

To apply the predictive power criterion objectively requires
comparison of the association between data produced by one
accounting method and the phenomena to be predicted with the
association between alternative accounting data and the object
of prediction. Beaver (1967), for example, tested the association
of various financial ratios (based on accounting data) with subsequent company failures. He found that the ratio of working-capital
flow from operations to total debt was more closely associated
with company success and failure in the subsequent five-year period
than was the current ratio, or any other familiar ratio. These
findings provided impressive (although not overwhelming) evidence that "funds revenues," "funds expenses," and debt (all
computed according to GAAP) were valuable for predicting failure.
Another example was Fama and Babiak's (1968) work on the
prediction of changes in dividends with the aid of earnings data.

In addition to direct tests of the association between accounting
data available at any specified date and subsequent events of interest
to a decision maker, a good deal of research has been done on
contemporaneous association, for example, between alternative
accounting data and share prices. Contemporaneous association
may indicate predictive power of accounting data on the assumptions that (a) future values of the accounting data are predictable,
and (b) the association will be stable. Contemporaneous association
can also indicate relevance in the sense of "used by decision makers."
Thus, observance of closer association of "flow-through" earnings
with stock prices than of "deferral" earnings with stock prices
would suggest that stock market actors prefer to base their decisions
on flow-through earnings. "If a model is an accurate representation
of empirical phenomena, it has predictive power" (Ijiri, 1975,
p. 7)—providing the relationships expressed in the model are

[14]Carsberg, Arnold, and Hope [Bryan Carsberg, John Arnold, and Anthony
Hope, "Predictive Value: A Criterion for Choice of Accounting Method," *Studies
in Accounting Theory*, 3rd ed., W. T. Baxter and S. Davidson, eds. (London: Institute
of Chartered Accountants in England and Wales, 1977)] argue "for the recognition
of the predictive value criterion as the primary means of choosing the most useful
of alternative methods of preparing financial accounting reports."

stable. Unfortunately, relationships of empirical phenomena pertaining to the social sciences are somewhat unstable. Examples are the "stock market's" cyclical shifts of emphasis between earnings and dividends, and its apparent tendency to learn, and become more "efficient," over a moderate period after a new method of doing business (e.g., leasing, franchising, or installment retailing of land) or a new accounting technique (e.g., pooling) comes along.

Predictive power is not a criterion that can be placed alongside the criteria discussed above. Usefulness in predicting is, of course, a desirable attribute of accounting outputs, but inasmuch as it encompasses several of the benefit criteria discussed above (attribute relevance, reliability, timeliness) it cuts across them. This duplication is disadvantageous only if it is used as a substitute for the encompassed criteria in appraising an accounting proposal. Thus, a difference between earnings before depreciation and earnings after depreciation with respect to their association with stock prices would not indicate a difference in relevance, or a difference in reliability, but only a difference in overall usefulness. Inability to attribute the difference to either relevance or reliability handicaps the profession in its search for improvements in accounting. It is also generally recognized that tests of association are, in a sense, also tests of the particular "loss function" (such as squared deviations) embodied in the association metric (e.g., one based on least squares methodology). Failure to find association is especially unrevealing because the weakness could be in the prediction model, the application of it, the relevance of the accounting data, or their reliability. In some cases, control samples can be used to eliminate one or more of these possible explanations. In sum, the predictive power criterion should be given a major role in accounting research, but it does not fit into the set of criteria for evaluating alternative accounting methods that is presented in this chapter.

APPLICABILITY OF THE CRITERIA

Decision making is an exercise in differential analysis: "What difference will it make whether we do this or that?" Events that are common to alternative courses of action cannot help the decision maker choose among them. That fact applies both to accounting decisions and to other economic decisions. In many accounting decision cases the evaluation procedure will disclose that there is no perceptible difference between method A and method B on several of the criteria, but that there are differences on other criteria. For example, if the accounting issue is one of choosing the wording for a line-item on the income statement, the alternatives may not differ on the criteria of attribute relevance, reliability, timeliness, optimal quantity, effects via other parties, and costs of producing accounting data, but they may differ on intelligibility, costs of utilizing, and comparability. On the other hand, a choice between historical cost and current market value for valuation of a security owned may be made primarily on the criteria of attribute relevance, reliability, comparability, and effects via other parties; the other criteria are insignificant in this case. But each of the criteria has its role. Consider the following list of criteria and accounting choices for which each criterion could be critical:

Relevance of the attribute being measured to the decisions of the user—any choice of a measurement method applicable to an asset or liability.

Reliability—many choices of a measurement method.

Comparability:

Interperiod comparability—any proposal to change an accounting method;

Intercompany and intracompany comparability—choices of classification schemes for reporting revenues and expenses;

Comparability of lengths of reporting periods—a decision whether to change the length of the reporting period.

Intelligibility—choice of descriptive terms, format, or presentation of a note.

Timeliness—choice of the length of interim reporting periods; a choice between a procedure which keeps records up to date daily and a procedure which requires substantial end-of-period work.

Optimal quantity—many decisions regarding possible aggregation for external reporting of data kept in separate accounts for internal needs.

Effects via other parties—choices of measurement methods.

Costs of producing accounting data—choices of data processing equipment and procedures; a choice whether or not to publish forecasts.

Costs of utilizing accounting data—format decisions; aggregation decisions; a choice whether or not to publish forecasts.

As we have pointed out before, these nine criteria are not mutually exclusive. We emphasize these particular criteria in order to cover fully the factors that affect accounting decisions. Several criteria that could have been merged might be neglected if not set out separately; otherwise the number of criteria might have been reduced to five or six. The several facets of comparability, for example, are fairly well covered by attribute relevance and reliability. Timeliness is closely related to optimal quantity; both are intimately involved with costs of production and costs of utilization. In addition to seeing possibilities for shortening the list of criteria, we see possibilities for adding to it. The reliability criterion could be split into verifiability and lack of bias; timeliness could be broken down into frequency and lag; predictive power could be appropriately included in some contexts. We encourage the accounting decision maker to organize the set of criteria according to the circumstances of his particular decisions.

PATTERNS FOR MAKING ACCOUNTING DECISIONS

Most major decisions are based on a mixture of objective evidence and subjective opinion. Some choices of accounting methods are heavily influenced by objective, measurable economic considerations; perhaps the best examples are found in tax accounting. But many choices in external reporting are based primarily on subjective judgments of the consequences of that choice. This does not, of course, mean that an organized technique of decision making is impossible; on the contrary, this book is based on the premise that accounting decision making can be more systematic than it has been in the past.

At this point, let's review the accounting decision process recommended in this chapter, illustrated in EXHIBIT III-2 and outlined on pages 37–38. Note that we recommended only the general pattern; different circumstances will determine precisely which groups need be considered, what uses they make of financial statement data, and even the particular set of criteria that is appropriate. Frequently, only one significant use by a user group need be considered; the analysis leading to the choice of method by one user group on a particular criterion may serve equally well as the basis for another group's choice if one evaluator represents more than one group, as in the case of the FASB or SEC. When a particular user or user group applies the technique, step 7 in the outline (and one level of the diagram) is eliminated. The general approach appears to be applicable to the making of accounting decisions on any level: society, industry, entity, or segment.

We recognize two serious limitations of our approach to making accounting decisions. One is the clarification of users' decision-making techniques that is required by step 4. Some accountants see it as a serious roadblock around which they must detour. To those of us who are oriented towards decision usefulness, it is a challenge which must be faced; to expect to be helpful to users without understanding their needs is fanciful. Even partial clarification of users' needs is to be preferred to overlooking them completely; chance is our only hope for hitting users' needs if we do not even take aim on the target.

The other limitation of this approach is that the preferences that must be identified, compared, and combined in steps 5, 6, and 7 are not quantified. Some readers may be tempted to use a point scoring system to convert preferences to numbers. For example, 100 points could be divided among the nine criteria in a particular fashion to represent the maximum significance of each criterion to a particular user group. Then the rating of an accounting method on a criterion would be expressed in a number between zero and the maximum permitted for that criterion. And/or weights could be assigned to the several user groups in order to permit aggregation of the preferences of some groups for a particular accounting method for comparison with the preferences of other groups for another method. But how could the weights assigned to groups, or to criteria, or the score given to any accounting method on one criterion by one user group, be defended? If I give method A nine points on the relevance criterion and you give it only five points, how can either of us justify our scoring?

The point scoring system for comparing two or more proposals could be modified if the decision involves whether or not to add an accounting procedure to those existing. For example, if the issue is whether to add supplementary statements in units of constant purchasing power (price level restatements), an evaluator could record his views by assigning a positive number of points to those criteria on which he thought the new technique would rate favorably and a negative number of points on those criteria on which he viewed the proposal as undesirable. If the sum of the points assigned were greater than zero, the evaluator would favor the proposal. Differences among the scoring sheets of several evaluators could provide a focus for continuing deliberations.

EXHIBIT III-8 illustrates how a weighting scheme might be reflected in a scoring sheet and shows hypothetical results of its use by two decision makers who were faced with the necessity of choosing between the deferral-amortization and the immediate expensing methods of accounting for research and development costs. The particular scheme illustrated here is based on the assumptions that the decision maker must recognize the rights of several interested groups and that the ratings on all of the criteria except relevance do not vary across groups. For example, the deferral-amortization method gets the same rating on the cost-of-production criterion by all groups of interested parties—an assumption that appears tenable if one independent party is doing the rating but would not be reasonable if each group were rating the methods as it saw them. (Note that the relatively low weight assigned to the effects via other parties criterion reflects the tendency of the effects recognized by different groups to cancel each other out, except for the managerial suboptimization effect, which is a net disadvantage to society. Weights assigned to this criterion may well be higher on scoring sheets designed for partisan use, such as by managers only or employees only.)

The example in EXHIBIT III-8 is designed to show that the use of a point scoring system cannot overcome the subjectivity of the decision makers' preferences. Even though the two individuals DM_1 and DM_2 are in perfect ordinal agreement, that is, have no disagreements about the rankings of the two accounting methods on any criterion for any interested group, they still disagree on the final choice. The source of their disagreement is in the differing strengths of their preferences for the deferral-amortization method on the relevance criterion and for the immediate expensing method on the reliability criterion.[15] Generally speaking, scoring sheets

---

[15] Incidentally, the ratings by DM_2 are my guess of the FASB's views, which led it to choose the immediate expensing method.

Exhibit III-8
EXAMPLE OF ACCOUNTING DECISION SCORING SHEET APPLIED BY TWO DECISION MAKERS
TO THE CASE OF ACCOUNTING FOR RESEARCH AND DEVELOPMENT COSTS

	Maximum Scores	Defer and Amortize		Expense Immediately	
		DM_1	DM_2	DM_1	DM_2
Relevance	40	30	25	5	15
To Owners	20				
To Long-Term Creditors	9				
To Short-Term Creditors	5				
To Managers	2				
To Employees	2				
To Public	2				
Reliability	20	8	3	18	20
Comparability	12	3	3	8	8
Effects via Other Parties	6	4	4	1	1
Intelligibility	6	3	3	5	5
Timeliness	4	3	3	3	3
Optimal Quantity	4	2	2	3	3
Cost of Production	4	3	3	4	4
Cost of Utilization	4	3	3	4	4
Total Scores	100	59	49	51	63

DM_1 and DM_2 are two hypothetical individuals who have the responsibility of choosing between the deferral-amortization and the immediate expensing methods of accounting for research and development costs.

may serve as check lists, as an aid to an individual in organizing his analysis, and as a basis for identifying the locus of disagreement among members of a decision-making group.

It is important that we recognize that the numbers on the scoring sheet, or on any similar scoring sheet, are lacking in objectivity, with the possible exception of the cost-of-production figures, where some data on which independent observers would agree might be obtained. Objective application of the criteria approach requires that we develop "public models" for rating accounting methods on the other criteria and for weighting the criteria and the interest groups. The subjective selection of numbers to represent personal opinions (private models) and subsequent arithmetic operations using those numbers do not make the procedure objective, and while the literature of multi-attribute decision making (e.g., Cochrane and Zeleny, 1973; Green and Wind, 1973) is relevant to the multiple-criteria approach to accounting choices, it does not have a solution to the problem of subjectivity. This does not mean that a decision-making procedure that calls for the recognition of uses, users, alternatives, and criteria cannot be helpful; it only means that the procedure cannot be shown to yield an unequivocably correct answer. When an objective (and otherwise suitable) procedure becomes available, the one suggested here should be set aside. In the meantime, the criteria approach to accounting decisions may play a useful role.

CONCLUSION

Maximization of social welfare is as appropriate a goal of decision making in the areas of external financial reporting as it is in any other public policy area but, unfortunately, it is also almost as difficult to quantify in the former domain as in others. Until a mathematical model of the social welfare approach becomes operational, if it ever does, those who are faced with accounting choices may be able to improve their decision-making techniques by identifying and applying a set of criteria of desirable accounting methods. This chapter has described such a set of criteria and suggested some techniques for its use in making accounting decisions.

Implementation of this approach depends heavily upon acquaintance with users' needs for accounting information. The next chapter consists of a general review of the decisions commonly made by the major external users of entity financial data and the types of data apparently called for by the common approaches to those decisions. That review provides a basis for applying the criteria to users' accounting choice problems—especially the criterion of relevance of the attribute being measured to the decisions of users.

ADDITIONAL READING SUGGESTIONS

Bedford, Norton M., *Extensions in Accounting Disclosure* (Prentice-Hall, 1973).

―――― and Toshio Iino, "Consistency Reexamined," *The Accounting Review* (July 1968), pp. 453–58.

Benston, George J., "The Value of the SEC's Accounting Disclosure Requirements," *The Accounting Review* (July 1969), pp. 515–32.

Bernstein, Leopold A., "Materiality—The Need for Guidelines," *The New York Certified Public Accountant* (July 1969), pp. 501–10.

Carsberg, Bryan; John Arnold and Anthony Hope, "Predictive Value: A Criterion for Choice of Accounting Method" in W. T. Baxter and S. Davidson, eds., *Studies in Accounting Theory*, 3rd ed. (London: Institute of Chartered Accountants in England and Wales, 1977).

Feltham, Gerald A. and Joel S. Demski, "The Use of Models in Information Evaluation," *The Accounting Review* (October 1970), pp. 623–40.

Financial Accounting Standards Board, "An Analysis of Issues Related to *Conceptual Framework for Financial Accounting and Reporting: Elements of Financial Statements and Their Measurement,*" *FASB Discussion Memorandum* (FASB, 2 December 1976), chapter 7.

Hendriksen, Eldon S., *Accounting Theory*, rev. ed. (Richard D. Irwin, 1970), chapters 4, 19.

Keller, Thomas F., *The Uniformity-Flexibility Issue in Accounting* (Prentice-Hall, 1974).

McCosh, Andrew, "Accounting Consistency—Key to Stockholder Information," *The Accounting Review* (October 1967), pp. 693–700.

Prakash, Prem and Alfred Rappaport, "Information Inductance and Its Significance for Accounting," *Accounting Organizations and Society*, No. 1, (1977).

Smith, James E. and Nora P. Smith, "Readability: A Measure of the Performance of the Communication Function of Financial Reporting," *The Accounting Review* (July 1971), pp. 552–61.

Sterling, Robert R. and Raymond Radosevich, "A Valuation Experiment," *Journal of Accounting Research* (Spring 1969), pp. 90–95.

1. Resolved, that the accounting profession should embark on a research program aimed at developing the aggregate social welfare approach to accounting choices to the point where it is practical.
   (a) Make the case for the affirmative.
   (b) Make the case for the negative.
2. What are the weakest links in the criteria approach to accounting decisions?
3. Can you suggest an objective procedure, or a quantitative technique, for implementing the criteria approach?
4. Give two alternative definitions of relevance (as applied in accounting) other than the one presented in this chapter.
5. Ijiri and Jaedicke define objectivity as follows:

$$\text{objectivity} = \frac{1}{n} \sum_{i=1}^{n} (x_i - \bar{x})^2$$

   How does this differ from McKeown's verifiability? Is it a more useful measure?
6. List those procedures in generally accepted product cost accounting that contribute to the unreliability of the result.
7. Is McKeown's concept of accuracy an operational one?
8. What is the justification for including comparability as a major criterion of valuable information alongside relevance and reliability? Do all five of the "types of comparability" described in the chapter fit logically under one heading?
9. To which of the other listed criteria does the intelligibility criterion closely relate?
10. What is the difference between optimal partitioning and optimal aggregation?
11. Explain how a historical report of a past transaction can influence that transaction.

12. The story is told in one English-speaking country that a firm resisted a governmental agency's requirement for data about its expenditures for one special purpose. After repeated requests turned to threats, the firm finally printed out data for all checks for the two years in question and sent them to the government agency. It was then able to insist that it had provided the data required by law but the agency was never able to get the information it wanted from the mass of data submitted. On which criteria did the company's reporting to the governmental agency rank low? Can you give other examples of poor reporting by these criteria?

13. Assuming you are a shareholder, on the criterion of effects via other parties would you prefer:
    (a) The FIFO or LIFO cost flow assumption for stocks of fungible goods?
    (b) Historical cost or current market valuation for securities owned?
    (c) Capitalizing and amortizing or immediate expensing of training costs?
    (d) Recording business combination as purchases or as poolings?
    (e) Flow-through or deferral of the tax credit on investments in new machinery and equipment?

14. What improvements in current GAAP do you think investors and their analysts would like on the criterion of cost of utilizing data?

15. Accounting for "self-insurance" has been an issue in accounting for a long time. On the criterion of effects via other parties, which method of accounting for "self-insurance" (really no insurance against certain risks on some property) would you expect managements to prefer?

16. What percentage of revenues are the accounting costs in firms with which you are acquainted? What changes in these percentages would you expect from making major changes in measurement practices?

17. Do you believe that managers and investors might reasonably give different weights to the criterion of reliability? For example, could you visualize managers arguing for method

A because it outranks method B by a modest margin on the criterion of relevance whereas method B has a modest margin of superiority on the criterion of reliability, but investors arguing for method B because they give more weight to reliability than managers do? Consider a proposal that all training programs costing more than $5,000 be capitalized and amortized over the number of years equal to the reciprocal of the annual employee turnover rate in the category of personnel involved. What opportunities are there for variations in the application of such a rule? Would you expect managers to have more confidence in the prospects for uniform, consistent, unbiased application of such a rule than investors would have? If the firm were organized on a product-line basis with each divisional profit-investment center including training and accounting activities, would you expect the top management of the company to see this accounting proposal the way divisional managers would see it? The way investors would see it?

18. When stocks of fungible goods are measured at historical cost determined on LIFO or FIFO cost-flow assumption or by specific identification, it is common for apparently identical units to be included at different values. Is this a defect in these methods? On what criterion?

19. On what criteria does lower of cost and market valuation of inventories rate low?

20. Give examples of accounting rules, methods, or principles that rate low on intracompany and/or intraline comparability.

21. If you were the benevolent dictator over the field of accounting to investors, what standards pertaining to timeliness would you impose?

22. Assuming you do not consider the list of criteria provided in this chapter to be perfect for the evaluation of accounting proposals, how would you change it?

23. The management of the Buckman Corporation was concerned about proper determination of the balances of its allowance-for-uncollectibles account and its merchandise inventory account, so it had six different members of its accounting department staff and four of the auditor's staff make separate

measurements of each item. The inventory was to be valued
at FIFO cost or market, whichever is lower. The following
measurements were made:

Measurer	Uncollectibles	Inventory
A	$ 9	$ 95
B	10	101
C	8	107
D	13	100
E	9	97
F	7	102
G	11	98
H	11	100
I	13	102
J	9	98

During the next year, all of the receivables ($500) were collected
except $12 which was written off as uncollectible, each of
the debtors involved being adjudged bankrupt.

(a) For the allowance for uncollectibles, what is its (i) verifiabi-
    lity per McKeown, (ii) verifiability per Staubus, (iii) objec-
    tivity per Ijiri and Jaedicke (see question 5 above), (iv)
    accuracy per McKeown?
(b) For the inventory, compute the four measures listed in
    (a), if possible.
(c) Which account balance has the greater verifiability per
    McKeown?
(d) Which account balance has the greater verifiability per
    Staubus?
(e) For which account balance did you obtain the larger
    numerical measure of objectivity per Ijiri and Jaedicke?
    What is your intuitive answer?
(f) Which balance is measured more accurately? Is there any
    limitation to the applicability of this concept in these cases?

24. Select an accounting issue and reach a decision on it by use
    of the criteria approach as described in this chapter.

25. Should consistency between ex ante analysis and ex post
    reporting be used as a criterion of good accounting? For
    example, if a budget is adhered to perfectly, should the actual
    income statement show the same income as the budget showed?

Or, if a capital investment analysis showed that investment in a new plant would yield a certain rate of return, assuming the detailed projections were realized to perfection, should the financial statements show that same rate of return? If not, what is wrong?

26. In a nonfinancial decision context for which accounting data are *not* likely to be helpful, give examples of contrasting degrees of relevance of attributes of an object to a decision at hand.

27. Do you think that managers of corporations and other entities might prefer one accounting method over another because of the possibility that the latter may be more likely to (1) induce adverse changes in tax laws, economic controls, environmental protection requirements, or other undesirable governmental actions; (2) encourage tough bargaining by union leaders; or (3) impact adversely on the managers' personal welfare through compensation plans tied to reported earnings or through an image of less successful management? Do you have any evidence of how managers make the tradeoffs between these conflicting incentives?

28. Please refer to Appendix III-iii, entitled "Examples of Potential Economic Consequences of Accounting Standards," and outline a program for gathering evidence of the potential and/or actual consequences mentioned for any one of the FASB projects listed there.

29. Effects via other parties involve an evaluator of alternative accounting methods who is affected by the accounting outputs and another party through whom the effect acts.
    (a) Outline and give examples of effects via other parties, using several groups of evaluators as the primary headings in your outline.
    (b) Outline and give examples of effects via other parties, using several groups of other parties that are of concern to stockholders as the primary headings.

30. Explain how market inefficiency, or differential perception, can lead to adverse economic side effects of an accounting decision. Assuming a highly perceptive (efficient) market and recognition of this market perceptiveness, what economic side effects are managers likely to exhibit concern about?

CHAPTER IV

USERS AND USES OF FINANCIAL DATA

In this chapter, we focus on users of financial data and classify them according to their relationship with the reporting entity. Specifically, we are concerned with the users' direct interests in accounting as a source of information that will help them in making decisions. Our objective is to identify economic attributes of objects, such as assets and liabilities, and events, including transactions, that are relevant to users' decisions and are, therefore, appropriate for the accountant to measure. In this chapter we do not discuss the variations within any given class of decision makers, or provide a basis for making all accounting choices. Rather, we consider general patterns, in a brief overview of users' information needs,[1] in order to indicate the types of analysis and research that can be helpful in implementing the criteria approach to accounting decisions.

DECISIONS AND PREDICTIONS

To make a decision is to choose one of two or more alternative courses of action; in the absence of alternatives there is no choice to be made. The rational basis for choice is the evaluation and comparison of the alternatives. A general term that is applied to alternatives in the literature of decision theory is "strategies." A choice among alternative strategies is made on the basis of predicted values of the "choice criterion." These values are com-

---

[1] The term "need" in this study refers to the lack of something desired or useful; my usage differs from that of commentators who say that decision makers do not have information "needs" because they can make decisions without information.

monly discounted expected values in monetary units; if the range of possible outcomes is material in relation to the decision maker's wealth, monetary values may be converted to a certainty equivalent by application of the decision maker's utility function.

Prediction is inherent in all decisions: all alternative strategies are to be undertaken in the future; the resulting outcomes, or "payoffs" in financial terms, depend upon future conditions, called "states of nature" or "state variables." In most business decisions, many state variables are usually relevant. For example, a decision regarding the level of plant production capacity may require a prediction of sales, available materials, and available labor; these are state variables, upon which the profitability of plant expansion may depend. Predictions must be made for each state variable; subjective probabilities may be assigned to each of several values of a variable (e.g., high, low, and most probable values), or a mean and a probability function may be selected to represent the prediction. EXHIBIT IV-1 illustrates this general description of a decision process. In general, the process requires that the decision maker work from left to right and then back from right to left. He first identifies the alternative strategies (A and B) and the crucial state variables (X_1, X_2, and X_3). Then he identifies the sources of the positive and negative payoffs (receipts and costs). He can then predict the states and payoffs, aggregate the payoffs, and convert them to the type of measure in which the criterion of choice is stated, such as expected net present value.

EXHIBIT IV-1 is an incomplete and oversimplified picture of the decision-making process. When the diagram is complete, each branch ends at the extreme right with a payoff box at the tip like a piece of fruit. Also, in a typically complex economic environment, the number of strategies will be greater than two, the number of important state variables greater than three, and the number of possible values for each state variable large, if not spanning a continuous range. Clearly, the tree and the amount of work required to fill it out can be immense. This is typical of decision making in a complex environment when the stakes are large.

The role of information in a decision process of this general type is to change the probabilities that the decision maker attaches to the alternative values of the state variables and the payoffs.

EXHIBIT IV-1

AN OUTLINE OF THE DECISION PROCESS

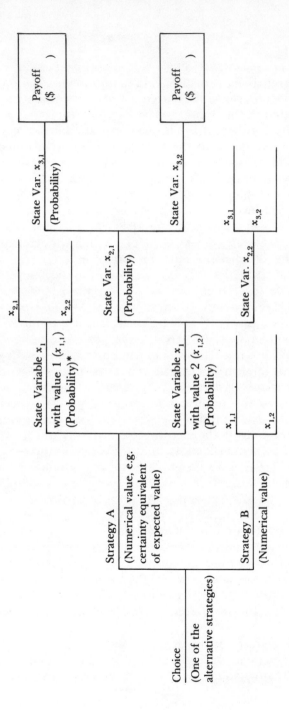

*As an example, if state variable x_1 is weather, value 1 is fair, and the probability of fair weather is .75, then $x_{1,1}$ = .75, and .75 should be entered in any space calling for $x_{1,1}$.

Assume that a decision maker has analyzed a problem, chosen feasible alternatives, and identified important aspects of the "state of the world" that bear upon his problem. Assume also that he has estimated the probabilities of realizing each alternative value of the state variables and payoffs at relevant future dates or over future periods. Now give him some information, such as a set of financial statements. The information provided will not affect his decision if it does not change his prior probability estimates of the value of the state variables or payoffs, or of which variables are relevant. Information is valuable to the direct user if it changes his "priors" and thereby improves his decision by causing him to elect a course of action with a higher payoff than the course he would have selected without the information. (Information may also be valued because it confirms a previous belief not held firmly.)

The brief review of decision making is designed to introduce the elements and the terminology common in the literature, and to illustrate the possible roles of accounting in the decision-making process. Accounting data, such as variances from standards or budgets, are often helpful in identifying a problem to be solved. In other cases, accounting data are said to be useful in identifying feasible strategies. But the more common role of external reports is to provide data that the decision maker uses to predict either state variables such as earnings, or payoffs such as dividends. In other words, the outputs of accounting systems are generally used as the inputs to prediction models.

Normative and Descriptive Decision Models

One unresolved issue in the relationship of accounting to decision models and prediction models is whether accountants should emphasize information for normative or for descriptive decision models. That is, should we concentrate on the way we think managers *ought* to make decisions or on the way they *do* make decisions? Sterling (1972, pp. 199–200) argues for emphasizing normative decision models:

> Decision makers are a diverse lot. They make their decisions on a wide variety of different bases. . . . Given this diversity, it is an economic, if not a physical, impossibility for us to

supply *all* the information that *all* decision makers want. Therefore, we must select and in the process of selection, we will fail to satisfy the wants of some decision makers. What we are arguing about then is the *basis* for selection.

The basis for selection that I prefer is to supply information for rational decision models. The modifier "rational" is defined to mean those decision models that are most likely to allow decision makers to achieve their goals. Since I don't believe that astrology allows people to achieve their stated goals, I am not interested in supplying them with an astrology report even though they use that kind of information in trading the market. For the same reason, I am not interested in supplying decision makers with some of the kinds of data now being included in accounting reports even though they use that data.

According to this view, some decisions are made by irrational methods; accountants should not contribute to such activities.

The contrary view is that accounting cannot be valuable if it supplies inputs to decision models that are not used. In addition, because accountants are not experts in decision making in fields such as security investments, marketing, production, and finance, they are in no position to decide which models are rational and which are not. Accountants should not become dictators of information: they should confine their investigations of decision making to "market research," in the sense that they should determine which potential accounting products are in demand by users. Advocates of descriptive decision models would agree with Abdel-khalik: "Perhaps it is the time for accountants to take cognizance of the concept of users' sovereignty" (1971, p. 470).

The normative advocates have some responses to those points:

1. If we only provide information for currently used decision models, improvements in decision making will be deterred because of a lack of data necessary to use new models. At best accounting could only begin to supply a new type of data after its usefulness, and a source of supply, had been established. Accounting would be put at a disadvantage in competition with other sources of information.

2. A survey of decision models in use is not likely to turn up models that require accounting-type data other than what is supplied by current accounting systems. Accounting

choices are effectively biased in favor of familiar methods; the novel accounting method does not seem to have a chance. On the criterion of attribute relevance, an attribute that is not now available would not be found to be used and if not used it is, according to the descriptive approach, not relevant.

3. If extant decision-making techniques are dysfunctional, contributing information for such uses may reduce the aggregate social welfare.

4. If we rely on descriptive models, changes in current accounting practice would be largely limited to:
   a. Elimination of duplication of information.
   b. Cost-reduction improvements in accounting methods.
   c. Adding the reporting of a type of information previously provided by another supplier and found to be in use.

On a broader level, the question may be raised whether it is more appropriate (1) to evaluate alternative accounting methods on the basis of current uses of accounting information, or (2) to evaluate alternative decision models on the basis of currently accepted accounting methods. Or do we need to assume that either the accounting outputs or the decision techniques are constant? The ideal ultimate solution might be to determine the information system and the decision model (or set of decision models for various uses) jointly, but this solution may be a long way off.

In the meantime, both accountants and decision makers must proceed with their daily work. As they do so, decision makers must rely heavily on the information that is routinely available to them; at the same time they may incur additional costs to obtain special information, while urging accountants and other suppliers of information to provide them with new types of data. Accountants, for their part, must attempt to meet the needs of current styles of decision making and respond to requests for new types of information to the extent it is feasible to do so. Different decision makers' demands for different information about the same object or event will continue to be a problem for accountants and decision makers. Fortunately, the evidence available at this time suggests that serious conflicts regarding which attributes of objects and events are relevant to decisions, due to use of different decision models for solving the same problem, are rare.

Accounting and Predictions

Some authorities who have emphasized the historical nature of accounting have tried to discourage accountants from concerning themselves with predictions. Bevis, for example, warned (1965, p. 68):

> A stockholder should bear in mind at all times that financial statements are not designed to predict the future, but to report on the past and present.

Chambers also has emphasized repeatedly that accounting deals with the past and the present, and excludes anticipatory calculations. For example (1966, p. 98):

> The word "account" has a commonly understood meaning which has persisted since its early appearance in the English language. It means to give a report of or to relate something that has happened. Now no one can give an account of something that has not yet happened, and something, indeed, which may not happen even if one sets out to procure its happening. To speak about accounting for the future is abuse of the language.

On the other hand, Sanders, Hatfield, and Moore observed that accounting must recognize the future (1938, pp. 21–22):

> . . . although accounting statements contain information about the past and the present, investors and credit agencies are constantly trying to read the future in them. While the accountant cannot make himself responsible for these prognostications, yet he must know that his statements will be put to such uses, and should not include anything which will definitely mislead a person of ordinarily intelligent familiarity with such matters, nor omit anything necessary to make the statements complete.

Their view is more consistent with the view taken in this book. Accountants unquestionably do, under current GAAP, make predictions and use the predictions of others as they prepare financial statements; examples include collectibility of receivables, lives of long-lived assets, and the longevity, turnover, and interest rate factors affecting pension costs. We recognize that the larger the role played by predictions the less reliable the resulting data.

However, perfect reliability is not possible; even the greatest reliability that may be feasibly attained may sometimes be sacrificed, justifiably, for the sake of the relevance of the attribute being measured. In view of this situation, there appears to be very little reason, other than the origin of the word "account," why accounting should be purged of all predictions. Extreme positions, including "accountants must never make predictions," ill become a professional field that is oriented towards service to many segments of society.

The more significant point, however, is that accounting is valuable largely because accounting outputs are useful in the prediction processes and models of *decision makers,* not those of accountants. Decisions always require predictions, if in no other way than to assume that the future will be like the past. For example, the most fundamental of all models of economic decision making, the comparison of incremental revenues and incremental costs of a proposed activity, requires future costs and revenue data. Past costs and revenues are not relevant to a decision about an activity except to the extent that they are useful bases for the prediction of future costs and revenues. The simplest prediction model is a simple extrapolation of past events: if it cost $x to perform a task the last time we did it, we may predict that it will cost $x to do it in the future.

More sophisticated prediction models include other parameters, but rarely do they exclude a past reading if it is available: in ongoing organizations the standard approach to budgeting starts with the most recent accounting data—past data—and makes adjustments for anticipated changes in state variables. It follows that the most directly useful accounting numbers measure attributes of objects and events, such as net realizable value (NRV) of an asset or operating cost in a department, that are the same as those required by decision models except for timing: decision models require future values of these attributes, while accountants are only able to report past or present values. Thus, accounting data on past sales are helpful to a manager who is deciding on expansion of production facilities to meet future demands of customers, that is, future sales. Similarly, an investor who is interested in predicting dividends will not ignore past dividends.

Many uses of accounting data for predictive purposes, however,

are not this simple and direct. Empirical researchers, in an effort
to compare the "predictive power" of accounting data produced
under alternative accounting methods, make tests of association
(e.g., correlation). In these tests researchers correlate accounting
numbers such as earnings, and events that decision makers seek
to predict such as dividends and stock prices. (For more on
predictive power, see chapter III, pp. 66–69.)

DECISIONS OF MANAGERS

The decisions made by entity managers at various hierarchial
levels are numerous and diverse. Although we shall not deal with
them in any degree of detail here, we will set forth a few of
their features.

The management role is often broken down by functions, such
as organizing, staffing, directing, planning, and controlling. In
discussions of the role of accounting in management, it is often
said that accounting data are most useful to managers in the
planning and control functions. If this is true—and we have no
basis for disagreeing—it raises the question discussed at the end
of chapter II: Does the decision-usefulness objective encompass
control? Consider Greenball's remarks:

> In my view, the role of accounting is to provide information
> in two quite different contexts: a) making *new* decisions and
> b) evaluating the quality of *past* decisions. These may be termed
> the planning (or ex ante) context, and the control (or "feed-
> back") or ex post context, respectively. Furthermore, account-
> ing is more likely to be useful in the control context rather
> than the planning context, in my opinion. . . . Cost and profit
> variances are computed and used to judge past performance
> and reward good past performance and division managers
> are rewarded and judged on the basis of past accounting
> measures of division performance.[2]

The uses of accounting data in planning and in controlling,
as Professor Greenball argues, should be distinguished. But both
planning and control involve decisions: a manager or management

---

[2] Melvin N. Greenball, letter to the author, 6 October 1972.

group makes control decisions, on the basis of feedback data, to investigate variances, change operating practices, reward subordinates (positively or negatively), or repeat activities that have paid off favorably.

Both planning and control decisions require predictions. We do not need to explain the relation between predictions and planning decisions, but a few comments about predictions for control decisions may be in order. We presume that a decision to investigate an unfavorable variance is based on a prediction that the variance will recur unless something is done about it. If the unfavorable variance is viewed as a one-shot, erratic event, nothing is done. But if the manager finds that the unfavorable variance is due to operating practices that he predicts will continue to produce excessive costs, he may decide to change operating practices. If a manager expects a subordinate's past superior or inferior performance to continue, he may decide to reward or remove the subordinate. And the repetition of past profitable activities typically is based on a prediction that similar activities will be profitable in the future. In all of these cases, if the historical accounting data have no predictive value, decisions based on them are likely to produce poor results. We conclude that the use of accounting data for both planning and control purposes requires predictive power.

One common category of information needed by managers is operating-cost data—the costs of doing things. In some cases, including cost-plus contracts and tax returns, accounting methods are specified by contract, regulations, or law; aside from these, managers typically use cost information to predict the costs of similar activities to be undertaken in the future. This suggests that accounting reports of operating costs should have high predictive value; it is particularly important because of the frequency with which activities are repeated, and because of the direct relevance of future costs to decisions about future activities. The better past activity costs are as surrogates for future costs, the better the basis for decisions. This point will come up again.

Many decisions of managers are aided by measures of management performance. What attributes of an entity's activities are relevant to such decisions? When information about management performance is sought, what can accountants contribute? The

concept of performance relates to carrying out a prescribed task
or meeting one's responsibilities: one "performs" when he accom-
plishes his objectives. The measurement of performance requires
that these objectives be quantified, a difficult step in some areas
such as learning an academic subject or improving product quality,
safety, training, research, employee morale, management development, and maintenance. Nonmonetary physical measures are
frequently used.

The measurement of an individual's *results* in such areas is also
difficult. If a manager has responsibilities in widely diversified
areas, such as safety, training, maintenance, product quality, and
product quantity, no single physical measure covers his performance adequately; several measures must be used for several areas
in which he performs, with the inevitable result that his overall
performance will be difficult to compare with that of another
person or another period. One answer to this is to convert
everything to a common denominator—money. For example, a
department manager's performance may be measured primarily
by the costs he incurs in comparison to a budget. Such a measure,
unfortunately, relates only to the inputs of resources and does
not encompass the quality of his output, or its quantity unless
the department adopts a flexible budget. The answer that many
firms have found is to decentralize operations in ways that give
a maximum number of managers responsibility for both inputs
and outputs, and for the difference—profit. But when profit is
computed in the conventional manner, the inputs of ownership
capital services are ignored. Return on owners' investment is a
measure that has been adopted to take this into account. But
emphasis on return on investment can lead managers of a highly
profitable division who have responsibility for capital expenditures
to pass up investments that would benefit owners but would lower
the average return on investment in the division. Therefore, the
residual income measure, after an imputed cost-of-capital charge
has been deducted, has been used for the sake of congruence
(see Dearden, 1961). The point is that we must expect that the
measure of management performance that is emphasized will have
a motivating influence; managers will strive for success by that
measure. If the measure is such that success for managers does
not contribute directly to success by the owners' criterion, this

lack of congruence can be expected to get poor results for the owners. (This point was discussed in chapter III under "Effects Via Other Parties.")

General recognition of the value of congruence of management and shareholder goals has led to widespread use of stock option plans and profit-sharing bonus plans as motivators of managers. The specter of the entrenched manager whose goals conflict with those of owners is occasionally invoked, but does not appear to be a common case. Let's assume, however, that such cases do occur. How might performance be measured in such a setting? What constitutes success for an entrenched management team that does not feel responsible for meeting owners' goals? Two types of managerial goals come to mind: (1) monetary rewards such as salary, bonus, and gains on stock options; and (2) direct utilities in the forms of prestige, satisfaction from work, and self-fulfillment. Because all of these benefits appear dependent upon the survival and financial growth of the firm, economic profit appears to be the central financial measure of entity success. Failure to cover costs, that is, to pay the returns necessary to attract resources, including equity capital, spells trouble for the entrenched (or any other) manager. Subject to the exceptions that (a) managers want to maximize their own salaries while owners classify manager's salaries among the costs to be minimized, and (b) managers want to minimize dividends while owners are interested in maximizing the value of dividends plus retained income (but not necessarily dividends alone), entrenched managers appear to have essentially the same view of costs, revenues, valuable resources, and claims against those resources as do the owners. For this reason we believe (but do not claim to have proven) that the attributes of entity resources and activities which are relevant to owners' investment decisions are also relevant to managers' judgments of their own, and their subordinates', performance. Now let us turn our attention to owners.[3]

---

[3] We are quite aware that this section has not done justice to the essence of managerial accounting; only the issue of attribute relevance has been given any serious attention, and that issue only in the context of the uses in which the relevant attribute has not been specified by agreement or law. This section's emphasis on prediction should not obscure the fact that information on events of the recent

DECISIONS OF OWNERS

The major classes of decisions made by owners and prospective owners are (1) investment decisions: to buy or not to buy, to sell or hold an ownership interest in the entity; and (2) voting decisions at shareholder meetings. Decisions that do not fall into either of these classes are likely to be minor in comparison.

Let's dispose of the voting decisions first. The voting issues that appear most frequently on the agendas of stockholders' meetings of American corporations, according to the author's informal survey, are (a) election of directors, (b) approval of the auditors, (c) approval of a management stock option plan, and (d) mergers. In some other countries, approval of the interim and proposed final dividends is common.

The question in which we are interested is: What types of financial accounting data can be useful in making these decisions? The general outlines of our answers are as follows:

(a) Election of directors—data helpful for appraising the performance of managers (including the directors themselves and their appointees).

(b) Approval of the auditors—no obvious financial accounting information.

(c) Approval of a management stock option plan—same as (a).

(d) Merger decisions—data helpful in comparing the investment value of the owners' interests in the company as it is and the value of their proposed interest in the proposed amalgamation.

(e) Approval of the dividend—data for predicting the return on capital in the hands of the company management (for comparison with its estimated return in other uses).

---

past is not only an excellent basis for predicting future events but, as it pertains to the bulk of two-party transactions, is almost always specified by contract or law as relevant to one or more purposes, e.g., fulfilling the terms of credit transactions (payables and receivables), completing payroll transactions and the related withholdings and filing payroll, property, sales, turnover, value-added, and income tax returns. In the major portion of the accounting department's daily work, which is tied to routine operating activities, attribute relevance is not an interesting issue, since there is no reasonable alternative to contractual amounts.

These answers appear to give no direct indications of the attributes of entity objects and events which are relevant to the voting decisions listed. But they do suggest that shareholder voting decisions for which entity financial data can be helpful may be reduced to two classes: (i) those for which information on *management performance* is helpful (a, c, and e), and (ii) those for which information for *investment decisions* is helpful (d). The former may be associated with decisions of managers, which have been covered in the previous section of this chapter; the latter will be dealt with in the next section.

The Classical View of Investment Decision Making

The present-value view of securities value has been recognized by finance scholars at least since Irving Fisher wrote, in 1906, that "the value of any capital-good, either of wealth or of property-rights, assuming that all future income is foreknown, is the discounted value of that income" (p. 223). This idea has become so widely accepted that Myron Gordon stated, more than half a century later, "The fundamental proposition of capital theory is that the value of an asset is the future payments it provides discounted at the appropriate rate" (1962, p. 3). The business school student learns this proposition early and repeatedly in either the undergraduate or graduate curriculum—in internal investment project analysis (capital budgeting), in bond valuation, and in the dividends and earnings capitalization models of stock valuation. Various editions of the Graham and Dodd classic, the traditional reference for security analysts, taught more than a generation of analysts to attempt to estimate the "intrinsic value" of a security for comparison with its current market price: "A general definition of intrinsic value would be 'that value which is justified by the facts, e.g., assets, earnings, dividends, definite prospects, including the factor of management' " (Graham, Dodd, and Cottle, 1962, p. 28). The objective of investment analysis is to find assets, such as securities, that are worth more than the price for which they can be purchased. In internal project analysis, the "net present value" criterion reflects the excess of the present value of future payoffs, discounted at the cost-of-capital rate or required rate of return, over the initial investment required. The same criterion is applicable to common stocks—if intrinsic value can be calculated.

The essence of the Graham and Dodd approach is to estimate the "average future earning power" and then apply "an appropriate 'capitalization factor,' " or multiplier, to it (p. 28). The multiplier will vary to reflect variations in (1) what is now called, in the jargon of security analysts, "the quality of earnings," which includes the degree of conservatism or lack thereof in the firm's accounting policies, and the extent to which nonrecurring credits or charges are included in earnings; (2) variability in earnings, especially "downside risk"; (3) growth of earnings; (4) percentage of earnings paid out as dividends; and (5) the required rate of return on common stock investments. This earnings capitalization model may be written

$$V = EM; \quad \text{if } V > P, \text{ buy}; \quad \text{if } P > V, \text{ sell}$$

where V is intrinsic value, E is the average annual future earnings projection, M is the multiplier or capitalization factor, and P is the current market price.

Another version of the classical valuation model is the dividends capitalization model:

$$V = \sum_{t=1}^{\infty} D_t (1 + r)^{-t}$$

Or, instead of capitalizing the entire stream of future dividends, a holding period, n years, may be assumed and the price at the sale date estimated:

$$V = \sum_{t=1}^{n} D_t (1 + r)^{-t} + P_n (1 + r)^{-n}$$

$$\text{where} \quad P_n = \sum_{t=n+1}^{\infty} D_t (1 + r)^{-t}$$

D_t is the dividend in any period, t; r is the required rate of return; and P is the market price of the security. A more sophisticated model, emphasizing net present value, is the one prepared by the AAA Committee on External Reporting in 1968. (See Appendix IV-ii.)

Now let's analyze these models in terms of the elements of the general decision process illustrated in EXHIBIT IV-1. The alternative strategies involve several securities (and perhaps other investment assets) in which the investor is seriously interested; the number may, of course, be much greater than two. The payoff variables are dividends (including liquidating dividends) and the market price, P_n, at a sale date. The state variables that need to be predicted, or estimated, are future earnings and an appropriate multiplier (for the earnings capitalization model); the future dividend series and the required rate of return (for the dividends capitalization model); and future dividends, future risk-free rates of return, the investor's certainty equivalent factor to adjust for risk, and the investor's marginal tax rate (in the case of the AAA Committee model).

The next step is to consider the information requirements for predicting or estimating the values of the state variables and payoff variables for the relevant periods or dates. The data needed may be divided into two categories: entity financial data and other data. The second category is outside the scope of the entity accountants' function; the first is his domain. EXHIBIT IV-2 tabulates what I consider to be the more obvious and pertinent types of data; the list may be revised if other information appears to be pertinent.

Note that information is needed about many *nonfinancial* variables with which accountants have very little to do. The types of *financial* data needed include several that are supplied in the normal course of events and do not involve measurement issues: accounting policies, separate disclosure of income charges or credits that may be classified as nonrecurring by the investor, stated capital, a five-year or ten-year summary of financial data, and data for the common ratios. Although these data all depend upon or follow from our solutions to the fundamental measurement problems, they contribute no insight that might be helpful in solving those problems. So let's focus on the basics—past earnings, evidence of cash flow potential, and past changes in cash flow potential.

The key issue of this chapter is: Do these decision models give accountants any clues as to which attributes of the entity's economic

Exhibit IV-2

Information Requirements of Classical Investment Decision Models

Variable to be predicted or estimated	Entity financial data that may be helpful	Other data that may be helpful
E (future earnings of entity).	Past earnings and revenues and expenses involved. Aspects of quality of earnings (conservatism of accounting, nonrecurring content, inflation effect).	Product demand schedule, future input prices, GNP, . . .
D (future dividends).	Present cash balance. Evidence of (+ or −) cash flow potential. Past changes in cash flow potential. Legality of dividends (stated capital).	Product demand schedule, future input prices, GNP, . . .
M (multiplier	Quality of past earnings.	Required rate of return.

applicable to earnings).	Variability of past earnings. Trend of past earnings. Past dividends/earnings ratio. Other financial relationships: debt/equity ratio, current ratio, times fixed charges earned . . .	
r (required rate of return).	None.	Yields on other investments.
P_n, I_{nk} (future price of stock).	Same as for D above except for more distant periods.	See D above.
α_{ik} (certainty equivalent factor to adjust for risk).	None.	None.
β_j (required risk-free rate of return before tax).	None.	Various.
m_{ik} (1-marginal tax rate of investor).	Data for predicting D and P_n (components of investor's taxable income).	Data for predicting D and P_n.

events and circumstances should be measured and reported to investment decision makers? Or, in more conventional accounting terminology, assuming that positive and negative stocks of economic resources (assets and liabilities) and changes in those stocks are to be measured, what measurement methods are most relevant to the decisions of investors? The Graham (earnings capitalization) formula emphasized future earnings and a multiplier; past earnings are listed as helpful for judging both. Does this relationship give accountants any insight as to *how to measure earnings?* We contend that it does not—except that it suggests that accountants should try to smooth earnings so as to yield a more stable series of earnings data. Such stability permits the analyst to put more weight on past earnings as a base for predicting future earnings. It could, in the absence of other guidelines, lead the accountant to all sorts of arbitrary smoothing gimmicks such as deferring all extraordinary gains and losses and amortizing them over five years, and generally spreading the effects of the economic events of one period over several periods. I do not believe that choosing a measure of earnings on the basis of its usefulness in predicting its own value in a future period will result in the choice of a measure that will be of greatest usefulness in predicting payoffs to investors. If that were true, it would seem wise to assume that each revenue and expense item was exactly the same as last period unless proof of a change could be presented, as this would help assure stability of reported earnings. Ability to predict itself does not appear to be a useful quality of a state variable in a decision model.

Another way of looking at earnings is to relate them to the Fisher and Gordon concepts of the value of a "capital-good" or "asset." The asset or capital good in question is the share of stock about which the investor is trying to decide. If the phenomenon called "earnings" is properly treated as a positive factor in the estimation of stock value, and if "stock value" means present value of future cash flows to the owner of the stock, then there must be a reason to believe that higher earnings will lead to higher cash distributions by the corporation, to earlier distributions, or to a reduction in the discount rate: these are the only ways to increase that present value. Earnings are, of course, related to all three of these factors. The discount rate, for example, might be reduced by reporting more stable earnings, because more stable earnings imply lower risk and a lower discount rate. But stability as a criterion of an earnings measure was rejected above. Surely a better reason for investors' interest in earnings is their association with the *amounts* and *timing* of future cash distributions to the shareholders. For this reason, we turn to the amounts and timing of future dividends as possible considerations in the design of a useful earnings measure.

The dividends that we are concerned with presumably are cash dividends. Distributions of other property are rare and would be relevant to most investors only to the extent of their cash equivalent; dividends on common shares "payable" in common shares are not payoffs to investors. Cash dividends require entity cash for payment: any prediction scheme ought to begin with this fundamental fact. Future cash dividends depend upon (1) the firm's capacity to pay cash, that is, its cash balance, at the proposed dividend date; (2) its legal right to pay dividends; and (3) the willingness of the board of directors to use its cash balance for immediate dividends. (Some alternatives to this third contingency are application to prior claims, investment in earning assets that are anticipated to yield at least a satisfactory return to shareholders, or holding as protection against the risk of insolvency.)

The firm's legal right to pay dividends is easily disclosed once it has calculated the owners' equity. Dividends are roughly the excess of owners' equity over stated capital. Owners' equity is computed, of course, when assets and liabilities are computed and compared. This line of thought leads to a dead end, too: recognition of the *need* to measure assets and liabilities does not help us determine *how* to measure them.

The directors' willingness to use the available cash for dividends depends upon their other needs for cash, after the dividend date. The information needed by one who seeks to predict directors' willingness to pay is of the same nature as that needed to predict capacity to pay as of the same date, but it is extended further into the future. If the analyst predicts that the firm will be *able* to pay $x at December 31, any prediction that the directors will be *willing* to pay an amount less than $x must be based on projections of firm needs for cash beyond December 31. Putting the two together, the time horizon for this information need is open-ended;

any information is relevant that helps predict any future cash flows of the entity. We shall use the term "cash flow potential" to mean any element of the wide pool of economic circumstances pertaining to the entity that has a potential impact on the entity's cash inflows and outflows. *Evidence of cash flow potential is the accountant's domain in relation to the investor's concern with predicting dividends.* Past changes in cash flow potential provide a starting point for predicting future changes in cash flow potential. If the accountant can measure any parts of the pool of cash flow potential consistently, and if he can also measure the changes in this pool, he has a chance of being helpful to the investor who is trying to predict dividends. This suggests that *the stocks of economic resources and obligations that accountants are concerned with are positive and negative cash flow potentials,* and that *the changes in economic resources and obligations are changes in cash flow potential.* The relevance of this conclusion to the definition and measurement of assets, liabilities, and income will be discussed in future chapters.

Portfolio Construction in Efficient Markets

A capital market theory has been developed in recent years which suggests that the investment strategy of selecting securities that will outperform the market average cannot be expected to be successful. Some of the key points in this theory follow:

1. The "market," that is, all buyers and sellers in the market, assimilates and processes all information made available to it almost instantaneously and in an unbiased manner.
2. Security prices at any time fully reflect all information available to the market. "A market in which prices always 'fully reflect' available information is said to be 'efficient,' " (Fama, 1970, p. 384; Fama also reviews the evidence supporting the hypothesis that securities markets are efficient.)
3. An individual investor cannot use publicly available information to obtain returns (dividends plus change in price) in excess of the average on the "market portfolio" (a portfolio consisting of all securities on the market) except by choosing more risky securities or by chance. Investors should not try to "beat the market" because they cannot do it.
4. A capital asset pricing model of the following general type

specifies the appropriate relationship between risk and expected returns (dividends and change in price, and hence future price based on known current price):

$$E(\tilde{R}_{i,t}) = R_{f,t} + \beta_i [E(\tilde{R}_{m,t}) - R_{f,t}]$$

$E(\tilde{R}_{i,t})$ is the expected return on security i in period t; $R_{f,t}$ is the known return available on a risk-free asset (generally thought of as a government security maturing at the end of period t); β_i reflects the extent to which returns on security i vary with returns in the market as a whole; and $E(\tilde{R}_{m,t})$ is the expected average return available in the market. The expected return on any security is the risk-free rate plus a risk premium that depends upon the volatility of the particular security. The risk premium on the market as a whole is the price that investors charge for taking the risks inherent in the typical investment, rather than settling for the risk-free investment. The risk premium is determined by the diverse tastes of all market participants in the same way as other prices are set in a competitive market. β_i is approximated by $\sigma(R_{it}, R_{mt})/\sigma^2(R_{mt})$ and has a value of 1 for any security that fluctuates to the same extent as the market as a whole. A more volatile security has a β value greater than 1; a less volatile security has a β between 0 and 1. A β value of zero implies no fluctuation whatsoever and so represents the risk-free security. EXHIBIT IV-3 depicts the relationship between risk and expected return at a given time. (The relationship can change over time as the market's taste for risk changes.) $E(\tilde{R}_m) - R_f$ is the risk premium that market participants attach to the average investment (which has a β of 1). $E(\tilde{R}_i) - R_f$ is the risk premium on security i (which has a β of .7).

5. Risk is divisible into two types. Systematic risk, measured by β above, is related to the fluctuations in the market; individual risk is peculiar to the firm and the specific security. The latter can be eliminated by diversification; the former cannot. The investor must decide for himself, based on his utility function, how much systematic risk he is willing to accept in exchange for greater returns. He may then choose securities that are consistent with his risk preferences. Financial data pertaining

EXHIBIT IV-3
RELATIONSHIP BETWEEN SYSTEMATIC RISK (β) AND EXPECTED RETURN

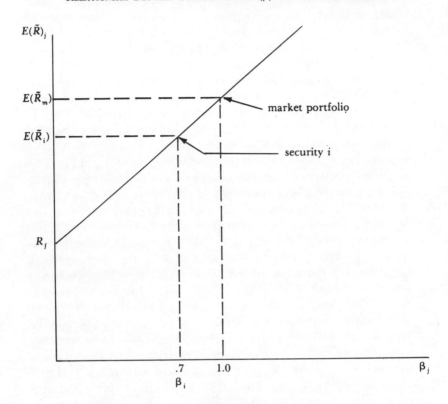

to the firm are helpful for this selection.

The implications of this capital market theory for the making of accounting decisions could be significant (Beaver, 1972). Some of the possibilities are discussed in the following paragraphs:

1. An individual investor could limit his use of financial data to use in estimating risk—if he cannot beat the market return.[4]

---

[4] In fact, if he is willing to accept the average market risk, the investor need not even estimate the risk in any specific security; he can buy a sufficiently large random sample of securities to represent both the return and the risk characteristics

At a minimum, portfolio theory puts greater emphasis on risk than does the classical theory of investment choice. Accountants might respond by providing more information that might be helpful to the investor in assessing risk. (See chapter XII.)

2. Many accounting issues involving alternative measurement rules are not very important because the efficient (perceptive) market will use the accounting method it prefers, provided that the necessary information is made available in some form from some source. *Disclosure* of the difference between LIFO inventories and FIFO inventories, for example, appears to serve the efficient market satisfactorily, regardless of which method is used in the financial statements. Several empirical research studies support this view (Kaplan and Roll, 1972; Sunder, 1973). "Bottom line fixation" is a disease to which an efficient market is immune.

3. In an efficient market, accounting researchers can test which of two or more widely understood accounting methods the market prefers; the method that produces numbers (such as earnings) more consistent with market behavior is presumably the method that the market prefers to rely upon. Once these preferences are disclosed by empirical research, accountants should provide the preferred data—as a minimum. Alternative data could also be supplied if there were some other strong reason, such as the requirements of a normative decision model, for doing so.

However, it does seem appropriate to warn of the possibilities of jumping to conclusions that are not warranted. For example:

1. We cannot conclude that accounting need not provide data for use in attempting to beat the market. The whole concept of market efficiency depends upon many investors trying hard

---

of the market as a whole. He does, however, need information about the return and risk offered by the market in order to determine his investment-consumption pattern over time. If the investor is not satisfied with the risk and return offered by the market as a whole, he could, adopting an alternative policy, seek an increased return (and accept the associated increase in risk) by borrowing additional funds to invest; or he could seek a reduced risk (and return) by investing part (or all) of his funds in a "risk-free" asset.

to earn superior returns; without their efforts the market would not be efficient and the resulting prices would not have the "fair game property" that they appear to have now. The opportunity to use public information to produce private information that permits superior predictions of return and/or risk gives the profit motive a role in the fair pricing of securities. If the profit motive is to have the effects that are generally claimed for it, information that is relevant to judging values would seem to be just as important in securities markets as in other markets. Market efficiency is fundamental analysis in action. The "let George do it" attitude of a few small investors (price takers rather than price makers) is quite acceptable as long as there are plenty of Georges trying to find securities that are worth more (or less) than their current prices. From the point of view of accountants, if we recommend that small investors ride on the coattails of an efficient market, we should take the steps necessary to assure that the market does price securities fairly. This seems to require information for predicting dividends to be paid on each stock. George cannot do his part in pricing a security fairly without firm-specific data that is relevant to the prediction of returns.

2. We cannot conclude that all accounting arguments can be acceptably settled by disclosure of results under alternative methods in case of doubt. Such disclosure is a valuable back-up system for occasional use, but if it is overused difficulties will arise on the optimal quantity criterion: one way of failing to communicate useful information is to report too much.

Decisions of Owners—Conclusions

As of this writing, the classical models of investment decision making appear to be popular; thousands of investors are trying to beat the market. But there is compelling evidence that the market for listed stocks in the United States can efficiently process *familiar* types of information *made available to it.* Small investors are thus unlikely to beat the market by enough to pay their transaction costs and analysis costs; their best protection may be in diversification, minimal trading (perhaps holding mutual fund shares), and relying on the efficiency of the market. Professional investors, on the other hand, might reasonably be expected to continue their search for new types of information and new interpretations of familiar data in an effort to beat the market. Such investors, on whom today's limited degree of market efficiency depends, must continue to estimate future returns as well as risks.

We conclude that market efficiency, or market perceptiveness, does not invalidate the classical models and the role of accounting in supplying information to them, but it does suggest that information pertinent to the estimation of risk should receive more emphasis than it has in the past. Market efficiency also suggests that an appropriate solution in some cases is to disclose information that would permit adjustment to an alternative accounting method. This solution should not be overused, however: it should be reserved for cases in which the heterogeneity of users' decision processes does not permit a single solution, and for other difficult cases.

The "accounting mission" is to make available to market participants the best possible set of information for use in making investment decisions. One step in accomplishing that mission is to ascertain the content of the information set the market is now using. In addition, normative decision models may provide a basis for including other data in the set to be provided, so that investors may choose between limiting themselves to the old data and supplementing it with the new.

DECISIONS OF LENDERS

Lenders include those parties who deliberately become creditors of the entity and wait for repayment in exchange for consideration known as interest. They include lessors and holders of the firm's debentures, mortgages, bonds, and promissory notes.

The basic decision made by lenders is the decision to make the loan or invest in debt securities. Potential lenders comprise, therefore, a major portion of the "lenders" category for the purposes of this analysis. Existing lenders have the choice of selling or assigning their claims, if they are negotiable; sometimes existing lenders are asked to renew their loan agreement. They may also have the opportunity to decide on the enforcement of certain provisions or restrictive covenants included in the original loan contract. Potential lenders also may have the opportunity to decide on any restrictive covenants to be included in the contract, or indenture, and to make decisions about such basic features as liens, mortgages, interest rates, maturity dates, and terms of partial or premature repayment.

The common decisions made by lenders may be divided into two groups: (1) the basic decisions—to lend or not lend, to sell or hold the debt security, and to renew or not renew the loan; (2) the secondary decisions—involving security arrangements, restrictive covenants, interest rates, maturity dates, prepayment arrangements, and other provisions of the loan contract. The first group of decisions clearly involves predicting the entity's capacity to pay, in cash, at the times and in the amounts called for in the contract. Willingness to pay is not as significant a factor as it is in the prediction of dividends, because creditors have substantially more power to force payment, although their power does have its limitations. The second group of decisions also involves predictions of the entity's capacity to pay. The greater the lender's doubt about repayment, the more restrictive covenants and liens he is likely to insist upon and the higher the interest rate he requires to cover the risk. In order to make his decisions the lender will need a great deal of information about the entity other than financial information. However, to the extent that his needs for financial information can be met by the entity, this information is likely to consist of evidence of the entity's future capacity to pay, that is, *evidence of its future cash flows and present cash resources.* This is the category of financial information about the entity that can help lenders predict the payoffs that will result from making a specific type of loan.

One may observe that lenders give a good deal of attention to concepts other than future cash flows and present cash resources. Lenders often use terms such as "current ratio," "debt-equity ratio," and "liquidity," and they give the underlying concepts heavy weight. It is important to recognize, however, that these concepts are important only to the extent that they are clues to the borrower's future ability to pay. Indeed, they are good examples of the indications of future cash flows in which decision makers are interested. But they are only as good as the underlying measurements that go into their computation.

The similarity between the financial information needed to make decisions about investing as a creditor and that needed to make decisions about investing as a shareholder is obvious. What are the differences? The major fundamental difference is the length of the period for which the entity's capacity to pay is of concern. At one extreme, a short-term lender need not be very concerned about the entity's cash flows and capacity to pay much beyond the few months of his loan term; the shareholder, however, must predict dividends for whatever period he will hold the security (usually unknown), plus a further period that is of interest to his successor (and perhaps his successor's successor). This difference in "horizons" usually does not result in conflicting views of the measurement of specified potential cash flows because if the time of the prospective flow is within the lender's horizon, he and the shareholder will have substantially the same interest in it; if the time is well beyond the lender's horizon he will have no interest in it at all. Lender and shareholder may, however, disagree on the significance of disclosing the time dimension of a potential cash flow. To the former, cash flows that are expected to occur prior to the date of termination of the loan differ markedly from those expected later; to the shareholder, whose interest in the firm has no definite termination date, timing is not critical as long as the amount is properly discounted.

Lenders and owners also have different interests in information regarding priorities among claimants if the firm cannot pay all. The owner or common shareholder knows where he stands without any specific data, but the holder of a preferred stock, a subordinated debenture, or a mortgage note, for example, expects the priorities within the capital structure to be clarified, so that he can judge the risk he is taking. These two special concerns of lenders—timing and priorities—have implications for the classification of balance sheet items; they should be taken into consideration when financial statements are being designed.

Decisions of Suppliers

Sellers of commodities and services on credit have a creditor's interest in their customers. The supplier's decision to sell to a particular company on credit requires that he predict the buyer's capacity to pay, just as in the case of a short-term lender. The role of accounting information in such a prediction of payoff and decision has been covered in the preceding section.

The supplier is also concerned with the viability of his relationship with the firm in many instances, particularly when long-term contracts involve a major portion of his output for several years as, for example, in the mining and aerospace industries. Even if the customer pays cash on delivery, the supplier gears up to provide the customer's needs on a continuing basis. The commitments that he makes are decisions and they must be based on predictions of the costs and revenues involved in the relationship for a considerable period of time. Thus, the supplier is greatly interested in the customer's financial stability, and in his prospects for continuing the type and volume of business on which the supply relationship depends. He might reasonably look to the customer's financial statements for evidence along this line. Information that is useful for this purpose includes two obvious categories: information on the customer's capacity to pay all of his debts as they fall due, that is, his solvency; and information on the stability of his volume of operations, as indicated by total sales within the category for which the supplier's product is used. A firm's financial report surely can, in some instances, be useful to its major suppliers when they make decisions regarding the volume, price, and other terms of long-term contracts, as well as when they decide on the extension of credit to the customer.

DECISIONS OF CUSTOMERS

The interest of customers in the economic affairs of an entity does not usually require that they predict its capacity to pay cash directly; rarely is a customer in a position of having a cash claim against its supplier, although advances by customers and returns of merchandise by customers provide occasional exceptions. Generally, the customer is concerned with product quality, quantity, and price, and with service, warranty follow-up, delivery details, and the maintenance of these features throughout a continuing relationship (such as a major, long-term contract). We can easily see how a supplier could provide financial information that would help a customer make a decision on a price, or make any decision in which the reliability of the supplier as a continuing source of supply is a factor. The type of financial information that would help the customer in price bargaining is the same type that the supplier uses in pricing decisions. This presumably includes some cost information and, perhaps, capacity data. The supplier's willingness to provide information that might help a customer judge the supplier's ability to execute a long-term contract and his reliability as a continuing source of supply appears to be the same as that discussed from the supplier's point of view in the previous section.

DECISIONS OF EMPLOYEES

Employees, and potential employees, are likely to be involved in two types of decisions about the entity for which financial information may be helpful. One is the decision to become or remain an employee. In this connection, an individual may use information pertaining to a firm's prospects for continuity (which is sometimes broken by an entity's inability to pay debts as they fall due), and for growth: these factors may affect the employee's prospects for continued employment, promotion, and remuneration through profit-sharing plans, stock options, and straight salary. The other type of decision is the wage or salary contract. The employee, or representative of a group of employees (union negotiator), may want to know the firm's or division's "profitability" and other factors that may affect its ability and willingness to grant wage increases to employees. In this use, the way profit is computed may not be important; the fact that it is perceived by *management* as profit is what makes it important to the union because the firm's profitability may affect management's willingness to yield to union demands.

DECISIONS OF OTHERS

The major interest to be considered under this heading is that of "the public" or society. Voters and their representatives, influenced heavily by information and opinions transmitted through the communications media, could be called the most significant group of decision makers. Changes in laws that affect business corporations occur fairly frequently; many of these changes involve consideration of factors that are, or could be, disclosed in financial reports. For example, legislators voting on requirements for expensive new pollution control equipment in a particular industry may want information about the profitability of that industry. Or legislation pertaining to the influence of insurance company investments on the share market may be more sensibly drafted if the legislators have information about the insurance industry's holdings of, and transactions in, securities. However, in view of the potential diversity of such uses of financial information about an entity's affairs, which involve specific decisions based on specific information, these possbile needs are not examined further.

CONCLUSION

Chapter III included definitions and explanations of a set of criteria that should be useful in evaluating alternative accounting methods. One of these criteria is relevance of the attribute being measured to the decisions of users of accounting data. In this chapter we have explored the nature of significant types of decisions by the major users of accounting data and, in the process, have identified some attributes of entity activities and status which are relevant to those decisions. Accounting is concerned with the measurement of those attributes and the communication of those measurements to decision makers.

Limited explorations of several common decision situations have suggested that the primary role of accounting data in these decision situations is to provide evidence useful to the decision maker in predicting the firm's future capacity to pay, that is, evidence of its present cash balance and of future cash flows. A simple version of the present shareholder's decision problem is:

The shareholder determines his payoff from selling "now" by obtaining a quotation from the share market, usually by telephoning a broker. He estimates the payoff from holding with the aid of a variety of techniques, some of which are aimed at the prediction of dividends and incorporate financial data that can be supplied by accountants.

The decisions of prospective shareholders, prospective lenders, prospective suppliers, customers, and employees may be diagrammed in a similar fashion. In each case, doing business with the reporting firm is one alternative, and accounting data have a chance of contributing to the decision by providing evidence of the firm's future capacity to pay.

We cannot expect accounting data to contribute significantly to the evaluation of every alternative of every decision of every party interested in the firm. It does appear, however, that accounting data can be helpful to some people in evaluating one alternative of certain decisions, and that the most significant contribution that accounting data can make to these decisions is to provide evidence that is useful in predicting the firm's future cash flows and, thereby, its future capacity to pay. In subsequent chapters we will focus on information for this purpose, which we shall sometimes refer to as information relevant to cash-flow-oriented decisions.

ADDITIONAL READING SUGGESTIONS

Archer, Stephen H., "The Structure of Management Decision Theory," *Academy of Management Journal* (December 1964), pp. 269–87; rpt. in Alfred Rappaport, ed., *Information for Decision Making* (Prentice-Hall, 1970), pp. 3–19.

Bierman, Harold, Jr., "The Implications to Accounting of Efficient Markets and the Capital Asset Pricing Model," *The Accounting Review* (July 1974), pp. 557–62.

Boothman, Derek, et al., *The Corporate Report* (Accounting Standards Steering Committee, 1975), sections 1–6.

Dyckman, Thomas R., David H. Downes, and Robert P. Magee, *Efficient Capital Markets and Accounting: A Critical Analysis* (Prentice-Hall, 1975), chapter 5.

Financial Accounting Standards Board, *Tentative Conclusions on Objectives of Financial Statements of Business Enterprises* (FASB, 2 December 1976).

Greenwood, William T., ed., *Decision Theory and Information Systems* (South-Western Publishing Co., 1969).

Kassouf, Sheen, *Normative Decision Making* (Prentice-Hall, 1970).

Lev, Baruch, *Financial Statement Analysis: A New Approach* (Prentice-Hall, 1974).

Lindley, D. V., *Making Decisions* (Wiley-Interscience, 1971).

May, Robert G. and Gary L. Sundem, "Cost of Information and Security Prices: Market Association Tests for Accounting Policy Decisions," *The Accounting Review* (January 1973), pp. 81–94.

Revsine, Lawrence, *Replacement Cost Accounting* (Prentice-Hall, 1973), chapters 1, 2.

Staubus, George J., *A Theory of Accounting to Investors* (University of California Press, 1961; rpt. Scholars Book Co., 1971), chapters 1, 2.

Wilson, Charles A. and Marcus Alexis, "Basic Frameworks for Decisions," *Journal of the Academy of Management* (August 1962), pp. 150–64; rpt. in William T. Greenwood, ed., *Decision Theory and Information Systems* (South-Western Publishing Co., 1969), pp. 63–82.

STUDY QUESTIONS

1. Do the decision processes of different members of a user group vary enough to affect the choice of accounting methods? Give examples. Do the varying needs within a user group necessarily conflict or can they all be met?
2. What elements are common to all decisions?
3. What is the role of information in decision making?
4. Define the following terms as used in decision theory: strategy, state of nature, payoff, expected value, risk, uncertainty, subjective probability.
5. On what grounds may an accountant argue in favor of supplying information other than what is called for by the current decision processes of users?
6. How is accounting related to the future?
7. How are decisions related to the future?
8. "To begin the discussion, it may be useful to point out that

all decisions are related to a choice of actions to be taken in the future. The clues are *all* from the past and the immediate task is to decide *what* events about the past promise to be relevant to probable choices to be made in the future" (Devine, 1971, p. 25). Do you agree? What implications does this position have for the development of accounting theory?

9. Do control uses of accounting information involve prediction? Generally? Always?

10. Describe a case in which the goals of top management and the goals of shareholders would be in serious conflict.

11. Give examples of issues on which shareholders are asked to vote, including some not mentioned in the chapter, and suggest the nature of the information requirements for voting on those issues.

12. Explain the relationship between earnings per share and shareholders' payoffs.

13. What are the determinants of the "quality of earnings"?

14. What is the relationship between the earnings capitalization model and the dividends capitalization model?

15. What information requirements of the AAA Committee on External Reporting investment decision model can be met by accounting? (See Appendix IV-ii.)

16. What revisions of EXHIBIT IV-2 would you suggest?

17. Is emphasis on "cash flow potential" as a state variable in the investment decisions of owners and others justified:
    (a) If the investor takes a classical valuation approach to investment decisions?
    (b) If the investor believes that securities are fairly priced and that he cannot beat the market?
    (c) If he believes that securities are fairly priced on the basis of information available to and generally understood by market participants but that it is possible to do superior analytical work which produces private information?

18. Define: business risk, financial risk, systematic risk, individual security risk.

19. Do you believe that the share market in your country is efficient at the semi-strong level? What evidence do you have?

20. If securities are fairly priced on the basis of publicly available information, can you see any likely ill effects from discontinuance of publication of corporate annual reports?

21. How do the information requirements of lenders differ from those of owners who are attempting to predict return and risk on individual securities? Does the efficiency of the market apply to debt securities in the way that it applies to equities?

22. "For example, consider the two major classes of users identified in the [Objectives Study Group] Report—creditors and investors. The payoff-relevant partition of future states will vary considerably between these two classes. The creditor is concerned with two basic events: default and no default, with finer partitions on the former. The investor [shareholder], on the other hand, is concerned with finer partitions of the no default event" (Beaver and Demski, 1974, p. 180). Do you agree?

23. Give examples of entity-supplier relationships such that the supplier would be vitally concerned with the entity's finances.

24. Give examples of entity-customer relationships such that the customer would be vitally interested in the entity's financial statements.

25. How do the interests of parties other than those given specific attention in this chapter relate to EXHIBIT III-1?

26. Do you agree that the measurement of an entity's cash flow potentials and changes therein is a reasonable primary measurement objective of accounting? Has the chapter made an adequate case for this position?

27. One way of summarizing the decision-usefulness basis for accounting decisions is to prepare a "users and uses matrix" which illustrates the importance to be attached to each category of users and the uses, states or payoffs in which they are interested by allocating 100 points over the various cells of the matrix. Here is an opportunity for you to use your imagination and understanding of users' needs: construct such a matrix.

CHAPTER V
STOCK CONCEPTS FOR USEFUL BALANCE SHEETS

The first four chapters have set the stage for a study of measurement in accounting. In particular, in chapter III an evaluative framework was developed that included a set of nine criteria that may be used in making choices between alternative accounting methods. Relevance of the attribute being measured to the decisions of the user was emphasized as the first criterion of useful information. Chapter IV included a survey of the common decisions of users of financial statements in an effort to isolate attributes of economic objects and events that (a) could be helpful to decision makers if known, and (b) can be measured and reported by accounting methodologies not drastically different from those with which accountants are now familiar. The results of that survey suggested that accountants should focus much of their attention on attributes relevant to the prediction of the firm's cash flows.

This chapter is devoted to the development of stock concepts that can be helpful in the type of accounting necessary to provide useful financial information to economic decision makers. The specific terms emphasized here are "financial position," "asset," "liability," and "residual equity." Defining these terms in this chapter will permit us to consider their measurement in the following three chapters.

AN APPROACH TO BALANCE SHEET CONCEPTS

We have used phrases such as "evidence of future cash flows" and "cash flow potential." We must now distinguish between "stock concepts" and "flow concepts." Stocks are existing quantities of things. Flows are movements of something, changes in stocks. In the analogous case of a tank storing a liquid, past inflows and outflows determine the present level of the liquid in the tank; the present stock represents a potential flow to another position. Balance sheet concepts are stock concepts. To the extent that cash movements are the future flows of interest to decision makers, the relevant stock concepts are cash flow potential, both positive and negative. Stocks of cash flow potentials are matters of fundamental interest to future-cash-flow-oriented decision makers. The stock concepts that are central to accounting must be measures of cash flow potential. In practice, however, we often must measure the present stock of cash flow potential by reference to the past flows that brought about the present position. The deficiencies in such "surrogate" measures are not visible in the liquid analogy because, except for expansion due to rising temperature or reduced pressure, the gallons of liquid in a tank, like cash itself, cannot grow except by means of inputs, whereas the cash flow potential of an accounting entity can grow "internally" by means of income.

After having emphasized the need for cash-flow-oriented stock concepts, we should note that, in a strict sense, an asset can be both valuable to its owner and significant to other users of financial statements even if it never contributes to anyone's cash flows. For example, a stock of one thousand cases of wine may be distributed to shareholders and consumed by them. Inclusion of such a stock as a corporate asset prior to its distribution is entirely appropriate. Assets with no cash flow potential may also exist in barter economies. These exceptions make it clear that definitions of asset and other stock concepts strictly in terms of cash flow potential would be a bit too narrow for general use; we should not require absolutely that a valuable economic resource be converted to cash to be considered an asset. Nevertheless, the limitations may be so slight that overlooking them for the sake of clearer exposition is justifiable. We do not feel obligated to allow for noncash payoffs to investors in our definitions of stock concepts.

Before discussing concepts of assets and liabilities, we should consider a more fundamental idea, the role of the balance sheet. Should we take it for granted that a balance sheet is to be presented? Why? What is the function of the balance sheet? An older approach may have emphasized the value of showing that the ledger balances and that there have been no obvious errors or omissions that raise questions about the honesty or competence of the accountant or management. But that narrow objective of balance sheet presentation is inconsistent with our approach. The primary function of the balance sheet, as a report to outside decision makers, must relate to the decision maker's need to predict the firm's capacity to pay. Could a balance sheet be viewed as a "statement of cash flow potentials"? Surely "balance sheet" provides only a tiny clue to the contents of the statement. Alternative terms, such as "statement of financial condition" or "statement of financial position" convey a great deal more information about the contents of the statement—if the reader sees some meaning in the term "financial condition" or in "financial position." Regardless of the name we give to the statement, let us tentatively accept the term "financial position" to signify the conglomeration of information that we intend to convey by means of a balance sheet.

FINANCIAL POSITION

The function of the balance sheet and the meaning of financial position have seldom been considered in depth. The classic pejorative remark by Canning (1929, p. 180) still applies to the state of accounting thinking: "Financial position is that which the balance sheet is intended to reflect." The APB was similarly ambiguous in 1970 (pp. 50–51):

> The financial position of an enterprise at a particular time comprises its assets, liabilities, and owners' equity and the relationship among them, plus those contingencies, commitments, and other financial matters that pertain to the enterprise at that time and are required to be disclosed under generally accepted accounting principles. The financial position of an enterprise is presented in the balance sheet and in notes to the financial statements.

Let's briefly review Canning's concept of financial position. After pointing out that "financial" pertains to finance and that "all recognized branches of finance have regard for both procurement and distribution of funds," he presented the following analysis:

Four Possible Meanings of "Financial Position."—A "position" to be "financial" must, therefore, be a position with respect both to fund procurements and to fund distributions. Fund procurements, with reference to any specified date, may be either past or future procurements; so also may distributions be past or future. There are, therefore, four possible pairings which may be shown schematically thus:

Fund procurements that: Fund distributions that:
1. Have occurred   1. Have occurred
2. Have occurred   2. Are expected to occur
3. Are expected to occur   3. Have occurred
4. Are expected to occur   4. Are expected to occur

To which of these pairings does the balance sheet most nearly conform? What role is played by assets? Clearly the first pair will not answer. If this pairing were adopted, the balance sheet would have to exhibit a sum equal to the total of cash receipts since the founding of the enterprise. Likewise, it would have to exhibit the total amounts paid to those who have been contributors, e.g., the totals paid to shareholders in the form of dividends and redemption of shares and to creditors, who have loaned funds, in the form of interest and principle payments. Nor will the second and third pairings answer; for each of them implies one of the cumulations implied in the first. There remains the fourth pairing. This is the one sought—not, to be sure, merely because it is the only one left, but for independent, positive reasons.[1]

In 1966 Chambers gave careful consideration to the concept of financial position and formulated a definition that is consistent with his liquidity-oriented theory of accounting (p. 101):

> Financial position is the capacity of an entity at a point of time to engage in indirect exchanges; it is represented by the relationship between the monetary properties of the means in possession and the monetary properties of the obligations of an entity.

Indirect exchanges are made through the medium of money; a firm's financial position, in Chambers' view, involves its immediate ability to raise cash and its needs to cover its obligations. Chambers'

---

[1] *The Economics of Accountancy* (1929, pp. 181–182). Copyright 1929. Renewed ©1957 by The Ronald Press Company, New York. Quoted by permission.

definition ties in with his preference for measuring assets at their "current cash equivalent," that is, at their "market selling price or realizable price" (p. 92).

It has been our experience that the term "financial position" is ordinarily used in a context such as this: a banker, a credit-rating agent, or an institutional investor who is concerned about or interested in a firm's financial position is thinking about the firm's ability to meet its debts as they fall due—both in the short run and in the long run. He checks cash on hand, the current ratio, and working capital as indicators of short-run ability to pay. He sees the debt-equity ratio and coverage of fixed charges as indications of the long-run risk of insolvency. The greater the confidence such a user of financial statements has in the firm's ability to meet its obligations, and the longer the period for which that confidence exists, the higher his regard for the firm's financial position. If he has no specific evidence of "financial difficulties" or a weak financial position, he assumes continuity rather than liquidation when he appraises a firm's financial position. But the concept of financial position may connote, in addition to the firm's prospects for remaining solvent, an ability to take advantage of opportunities that may arise and that require cash. Such an ability requires liquidity and/or borrowing capacity; it is usually appraised under the assumption that the firm's existing activities will continue, unless evidence to the contrary is available. Finally, liquidation values are often of great interest to the evaluator of financial position when he is considering the possibility of insolvency.

Now let's see if we can spell out the concept of financial position. In the first place, it is future-oriented; information about financial position must be relevant to the future if it is to be useful to decision makers. A report of past receipts and disbursements, for example, tells us little about financial position except the cash balance. Secondly, financial position must deal with current stocks of some wealth-related items in general, emphasizing those items of wealth with relatively direct (positive or negative) cash flow potential, if the concept is to be useful in predicting the firm's capacity to pay. Finally, although the relevant time horizon over which the wealth-related items may affect the firm's capacity to pay is indefinite and long, the timing of the benefits must be encompassed within the concept. Taking all of these points into account, we may define *financial position* as an *entity's cash flow potentials, their distribution over time, the relationships between their positive and negative elements, and their risk and uncertainty attributes.* Assets and liabilities are parts of a firm's financial position.

ASSET, LIABILITY, AND RESIDUAL EQUITY

A good starting point for a study of the meaning of "asset" is a review of some historic milestones in the literature. In 1908, Charles Ezra Sprague showed a far deeper understanding of the concept of assets than was generally reflected in the literature of his time (pp. 47–48):

> . . . the assets comprising the debit side of the balance sheet may be considered in one or more of the following ways:
>
> 1. As things possessed, directly or indirectly, or physical assets.
> 2. As rights over things and persons, for use, for services, or for exchange.
> 3. As incomplete contracts, whereof our part has been performed in whole or in part; or contractual assets.
> 4. As the result of services previously given, or *cost.*
> 5. As the present worth of expected services to be received.
> 6. As capital for the conduct of business operations.
> 7. As investment in the hands of another who uses it as capital.

The very breadth of Sprague's listing of views of assets, however, indicates a potential for confusion, and Sprague did not emphasize any one view enough to dispel it.

Canning, as indicated by his approach to financial position, preferred a future-oriented view of assets (p. 22):

> An asset is any future service in money or any future service convertible into money (except those services arising from contracts the two sides of which are proportionately unperformed) the beneficial interest in which is legally or equitably secured to some person or set of persons. Such a service is an asset only to that person or set of persons to whom it runs.

Here we see a clear-cut emphasis on future service—a view that is entirely consistent with our interest in future payoffs to investors.

Paton and Littleton introduced the term "service potentialities" in their discussion of the subject matter of accounting (1940, p. 13):

> It is not "money" that is significant; it is not "price" that is significant. "Service" is the significant element behind the accounts, that is, service-potentialities, which when exchanged, bring still other service-potentialities into the enterprise.

It was William J. Vatter, however, who set the pattern for modern definitions (1947, p. 17): "Assets are service potentials, not physical things, legal rights, or money claims." Service potential is now commonly accepted as the central characteristic of assets.

For the sake of comparison, let's look at a pair of prominent definitions that we have not found helpful. First, the Committee on Terminology proposed (1953, p. 5) that:

> . . . the term asset, as used in balance sheets, may be defined as follows:
>
> Something represented by a debit balance that is or would be properly carried forward upon a closing of books of account according to the rules or principles of accounting (provided such debit balance is not in effect a negative balance applicable to a liability), on the basis that it represents either a property right or a value acquired, or an expenditure made which has created a property right or is properly applicable to the future. Thus, plant, accounts receivable, inventory, and a deferred charge are all assets in balance-sheet classification.

I object to this definition because it requires (a) double-entry accounting, (b) knowledge of which debit balances are properly carried forward after closing according to the principles of accounting, and (c) knowledge of what constitutes a contra liability. It appears to be clearly interpretable only by fully qualified accountants, and may not exclude anything that can be rationalized as "properly applicable to the future."

In 1970 the APB (pp. 50–51) also attempted to define asset, but without improving upon the 1953 definition:

> Assets—economic resources of an enterprise that are recognized and measured in conformity with generally accepted accounting principles. Assets also include certain deferred charges that are not resources but that are recognized and

measured in conformity with generally accepted accounting principles.

According to this definition, an asset may, or may not, be an economic resource; if we are acquainted with generally accepted accounting principles we are expected to be able to identify which economic resources should be included, and which excluded, and which deferred charges that are not economic resources should be included. It is not a suitable working definition.

A working definition of asset, or of any other practical accounting concept, should assist the accountant in making decisions on the job. As he examines any economic object that appears to have some possibility of being an asset, whether recorded in the accounts or not, he should be able to refer to a set of criteria that, if met by the object in question, justify its classification as an asset. The following criteria are candidates for inclusion in such a set:

1. *Service potential,* or some other attribute related to value. Positive cash flow potential is a more practical version of this attribute for ordinary business situations, but the broader term, which encompasses capacity to yield benefits in any form, may be preferable. In any event, we must make clear that the first criterion of an asset is some quality related to economic resources, wealth, utility potential, goodness, or desirability.[2]

2. *Association with the entity,* or perhaps its owners. To be an asset, an item of wealth must be expected to serve the particular entity (or its shareholders). A society may have some items of wealth, such as climate or water supply, that are not tied to a specific entity within that society; they could, however, be classified as assets on a societal balance sheet.

3. *Measurability.* Some property (or attribute) of the item

---

[2] Indeed, the desirability of assets is one possible starting point for explaining double-entry bookkeeping. Because all assets are desirable, someone will claim them. The portion of total assets not claimed by parties with specific claims (creditors) will be claimed by someone entitled to the residue (residual equity holder). Hence, assets equal equities. Once we have established that the quantities of things in which parties are interested can be expressed in equation form, we have the basis for double-entry because an equation cannot be maintained through changes without a set of equal and opposite "entries" each time anything is recorded.

which has a demonstrable relationship to service potential must be subject to measurement in monetary terms with acceptable reliability. (Cash flow potential is the most obvious such property but there are several substitutes, or surrogates, for it, as we shall see subsequently.) This criterion is probably the most difficult to apply, but it does seem necessary. We do not believe any of the entity's assets should be omitted from the balance sheet, although we know that many objects which have service potential to the entity cannot be quantified satisfactorily. Even if the asset category were defined so broadly as to encompass "off-balance-sheet assets," we would still be faced with the necessity of establishing criteria for distinguishing between balance sheet assets and off-balance-sheet assets. It seems preferable to limit assets to those to be included on the balance sheet at positive values. This requires measurability.

We have no suggestions regarding what level of reliability should be considered acceptable. Indeed, we are not certain how reliability, as a whole, should be measured although we have suggested a measure for verifiability (see chapter III). This is just one more example of need for the best judgment of a well-qualified and unbiased professional accountant.

4. Another criterion that may be needed is *measurability of any obligation* established by the contract that provides the basis for the asset. "Executory" contracts (which are substantially unperformed by both parties) typically involve valuable rights and burdensome obligations. The value (to decision-making readers) of including such rights as assets would appear to be seriously limited unless the related obligations are also included among the liabilities. However, rights and obligations that are considered equal at the date of making a contract may become unequal at a later date, thereby affecting the shareholders' equity and income; such a possibility makes the inclusion of such rights and obligations in the accounts a significant issue. There may be cases in which one side is measurable with barely acceptable reliability, and the other is measurable only by setting it equal to the measurable side. Such a weak, dependent measurement may be rejected as submarginal on the combination of relevance and reliability, so the whole transaction may be omitted from the accounts.

5. *Severability* is a criterion that Professor Chambers uses (1966, p. 130). In his opinion, if you cannot sell it separately—without selling the business as a whole—it is not an asset. This criterion appears to omit such general intangible items as goodwill, although one may throw them out on the measurability criterion anyway. But why should we want to require severability? If something will provide measurable service potential to the owners only in its existing setting, why should it not be included as an asset?

6. Sprouse and Moonitz (1962, p. 20) included "acquired by the enterprise as a result of some current or past transaction" in their definition of assets. If the term "transaction" omits such economic events as discoveries and births of livestock, one may question whether exclusion of such objects of wealth is warranted. If "transaction" is broad enough to include such events, what is excluded by this criterion? If nothing is excluded, the criterion does not help.

Which of these possible criteria should we accept and which should we reject? Perhaps there are other candidates. My own choice is to include the first three of the above. If a one-sentence definition is desired, perhaps the following will serve:

AN ASSET OF ANY ENTITY IS ANY ECONOMIC RESOURCE THAT IS CAPABLE OF PROVIDING SERVICES TO THE ENTITY AND THAT IS PRESENTLY MEASURABLE IN MONETARY TERMS.

The primary characteristic of a *liability* is its "negative value," or its requirement for the conveyance or disposition of assets. A liability must pertain to the entity and be measurable but the residual equity must be excluded. The following statement covers these criteria:

A LIABILITY OF ANY ENTITY IS ANY EXISTING RELATIONSHIP THAT WILL RESULT IN THE DISPOSITION OF PRESENT OR FUTURE ASSETS OF THE ENTITY, AND THAT IS PRESENTLY MEASURABLE (INDEPENDENTLY OF TOTAL ASSETS) IN MONETARY TERMS. [3]

Every entity has residual equity holder(s). The residual equity in an entity is the "right to receive any services that the entity is capable of providing in excess of those required to satisfy the definite, enforceable rights of related parties" (Staubus, 1961, p.

---

[3] For another perspective of liabilities, see Moonitz (1960).

19). We compute the amount of the residual equity by deducting total liabilities from total assets. If liabilities exceed the assets, the lowest ranking claimants in the liability category become residual equity holders. Participating preferred stock and convertible preferred issues are generally interpreted as part of the residual equity, while "straight" preferred must be associated with the liabilities for some purposes. It seems best to avoid generalizing about the classification of preferred stock.

ADDITIONAL READING SUGGESTION

Financial Accounting Standards Board, "An Analysis of Issues Related to *Conceptual Framework for Financial Accounting and Reporting: Elements of Financial Statements and Their Measurements*," *FASB Discussion Memorandum* (FASB, 2 December 1976), chapters 1–4.

STUDY QUESTIONS

1. Define financial position. Explain the role your concept plays in the type of accounting that you think is most valuable.
2. Define asset. Are the following things assets by your definition?
   (a) Purchased goodwill.
   (b) Internally developed goodwill.
   (c) Prepaid interest.
   (d) Unamortized bond discount.
   (e) Net operating loss carry forward.
   (f) Income tax "prepaid" in the sense that it relates to income not yet recognized in the books.
   (g) A loyal and competent employee group.
   (h) A baseball player "purchased" for a cash sum from another club.
   (i) Rights to the use of leased property for which rent has not yet been paid.
   (j) Patents, models and knowledge developed by the company research department.
   (k) Future cost reductions expected from a recent rearrangement of productive facilities.
3. Define liability. Are the following things liabilities by your definition?

    (a) Reserve for self-insurance.

    (b) Obligations on product warranty.

    (c) Income tax expected to be paid on income booked but not yet subject to tax.

    (d) Credit balances in standard cost variance accounts.

    (e) Football club's obligation on a player contract for the remainder of the year.

    (f) Payments to be made on lease contract for services not yet received.

4. The following account title appeared in the balance sheet of the American Electric Power Company in its 1962 *Annual Report.* Is it a liability?

    "Accumulated amortization invested in the business equivalent to the reduction in federal income taxes resulting from accelerated amortization and liberalized depreciation, which is recorded as earned surplus restricted for future federal income taxes in accounts maintained pursuant to state regulatory requirements."

5. Is "cash flow potential" an appropriate test of an asset or is a broader term more fitting? Give examples of assets which do not have cash flow potential—if you can.

6. Is "severability" an appropriate test of an asset's existence?

7. Which form of the accounting equation do you prefer and why?

8. What is the function of the balance sheet? Do you prefer an alternative name?

9. Is measurability an operational test of the existence of an asset?

10. Is measurability of a related obligation an appropriate test of an asset's existence?

11. Give examples of features of capital stock that would warrant classifying the shares as residual equity.

12. As a practical matter, what difference does it make to users of financial statements whether the rights and obligations specified in executory contracts, such as leases, contracts to purchase, and contracts to sell, are included in or excluded from the asset and liability sections of balance sheets?

CHAPTER VI
MEASURES AND MEASUREMENT

The stocks concepts most fundamental to the accounting process have been defined. The next step is to determine how to measure the objects referred to by those concepts. Three chapters are devoted to this subject. We begin with some musings on the semantics of our subject. What are the roles of accountants in valuation and measurement? Which work—valuation or measurement—is more appropriate? Do accountants measure stocks and flows, only stocks, or only flows?

We proceed to argue that the accountant's major role in measurement is finding various types of evidence of the amounts of assets and liabilities and selecting and combining those bits of evidence which yield the best measure of the particular net asset item in the circumstances. The classification of types of evidence leads us to the most important part of the chapter—descriptions and presentation of the merits of each of nine measurement methods. The following two chapters will deal with choosing a measurement method within the framework of the set of criteria presented in chapter III.

MEASUREMENT IN ACCOUNTING

The first issue to be considered in this section is terminological. Is "measurement" the appropriate term for use in accounting or would "valuation," or perhaps "quantification," serve better? "Valuation" has been used extensively in the accounting profession. Our textbooks, for example, commonly refer, sometimes in chapter titles, to inventory valuation or the valuation of receivables. This usage is still common despite such disclaimers as Maurice Peloubet's (1935, p. 209): "Valuation in any true or important sense is not a matter for the accountant and the more completely this is recognized by accountant and client the better it will be for all concerned." This strong statement was emphasized by being placed at the end of the article, but many of Peloubet's preceding remarks did not support the wording of his conclusion. In fact, his immediately preceding sentence probably would be accepted by more accountants. "Any accountant who attempts to make valuations *other than those indicated by the accounts, or by some definite index, such as a market price,* is coming dangerously close to the boundary of his own field and is preparing to step over into that of the economist and engineer" (emphasis added). And on the preceding page: "While the accountant cannot make valuations, it is true that his experience, which puts him in the position of a particularly well-informed layman, so far as engineering, economic and legal facts are concerned, makes him a competent critic of such valuations and should enable him to detect anything grossly or substantially inaccurate." Valuation, then, may well be "a matter for the accountant" to be concerned with even though he minimizes the extent to which he injects his own valuations of assets and liabilities into his work. Accountants are constantly working with valuations made by others, especially buyers and sellers of goods (including services), but making valuations of net asset items (assets and liabilities) is not their primary duty.

"Measurement is the core of accounting," according to Ijiri (1967, p. x). The accountant does little that does not rely upon measurements (and upon valuations, for that matter). But Churchman (1971, p. 57) questions whether accounting is a system of measurement: "To be sure, accounting is a systematic method of gathering data. . . . But to be systematic in gathering data does not mean to measure, under the assumptions that I have made." He may be right. Those who play major roles in setting prices—buyers and sellers—surely do more to measure assets. If measurement is the "assignment of numbers to objects" (Ijiri, 1967, p. 22), accountants clearly play a secondary role in most cases. They select one of several numbers that have already been assigned to the object by someone else.

An alternative term, if we do not feel justified in denoting the accountant's role in determining the amounts of financial properties as "measurement," is "quantification" (Ijiri, 1967, p. 3):

> Accounting is a system for communicating the economic events of an entity. Communication is based primarily on quantitative information. Therefore, our study is directed toward understanding the substance of the economic events of an entity and the rules of quantifying them as well as the relationship between accountants and users of accounting information.

If this can serve as the opening paragraph of *The Foundations of Accounting Measurement,* and if quantifiability is properly included as one of the four standards to be used as criteria in evaluating potential accounting information (AAA, 1966, p. 7), perhaps "quantification" is the term we are seeking. According to the handiest Webster, "quantify" means "to determine, express, or measure the quantity of," a definition that seems well suited to the accountant's role in determining amounts. But, on the other hand, one meaning of "measure" is "to ascertain the quantity, mass, extent or degree of in terms of a standard unit or fixed amount" (Webster). "To ascertain the quantity" would seem to mean approximately the same as quantifying. If so, the accountant's definition of "measurement" could be "ascertaining the quantity of an economic attribute of an object or event." Perhaps quantification and measurement in accounting are synonomous.

We believe that the accountant finds, selects, accumulates, and reports evidence of valuations (made by others). The evidence he typically selects may be presumed to be ordinally related to valuations. For example, when the accountant selects a price paid by a buyer he is selecting a measure of value that is typically less than the valuation (usually subjective) placed on the asset by the purchaser, but greater than that of the seller. The accountant also plays various roles in quantifying economic objects and events, so we should not hesitate to use the term "quantification" for a portion of accounting activities. But, all things considered, we prefer the term "measurement" as a name for the activities of accountants and others which are involved in the determination of the amounts to record in accounts and report on financial statements. We suspect that most accountants will disagree with Churchman and will conclude that *accounting is a measurement system.*

Measurement of Stocks and Flows

All accounting entries record flows, i.e., changes in stocks, and all stocks are the result of flows. An entry inconsistent with available evidence of the change in a stock is, at a minimum, suspect if not obviously erroneous. Although one could also argue that a recorded stock that is inconsistent with available evidence of the net of all prior flows is suspect, difficulties in accumulating convincing evidence of all prior flows—how can one be certain none has been overlooked?—are likely to lead the accountant to rely on the stocks evidence rather than on the flows evidence if the two conflict.

Stocks frequently are verifiable independently of flows, e.g., physical counts of inventories; the related flow, e.g., inventory shrinkage, may be inferred from the existence or absence of some portion of the stock. Flows usually cannot be observed to the satisfaction of accountants without also observing stocks. Statements about flows are almost always more convincing if they are corroborated by evidence of stocks before and after the flow. But existence of a stock can convince one that a flow did occur in the past as can the absence of a stock previously observed, even if no flow was observed.

In sum, skeptical independent parties often can be convinced of the occurrence of flows without observing them while skeptical independent parties are not likely to be convinced of the existence of stocks without observing them. Belief in existence may require direct evidence; belief in events may not. Therefore, in cases of apparent inconsistency between evidence of stocks and evidence of flows, the former governs. For this reason, the remainder of this chapter will focus explicitly on the measurement of stocks (assets and liabilities); the determination of which flows should be included in the calculation of profit will be discussed in a subsequent chapter.

TYPES OF EVIDENCE OF ASSET AND LIABILITY AMOUNTS

In this section we are concerned with the nature of the available evidence of asset and liability amounts. The *existence* of an asset or liability is not an issue at this point; we are dealing with items that are assumed to have been identified as assets or liabilities in accordance with the definitions in chapter V. The question is: What types of evidence may be used as bases for the calculation of asset and liability *amounts?*

As we noted in an earlier chapter, objectivity has always been sought by accountants. Accountants prefer relatively objective, impersonal evidence as inputs to the accounting process. Kohler (1970, p. 299) defined "objective" as "Having a meaning or application apart from the individual, or the peculiarities of his experience or of the environment . . ." Accountants are reluctant to use their own judgments or those of entity personnel as starting points for the measurement of financial statement items, although they do make exceptions if the judgment comes from a skilled technician or professional such as an engineer, or if the circumstances offer extremely unattractive alternatives. For example, the alternatives to accountants making their own judgments of uncollectible receivables often are too distasteful for accountants to accept. Even in such cases, though, the accountant does seek objective evidence, such as the record of write-offs in previous years, as a starting point for his judgment. EXHIBIT VI-1 illustrates the most common types of objective evidence available to accountants as starting points for the determination of amounts of assets and liabilities.

A few explanatory comments may be helpful. The amount stated on the face of coins, currency, checks, and some types of notes and certificates is good evidence of their amounts. Contractual evidence may be found in documents, such as invoices, which describe some of the terms of explicit or implied contracts. Accountants typically are able to obtain contractual evidence of accounts and notes receivable and payable, some other assets in the claims-to-cash category, and some other liabilities. Exit prices are prices in the market in which the entity would sell; entry prices are prices in the market in which it buys. These could be the same, as in the case of listed securities. The meanings of current prices, past prices, and entity involvement seem clear. Historical cost, for example, is based on category III-B-2-a, past entry price in which the entity was involved. Bank statements and financial statements of "investees" (for the equity method) are included in category V. Bad debts experience, a plant engineer's

EXHIBIT VI-1

TYPES OF EVIDENCE OF ASSET AND LIABILITY AMOUNTS

```
    I.   Face or nominal amount
   II.   Contractual evidence
  III.   Market prices
         A. Exit prices
            1. Current
               a. Entity involved in establishing price
               b. Entity not involved
            2. Past
               a. Entity involved in establishing price
               b. Entity not involved
         B. Entry prices
            1. Current
               a. Entity involved in establishing price
               b. Entity not involved
            2. Past
               a. Entity involved in establishing price
               b. Entity not involved
         C. Price indexes
            1. Specific (narrow) index of current entry prices
            2. General (broad) measuring unit index
   IV.   Physical observation and count of quantities
         A. By entity personnel
         B. By external personnel as reported to entity
    V.   Records of other entities
   VI.   Miscellaneous statistical evidence
         A. Provided by entity personnel
         B. From external sources
```

records of machine lives, and the unamortized cost of an asset for tax purposes are examples of evidence falling in category VI. While one might think of such documents as newspapers and vendors' price lists as categories of evidence, these are better regarded as media, or transmission devices, for evidence.

Another feature of EXHIBIT VI-1 may not be obvious. The categories of evidence listed not only provide the bases for the measurement of assets, but also cover liabilities. The basic evidence for the quantification of most liabilities falls into category II, but market prices for goods and services are sometimes used, especially in connection with obligations to deliver goods or render services. Data from categories V and VI are often helpful too.

These types of evidence of asset and liability amounts are the raw materials for the accountant's role in measurement. Accountants do not rely heavily on their own opinions of asset values but they do rely upon their own judgments of various types of evidence of value. If the accountant has any area of expertise pertaining to value, it is in the field of evidence of value. The professional accountant uses his greatest skill, his most professional judgment, when he selects the types of evidence on which he will rely in ascertaining the amount of a specific asset or liability. He typically combines several bits of evidence in arriving at an acceptable measurement of an item, but he does not create the evidence out of thin air. Types of evidence, such as those listed in EXHIBIT VI-1, constitute the building blocks from which measurement methods are constructed.

MEASUREMENT METHODS FOR ASSETS AND LIABILITIES

In accounting, a *measurement method* is a procedure for utilizing one or more types of evidence in ascertaining the amount of an asset or liability. A *measurement* is both the act of measuring and the specific number resulting from the application of a measurement method to an object (asset or liability) in a particular case. A *measure,* in the sense of an instrument for measuring, is essentially synonomous with a measurement method. The phrases used to identify measures, and variations thereof listed in EXHIBIT VI-2, may also be used as short symbols for the related measurement methods. Thus, net realizable value (NRV) is a common measure of asset amounts and is a measurement method that requires evidence of the physical quantity of goods on hand, the current entry prices for services required to sell those goods, and the current exit price of the commodity. If an accountant finds evidence of 1,000 units of a commodity on hand, an exit market price of $8 and costs of selling of 50¢ per unit and makes the calculation $1,000(\$8.00 - .50) = \$7,500$, his measurement method is NRV and his measurement of the stock of this commodity is $7,500. NRV is also the measure of asset amount the accountant has

Exhibit VI-2

Measures of Assets and Types of Evidence Utilized

Measures		*Types of Evidence Utilized (see EXHIBIT VI-1)*
1	Face value	I — Face or nominal amount
2	Future cash flows, subject to recognized uncertainties	II — Contractual evidence of future cash flow
		VI — Miscellaneous statistical evidence
3	Discounted future cash flows	II
		VI
		III-B-1 — Market price for use of money
4	Current market price	III-A-1 — Current exit market price
		III-B-1 — Current entry market price
		IV — Physical observation and count of quantities
5	Net realizable value (NRV)	III-A-1
		III-B-1 — Current entry price for services required to sell
6	Replacement cost	IV
		IV

Item	Code	Evidence
a. Based on specific market prices —		
i. Amortized _____	III-B-1	Miscellaneous statistical evidence of quantities
	VI	
ii. Not amortized _____		
b. Based on a specific price index —		
i. Amortized _____	III-C-1	Specific price index
	VI	
ii. Not amortized _____		
7 Restated historical cost* _____	III-B-2-a	Past entry price involving the firm
	III-C-2	General measuring unit index
	VI	
a. Amortized _____		
b. Not amortized _____		
8 Original historical cost* _____	III-B-2-a	
	IV	
	VI	
a. Amortized _____		
b. Not amortized _____		
9 Equity method _____	V	Records of other entities, plus all other types of evidence (indirectly)
a. Pure _____		
b. Cost-based _____	III-B-2-a	

*While the evidence on which restated historical cost and original historical cost measurements are based is contractual, it is not contractual evidence of cash flow potential as it is in the cases of receivables and payables. However, we would not quarrel with anyone who chooses to relate the historical cost methods to contractual evidence.

chosen to use. EXHIBIT VI-2 lists several measurement methods that are either commonly used in accounting practice or widely discussed in the literature, and it ties each method to one or more types of evidence listed in EXHIBIT VI-1.

It is essential that the reader be thoroughly familiar with the alternative measurement methods if he is to be free to choose among them in an informed manner. If one is ignorant of an alternative, or lacks full understanding of it, he is not genuinely free to choose. In this section we shall describe nine different measurement methods and give sufficient explanation and justification for each method's use to make it a credible candidate for acceptance by the accounting profession for at least occasional use. As we do this, it may appear that we are adopting an advocacy position; in fact, our intention is not to advocate any method as best but rather to present a strong case for each so that it will not be rejected by the reader at this stage of the investigation. Evaluation will follow in succeeding chapters.

Face Value

Face value is the traditional basis for stating the amounts of coin, currency, checks, drafts, money orders, and a few other types of items which meet the criteria of cash on hand. Its use requires reading the nominal amount appearing on the object itself, counting the number of such identical objects, and using arithmetic processes to aggregate these data. Some accountants may question the inclusion of face value, or counting face value, as a measurement method, but its exclusion would appear to leave some assets unmeasured—a rather awkward status in the present context. The issue is not a momentous one.

Future Cash Flows

Contractual evidence and documentary evidence from other entities are relied upon in calculating future cash flows. Future cash inflows from customers are rights provided for in the contract of sale, whether written, oral, or implied. Copies of internal documents, such as sales invoices, the contract itself (if written), and confirmations from debtors are examples of evidence used by accountants to establish the amounts of claims against debtors.

Similarly, obligations to trade creditors are measured by reference to purchase invoices, copies of internal documents, and contracts. But in the case of debtors, the estimation of future cash flows requires that consideration be given to bad debts, or uncollectible accounts. The evidence used in estimating the provision for doubtful debts may be varied but often includes write-offs, the credit ratings of customers, the age of outstanding balances, and current macroeconomic statistics. The subjectivity of the process is undeniable, but so is its relevance. The measurement of receivables and monetary obligations on the basis of future cash flows is one of the oldest techniques in accounting; indeed, the terms "debit" and "credit" are thought to have entered the vocabulary of accounting when, during the Renaissance, Genoese and Venetian merchants and bankers recorded the amounts owed to them by debtors and by them to creditors.

Discounted Future Cash Flows

Adjustments of future cash flows are sometimes made in order to obtain a better estimate of the present significance of the claims to cash. For example, future collection and bookkeeping costs may be deducted from a sum of receivables made up of many small amounts, especially if the payments are to be made over a long period. Similarly, receivables not due in the near future may be discounted for an interest, or cost-of-capital, factor in order to recognize the difference in financial significance between a dollar due tomorrow and a dollar due a year hence. Material amounts of unearned interest are not included in the amounts at which long-term accounts and notes receivable and other debt instruments owned are shown in the accounts. Nor are material amounts of unaccrued interest shown as liabilities. For example, a 5-year, 8 percent, interest-bearing note with principal value of $1,000 is a contract calling for a total of $1,400 in cash. But it would be valued, at a balance date 4 ½ years prior to maturity, at $1,040—as an asset on the holder's balance sheet and as a liability on the maker's statement. The use of money is viewed as a service rendered, over the period of the credit relationship, by the lender to the borrower. The lender does not record his revenue and receivable for this service until the service is rendered, and the borrower omits the expense and liability until the service is received. Partial performance is recorded in accordance with the accrual concept (of which accounting for interest is a prime example).

Measuring assets and liabilities on the basis of future cash flows less unaccrued interest is a universal practice if the interest rate is explicitly stated; the valuation principle involved is accepted by many accountants even in the absence of an explicitly stated rate or if the explicit rate is out of line with current market rates for similar credit arrangements. We shall use the term "discounted future cash flows" to apply to anticipated future cash receipts and disbursements net of an interest allowance for the waiting period, whether the computation is made by simple deduction or by the calculation of true present value based on a discount factor, and regardless of the explicitness of the interest (discount) rate. The true discounted (present) value of a future cash flow is the amount that, with the addition of compound interest, will grow to the maturity amount or amounts at the future payment date or dates. We do not, of course, visualize the application of the discounted future cash flow method to any asset or liability except those providing contractual evidence of future cash flows. While it is reasonable to argue that discounted future cash flow is a *relevant attribute* of any asset, it is also reasonable to adopt the view that, if discounted future cash flow is to be *acceptably reliable,* the bulk of the future cash flows involved must be specified by contract, that the remaining costs to be netted off must not be large, and that the obligor must meet some standard of credit worthiness.

A short digression on the history of discounted value (adapted from Staubus, 1967a) may be useful at this point. The main idea in the concept of capital value is that the value of any asset is the present value of all future benefits obtainable from it, discounted at the required rate of return. This viewpoint now permeates the thinking of the professional investors in the financial centers of the world, and has been generally accepted in the academic literature of finance for at least several decades. Perhaps the most frequently quoted work is *The Theory of Investment Value* (1938) by John Burr Williams. He defines investment value "as the present worth of the future dividends in the case of a stock" (p. 6). Earlier,

Robert F. Weise had written: "The proper price of any security
. . . is the sum of all future income payments discounted at the
current rate of interest in order to arrive at the present value"
(1930, p. 5).

These writers probably would not want to take much credit
for the present value concept of securities value, for they undoubtedly were familiar with the writings of Irving Fisher, who, in
The Nature of Capital and Income (1906, p. 223), concluded "that
the value of any capital-good, either of wealth or of property-rights,
assuming that all future income is foreknown, is the discounted
value of that income." Fisher, in turn, must have been acquainted
with the views of von Bohm-Bawerk (1891, pp. 342–43):

> A material service, which, technically, is exactly the same as
> a service of this year, but which cannot be rendered before
> next year, is worth a little less than this year's service; another
> similar service, but obtainable only after two years, is, again,
> a little less valuable, and so on, the value of the remote services
> decreasing with the remoteness of the period at which they
> can be rendered. Say that this year's service is worth 100,
> then the next year's service—assuming a difference of 5
> percent per annum—is worth in today's valuation only 95.23;
> the third year's service is worth only 90.70; the fourth year's
> service, 86.38; the fifth, sixth, seventh year's services, respec-
> tively, worth 82.27, 78.35, 74.62 of present money. . . . That
> the figures should alter according as the date of the valuation
> stands nearer or farther from the date of obtaining the utility,
> is an entirely natural thing, and one *quite familiar in financial
> life*. The value of paper—which is just a "durable good" with
> annual uses—always stands a little higher shortly before the
> interest or dividend terms than some time before. I may note
> that the above figures are taken as before from Spitzer's Tables
> and are based on an interest rate of 5 percent. [Emphasis
> added.]

The valuation of financial claims by discounting the future cash
flows they promise, with the aid of present value tables, was a
common practice in the time of Bohm-Bawerk and Simon Spitzer,
whose first edition of interest tables appears to have been published
in 1865 in Germany. Spitzer, however, did not have to make
all the computations himself; many earlier volumes were available
to him, especially in English. For example, the first of many editions

of Sir Isaac Newton's *Tables for Renewing and Purchasing the Leases of Cathedral-Churches and Colleges,* published in London in 1686, included present value of annuity and related tables, as did John Playford's *Vade Mecum,* or the *Necessary Companion,* the third edition of which was published in London in 1683. Playford's pocket-sized manual included such handy tables as weights and measures, world coin equivalents, multiplication tables showing the products of unit prices and quantities, post rates, and fares of coachmen, carmen, and watermen, so it was obviously intended for the daily use of London merchants. The inclusion of present value tables strongly implies that they were considered relevant to the business affairs of seventeenth-century England. Professor Robert Parker (1969) has traced compound interest and present value tables to Simon Stevin (Antwerp, 1582), Jean Trenchant (Lyons, 1558), and Pegolotti (Florence, 1340). This background suggests that the present worth concept of asset value is a practical approach of long standing.

Jumping from the fourteenth century to the twentieth, we note that the concept of discounted value also has direct application in current accounting practices. Six *Opinions* of the APB (*Nos. 5, 7, 8, 12, 21,* and *27*) have required or permitted use of present value in the measurement of assets or liabilities. These include the 1971 *Opinion* on "Interest on Receivables and Payables," which recognized the general idea that future cash flows must be discounted even if an "imputed" rate must be selected because of the lack of a reasonable explicit rate.

Current Market Value

The current market price of some types of assets is readily obtainable and, in the cases of some other assets, it may be obtained with modest or substantial effort. The best example is a listed security. Common bulk commodities, such as agricultural and mineral products, and some types of equipment (construction equipment, trucks, and automobiles) are additional examples in which an owner of an asset may be able to obtain an independent expression of current market value. In still other cases, the owner is able to ascertain either the price at which he is offering to sell the asset (finished goods and merchandise intended for sale) or the selling price of another vendor. It should be clear that these various market prices are not of equal reliability so may not be equally acceptable to an accountant; this issue will be discussed in chapter VIII. Nor are they of equal relevance—a matter to receive attention in chapter VII.

Current market values are sometimes usable in the measurement of liabilities, as well as assets, one example being outstanding debt securities (bonds payable), which are traded and quoted in a securities market. When a change in a market price is recorded in an asset or liability account, the offsetting entry is made in a positive or negative income account which may be called "holding gain or loss on [the asset or liability involved]" or "revaluation of [the item involved]."

The merits of current market price as a measure of asset amount are greatest and most clearly recognizable when the market is perfectly competitive. Under these conditions, the most recent market price reflects the combined opinions of many knowledgeable buyers and sellers, each attempting to act in his own best interest. Each prospective buyer makes a judgment as to whether the good is worth more or less than its current price; if he judges it to be worth more, he will want to buy. Similarly, each prospective seller attempts to judge whether the good is worth more to hold, perhaps for personal or business use or for future sale, than the current price at which he could sell. If any of these parties does not contemplate immediate use or consumption of the good, he must consider possible future prices of the good and future payoffs from holding and using it. Any predicted future price or other payoff must be discounted for the waiting period. The result when many prospective buyers and sellers, usually including those most knowledgeable with respect to the particular market, intently strive to maximize their own welfare is the establishment of a market price that independent observers typically respect as the most accurate judgment of the value of that good at that time. To "second guess the market" by insisting that some other price is a better expression of current value would appear extremely foolhardy—especially if the disbeliever were unwilling to enter the market, on whichever side his judgment dictated, to act on his allegedly superior judgment to make a speculative profit. Surely the only type of person who

could expect others to accept his personal judgment over that
of the competitive market would be one who has a proven record
of success (beyond that due to chance) in judging the market—a
successful speculator. Current prices in competitive markets are
hard to beat as evidence of current service potential of an asset.
However, we must remember that the case for market prices,
current or otherwise, weakens as we consider less than perfect
markets, especially if the entity whose assets are being measured
plays a big role in the establishment of the price. But the alternative
to using prices in imperfect markets may be even less acceptable.

The advantage of the most recent price over an older price
becomes apparent when we recognize the promptness and accuracy
with which a competitive market processes information that becomes available and adjusts the price accordingly. Studies of the
efficiency of securities markets have indicated that prices adjust
to new information quickly. The same can be said for basic
commodity markets and, to a lesser extent, for markets for other
common goods. If any relevant information has become available
since yesterday, today's price tends to reflect it. At worst, the
most recent price reflects as much information as any older price;
at best, it utilizes the additional information that has become
available between the two dates.

So that we may avoid a common misapprehension, let's make
it clear at this point that the merits of current market value are
not limited by the presence of a large quantity of an asset and
the inability of the market to absorb the entire quantity immediately
without a reduction in the price. Current market price is not
included here because it reflects immediate liquidation value. On
the contrary, the current price is appreciated because it reflects
the best judgment of market actors who are attempting to maximize
their own welfare, whether that requires waiting or not. On the
assumption that the entity for which we are accounting is also
attempting to maximize the payoff from ownership of an asset,
whether by immediate or delayed action in the market, the price
at which the entire quantity could be sold immediately, if that
price is below the quoted market price, would appear to be
acceptable to neither the management (for action) nor the accountant (for reporting as a primary measurement of the asset), even
though one could envision a set of circumstances under which

the management might "sacrifice" the asset. Similarly, the observation that free market prices fluctuate provides no support for an older price in the absence of evidence of a reversion pattern in market prices, as opposed to the generally accepted random walk pattern. Since the most recent price reflects more information than any older price, it appears to be the best available estimate of discounted future prices.

It seems safe to say that market prices constitute the most important class of evidence of asset and liability amounts and that current market prices are an important subset of that class. Not only is current market price a measurement method in its own right, but it is the primary component of two other measurement methods: net realizable value and replacement cost.

Net Realizable Value (NRV)

We use the term "net realizable value" to mean a current valuation (at the balance sheet date) based on the *current* price at which the asset could be sold less the current costs of selling and collecting the sales price. (While the term "net realizable value" is sometimes used to mean estimated *future* net proceeds from disposing of an asset, we must classify such a procedure as a version of the future cash flow method of measurement.) NRV is based on the price in the market in which the firm would normally sell the asset (an exit price) and on the current entry prices of the commodities and services that must be consumed in making the sale, delivering, collecting, and so on. In order to minimize the possibility of misinterpretation, we should emphasize the wide variation in availability of clear-cut current market prices and in difficulties encountered in estimating the remaining costs to be deducted. Such problems result in variations in the reliability of measurements of NRV in different circumstances.

NRV is a widely used measurement method, especially in conjunction with historical cost in the traditional approach to the measurement of current assets at the lower of cost and market and in the write-down of obsolete noncurrent assets. (Note, however, that "market" in the phrase "lower of cost and market" often means replacement cost rather than net realizable value.) NRV is also commonly applied to the finished stocks of some industries, especially in nonferrous metals and agriculture, without consideration of cost. The prevalence of these practices suggests that accountants are familiar with the concept of NRV and have a good deal of experience with its application.[1]

Liabilities can be measured at negative NRV. If net realizable value (the net effect that the liquidation of an asset at current prices would have on the firm's cash balance) is sometimes an appropriate measure of assets, then the net effect that the liquidation of a liability at current prices would have on the firm's cash balance may also be an appropriate measure of a liability in some cases. For example, an obligation to deliver certain merchandise or other stocks could be measured by the cash outlay, including fringe costs, that would be required at the balance sheet date to acquire and deliver the goods. Or bonds payable could be measured at their current market price plus commission.

One of the most significant potential applications of NRV is to a finished stock of a commodity for which an independent market price quotation is regularly available. The availability of such a quotation permits the accountant to measure output at market value without waiting for a sale, thus recording the

---

[1] The use of NRV without regard to cost is permitted in American GAAP by ARB No. 43, chapter 4, Statement 9 (AICPA, 1953), which is based on *ARB No. 29* (1947): "Inventories of gold and silver, when there is an effective government-controlled market at a fixed monetary value, are ordinarily reflected at selling prices. A similar treatment is not uncommon for inventories representing agricultural, mineral, and other products, units of which are interchangeable and have an immediate marketability at quoted prices and for which appropriate costs may be difficult to obtain. Where such inventories are stated at sales prices, they should of course be reduced by expenditures to be incurred in disposal, and the use of such basis should be fully disclosed in the financial statements."

A survey by Higgins (1964) disclosed that a majority of the U.S. and Canadian processors of cereals and grains valued commodity inventories at some version of current market value and that a large minority of lead-zinc miners and uranium miners followed similar practices. Foster (1969) reported that Australian mining companies valued 35 out of 55 inventory accounts on a current market price basis.

In the measurement of inventories at lower of cost and market, American practice places greatest emphasis on replacement cost as the meaning of "market," subject to exceptions for which NRV or NRV less a normal profit margin are acceptable, while *Standard No. 2* of the International Accounting Standards Committee calls for NRV as the measure of market value.

management's production achievement in the period of production rather than in the period of sale. The impact of this method on periodic profit or loss can be taken into account most simply either by adjusting the ending inventory of the commodity to NRV, if the firm uses a cost accounting system that includes a finished stock account at cost, or by setting up the ending inventory at NRV if no cost accounting system is in use. In either case the credit would be to the main revenue account which includes sales for the year. The sum, less the NRV of the beginning inventory, would be reported in the income statement as the market value of the year's output.

But if the accountant prefers to use the NRV method in a manner which distinguishes between revenue from production and holding gains and losses, and if a "perpetual" (i.e., up-to-date) stock accounting system is used, a set of entries along the following lines would be appropriate (if the product is copper bars):

Dr. Cost of copper bars produced (expense)   X
   Cr. Work in progress   X
      To record cost of product completed.

Dr. Finished stock   X
   Cr. Market value of copper bars produced
   (revenue)   X
      To record value of output.

Dr. Accounts Receivable   X
Dr. or Cr. Loss or gain on holding copper stocks   X or X
   Cr. Finished stock   X
      To record sale of copper and difference
      between market price when produced and sale
      price.

In practice the last entry would probably exclude the gain or loss, and finished stock would be credited for the selling price. In these circumstances whatever adjustment was required at the end of the period to state the closing stock at market value would automatically record the net holding gain or loss for the period. For example, if prices have been rising during the period, sales would result in crediting the finished stock account with prices higher than those at which the product was charged to finished stock, so a debit adjustment of the finished stock account, offset by a credit to "gain on holding copper stocks" account, would be in order. The cost of copper produced would be deducted from the market value of output in the income statement. The holding gain or loss would be shown separately. Shipping and other post-production costs could be charged to expense as incurred except for the estimated costs of disposing of the closing stock, which could be recorded by crediting a contra stock account as follows:

> Dr. Shipping expenses   X
>   Cr. Finished stock—provision for future costs   X
>   To provide for remaining costs of disposing of
>   closing stock.

This leaves closing stock at NRV, and the estimated post-production costs (e.g., shipping) are matched with the market value of the output for the period. The income statement reflects the profit or loss from producing a saleable commodity, as well as the net gain or loss resulting from holding stocks of the product while the market fluctuates. This separation may give the reader a better basis for predicting future results.

Replacement Cost

The current entry price of an asset, including fringe acquisition costs such as transportation and commissions, is a widely used measurement method, especially as an expression of "market" in the lower of cost and market method. It is also applied to long-life assets, sometimes through the use of specific indexes of the prices of narrow categories of fixed assets. The Philips Lamp Companies follow this practice. Some British and Australian firms that make occasional revaluations of long-term assets also use the replacement cost version of current value.

Replacement cost differs from NRV by being based on the market in which the firm buys (e.g., the wholesale market), whereas NRV is based on the market in which the firm sells (e.g., the retail market). Even if the two markets are the same (e.g., the listed share market), replacement cost technically includes the fringe costs of acquisition as additions to market price, whereas NRV is market price less selling costs such as commissions. The spread between replacement cost and NRV in the one-market case can be substantial for some types of assets, such as used automobiles.

The measurement of stock items in the categories of raw materials, supplies and merchandise purchased and held for sale on a replacement cost basis poses few peculiar problems. Current quotations from suppliers of the commodity and of the transportation and other fringe services typically are readily available. Manufacturing work in process and finished goods can be measured on the basis of up-to-date standard costs of production. Several methods of calculating replacement cost of plant assets are used:

1. Direct pricing by obtaining a quotation for the specific model of asset on hand.
2. Indexing of historical cost, using the percentage change in a specific price index for the type of asset being measured.
3. Unit pricing of the basic physical feature of the asset, such as square feet of a building or lineal feet of lines and pipes, based on recent construction costs of similar items.
4. Functional pricing in cases in which the model of asset held is no longer in production but a new model which will perform the same function is available. If the new asset has a different productive capacity, the relative capacities of the old and the new must be taken into consideration.

The value of limited-life long-term assets that decline in service potential must be reduced by amortization (a term used here to include depreciation in the case of tangible assets). Replacement cost less amortization is not, however, listed as a separate measurement method, since the basic replacement cost method is considered applicable to the remaining stock of services embodied in a fixed asset. Such application typically requires determination of replacement cost new and the portion of the original package of services that remain available to contribute to future cash flows of the firm.

"Replacement cost used" is an alternative version of replacement cost; it may be useful in those cases in which market prices of used assets are available. Some computers, automobiles and trucks, aircraft, machine tools, and looms fall in this category. If the asset is of a type that is no longer the most efficient source of the services it provides, as in the case of supercession by a new, more efficient model, replacement cost new should be interpreted to mean the current cost of acquiring equivalent services, not the "reproduction cost" of a physically identical asset. Variations in output rate and operating costs can make the estimation of the cost of equivalent services via a technologically improved asset highly subjective. If the market for used assets of the type actually held is well developed, used asset prices would appear to be a preferable approach to the measurement of out-of-date assets held. (See chapter XIV for more on this subject.)

The additional entries required to account for assets at replacement cost are very simple. In fact, if replacement cost is used as the sole valuation of an asset (with no retention of historical cost data for some purposes), the only special entry would be a debit or credit to the asset to adjust it to the current replacement cost, an adjustment of the accumulated depreciation account by the same percentage but in the opposite direction, and a credit or debit to a holding gain or loss account for the difference. Subsequent entries to record the consumption or sale of the asset (including depreciation of fixed assets) would be based on the revised asset amount. If, on the other hand, cost data must continue to be provided for some purposes, the revaluation entry would require special asset and accumulated depreciation accounts for the difference between cost and replacement cost. In those firms in which depreciation and consumption of materials and supplies are charged to work in process and finished stock, maintenance of these latter accounts on two bases would be somewhat more difficult, but basic replacement cost records probably could be adjusted to an historical cost basis with acceptable accuracy by the application of estimating techniques that would not require detailed cost-based records.

The isolation of the holding gains and losses associated with assets involved in the basic operating cycle is commonly viewed as a major advantage of replacement cost measurements, not primarily because of the value of information on such gains and losses, but because it results in "current matching" of the costs and revenues used in computing the operating margin by "costing out" resources consumed in earning revenues at their current entry market prices. This current matching is thought by many accountants to give the reader a better indication of the profit margin that can be maintained through all types of price movements. In terms of inventory items, this means that the "inventory gains and losses," as they are sometimes called, should be removed from the operating margin accounts in order to allow the latter to reveal current operating margins.

In fact, however, we should recognize that the same thing could be accomplished wtihin the context of the historical cost measurement of ending inventory if goods used or sold were "costed out" at replacement cost and the ending inventory were adjusted to historical cost. Assuming prices increased during the period, the adjusting entry would involve a debit to inventory and a credit to the holding gain account. The latter would then offset the higher cost-of-sales figure to yield a net profit based on historical cost. The only difference between the historical cost income statement with "inventory profits" segregated and the income statement based on replacement cost measurement of inventories would be that the latter would report the unrealized holding gains or losses on the ending inventory and exclude those from the beginning inventory.

Finally, we should mention that the counterpart of replacement cost may be considered applicable to liabilities that involve obligations to deliver commodities or services. Perhaps it should be called "negative replacement cost," "replacement receipt," or "replacement proceeds." If, for example, a liability has been established at the selling price of goods but the selling price changes before the goods are delivered, the liability could be adjusted to the current selling price of the goods, just as an asset could be adjusted to the current buying price of the goods—replacement cost. Note that we are not necessarily recommending this practice; we are only describing it in order to provide a more complete coverage of measurement methods that could be applied to liabilities.

Historical Cost

Historical cost is a past entry price in which the firm was involved (category III-B-2-a in EXHIBIT VI-1). As a type of market price, it reflects the market's judgment of the asset's cash flow potential, in a general sense, at the date of the transaction. Sellers at that price believe that the asset has no greater cash flow potential to them; buyers at that price believe that the asset has a cash flow potential to them of not less than the market price. In particular, the acquisition price reflects the judgment of the management of the buying firm that the asset is worth at least its cost in the use visualized at the time of acquisition. Historical cost includes any fringe costs of acquisition.

In addition to reflecting the market's judgment of value as of an asset's acquisition date and shortly thereafter, historical cost often rates high on both the reliability and cost of accounting criteria. Regarding the latter, when an asset is purchased directly from another entity with immaterial fringe acquisition costs, a minimum of accounting effort is required to debit to the asset account the amount of the cash disbursement made to acquire it. In such cases, the cost valuation would be highly verifiable and free of bias. In other cases, especially the finished goods inventory of a manufacturer, the cost of accounting on the historical cost basis becomes relatively high and the reliability may be extremely low because of the large number of calculations and judgments that are involved in "product cost accounting," especially if a major material input contributes to several products (the joint products case). It is essential that we recognize the wide range of reliability of historical cost data.

The historical cost of limited-life assets that decline in service potential is commonly amortized or depreciated in order to value the asset at the cost of the remaining stock of services. The amortization procedure detracts substantially from the reliability of historical cost because of the difficulties and judgments involved in estimating the asset's life and salvage value and in selecting a pattern of depreciation.

Historical proceeds or receipt—the counterpart of historical cost—is often applied to liabilities. For example, nonmonetary liabilities such as obligations to deliver goods, provide the use of property, or provide insurance protection may be measured by reference to the amount of money received for the goods or services remaining to be provided, when the liability was established.

Restated Historical Cost

Original historical cost is "restated" when it is adjusted for the change in the purchasing power of the monetary measuring unit, as measured by the change in a general price index between the asset's acquisition date and the balance date. If an asset was purchased for $100 five years ago, and the general price level has risen 40 percent since that date, we can restate the acquisition cost of this asset at $140. An alternative term for this measure is "historical real cost," as distinguished from "historical money cost."

The major argument for this method is that a reader of financial statements has a clearer impression of the significance of the current dollar in terms of the purchasing power it represents than he has of any other dollar. If so, the amount of the sacrifice that was made to acquire an asset can best be conveyed to the reader if that sacrifice (cost) is expressed in terms of the number of "current" dollars that have the same purchasing power significance as the number of "acquisition date" dollars that were paid for the asset. Historical cost stated in current dollars is viewed as a more accurate expression of the sacrifice made to acquire the asset than historical cost stated in dollars used at an earlier date. Restated historical cost is a version of cost; it is not a current value method. It is subject to amortization in the same circumstances as historical cost. Its mirror image (restated historical receipt) could be applied to nonmonetary liabilities. Restated historical cost is recorded in the accounts by an entry in the asset and accumulated depreciation account and by an offsetting entry to a special shareholders' equity account that is not included in the calculation of income. Aside from this difference, the comments above pertaining to the recording of replacement cost apply also to restated historical cost.[2]

Equity Method

Two versions of the equity method should be discussed. The *pure equity method* of asset measurement means showing securities owned, generally ordinary shares, at their "book value" as reflected in the balance sheet of the issuing company (the investee). The *cost-based equity method* begins with the historical cost of the shares

---

[2] See chapter IX for a more comprehensive treatment of accounting under inflationary conditions.

when acquired by the owner and then adjusts for all subsequent changes in their book value as reported in the financial statements of the investee; any acquisition-date discrepancy between investor and investee valuations is preserved. Variations are often applied for the sake of conservatism, or to adjust the share of investee's earnings included in the investor's income to the amount that would be shown if the investee's accounts had been consolidated with those of the investor. In both versions of the equity method the investor reports its share of the investee's earnings or losses in its own profit and loss account, while dividends received are treated as reductions in the asset. *(APB Opinion No. 18* deals with the equity method.)

Supporters of the equity method contend that it is the only way of accounting for the investor's interest in the investee that is consistent with the investee's accounting. If the investee uses the best accounting methods available, one could question any method of accounting for the investment which conflicts with those methods. The cost-based equity method is, from this point of view, a compromise in that it utilizes only the investee's current earnings report and not its current balance sheet. That discrepancy opens the cost-based equity method to the criticism that cost may be greater than book value at acquisition date because the investor anticipates, and pays for, future earnings in excess of a normal rate of return on book value; if these future earnings are then added to the investment account when they appear, they are double-counted. Perhaps the cost-based equity method could be amended to meet this criticism.

Income Tax Allocation and Measurement

One more measurement technique deserves some attention in this chapter. It can be argued that an asset's (or liability's) tax "basis" affects its cash flow potential, so the basis should be considered in its measurement. If two assets are identical in every respect except for differing bases, they differ in cash flow potential, because an asset's basis will contribute to cash flow an amount equal to the basis times the company's incremental tax rate in the period or periods when the asset is deductible in computing taxable income. With a 48 percent tax rate, for example, an asset with a basis of $1 will be worth at least $.48 even if it makes no contribution to cash flow except by reducing the tax liability. But note two caveats: this value depends on the future occurrence of taxable income and is subject to discounting for the waiting period.

Following that line of reasoning, suppose that an asset is valued at $100 (by any one of the methods discussed above, e.g., NRV) but has a tax basis of $150. If the asset were sold tomorrow for its balance sheet value of $100 and if a $50 deductible loss saves $24 in income tax, the asset contributes $124 to the firm's cash balance and $24 to net income. Any asset which is shown on the books at an up-to-date market price less than its basis therefore carries with it a pool of instant earnings and any asset valued at a price above its basis bears the burden of an instant loss. The indicated solution is to adjust the valuation otherwise chosen by the marginal tax rate times the difference between that valuation and the basis. A higher basis calls for a positive adjustment of the valuation; a lower basis requires a subtraction. A similar adjustment procedure is applicable to liabilities. Note that this technique is an application of the principle of comprehensive tax allocation and includes the usual cases (such as a difference between book and tax depreciation). It is an alternative to the use of separate accounts for deferred tax liability or income taxes paid in advance. (See chapters VIII, IX, and XIV for more on this subject.)

Conclusion

We have described nine methods of measuring assets and liabilities, and have discussed the possibility of adjusting any of them by the value of the tax advantage or disadvantage associated with a difference between the value otherwise determined and the valuation basis used in determining taxable gain or loss. While we have presented a positive case for each method, we do not argue that any one of them is the universal solution to measurement problems; we believe that we have made such a good case for each method that it is entirely conceivable that practicing accountants may find roles for all of them somewhere in their work. In fact, all of them are now in use.

Our study, then, has reached the stage where we know what we want to accomplish and we have a set of criteria for evaluating alternative proposals. We have concluded that the major external use of financial statements is in predicting the firm's capacity to pay. The concepts of financial position, asset, liability, and residual equity appear to be useful in thinking about cash flow potential (and any other potential service to owners). We are familiar with nine different ways of quantifying positive and negative service potential. The next question is: When do we use which method?

ADDITIONAL READING SUGGESTIONS

American Accounting Association, Committee on Accounting Valuation Bases, "Report of the Committee on Accounting Valuation Bases," *The Accounting Review* (Supplement 1972), pp. 535–73.

Boothman, Derek, et al., *The Corporate Report* (Accounting Standards Steering Committee, 1975).

Chambers, R[aymond] J., "Measurement in Accounting," *Journal of Accounting Research* (Spring 1965), pp. 32–62.

Edwards, Edgar O. and Philip W. Bell, *The Theory and Measurement of Business Income* (University of California Press, 1961).

Financial Accounting Standards Board, "An Analysis of Issues Related to *Conceptual Framework for Financial Accounting and Reporting: Elements of Financial Statements and Their Measurements,*" *FASB Discussion Memorandum* (FASB, 2 December 1976), chapter 8.

Ijiri, Yuji, "Theory of Accounting Measurement," *Studies in Accounting Research, No. 10* (AAA, 1975).

McKeown, James C., "Comparative Application of Market and Cost Based Accounting Models," *Journal of Accounting Research* (Spring 1973), pp. 62–99.

Revsine, Lawrence, *Replacement of Cost Accounting* (Prentice-Hall, 1973).

Vancil, Richard and Roman L. Weil, *Replacement Cost Accounting: Readings on Concepts, Uses and Methods* (Thomas Horton and Daughters, 1976).

STUDY QUESTIONS

1. Is valuation a term that is properly used in connection with determining the amount of an asset or equity?

2. Compare the process of measurement in accounting with measurement in physical sciences. Analyze the process of measurement in accounting.

3. Name and describe the forms of evidence of value that are most useful in accounting. Should we replace the term "value" in this sentence?

4. Compare the following terms: basis of valuation, measurement method, type of evidence of value, measure (noun), property of an asset, economic attribute.

5. What properties of assets are measurable?

6. "Any accountant who attempts to make valuations other than those indicated by the accounts, or by some definite index, such as a market price, is coming dangerously close to the boundary of his own field and is preparing to step over into that of the economist and engineer. Valuation in any true or important sense is not a matter for the accountant and the more completely this is recognized by accountant and client the better it will be for all concerned" (Peloubet, 1935, p. 209). Do you agree? Why?

7. United Airlines, according to an employee, capitalizes large amounts of interest cost on advances to equipment suppliers. Is this a proper inclusion in acquisition cost? On which criteria does this accounting method rate low?

8. Give examples of the availability of current market values, net realizable values (NRV), or replacement cost data for used plant assets.

9. Referring to the outline of types of evidence in EXHIBIT VI-1, show which types of evidence are used in the following measurement methods:
   (a) Discounted future cash flow.
   (b) NRV.
   (c) Restated (for changes in the measuring unit) historical cost.

(d) "Historical receipt" applied to a deferred credit to revenue.
(e) Replacement cost.

10. How does the justification for the equity method of accounting for investments in common stock as given in this chapter differ from that provided in *APB Opinion No. 18?*

11. Is accounting a measurement system?

12. It has been alleged that revenues and expenses are not measured directly but can only be determined after the amount of an associated asset or liability has been measured. Are sale and purchase transactions at specified prices exceptions to this statement? Do adjustments for uncollectible receivables and cash discounts indicate whether the allegation is true or false?

13. Can you suggest any improvements in the outline of types of evidence of asset and liability amounts as presented in EXHIBIT VI-1?

14. Give examples, from currently acceptable accounting practices, in which an asset or a liability is stated at the undiscounted amount of future cash flow promised. At discounted future cash flows.

15. Give examples from current practice of the use of current market values without any adjustment.

16. Give examples from current practice of the use of NRV.

17. Give examples from current practice of the use of replacement cost.

18. Describe a production situation in which you believe it is feasible (although not necessarily desirable) to measure finished goods inventory at net realizable value. Prepare a set of pro forma (without amounts) journal entries for production costs, completion of production, sale, and related expenses.

19. Explain why the recording of the restated historical cost of an asset does not involve income.

20. Argue both sides of the proposition that the tax basis of an asset is an attribute which should be taken into consideration in its measurement.

21. Which of the nine measurement methods described in this chapter are, according to generally accepted accounting prin-

ciples, applicable to inventories of commodities? Explain and give examples.

22. Design a simple income statement based on measurement of finished goods inventory at NRV (and recognition of revenue at completion of production).

23. North American Properties, Inc. (NAPI) purchased an apartment house from Berkeley Investment Company (BIC). BIC had asked $1,000,000 for the property but the sale contract provided for payment of $200,000 in cash, $100,000 at the end of each year for seven years, and $300,000 in eight years, the delayed payments to be backed by mortgage notes. NAPI had proposed this arrangement because it would have had to borrow most of the purchase price, at an interest rate of approximately 8% if BIC had insisted on full payment in cash. NAPI assigns 20% of the purchase price to the land.

    Record the purchase on the books of NAPI.

24. Prepare simple numerical examples showing, with the aid of "T" accounts or journal entries, how current matching of the replacement cost of resources consumed with current revenues and the isolation of holding gains and losses on inventories can be achieved (a) with replacement cost measurement of inventories and (b) with historical cost measurement of inventories.

25. This is an exercise in measurement of assets and income per discounted future cash flows.

    Al Revsine's only asset is a fishing boat which he has leased to Larry Rappaport for 15 years at an annual rental of $5,000 per year payable at the end of each year plus an additional $10,000 at the end of 15 years. At the latter date the boat is to become the property of Rappaport regardless of its value or condition. Local banks are making similar financing arrangement on a 10% yield basis, compounded annually. Revsine applies all incoming cash to consumption expenditures so has no "business assets" other than the leased boat.

    (a) What is Revsine's net worth at the beginning of the lease period?

    (b) What is Revsine's net income in the first year of this arrangement?

(c) What is Revsine's income in the fifteenth year of the lease?

26. Consider cases in which a firm holds a large quantity of an asset, e.g., a large block of shares or a large stock of a commodity. In the valuation of such an asset, do you believe it is necessary to take into account the prospect that a quick sale of the entire quantity might depress the market, if there is no evidence that a quick sale is likely?

27. A and B are related entities which are not permitted to report income or loss on sales to each other. When such sales occur the basis of the asset transferred is the same in the hands of the buyer as it was in the hands of the seller.

    Assume A has an asset with a tax basis of $40 and a quoted market value of $60. A tax rate of 25% would apply to gains on this asset by either A or B.

    If A and B enter into arms-length negotiations regarding the sale and purchase of this asset and if you are negotiating on behalf of A, what would you set as a minimum fair sale price? What is the maximum purchase price that would be fair to B?

    What implications does this case have for interperiod tax allocation or for consideration of income taxes in asset valuation? What solution do you recommend—and why?

28. The Sprouse Investment Company is a corporation which has specialized in making substantial loans to "small businesses" with promising futures. It has been the practice to discount non-interest-bearing first mortgage notes when such loans are granted. The Company has obtained some of its working capital by borrowing at favorable interest rates from individuals and banks and has usually followed the practice of issuing, at a discount, non-interest-bearing notes in evidence of these obligations.

    Selection and approval of loans has been the responsibility of the corporation's president, who has also been the major stockholder. The president is now deceased and the other stockholders agree with the president's heirs that the corporation should be dissolved. Some of the assets have been liquidated and some of the outstanding obligations have been settled.

On January 1, 1977 there remains, however, some assets which it has been agreed should be sold at a fair price to Horngren, one of the surviving stockholders who has also been an officer of the corporation, *provided* he also assumes the remaining liabilities.

The remaining assets consist of four of the non-interest-bearing first mortgage notes. They have maturity values of $40,000, $50,000, $80,000 and $50,000 and are due on December 31, 1977, December 31, 1978, December 31, 1979, and December 31, 1980, respectively.

The liabilities to be assumed also consist of four non-interest bearing notes. The maturity values are $25,000, $30,000, $45,000 and $30,000; they fall due on the last day of 1977, 1978, 1979 and 1980 respectively.

Horngren purchases the assets and assumes the liabilities. He decides to keep a separate set of accounting records on the accrual basis for this investment.

REQUIRED: Prepare journal entries to record Horngren's transactions from January 1, 1977 through December 31, 1980, inclusive, based on the price he should pay in order to earn a 6 percent return on his investment. The books are to be closed each December 31. Assume all notes are paid in full on their due dates and that Horngren withdraws any cash balance at the end of each year.

CHAPTER VII

MEASUREMENT METHODS AND THE RELEVANCE CRITERION

Nine methods of measuring assets and liabilities have been described. The reader is encouraged to look at these nine measurement methods as tools for use in making valuable financial data available to those who need it. Each tool has been described and its merits extolled. But little has been said about how to choose the best tool for the job at hand as the circumstances vary.

The set of criteria discussed in chapter III gives us a basis for choosing a measurement method. Generally speaking, those criteria cannot be applied without knowledge of the specific conditions of a particular case. For example, we can not say, in general, which measurement method produces the most reliable results. The historical cost of securities owned frequently can be determined with a high degree of reliability, but if the security were acquired in the purchase of a going business and is unlisted, or if the asset is not securities but an internally developed patent, historical cost may be an unreliable measure. *The criterion of attribute relevance, on the other hand, is subject to general application to measurement methods, once we have specified that the principal attribute that we seek to measure is cash flow potential.* On the assumption that the merits of such a measurement objective have been established in chapter IV, the present chapter is devoted to an evaluation and ranking of the nine measurement methods on the criterion of the relevance of the specific attribute measured to cash-flow-oriented decisions. The roles of other criteria in the selection of measurement methods are discussed in the next chapter.

PRINCIPALS, SURROGATES, AND RELEVANCE

An attribute of an object or event is relevant to a decision if knowledge of its quantity, degree, or existence will help the

162

decision maker either (a) identify promising alternative courses of action and judge their feasibility, or (b) identify and evaluate possible outcomes of available courses of action. In chapter III we suggested that (a) is a minority use and rarely involves information on such illiquid assets as long-term plant assets and inventories not held for sale in their existing form. In chapter IV we pursued the (b) branch of attribute relevance and concluded that evidence of a firm's future capacity to pay *could* be helpful to owners, lenders, managers, suppliers, customers, and employees in predicting their payoffs from an association with the firm. *We use the term "cash flow potential" to mean the present significance, considering prospective timing and amount, of any existing capacity to produce a cash inflow or outflow.* Cash flow potential is, then, the *principal* attribute that we seek to measure. In this chapter, *we use the term "attribute relevance" to mean the relevance of an attribute to cash-flow-oriented decisions.*

The cash flow potential of most assets and liabilities cannot be measured directly. This problem typically is approached by measuring an alternative attribute that has a demonstrable economic relationship to cash flow potential and so can serve as an estimate of it. We call such a related attribute used in lieu of cash flow potential a "surrogate" attribute. Thus, an asset's current market value, or perhaps its acquisition cost, may be accepted as a surrogate for cash flow potential when a direct measurement of cash flow potential—the principal—fails to meet some of the criteria established in chapter III, especially reliability. We will evaluate all of the measurement methods described in chapter VI as surrogates for cash flow potential.

An analogy may illustrate the use of surrogate measurements. The road mileage between two coastal cities normally differs from the sea route mileage, but in some circumstances a traveller or shipper may find one of these measures useful as a surrogate for the other (unknown). Typically a surrogate is not a perfect substitute for its principal, and sometimes it may be so poor as to be useless. Often, however, a surrogate measure (or measurement of a surrogate property) is of some value to the user who is unable to obtain a direct measurement of the principal—cash flow potential in our case. But we must make certain that a relationship exists which justifies the acceptance of one measure as a surrogate for another: "Surrogates are an appropriate response to a lack of data, but not to a lack of theory" (Thomas, 1969, p. 12).

A word about the relevance of principals and surrogates may be helpful. Our analysis in chapter IV indicated that information on cash flow potential is much needed by external decision makers. While we hesitate to say that cash flow potential is perfectly relevant to any decision in the sense that it is the economic attribute that is specifically called for in a decision model, it does seem clear that it is closer than any other attribute to being perfectly relevant to cash-flow-oriented decisions. We shall speak of cash flow potential as being "directly relevant" to cash-flow-oriented decisions. Surrogates for cash flow potential are "indirectly relevant" to such decisions. Recognizing that some measures are better surrogates for cash flow potential than others, we argue that different measures have different degrees of relevance to decisions. Relevance is not a quality of economic attributes, or of measures of them, that can only be dichotomized (all or nothing); it comes in various degrees. Recognition of this fact is important to our subsequent discussion of alternative measurement methods.

Finally, we should recognize the generality of relevance. In general usage, the term "relevant" is open-ended until the phrase "relevant to . . ." is completed. In accounting there has been some tendency to use the term without the accompanying object phrase. Such usage is to be deplored, unless the object may be understood from the context. In this chapter, we discuss the relevance of various economic attributes, and measures of them, to cash-flow-oriented decisions. Once we have narrowed the application of accounting information to use in making cash-flow-oriented decisions, we may speak of certain attributes and measurement methods as being more relevant than others. Within such a context, the relevance of attributes is general; in a broader context, the relevance of an attribute varies with the decision setting.

DIRECT MEASUREMENTS OF CASH FLOW POTENTIAL

We consider three measurement methods in this section: face value of cash items, future cash flows, and discounted future (or promised) cash flows. These methods are referred to as "direct" methods because they rely on direct evidence of present or future cash amounts. They differ from methods that are based on what has happened in the past (historical cost and restated historical cost), or on what could have happened at the balance sheet date (replacement cost or net realizable value [NRV]). It follows that future cash flow methods are only applicable when firm evidence of future cash receipts or payments (normally contractual evidence) is available. It should be intuitively obvious that these "direct" measurement methods yield results more relevant to cash-flow-oriented decisions than do the "indirect" methods.

Within this trio of methods, the technique of counting the face value of coins, currency, checks, money orders, and perhaps a few other "cash items" yields data that are more relevant to cash-flow-oriented decisions than any other data that accountants can report about asset items. Assuming possible imperfections in this method (counting and arithmetic errors, counterfeit money, bad checks, or inflation before the money is spent) are insignificant, face value ranks at the top of the list of cash-flow-relevant measurement methods.

The first substantive issue of this section is: Do future cash flows (receipts and disbursements) need to be discounted? If we have solid evidence that a debtor will pay the firm $1,000 one year from the balance date, do we need to discount the $1,000 or reduce it by unearned interest, in obtaining the amount to be shown as an asset? Inflation apart, is $1,000 to be received one year from now as large an asset as $1,000 to be received tomorrow? We believe that most businessmen and accountants would answer no to the last question: $1,000 to be received tomorrow and $1,000 to be received a year hence are not equal and do not add to $2,000 of assets. No practical businessman or investor would be willing to pay the same amount for these two assets, nor would he like to base an investment decision on a balance sheet that includes both of them at maturity values. We all know that the $1,000 to be received tomorrow could be invested to mature to a sum greater than $1,000 one year hence, and is therefore a preferable asset. Similarly, $1,000 due tomorrow is a more burdensome obligation than $1,000 due a year hence. Accounting practices that ignore such differences do not measure up to the relevance criterion. The discounted future cash flow method yields more relevant information than does the undiscounted future cash flow method.

The example depicted in EXHIBIT VII-1 illustrates the importance of discounting. Assume that Companies R and S each have notes receivable with aggregate maturity amounts of $100,000 and notes payable with maturity amounts of $90,000. Their balance sheets are identical on the future cash flow basis of measurement. Now consider discounting. Assume that Company R has long-term notes receivable (with maturities averaging close to three years) and short-term notes payable (with maturities averaging about three months). Company S, on the other hand, has "borrowed long" and "loaned short"; its receivables average one year in maturity while its liabilities mature in about three years. The balance sheets based on discounted cash flow measurements are quite different. If the accountant says that the two companies are in the same financial position and have the same net worths, he is treating unlike things alike, and thus ignoring the criterion of comparability, and the resulting data are not as relevant to cash-flow-oriented decisions as they could be. The addition or subtraction of measurements of different attributes yields a sum or difference that is not subject to clear interpretation; it should be avoided if possible. (Note, however, that the resulting number is not necessarily useless; see p. 203.) The timing of a prospective cash flow must be taken into consideration in measuring the amount of the cash flow potential. To quote a prominent CPA (Defliese, 1973, p. 13): "Today, discounted cash flow has become the yardstick of comparison of all values."

At this point several warnings may be appropriate. First, the test of materiality may permit use of either the future cash flow measure or the discounted future cash flow measure in cases in which there is some consideration that favors the former—for example, the cost of calculating the discount or difficulties in agreeing on the appropriate discount rate. Second, both of these measures require reliable evidence of future cash flows; if that evidence is lacking, a surrogate measure should be chosen. We certainly do not want to encourage accountants to guess at future selling dates and prices of inventories on hand and include those inventories on the balance sheet at discounted values. Fixed assets are even further removed from the direct cash flow measurement

EXHIBIT VII-1

COMPARISON OF UNDISCOUNTED AND DISCOUNTED CASH FLOW MEASUREMENTS

MEASUREMENT OF MONETARY ITEMS AT FACE VALUE

Companies R and S
Balance Sheet
December 31, 1975

Notes Receivable, at Maturity Values	$100,000	Notes Payable, at Maturity Values	$90,000
		Owner's Equity	10,000

MEASUREMENT OF MONETARY ITEMS AT DISCOUNTED VALUES

Company R
Balance Sheet
December 31, 1975

Notes Receivable, at 12% Discounted Values [3-year maturity]	$71,000	Notes Payable, at 10% Discounted Values [3-month maturity]	$88,000
		Owners' Equity	(17,000)

Company S
Balance Sheet
December 31, 1975

Notes Receivable, at 12% Discounted Values [1-year maturity]	$89,000	Notes Payable, at 10% Discounted Values [3-year maturity]	$67,000
		Owners' Equity	22,000

picture. On the other hand, it is possible that a stock of merchandise or finished goods on hand is covered by a contract to sell which *does* provide reliable evidence of a future cash flow. Similarly, a lease contract might, in some circumstances, provide a lessor with sufficient basis for measuring machinery or even real property on a discounted future cash flow basis. In general, however, direct measurement of assets and liabilities on the basis of future cash flows should be limited to monetary assets and monetary liabilities—cash, claims to cash, and obligations to pay cash. Nonmonetary assets that are expected to contribute to future cash flows through the operating cycle—conversion to saleable goods or services, to receivables, and then to cash—are unlikely to be measured on a cash flow basis. Even if the selling price of the product is "assured," the portion of that selling price attributable to the particular input under examination—a raw material, an item of supplies, a machine—cannot be determined in any objective way. This "allocation problem," as it is often called, is, under such circumstances, a weakness in the reliability of the discounted future cash flow method; discounted future cash flow information certainly would be relevant to cash-flow-oriented decisions.

Relevance of Other Measurement Methods

We may analyze the remaining measurement methods more effectively if we divide our subject matter—assets other than cash and receivables, and liabilities—into four categories on the basis of their future roles in the firm:

1. Assets held for *sale* in their present form (e.g., merchandise inventories, finished goods held by manufacturers, and obsolete plant assets).
2. Assets held for *use* as inputs to production processes, or for use in operations (e.g., raw materials, work-in-process inventories, and plant assets in use).
3. Assets held as *investments* to yield income and/or appreciation (e.g., securities).
4. Liabilities.

Our analysis of the measurement of these classes of assets and liabilities is based on the incremental approach to value. Accordingly, we view the cash flow potential, or value, of one unit of an asset as the difference between the value of the firm when the unit in question is included and the firm's value when that unit is excluded. We shall consistently focus on the question: "What difference would it make to the firm if one unit of this asset (out of several on hand) disappeared (with sufficient notice to permit the most economical adjustment)?" In taking this approach, we realize that the sum of the individual asset values, regardless of which measurement method (or combination of methods) is used, does not yield the overall value of the firm. This is unfortunate from the standpoint of investors, but a reliable measurement of the value of the firm is simply out of reach of accountants at the present time, although they can help investors in their inevitable quest for this information. Accountants must work with specific asset units—a machine, a square meter of material, a building—not with the production facilities of a company in one location or the value of a division of a company. In view of accountants' great respect for and necessary dependence upon market prices as evidence of value, their first choice of evidence of the value of the whole firm would have to be the market price of its shares (if available). However, investors are not likely to be willing to pay accountants much for that information. So we must concentrate on the incremental values of individual assets in sizes that are commonly bought and sold. The failure of the sum to represent a measure of the value of the whole firm (additivity failure) is a limitation of accounting that we do not know how to overcome. Our reliance on the incremental approach is based on the premise that although this limitation represents a serious imperfection, it does not completely invalidate the results.

Assets Held for Sale

We begin with the proposition that users of financial statements want to know the discounted net cash receipt that will result from the disposition of an asset. In the absence of reliable direct evidence of a future cash receipt, the cash receipt that could be enjoyed at the balance sheet date less the prices (in the entry market) of whatever services or commodities are needed to sell the asset, that is, NRV, is in many cases a good surrogate for the discounted future cash flow that will result from the disposition of the asset. We may better understand the potential role of this measurement method if we note its possible weaknesses. First, we may not be able to identify the one, clear-cut, objective, independent market quotation. Many securities, basic products of mines, the sea, and the land, and standard, graded manufactured products are traded in markets that provide quotations meeting the accountants' reliability standard; however, many assets in the categories of plant, work in process, and finished stocks of branded, technical, and fashion goods do not. But the weaknesses of NRV in the latter cases must not be used as an excuse for not applying it in some of the former. Accountants must take the responsibility of selecting the most appropriate method to use consistently in the particular case—one type of asset in one firm. The inappropriateness of that method in other cases is irrelevant, except to the extent that comparability must be considered as one criterion of useful information. (Comparability, however, does not require the same treatment of items in significantly different circumstances.)

Other possible weaknesses in NRV as a surrogate for discounted future cash flow are changes in the market price between the measurement date and the sale date, a change in the management's plans for sale, and errors in the calculation of the costs to be deducted from current selling price to obtain NRV. These potential weaknesses clearly apply unevenly to different assets. The individual accountant, the group of accountants concerned with a particular industry, and the accounting profession as a whole must use professional judgment to discriminate between those cases in which the weaknesses are disabling and those in which they are only imperfections.

The *market value* of an asset, without any deduction for costs of selling or addition of fringe acquisition costs, may relate to a market in which a firm buys, to one in which it sells, or to both (in one-market cases such as securities). It would appear to be a good surrogate for NRV if the necessary selling costs are immaterial, for current replacement cost if fringe acquisition costs are immaterial, or for discounted future cash flow under certain circumstances.

Current replacement cost may be a good surrogate for the NRV of assets held for sale. The justification for this assertion lies in one of the most generally accepted ideas in economics: the selling price of an article tends to cover its full economic costs, including a return on capital, when a competitive market is in equilibrium. This tells us that there is a relationship between NRV and replacement cost. But we all know that this relationship is a fairly general one; it may not be very close for any one commodity at any one time. Lack of competition among buyers or sellers and various short-run factors can make substantial differences. Furthermore, the problems of ascertaining the full, current cost of producing or acquiring any asset, including incremental administrative and overhead costs and cost of capital, are often formidable. As a consequence, we are forced to recognize that the suitability of replacement cost as a surrogate for NRV is seriously impaired in many cases. But again, we insist that its unsuitability in some cases need not preclude its use in other cases in which its limitations are minor compared with those of alternative methods.

EXHIBIT VII-2 diagrams the relationship between NRV and replacement cost. This "gap chart" reflects the various stages in the operating cycle of a manufacturing firm (laid out along the horizontal axis) and the major components of the selling price (on the vertical axis). (The operating cycle of a merchandising firm would include only one stage for inventories, and conversion costs would be omitted from the costs.) The cost accumulation approach to the measurement of operating cycle assets accumulates the amounts of all sacrifices made to obtain resources used in the cycle activities, conceivably all the way to the ultimate step, cash realization. This approach takes into consideration an asset's

EXHIBIT VII-2
RELATIONSHIP BETWEEN NRV AND REPLACEMENT COST

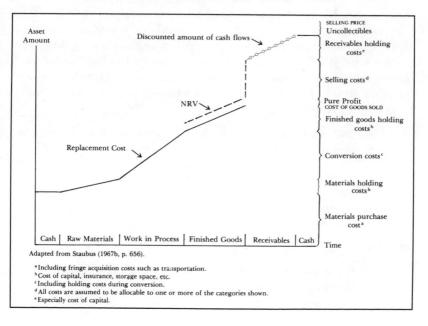

Adapted from Staubus (1967b, p. 656).

[a] Including fringe acquisition costs such as transportation.
[b] Cost of capital, insurance, storage space, etc.
[c] Including holding costs during conversion.
[d] All costs are assumed to be allocable to one or more of the categories shown.
[e] Especially cost of capital.

history. The future-oriented NRV approach, on the other hand, is based on future steps in the operating cycle and the amounts of cash flows associated with them. Thus, all sacrifices that must be made in the future are deducted from the selling price to obtain the NRV. As the term is used in this book, NRV is future-oriented only with respect to the activities that are expected to occur; the amounts attached to them are based on current market prices of both the final product and the remaining inputs. When the cost accumulation approach is applied on a genuinely full-cost basis, including cost of capital and all allocations, and when the NRV approach deducts all remaining costs on the same basis, current replacement cost equals NRV in competitive equilibrium. If the two values are not equal, a pure economic profit or loss occurs; it is reflected in a gap between the two lines. In traditional accounting terminology, the accountant is said to "recognize revenue" when he switches from one measurement approach to the other; we call this "jumping the gap." Note that the gap is likely to be positive (a gross profit) if some items of cost, such as cost of capital and general administrative costs, are excluded from both the accumulated costs and the remaining costs to be deducted from selling price in computing NRV. The chart would look very much the same whether the cost accumulation approach were applied on a current replacement or historical basis. Also, it becomes apparent that the discounted future cash flow view of receivables is identical to a future-oriented version of NRV in which cost of capital is deducted as a remaining cost.

If it is accepted that:

(a) NRV can be justified as providing evidence of future cash flows on the basis that current selling price is a good surrogate for future selling price, and

(b) replacement cost can be justified as a surrogate for NRV, and

(c) historical cost can be a reasonable surrogate for replacement cost,

it follows that

(d) historical cost may, in some circumstances, be a surrogate (albeit twice removed) for future cash flow potential. (Surrogacy is a transitive quality.)

That *historical cost* can be a reasonable surrogate for replacement cost may be explained as follows: the major difference between them is in the date of the market price involved, and there is a high statistical correlation between the prices of a sample of goods at one date and the prices of that same set of goods at another date not far removed from the first. This association links historical cost to replacement cost, which has already been linked to NRV, which in turn is a surrogate for discounted future cash flows.[1] The surrogate chain is beginning to take shape.

With the assistance of James Salven, I once gathered some empirical data relevant to the hypothesis that the association of the prices of a set of goods at date d_1 with the prices of the same set of goods at date d_2 increases as d_1 approaches d_2. The goods chosen for the test were those commodities for which wholesale prices are quoted daily in the *Wall Street Journal;* data were available for 47 commodities. The test focused on 1971 year-end reporting on the alternative assumptions (1) that inventories held at that date would be sold at random 1972 dates, and (2) that the year-end inventories would be sold at the beginning of April 1972. Prices were obtained for dates one year, six months, three months, and one month before the year-end, and for the last business day of the year. The coefficient of correlation was computed for each· of these five sets of prices and (1) the random-date set of 1972 prices and (2) the April 1972 prices. The results, plotted in EXHIBIT VII-3, support our hypothesis that the longer the time lag between d_1 and d_2, the lower the degree of association. Calculations of mean percentage error of earlier prices as predictors of later prices confirm these results; the less the time lag, the closer the relationship. These data support the view that historical cost may be accepted as a surrogate for current replacement cost (or even future replacement cost); the more recent the cost, the better the surrogate.

Before leaving historical cost, a word should be said about differences in the circumstances surrounding the acquisition of an asset. One difference is between (1) an asset which was acquired

---

[1] See Barton (1974), for a development of the argument that replacement cost is *not* closely enough related to discounted future cash flow to justify using the former as a surrogate for the latter.

Exhibit VII-3
Correlation of Prices of 47 Commodities at Two Dates

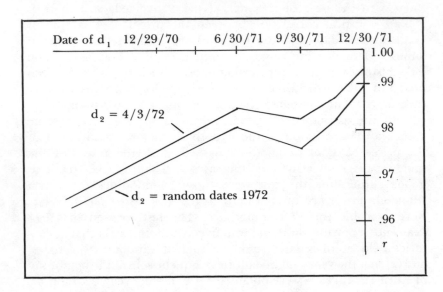

in substantially its present form for an agreed price, as opposed to (2) an asset which was constructed, manufactured, or otherwise assembled from a combination of separately acquired and independently priced inputs. The cost of assets in the first category typically represents a more objective market evaluation because other buyers and sellers probably were involved, in some sense, in the market for that particular form of asset. A "self-constructed" asset that is unique has not been appraised by the market as a unit; only the firm's management has judged that the asset will be worth, when completed, at least its estimated cost. The actual acquisition cost would appear to be a less relevant measure of cash flow potential in the latter case.

This case also suggests another difference in circumstances of acquisition: the difference between expected costs and realized costs. Only the former are included in management's minimum judgment of the value of the new asset. Actual historical cost of internally assembled assets does not seem to warrant as much support, on the ground that management judged the asset to be worth at least its cost, as (1) the estimate of cost on which the judgment was made or (2) actual historical cost in "simple purchase" acquisitions. These considerations appear to detract from the merits of historical cost and adjusted historical cost of such possible assets as capitalized research, development, and exploration costs; other self-developed intangibles; and, to a lesser extent, self-constructed plant assets, work in process, and finished stocks. We are not suggesting that these items should not be measured at cost, but we do suggest that this possible weakness be considered when comparing the historical cost method with alternatives for use in such cases. In this context, standard cost appears to have considerable merit, where applicable, because it excludes unanticipated costs.

Restated historical cost is a version of historical cost that appears to be a better surrogate for replacement cost than historical cost expressed in the measuring unit in effect at the acquisition date. Consider this example: Item x was purchased ten years ago for $300. A general price index representing prices in the entire economy has risen 50 percent since then. What is the best guess of the current price of x, if one does not know the nature of x? Since most prices have risen and the average rise has been 50 percent, an estimate of $450 would appear to be safer than an estimate of $300. For this reason we rank adjusted historical cost over original historical cost as a surrogate for replacement cost.

We may use a variety of types of price indexes for adjusting historical cost in order to obtain a better surrogate for replacement cost. The price of an asset (i) at any date is a function of its price at an earlier date:

$$P_{i,2} = f(P_{i,1}).$$

When index numbers are used to express the relationship, we may write:

$$P_{i,2} = \left(\frac{I_2}{I_1}\right) P_{i,1} + e.$$

That is, the later price may be estimated, subject to an error term (*e*), by applying the change in an index to the earlier price. The nature of the index makes a great deal of difference, of course. An index of all prices in the economy typically can be used to adjust an older price (e.g., historical cost) towards a later (e.g., current) price. Such an adjustment, however, could be in the wrong direction, since a few prices can be expected to move against the trend, especially if the overall change is modest. But if the general price index has doubled, price declines are likely to be rare.

Goods can be divided into classes for greater uniformity of price changes. For example, the prices of several grains tend to move together much more uniformly than do farm prices in general or all wholesale prices. The prices of automotive products probably move more uniformly than do the prices of all durable goods. This suggests that the narrower the classification of goods included in the index, the better an index-adjusted price will serve as a surrogate for the current specific price. EXHIBIT VII-4 illustrates this point. The variety of indexes listed there range from one that reflects the average of all prices, so may be used as a measure of the change in the significance of the monetary unit used in the economy, to one that is likely to yield a close surrogate for

EXHIBIT VII-4

SURROGATE RANKING OF MEASURES OF PRICE CHANGES FOR USE IN ADJUSTING AN OLD
PRICE OF AN ASSET TO ITS CURRENT PRICE

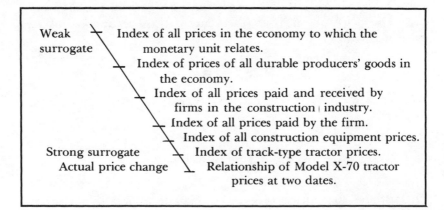

Weak surrogate — Index of all prices in the economy to which the monetary unit relates.

Index of prices of all durable producers' goods in the economy.

Index of all prices paid and received by firms in the construction industry.

Index of all prices paid by the firm.

Index of all construction equipment prices.

Strong surrogate — Index of track-type tractor prices.

Actual price change — Relationship of Model X-70 tractor prices at two dates.

replacement cost when the change in the index is applied to historical cost. The latter (narrow) index is not appropriate for restating historical cost in the current-size measuring unit, nor is the general price level index a very good basis for estimating replacement cost, although it is likely to be of moderate value for this purpose. The prompt periodic computation and publication of many narrow product-group price indexes would greatly facilitate the application of the specific index version of the replacement cost measurement method. (Note that this discussion is concerned only with asset measurement at a specified date such as a balance sheet date; the comparison of asset measurements that is involved in computing income will be discussed in chapter IX in the context of changing price levels.)

To summarize, measurement methods may be ranked on the relevance criterion for application to assets (other than investments) held for sale as follows:

1. NRV (in the market in which the asset is expected to be sold).
2. Current replacement cost.
3. Restated historical cost.
4. Historical cost.

Assets Held for Use

The category of assets held for use includes raw materials to be used in production, supplies of various sorts, work in process, limited-life plant assets such as machinery and buildings, and land. The critical practical limitation is the absence of direct evidence of the contributions that these assets will make to the firm's future cash flows. This circumstance again forces accountants to turn to a surrogate for direct measurement of future cash flows.

Using the incremental test of asset value (see p. 168), the most useful question to ask appears to be: What difference would it make to the firm's future cash flows if a unit of the asset disappeared? The answer depends upon differences in noncash events. There are three major possibilities:

1. A change in quantity on hand may result in a change in future acquisitions:

    a. By purchase, if the asset is normally acquired in its existing form.

    b. By production, if the asset is of a type that is produced within the firm.

2. A change in quantity on hand could result in a change in future usage of the asset (resource) in production:

    a. Change usage by changing the output and sales of the firm's product.

    b. Change usage by substitution of this resource for another or vice versa.

3. A change in quantity on hand could result in a change in the direct sales of the asset itself—if it is held for use but is effectively obsolete from the point of view of the firm and its present activities, and so is available for sale. (Examples might include machinery which is in use but is out of date and therefore would not be replaced if it became unserviceable, or a stock of material which was purchased for other circumstances but is being "used up" because it is on hand.)

These possible consequences of changes in the quantity of an asset on hand may be associated with measures of assets as follows:

1. If one less unit on hand means that the firm must acquire one more unit in the future, then the presence of a unit of the asset saves the firm the future incremental acquisition cost (by purchase or production) of a unit. Current replacement cost is a reasonable surrogate for future acquisition cost.

2. Consequences of changes in future usage:

    a. If the incremental asset affects future output and sales, then the financial consequence of its disappearance would be the change in the future sales of the final product, less the saving by not incurring the cost of other resources used to make the product. We shall designate this type of valuation as "completed-cycle NRV." It is related to the concept of "value in use."

    b. If the availability of one less unit of the asset would require the consumption of more of another resource (assuming substitutability), then the significance of a unit of the asset would be measurable by the cost of the substitute.

3. In the case of the out-of-date asset, a change in the quantity

on hand presumably would not affect future acquisitions of the same type of asset, but might well affect the future sales of retired or unneeded assets. The "as-is NRV" (if sold in their present form rather than continuing through the operating cycle) of such assets appears to be a better indicator of their current significance to the firm.

The preceding analysis is summarized in EXHIBIT VII-5 for ready reference. Our next step is to consider the probable frequency of occurence of each of the possible responses to a change in the stock of the asset, so that we can determine the applicability of the various measurement methods under discussion in this chapter to assets held for use. Experience suggests that the first response listed—change in future acquisitions—is by far the most frequent one. The frequency of response 2a—change in output and sales—is hard to judge; the presence of stocks of the asset itself and of assets in later stages of the production cycle sometimes prevents a small change in the quantity of an asset on hand from

EXHIBIT VII-5

APPLICATION OF THE INCREMENTAL TEST OF ASSET VALUE TO ASSETS HELD FOR USE

Difference in Actions	Financial Consequences	Relevant Surrogate Measure
1. Change future acquisitions		
a. By purchase	Change future purchase costs	Current replacement cost by purchase
b. By production	Change future production costs	Current replacement cost by production
2. Change usage		
a. Change output of product	Change future sales receipts and costs of other inputs	Completed-cycle NRV
b. Change other (substitute) inputs	Change in cost of substitute	Current replacement cost of substitute
3. Change direct sales of asset	Change future receipts and selling costs	As-is NRV

This EXHIBIT is based on an analysis in Staubus (1971a) and is adapted from an exhibit in Staubus (1971b, p. 58).

affecting sales of the firm's product and the cash receipts that follow sales. Response 2b may be more likely but probably does not happen in more than a small minority of cases. Response 3 is only relevant to out-of-date assets.

We conclude that (1) as-is NRV is a relevant measure of out-of-date assets held for use; (2) completed-cycle NRV and current replacement cost of a substitute are sometimes relevant measures of assets held for use (but rarely are they acceptably reliable); and (3) replacement cost is the most frequently relevant measure of assets held for use. Our conclusion regarding replacement cost is, we believe, consistent with the experience of the average businessman. With respect to most assets held for use, the greater the stock on hand, the smaller the quantity to be purchased in the future. Every unit on hand saves the firm a future cash outflow in the amount of future replacement cost, and present replacement cost appears to be the best surrogate for future replacement cost. On this basis, we conclude that replacement cost is the most frequently relevant measure of up-to-date assets held for use.

This conclusion is based on the incremental test of asset value applied to normal circumstances. It is not based on such tests as: What would a motorist pay for a tire if he were stranded in the desert? Or, what would a manager pay for a unit of material if his entire stock suddenly disappeared so that his production line must be closed down? Or, what would a manager pay for a new conveyer belt which is necessary to permit his plant to operate? These are not normal valuation situations. While assets may be "worth" many times their replacement cost in emergencies, we believe that the typical significance of an asset held for use is that it saves its owner its future acquisition cost. Replacement cost is the obvious surrogate for future acquisition cost.

Two versions of NRV have been introduced in this section: completed-cycle NRV and as-is NRV. How do they rank on the criterion of relevance to cash-flow-oriented decisions? No simple answer is suitable. Completed-cycle NRV (which approximates value in use) is highly relevant if the asset is to be used in the operating cycle and its absence would result in loss of sales. But if it is to be sold "as-is," what it *could have* contributed to operations is not directly relevant to a decision being made on the basis of predictions of the firm's future cash flows. In other words, the asset's cash flow potential in its most likely use—presumably its best use—is highly relevant to cash-flow-oriented decisions; cash flow potential in an unlikely use is of little relevance. This suggests that a more useful breakdown of NRVs would distinguish "best-use" NRV from "secondary" NRV. Best-use NRV is completed-cycle NRV in case 2a of EXHIBIT VII-5 but is as-is NRV in case 3. It appears, then, that best-use NRV should be ranked high in some circumstances, while secondary NRV (cash flow potential in an unlikely course of action) is an attribute of substantially less relevance to cash-flow-oriented decisions. Transaction costs, transportation costs, location disadvantages, and potential buyers' uncertainties about the condition of the asset can cause such a large gap between completed-cycle NRV and as-is NRV that we hesitate to suggest that either is a close surrogate for the other—and such a surrogate relationship is required if secondary NRV is to be a close surrogate for best-use NRV. Consequently, we are unwilling to rank secondary NRV as a surrogate for cash flow potential. Furthermore, both completed-cycle NRV and as-is NRV pose serious reliability problems in application to many assets held for use.

Note also that a case-by-case application of this analytical approach requires the labelling of each asset as up-to-date or out-of-date. While some readers may dismiss this as a routine feature of good asset management, from an auditor's point of view it provides an opportunity for manipulation. (Remember that current GAAP require the writing down of obsolete assets.) At what stage of an asset's life (especially that of a fixed asset) should it be switched from the up-to-date to the out-of-date category and written down from replacement cost to as-is NRV? (Completed-cycle NRV for plant assets is presumably out of the question on the reliability criterion.) In the jargon of contemporary American used car trading, this is the question of when to switch from "high blue-book" (or black book, or red book) to "low blue-book" value, where high blue book is the dealer selling price and low blue book is the dealer buying price. (Of course, replacement cost used is not available with reasonable reliability for most other fixed assets; depreciated replacement cost new is the more commonly available version.)

This switching issue is a classic case in which the accountant must make the trade-off between relevance and reliability; occasional differences in judgment are inevitable. The problem may be clarified if we diagram the possible relationships between replacement cost (RC), completed-cycle NRV (CCNRV), and as-is NRV (AINRV), and the indicated management action and measurement method. (CCNRV of assets held for use is assumed to be excluded as an accounting basis on the reliability criterion.)

(a)	CCNRV > RC > AINRV	Up-to-date asset; subject to replacement; measure at replacement cost.
(b)	RC > CCNRV > AINRV	Out-of-date asset; hold for use but do not replace; measure by as-is NRV.
(c)	AINRV > CCNRV	Obsolete asset; sell; measure by as-is NRV.

The listing highlights the two difficult judgments that are necessary to apply this analysis: (1) ordering the measures for classification of the asset as up-to-date or either out-of-date or obsolete; and (2) measuring the asset by the method indicated by the ordering. Both difficulties, of course, stem from the unreliability of the measurement methods listed, especially completed-cycle NRV and as-is NRV, in these circumstances. The easier option of selecting depreciated replacement cost new for all limited-life plant assets is a tempting one when the reliability and comparability criteria are taken into consideration, but best-use NRV is entitled to a high ranking on the relevance criterion—the focus of this chapter.

The valuation of assets held for use in accordance with the analysis summarized in EXHIBIT VII-5 is consistent with the costing technique of charging operating activities with the *cost of using resources*. When assets are carried at the amount of the sacrifice occasioned by their disappearance, recording their usage by debiting the appropriate operating activity account and crediting the asset account with this amount results in relevant costing of activities. Historical cost accounting when prices are changing involves charging operations for the cost of acquiring resources rather than the cost of using them, and so does not provide the information needed by managers in deciding how to accomplish their objectives—that is, what combination of resources to utilize. If, for example, materials were purchased when the price was $3 per pound but the price is now $4 per pound, and if the management is making a decision involving alternative courses of action that would require different quantities of this material, the current cost of using this item, if it is classified as up-to-date, is $4, and the wrong decision could be made if this figure were not used. An accounting system which routinely records the current cost of using resources appears to provide a better basis for managerial decisions than does a system based on historical cost (see Staubus, 1971a).

The above interpretation of the cost of using resources appears to be the single-firm version of the economic concept of opportunity cost. According to the latter concept, the cost to an economy of using resources in a specified application is their value in the next best alternative use in the economy. From the point of view of the management of one firm, the cost of using resources is the alternative sum of money the firm could have had; this often is future replacement cost of stocked resources but could be one of several other measures.

To summarize this section, we may rank measurement methods on the relevance criterion for application to up-to-date assets held for use (on the assumption that completed-cycle NRV is not available) as follows:

1. Current replacement cost.
2. Restated historical cost.
3. Historical cost.

Out-of-date assets held for use (as well as obsolete assets) should, on the relevance criterion, be measured at as-is NRV.

Assets Held as Investments

The category of assets held as investments includes debt securities, shares, real property, and personal property (such as art objects) that are held for regular income and/or capital appreciation. Direct contractual evidence of future cash flows is normally available for debt securities. These flows can be discounted at the appropriate current market rate of interest. Current market value appears to be a second choice until we recognize that discounting at the current market rate of interest yields a result that is identical with current market value, since the yield rate that active buyers and sellers of securities use to calculate the price at which they are willing to buy or sell is the market rate of interest at the time. Thus, as a practical matter, we may speak of the valuation of debt securities at market value without departing from the discounted future cash flow goal.

Direct evidence of future cash flows from shares of common and preferred stock is not available, so market value would be the most relevant measurement method practically available for application to such assets. NRV (market price less commission and tax) and replacement cost (market price plus commission) do not appear to be as good surrogates for discounted future cash flows as the market price; the latter averages buyers' and sellers' judgments of the present value of the future cash flows to be enjoyed by the owner of the shares. The basic dilemma faced by the accountant when measuring an asset that is bought and sold in the same market is when to absorb the commissions (and other transaction costs). If we assume no change in the market price, carrying a security at full original or replacement cost would result in charging both the buying and selling commissions to the period of sale, whereas the use of NRV charges both commissions to the period of purchase. When market value is used, the purchase commission is charged to the period of purchase and the sale commission is assigned to the period of sale, while all market price changes are reflected in income as they occur. This seems to be the most equitable solution.

Replacement cost may have a role in the valuation of real property investments; one version of professional appraisals of buildings is "replacement cost new" from which depreciation is then deducted. We rank replacement cost immediately after market value for application to investments.

Historical cost has the same basis for use as a surrogate for current market value of investments as it has with assets held for sale. Similarly, historical cost adjusted by a general price index has the usual advantage over historical cost. This brings us to another method that is related to historical cost and which is applicable to shares owned—the *equity method.* (The justification for its application—in either of two versions—was given in the previous chapter and so will not be repeated here.) We must recognize it as a method that takes into account changes in the value of the investment, as measured on the books of the issuing company (the investee) since acquisition date. This updating procedure results in a measure that is more future-oriented than is historical cost, so it would appear to be a better surrogate for discounted future cash flows and more relevant to decisions regarding investments in the company owning the shares. We therefore rank it ahead of historical cost and adjusted historical cost, but behind current market value in typical circumstances.

Liabilities

Accountants typically perceive the measurement of liabilities as less difficult than the measurement of assets. The availability of direct evidence of the future cash flows required by the majority of liabilities is a good reason for this perception. This evidence permits accountants to show liabilities at the sum of the future cash payments called for in the contract, less unearned interest— that is, at discounted future cash flows. Alternatively, if discount is immaterial because the payment date is near at hand, accountants record undiscounted future cash flows. The reader who has followed the argument that future cash flows are relevant to investment decisions is likely to agree that the discounted future cash flow method and the future cash flow method, if the waiting period is short, rank first and second, respectively, for application to liabilities.

The market value group of methods, including NRV and replacement cost, may also have some applicability to liabilities, but there are dangers in measuring the firm's own debt at its market value. The market value of a firm's debt may change for various reasons, the most common being changes in the market rate of interest and in the risk associated with the issuer. A change in risk is a change in the probability distribution of future payoffs. To the extent that a change in risk affects the debt's market value, any revision of the liability amount would result in an offsetting change in the shareholders' equity in the direction opposite to that implied by the market's changing view of the firm's prospects. For example, if the market lowered its opinion of the firm's future, it might mark down the firm's debentures. If the accountant for the issuing firm reduced the liability amount and recorded the offsetting credit as an increase (of any type) in the shareholders' equity, the balance sheet might be made less relevant to investors' decisions. This would be similar to providing for bad debts on the books of the debtor. This danger suggests the possibility of changing the discount rate applied to debt only to the extent of changes in the market rate for the original risk class of the debt at its issue date, and not for changes in the discount rate applied by the market to the issuer's securities because of changes in the perceived risk associated with the issuer itself.

The alternative view is that to discount future cash outflows at the original issue discount rate is to recognize the degree of risk that the market perceived at issue date. Valuation of the debt at its current market value, however, takes into account the degree of risk that the market perceives currently. Which is preferable, the risk perceived at the earlier date or that perceived at the later date? The answer most acceptable to future-oriented accountants is likely to be the risk at the later date. Still another possibility is the use of a risk-free rate; however, discounting at the lower risk-free rate would seem to involve recognition of a loss on issue of the debt, a step that is not consistent with any view of borrowing with which we are familiar.

The answer to this problem seems to lie in recognition of the probability distribution of future payoffs on which the expected value of both equity and debt securities is based. In every risky undertaking there is some probability that the creditors will not be paid in full and, therefore, some probability that owners won't be paid at all. When this probability increases and the value of the ownership interest declines, the value of the debt moves in the same direction. To lower the value assigned to the debt would be reasonable if the accountant treated the circumstances that resulted in the market lowering its assessment of the expected value of the debt as a loss of assets and as a corresponding reduction in the value of the owners' equity. This means that a major decline in the value of assets reduces the expected value of both the creditors' claims and the owners' interests. This view is illustrated in EXHIBIT VII-6 by the distribution of aggregate payoffs

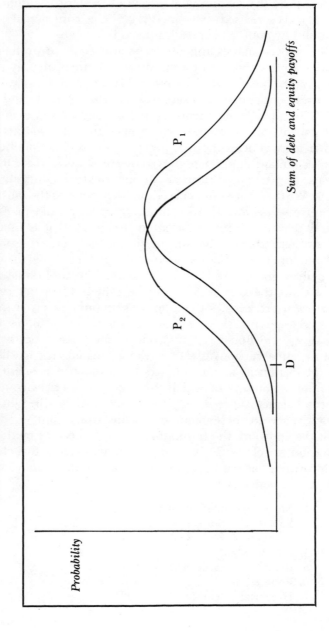

EXHIBIT VII-6

MARKET'S REASSESSMENT OF PROBABILITY DISTRIBUTION OF FUTURE PAYOFFS TO INVESTORS expected by the market at the time of issue of the debt, P_1, and the market's revised assessment, P_2. The contractual payments required by debt instruments sum to D.

The above analysis appears to be applicable to preferred stock as well. In the absence of a maturity date, the only way preferred stock can be measured at discounted future cash flows is to assume the preferential dividend rate will be paid regularly and perpetually. The appropriate discount rate (capitalization rate) must reflect the risk of failure to pay. We believe that the market price of the security reflects the risk and pure interest factors better than any accountant's judgment can, so we see no need to discuss further the use of discounted future cash flow measurements of preferred stock. We therefore rank current market value as the most relevant measure of preferred stock. Issue price, as an old market value, is less relevant to future-oriented decisions. If it is used, should it be restated for changes in the size of the measuring unit?

Nonmonetary liabilities, such as obligations to perform services or deliver goods, are a different story. The traditional approach is to show them at what could be called "historical receipt" or "historical proceeds"—the amount of money received in advance in exchange for the services or commodities to be provided. However, we should call attention to the possibilities of applying the negative versions of NRV (the estimated cost of discharging the obligation as at the balance date) and replacement cost (the amount of money for which the goods or services could be sold at the balance sheet date). We do not feel justified in devoting much space to these methods in this study, but we do believe that they outrank the traditional historical receipt method on the criterion of relevance—our only consideration in this chapter.

Measurement methods applicable to liabilities may be ranked, on the relevance criterion, as follows:

1. Discounted future cash flows.
2. Future cash flows, if waiting period is short.
3. Current market price.
4. Negative NRV.
5. Replacement receipt (or proceeds).
6. Restated historical receipt (or proceeds).
7. Historical receipt (or proceeds).

SUMMARY OF RELEVANCE APPRAISALS

The preceding analyses of the relevance of measurement methods to cash-flow-oriented decisions is summarized in EXHIBIT VII-7. Consolidating the partial conclusions reached in relation to assets held for sale, assets held for use, and assets held as investments results in some discontinuities. For example, current market price is ranked above best-use NRV for application to investments that are bought and sold in the same market, but it defies ranking for application to assets held for sale because of variations in the significance of deductible costs. And the equity method ranks between current market value and restated historical cost for equity investments, but it is not applicable to any other asset category. In the case of up-to-date assets held for use, the first five methods are unlikely to be reliable enough even to be thought of as possibilities. In sum, while EXHIBIT VII-7 is only a rough guide to the relevance of measurement methods for application to assets in general, it is intended to illustrate the linkages that are the heart of the surrogate chain. These linkages may be summarized in a series of brief statements as follows:

1. The measurement of cash items at their face value is assumed to be the ultimate in the measurement of financial attributes relevant to cash-flow-oriented decisions.
2. We assume that the amounts and times of cash flows promised by or to the entity can be combined with the aid of a discount rate to yield the most relevant measure of cash flow potential for noncash assets. Undiscounted future cash flows can, if the waiting period is short, yield a close surrogate for discounted future cash flows.
3. NRV—the net proceeds that could be obtained by selling a unit of the asset (a) in its "best use" and (b) employing market prices prevailing at the measurement date—is a close surrogate for the present value of the flow that will be realized if the market is competitive and well informed.
4. The tendency of full cost to equal selling price in a competitive market makes replacement cost a close surrogate for NRV in many cases.
5. Restated historical cost—an old market price adjusted by the average change in market prices during the holding

Exhibit VII-7

Measurement Methods Ranked by Relevance to Cash-Flow-Oriented Decisions (The Surrogate Chain)

Measurement Method	Relationship Justifying Use	Variance from Related Method
1. Face value of cash		
2. Discounted future cash flows	Direct measurement of cash flow potential	Vs. cash, uncertainties introduced: timing, amount, discount rate
3. Future cash flows, if short term	Direct measurement of quantity dimension of cash flow potential	Ignores timing of flow
4. Current market price of single-market assets	Competitive market price is based on actors' judgments of present value of future cash flows from asset. Current price≈future cash flow from sale	Imperfections in market
5. Best-use NRV	Good surrogate for discounted future cash flows per (4) above	Vs. discounted future cash flow, imperfections in market; uncertainty of costs deducted

6. Current replacement cost		
a. If incremental unit affects sales	Surrogate for (5): full replacement cost equals NRV in competitive equilibrium	Pure profit (±) due to market imperfections
b. If incremental unit affects future acquisitions	Surrogate for incremental future cash flows via reduced future purchases	Vs. discounted future cash flow, imperfections in market
7. Equity method	Improves upon cost methods by updating per investee's accounting methods	Vs. market, all limitations of investee's accounting. Vs. cost, recorded value changes since acquisition
8. Restated historical cost	Estimate of replacement cost	Differs from replacement cost by real price change
9. Historical cost	Surrogate for replacement cost or restated historical cost	Differs from replacement cost by nominal price change

period to date—is a reasonable surrogate for replacement cost—an old market price adjusted by the change in the price of the specific commodity.

6. Historical cost is the equivalent of restated historical cost expressed in a different (older) measuring unit. If the change in the measuring unit between the two measurement dates has not been great, historical cost may be an acceptable surrogate for restated historical cost. Historical cost is also a surrogate for replacement cost, the only source of difference being in the timing of the entry market prices used.

7. A set of statements similar to 2 through 6 above can be written so as to apply to liabilities.

The reader must see clearly that the ranked list presented here is not a full guide to the choice of a measurement method because it reflects only one criterion—relevance. It does, however, provide a basis for stating our general procedure for choosing a measurement method for application in circumstances calling for information relevant to cash-flow-oriented decisions. *Starting at the top of the list in EXHIBIT VII–7, evaluate each measurement method on the basis of the other eight criteria presented in chapter III (especially reliability, effects via other parties, and cost of production) until a method is found which is acceptable on those other criteria. Choose that method.*

Another way of reviewing the relationships between measurement methods is to start with historical cost and consider its weaknesses and how to improve upon it. Following this pattern, we can step on up the ladder to discounted future cash flows as follows:

1. The first readily available measure of a newly acquired noncash asset is its acquisition cost, or *historical cost*—its market price at acquisition date. But with the passage of time and changes in the purchasing power of the monetary unit, the sacrifice made to acquire an asset may be communicated more effectively if we state it in the current measuring unit.

2. This leads us to *restated historical cost,* which permits us to add the costs of all assets in terms of the same measuring unit.

3. But rather than measure the asset at its old entry market price (expressed in current measuring units), why not

update the measurement to current entry market price—
current replacement cost—including fringe acquisition costs,
of course? Of all the past market prices that are available
for use, the most recent one is the most relevant to
future-oriented decisions.

4. If the asset is available for sale and its NRV in the market
   in which it is likely to be sold can be calculated, we should
   make use of this evidence of the cash flow that could be
   received at the date of the measurement by committing
   the asset to its most valuable use. Current price in an exit
   market is more future-oriented than current price in an
   entry market if the asset's presence is expected to affect
   future sales.

5. The only measure of an asset that is more relevant to
   cash-flow-oriented decisions than the cash flow that could
   be enjoyed at the measurement date is direct contractual
   evidence of the cash flow that will occur. Considering the
   waiting period, or financing cost during the holding period,
   discounted future cash flow is the ultimate relevant measurement of a noncash asset.

This chapter has dealt with the relevance of measurement
methods to cash-flow-oriented decisions. We have attempted to
explain those linkages between measurement methods that provide
the economic basis for acceptance of surrogates for discounted
future cash flows. If this approach seems complicated, you can
fall back on two simple tests of the relevance of financial information:

(a) If you were a partner in a business and had an agreement
    to either buy your partner's interest or sell your interest
    to him at book value according to the balance sheet, which
    measurement method would you consider most equitable
    for application to any particular asset? Your sense of equity
    will rarely lead you to an irrelevant measurement method.

(b) If you were the manager of the business for the current
    period only, which measurement method should be used
    for determining the beginning and ending values on which
    the calculation of income is based, assuming that your
    performance is appraised on the basis of reported income
    and that you are honest?

In the next chapter, the discussion of measurement method

choices will be expanded to take into consideration criteria other than relevance.

ADDITIONAL READING SUGGESTIONS

Baxter, W. T., *Depreciation* (Sweet & Maxwell, 1971), chapter 4.

Canning, John B., *The Economics of Accountancy* (Ronald Press, 1929), chapters 11, 12, 13.

Chambers, Raymond J., *Accounting, Evaluation and Economic Behavior* (Prentice-Hall, 1966; rpt. Scholars Book Co., 1974), chapters 4, 5, 7, 9, 10.

———, *Securities and Obscurities* (Gower Press, 1973).

———, *Accounting for Inflation* (Department of Accounting, University of Sydney, 1975).

Edwards, Edgar O. and Philip W. Bell, *The Theory and Measurement of Business Income* (University of California Press, 1961).

Revsine, Lawrence, *Replacement Cost Accounting* (Prentice-Hall, 1973).

Ross, Howard, *Financial Statements: A Crusade for Current Values* (Pittman Publishing Corp., 1969).

Sterling, Robert R., *Theory of the Measurement of Enterprise Income* (University Press of Kansas, 1971).

———, "Decision Oriented Financial Accounting," *Accounting and Business Research* (Summer 1972), pp. 198–208.

STUDY QUESTIONS

1. Is an attribute of an object or event either clearly relevant or clearly not relevant to a decision, or is relevance a matter of degree? How do the concepts of principal and surrogate relate to relevance?

2. The following exercise is designed to give you experience in thinking of principal-surrogate relationships. Fill in the blanks.

Principal	*Surrogate*
(a) Cash flow potential	NRV
(b) Intelligence	

(c) _____   Grade in course
(d) Risk associated with a
    security investment   _____
(e) _____   Current market price of
                                bonds payable
(f) Future costs of an activity _____
(g) _____   Future money receipts by an
                                investor
(h) Replacement cost of an
    asset   _____

3. "In the measurement of assets held for use, replacement cost frequently is a closer surrogate for discounted future cash flows than is the most readily available version of NRV." Explain.

4. Consider the inventory cost flow assumptions, LIFO and FIFO:
   (a) Which cost flow assumption yields balance sheet information more relevant to cash-flow-oriented decisions?
   (b) Which measures the cost of using materials most relevantly?
   (c) Are your answers to (a) and (b) consistent or reconcilable? Explain.

5. What property(s) or attribute(s) of an asset are relevant to a decision:
   (a) to sell the asset now or hold it for future sale?
   (b) to sell a money claim type of asset (bond, note or account) now or hold it until maturity?
   (c) to use material A or material B in manufacturing product Y when both A and B are on hand?

6. It is alleged that the concept of "cost of using a resource" is central to the field of "cost accounting." Define "cost of using." How are asset measurement methods related to the cost of using a resource?

7. What are the prerequisites to arraying measurement methods in order of relevance?

8. Consider the problem of measuring liabilities. Prepare an array of measurement methods applicable to liabilities in order of their relevance to residual equity investment decisions.

9. For each of the following cases, which of the available measures is most relevant to common stock investment decisions made

by the model or process you recommend (and which you may feel obliged to specify)?

(a) Two $1,000 notes receivable made by American Telegraph and Telephoto Corporation, one due in 1 day, one due in 366 days. Comparable notes yield 8%.

(b) Ten thousand bushels of No. 2 soft red winter wheat are stored in a Chicago elevator. This grade of wheat is quoted at $3.45 on the Chicago Board of Trade spot market. The owning firm has contracted to sell it to General Pellsbury Mills at a price of $3.30 per bushel FOB its present location four months from the balance sheet date.

(c) The CV firm, a minor producer of common copper ingots, has 60,000 lbs. of finished product on hand. The quoted local market price is 65¢ per pound. The firm's standard cost of production is 57¢, subject to variances not greater than ±2% in recent months.

(d) The Multiversity Book Store has on hand 3,000 copies of Noah's Seventeenth Old Collegiate Dictionary which it purchased at $5 each in anticipation of a price rise. The publisher is now selling them for $5.50. Both this store and its competitors are now selling this dictionary for $6.95 to provide a normal markup on the $5.50 list price.

(e) The Metropolitan Press has two model AH Allis-Warner presses, one recently installed at a cost of $45,000, the other purchased two years ago at a cost of $36,000 and with an estimated useful life of 10 years. Since the first press was purchased, the general price index has advanced from 120 to 132. The new press had been installed in Metropolitan's Upstate Plan which provides early delivery to readers in that area. It is under the direction of Dan Clay, plant manager. The 2-year old press is located in Henry Webster's City Plant.

(f) One of the company's properties is a 380-acre undeveloped island lying a mile off the central California Coast. It was purchased for $2,000 in 1916 when the general price index was 33 as against today's 165. There is no comparable piece of property anywhere.

(g) Wallakang Woolen Mills of Adelaide has on hand 80,000

pounds of No. 1 three-inch native wool which it purchased at auction in Cunnamulla for an average of $1.50 per pound. It then paid $1,200 to get the lot trucked to Adelaide. While Wallakang has not thought of selling this wool as it will need every bit of it in its own spinning operations in the coming season, if it were to sell it the Cunnamulla auction would be the best market. The latest price for this grade in Cunnamulla is now $1.51.

10. Design an empirical test of the hypothesis that the association of prices at date *m* with prices at date *n* increases as *m* approaches *n*. State the sources from which you would obtain the necessary data, sample content, statistical tests to be used and the possible applicability of your conclusion.

11. How should *APB Opinion No. 18* on the equity method of accounting for investments in common stock be changed to make it consistent with the suggestions of this chapter?

12. What is the justification for accepting best-use NRV as a surrogate for discounted future cash flow?

13. What is the justification for accepting current replacement cost as a surrogate:
    (a) for discounted future cash flow in the case of up-to-date assets held for use?
    (b) for NRV in the case of assets held for sale?

14. On what grounds can it be argued that current replacement cost is a closer surrogate for discounted future cash flow than is historical cost?

15. On what grounds can it be argued that restated historical cost is a closer surrogate for current replacement cost than is historical cost?

16. Referring to the "gap chart" illustrated in EXHIBIT VII-2, what circumstances may cause the gap to be positive, i.e., NRV greater than replacement cost? What could make it negative?

17. Is the incremental test of asset value, as applied in this chapter to assets held for use, an appropriate test for selecting a surrogate measurement method?

18. Is ranking measurement methods on the criterion of the

relevance of the attribute being measured to cash-flow-oriented decisions worthwhile? Is it clear that cash-flow-oriented decisions constitute the major group for which financial statement data can be helpful?

19. "According to my experience, analysts give very little consideration to book value of shares according to the balance sheet so there is not much point in accountants worrying about book value." Comment.

20. Evaluate *FASB Statement No. 12.*

21. Explain how different forms of NRV can vary widely in their relevance to cash-flow-oriented decisions.

22. Pacific Gas and Electric Co. has the following bond issues, among others, outstanding:

Series	Year of Maturity	Nominal Interest Rate	Issue Price	Year of Issue	Estimated Net Book Value	Estimated Market Value
II	'95	$4^{1}/_{2}$	100	1962		
00	'99	$5^{1}/_{2}$	$100^{3}/_{4}$	1967		
PP	'99	$6^{7}/_{8}$	101	1967		
QQ	'00	$6^{5}/_{8}$	100	1968		
TT	'01	9	102	1969		

Consider questions (a) through (e) in relation to the issuer of bonds.

(a) Estimate the net book value of each issue on the basis of GAAP.

(b) On which criteria does GAAP accounting for these bonds rank high?

(c) On which criteria does GAAP accounting for these bonds rank low?

(d) As of this writing, the $4^{1}/_{4}$s of '95 are quoted at 58 and the 8s of 2003 at 94. Estimate the market value of the other issues.

(e) Consider the possibility of presenting these liabilities on the balance sheet at their market values. On which criteria does market value rank high? Low?

CHAPTER VIII
MEASUREMENT METHODS AND OTHER CRITERIA

Nine measurement methods were appraised and ranked on the criterion of attribute relevance in chapter VII. This was feasible because the relevance of the attribute emphasized by each measurement method was related to cash-flow-oriented decisions. Those appraisals do not apply to other types of decisions. But since our analyses in chapter IV suggested that financial statements are used primarily in making cash-flow-oriented decisions, our conclusions in chapter VII are generally (but not universally) applicable when an accountant is applying the relevance criterion in making accounting decisions.

Unfortunately, such a general assessment of measurement methods on the other criteria is not feasible. For example, the reliability of a measurement method depends upon the measurer and the object being measured, rather than upon the user and his decision process. Intercompany comparability of a method depends upon the methods used by those other companies with which comparisons are to be made. Intelligibility depends upon the readers. Cost of producing the accounting data depends upon the availability of evidence, volume of transactions, and so forth. Consequently, we are unable, in this study, to analyze measurement methods on other criteria in a systematic manner comparable to our analysis of relevance in chapter VII. Instead, we offer some loosely related comments that should stimulate your thinking about the application of all of the criteria in making final selections of measurement methods. In this sense, we begin to confront the complexities of making accounting decisions in the real world.

RELIABILITY

While the relevance of a financial datum depends upon the
circumstances of its use, the reliability of a datum depends upon
the circumstances of its gathering. Anyone attempting to evaluate
an accounting method for application in a particular case must
judge the reliability of the resulting data in those particular
data-gathering circumstances. However, it is possible to generalize
to a limited extent on the subject of reliability of measurement
methods. For example, we may attempt to rank measurement
methods for application to the finished goods inventory of manufacturers of ladies' clothing. Our conclusions, if based on familiarity
with the industry and with the alternative measurement methods,
may be applicable to this one asset category in all firms in the
industry. "The usefulness of a measure cannot be determined
until a specific use is given, whereas the objectivity of a measure
can be determined independently of its use" (Ijiri and Jaedicke,
1966, p. 478), but not independently of the circumstances in which
the specific measurement is made. When we recognize this we
see why measurement methods cannot be ranked on the basis
of usefulness for general application. Selection of the measurement
method for use in specific balance sheet areas or in special industries
must be left to accounting authorities such as the FASB, the
Accounting Standards Executive Committee (of the AICPA), or
industry committees; in special circumstances, the professional
judgment of the accountant on the job may require that all
generalizations be overridden. In making these choices, the accounting decision maker might well start with the relevance
criterion, which can be applied without knowing the specific
circumstances, and then proceed to a consideration of reliability,
comparability, cost, and other criteria.

There is a tendency among some people to confuse reliability
with relevance. When we question the reliability of, for example,
historical cost measurements, we are not asking if we would want
to use such measurements but only if accountants can determine
historical cost in such a manner that we can rely upon the result
as representing historical cost. We do not expect it to equal
discounted future cash flow or some other measure of the asset.
We are not using the term "reliable" to mean anything similar

to "a reliable predictor of discounted future cash flows." To take another example, a discrepancy between NRV (net realizable value) at the balance sheet date and eventual proceeds from sale is a relevance weakness whereas differences among various accountants' measurements of NRV as of the balance sheet data constitute a reliability weakness. This distinction permits us to use relevance and reliability as separate criteria of accounting methods and thus to break down and isolate the source of our preference for one method over another.

The more detailed the specification of rules for applying any accounting principle, the greater the probable reliability of the results. Consider, for example, the lower-of-cost-and-market principle as applied to inventories. (a) If several accountants understand that they are to measure an inventory at lower of cost or market, with no further specification of the method, there is likely to be a great deal of dispersion in their measurements. (b) If the accountants are told to use lower of FIFO cost or market, the dispersion is likely to be reduced. (c) If they are told to use lower of FIFO cost or market under the following conditions, it will be further reduced: cost includes inbound transporation and excludes all available cash discounts; market is to be replacement cost (computed on the same basis as the original cost), unless replacement cost is above current NRV (in which case NRV is to be used) or below NRV less a normal profit margin (in which case the latter is to be used). This approach was used by the APB in, for example, the business combinations area in an effort to "narrow the areas of difference" among the accounting practices of American companies. There is, of course, another approach to narrowing the areas of difference: setting fundamental objectives and standards which clarify what financial statements in general are expected to accomplish.

The reliability of any one measurement method may vary remarkably in different applications; the tabulation in EXHIBIT VIII-1 should make this clear by indicating some fairly general cases in which a measurement method may be relatively reliable, of doubtful reliability, and relatively unreliable, respectively. In addition to the types of variations in reliability illustrated, there can also be differences within any one case listed there. For example, the amortized historical cost of an intangible asset with an original

legal life of five years can be measured with greater reliability
than the amortized historical cost of goodwill. We suggest that
accountants do, and must, set some sort of minimum level of
reliability below which measurements should not appear on financial statements, regardless of the merits of the measurement based
on other criteria.

COMPARABILITY

Five different aspects of comparability were listed in chapter
III. Inasmuch as financial data are rarely used in isolation, a
very good case could be built for the proposition that solutions

EXHIBIT VIII-1

EXAMPLES OF POSSIBLE APPLICATIONS OF MEASUREMENT METHODS WITH DIFFERENT
LEVELS OF RELIABILITY

Measurement Method	Relatively Reliable Applications	Applications of Doubtful Reliability	Relatively Unreliable Applications
Discounted future cash flows	Claims against debtors of good credit standing	Claims against debtors of poor credit standing	Work in progress; plant assets
NRV or market value	Listed shares; stocks of saleable metals	Real property with specialized improvements	Patents; copyrights
Replacement cost	Common grades of lumber, sheet steel and other materials	Land; old buildings	Patents; copyrights
Historical cost	Securities; commodities purchased on a delivered price basis	Joint products; trade receivables; amortized intangibles; depreciated buildings	Self-developed goodwill

to all of our comparability problems would go a long way towards making financial statements more useful. If we set high standards of comparability, we would have to eliminate the historical cost and restated historical cost measurement methods, do something about the price level (measuring unit) problem, give up multiple-choice accounting (where we can choose from alternative generally accepted methods), and minimize the use of methods that permit the injection of varying personal bias. As we mentioned in chapter III, if we wanted to minimize the number of different criteria that are to be considered by accountants in evaluating alternative accounting methods, we could treat the several aspects of comparability as parts of relevance and reliability. We prefer, however, to emphasize it by separate recognition.

Some accountants believe that there is something wrong with mixing several measurement methods in the same set of financial statements. Their concern has been associated with the conventional mixture as well as with the type of combination suggested in this book. The basic problem: "There is no way of equating or relating property a with property b if a and b are independent properties" (Chambers, 1965, p. 35). For example, the sum of, or the difference between, five pounds and three feet is meaningless. But, as we took pains to point out in chapter VII, the properties, or attributes, measured by the nine measurement methods appraised there are *not* independent properties; *they are related properties.* The addition of assets, or liabilities, measured by different methods is not a crippling defect in financial statements as long as all of the methods used yield measurements of cash flow potential or a surrogate for it. This gives them a common base. Analogously, the sum of the area of one piece of land computed by aerial photography and the area of another parcel determined by ground survey may be usefully accurate despite its imperfection.

We must make it clear that use of several measurement methods does not imply random choice or repeated changes. Consistency of accounting methods over time is one of the important aspects of the comparability criterion, as is uniformity of methods among entities that hold the same types of assets in similar circumstances. Comparability requires that like objects and events be reported as like and that the differences among items be reflected in the statements.

Additivity

Additivity has a technical meaning as applied to a property or attribute of an object. A property is additive if the sum of the measurements of the quantities of that property associated with two separate objects equal the single measurement of the quantity of that property associated with the combination of the two objects. When one quart of water of 40°C is poured into a vessel containing three quarts of water of 50°C, the combination consists of four quarts of water but its temperature is neither 90° nor 190°. The property "volume" is additive; the property "temperature" is not. No economic property is perfectly additive— not cash flow potential, not historical cost, not current market value, not discounted future cash flows, although the latter appears to be the closest to being additive. For that matter, the volume property of water is not perfectly additive because when many one-quart containers of water are combined, the pressure will increase the density of the water and reduce the space it occupies. But it is close enough to being perfectly additive to yield useful information in most cases. The same can be said for cash flow potential.

In addition to the requirement of additivity, measurements should be added and subtracted with a common scale and, of course, a common basic property (as illustrated on p. 203). The common scale requirement is violated when meters are added to yards, Australian dollars are added to U.S. dollars, or when 1965 U.S. dollars are added to 1975 U.S. dollars (if the fundamental property being measured by monetary units is potential purchasing power, not numerosity of pieces of paper). This measuring unit problem will come up again in chapter IX.

OTHER CRITERIA

The *intelligibility* criterion could affect the accountant's choice of a measurement method if he judges that one method, or his explanation of it in the reports, would be less easily understood than another method. The accountant's own understanding, however, may be a more critical basis for choice of measurement method. If he does not know how to apply, or does not feel comfortable with, one method, his choice of method may be biased. For this reason, we suggest that an accountant is properly trained for positions involving responsibility for choice, or approval, of measurement methods *only* if he is thoroughly familiar with a wide range of possibilities.

While we have no specific comments to add here on the criteria of timeliness and cost of utilizing information—see chapter III for the original discussions—we do want to say something about *the relative importance of the several criteria.* Attribute relevance and reliability are the key criteria involved in the choice of measurement methods but other criteria may also play supporting roles. In other accounting decisions, about terminology and format choices, for example, other criteria—especially intelligibility—are relatively more important. When we are evaluating any particular accounting practice, we must recognize that we will rarely judge a method to be perfect on any criterion, but we must reject it if it fails completely on any criterion. A minimum acceptable rating on each of the nine criteria set out in chapter III is a necessary but not sufficient condition for accepting a proposed accounting method.

Multi-Valued Statements

One general type of measurement proposal that has appealed to people who see merit in several methods calls for multi-valued financial statements. For example, the AAA committee recommended the use of historical cost and "current cost" in *A Statement of Basic Accounting Theory.* We can understand how an accountant might have difficulty in choosing a measurement method in a case in which one method is superior on one or more criteria and another method is superior on other criteria. The use of two or three methods on a comprehensive basis, however, is difficult to justify for these reasons:

1. The cost of production criterion may become significant. It may be, for example, that the cost of obtaining the valuation data for historical cost, replacement cost, and NRV would be six times what it would be under the single-valued approach advocated in the previous chapter, because cost and availability of data are considered in

choosing the one value to report. The second and third values often would entail substantially more difficult measurements.

2. The optimal quantity criterion could favor multi-valued statements only if specific users wanted more than one set of values. Otherwise, all users would be handicapped by the superfluous data.

3. Comprehensive application of any one method throughout the balance sheet requires accepting relatively unreliable measurements in some cases. Comprehensive application .·of second and third choice methods would involve still less reliable measurements. In other words, given that a major objection to measuring all assets and liabilities by one method is that acceptably reliable evidence of one type is not available for all items, and that reliability presumably would be a criterion in choosing the one method, then if we insist on applying two or three methods to every item, the average reliability of the measurements would be reduced.

4. While historical cost data may have to be available for some use for which it is specified (such as taxation), the accountant may select a current value measure for application to a specific asset for general reporting without having to disclose cost or to distinguish between realized and unrealized gains and losses. Current value is an indicator of future cash flows, but the partitioning of current value into cost and unrealized gain or loss is not helpful for this purpose (providing that the tax allocation aspect has been taken into consideration; see pp. 154–155).

Single-Valued Statements

Auditors sometimes tend to overemphasize reliability and objectivity at the expense of relevance. They also sometimes prefer to try to apply one measurement method to everything. Thus, we occasionally hear it said that accountants should stick to historical cost because it is objective. We have several objections to this statement: (a) It implies that all assets are measured at historical cost under current GAAP (in the face of the obviously noncost measurements of receivables, cash, and written-down assets). (b) It implies that historical cost is uniformly objective (despite the wide variations in judgments of cost inclusions at acquisition, manufacturing cost accounting methods, and amortization methods for limited-life assets). (c) It overemphasizes the merit of trying to apply one measurement method to all assets. (d) It specifies the choice of the measurement method that ranks lowest on the criterion of relevance to cash-flow-oriented decisions. (e) It neglects criteria other than objectivity. (f) It neglects liabilities. "There is no virtue in persisting with one method of approximation if another and better method becomes available. Consistency in objective is to be preferred to consistency in method" (Chambers, 1966, p. 260).

Another group of single-method advocates, including some of our most respected accounting theorists, such as Chambers and Sterling, argue for *uniform use of as-is NRV* or a closely related method sometimes described as *current exit value*. The intention is to measure every asset at the cash flow that could be obtained for it by direct sale. One argument for this approach is that it informs investors of the minimum payoffs that they can count on, because the management should only continue operating if it foresees higher (than liquidation) payoffs thereby. In terms of the analysis in chapter IV, this minimum payoff is one end of the probability distribution of future payoffs, but there is no basis for considering it to be the most likely payoff to investors. Our analysis gives more attention to providing information for estimating the remainder of the distribution.[1] Another argument for as-is exit values is that shareholders need to know the break-up value of their company so that they can decide for themselves (as a group) whether to continue operations or liquidate. We believe that accounting can be more valuable to investors if it is aimed primarily at the decision to sell-or-hold (and buy-or-not-buy) the firm's securities, as explained in chapter IV.

---

[1] Sterling (1972, p. 206) argues, quite plausibly, that the difference between the current market price of a security and the distribution to its holder if the firm were to be liquidated currently is a measure of the riskiness of that security. Similarly, the difference between an asset's acquisition cost and its NRV at acquisition date is an indicator of the risk involved in the purchase of any asset.

On Discounted Future Cash Flows, Future Cash Flows, And
Face Value

The uneven effect on the income statement is an undesirable consequence of failing to discount future cash flows. For example, if a lender reported a constant amount for a receivable at various dates over its life (assuming no interim interest payments were involved), all of the interest income on the loan would have to be reported in either the period in which the loan is made or the period in which it matures. Either method rates poorly on the criterion of effects via other parties as well as on attribute relevance. Imagine a seller allowing three years to pay with no explicit interest but the financing cost included in the nominal selling price. Recording the full amounts of such selling prices as revenue would involve extreme "front-end loading" of income, would reduce the usefulness of the balance sheets as well as income statements, and would offer a great opportunity for managerial manipulation.

Sterling (1972, p. 203) has objected to the use of discounted values in financial statements on the ground that discount rates are personal to each individual, that the relevant rate is the investor's unique rate, and that discount rates cannot be used by the accountant because they are both unknown to him and vary among the firm's several investors. The answer to this reasoning is that the accountant must use the market discount rate, not that of any one investor, and that the investor's personal choice of rate for the type of asset or liability in question cannot be significantly higher than the market's or he will have no investment. As much as I may want to earn double the market rate of return, if I insist on it I am not likely to do much investing, especially in an efficient market. Nor am I willing to accept less than the available market rate. In the interest of reliability, the accountant must choose a publicly known market rate. If he does, we can expect that it will vary insignificantly from the personal effective rates of investors.

To be consistent, if we are reluctant to use the market discount rate in discounted future cash flow computations for financial statements, does it not follow that we should also be reluctant to use current market prices of commodities? Inasmuch as buyers and sellers of machines or bonds attempt to take into account the waiting periods before they receive the payoffs from ownership, discount rates are built into market prices of all durable goods and securities. If we dislike such discount rates, we must reject current market values. The value of any asset to its owner may be greater than its current market price, thus providing the owner with a type of "consumer's surplus," or "owner's surplus." This discrepancy may even be due to the owner's willingness to accept a lower discount rate. Thus, we must recognize that the current market value of an asset may be less than its value to the owner and that a current market discount rate may be higher than the minimum that an investor would accept if necessary. Both discounted future cash flows and current market value are measurement methods which must be based on currently available objective evidence of the expectations of market actors. In fact, in cases in which both are readily available, such as quoted bonds, discounted future cash flow equals current market value. So we cannot detect any difference in the underlying legitimacy of these measurement methods. Furthermore, since under perfect market conditions NRV equals full replacement cost, it is apparent that discounted future cash flows, NRV, and replacement cost can be equal. Their differences depend upon the particular market imperfections involved in a specific case.

Sterling has also argued (1968, p. 498) that accountants cannot measure future cash flows or discounted future cash flows because a magnitude that lies in the future cannot be measured. The answer to this point is that the use of present contractual and market evidence that is relevant to future events is not the measurement of a nonexistent object. When space scientists base their calculations of the distance between heavenly bodies as of a future date on current and past evidence, the usefulness of such a calculation depends upon the bodies continuing in their orbits as predicted. Similarly, when an accountant reports discounted future cash flow, NRV, or the historical cost of an asset, the value of these data to decision makers depends on the relationship between the amounts reported by the accountant as of the balance sheet date and the future cash flows of the firm. For example, the 12/31/×1 market value of an asset is not directly relevant to an investment decision being made by an investor as he receives the financial statements on February 15, 19×2. The data are relevant only if they assist the decision maker in evaluating an outcome of a course of action that is available to him; selling the firm's assets last December 31 is not a possible course of action in ordinary circumstances. The value of December 31 data depend on their prediction usefulness just as do the value of the astronomer's calculations to scientists planning a space trip. The accountant who accepts contractual evidence of future cash flows and discounts them at the current market rate of interest is not "predicting" in any sense different than that in which the accountant who reports current market value is "predicting." Neither is reporting data relevant to an investor's decision unless there is a relationship between the data reported and future cash flows of the firm. If these procedures are not measurement, it is clear that accountants must not be limited to reporting measured amounts. They certainly constitute useful quantification.

In order to promote congruence between the goals of managers and shareholders—an important aspect of the effects via other parties criterion—the measurement of management's performance on behalf of shareholders must be as accurate as possible. When we think of business activities as centering on the series of events which make up the operating cycle and recognize that profit or loss is the difference between the cost of inputs and the value of outputs as measured by receipts from customers, the question arises as to the appropriate stage in the cycle for recognizing the profit or loss. One view is that the profit or loss builds up steadily through all stages of the cycle. Alternatively, it can be argued that a particular enterprise may perform some activities exceptionally well (and profitably) while it may perform poorly in other phases of the cycle. It is not obvious that one of these views is more logical than the other. But most accountants appear to feel that they want fairly clear evidence before they recognize that any activity has been either profitable or unprofitable. Until the evidence indicates otherwise, accountants traditionally assume that business transactions are break-even events. Thus, we record the acquisition of resources as a break-even transaction and we continue to record the use of resources as break-even transactions—that is, the cost incurred is assigned to the asset acquired—until we have independent evidence for a departure from cost—

that is, for "jumping the gap" to a noncost measure. The measurement of newly acquired resources at as-is NRV contradicts this view. Since it typically involves recording a substantial loss on acquisition, and so discourages managers from purchasing resources, it rates low on the effects via other parties criterion. This is a serious objection to the use of as-is NRV for newly acquired assets (and completed-cycle NRV is rarely available for assets going into the operating cycle). On the other hand, the earlier the stage in the operating cycle at which the accountant can "jump the gap" to an independent, forward-looking measurement (completed-cycle NRV, discounted future cash flows, or future cash flows), the higher the level of attribute relevance. This step is usually heavily dependent upon the reliability criterion.

On NRV, Replacement Cost, and Historical Cost

The limited relevance of the attribute "as-is NRV" when it is not the same as best-use NRV deserves additional attention. We must recognize that an individual who has the power to make the sell-or-hold decision regarding an asset—for example, the investor holding shares or the enterprise manager—must have information about the proceeds he could realize by selling the asset at the time he is contemplating selling it as well as information pertaining to the payoffs he could enjoy by holding the asset. The shareholder, therefore, wants quick access to stock market quotations; he usually turns to his broker for such information. But the manager who is contemplating selling a used machine typically has a more difficult time ascertaining the price at which he could sell his asset. He may telephone machinery dealers, refer to detailed records of past sales of similar assets, or talk to other users of similar assets, but we would not recommend that he expect his accounting system to carry this information on each existing asset. The magnitude of the task of maintaining up-to-date and reliable data on the as-is selling prices and costs of selling for every asset the firm owns is likely to result in rejection of as-is NRV on the cost-of-production criterion. Nor is it likely, in our opinion, that accountants can provide reliable information on the "holding value," or value in use, of a machine or other "complementary" asset used in a firm. So we suggest that accounting should not be expected to contribute much to the manager's sell-or-hold decision in the case of a complementary asset held for use. And since the probability that the as-is NRV of such assets represents the type of cash flow contribution that the asset actually will make to the firm typically is low, as-is NRV ranks low on the criterion of relevance to the hold alternative of securities investors. In addition, it is usually *unreliable* when applied to plant assets and work in process.

The above comments on complementary assets do not apply to *"solitary" assets held for use or investment,* that is, assets that produce a cash flow with very little assistance from other assets or that could be used in this way. For example, the current market value of an office building or an apartment building may rank quite high on the attribute relevance criterion. (Whether costs of selling should be deducted [leaving NRV] or fringe acquisition costs added [yielding replacement cost] is not clear; we lean towards the straight market value in the absence of evidence of quick sale prospects.) It could be argued that there is no such thing as a completely solitary asset. In any event, one could take the position that the larger the asset being measured as a proportion of total inputs to an activity yielding a specific cash inflow, the more appropriate it is to measure that asset by starting with a measure of the total future inflow and deducting the costs of other inputs. On the other hand, the larger the remaining inputs in relation to the asset on hand, the less suitable is a measure of prospective inflow, such as NRV or discounted future cash flow, and the more suitable is a measure of inputs to date, such as replacement cost or historical cost. The latter approach (cost accumulation) attributes no profit to the inputs to date. The former (a future-oriented measurement) attributes all of the profit to the inputs to date. While neither approach is perfect, choosing between them on the basis discussed here would appear to minimize the extent of the "error" in profit attribution.

To the extent that an organized and competitive market exists for *used assets* and relatively objective quotations can be obtained, current market values may be useful in accounting. Examples are the quotations on used car prices available in the *Kelly Blue Book* and similar publications and those on data processing equipment in the *Price Guide for Used Computers.* Satisfactory quotations may also be available for some categories of construction equipment, trucks, common machine tools, and aircraft. But as long as the asset is classified as up-to-date, we would choose to record the price the firm would have to pay to acquire a similar asset plus fringe acquisition costs—that is, replacement cost—and not the price it could receive if it were to sell (less selling costs). If the asset were classified as out-of-date, as-is NRV would be appropriate. This procedure has the major advantage of substituting the market's judgment of depreciation for the personal judgment of the accountant or other firm personnel, and so it could be rated as preferable to depreciated historical cost on both relevance and reliability. We foresee a valuable role for independent reporting services working in various used asset areas. We suspect that more such services would be offered if the need for them were made known. See McKeown (1971) and Beidleman (1973) for interesting empirical work on the use of market prices for used plant assets.

Some writers (e.g., Baxter, 1971, chapter 4) have suggested that the lower of replacement cost and NRV is generally suitable for measuring *nonmonetary assets*. They argue that an asset cannot be worth more than what it would cost to replace it, nor can it be worth more than what it can be sold for. This seems to be an arbitrarily conservative approach to valuation. From the point of view of investors, it seems more appropriate to select the *higher* of any two available measures on the ground that management would normally use an asset in its more valuable use, not in its less valuable use. Inasmuch as an objective of business activities is to produce assets worth more than their replacement cost, it seems strange to deny that this can happen. NRV of newly acquired assets is, as we have seen, normally below replacement cost by the costs of selling plus the fringe acquisition costs—even for a commodity-type asset. For specialized and self-constructed assets, as-is NRV is typically far below replacement cost while completed-cycle NRV is simply unavailable. The proposal to use the lower of replacement cost and NRV is rejected.

Lenders, it is often said, are more concerned with exit values of assets than are owners. A possible explanation for this difference in interests is that lenders have little difficulty in predicting their maximum returns; the returns provided for in the contract typically are the maximum. Relatively more of a lender's attention must be focused on business failure and liquidation—the low end of the probability distribution of future entity payoffs. Exit prices are highly relevant to such predictions.

The replacement cost measurement method faces some serious problems in application to *assets held for use*. One problem area involves machinery that is no longer manufactured or that would not be replaced in kind if it were lost. Perhaps a much improved, and more expensive, model has come on the market, which makes the model used by the entity semi-obsolete but still worth using. The current entry price for the improved model clearly is not suitable as the replacement cost of the old, since it is likely to be more expensive than the old model because of the new features incorporated in it. If the purchase cost of the new were substituted for the current cost of the old when the new becomes available, it would typically result in an increase in the asset amount just at the time when the existing asset becomes obsolete or semi-obsolete. While estimates of comparative operating costs could be made and discounted to indicate an estimated value of the existing unit, the reliability of such calculations may leave a good deal to be desired. If an active market for used units exists, it may provide a suitable measure of either replacement cost or NRV; the latter may well be the better choice in these circumstances. In the absence of a suitable used market, replacement cost based on a specific price index should be considered. While a switch to NRV probably should be made at some stage in a plant asset's life, the timing of the switch probably should be related to the quality of the used asset market. We would be more eager to switch to as-is NRV if the market were active and reflected demand for use rather than for scrap.

Replacement cost also poses problems in the measurement of *natural resources and raw commodities*. Consider, for example, the measurement of replacement cost of standing timber or petroleum reserves based on growth or exploration and development of reserves. The difficulties are formidable. The solution may be to apply a different version of NRV: NRV at the next stage in the operating cycle at which a ready market exists for the raw or intermediate commodity. Thus, a firm that normally cuts its timber and then saws it into lumber could measure its standing timber at the NRV of logs. Of course, in some locations, the NRV of standing timber would be a feasible measurement. Or an integrated oil company could measure its underground reserves at their NRV in the crude oil (on the surface) market even though it usually refines its own crude. Similarly, an inventory of self-produced logs or crude oil held for processing may be measured at replacement cost in the log or crude oil market rather than at replacement cost by growing timber or finding and lifting oil. These points can be consolidated into the generalization that NRVs and replacement costs based on markets for commodities at stages of production near that of the asset being measured can be useful versions of current value in vertically integrated companies. These methods should be given careful consideration by companies in commodity-oriented industries.

Historical Cost

Historical cost (as pointed out on p. 152) represents a minimum judgment by management of the value of the asset's potential contribution to the firm's cash flows. One could use this point to argue that historical cost is relevant to the circumstances of the particular firm because the firm's own management—not just other buyers and sellers—participated in the establishment of the price. But this interpretation of historical cost implies unreliability—especially bias. In fact, in the cases of (1) unique assets, such as real property, or (2) any asset purchased in an auction market, the purchaser could be the only person in the world who thinks the newly-acquired asset is worth as much as he paid for it. To the extent that accountants are reluctant to rely upon values based on the opinions of entity personnel, but respect independent market prices, historical cost is the least objective of all market prices. It is, nevertheless, highly verifiable in cases of simple purchases (as opposed to construction or manufacturing); invoices and cancelled checks provide documentary support for the recorded cost.

The term "stewardship" often has been associated with historical cost. Many people apparently have been concerned that if the accounts do not continue to show historical costs, when the asset is sold or consumed cost will not be matched with revenue and the management's success revealed. This is a venture-oriented view of financial reporting. If we want to know how much profit we made on an asset from the time we bought it to the time we sold it, acquisition cost must be compared with the selling price. But under the periodic reporting convention, if we want to calculate periodic profit, we must know the net assets at the beginning of the period and the net assets at the end of the period. When periods are important, the measurement of assets and liabilities at the beginning and end of the period is comparable to transfer pricing (between divisions); the end-of-period valuation is a credit to the manager of that period and a charge to the new manager who is taking over at the beginning of the next period. Reporting on periodic stewardship when the steward's objective is to increase the value of the owners' equity requires that the beginning and ending measurements reflect the owners' concept of value—presumably something similar to the present value of future returns. Note, also, that the old concept of matching historical cost with selling price to reflect success requires a stable measuring unit—if success means making the owner better off.

Historical cost is clearly the bookkeeper's choice of measurement methods because it is by all odds the easiest basis for recording purchases of assets when the cash disbursement is being recorded in a double-entry system. Departures from acquisition cost require some other form of evidence. A similar point applies to the recording of liabilities at historical receipt.

In the simplest of circumstances, historical cost is an extremely low-cost measurement method, and its low cost may well justify a role for it in any future measurement system even though more relevant measurement methods are emphasized. The incremental cost of substituting replacement cost for historical cost may exceed the incremental value of replacement cost's greater relevance when the asset amounts involved are small and the holding period is so short that major changes in prices are rare.

The term "historical production cost," when applied to work in process and finished goods inventories, could be defined to mean the sacrifices made in the production of the product, that is, the sum of the costs of *using* the resources that were devoted to its production. As we pointed out on page 183, the sacrifice entailed in using a resource which has been held for a period prior to use may be quite different than the sacrifice involved in its acquisition. Subsequently, however, both may be referred to as historical data. Information about acquisition costs constitute only a small part of the historical data pertaining to a firm's operations.

According to information theory, any period-end number that was known at the beginning of the period does not provide information. Information reduces uncertainty; the receipt of a report which includes only numbers that were already known does not reduce uncertainty. On this basis we can question the value of those balance sheet and income statement numbers which reflect the amortization of old amounts by a predetermined pattern such as straight-line calendar, sum-of-the-years-digits, or constant percentage of diminishing balances. However, we can argue that a bit of information is provided if the recipient of the report did not know whether the asset being amortized had been disposed of or not. But "use" methods of depreciation, such as units-of-production, and the use of current market values of used assets do have the potential of providing more information to readers of financial statements than is conveyed by numbers based on predetermined amortization patterns.

Defenders of the historical cost measurement method have argued that the actual use of historical cost data by a variety of decision makers is evidence that the data are useful. According to this view, historical cost data should be provided because they are used. But it is not clear which is cause and which is effect. Perhaps historical cost data are used primarily because they are provided. Some people also follow the practice of rubbing a rabbit's foot every morning, but we need not conclude that such a practice affects subsequent events. But how can we be sure? Scientists frequently have belatedly found evidence supporting old wives' tales and other customs which previously had been classified as superstitions. A tea made from the roots of abracadabra plants found growing on the north side of a rock may well have some healing properties. But penicillin may be more effective by a wide margin. Similarly, historical cost data may have some value, as argued in chapter VII, but more relevant methods may provide much more valuable data.

TAX ASPECTS OF MEASUREMENT

When applying measurement methods other than acquisition cost (which typically is consistent with the tax-deductible bases of assets), we should remember to make provision for the "tax allocation" aspect as discussed on pages 154–55. There we suggested that the tax basis of an asset (or a liability) was an integral part of its service potential and that, other things remaining equal, two assets with different tax bases have different cash flow potentials. We can look at tax adjustment valuation in either of two ways. If we think of adjusting the market value by the amount of tax that would have to be paid upon sale, the tax-adjusted market value is $A_{TA} = M - (M - B) T$ where M is market value, B is tax basis and T is the incremental tax rate(s) that is applicable. Alternatively, if we think of adjusting the basis by the appreciation that can be retained after paying tax on the appreciation, $A_{TA} = B + (M - B)(1 - T)$. These two expressions yield equal tax-adjusted asset values. We suggest that the association of tax adjustments with the general category of assets or liabilities to which they pertain (although not necessarily with the individual asset or liability item) is helpful to the analyst who is concerned with such relationships as working capital, current ratio, debt-equity ratio, and the like. It appears that a single liability (or asset) account derived from comprehensive tax allocation is not subject to clear interpretation when computing debt-equity ratios or return on capital employed. The alternative of stating each line item on the balance sheet on a tax-adjusted basis (if applicable) may be preferable on the criteria of comparability and intelligibility.

The asset and liability adjustment approach to tax allocation involves some issues that are glossed over in the deferral approach, which is generally accepted in the U.S. One such issue is the possibility that the applicable tax rate will change. While most of us may be reluctant to predict any change in tax rates, we presumably would want to revise the tax adjustments of values as the law is changed. Another prediction problem relates to the uncertainty as to which tax rate will apply in the case of capital assets that have not yet been held long enough for any gain or loss to qualify as long-term. Will they be sold for a short-term gain or loss or for a long-term gain or loss? The occurrence of other gains and losses in the tax year, or carried forward, can also affect this matter. Finally, there are the questions of whether to discount the tax adjustment and if so, how to determine the timing of the cash flow involved. One answer to this problem is to divide the net asset items into three classes: (1) current assets and liabilities; (2) noncurrent items with an established and scheduled life, such as depreciable assets; and (3) noncurrent assets with no known tax life, such as land. The tax-adjusted value of the first group could be computed without discount (on grounds of materiality and uncertainty). The tax adjustment applicable to the second group could be discounted for the known waiting period at a cost-of-capital rate. The tax adjustment on the third group could be ignored on the basis that it is likely to fall so far in the future that the present value of the tax effect approaches zero.

DISTINGUISHING BETWEEN USEFUL AND USELESS MEASUREMENTS

We recommend that accountants give more consideration to the concept of a cutoff between useful and useless measurements. If we evaluate a particular measurement on the three criteria of relevance of the attribute being measured to cash-flow-oriented decisions, reliability, and comparability, a composite evaluation may, in some cases, indicate that the measurement is not of any significant value to any decision maker for whom the accounting data are intended. Since decision makers presumably use accounting data for predicting state variables and payoffs, as suggested in chapter IV, we must raise the question (in any borderline case) of whether or not the measurement has any predictive power. The composite evaluation of the measurement on the relevance, reliability, and comparability criteria, perhaps with the occasional inclusion of timeliness, can be accepted as a judgment of the predictive power of the measure, or the lack thereof. Thinking of familiar balance sheet accounts and of usefulness in predicting the firm's future capacity to pay, we would rate measurements of cash as best, with discounted future cash flow measurements of payables and low-risk receivables close behind. Quoted securities stated at market value as of the measurement date would also receive a high rating, although the tendency of securities markets to fluctuate rapidly would make timeliness a more important element in the evaluation of the prediction usefulness of this measurement than in other cases. The NRV or replacement cost of regularly quoted, standard grade commodities would probably receive a good rating. Replacement cost of familiar, general purpose, portable plant assets would follow and replacement cost of the more specialized and immobile plant assets would get a lower rating. If these measurements are made on the basis of replacement cost new less depreciation, the latter feature would likely be perceived as a weakening one. Intangible assets and deferred costs of research, development, exploration, and so forth would be near, if not beyond, the cutoff point on the scale of prediction usefulness. Such items have the severe handicaps of minimum attribute relevance (historical cost), low reliability of the originally capitalized amounts (if not purchased intact), room for bias in the choice of amortization pattern and estimated life, and lack of comparability across companies. These weaknesses must have been recognized by the FASB when it outlawed the capitalization of research and development costs in 1974.

SOME OBSERVATIONS ON CURRENT PRACTICES

Variations in the predictive power of measurements are reflected in the practices of analysts and investors. As an example, Standard & Poor's Corporation regularly reports "Cash & Equiv.," "Curr. Assets," "Curr. Liabs.," and "Long Term Debt" (but not noncurrent assets) for every company listed in its *Stock Guide.* Its *Bond Guide* shows the ratio of debt to net property; intangibles are omitted from this calculation. Security analysts and investment advisory services, such as *Value Line,* give some attention to "cash flow," or earnings before deducting depreciation and amortization, thus expressing a lack of faith in the accountants' measurements of fixed and intangible assets. In real estate circles, depreciation is given relatively little attention (except on a tax basis); property values are often expressed as a multiple of either gross rentals or cash flow. (Tax deductible depreciation is treated as a source of cash flow.) Accountants should give more attention to variations in the predictive power of their measurements and to the hard choice of labelling some measurements as useless.

APB Opinion No. 16 (paragraph 88) provides an example of the use of several measurement methods in that it suggests how the various assets and liabilities of an acquired company may be recorded on the acquiring company's books by the purchase method. Some of the suggestions are: marketable securities at current NRVs; receivables at present values of amounts to be received determined at appropriate current interest rates, less allowances for uncollectibility and collection costs, if necessary; finished goods and merchandise at estimated selling prices less selling costs and a normal profit margin; work in process at estimated selling prices less remaining costs and an allowance for profit; raw materials at current replacement costs; plant and equipment to be used, at replacement cost for similar capacity; plant and equipment to be sold or held for later sale rather than used, at current NRV; specific intangible assets, at appraised values; current liabilities and accruals at discounted amounts.

No single-measurement-method system of accounting is feasible in typical real-life firms without omitting major segments of the asset category as we now know it. A policy of uniform application of either historical cost or replacement cost encounters difficulty with receivables and with finished products produced jointly with others. Exit values are costly and unreliable in cases of specialized and immobile plant assets and work in process. Future cash flows from plant assets and raw materials inventories cannot be ascertained with acceptable reliability. Surrogates are bound to remain popular through the foreseeable future. The multi-measurement-method system is here to stay.

ADDITIONAL READING SUGGESTIONS

Chambers, R[aymond] J., "Measurement in Accounting," *Journal of Accounting Research* (Spring 1965), pp. 32–62.

Financial Accounting Standards Board, "An Analysis of Issues Related to *Conceptual Framework for Financial Accounting and Reporting: Elements of Financial Statements and Their Measurement,*" *FASB Discussion Memorandum* (FASB, 2 December 1976), chapters 9, 10.

Larson, Kermit and Schattke, R. W., "Current Cash Equivalent,

Additivity, and Financial Action," *The Accounting Review* (October 1966), pp. 634–41.

Lemke, Kenneth W., "Asset Valuation and Income Theory," *The Accounting Review* (January 1966), pp. 32–41.

McKeown, James C., "An Empirical Test of a Model Proposed by Chambers," *The Accounting Review* (January 1971), pp. 12–29.

STUDY QUESTIONS

1. Give examples of assets and their environments in which:
   (a) Historical cost is likely to be more reliable than NRV.
   (b) The opposite of (a)—NRV is likely to be more reliable than historical cost.
   (c) Replacement cost is likely to be more reliable than NRV.
   (d) Discounted future cash flow is likely to be more reliable than historical cost.
   (e) Discounted future cash flow is likely to be more reliable than NRV.
   (f) The opposite of (e)—NRV is likely to be more reliable than discounted future cash flow.

2. For each of the following liabilities, select the measurement method you think would yield the most *useful* information to major users of financial statement data:
   (a) Bonds payable which were issued at a discount to yield 7.1%. The coupon rate is 7%; at the current market price of 92 they yield 8%.
   (b) Unearned subscription revenue of a magazine publisher. These subscriptions were sold at $12 per year but the current subscription price is $13.20.
   (c) An advance of $700 by a customer in full payment for goods on hand costing $500 which are to be delivered to the customer in the near future.

3. El Monte and Stokely Van Carmichael are competitors in the pea canning business in Minnesota. This canning season El Monte paid farmers $100 per ton, cash on delivery, to the cannery and financed its inventory with bank loans. Stokely considered 10% bank financing too expensive so it offered farmers $102 per ton, payable at the beginning of the next

growing season (nine months later) when the farmers needed money to pay for seed, fertilizer, equipment, labor, etc.

How would you measure (a) Stokely's liability to farmers at the end of the canning season, (b) Stokely's inventory of canned peas (specifically, the cost of the raw materials used)? Note: assume that pea canners make about 4% profit before taxes—as a percentage of sales.

4. For each of the following cases, *select the measurement method* you think would be most *useful* to investors:

(a) Federal Reserve Notes (legal tender) on hand totalling $100 which had been received in exchange for merchandise which had cost $80.

(b) A roll of 20 JFK half-dollars which had been purchased as an investment for $14. Coin dealers are now bidding $15.00 per roll for such coins.

(c) A specially designed conveyor system the installation of which has just been completed at a total cost of $38,000, including $30,000 paid to the manufacturer and $8,000 labor cost for installation by our own men. If it were to be removed and sold now it would bring $5,000 in the used equipment market after removal at a cost of $1,500.

(d) Fashionable ladies' dresses held by (1) their manufacturer, (2) a retailer.

(e) Bonds owned for which no quotation is available.

(f) A five-year old apartment building.

(g) One hundred shares of IBM stock; today's close on the NYSE was $225. Sale on the NYSE would require payment of a commission of $98 and payment of the New York stock transfer tax of $5. The same commission, but no tax, would be paid upon purchase.

(h) For many years Owens-Illinois Glass Company and Corning Glass Works each owned 33.4% of the common shares of Owens-Corning Fiberglas Corporation. The shares were listed on the NYSE. Which measurement method would you use for Owens-Illinois' or Corning's interest?

(i) The firm has in use a 4-year old Figure Control 4600 central processing unit and a combination of peripheral equipment which was purchased for $2,000,000 and has a total estimated life of 8 years. While this model is no longer in production, the most economical combination with comparable operating characteristics would cost $1,500,000 with an estimated life of 4 years. The equipment on hand has a "blue-book" price of $1,200,000 according to the *Price Guide for Used Computers,* published by Time Brokers, Inc., New York.

(j) Land used by the firm as a plant site.

(k) Automobiles used by company personnel.

(l) A promissory note calling for payment of $50,000 in two years which was received one year ago from a maker with an excellent credit rating in exchange for a quantity of branded and differentiated products of the firm which would normally have sold for $37,500 in cash but which cost the firm $26,000 to produce.

5. Do long-term investments in common stocks of affiliated companies pose any peculiar measurement problems? What methods would you consider?

6. A few years ago a balance sheet of Owens-Illinois Glass Company showed, among the current assets, stock of Owens-Corning Fiberglas Corporation at cost, approximately $1,400,-000. A note accompanying the financial statements disclosed that the market value of that stock at the balance sheet date was over $109.million. If the shares had been sold at their market value, the gain of some $108 million would have been subject to tax at the 25% rate applicable to long-term capital gains. If you were asked the value at which this asset should be stated in a balance sheet relevant to cash-flow-oriented decisions, what amount would you select?

7. As you look at current accounting principles and business practices, what evidence do you see to indicate that measurement methods actually are selected on the basis of relevance and reliability? Do you see more evidence that is inconsistent with this view?

8. Once upon a time male twins were born to a famous merchandising magnate. As they reached manhood their father refused to take them into the business because they quarrelled incessantly. So I. Magnate and J. Magnate each, independently,

decided to start their own businesses. The similarity of their backgrounds resulted in their making identical decisions in forming and operating their businesses except that I. Magnate selected "Shorty" Financio as his financial vice-president while J. hired "Slim" Financio. Shorty talked I. into a major one-year bank loan at 6% because he thought interest rates would fall, while Slim convinced J. that the issuance of 20-year bonds at 6% was the way to go because interest rates were going to rise.

Lo and behold! Interest rates rose and Shorty issued 8%, 19-year bonds at the end of the year to replace his 6% bank loan.

Query 1: Which financial manager was most successful in year 1? How should this be reflected in the financial statements just before Shorty's refinancing?

Query 2: Immediately after Shorty's refinancing, is there a difference in the obligations of the two companies? If so, how should it be reflected?

9. Imagine that you have found a small tribe of New Guinean aborigines who have a hidden gold mine. They are willing to sell you pure gold for one 1971 JFK half-dollar per ounce. How would you account for your acquisitions of gold and its subsequent resale in the London gold market?

10. The Lessor Company has only one asset—a specially constructed ship equipped to haul frozen thingamajigs—which is leased for its remaining life to the only firm in the world that is interested in transporting frozen thingamajigs on the high seas. The lease gives the Lessee Company the option to purchase the ship for one dollar at the end of the lease period and is nontransferable, i.e., is subject to cancellation by the lessor if the lessee assigns its interest in the contract.

While the Lessee Company has a top credit rating and is in excellent financial condition, and is making a satisfactory return on frozen thingamajigs, it now has excess capacity in its fleet and has requested Lessor Company to cancel the lease. The lessor, of course, refuses.

The lease calls for rentals of $60,000 per month for eight more years. A large scrap metal processor in the ship's home port issues a weekly list of prices it will pay for various types of scrap. The most recent list showed "Ships of welded steel construction, 5,000 dead-weight tons and up, $48 per ton." The ship in question meets this description, weighing 7,000 tons. An investigation discloses that there is no other demand for this ship.

If you had a half interest in the Lessor Company and had the opportunity to either sell your half or buy the other half at book value, what measurement method would you consider most equitable for determining book value of the owners' equity?

11. *"Liabilities* should be stated at their current value at incurrence or issuance. . . . However, it is not appropriate to adjust liabilities because of subsequent changes in the market's evaluation of those liabilities. To change liabilities because of changes in the market rates at which a particular security may be issued, or because of changes in other conditions affecting the capital markets, tends to introduce the marketplace's on-going evaluation of the business into the financial statements" (Arthur Andersen & Company, 1972, p. 117).

   Do you agree? Why?

12. Is the subtraction of liabilities from assets just as illogical as the subtraction of three oranges from five apples? What is required to make the remainder meaningful in either case?

13. The LIFO, FIFO, and specific identification versions of historical cost can result in showing apparently identical units of a commodity at different amounts. It is sometimes said that this is a defect in the historical cost measurement method. If units of a commodity, or shares of a security, which cost different amounts, are revalued at tax-adjusted NRV, they will also be stated at different amounts. Is this a defect in tax-adjusted NRV? Explain.

14. Which measurement methods would you rank low on the criterion of comparability? Explain the type of comparability that is involved and the circumstances.

15. Which measurement methods would you rank highest on the criterion of intelligibility?

16. Which measurement methods would you, as a stockholder, rank low on the criterion of effects via other parties?

17. Define additivity. What is the significance of additivity in the context of accounting measurement? How serious are the additivity defects in (a) conventional balance sheets and income statements and (b) statements based on the recommendations in chapters VII and VIII of this book?

18. Give arguments for and against the proposition that the use of more than one measurement method on the same balance sheet is unacceptable because it violates the additivity requirement.

19. Now that you have had more experience thinking about criteria of good accounting methods, do you agree that all of the criteria discussed in chapter III must be satisfied to some degree? That is, is every one of the criteria so powerful that a terrible rating would cause rejection of an accounting method even though it is satisfactory on all of the other criteria?

20. If several specific measurements of relatively irrelevant attributes are combined is the resulting sum *unreliable*?

21. In January 1976, an AICPA task force circulated a working draft of a proposal regarding "Valuation of Real Estate and Loans and Other Receivables Collaterized by Real Estate." One feature of the proposal required writing down investment property, particularly projects not yet completed and substantially fully rented, to estimated future NRV less carrying costs including interest.

    The following paragraphs are excerpts from a banker's response to this proposal. Evaluate the proposal and the banker's response using a set of criteria of your choice.

    Dear Mr.

    We have recently received a copy of your working draft dated January 27, 1976, entitled "Valuation of Real Estate (Other Than Long Term Investments in Real Estate) and Loans and Other Receivables Collateralized by Real Estate, a Proposed Recommendation to the Financial Accounting Standards Board."

    It is our understanding that this draft will be applicable to all industries. This statement, if adopted, will have a great and unfavorable impact on the banking industry and on those who are involved and concerned with the well-being of that industry: its present and future owners, depositors, and other creditors. My views on this matter are shared by my associates, who include three professional accountants holding the CPA certificate, and by a host of bankers with whom I have discussed this matter. I hope very much you will take our concerns into account in your deliberations.

The concept of "present value" appears to be strongly supported by the public accountant profession. There is little question that its application results in the most conservative income results and the most conservative balance sheet presentation. In a litigious environment this is a very desirable result for certain groups. However, it seems to ignore fair presentation and full disclosure concepts and certain public interest questions which are involved.

With respect to the public interest, one should consider the literature on bank failures in the 1930's. The agreement of the regulatory agencies in 1937 to carry sound bank assets at amortized book value rather than current market value came about because of present-value accounting. The use of the concept by the authorities in the early 1930's rendered many banks insolvent and forced property liquidation in adverse markets. Most informed observers would agree that this was a serious mistake. Adoption of this concept now would significantly impact the capital position of many banking institutions, resulting in impairing dividend payment, reducing access to long term capital markets, and encouraging the sale of real estate at bargain prices.

The accounting principle enunciated in this position paper which represents the most significant departure from present accounting practice is the requirement that in the determination of net realizable value, estimated interest carrying costs should be included. While the shift from recognizing interest expense as a period cost to a more theoretical computation appears more scientific it, in fact, only adds another subjective determinant to a procedure which already involves a number of subjective determinants, i.e. the future price at which the property can be sold, the year in which it will be sold, etc. This process introduces into the determination of net income what, in our opinion, is an unreasonable degree of subjectivity. It is highly probable that the results would be less accurate than those results obtained under present accounting procedures.

We subscribe to the present accounting concept that future reductions in interest income should be recognized in future years and not in the current year. Providing an allowance in the current year in those circumstances merely results in a shifting of income from current year to future years; in this respect it is quite different from a bad debt allowance which is designed to reflect the fact that a portion or all of the principal will not be collected.

In our opinion, more can be accomplished for the benefit of investors and creditors in the area of possible losses related to real estate by full and complete disclosure. For example, investment in real estate, particularly troubled real estate, should be categorized by type of project, state of completion, an indication as to present expectations as to when the demand for such real estate is expected to come about, etc. This type of disclosure is very much in accord with the Securities and Exchange Commission's requests for disclosure as to financial asset quality, maturity characteristics, etc. It would be up to the reader of the financial statements to decide for himself what set of future economic and market assumptions are most likely and then to draw conclusions therefrom. We do not believe accountants and financial people can do a better estimating job in this area. Further, these assumptions and conclusions are subject to continuing change. To attempt to reflect a dynamic situation in a single net income figure is not realistic.

Present value accounting for bank assets introduces major new conceptual considerations. Such a move should be preceded by the public dialogue required to form basic accounting principles, for accounting principles can be effectively administered only if there exists a broad understanding and consensus thereon. Present value accounting does not have this conceptual foundation.

Sincerely yours,

Thomas I. Storrs
NCNB Corporation   [Quoted by permission.]

(a) What criteria did Mr. Storrs use in evaluating the AICPA proposal?
(b) Which of the criteria presented in chapter III of this book did he not use?
(c) Considering the accounting alternatives under discussion in the letter, would you say that Mr. Storrs believes in market efficiency in the sense described in chapters I and IV of this book?

(d) Whose interests (in financial reporting) does Mr. Storrs appear to be representing?

(e) Do you believe that current value accounting by banks could cause bank failures? Is it in the public interest or contrary to it?

CHAPTER IX

COMMON UNIT ACCOUNTING

A wide range of asset and liability measurement methods were discussed in chapters VI and VII. The emphasis was on selecting, for application to the asset or liability being measured, the measurement method that best reflected the item's cash flow potential. The approach was designed to produce a balance sheet which reported the residual equity interest in the firm's cash flow potentials. Measurement of this current stock of cash flow potentials was advocated as the key to providing information useful for cash-flow-oriented decisions. Measurement of the current stock was also considered essential to the measurement of flows, or changes in stocks of cash flow potentials over time. The group of measurement methods discussed in those chapters, including restated historical cost, appear to be useful in accounting for stocks and flows of cash flow potentials. But there is one serious flaw in that measurement system, and that flaw is the subject of this chapter.

Measurements of flows, such as the revenues, expenses, gains, and losses that constitute business income, often require comparisons of measurements of stocks at two points in time.[1] Some expense measurements, for example, involve adding a beginning balance and purchases, then subtracting an ending balance. For the result to be clearly interpretable the three measurements must be made in a common unit. And when different line items are added and subtracted on an income statement, common units are also desirable.

Accountants traditionally have considered all units of money that are denominated in the same currency to be comparable. Thus, all monetary amounts expressed in deutsche marks are

---

[1] Portions of this chapter are adapted from Staubus (1975b).

considered subject to addition and subtraction without any adjustment: "A DM is a DM is a DM." This means that our focus is on the number of monetary units; what the money units will buy we ignore. The alternative view is that deutsche marks, and lire, and U.S. dollars are significant because of what one can buy with them, and since this—their purchasing power—varies over time, "A DM is not a DM is not a DM." The size of the monetary unit actually varies so that adjustments must be made to express measurements relating to different dates in a common unit. Preparing financial statements in monetary units adjusted for the changes in a purchasing power index, or price level index, may be called "price level accounting," "general purchasing power accounting," "current purchasing power accounting," "common dollar accounting," or "common unit accounting." We will use the latter term here to signify the currency of any country, to avoid implying the use of a particular type of index, and to express the basic objective of the procedure in a short phrase. Under whichever name one may prefer, common unit accounting is, in the mid-1970s, under serious consideration in major English-speaking countries as an alternative to accounting in numbers of monetary units of varying sizes.[2]

Common unit accounting is intended to make all monetary amounts appearing on any one financial statement, and on any articulated set of financial statements presented at one time, comparable in terms of purchasing power. Thus, if $95 is subtracted from $100 the remainder can be read as $5 with the purchasing power that dollars have as of the date of the financial statement. Application of the current value measurement methods (excluding historical cost) discussed in chapters VI and VII does express all measures on one balance sheet in monetary units of the same purchasing power; such a measurement system, however, does not achieve common purchasing power measurements on an income statement or on comparative balance sheets. We must make a "scale adjustment" for changes in our measuring instrument—the monetary unit—in order to achieve purchasing power comparabi-

---

[2] Rough general purchasing power restatements have been made, and required for income taxation, in Brazil for several years. Chile adopted a more comprehensive system in 1974.

lity of measurements that are made at different times under inflationary conditions.

COMMON UNIT ACCOUNTING AND THE RELEVANCE CRITERION

The mathematical basis for common unit accounting has been explained but the relevance of the resulting data to the decisions of users of financial statements has not. A simple example may help us think about this aspect of the problem.

An Exercise in Current Value and Common Unit Measurement

At the beginning of period one, when a general price index stands at 100, Jane Doe purchases a share of X Company stock for $100. At the end of period one, Doe still holds the stock, its market price is $108, and the price index is at 110. Early in period two, while the price index is still at 110, Doe sells the stock for $106.

What is her income in period one? In period two? For the venture? Make these income calculations under several different measurement methods. Which measurement method yields asset and income numbers that appear to be most relevant to (a) a prospective lender's decision whether to lend money to Doe, (b) a judgment of Doe's performance as a portfolio manager, (c) the taxation of Doe's income, and (d) Doe's decision as to how much she can consume and still be as well off at the end of each period as she was at its beginning? (The common unit principle requires that 100 purchase-date dollars be restated as 110 end-of-period-one dollars.)

	Variable Units		Common Units	
	Historical Cost	Current Market	Historical Cost	Current Market
Period one				
Beginning	$100	$100	$110	$110
End	100	108	110	108
Income	$ 0	$ 8	$ 0	$ -2
Period two				
Beginning	$100	$108	$110	$108
End	106	106	106	106

Income	$ 6	$ −2		$ −4	$ −2
Venture Income	$ 6	$ 6		$ −4	$ −4

Now consider the following comments pertaining to this exercise:

1. The choice between historical cost and current market value affects the *timing* of the reported income.
2. The choice between traditional variable unit accounting and common unit accounting affects the *total income* over the life of the venture.
3. Common unit accounting changes reported income by changing beginning (old) balance sheet amounts, not by changing ending balance sheet amounts.
4. The difference between common unit and variable unit income over the life of the venture is $10, which is equal to the percentage change in the general price index times the beginning owner's equity stated in beginning dollars. (See chapter X for a more precise expression of the difference between variable unit and common unit income.)
5. The exercise may be considered a simple test of the relevance of data produced by different measurement methods—relevance to the types of uses suggested just before the solutions were tabulated. Assuming that no serious qualifications on grounds of cost, reliability, and so forth are warranted in this simple case, your choice of solutions indicates your view of the relevance of the alternative sets of data to the types of decisions listed. I believe that the common units, current market column includes the most relevant information. Doe's investment does not appear to have been successful in either period one or period two and she should not be required to pay any income tax on her venture.

In chapter IV we said that an attribute of an object or event is relevant to a decision if knowledge of its quantity will help the decision maker evaluate possible outcomes of available courses of action. In the next section of this chapter, we argue that the attribute of wealth that is most helpful to an individual in evaluating the outcome of a particular consumption-investment policy is the purchasing power into which that wealth can be converted over time. A change in the purchasing power potential of an individual's wealth is the measure of wealth that is most relevant to his consumption-investment decisions.

THE INDEX CHOICE AND CAPITAL MAINTENANCE

We have discussed the general objective of common unit accounting—to report in units of equal purchasing power. Now we need to examine the specifics of that objective, and to face up to such questions as "Whose purchasing power?" and "Power to purchase what?" Since we need to restate nominal units as purchasing power units in order to compute *income* rather than to prepare a balance sheet, we may find it helpful to distinguish between *capital* and *income*. The term "capital" has many meanings, but all of them relate to stocks of wealth (or interests in such stocks); "income," however, relates to changes in stocks of wealth, or flows of wealth. The term "capital maintenance" means having the same amount of capital at the end of a period as at its beginning so that the entity may "break even," or have zero income. Once we have clarified what it means to maintain capital at its previous level, the computation of income follows. Income is the excess of ending capital over the amount needed to maintain beginning capital at a constant level. To paraphrase the definition by J. R. Hicks (1946), income is the amount one can consume during a period and still be as well off at the end of the period as at the beginning. Or, income is the amount an individual can consume or a corporation can distribute and still maintain the original amount of capital intact.

What *is* required to maintain the original amount of capital intact? How much must we have at the end of the period in order to feel that we have maintained our capital? One possible answer to this is the *money capital* concept of capital maintenance: if the net assets of the firm are worth as many dollars at the end of the period as the firm's net assets were worth at the beginning, capital has been maintained. But, having as many dollars at the end of the period as we had at the beginning is not the same as being as well off—if the purchasing power of the dollars has changed. We implicitly rejected the money capital concept when we turned to the purchasing power concept at the beginning of this chapter, and we assume hereafter that it is unacceptable.

Maintenance of Physical Capital

Another possible concept of capital maintenance is *physical capital* maintenance. In this view, if we have on hand as many units of materials, finished products, and machine services as we had at the beginning of the period, or if we have enough cash to buy such equivalent physical assets, we have maintained our capital. By this approach, income realized by the sale of an asset may be computed by deducting from its selling price the number of monetary units that it would take to replace that asset. This concept of capital maintenance requires the use of the replacement cost method of measuring expenses and would require that the holding gain (or loss) be excluded from income. Thus, if two widgets were purchased at the beginning of the period for $6 each, one was sold for $9 when its replacement cost was $7, and the other is still on hand at the end of the period with a replacement cost of $7.50, the income for the period would be $9 less $7, or $2. No income would be recognized on the unsold widget. In circumstances that would make it difficult to determine and record the replacement cost of each commodity, we could use a narrow (specific) price index that reflects price changes in the categories of commodities being measured in order to approximate specific replacement cost.

Now let us consider the implications of physical capital maintenance. If the cost of goods sold is determined by replacement cost, how does a trader who buys and sells securities, or a commodities speculator, earn any income? If a trader buys and sells in the same market, replacement cost at the time of sale (the measure of cost of goods sold) must be the same as selling price, so no income is ever recognized. Or, consider the case of the two trading companies, X and Y. Suppose X invests in commodity A, which rises in price, and Y invests in commodity B, which falls. If the costs to be matched with revenues upon sale are replacement costs, A and B may appear to have performed equally well; that is, they could show equal incomes: zero. In effect, if capital maintenance means that we must be able to replace what we sold or consumed in the course of business, it makes no difference which assets we buy and hold. But surely we are better off holding assets that rise in price than we are holding assets whose prices fall! It is difficult to imagine anyone choosing a physical concept of capital maintenance in the face of this evidence.

A variation on the physical concept of capital maintenance is the *firm purchasing power* concept. It calls for the use of an index of prices of commodities that the firm purchases (including raw materials, or merchandise, and plant assets such as machinery and buildings). Such an index would measure changes in the power of the monetary unit (e.g., dollar) to purchase the things necessary for the firm to stay in business. Such a concept of purchasing power might appear appropriate for implementing the general purchasing power restatement proposal. On closer examination, however, the concept is essentially a physical capital maintanence approach and is subject to the evaluation in the preceding paragraph. If it were adopted, a firm holding a set of assets that fell in price would look just as good as a firm holding a rising "portfolio" of assets.

Some writers argue that a firm does not have income until it has provided for maintaining the same productive capacity and carrying the same inventories as it had at the beginning of the period. According to this argument, if prices pertaining to our industry rise faster than do average prices in the economy, and if income taxes and dividends are based on a computation of income that does not provide for replacing the physical assets (or their services) consumed, then 100 percent payout of reported income would require either borrowing more money or contracting the physical operations of the firm. But could not a firm be driven out of business by such policies?[3]

The argument favoring physical capital maintenance does not recognize that *maintenance of physical capacity is not necessary to maintain the real earning power and investment value of the firm.* A phenomenon associated with mobility of capital is the tendency towards a common rate of return on capital in firms with similar risk levels, if there is freedom of entry and exit. Thus, assume that Companies X and Y start out with equal capital, that X's

---

[3]An excellent statement of this position has been made by Revsine and Weygandt (1974). Another prominent advocate of the specific entity capital maintenance concept is R. S. Gynther (1974 and earlier works).

assets rise in price more than Y's, and that owners' capital is
retained (or added) to permit the financing of the higher priced
assets; then, further assuming fluid capital markets and competitive
conditions, X's earnings must rise more than Y's if the rates of
return on investment in the two firms are to be equal. Otherwise,
capital would tend to flow out of one industry and into the other.
In other words, maintenance of physical capital in a more inflationary industry will tend to increase the industry's real earning power.
If the capital has greater earning power, it is a larger quantum
of capital, so capital has been more than maintained. The firm
purchasing power concept of capital maintenance is rejected.[4]

Another perspective from which to analyze the capital maintenance issue is that of project investment analysis, or capital
budgeting. How can one measure the success, or income, of a
project over its lifetime? If the measuring unit is stable, and
assuming all equity financing and no income tax, an investment
project yields a lifetime income if it produces cash inflows greater
than the cash outflows associated with it. If the measuring unit
is not stable, some adjustment must be made in order to net
out the various cash flows. But surely that adjustment would have
nothing to do with the investment required to undertake a similar
project as a successor to the first. The success of the first project
has nothing to do with the cost of its successor. An investor would
not consider rejecting an otherwise profitable investment opportunity because he foresaw a great increase in the investment required
to replace the first asset.[5]

Maintenance of Investors' Consumption Purchasing Power

We have not mentioned the decision-usefulness approach to
accounting issues in our discussions of possible capital maintenance

---

[4]As an aside we may observe that if the price of a commodity rises faster than
a general price index over a considerable period (presumably due to a supply
constraint), its sales volume typically will decline (if there is any elasticity of demand),
so the company may be able to maintain its share of the market without maintaining
the same physical volume of operations. In any event, a company's "right" to
maintain its physical level of operations surely is weak compared to its duty to
maintain the amount of consumer purchasing power that its shareholders have
entrusted to it.

[5]A conversation with Jack Hanna helped me see this point.

concepts. When we associate the Hicksian concept of income with the *objective of producing accounting data that are useful to the readers of financial statements,* it becomes apparent that it is the users' purchasing power with which accountants should be concerned. If we agree that the managers are working for the owners and that employees make only limited use of financial statements, then the major groups of users who appear to warrant substantial consideration here are investors (owners and creditors, including suppliers) and taxing authorities. It is investors' well-offness that managers are trying to maximize and that governments are trying to tax.

People invest in enterprises in order to increase their real wealth—to have greater purchasing power than they would otherwise have. The ultimate objective of all investment activities is consumption of goods by people. Investors like to know their income so they can know how much they can consume without eating into their capital. From a longer-term perspective, an individual needs to know his beginning capital and predict his lifetime income if he is to spread his consumption and bequests in a pattern that equalizes marginal utility and maximizes total utility. Knowledge of his income in the recent past and knowledge of his present capital (including income to date) are helpful in predicting future returns available for consumption expenditures. If an investor owning an interest in a business is taxed on a return of capital by a taxing authority who intends to be taxing income, or if the investor spends for personal consumption a cash return that he believes to be income but is in fact a return of capital, then accounting is not providing the information that is most relevant to those decisions, namely the change in the purchasing power potential of his wealth. For investor's multiperiod investment-consumption decisions, for income taxation decisions, and for decisions regarding managers' success in achieving owners' objectives—for all of these basic uses of income information, *capital is maintained when the investor has end-of-period wealth with the same consumption purchasing power as he had at the beginning of the period, and income is an increase in the investor's stock of consumption purchasing power.*

The argument has been advanced (Sandilands Report, 1975) that the use of a retail price index for restatement of corporate accounts is inappropriate because such a general index does not accurately measure the changing purchasing power of the monetary unit in the hands of individual shareholders who do not purchase the same "market basket" of goods as that used in constructing the index. According to that argument, the general index is imperfect for most shareholders. But if we think for a moment of the degree of perfection that is involved in other aspects of accounting, we are likely to conclude that a general index is accurate enough to be acceptable—a judgment confirmed by the millions of people (union members with cost-of-living adjustment clauses in their contracts, businessmen, and others) who rely on such indexes.

The appropriate index to use in restating accounting measurements in units of purchasing power is an index of prices of goods consumed by investors. To my knowledge, no such index has been constructed and maintained in any country. The best-known consumer price index in America is an index of prices paid by factory wage earners and clerical employees, so it is not ideal for price level restatements. Fortunately, the Labor Department plans to commence publication of a new consumer price index in February 1978. It will reflect prices paid by a broader segment of the population but will not be specifically aimed at the investor segment. Still another index appears to be needed.

In practice, the Accounting Standards Steering Committee has chosen the British retail price index and the Irish consumer price index for use in common unit accounting. The FASB, on the other hand, has, as of this date, selected an economy-wide index—the gross national product implicit price deflator—and similar indexes have been suggested for use in Australia and Canada.

Note that the extent of price change reflected by the chosen index establishes "par" for changes in specific prices. Assuming that assets are measured at their current values, if the price of a particular asset increases by the same percentage as the index, no real gain or loss occurs; only a greater-than-average or less-than-average increase would be recognized as an income item. Thus, under a *physical* concept of capital maintenance, no gain or loss would be recognized when assets were revalued to current replacement cost; the offsetting entry would be treated as a restatement of owners' equity. But if an investor purchasing power concept of capital maintenance were accepted, revaluations of specific assets other than in proportion to the change in the chosen index would result in a holding gain or loss on the asset. The chosen index is also used for measuring both the loss from holding cash and other monetary assets and the gain from being in debt during inflation.

One other point relating to capital maintenance needs to be made here. Our standard of capital maintenance must be consistent across all balance sheet items if the sums and differences reflected in the residual equity are to be clearly interpretable. For example, we must not apply different indexes in restating monetary and nonmonetary items. If a monetary asset must increase in nominal units by the percentage increase in the consumer price index in order to maintain its real value, the same is true of a nonmonetary asset. If, on the other hand, an entity purchasing power index is applied to restate nonmonetary items, it should also be applied to monetary items. A loss or gain is then reported in the amount of any difference between the restated beginning measurement and the ending measurement, whether the item is monetary or nonmonetary, an asset or a liability.

COMMON UNIT ACCOUNTING PROCEDURES

The problem that common unit accounting is intended to solve is that of adding, subtracting, and otherwise comparing measurements made in monetary units of various sizes. The first step towards the solution is the selection of the unit in which all of the measurements in question are to be stated. Since the current purchasing power of the local currency is more familiar to readers of financial statements than any other unit, the end-of-period unit is normally chosen as the base. Accordingly, all measurements pertaining to earlier dates are "rolled forward" by multiplying them by one plus the percentage change in the index between the two dates. Thus, "dating" the old measurements is a key step. The objective of roll-forward computations is to calculate the number of current units that equals—in purchasing power—the number of old units reflected in the old measurement. If, for example, the old measurement was made at a date when the purchasing power index was at 120 and it is now at 132, and

if the old measurement was $60, the roll-forward computation
is $60(132/120) = $66.

The increase in number of monetary units from 60 to 66 in
this case is not a gain or any form of income; it is simply a
"restatement" of the old amount in the current measuring unit.
*A gain or loss on an asset or liability is recorded, however, if its amount
as measured for reporting on the current balance sheet differs from the
restated old amount.* The possibilities may be outlined as follows:

A. Measurement of an asset or liability at the *restated old amount.*
   In this case, no gain or loss is recognized. This procedure
   (described in chapter VI) is commonly applied to many
   "nonmonetary" items such as inventories, plant assets, and
   deferred credits to revenue. When applied to an asset
   that was previously measured at historical cost, it is called
   "restated historical cost." The comparable term for measurement of a liability is "restated historical receipt."
B. Measurement of an asset or liability *independently* of its
   restated measurement, thus recording a gain or loss.
   1. Measurement at the *old numbers of dollars* (the usual
      treatment of "monetary" items such as cash, receivables,
      and payables). For example, if the firm has held $100
      in currency from the old measurement date to the
      current date, a restatement, under inflationary condi-
      tions, would show a number greater than 100. Showing
      this currency on the current balance sheet at only $100
      would reflect a loss, precisely what we believe has
      happened to its purchasing power. If a liability were
      restated from $200 to $220 in current units, but a
      current measurement puts it back at $200, then a $20
      gain is recorded—a gain from being in debt during
      inflation. In a period of *deflation,* a gain would be
      recorded on holding cash and receivables, and a loss
      on liabilities would appear.
   2. Current measurement of an asset or liability at neither
      the restated old amount nor the original old amount
      would show a gain or loss—the difference between the
      new measurement and the restated amount. Use of
      current value measurement methods, such as NRV and
      replacement cost, would normally produce such a gain
      or loss.

Now let's look at a simple illustration. The Static Company begins a year with nonmonetary assets, perhaps land, valued at $100, monetary liabilities of $40, and a residual equity of $60. The price level index used for restatements rose by 10 percent during the year and the company engaged in no transactions. The accompanying comparative balance sheets (EXHIBIT IX-1) include the old values in old units in the first column and the old values in new units in the third column; the difference represents restatements. For the ending balance sheet (column 5), the nonmonetary assets are reported at their restated beginning values while the monetary liabilities are revalued downwards to the future cash flow basis (which is the same number of nominal dollars that was recognized at the beginning of the year). Thus a gain of $4 is recorded on the debt. The residual equity shows the gain on debt as the difference between the restated beginning balance sheet amount and the ending balance sheet amount.

This EXHIBIT is a very simple example designed to illustrate the essence of common unit accounting. In this case, we measured the nonmonetary assets at the end of the period at restated historical cost, $110. While that number of dollars exceeds the beginning number by 10, it does not represent a gain or any form of increase

EXHIBIT IX-1

STATIC COMPANY

BALANCE SHEETS

19X2 AND 19X1

	12/31/1 in 12/31/1 $	Restate- ments	12/31/1 Restated in 12/31/2 $	Revalu- ation	12/31/2 in 12/31/2 $
Nonmonetary assets	100	10	110	0	110
Monetary liabilities	40	4	44	(4)	40
Residual equity	60	6	66	4	70

in the residual equity. The monetary liabilities, on the other hand, are shown at the same number of dollars at the end of the period as they were at the beginning, but a gain of $4 is recorded and it increases the residual equity from its restated amount of $66, to $70. Thus, when we compare the ending balance sheet with the beginning balance sheet in old units, we find *that the nonmonetary assets are shown at a larger number but no gain is recognized, while the monetary liabilities are shown at the same number but a gain is recognized.* If the nonmonetary assets had been measured by any method other than restated historical cost, a gain or loss would have been recognized in the amount of the difference between restated historical cost and the new measurement.

Now let's move on to a case with transactions during the year. The Two-Transaction Company, an art investor, begins the year with the balance sheet shown in the first column of EXHIBIT IX-2. The index is at 100 at the year's start, at 103 when asset A is sold for $42 on April 30, at 108 when an appraisal fee of $10 is paid on September 30, and at 110 at year-end. The year-end cash balance (monetary assets) is $52. The residual equity balance shows an income of $1.

All income statement items have been restated in $12/31/\times2\$$. The sale was made when the index was at 103; multiplying the original selling price by 110/103 restates it in the size of units that prevailed at year-end when the index was at 110. Those year-end dollars could be symbolized by 110$. Thus, 103$42 = 110$44.85. The asset that was sold had a year-start valuation of $30 which, when multiplied by 110/100, yields 110$33. Similarly the appraisal expense, 108$10, is equal to 110$10.19.

The loss on net monetary assets can be computed in two ways. We know intuitively that the loss occurs because of the shrinkage in the purchasing power of monetary assets held, or a gain occurs due to the shrinkage in the real burden of debt as the level of prices changes. The amount of debt owed (net of monetary assets), or the amount of monetary assets held (net of monetary liabilities), times the change in the index, determines the gain or loss on net monetary position. When the net monetary balance (or position) changes during the accounting period, the gain or loss may be computed for each portion of the period (subperiod) that the balance held steady; then that gain or loss should be rolled forward

EXHIBIT IX-2
TWO-TRANSACTION COMPANY
BALANCE SHEETS
19X2 AND 19X1

	12/31/1 in 12/31/1 $	12/31/1 in 12/31/2 $	12/31/2 in 12/31/2 $
Nonmonetary asset A	30	33	
Nonmonetary asset B	50	55	55
Monetary assets	20	22	52
Monetary liabilities	40	44	40
Residual equity	60	66	67

TWO-TRANSACTION COMPANY
INCOME STATEMENT
19X2 (12/31/2 $)

Sales [42 (110/103)]		$44.86
Less, Cost of goods sold [30 (110/100)]	$33.00	
Appraisal expense [10 (110/108)]	10.19	43.19
Net operating income		$ 1.67
Loss on net monetary position[a,b]		.67
Net income		$ 1.00

[a]Loss calculated on net monetary *balances* (balance times fractional change in index, then rolled forward to year-end):

$1/1–4/30$: $(40 - 20)(3/100)(110/103)$ $= \$ .64$
$5/1–9/30$: $(40 - 20 - 42)(5/103)(110/108)$ $= -1.09$
$10/1–12/31$: $(40 - 20 - 42 + 10)(2/108)$ $= - .22$

Loss on net monetary position $110\$(.67)$

[b]Loss calculated by comparing monetary *transactions* in 12/31/2 units and in original units:

	Original $	Index Factor	12/31/2 $
Net liability balance 1/1	$20.00	110/100	$22.00
Receipt 4/30	(42.00)	110/103	(44.86)
Disbursement 9/30	10.00	110/108	10.19
Computed ending balance (asset)			(12.67)
Measured ending balance	$(12.00)		(12.00)
Difference: Loss on net monetary position			$110\$(.67)$

from the end of the subperiod to the reporting date. These calculations are illustrated in note *a* of EXHIBIT IX-2; the computation procedure may be called the *balances method.*

An alternative method of calculation that achieves the same result and may be more convenient under some circumstances is to roll forward the beginning net monetary balance and every change in it (thus computing an ending balance that would have existed if the monetary items could have kept pace with inflation), and then deduct the ending monetary balance as actually measured. This method—the *transactions method*—is shown in note *b* of EXHIBIT IX-2. In practice, either method of calculation may be applied so as to recognize no more than twelve changes in balance each year in order to relate to monthly financial reports and monthly price index reports. There is no need to aim at a literal level of absolute accuracy. But we can conclude from this exercise that Static Company procedures are not adequate in active firms; it is not feasible to compute price level gains and losses by restating the beginning balance sheet and comparing it with an ending balance sheet on a mixed measurement basis.

Common unit accounting is likely to be limited to supplementary reporting for the foreseeable future. If so, ledger accounts are not likely to be adjusted to a common unit basis. Nevertheless, accountants who are accustomed to thinking in terms of a self-balancing double-entry system may want to visualize common unit accounting in terms of entries in the accounts. Such a set of illustrative entries has the advantage of showing how the procedure fits into a familiar framework. The Two-Transaction Company example will be cast into a double-entry format for this purpose. While this example includes no preferred shares, no dividends, and no nonmonetary liabilities, the entries that would be required to restate those items are also illustrated. For convenience, a "common unit restatements" account is used to assemble the offsetting (and balancing) entries associated with each restatement. (ΔI_t is the symbol for the fractional change in the price index during the period.)

(1) Dr. Loss on net monetary assets	$ .67	
Cr. Common unit restatements		$ .67
(See EXHIBIT IX-2 for details of computation.)		

(2) Dr. Common unit restatements   6.00
    Cr. Residual equity accounts   6.00
    (ΔI_t) beginning balance
(3) Dr. Nonmonetary asset accounts   5.00
    Cr. Nonmonetary liability accounts   0
      Cr. Common unit restatements   5.00
      (ΔI_t) ending balance
(4) Dr. Common unit restatements   0
    Cr. Preferred stock—inflation   0
    shrinkage(ΔI_t) ending balance
(5) Dr. Expense accounts (3.00 + .19)   3.19
    Dr. Dividends declared   0
    Cr. Common unit restatements   .33
    Cr. Revenue accounts   2.86
    Original amount times change in index
    from "date basis" to end of period.

The following additional observations may now be made regarding this procedure:

a. If all calculations are made precisely, the entries in the common unit restatements account will net out to zero, as in this example; under typical circumstances, a small balance will remain, which should be buried in the loss or gain on net monetary position.
b. When the common unit accounting procedure is applied with GAAP, the lower of cost and market test must be made after nonmonetary assets are restated; a write-down to income may be required.
c. All of the restated balances are to be used in the preparation of common unit financial statements. The usual types of closing entries should then be made, including the closing of the loss on net monetary assets in the same way as revenues and expenses. The account for "preferred stock—inflation shrinkage" is not an income account and should be closed directly to retained earnings along with dividends.
d. If the capital structure had included preferred stock (with the same total assets), either entry (1) or entry (2) would have been reduced by the amount of entry (4).
e. If dividends had been paid before the year-end, the Dr. to dividends in entry (5) would have been offset by a smaller loss on net monetary assets in entry (1) since the cash

balance would have been lower for part of the year.

In contemporary practice, these entries are not likely to be journalized or posted to ledger accounts, but may well appear on a work sheet used in the preparation of common unit financial statements. EXHIBIT IX-3 illustrates how such entries may adjust traditional variable unit data to common unit data. Each debit or credit to an account other than the common unit restatements account would be supported by a schedule showing the calculation of the amount. Such calculation schedules are illustrated in several readily available reports (AICPA, 1963, 1969; FASB, 1974), but without being tied to a complete double-entry work sheet. (Consult those sources for additional assistance.)

Common unit accounting may be done as accurately and in as much detail as is appropriate in the circumstances, including a consideration of the costs of doing it. At one extreme, rough restatements may be made on the basis of published financial statements. Or, computer programs could provide for dating every entry made in variable unit accounts; then, when index data become available, the dated variable unit data could be retrieved and restated. A compromise that is likely to be popular is to restate monthly totals of transactions if the index chosen is available monthly (or quarterly summaries of transactions if the index is only available quarterly), along with common unit data from the beginning of the month.

Examples of procedures for restating published data are available (Cutler and Westwick, 1973; Davidson and Weil, 1975a). The most difficult step is ascertaining the "date basis" of the nonmonetary items. Once this has been done in some fashion, the nonmonetary assets and liabilities, the fixed portions of the residual equity, and the temporary (income and residual equity) accounts may be restated by multiplying the variable dollar amounts times the index factor (index at end of period over index at base date). The gain or loss on net monetary position can be computed for interim periods using the average balance, computed as accurately as desired, and the fractional index change during the interim period. Small errors need not be a matter for concern. The reader is encouraged to experiment.

EXHIBIT IX-3

TWO-TRANSACTION COMPANY WORKSHEET FOR COMMON UNIT FINANCIAL STATEMENTS
12/31/X2

	Data for Variable Unit Statements		Common Unit Restatements		Data for Common Unit Statements	
	Dr.	Cr.	Dr.	Cr.	Dr.	Cr.
Nonmonetary asset B	$ 50		(3) 5.00		$ 55.00	
Monetary assets	52				52.00	
Monetary liabilities		$ 40				$40.00
Residual equity (1/1/X2)		60		(2) 6.00		66.00
Sales		42		(5) 2.86		44.86
Cost of goods sold	30		(5) 3.00		33.00	
Appraisal expense	10		(5) .19		10.19	
	$142	$142				
Loss on net monetary position			(1) .67		.67	
Common unit restatements			(2) 6.00	(1) .67	0	0
				(3) 5.00		
				(5) .33		
			$14.86	$14.86	$150.86	$150.86

MONETARY AND NONMONETARY ASSETS AND LIABILITIES

A distinction must be made between "monetary" and "nonmonetary" net asset items if we are to compute the gain or loss on net monetary position, a key information output from a common unit accounting system. We should, therefore, clarify the meaning of these terms. A *monetary item* (asset or liability) is one that will entail future cash flows in nominal amounts that are not affected by inflation. The purchasing power value of monetary items to owners varies with inflation. Such cash flows typically are fixed by contract but they need not be. *Nonmonetary items* are all other assets and liabilities.

One common misconception about the monetary-nonmonetary distinction is that any item measured at historical cost or historical receipt should be restated to the current number of measuring units equivalent to the historical number and is, therefore, a nonmonetary item. But the measurement method applied to an asset, or the attribute that is measured, does not determine whether the item is monetary or nonmonetary; some nonmonetary items are measured by current value methods. There are some cases in which conventional accounting practice appears to involve measurement on a historical basis, but a little thought shows restatement of such a measurement to be obviously inappropriate. One example would be a note receivable recorded at its cost which is not equal to its face value, and on which interest is not being accrued because of doubtful collectibility. Another would be an asset or liability recorded in a tax allocation entry. This case will be discussed below.

Superimposing common unit accounting on GAAP involves measuring those items that are reported under GAAP at historical cost (most nonmonetary assets) or at historical receipt (most nonmonetary liabilities) by restating those old measurements. This means that no gain or loss is reported on those items prior to their use or liquidation; an exception is the write-down of an asset under the lower of restated cost and market rule. Monetary items, on the other hand, are normally adjusted from restated old measurements to face value, some form of future cash flow measurement, or current market value, so gains and losses on them are reported. One result is that *an error in classifying an item will affect the currently reported net gain or loss on monetary items with an offsetting error in income in the period of liquidation of the item.* For example, if a note payable were classified as nonmonetary, it would be restated upwards in a period of inflation and the gain on its real shrinkage during the period would be omitted from income. When it is paid at the nominal maturity value, a gain on settlement of the liability would be recorded. We conclude that misclassification can be a serious error.

Monetary-Nonmonetary Classification Problems

Not all assets and liabilities are easily classified as monetary or nonmonetary. In the case of convertible securities owned or issued, for example, neither classification seems generally appropriate. We would like to classify a convertible security as monetary if it is selling near its investment value as a fixed income security, and as nonmonetary if it is priced primarily on the basis of its common share equivalent. Unfortunately, that solution leaves a gray area; the call on common shares that the conversion privilege represents is always worth something, so a convertible security normally sells at a price that is at least slightly above its investment value. Drawing a line through the gray area would be extremely difficult because (1) the investment value of a convertible security is difficult to quantify, and (2) any premium of market price over investment value that would be permitted for a monetary security could only be determined arbitrarily. Consequently, it is tempting to hypothesize that both issuer and holder expect convertible securities to have, or come to have, value as a residual security, so both issuer and holder should uniformly classify them as a nonmonetary item in common unit financial statements. Is that an acceptable solution, or should we refrain from predicting conversion and treat convertibles as monetary? We could avoid the issue by measuring the attribute most relevant to cash-flow-oriented decisions—current market value—and then record a gain or loss for the difference between the restated beginning amount and the ending market value.

Cash, receivables, and payables denominated in a foreign currency are sometimes questioned. It seems clear, however, that their purchasing power is also subject to change with inflation;

since whether inflation occurs in the domestic economy or in
another country will affect the amount but not the principle,
monetary classification seems appropriate. However, to the extent
that the monetary classification is significant because it includes
all of those items on which a gain or loss can be computed by
simply applying the domestic inflation factor, foreign currency
items must be segregated for separate treatment similar to that
accorded to bonds carried at current market value. The loss or
gain on a constant balance would be the difference between the
restated beginning translated amount and the newly translated
balance (at the end-of-period rate). For example, $100 of lire
at the beginning with a 10 percent dollar inflation rate and a
5 percent decline in the lire would yield a $15 loss and a $95
ending balance (if the lire were held through the period).

Credit or debit balances related to income tax allocation appear
to be monetary because the addition to or deduction from future
tax payments can be expected to vary only due to changes in
the tax law, a change in the taxpayer's "bracket," or lack of taxable
income, but not due to changing price levels. One way of testing
whether an item should be classified as monetary or nonmonetary
is to consider whether restatement of the item would result in
its valuation at an amount that appears to be out of line with
the expected future cash flow associated with the item so that
a gain or loss would be taken on it when it is liquidated. Clearly,
in a simple deferred tax case (e.g., one involving use of the
installment sales method), restatement of the liability would put
it at a figure larger than is needed to pay the tax due when
the installment receivables are collected, so a gain would be
recorded. A deferred tax liability, or asset, is a monetary item.

One final point about monetary items: ordinary preferred stock
is a monetary owners' equity item. The common shareholders
benefit from its decline in real value with inflation, but since
that benefit does not change the total owners' equity, it is not
income. It should be offset against the preferred dividend when
the earnings available to the common shareholders are computed.

The Gain on Long-Term Debt

We have seen earlier in this chapter that common unit accounting
treats the loss of purchasing power of monetary assets held as

an income statement item; we have also seen that the reduced purchasing power significance of monetary liabilities due to decreased purchasing power of the monetary units to be paid out in the future is a positive component of income. We must recognize, however, that some accountants have disagreed with the way in which common unit accounting treats the gain on long-term debt as its purchasing power significance decreases. Individual members of two of the national standards-setting bodies have taken the position, in private correspondence, that the restatement of long-term debt is not an income item on a current basis. The best-known application of common unit accounting in the United States—that at the Indiana Telephone Company—defers the recognition of such income until the debt is retired. Another position (Saunders and Busby, 1976) is that the controversial "gain" on debt and preferred stock should be deferred as a "nonmonetary liability" (owed to whom?) and amortized at the composite rate of depreciation being applied to "property, plant and equipment" on the grounds that "treating the inflation effect of sources of property investment on the same basis as the inflation effect of the property it finances results in a realistic presentation for evaluating the overall impact of inflation" (p. 19). Since it is likely that others question the propriety of the majority view, let us consider a simple example.

The Debt and Debtless Companies

A static firm, the Debt Company, holds 1,000 units of a commodity through a period when the price index increased by 10 percent. The conventional balance sheet looks like this:

DEBT COMPANY
BALANCE SHEET
During 19x1

Commodity: 1,000 units	$100	Debt	$40
		Residual equity	$60

Upon restatement and revaluation of the debt, the balance sheet reflects income of 4 end-of-period dollars; that is, a residual equity amount $4 greater than is necessary to maintain the residual equity holders' purchasing power. The income is derived from a gain on the debt.

DEBT COMPANY
BALANCE SHEET
Restated and Revalued
12/31/x1

Commodity: 1,000 units	$110	Debt	$40
		Residual equity	$70

Is this $4 income distributable (without impairing capital)? Yes, it is if it is real at all. If the market selling price of the commodity is now $.11 per unit, the firm can sell 36 units for $3.96 and pay a cash dividend of that amount, or it can pay a dividend in kind by distributing 36 units of the commodity, leaving the following balance sheet at the start of the next period:

DEBT COMPANY
BALANCE SHEET
1/1/x2

Commodity: 964 units	$106.04	Debt	$40
		Residual equity	$66.04

If the price level again increases 10 percent, a restatement and revaluation of the debt to $40 would leave an income of $4, which could be distributed in the same manner. This practice can continue as long as the price level increases, the price of our commodity keeps pace, and the commodity is divisible enough to permit carving off a portion for sale or distribution. The earning power of the company is not reduced below its beginning-of-period level by such distributions. But note two things that common unit accounting does not do: (1) It does not, by itself, account for unrealized gains or losses due to specific price changes different than the index; current value accounting, along with common unit accounting, is needed to reflect this properly. (2) It does not report on liquidity any more than other accrual accounting systems do; a liquidity-oriented funds statement is needed for this purpose.

Now compare the Debt Company's results with those of the Debtless Company, which differs only in its capital structure.

DEBTLESS COMPANY
BALANCE SHEET
During 19x1

Commodity: 1,000 units	$100	Residual Equity	$100

Restated
12/31/x1

Commodity: 1,000 units	$110	Residual Equity	$110

Note that the residual equity in this company has only remained constant in real terms at $110 end-of-period dollars, which are equal to 100 beginning dollars. When this outcome is compared with the increase in real value of the residual equity in the Debt Company, in an amount equal to the 10 percent rate of inflation times the debt, it is clear that residual equity holders gain from debt during inflation. Under common unit accounting, the gain is recorded on an accrual basis; under variable unit accounting it is recorded upon realization of the assets. It seems impossible for any double-entry version of common unit accounting to avoid recognition of the $4 increase in the real amount of the residual equity in the Debt Company. It is, of course, possible to define income so as to exclude this particular source of "better-offness" of the owners.

To summarize in other words, a price level gain on debt represents "better-offness" of owners and is distributable to them without impairing capital. Like any other accrual basis income, it does not assure liquidity. The potential problem of a profit accompanied by a cash shortage is a risk involved in computing income on any noncash basis. But it is difficult to see how the use of cash to pay off the debt would make the gain any more distributable (as is implied by "deferring" it). Nor does paying off the debt change the exposure to inflation as the reductions in cash and debt offset each other, leaving the net monetary position unchanged. How could debt retirement (and *disbursement* of cash) be considered a realization event related to a gain? The date of realization of a gain or revenue is the date of the cash (or near-cash) receipt, which occurs, in this case, when the larger dollars are borrowed, not when the smaller dollars are repaid.

We must realize that a complete, systematic approach to common unit accounting requires recognition that the purchasing power significance of nominally constant debt and monetary assets changes with inflation; we cannot recognize restatement on unbalanced parts of the balance sheet and still have a balancing statement. The idea that debtors gain currently from inflation is as widely accepted and understood as any aspect of inflation accounting. Failure to report it as a gain would be hard to explain. Within the context of an $A = L + P$ balance sheet and income as the change in net assets other than by transactions with owners, there simply is no mathematically acceptable alternative to treating the change in purchasing power related to debt as income.[6]

Common Unit, Current Value Accounting

The two immediately preceding sections of this chapter have been devoted to common unit accounting in relation to GAAP. Now it is time to discuss common unit accounting combined with current value measurement methods.[7] To illustrate this combination, let's take the case of the Two-Transaction Company (see pp. 244–49) and add two bits of information: (1) the replacement cost of asset A at the time of its sale was $35, and (2) the replacement cost of asset B at year-end was $48. Now let's review the journal entries on pages 246–47. Entry (1) is unchanged because the monetary items are unchanged. Entry (2) is also the same as before. Entry (3), however, is revised to record the revaluation of (a) the outgoing asset A from $30 to $35 at the date of its sale, and (b) the remaining nonmonetary asset from $50 to $48 as of year-end. That makes entry (3):

---

[6] In chapter XIII we will suggest that the inflation gain on interest-bearing liabilities be deducted from nominal interest expense, that the inflation loss on interest-earning assets be deducted from interest earned, and that the inflation gain or loss on the net amount of cash, non-interest-earning receivables, and non-interest-bearing monetary liabilities be shown separately on the income statement.

[7] The common unit, current value accounting system described here is the same (in substance) as that in Staubus (1961) and is presented here through the courtesy of the copyright holder.

(3-a) Dr. Nonmonetary asset A $5.00
     Cr. Revaluations and restatements $5.00
(3-b) Dr. Revaluations and restatements 2.00
     Cr. Nonmonetary asset B 2.00

(The common unit restatements account has been retitled to reflect its new role.) Entry (4) is still blank because there is no preferred stock. Entry (5) is changed because the cost of goods sold is changed to $35 as of the sale date. The $35 rolled forward from 103$ to 110$ is $35(110/103) = 110$37.38, which requires an adjustment of $2.38. Added to the $.19 adjustment of the appraisal expense, the expense restatement becomes $2.57. Entry (5) is:

(5) Dr. Expense accounts $2.57
    Dr. Revaluations and restatements .29
     Cr. Revenue accounts $2.86

When these entries are posted to the revaluations and restatements account, along with a closing entry (6), we have:

Revaluations and Restatements

(2) Restatement of beginning residual equity	$6.00	(1) Loss on net monetary assets	$0.67
(3-b) Write-down of asset B	2.00	(3-a) Write-up of asset A	5.00
(5) Restatement of revenues and expenses	.29	(6) Loss on revaluation of nonmonetary assets	2.62
	$8.29		$8.29

You may question the accuracy of the description of entry (6). How can this "plug" figure turn out to be the *amount by which the nonmonetary assets failed to keep pace with the change in the general price level* as reflected in the index used to restate the accounts to common units? One explanation is that entries (3-a) and (3-b) have replaced entry (3), which reflected the index-based restatement, with the actual change in asset prices; the difference is, of course, the "real" loss (or gain). We should also remember that entry (5) was changed because the cost of goods sold was changed, but it still serves the same purpose.

If you still doubt the authenticity of the $2.62 loss on revaluation, consider the following proof:

	Required to keep pace with inflation	Actual Current Valuation	Gain or loss
Asset A—30(103/100)—at sale date	$30.90	$35.00	$4.10
Rolled forward to year-end (multiplied by 110/103)	33.00	37.38	4.38
Asset B, end of year—50(110/100)	55.00	48.00	(7.00)
Net loss on revaluation, in 110$			$(2.62)

So the revaluation loss on nonmonetary items is indeed $2.62 in year-end dollars. *Restating everything except the nonmonetary assets and liabilities while revaluing the nonmonetary items to current values discloses the gain or loss due to the nonmonetary items changing in real value.*

Several aspects of this procedure deserve additional discussion. One is the calculation of the revaluations of nonmonetary assets. In this case we distinguish between the revaluation of an outgoing asset and the revaluation of one on hand at year-end, but this distinction is not necessary. Consider, for example, an inventory account that has substantial activity during the year. If it is feasible to maintain up-to-date information on the current cost of acquiring an item (by purchase or production); if current acquisition price is always used to credit the inventory account when the outgoing goods are being charged to cost of goods sold or to other accounts; and if the beginning and ending inventories are stated at current values as of the beginning and end of the year, respectively; then the revaluation gain or loss can be computed as the one unknown in the "account equation." While the Two-Transaction Company does not provide an ideal example because it acquired no inventory items during the year, it can illustrate the idea of solving for the revaluation in any account. Assume that assets A and B were recorded in one inventory account:

Inventory			
Beginning inventory at current value	$80	Outflows at current value	$35

Acquisitions	0		
Revaluations		Ending inventory at	
(last entry)	3	current value	48
	83		83

With no revaluations, there are normally four types of entries in a ruled and balanced inventory account: beginning balance plus acquisitions on the debit side, and outflows plus ending balance on the credit side. Revaluations make a fifth type. If we know four of the five, we can solve for the unknown—the total revaluations. (However, physical shrinkage must not be overlooked.) That makes it very easy to calculate the *nominal* revaluation gain or loss in any account for which current value information has been constantly available. The *real* gain or loss is then computed in the revaluations and restatements account as previously illustrated.

The restatement of the revenue and expense accounts becomes very simple under current value accounting because all costs of asset consumption (cost of goods sold, depreciation, depletion, amortization), as well as any previously deferred revenues, are stated in current monetary units as of the interim date when the consumption takes place. That makes them well matched with the current revenues. Both revenues and expenses can then be rolled forward uniformly to the end of the reporting period. The net effect on income is due to the rolling forward of the difference, that is, rolling forward interim income numbers to year-end. Omission of this step may not cause a material error if the profit margin is thin. Using the revaluations and restatements account to accumulate the related entries, we see that omission of the restatement of revenues and expenses—entry (5)—would cause an offsetting error in the "plugged" entry: the loss or gain on revaluation of nonmonetary assets. That error results in a mis-classification affecting operating income and revaluation gain or loss.

Failure to obtain current ending values or current values of outgoing items will require the substitution of restated previous measurements, such as restated historical costs (or restated historical receipts for nonmonetary liabilities), if we are to achieve common unit accounting. This involves the assumption that such assets (and liabilities) are still worth their original valuations in old units. That assumption could, of course, be wrong, just as the traditional historical cost valuation assumption could be wrong.

In view of the obvious difficulties that the accounting professions and businessmen in many countries have had in settling on a system of inflation accounting, it may be worthwhile to recapitulate the potential contributions of common unit accounting and current value accounting to the goal of reporting more useful information to those who rely on financial statements.

A. The adoption of *common unit accounting* means substituting either a consumer purchasing power or general purchasing power concept of capital maintenance for the montary capital maintenance that is incorporated in GAAP. It can accomplish the following:

1. *For the balance sheet as of a single date:* more relevant measurements of nonmonetary assets (and liabilities). As explained in chapter VII, adjusting the historical cost of an asset by the average percentage change since acquisition date in all prices included in the index typically will yield a price closer to the current price of the asset than was the historical cost without restatement. The broader the sample of assets being restated on a particular balance sheet, the closer we can expect the resulting total asset number to be to its current value equivalent. Therefore, price level restatement of nonmonetary assets tends to approximate current valuation; the more comprehensive the balance sheet, the closer the approximation. The results can be quite good for a national balance sheet, moderately good for the consolidated balance sheet of a large group, and poor for a specialized division or small company. The latter observation may be one reason why operating managers tend to be more interested in current value accounting than in common unit accounting.

2. *For comparative balance sheets of an entity:* the roll-forward procedure that is applied to old balance sheets, as explained in the FASB and other write-ups, makes a big contribution to the comparability of balance sheets at different dates.

3. *For the periodic income statement:* the common unit accounting system removes the inflation factor so as to

yield what economists recognize as real income over the lifetime of the entity, so the typical periodic income number is likely to be closer to real income. Putting it another way, common unit accounting "gets the income right" in the long run. Assuming that the system were adopted by all users, this feature has significant implications for an economy in which an income tax is used heavily and private sector real savings are depended upon for improvement in the standard of living.

4. *For comparative income statements:* the roll-forward feature of common unit accounting procedures makes a big contribution to the comparability of income statements and the interpretation of trends over time.

B. The adoption of *current value accounting* means measuring all assets and liabilities without use of historical cost, restated historical cost, historical receipt, restated historical receipt, or discounted values based on noncurrent discount rates; matching current costs with current revenues on the income statement; and including both unrealized and realized holding gains and losses in income. It would tend to accomplish the following:

1. *For the balance sheet:* produce the most relevant measurements of assets, liabilities, and residual equity that are possible. If added to common unit accounting, current value accounting would improve the relevance of the measurements on the single balance sheet.

2. *For the periodic income statement:* improve the timing of income by reporting it when market prices change rather than upon realization. When superimposed on common unit accounting, the result would be both proper timing and an accurate representation of long-run real economic income. Without common unit accounting, the timing would be fine, but the long-run total would be based on comparing costs and revenues in different sizes of units.

C. Looking at the whole picture, in view of the general understanding that common unit accounting procedures are much less costly and much more reliable than comprehensive current value accounting, it seems clear that the former is a much better bargain as a step towards improving financial accounting in times of inflation. In addition, it

would appear that we could have the additional advantages
of current value accounting for the particular assets and
liabilities (and associated income statement items) for which
the reliability and cost criteria can be met acceptably,
perhaps adding categories of net asset items as we gain
experience. Note that vertical comparability on a financial
statement would not be impaired (relative to GAAP) by
such partial adoption of current valuations, as there is
a lack of comparability now. Needless to say, we assume
that steps towards current valuations would be made
uniformly across firms in similar circumstances.

In summary, the combination of current value accounting and
common unit accounting can work out beautifully—if the current
value information is readily available. Common unit accounting
is much easier when combined with current value accounting
because it no longer is necessary to date and restate each nonmonetary asset or liability. Restatement of the income statement is also
easier because all amounts appearing on any interim statement
are stated in the prevailing unit of that interim period. Furthermore, the absence of current value data for a few nonmonetary
assets does not seriously affect the desirability of the combination,
provided that the restated historical measurements of the remaining items are actually entered in the accounts and kept up-to-date.
The combination provides by far the most relevant information
for users' needs and at a very modest cost over either system
alone.[8]

---

[8]Accountants would be wise to avoid the procedure, suggested by some writers,
of deducting a "capital maintenance charge," computed by applying the fractional
index change during the period to the beginning residual equity, in the computation
of net income for the period. These writers also include the gross revaluations
of nonmonetary items in income. In the Two-Transaction Company, the capital
maintenance charge would be our restatement of residual equity, $6. Together
with the gross revaluations of $5 credit and $2 debit, the net effect on income
is a $3 debit, and same as our $2.62 revaluation loss, $.67 monetary items loss,
and $.29 credit for restatement of income statement items. The information
communicated, however, is quite different. The procedure that we would avoid
says that the company gained $3 on holding nonmonetary assets (which directly
violates the idea of common unit accounting) and suffered a loss of $6, which
is described as a "capital maintenance charge." No gain or loss from being in
debt or holding money is even mentioned. I defy anyone to explain to financial

INCOME TAXATION AND COMMON UNIT ACCOUNTING

As long as common unit accounting is not accepted for computing taxable income, and assuming that the principle of comprehensive tax allocation is accepted, how should it be applied under common unit accounting? Neither the provisional standard on "Accounting for Changes in the Purchasing Power of Money" in Britain and Ireland nor the FASB exposure draft on "Financial Reporting in Units of General Purchasing Power" (1974) provides for tax allocation related to the monetary gain or loss or to the restatement of nonmonetary items. Is this appropriate? (I mentioned earlier in this chapter that the FASB treats the liability for deferred taxes as a nonmonetary item and I disagreed with that treatment.)

To test the various possible treatments of income taxes in connection with common unit accounting, let's take the example of the Land Company: at the beginning of period one, it purchased land for $200 and financed it with debt of $50 and equity capital of $150. Assume that the land was held until the beginning of period two, when it was sold for its restated book value of $220, after a 10 percent rate of inflation in period one was recognized. A tax rate of 50 percent applies to the $20 taxable gain. EXHIBIT IX-4 shows the income calculation under GAAP and under four different combinations of common unit accounting and tax accounting. The "no tax allocation" column is consistent with the FASB exposure draft. The next column reflects results under the conventional income statement approach to tax allocation by which tax is provided on any reported income unless it will never be taxed. I consider an excess of common unit accounting income over GAAP income to be taxable eventually because, as I show in chapter X, a company's lifetime income under common unit accounting is less than under GAAP (assuming inflation), so any temporary excess of common unit accounting income over GAAP income will be more than offset by future reversals. Consequently, in the long run there will be no untaxed common unit accounting

---

statement readers exactly why a "capital maintenance charge" should be deducted on an income statement. The idea that income can be affected by a loss on the residual equity is inconsistent with the generally accepted idea that income is a change in the net assets. I emphatically reject it.

EXHIBIT IX-4
LAND COMPANY
BALANCE SHEET
JANUARY 1, PERIOD ONE

| Land | $200 | Note payable | $50 |
| | | Residual equity | 150 |

LAND COMPANY
INCOME CALCULATIONS

| | | | Common Unit Accounting | | |
| | | | Tax Allocation By— | | |
	Per GAAP	*No Tax Allocation*	*Conventional I/S Approach*	*Asset Valuation Approach*	*Asset Split: Mon'y/ Nonmon'y*
Period One					
Gain or (loss) on monetary items	$ 0	$ 5	$ 5	$ 5	$ (5)
Income tax	0	0	(2.5)	(10)	0
Net income	$ 0	$ 5	$ 2.5	$ (5)	$ (5)
Period Two					
Gain on sale	$20	$ 0	$ 0	$ 0	$10
Income tax	(10)	(10)	(7.5)	0	(10)
Net income	$10	$(10)	$(7.5)	$ 0	$ 0
Venture					
Net income	$10	$ (5)	$(5)	$ (5)	$ (5)

gain. The fourth column is based on tax allocation by adjusting the asset value (perhaps via a contra account), as explained in chapter VI. The general principle of this fourth approach is that any difference between an asset's book valuation and its tax basis requires an adjustment of the former so that the net valuation of the asset (or liability) will be equal to the after-tax proceeds that would be enjoyed if the asset were sold for its preadjustment valuation. In other words, no instant gain or loss due to taxation should be built into an asset's valuation. The tax adjustment contra account is a monetary item.

The final column of EXHIBIT IX-4 shows the income calculations under the view that a nonmonetary asset can be divided into two parts representing two sources of cash flow potential: (1) a cash flow contribution by saving taxes, and (2) a cash flow contribution due to its basic services. The first part could be classified as a monetary item because its nominal monetary amount has been substantially fixed by the asset's purchase price and will not vary because of inflation. The latter portion, on the other hand, is a conventional nonmonetary item. If so, a purchasing power loss of $10 is suffered on the monetary portion ($100) and it more than offsets the $5 gain on the debt. The nonmonetary portion is restated from $10 to $110. This gives the asset a total restated valuation of $210 so that its sale for $220 yields a gain of $10, a taxable gain of $20, and income tax of $10.

Note that only the last two methods set up the asset valuation so that no instant net income or loss is reported when the asset is sold for its restated historical cost of $220 on the first day of period two. I prefer one of these methods. The penultimate one—tax allocation via asset valuation—may be most easily interpreted. The layman might interpret the results from period one like this: "We assume that our investment kept pace with inflation and we gained on our debt, but if we sell the land the tax collector will sock us for $10 tax, which puts us in the hole. We can postpone the tax, but sooner or later we'll have to pay it, unless our investment goes bad first, so we may as well recognize it now. It has not been a good year." Do you agree?[9]

---

[9]Cf. p. 180.

Now let's look at the tax aspect of current value accounting combined with common unit accounting. Suppose that the Land Company's assets were revalued to $250 at the end of period one and were sold for that price at the beginning of period two. Following the asset valuation approach to tax allocation, a potential selling price of $250 would involve a tax of $25 (at the assumed 50 percent rate). A potential selling price of $250 also implies a revaluation gain of $30 before tax, since it would take $220 current dollars to break even in purchasing power. The other income effect is the $5 gain on the debt. The income calculations may be summarized as follows:

Period One

Revaluation gain, before tax	$30
Monetary gain	5
Income tax provision	(25)
Net income	$10

Period Two

Gain on sale	$ 0
Income tax	0
Net income	$ 0

Venture

Net income	$10

Now consider the asset valuation approach to tax allocation as applied to a going concern that reports to its shareholders on a common unit accounting basis and pays income taxes on a GAAP basis. The gain or loss on net monetary position may be ignored when the income tax adjustment on net asset values is calculated because that income item will never affect the tax paid; only restatements of old GAAP measurements of nonmonetary items need be considered. The simple generalization from chapter VI still holds. We must adjust the valuation (e.g., restated historical cost) made without consideration of taxation, by the marginal tax rate times the difference between the valuation and the asset's basis. (The possibility of grouping net asset items according to their lives, and treating each group differently, was discussed on p. 219.)

WHAT DIFFERENCE DOES IT MAKE?

In this section of the chapter we want to discuss the importance of the common unit–variable unit controversy. Assuming that a logical case has been made for common unit accounting, are the differences really material? Does anyone care? Should accountants and others be concerned? These types of questions deserve some attention before we make a decision on this issue.

First, let's consider the question of materiality. It is apparent that restatement of long-lived assets will have a material effect upon the total assets in companies with large amounts of such assets. Similarly, the restatement of the residual equity typically will be substantial. Since debt is not restated, debt-equity ratios will be reduced. But our greatest interest is likely to be in the net income number. Fortunately, we have the results of three major studies completed in the 1970s which provide us with some evidence on this point. (The substantial number of individual company data accumulated over the preceding quarter-century will not be discussed because the variations in rates of inflation and in capital structures over the decades make such data somewhat less interesting.)

One interesting study was done by the Mechanical Engineering Economic Development Committee (1973) in Britain and covers 126 companies and the years 1966–71. This study reported that aggregate profit (after interest and profits taxes) of the 126 companies, computed on a common unit accounting basis, ranged from 62 percent to 78 percent of the aggregate variable unit profit, for the six different years. Restatement of cost of goods sold was the largest factor in the differences between the two sets of profit numbers. In the early years of the period studied, when inflation rates were modest, restatement of depreciation was the second most significant factor, but as both the companies' debt and inflation increased in 1970 and 1971, the gain on net monetary liabilities more than offset the increase in depreciation. After taxes and dividends, the aggregate retained profit for the six years was £10 million on a common unit basis compared with £124 million on a variable unit basis.

The Cutler and Westwick (1973) study covered 137 companies representing approximately 75 percent of the market value of all U.K. companies quoted on the London share market. The authors have not identified the year covered, but it was probably 1971. They computed common unit income by making rough adjustments of published data. The results showed that common unit income differed from variable unit income by more than 10 percent in 107 of the 137 companies, by 50 percent or more in 34 of the companies, and by more than 100 percent in 11 companies. The three major adjustments—gain or loss on net monetary position, cost of goods sold, and depreciation—were of roughly equal significance.

Davidson and Weil (1975a) used published data to adjust the incomes of the 30 companies included in the Dow Jones Industrial Average and 30 other companies selected from the *Fortune* 500 industrials. Their data related to 1973 earnings and showed that 32 of the 60 companies had common unit income that differed from their variable unit income by at least 10 percent and 17 of the 60 showed differences of more than 25 percent. The median difference in the Dow Jones companies was 11 percent, in the other companies, 12.5 percent. The smaller discrepancies in the U.S. companies (as compared with the U.K. companies) may be due to a more sudden increase in the rate of inflation in 1973 as compared with previous years. (See chapter X for an explanation of why a sudden increase in the rate of inflation tends to increase common unit accounting earnings relative to variable unit accounting earnings.)

Variable unit accounting, according to these statistics, yields income numbers that are materially different from those that would result from common unit accounting. What difference does this make to the various parties who have an interest in the financial results of enterprise operations? Reported earnings numbers are relied upon heavily as a basis for major decisions that affect the distribution of the rewards and burdens of participating in our society. The income taxes paid by corporations and the owners of unincorporated businesses depend on a method of computing income. Reported profits are believed to have some effect upon the expectations of employees and other parties who sell goods and services to the firm. Customers and the public, sometimes through elected officials, are bound to be influenced, at least to some extent, by their perception of the profitability of specific businesses and industries, and of the business sector of the economy. All of these parties—the tax collector, employees, suppliers, customers, and the remaining public—are likely to expect more from a profitable enterprise than from an unprofitable one. We hypothesize, therefore, that the future taxes, wages, and other costs of an enterprise will be increased by increasing the *reported* profits of enterprises. If so, the overstating or understating of profits *does* make a difference. And, let's not forget, the "error" in variable unit accounting varies widely among companies.

A shift to common unit accounting as the primary evidence of enterprise success might be greeted with varying degrees of enthusiasm or antipathy by the different parties that are affected by financial statements. We should not be surprised to find managers in companies whose common unit income would be lower than their variable unit income resisting the changeover, because managers typically prefer to report successful results (of their management). Owners of closely-held businesses, on the other hand—at least those who understand the alternatives—could be expected to favor common unit accounting, especially for tax purposes. People whose rewards are tied to the stock market may resist common unit accounting on the assumption that "bottom-line fixation" would result in a reduction in share prices commensurate with the typical reduction in reported earnings. Those who believe the market is roughly efficient on this issue may not feel strongly either way.

Union officials are likely to oppose the change because they would anticipate that the reduction in profit that would be reported by most firms in the short run and by all firms in the long run (1) would strengthen managers' resistance to demands for wage increases, and (2) would eventually result in a reduction in the income taxes collected from businesses, which would have to be offset by increases in personal taxes. My own guess is that any major decrease in the collection of income taxes from business would be offset by a value-added tax, or something similar. This would be favored by those who believe that income taxes, especially on business income, encourage waste and tax evasion or avoidance. In sum, citizens and elected officials can be expected to take positions for or against a switch to common unit accounting on the basis of their appraisals of the consequences that the change would have on their own economic interests, not on the basis of the quality of the resulting accounting data as evidence of real economic results and as bases for making decisions. (Readers who recall chapter III may recognize that this paragraph implies that effects via other parties would be a key criterion in any evaluator's choice of sides on the common unit accounting issue.)

One of the simplest and most important possible applications of common unit accounting could be in the computation of taxable income from securities investments. If the tax basis of a security were increased by the amount required to keep pace with inflation or if nominal income from a security were only taxed when, on a cumulative basis since acquisition, it exceeded the cumulative restatement, the "income tax" would tax only the real income of securities investors rather than taking part of their originally invested purchasing power. Whether the tax law is changed or not, securities investors are advised to take the loss of purchasing power of money into consideration in computing the rate of return they earn on their investments. The simplest way to approximate a CUA rate of return (before tax) is to compute the return in the usual way—dividends or interest plus appreciation—convert it to a percentage of beginning-of-period market value, then subtract the inflation rate for the period. If the investor wants to know his after-tax rate of return he must deduct from his gross return the taxes he pays on the dividend and a tax provision for the capital gain, whether the gain is realized or not. If a more refined calculation is desired, one could (1) relate the return to the average investment during the period instead of to the beginning value, (2) take the inflation rate into account by restating the beginning market value in the computation of both the appreciation and the investment base, instead of simply subtracting it from the rate of return, (3) restate dividends, or interest, and taxes in end-of-period monetary units, and (4) use tax-adjusted market values in the denominator.

If this approach to the computation of an investor's real return is appropriate, then it is obvious that traditional computations based on variable units seriously overstate such returns. In fact, inasmuch as returns on securities are customarily computed on a current value basis, the percentage overstatement each period is equal to the percentage increase in the consumer price index.

Now let's see just what this means in a real case—a typical one from recent history that has been wound up. In January 1970, TRW, Inc., issued $50 million of five-year, 8 3/4 percent notes at par. These securities offered one of the highest interest rates the American market had ever seen on obligations of that quality (Standard & Poor's A). Did this represent a bonanza for investors? Suppose that the typical buyer of these securities was in the 50 percent tax bracket including state and federal income tax rates. This means that his after-tax nominal return was 4 3/8 percent. Now compare that with the rate of increase in the U.S. Consumer Price Index published by the Bureau of Labor Statistics. The percentage increases in each year were as follows:

1970	5.2%
1971	3.4%
1972	3.7%
1973	9.4%
1974	11.7%

In only two years out of the five-year life of this issue did the investor have a positive real return, and the average real annual return for the life of the issue was −2.3 percent. An after-tax annual return of 6.7 percent would have been required to break even. This translates into a before-tax nominal interest rate of 13.4 percent. This case illustrates how a tax that is intended to be an income tax can take a slice of capital in inflationary periods with variable unit tax accounting.

The above example illustrates the importance of "indexing" the input amounts that are used in the computation of investment returns to a securities holder. But does a bond holder care whether the *issuing company* adopts common unit accounting or variable unit accounting? Revsine (1973, pp. 6–7) has argued that he does not:

> . . . the creditor's potential return is fixed. Irrespective of the extraordinary profitability of the firm, the lender will receive only the agreed on interest and the principal repayment. The lender should have already adjusted for anticipated inflation in setting his required interest rate. Thus, his prime concern is whether the firm can maintain or improve its existing *nominal* dollar position. If it can, payment of both principal

and interest is likely. If it cannot, payment is jeopardized. Notice that the creditor is not harmed by a weakening in the firm's real net asset position so long as the nominal net asset position is maintained.

This position seems reasonable—at first glance. After all, the borrower has only agreed to pay back a specified number of units of money, not a fixed amount of purchasing power. But does this view really reflect the creditor's interest in financial information from the firm? One reason for a short-term creditor to be less interested in the calculation of the firm's income is that liquidity is more important than profitability to him. But a long-term creditor who uses financial statements to provide information to help him predict the firm's capacity to pay its debts as they come due must consider risk. The debt-equity ratio is an important indicator of risk. A typical firm that strives to maintain its level of physical operations during an inflationary period must increase its money capital. If its management, shareholders, and tax collectors believe that its nominal income is real, and so take it all in the forms of taxes and dividends, the increased total capital must come from debt. The result is an increase in the debt-equity ratio and a decrease in the probability of the firm repaying its creditors. I conclude that creditors may have a strong interest in the adoption of common unit accounting by borrowers and in its acceptance by taxing authorities. The following example illustrates what can happen in extreme circumstances:

> Joe X invested $4,000 of his own money in a Guzzlemobile and went into the taxi cab business. His accountant computed depreciation in accordance with GAAP and Joe set aside a cash replacement fund in the amount of his accumulated depreciation, confident that he could consume the income his accountant reported to him without fear of harming his "business." At the end of the car's life, he found that the replacement cost of a Guzzlemobile, along with the general price level, had doubled. So he went to his friendly banker and borrowed $4,000 to add to the $4,000 he had set aside, promising to pay the debt in installments. This he did, but when replacement time came around once more he again found that inflation made him unable to finance his new equipment out of his own capital so he borrowed again, except

this time he had to borrow $12,000. When he attempted to repeat the cycle the fourth time, his banker was less friendly. In fact, he refused to lend Joe the necessary $28,000 because Joe's equity would have been only 12.5 percent. Joe was out of business. Of course, he still had his $4,000, but it would buy very little. The accompanying condensed balance sheets show the essence of his financial position at the beginning and end of each asset cycle.

JOE X

BALANCE SHEETS

	First Car Beg.	First Car End	Second Car Beg.	Second Car End	Third Car Beg.	Third Car End	(Pro Forma) Fourth Car Beg.
Cash	$0	$4,000	$0	$4,000	$0	$4,000	$0
Car	4,000	0	8,000	0	16,000	0	32,000
Debt	0	0	4,000	0	12,000	0	28,000
Equity	4,000	4,000	4,000	4,000	4,000	4,000	4,000

The moral of this story is that if income is computed on a variable dollar basis, and if that income is taxed and consumed, a long period of inflation will require either new equity capital (and dilution) or an increase in the amount of debt financing required to maintain the earning power of the enterprise. Failure to maintain the earning power is likely to make it difficult for the firm to pay its debts while the alternative of increasing the debt-equity ratio increases the risk that a period of poor performance or poor business conditions will lead to bankruptcy. Long-term creditors should prefer common unit accounting.

The plight of lenders has been given substantial attention. But what about the effects of inflation on borrowers? If lenders' returns are overstated and overtaxed, are not borrowers' profits understated, and perhaps undertaxed? Indeed, they are. TRW, Inc., which borrowed at 8³/₄ percent, was able to deduct the nominal interest expense on its tax return. If its tax rates aggregated to 50 percent, its after-tax cost was only 4³/₈ percent. If it paid back dollars that had been shrunk by inflation at the average annual rate of 6.7 percent, it incurred a negative real interest cost. Under these circumstances, it seems reasonable to say that the Internal Revenue Service took part of the lenders' capital and gave it to the borrower. Can we conclude from this case that the team of inflation and the income tax collector are bound to take from the lender and give to the borrower? Not necessarily. Lenders could conceivably insist on high enough interest rates to cover both inflation and the tax and still have a real return left. For example, if lenders predict a 10 percent rate of inflation and a 50 percent tax rate and want a 4 percent real, after-tax return, a nominal interest rate of 28 percent would meet their goal. Under such circumstances, the borrower would also be paying a real, after-tax rate of 4 percent, if his tax rate is 50 percent. But it should be clear that nominal interest rates in the U.S. have not, in recent years, approximated levels required to give a lender in a typical tax bracket the 3 to 4 percent after-tax real rate of return that some people consider normal. A look at EXHIBIT IX-5 should make this point clear. Nor has this pattern been limited to the 1970s. Data accumulated by Ibbotson and Sinquefield (1976) show that investors in long-term corporate and U.S. Government bonds have earned a negative *before-tax* return for the

EXHIBIT IX-5

BOND YIELDS, PURCHASING POWER LOSSES, AND REAL RETURNS IN THE U.S.

Year	Nominal AAA Corporate Bond Yields*	Investor's Costs Loss on Purchasing Power	50% Tax	Net Real Return	Nominal Yield Required to Net 4% Real (in 50% bracket)
1970	8.0	5.2	4.0	(1.2)	18.4
1971	7.4	3.4	3.7	.3	14.8
1972	7.2	3.7	3.6	(.1)	15.4
1973	7.4	9.4	3.7	(5.7)	26.8
1974	8.6	12.2	4.3	(7.9)	32.4
1975	8.8	7.0	4.4	(2.6)	22.0

*Source: *Moody's Bond Survey*, various dates.

forty-year period ending in 1974. What has the accounting profession done to make the average citizen, or investor, aware of this pattern?

If both borrower and lender correctly predict the rate of inflation, they have the opportunity to reach agreement. The borrower, in effect, sells his tax advantage to the lender to offset his tax disadvantage. It is unexpected rates of inflation that result in transferring wealth between lending and borrowing groups. Since reaching agreement on the rates of inflation that will prevail during the life of a loan is very difficult, indexing both the contractual interest rate and the tax basis of debt owned and owed would appear to be a superior solution. Until this is done, the high and unnecessary risks involved in borrowing-lending relationships are likely to impede the functioning of the capital markets.

REASONS FOR DELAY IN ADOPTION OF COMMON UNIT ACCOUNTING

As of April 1976, common unit accounting has been used regularly by only one public company in the U.S.—Indiana Telephone Corporation. The failure of all other publicly owned, profit-seeking companies to adopt this method needs some explanation, which we can begin to provide by looking at the following areas of concern.

First, there was no demonstrable need for common unit accounting until inflation rates began to rise. Inflation was at a low enough rate through the period from 1952 to 1967 that the accounting profession and the business community did not perceive it to be a great problem. For these fifteen years, the rate of inflation did not exceed 4 percent per year and even through 1972 the inflation rate was under 6 percent in the U.S.

Secondly, common unit accounting has practical restrictions. It is costly because of the detailed work involved. It is also unacceptable for calculating taxable income. This, of course, represents the absence of a strong positive reason for adopting the method.

Third, common unit accounting is still only imperfectly understood. It has been confused with current value accounting in the minds of many people, so they have not obtained a clear perception of its effect. As a group, accountants have failed to study common unit accounting, understand its problems, learn the methodology, and prepare to apply it. Common unit accounting has not been taught generally and effectively in the accounting programs at the university level. Such imperfect and limited understanding naturally breeds mistrust: investors and analysts alike have not understood the methodology and so have not trusted it. The methodology itself is still imperfect. The ideal index is not available now; it is not even clear which index *should* be used. Nor does the methodology solve all of our price change accounting problems.

The financial community has feared, in addition, that common unit accounting would result in reporting lower earnings, which would be translated into lower share prices by an "inefficient" market. Management is reluctant to report the lower earnings that common unit accounting does yield in a majority of cases. At the same time, however, management is reluctant to report the higher earnings that common unit accounting often yields in regulated utilities. As discussed in the next chapter, a low turnover of nonmonetary assets combined with high net monetary liabilities can cause common unit income to exceed variable unit income in some periods. The managements of public utility companies may be reluctant to report to their regulatory commission on this basis because the commission may, as a result, not allow utility rates as high as they would otherwise permit. The peculiar problem of regulated industries is that the earning-power values of their assets fail to keep pace with inflation when the regulatory commissions limit their earnings to a prescribed rate of return on "invested cost," that is, historical cost of assets. This means that the current value to the company of the old assets is less than depreciated replacement cost. The proper accounting response to this limitation is to restate the cost of the nonmonetary assets on a common unit basis, then take a loss and write the assets down to historical cost—the value that the regulatory commission allows the company to recover. On this basis, Davidson, Sidky, and Weil (1976) found that only 7 of the 24 utility companies included in the Dow Jones and Standard & Poor's utilities averages had positive net income in 1974, and none had common unit accounting income in excess of 55 percent of variable unit accounting income. If, on the other hand, the commission permits the use of restated historical cost for rate making, then no such loss and write-down need be recorded.

A final clue to the failure of publicly owned, profit-seeking companies to adopt common unit accounting is to be found in the traditional unspoken doctrine of user subordination and management and accountant domination. Most external reporting decisions traditionally have been made by those who feel the costs of accounting, rather than by those who stand to benefit from it and who actually bear the costs—the investors. There is some question as to whether we have a right to expect good decisions in accounting, or in any other field, until the decision makers are able to match the relevant costs and benefits on a one-dollar, one-vote basis.

APPRAISAL OF COMMON UNIT ACCOUNTING ON THE CRITERIA OF
CHAPTER III

In chapter III we discussed nine criteria by which competing accounting proposals could be appraised. It seems appropriate to apply those criteria to the proposal to prepare common unit financial statements for all major uses.

1. *Relevance* of the attribute being measured to the decision processes of users. Our discussion early in the chapter indicated that real income is more relevant to the decisions for which income data are used than is nominal money income. Common unit balance sheet data are more relevant, too.

2. *Reliability.* The present unavailability of perfectly accurate and appropriate indexes, together with possible disagreements on the monetary-nonmonetary classification of a few items, can be tallied as potential deficiencies in the reliability of common unit financial statements as compared with variable unit statements.

3. *Comparability.* A vast improvement in comparability results from eliminating the variability in the measuring unit.

4. *Intelligibility.* A modest additional effort is required to understand common unit statements.

5. *Timeliness.* Financial statement preparation could be delayed until the desired index is published. If the delay is serious, the accountant may choose to base the statements on a reading of the index for a date prior to the end of the period.

6. *Optimal quantity* of information. It is not clear whether the addition of supplementary, common unit statements results in a total quantity of information that is closer to, or further from, the optimum.

7. *Effects via other parties.* From the point of view of *investors,* the effect via the Internal Revenue Service (if it also uses common unit statements) would be most welcome. Managers, too, could be expected to act more in the interests of investors. From the point of view of *professional managers,* use by the Internal Revenue Service would also be desirable. Use by investors, however, assuming lower common unit income and an "inefficient market," would be undesirable.

8. *Cost of utilizing accounting data.* An analyst would do more work, costing more money, if he wanted to make calculations on both variable unit and common unit bases. But if he now tries to allow for inflation, his work would be eased by the availability of common unit statements.

9. *Cost of producing accounting data.* The cost would be increased moderately.

As pointed out in chapter III, the final decision on this issue (or any other) depends upon the weighting of the various criteria and the degree of superiority possessed by a method on a given criterion. We leave this decision to the reader.

SUMMARY

1. The computation of income requires the comparison, addition, and subtraction of measurements made at different times. Analytical techniques applied to comparative balance sheets require similar mathematical operations.

2. Defining and calculating income as an increase in the purchasing power of the owners of a business is consistent with the accounting objective of providing information useful to owners and those interested in the returns of owners.

3. When the general price level changes, the purchasing power of the nominal monetary unit changes. Such variation prevents the operations of addition and subtraction of nominal monetary units from accomplishing what is required to achieve the objectives of accounting. Common unit accounting is an adjustment technique designed

to permit more useful computations with monetary units in periods of inflation by utilizing units of equal purchasing power instead of nominal monetary units.

4. Common unit accounting requires choosing a purchasing power unit existing as of a certain date (typically the financial statement date) as the measuring unit. All measurements used in the financial statements which are not stated in that unit are adjusted to it.

5. Balance sheet items may be measured by any method desired. When they are not measured at their restated beginning amounts, a gain or loss is recorded under common unit accounting. This is normal with monetary items and with nonmonetary items measured by any current value method.

6. A monetary item is one that will entail future cash flows in nominal amounts that are independent of inflation. All other balance sheet items are nonmonetary. An entity gains or loses on its net monetary position from inflation alone, regardless of other economic events.

7. A gain on net monetary position is as "distributable" as any gain on revaluation of assets or liabilities; i.e., it is subject to the acceptability or convertibility of existing net asset items at their book values.

8. Common unit accounting is much simpler when combined with comprehensive current value accounting (as compared with the common unit–GAAP combination).

9. Income tax should be recognized on restatements of nonmonetary assets and liabilities in order to avoid valuations that cause major income effects in future periods.

10. The difference between variable unit income and common unit income typically is material.

11. The attitudes of various groups towards common unit accounting can be expected to reflect their economic interests.

12. Unexpected inflation transfers wealth from the lender to the borrower. Overestimates of inflation tend to reverse this transfer. Indexing contractual interest rates and the tax bases of securities owned and of debt outstanding can solve this problem.

13. Common unit accounting appears to be distinctly superior to variable unit accounting on the criteria of relevance, comparability, and effects via other parties but is, or may be, inferior on other criteria.

We close this chapter with two paragraphs from "The Credibility of Corporations" by Irving Kristol (1974, p. 12):

> . . . what is one to make of a corporation which proudly announces that it has just completed the most profitable year in its history—and then simultaneously declares that its return on capital is pitifully inadequate, that it is suffering from a terrible cost-squeeze, etc., etc.? In 1973, most corporations were engaged in precisely this kind of double-talk. Is it any wonder they created so enormous a credibility gap?
>
> Now, the truth is that 1973 was not so profitable a year for our large corporations. One would see this instantly if corporations reported their profits in *constant dollars*—i.e., corrected for inflation. Trade unions do this when they report their members' earnings to the world at large—*they* don't want to look like "profiteers" when they sit down at the bargaining table. Corporations, in contrast, do seem to be under a compulsion to look like "profiteers"—even when they are not, in fact, operating at a particularly profitable level.

ADDITIONAL READING SUGGESTIONS

Accounting Standards Committee, "Current Cost Accounting," *Proposed Statement of Standard Accounting Practice*, ED18 (Accounting Standards Committee, 30 November 1976).

Accounting Standards Steering Committee, "Accounting for Changes in the Purchasing Power of Money," *Provisional Statement of Standard Accounting Practice, No. 1* (June 1974).

American Institute of Certified Public Accountants, Accounting Principles Board, "Financial Statements Restated for General Price-Level Changes," *Statement of the Accounting Principles Board, No. 3* (AICPA, 1969).

American Institute of Certified Public Accountants, Accounting Research Division, "Reporting the Financial Effects of Price-Level Changes," *Accounting Research Study No. 6* (AICPA, 1963).

Backer, Morton, *Current Value Accounting* (Financial Executives Research Foundation, 1973).

Basu, S. and J. R. Hanna, *Inflation Accounting: Alternatives, Implementation Issues and Some Empirical Evidence* (Society of Industrial Accountants of Canada, 1975).

Bradford, William, "Price-Level Restated Accounting and the Measurement of Inflation Gains and Losses," *The Accounting Review* (April 1974), pp. 296–305.

Burton, John C., "Financial Reporting in An Age of Inflation," *Journal of Accountancy* (February 1975), pp. 68–71.

Chambers, Raymond J., *Inflation Accounting* (University of Sydney, Department of Accounting, 1975).

Davidson, Sidney, Clyde P. Stickney, and Roman L. Weil, *Inflation Accounting* (McGraw-Hill, 1976).

Gynther, R. S., *Accounting for Price-Level Changes—Theory and Procedures* (Pergamon Press, 1966).

Moonitz, Maurice, "Price-Level Accounting and Scales of Measurement," *The Accounting Review* (July 1970), pp. 465–75.

———, *Changing Prices and Financial Reporting* (University of Lancaster, International Centre for Research in Accounting, Arthur Andersen & Co. Lecture Series, 1973; rpt. Stipes Publishing Co., 1974).

National Council of the Institute of Chartered Accountants in Australia and General Council of the Australian Society of Accountants, "Current Cost Accounting," *Statement of Provisional Accounting Standards,* DPS 1.1/309.1 (Institute of Chartered Accountants in Australia and Australian Society of Accountants, October 1976).

———, "The Basis of Current Cost Accounting," *Explanatory Statement,* DPS 1.2/309.2 (Institute of Chartered Accountants in Australia and Australian Society of Accountants, October 1976).

Raby, William L., "Tax Allocation and Non-Historical Financial Statements," *The Accounting Review* (January 1969), pp. 1–11.

Rosen, L. S., *Current Value Accounting and Price-Level Restatements* (The Canadian Institute of Chartered Accountants, 1972).

Sterling, Robert R., "Relevant Financial Reporting in an Age of Price Changes," *Journal of Accountancy* (February 1975), pp. 42–51.

Sweeny, Henry W., *Stabilized Accounting* (Harper & Brothers, 1936; rpt. Holt, Rinehart and Winston, 1964).

Tracy, John A., "A Dissent to the General Price-Level Adjustment Proposal," *The Accounting Review* (January 1965), pp. 163–75.

STUDY QUESTIONS

1. What concept of capital maintenance is most suitable for general use in corporate reporting to shareholders? (What version of cost must be covered before any income can be recognized?)

2. Assuming that the general price level rises, in what circumstances would it increase the real amount of the owners' equity? In what circumstances would it decrease the owners' equity?

3. What types of decisions might be improved by reliance on price-level-restated financial data instead of on conventional statements?

4. Assuming that financial statements are taken at face value, that is, that the income and book values are accepted as representing what a layman might naturally expect, which groups in society may be harmed and which benefited by conventional statements as opposed to price-level-restated statements?

5. Outline a set of instructions for first-time restatement of financial statements based on GAAP to allow for the change in the measuring unit.

6. Outline a set of instructions for the preparation of price-level-restated statements and updating the ledger accounts on the assumption that the accounts were restated in the measuring unit of the previous year-end and that they are to be restated annually and "booked."

7. Do you see any relationship between an inflation gain on debt and the nominal cost of capital? Explain.

8. Do income statement items need to be adjusted from the date of occurrence of the revenue or expense to the reporting date? Under what circumstances are such adjustments most important?

9. What is the fundamental objective of common unit accounting?

10. Here is a test of your acceptance of common unit accounting:
    (a) John Doe buys a share of X Company stock for $100 when the index of prices included in Doe's expenditure pattern stands at 100. At the end of the period, Doe still

holds the stock and it has a quoted market price of $116. The price index is at 110. What is Doe's income for the period? In what measuring unit do you express it? What measures (or measurement methods) are used in calculating it?

(b) Doe sells the X Company stock in period two for $118 when the price index is at 121. What is Doe's income in period two? In what measuring unit is it expressed? What measures are used in calculating it?

(c) What is Doe's income for the venture, in 121$?

11. Are the following items monetary or nonmonetary?
    (a) Deferred tax liability due to interperiod tax allocation.
    (b) Cumulative, nonparticipating preferred stock outstanding.
    (c) Estimated liability on product warranties.
    (d) Liabilities denominated in a foreign currency.
    (e) Liability for losses on firm purchase commitments.
    (f) Deferred investment tax credits.
    (g) Advance to supplier on purchase contract.
    (h) Common stock owned.
    (i) Convertible preferred stock owned.
    (j) Inventory of gold bullion.
    (k) Unexpired insurance.
    (l) Deferred rental revenue (for rent collected in advance).

12. The controller of a group of insurance companies questioned the following items when beginning to apply common unit accounting. Are the items monetary or nonmonetary?
    (a) Life insurance policy benefit reserves.
    (b) Unearned premiums (received in advance) on fire and casualty policies.
    (c) Fire and casualty "case reserves" for estimated settlements of past losses.
    (d) Unearned premiums (received in advance) on life insurance policies.

13. What possible defects could a conventional revenue figure have that could be remedied by price level restatement?

14. Would it be more appropriate to measure an entity's net monetary position (for computing the gain or loss on it) by using the amounts of future cash flows called for in the

contracts rather than by using discounted future cash flows?

15. Assume that we have made irresistible cases for both current value measurements of assets and liabilities and for common unit accounting:
    (a) What is accomplished by adopting common unit accounting if (restated) historical cost is used for many nonmonetary assets?
    (b) What is accomplished by adopting current value accounting without adopting common unit accounting?
    (c) Can we accomplish the objective of common unit accounting by deducting (on the income statement) an amount equal to the change in the chosen general index times the beginning owners' equity,
       i) if we continue to use noncurrent values?
       ii) if we use current value accounting?

16. Prepare common unit financial statements for a company of your choice using publicly available variable unit data and an index of your choice. Outline the procedures you follow.

17. Can you suggest any variations on the method of computing a securities investor's rate of return that was suggested on page 270?

18. Present arguments for and against the proposition that the U.S. income tax law is a tax on capital.

19. It has been alleged that under at least one concept of capital maintenance a securities trader or commodities trader would never have income. Explain.

20. Explain how an enterprise can have income in the sense of making the owners better off without distributing assets to the owners or having cash available to distribute.

21. The following information is available regarding the net monetary position of the Sterling Company in 197x:

	Date	Index Number
Net position, $60,000—liability	Jan. 1	120
Sale of land for $20,000 on account	Mar. 1	122
Payment of expenses, in cash, $10,000	July 1	125
Collection of receivable, $20,000	Sept. 1	126

| Payment of dividend, $5,000 | Dec. 9 | 129 |
| Net position, $55,000 | Dec. 31 | 130 |

Compute Sterling's gain or loss on net monetary position in 197x, expressed in 130$.

22. The chief accountant of the Revsine Company made an error by classifying a monetary liability as a nonmonetary liability. This item came into the firm when the price index stood at 100. The index was at 110 at the end of the first year and the liability was paid at face value in the second year when the index was at 115. The error was never discovered. What errors in common unit financial statements were made? (Ignore interest.)

23. In what sense is a gain on net monetary position distributable income?

24. What circumstances are likely to cause variable unit period income to be higher than common unit income? What circumstances would tend to reverse the relationship?

25. Explain how common unit accounting can be combined with current value accounting to disclose the loss or gain that results when nonmonetary items do not change in nominal value in proportion to the change in the price index.

26. Is interperiod tax allocation needed in relation to restatements on nonmonetary items in common unit accounting? Is it needed with respect to gain or loss on net monetary position?

27. Compute the real, after-tax income of an investor in the 50% tax bracket who held any actual security of your choice over a several-year period.

28. What objections to common unit accounting do you think have been most important in delaying its adoption in your country?

29. According to Saunders and Busby (1976), Toledo Edison Company—an electric utility—prepared a set of financial statements for 1974 on a general price-level restated basis. The preparers declined, however, to follow the FASB recommendations on treatment of the purchasing power gain on debt as a component of income, and on treatment of the purchasing power gain on preferred stock outstanding as an

increase in earnings to the common equity. Instead, these two items were credited to an account entitled "Accumulated inflation effect from financing sources other than common stock equity," which was treated as a noncurrent, nonmonetary liability to be amortized as an offset to depreciation by applying the composite rate of depreciation on all property, plant and equipment (presumably including land) to the balance of the liability account.

Comment on this procedure. Consider such questions as these: Is this new type of account a liability? What alternative classifications of it could be considered, and what do the alternatives imply with regard to the basic issue? Is there a gain to equity holders from being in debt during inflation? If so, when does that gain occur.

30. "It has been suggested that with enough debt outstanding, a firm can report profits (on a general price level adjusted basis, including monetary gains) right up to the time it goes bankrupt" (Davidson and Weil, 1975a, p. 77).

Do you consider this point to be a valid objection to the inclusion of the "gain on debt" and "gain on preferred stock" from price level restatement in earnings to the common equity? What does the quotation imply with respect to the wisdom of being in debt during inflation or the comparative advantage of debt versus equity financing during inflation? To the extent that nominal interest costs include an inflation premium, how accurately is real interest cost reported if the offsetting credit reflecting the purchasing power gain on debt is omitted?

31. Mr. Larson purchased a share of Zeff Co. stock for $100 at the beginning of period one when the consumer price index was at 100. The stock paid no dividend in the first year and was quoted at $80 at year-end when the CPI stood at 110.

In year two, Larson received a dividend of $6, and the stock was priced at $95. The CPI was at 121. Larson is in the 60% tax bracket for incremental dividends and expects to pay a long-term capital gain tax of 30% on his net gains (which he normally has).

Make the most refined calculation of Larson's rate of return on investment in year two that you know how to make.

CHAPTER X

THE VARIABLE UNIT
ACCOUNTING–COMMON UNIT
ACCOUNTING EARNINGS
DIFFERENCE

A number of studies have been made in order to estimate effects of common unit accounting on popular financial parameters, especially those involving income.[1] The reported results may well confuse the issue until sufficient evidence is gathered and summarized to permit some generalizations about the differences between variable unit accounting (VUA) earnings and common unit accounting (CUA) earnings. We begin by summarizing some key results of specific studies:

1. Petersen (1973) reported slightly larger net income numbers, on the average, on the CUA basis—compared with VUA income numbers—and suggested that ". . . to the extent that this (displacement) effect is stable over time and across industries, investors might very well be able to 'adjust' for general price-level movements when using published financial information for decision making" (p. 43).

2. The British study by the Mechanical Engineering Economic Development Committee (1973) showed that aggregate CUA profits for the industry ranged from 62 percent to 78 percent of VUA profits for the six different years studied, and that earnings exceeded dividends by £124 million on

---

[1]This chapter has been adapted from Staubus (1976a) and is published here with permission. The author acknowledges significant assistance from Robert Hamilton, Yuji Ijiri, Shahid Waheed, and Roman L. Weil.

VUA, and by only £10 million under CUA over the six-year period.

3. Davidson and Weil (1975a) reported that the median CUA/VUA income relationship in 1973 was 92 percent for the 30 Dow Jones Industrials and 99 to 100 percent for 30 other companies.

4. Cutler and Westwick (1973) reported a VUA–CUA difference (as a percentage of VUA earnings per share) of more than 10 percent in 107 of 137 British companies, more than 50 percent in 34 of these companies, and more than 100 percent in 11 companies.

5. Basu and Hanna (1975) estimated the aggregate CUA earnings available to the common equity of 368 companies in 1974 was 91.9 percent of aggregate VUA earnings.

6. Paul Rosenfield (1969) reported GAAP earnings differing from restated earnings by 10 percent or more in 22 of 29 cases.

These widely varying results may well leave the typical concerned observer not only confused as to the general effects of CUA but also unable to judge its potential impact on the firm, industry, or economy under the conditions and for the period of time with which he is concerned. Are the earnings differences significant or not? Under what circumstances might they become significant? Do they follow a simple pattern? What causes the variations? This chapter works towards answers to these questions.

ANALYSES AND RESULTS

We begin with a series of brief statements about the differences between VUA earnings and CUA earnings in order to outline the terrain that we cover and the conclusions that we reach in the body of this chapter. We support these statements with algebraic analyses and simple numerical examples in subsequent sections.

(1) Balance sheet items may be divided into four classes that are relevant for the analyses made in this chapter: (a) fixed monetary items, (b) revalued monetary items, (c) revalued nonmonetary items, and (d) entry price nonmonetary items. Classes (a), (b), and (c) are measured in the monetary unit existing at the balance date so are

called "current unit items" (CUI). Class (d) items are "old unit items" (OUI).

(2) *The VUA–CUA lifetime earnings difference.* The lifetime earnings of an entity, or on an investment, as of the dates originally recorded, are larger under VUA than under CUA by the sum of the products of periodic inflation rates and periodic, common unit owners' equity amounts. In the case of an investment in one entry price nonmonetary asset, this difference is equal to the inflation rate during the investment's life times the original cost in original money units. Neither balance sheet composition nor turnover affects this conclusion.

(3) *The lifetime earnings difference as "rolled forward."* When CUA earnings are "rolled forward," that is, restated in inflated units at a later date, such as the end of an accounting period, after several accounting periods, or at the end of the entity's life, the difference between the two earnings numbers typically is less than that stated in (2) above. In fact, when cumulative dividends exceed contributed capital, it is possible for rolled-forward lifetime CUA earnings to exceed VUA earnings not rolled forward.

(4) *Effects of balance sheet composition on the lifetime earnings difference.* Neither the debt-equity ratio nor the net monetary (asset or liability) position affects the VUA–CUA lifetime earnings difference on a given residual equity base.

(5) *Difference in periodic earnings.* Common unit accounting earnings may be either more or less than variable unit accounting earnings for any period less than an entity's lifetime (e.g., a day, a year, or from inception to the present date), and by almost any amount.

(6) *Causes of the difference in periodic earnings.* The difference in periodic earnings depends on: (a) the CUI–OUI composition of net asset items—see (1) above; (b) the turnover and realization of OUI; (c) profitability; (d) the length of the reporting period; and (e) rates of inflation in both the reporting period and the holding periods of all OUI "realized" in the reporting period.

(7) *Effects of leverage on the periodic earnings difference.* With steady turnover of OUI of at least once per period, the difference in periodic earnings is not affected by leverage.

With turnover of less than one on any old unit asset item, which is typical of "fixed assets," monetary leverage reduces the excess VUA income, as restatement charges associated with old unit assets are deferred but restatement credits on net debt increase income immediately.

(8) *Effect of turnover and realization on the periodic earnings difference.* The timing of the earnings difference due to charging the costs of old unit assets to expense lags in relation to the turnover period, because slow turnover results in a deferral of the charge to expense resulting from restatement.

(9) *Effect of a change in the rate of inflation on the periodic earnings difference.* A sharp increase in the rate of inflation (as in the 1973–74 U.S. economy) after a long period of modest inflation can boost CUA earnings substantially if the firm has net current unit liabilities and/or is profitable. Thus, increasing inflation can eliminate (temporarily) the typical periodic excess of VUA earnings over CUA earnings.

(10) *Effect of profitability on the periodic earnings difference.* Revenues and expenses are rolled forward to the end of the reporting period; hence, the greater the profit, the greater the absolute amount of the roll-forward effect.

(11) *Effect of the length of the reporting period on the periodic earnings difference.* Other things remaining equal, the longer the reporting period the greater the roll-forward effect on CUA earnings.

(12) The influences listed in (6) above combine, interact, and vary over companies and periods in such complex ways that simple rules do not permit accurate estimates of the effects of CUA on earnings.

THE CLASSIFICATION OF BALANCE SHEET ITEMS

The monetary-nonmonetary basis of classification of balance sheet items is familiar to the reader. Another basis of classification that is relevant to the ideas in this chapter is whether or not the item is revalued under variable unit accounting. Use of these two bases of classification and two classes on each basis results in four classes:

1. Fixed monetary items, such as cash and short-term receivables and payables.

2. Revalued monetary items, such as bonds owed or owned, that are carried at current market values, or at values computed by discounting at the current market rate of interest.
3. Revalued nonmonetary items, such as inventories carried at current values.
4. Entry price nonmonetary items, such as inventories or long-lived plant assets carried at historical cost under VUA and restated historical cost under CUA.

The monetary-nonmonetary dichotomy is significant because monetary items automatically lose value during inflation. During a reporting period, the difference between average monetary assets and average monetary liabilities, which is called the "net monetary position" (NMP), may be multiplied by the inflation rate to determine the inflation gain or loss on net monetary position. When class 3 (revalued nonmonetary items) is added to the monetary classes, the combined group may be called "current unit" items (CUI), because they are all measured by methods that rely on the current monetary unit, not an old unit. Cash, receivables, and payables are all measured at the balance date in the unit in existence at that date; no old dollars are on hand or are to be transferred. Market prices to which revalued items are adjusted are also expressed in current dollars. Assets or liabilities measured at their historical entry price (cost or receipt), on the other hand, were measured at an earlier (entry) date in the measuring unit in use at the time. They are called "old unit items" (OUI) and constitute class 4 above. The CUI–OUI dichotomy is important in some of the analyses in this chapter.

THE LIFETIME EARNINGS DIFFERENCE AS ORIGINALLY RECORDED

The essence of the common unit accounting methodology is the *restatement* of all "earlier" measurements that are to be compared with "later," that is, current, measurements.[2] The comparisons may involve multiple balance sheets or an income statement where earlier (deferred) costs are often compared with later revenues

---

[2]See the "Common Unit Accounting Procedures" section of chapter IX for a description of this methodology.

and, in some cases, earlier (deferred) revenues are compared with later costs. All balance sheet items are subject to restatement, and all restatements of assets and liabilities affect income (eventually). Restatements of nonmonetary items affect income when the asset is sold (or the liability is eliminated), and the restated amount is compared with the proceeds (or costs of eliminating the liability), or when the item is revalued. Restatements of monetary items are reported immediately as purchasing power losses or gains. The differences between VUA earnings and CUA earnings are due to restatements of net asset items.

Consider *an entry price nonmonetary asset* costing $100 which is held through two periods of 10 percent inflation and then is sold (for any amount). Its restated cost is $121, which changes the gain or loss on sale by $21, which in turn is equal to 10 percent of the first period's starting value ($100) plus 10 percent of the second period's CUA beginning value ($110). Now consider a $100 *fixed monetary* asset held for two periods of 10 percent inflation. At the end of the first period, we record a purchasing power loss of $10, which is 10 percent of the beginning value in beginning-of-period dollars. At the end of the second period another $10 loss is recorded based on identical calculations. In each period, the $10 loss is equal to the $10 restatement of the beginning value. A third example is that of a revalued item, which could be monetary or nonmonetary, that is held through two periods of 10 percent inflation. It cost $100 at the beginning of period one, is revalued to $120 at the end of period one, and is sold for $150 at the end of period two. The VUA income is $50. Under CUA, the period-one income is the $120 ending valuation less the $110 restated entry price, or $10. In period two the $150 selling price is matched with a restated beginning-of-period amount of $120 × 1.10, or $132, so the income is $18. The CUA income for the venture is $28, which differs from the VUA income by $22, which in turn is equal to 10 percent of the period-one beginning valuation plus 10 percent of the period-two beginning valuation. What do these three cases have in common? While the aggregate two-period restatements vary ($21, $20, and $22, respectively), we can state the lifetime earnings differences in all three cases as follows:

$$Y_l - Y_l^* = \sum_{t=1}^{m} (Y_t - Y_t^*) = \sum_{t=1}^{m} A_t^* \, r_t = \sum_{t=1}^{m} E_t^* \, r_t \qquad [1]$$

Notation:

* denotes a CUA parameter; VUA parameters have no *.

E is the equity (either owners' or residual) in an entity.

Y is the earnings on the above equity (E).

A is the amount of a net asset item—an asset or a liability.

r is the inflation rate in a period.

t is a subscript denoting a period of time during which E remains constant.

m is the last period in the life of an entity or net asset item.

l is the entire life span of an item or entity.

It is important to note that restatements of entry price nonmonetary items are compounded; restatements of fixed monetary items relate to the same base each period through the life of the item; and restatements of revalued items relate to their current values. Furthermore, it should be apparent that the lifetime earnings difference is *not* equal to the sum of the products of the periodic inflation rates and VUA equity amounts because the restatements of entry price nonmonetary items in periods subsequent to the first holding period are based on previously restated amounts, not on variable unit amounts. When $A \neq A^*$ and $E \neq E^*$, the restatements, and the resulting earnings difference, relate to the previously restated base. Finally, it should be apparent that neither multiple assets nor the presence of both assets and liabilities affects the general conclusion that *the lifetime VUA–CUA earnings difference, as of the dates originally recorded, is equal to the sum of the products of the periodic inflation rates and the beginning-of-period, common unit equity amounts.*

Restating this analysis, if we assume that (1) there are no deferred credits to revenue, (2) the gain or loss on net monetary assets is computed by comparing restated beginning amounts and new items (as costs) with ending amounts and liquidations, and (3) there are no roll-forward restatements, it follows that (a) the difference between VUA and CUA income numbers is due entirely to differences in costs used in computing income, (b) the differences in costs are due to restatements of *all* net asset items, and (c) these restatements of net asset items equal the restatements of the residual equity. Therefore, the sum of the periodic income differences is equal to the sum of the periodic restatements of the residual equity. Letting c symbolize costs, we can write

$$ Y_t - Y_t^* = \sum_{t=1}^{m} c_t^* - \sum_{t=1}^{m} c_t = \sum_{t=1}^{m} A_t^* r_t = \sum_{t=1}^{m} E_t^* r_t \qquad [2] $$

Relaxation of assumption (1) would require the inclusion of revenue terms in the second part of equation [2].

The period concept that is used here (the time during which E remains constant) is an unusual one. Its choice is dictated by the fact that a change in the net asset values exposed to inflation is a change in the base on which restatements are computed and in the difference between VUA earnings and CUA earnings. The shortest period recognized for most accounting purposes is the day, so daily revisions of the base (E^*) appear to be the practical limit, although some readers may want to consider stating the earnings difference under the assumption that E^* changes continuously. For a reasonably accurate approximation, we may say that the VUA–CUA earnings difference is based on the average CUA equity in each accounting period.

EXHIBIT X-1 is a simple example based on a 10 percent rate of inflation each period. The entry price nonmonetary asset was purchased for $100, held for two periods, and sold for $121.

These calculations compute an entity's lifetime VUA–CUA earnings difference by summing periodic differences as they would actually be reported each period under the respective accounting systems, that is, in the monetary units of the respective periods. Given the fundamental premise of common unit accounting—that monetary units which differ in purchasing power should not be added or subtracted—such a calculation is improper. But, on the other hand, variable unit accounting is based on the premise that varying purchasing power can be ignored. When one number is produced by one system and one is produced by the other, it is not clear how the two should be compared. The view

EXHIBIT X-1
TWO APPROACHES TO THE COMPUTATION OF LIFETIME VUA–CUA EARNINGS
DIFFERENCE

Beginning Balance Sheet			
Fixed Monetary Asset	100		
Entry Price Nonmonetary Asset	100[a]	Equity	200

[a] Held through two periods of 10 percent inflation, then sold for $121.

Difference via Income Statement Approach			
	Y	Y^*	$Y - Y^*$
Period one:			
on monetary item	$ 0	$-10	$10
on nonmonetary item	0	0	0
Period two:			
on monetary item	0	-10	10
on nonmonetary item	21	0	21
Lifetime totals	$21	$-20	41

Difference via Equity Approach			
	A_t^*	E_t^*	r_t	$E_t^* r_t$
Period one:	$100 + 100	$200	.10	$20
Period two:	100 + 110	210	.10	21

$$\sum_{t=1}^{m} E_t^* r_t \qquad \$41$$

encompassed in the present approach is that the periodic earnings under the two systems should be compared each period and the differences summed over the life of the entity. Alternatively, the periodic earnings computed by VUA could be summed and compared with the sum of periodic, rolled-forward earnings computed by CUA. This would yield a substantially different lifetime discrepancy. The calculation presented here appears to be most relevant to the decisions made by users of financial statements because the earnings on which they base their decisions are recently reported periodic earnings rather than lifetime earnings expressed in end-of-life units. Thus, if CUA were really relied upon, tax rates would be applied to earnings as reported at the end of each period rather than on earnings rolled forward to the death of the firm, price/earnings ratios presumably would be based on recently reported earnings, and wage negotiations could be influenced by recently reported earnings.

THE LIFETIME EARNINGS DIFFERENCE WHEN ROLLED FORWARD

The FASB (1974) methodology calls for rolling forward prior periods' earnings when comparative statements are being prepared, and also for rolling forward the cumulative earnings less cumulative dividends that make up the current retained earnings. This suggests that it is appropriate to measure lifetime CUA earnings in end-of-life monetary units, that is, in units rolled forward to the end of the entity's life. It should be clear that the results from comparing two series when one is restated to a single date and the other is not depend heavily on the single date chosen. Consider the comparison of a simple venture profit stated in VUA and in CUA terms. Assume that you purchased a parcel of land for $1,000 on January 1 when the price index was at 100, sold it for $1,500 on July 1 when the index stood at 110, reported it on your tax return immediately after the end of the year when the index was at 121, and restated the results for comparison with the results of another venture at the end of year 2 when the index was at 145.2. The following calculations show four different earnings numbers.

	Common Unit Accounting	Variable Unit Accounting
Selling price	$1,500	1,500
Cost	1,100	1,000
VUA profit		$500
CUA profit in 110$	$400	
CUA profit in 121$ at year end	440	
CUA profit in 145.2$ one year later	528	

Yuji Ijiri (1976 and in conversation with the author) has pointed out that the rolled-forward lifetime CUA earnings can exceed the lifetime VUA earnings as originally reported. This can be explained as follows (using the notation of the previous section and letting C, D, and Y represent contributed capital, cumulative dividends, and cumulative earnings, with restated items rolled forward):

$$A = C - D + Y \qquad [3]$$

$$A^* = C^* - D^* + Y^* \qquad [4]$$

Upon termination, when all assets have been turned into cash, $A = A^*$. Therefore, by subtraction,

$$0 = (C^* - C) - (D^* - D) + (Y^* - Y). \qquad [5]$$

Rearranging,

$$Y^* - Y = (D^* - D) - (C^* - C); \qquad [6]$$

therefore, $Y^* - Y$ is positive when $(D^* - D) > (C^* - C)$. That is, lifetime CUA earnings exceed lifetime VUA earnings when the restatement of lifetime dividends exceeds the restatement of contributed capital. This requires that dividends exceed capital during sufficient inflation to yield an excess dividends restatement large enough to offset the excess capital restatement in the early periods of the entity's life when $C > D$.

Another way of stating the conditions under which rolled-forward cumulative CUA earnings can be larger than cumulative VUA earnings is based on conclusion (1) on page 288 regarding the general tendency of VUA earnings to be larger by the inflation rate times the CUA equity. The roll-forward effect on all prior earnings can exceed the inflation rate times residual equity in any period in which all prior earnings exceed the residual equity, that is, when cumulative dividends exceed contributed capital. If this effect persists, it eventually can overtake the earlier difference in the opposite direction.

These circumstances are illustrated in EXHIBIT X-2, which is based on an inflation rate of 10 percent per period, purchase

EXHIBIT X-2

ILLUSTRATION OF LIFETIME CUA EARNINGS ROLLED FORWARD EXCEEDING LIFETIME VUA EARNINGS AS REPORTED

	Period One		Period Two		Lifetime Earnings		
	VUA	CUA	VUA	CUA	VUA	CUA Reported	CUA Rolled to End[a]
Land (beginning)	$500	$500	$500	$500			
Debt	400	400	400	400			
Contributed Cap.							
Beginning	100	100	100	110			
End		110		121			
Retained earnings (end)		−10		−121			
Sale	1,000	1,000	1,000	1,000	$2,000	$2,000	$2,100
Cost	500	550	500	550	1,000	1,100	1,155
Gain on Sale	500	450	500	450	1,000	900	945
Gain on Debt		40		40		80	84
NET INCOME	**500**	**490**	**500**	**490**	**1,000**	**980**[b]	**1,029**[c]
Distributions	500	500	600	600	1,100	1,100	1,150

[a] All CUA flow data of period one are multiplied by 1.10 and added to period two data to obtain the numbers in this column.

[b] The originally reported income difference is $Y_i - Y_i^* = \sum_{t=1}^{m} E_t^* r_i = 100(.10) + 100(.10) = 20.$

[c] Note that
$$Y^* - Y = (D^* - D) - (C^* - C)$$
$$1029 - 1000 = (1150 - 1100) - (121 - 100) = 29.$$

of land for $500 at the beginning of each period and sale for $1,000 at the end of each period, and the payments of dividends of $500 and $600 at period-ends. In this case, CUA income is lower than VUA income each period, but it is higher when rolled forward and added. If CUA income were taxed, the cumulative income taxes could be higher after rolling forward, but lower each period, than under VUA taxation; however the taxpayer is not likely to prefer VUA taxation. If we accept the CUA premise and reject the traditional idea, the comparison of results should be made on CUA terms rather than by rolling forward one series but not the other. If both income series are rolled forward, VUA lifetime earnings will exceed CUA lifetime earnings, assuming inflation.

EFFECT OF LEVERAGE ON THE LIFETIME EARNINGS DIFFERENCE

Some of the literature reporting results of empirical studies (Cutler and Westwick, 1973; Davidson and Weil, 1975a) may have given the impression that the CUA lifetime earnings are increased, relative to VUA earnings, by the existence of debt in the firm's capital structure. I disagree.

Let's assume, just for this discussion of leverage, that no balance sheet items are revalued; all monetary items are fixed and all nonmonetary items are carried at their entry prices. If a monetary item remains on the balance sheet for m periods,

$$\sum_{t=1}^{m} (Y_t - Y_t^*) = \sum_{t=1}^{m} A_t r_t \qquad [7]$$

with A_t constant, whereas, a nonmonetary item or series (including replacements) disposed of at the end of m periods would produce the following difference:

$$\sum_{t=1}^{m} (Y_t - Y_t^*) = \sum_{t=1}^{m} A_t^* r_t \qquad [8]$$

with A_t^* growing and compounding with the accumulated restatement. Thus, if debt is used to finance additional nonmonetary assets, the increase in monetary gain on the negative monetary net asset item (debt) is less than the decrease in gain on sale of the restated nonmonetary asset because the latter is compounded. It appears that leverage tends to *augment* the normal lifetime excess of VUA earnings over CUA earnings as originally reported. Actually, however, this augmentation is dependent upon a larger equity base after the first period if the early gains on debt are plowed back via continued holding of the same (or equivalent) nonmonetary assets (as in the example in EXHIBIT X-3). With strict maintenance of CUA owners' equity, there would be no increase in $Y - Y^*$ due to leverage. The example in EXHIBIT X-3, based as usual on a 10 percent periodic rate of inflation, illustrates these effects as well as adherence to the rule of conclusion (2) on page 289. The difference between cases I and III would be wider over a longer holding period due to the widening discrepancy in the equity amounts.

DIFFERENCES IN PERIODIC EARNINGS

According to rule (2) on page 289 VUA earnings should tend to exceed CUA earnings under inflationary conditions. Yet Davidson and Weil (1975a) found that more than one-fourth of the companies they studied had higher CUA earnings than VUA earnings in a year of 7.4 percent inflation. In a similar British study, Cutler and Westwick (1973) obtained similar results. In the two-period examples in EXHIBITS X-1 and X-3, the earnings differences ranged from −10 percent to +27 percent under 10 percent inflation. It is apparent that periodic earnings differences do not adhere to the lifetime rule. Why not?

A look at the components of the periodic difference may be instructive. For this purpose, we can organize the income statement effects of the restatement methodology as in EXHIBIT X-4. (The term "old unit expenses" indicates the consumption of old unit assets while "old unit revenues" are those which involve reductions in old unit liabilities, such as deferred credits to revenue.) It is possible for any one of the four pairs of effects to net out to either a positive or negative adjustment of VUA income, but the most common effects are positive for (1) and (4) and negative for (2) and (3). While it may be more convenient to compute depreciation directly in end-of-period units, consistency with conclusion (2) on page 289 requires that nonmonetary income items, like monetary revenues and expenses, be stated first in the monetary unit of the interim transaction date and then rolled forward to the end of the period, if roll-forward effects are to be isolated.

A review of the calculation of these adjustments discloses the factors that influence their amounts:

1. The gain or loss on net monetary position is influenced by (a) the *inflation rate during the period* and (b) the *balance of net monetary items during the period*. The relative contribution of factor (b) to the periodic difference depends upon the relationship of net monetary assets (and therefore net nonmonetary assets) to the residual equity. This may be called the "monetary-residual equity ratio."

2. The process of restating revalued nonmonetary items affects the CUA income by the *inflation rate* times the *balance of nonmonetary items being revalued*. For example, if a nonmonetary asset costing $100 is revalued to $107 with 10 percent inflation, restatement of the $100 converts a $7 VUA gain into a $3 CUA loss. The difference is 10 percent of $100. The relative weight of this category of restatements as a component of the overall VUA–CUA earnings difference depends upon the relationship of revalued nonmonetary items (RNI) to the residual equity. This may be called the "*RNI–residual equity ratio.*"

3. The restatement of old unit revenues and expenses depends on (a) the total *inflation percentage during the holding periods of the OUI that* "hit the income statement" in the given period and (b) the original amount of these old unit income items. The total inflation percentage during the holding period is dependent upon the length of the holding period and the rate of inflation in each calendar period making up the total holding period.

   If the holding period factor in (a) is combined with (b) (the amount of old unit expenses and revenues), the group (3) influences can be described as inflation rate and "sum of the products of ages and amounts of OUI realized during the period," or "dollar-periods" (e.g., dollar-years), of OUI realizations. Although it does not describe this latter influence perfectly, the term "turnover-realization factor" (TOR)

EXHIBIT X-3
EFFECT OF LEVERAGE ON LIFETIME EARNINGS DIFFERENCE

	Monetary Assets	Land	Monetary Liabilities	Equity
CASE I—NET MONETARY ASSETS				
Period One:				
Beginning	$ 50	$50		$100
Restatement	5	5		10†
Monetary Loss	-5			-5
End	50	55		105
Period Two:				
Restatement	5	5.5		10.5†
Monetary Loss	-5			-5
Sale (VUA gain, $10.5)	60.5	-60.5		
End	$110.5	0		$110.5

$$\dagger \sum_{t=1}^{m} E_t^* \, r_t = 10 + 10.5 = 20.5 \qquad Y_i - Y_i^* = 10.5 - (-5 - 5) = 20.5$$

	Monetary Assets	Land	Monetary Liabilities	Equity
CASE II—NO NET MONETARY POSITION				
Period One:				
Beginning		$100		$100
Restatement		10		10‡

End			110	110
Period Two:				
Restatement			11	11‡
Sale (VUA gain, $21)	$121		-121	
End	$121		0	$121

‡ $\displaystyle\sum_{t=1}^{m} E_t^* r_t = 10 + 11 = 21$ $Y_l - Y_l^* = 21 - 0 = 21$

CASE III—NET DEBT

Period One:				
Beginning		$200	$100	$100
Restatement		20	10	10§
Monetary Gain			-10	10
End		220	100	120
Period Two:				
Restatement		22	10	12§
Monetary Gain			-10	10
Sale (VUA gain, $42)	$242	-242		
Debt Retirement	-100	-100		
End	$142	0		$142

§ $\displaystyle\sum_{t=1}^{m} E_t^* r_t = 10 + 12 = 22$ $Y_l - Y_l^* = 42 - 10 - 10 = 22$

EXHIBIT X-4

ADJUSTMENTS OF VUA INCOME WHEN CUA IS APPLIED

Item Affected	Direction of Effect
(1) Gain or loss on net monetary position:	
a) Gain on monetary liabilities	+
b) Loss on monetary assets	−
(2) Restatement of revalued nonmonetary items:	
a) Assets	−
b) Liabilities	+
(3) Restatement of old unit income items:	
a) Old unit revenues	+
b) Old unit expenses	−
(4) Roll forward of interim flows:	
a) Revenues	+
b) Expenses	−

suggests the general idea and will be used hereafter.

4. While it is possible that large lumps of expenses or revenues may "hit the income statement" relatively early or late in the period, if we assume that they fall at midperiod, on the average, the factors influencing the difference between the revenue roll-forward and the expense roll-forward are the difference between revenues and expenses, or profitability; *the length of the reporting period* (one-half of which is the roll-forward period); and the *rate of inflation during the roll-forward period.*

The italicized factors identified in the preceding four enumerated paragraphs may now be consolidated. First, we may combine the monetary-residual equity ratio mentioned in (1) with the RNI–residual equity ratio mentioned in (2), and call the combination the CUI–residual equity ratio, because monetary items plus revalued nonmonetary items constitute all current unit items. Then we may group the factors into five categories: (a) the CUI–residual equity ratio (an aspect of balance sheet composition); (b) the turnover-realization (TOR) ratio; (c) rates of inflation during the periods from acquisition of the oldest old unit item realized during the period through the end of the reporting period; (d) profitability; and (e) the length of the reporting period. The studies by Cutler and Westwick (1973) and Davidson and Weil (1975a, b, and c) show that the combined effect of these factors varies so much across companies and among years that there is no simple rule for approximating the difference between CUA earnings and VUA earnings for specific calendar periods. Subsequent sections will be devoted to achieving a better understanding of each of these factors.

EFFECT OF NET MONETARY POSITION ON THE PERIODIC EARNINGS DIFFERENCE

"The results for Trans Union and Loews, like the results for AT&T from the Dow list, indicate that when monetary gains are recognized, firms with large amounts of debt outstanding may do very much better in times of increasing prices than is shown on historical dollar accounting statements" (Davidson and Weil, 1975a, p. 28). Other writers and speakers have expressed similar views. Under what circumstances is this statement true?

To simplify the analysis in this section, let's assume away all revaluations; assume all monetary items remain at fixed amounts and that all nonmonetary items are carried at entry prices. It turns out that the effect of the monetary-residual equity ratio interacts with the turnover-realization factor in such a way that the latter cannot be ignored in this section. Let's begin by defining the TOR ratio for an accounting period as the dollar-years of NMA realizations divided by the average NMA.[3] Thus, the TOR ratio would be one in any period in which the firm's only NMA holding was acquired at the beginning and sold at the end. Similarly, if the only realization during the period were half of the NMA that had been held for two accounting periods, the TOR ratio would be one. It must be computed using VUA numbers.

Now, consider the effect of variations in the net monetary position (MP) when the TOR ratio is one and "current," that is, when

---

[3] But note that relaxation of our assumption of absence of revalued nonmonetary items would require that we substitute OUI for NMA in defining TOR.

there is no carry-over of old NMA at the beginning of the period
or at the end of the period. Since this is a complete cash-to-cash
cycle in one accounting period, the lifetime rule applies: $Y -$
$Y* = E*r$. Neither the sign nor the size of MP matters. Since
NMA + MP = E, the difference between VUA earnings and
CUA earnings because of the restatement of MP (treating an asset
position as positive) plus the restatement of NMA equals Er. Given
a level of E, any change in NMA must be offset by a change
in MP, so the absolute levels do not matter; only the algebraic
sum (E) is significant. (This point is illustrated by both periods
of the example in EXHIBIT X-2.)

If the periodic earnings difference (excluding the roll-forward
effect) is to be anything other than $E*r$, the restatement of
nonmonetary income statement items must vary from $NMA_t^*\ r_t$
because the $NMP_t^*\ r_t$ factor always plays its role (in making the
earnings difference equal to $E*r$). If the TOR ratio is not one,
the restatement of nonmonetary income items will not be equal
to $NMA_t^*\ r_t$ because the "dollar-periods" of asset items that hit
the income statement will not equal all nonmonetary items held
(NMA_t^*). If TOR is not current, the inflation percentage used
in restating nonmonetary income items (the inflation percentage
during the holding period of the items being "realized") will not
equal r_t, unless the inflation rate is constant. This means that
the restatement of nonmonetary income items will not play the
role that is necessary to make factors (1) plus (3) of EXHIBIT
X-4 equal to $E_t^*\ r_t$. Under such circumstances, the level of NMP
makes a difference. At one extreme, if TOR = 0, factor (2) is
zero, so the monetary-residual equity ratio completely determines
$Y_t - Y_t^*$ (aside from the roll-forward element and assuming no
revaluations). The TOR = 0 case is illustrated in EXHIBIT X-3,
cases I, II, and III, period one.

With a TOR ratio of greater than one and no nonmonetary
items remaining on the balance sheet at the end of the period,
the monetary-residual equity ratio during the period is not a factor;
the earnings difference is $E_t^*\ r_t$ plus accumulated, unrealized
restatements $(A_t^* - A_t)$ as of the beginning of the period. However,
the monetary-residual equity ratio during prior periods affects
the accumulated unrealized restatements of NMA in relation to
E, so it can affect the periodic earnings difference even with

complete turnover. The results of the *second period* for the three cases of EXHIBIT X-3 illustrate this effect. The fact that $Y_t - Y_t^* = E_t^* r_t + (A_t^* - A_t)$ in these three cases is shown as follows:

CASE I

$$E_t^* r_t \quad = 105(.10) \qquad = 10.5$$
$$A_t^* - A_t = 55 - 50 \qquad = \underline{5.}$$

$$Y_t - Y_t^* = 10.5 - (-5) \qquad = \underline{\underline{15.5}}$$

CASE II

$$E_t^* r_t \quad = 110(.10) \qquad = 11$$
$$A_t^* - A_t = 110 - 100 \qquad = \underline{10}$$

$$Y_t - Y_t^* = 21 - 0 \qquad = \underline{\underline{21}}$$

CASE III

$$E_t^* r_t \quad = 120(.10) \qquad = 12$$
$$A_t^* - A_t = 220 - 200 \qquad = \underline{20}$$

$$Y_t - Y_t^* = 42 - 10 \qquad = \underline{\underline{32}}$$

In sum, the monetary-residual equity ratio affects the periodic earnings difference whenever the deferred (unrealized) restatement of NMA changes during the period, that is, in all but the most exceptional circumstances, under GAAP.

This may be the best place to point out that a complete current value accounting system, in which all assets and liabilities are CUI, results in a TOR ratio of one. If all nonmonetary net asset items are revalued to current prices, those assets are given essentially the same treatment as monetary items; and the sum of these individual, nominal revaluations, less $A_t r_t$, would be an income item in a current value, common unit accounting system. This means that at the beginning of the next period, A would equal A^* and the periodic CUA–VUA earnings difference, excluding any interim profit roll forward would be $E_t r_t$. Such a system has the distinct cost advantage that no restatements of individual assets need be made. If the holding gain or loss account is debited with the periodic restatement of the residual equity and is debited or credited with nominal revaluations of the nonmonetary items, its balance will be the net real holding gain, including the gain or loss on net monetary position. If, by coincidence, all nonmonetary items were revalued by the general inflation percentage, the net holding gain or loss would be the gain or loss on net monetary position. (See the "Common Unit, Current Value Accounting" section of chapter IX for more on this point.)

EFFECTS OF VARIATIONS IN THE TURNOVER-REALIZATION FACTOR

Variations in the TOR ratio probably account for more of the variation across companies than any other factor. However, first we should recognize that increasing the asset turnover beyond one per period, on a given base, has no effect on the VUA–CUA earnings difference because it does not change the TOR ratio. If $1,000 of inventory were turned over six times a year, each charge to cost of goods sold would have two months of inflation to be removed; if it were turned over only once, the $1,000 cost would have twelve months of inflation to be removed. In either case, the TOR ratio is one, and the effect on the aggregate restatement is the same. If, on the other hand, turnover were increased by decreasing the inventory level, the periodic earnings difference would be affected by the change in the monetary-residual equity ratio; the TOR ratio again would be unchanged.

The effects of the TOR ratio can be seen more clearly if we think of an example in which it changes drastically over time. EXHIBIT X-5 gives the general idea without stretching out the major investment in nonmonetary assets over many periods. Note that the *lifetime* difference rule holds up once more, but that the *periodic* difference varies sharply and even shows an excess of CUA earnings over VUA earnings in the absence of turnover. But in period three, the TOR ratio of 3 has a dramatic effect. In a hypothetical forty-period example of a company owning one heavily-leveraged piece of rental property, the VUA–CUA earnings difference ranges from −20 percent to +85 percent with a 10 percent inflation rate. Low TOR ratios, together with large net debt positions, were undoubtedly the cause of the higher CUA earnings that Cutler and Westwick found for the property (real estate investment) companies in their sample. Such discrepan-

Exhibit X-5

Effect of Turnover-Realization Factor on Income Differences

Date	Common Unit Balance Sheet			Inflation Rate X Equity	Income Differences	
	Land	Debt	Equity		Monetary Gain	"Cost of Sales" Dif.
1/1/1	$500	$400	$100			
Period One				$10	$(40)	
1/1/2	550	400	150			
Period Two				15	(40)	
1/1/3	605	400	205			
Period Three				20.5	(40)	
12/31/3†	665.5	400	265.5			$165.5
				$45.5‡	$(120)	$165.5

† Assume the land is sold at this date (at any price).

‡ $\sum_{t=1}^{m} E_t^* r_t = 45.5 = 165.5 - 120.$

cies—CUA earnings greater than VUA earnings during inflation—must be recognized as a "temporary" phenomenon; assuming the investment has a finite life, a very large VUA "overstatement" of earnings looms ahead. Is this overhanging "obligation" similar to the deferred tax liability and routine accounts payable that will come home to roost upon contraction of the scale of operations?

It is apparent, then, that the periodic income differences related to entry price nonmonetary assets tend to lag behind what would be true if the basic lifetime earnings difference rule—a balance-sheet-based rule—were applicable to periodic earnings, because the income effect does not show up until asset costs are charged to expense. At one extreme, an asset purchased today and sold tomorrow affects the income statement tomorrow. At the other extreme, land used as a plant site may not affect the income statement, nor its restatement affect the income difference, for many years. Whether the entry price nonmonetary asset is a fast-turnover stock item that is held a week or land that is held a century, it does not affect the income difference until it is deducted in the computation of income while it affects the balance sheet from acquisition date to disposition date. *As long as any unrealized restatements of nonmonetary assets are carried forward on the balance sheet, the cumulative earnings difference to date will be less than the sum of the products of periodic inflation rates and restated residual equity amounts.*

This lag effect means that the difference in depreciation expense (under the two accounting systems) is less than the inflation rate times the CUA book value of the assets during growth periods (when the deferred restatements are increasing) and greater during contraction periods. Even during periods in which the restated amounts of assets remain constant, the income difference is less than A_t^* due to the compounding effect of inflation on restated amounts of nonmonetary assets. For example, if the nonmonetary assets consist of five machines with five-year lives, each purchased at the beginning of a different year, the TOR ratio under a steady 10 percent inflation rate is only .88 instead of the 1.0 that would be experienced under constant prices. Under constant prices, the weighted average of the TOR ratios of the five separate machines would be 1.0, but with inflation the higher prices of the newer, low-turnover machines reduce the weighted average TOR ratio.

Thus, even during a steady physical state, the depreciation difference lags and the earnings difference is reduced.

EFFECTS OF CHANGES IN THE RATE OF INFLATION

The change in the gross national product implicit price deflator—the index proposed for restatements in the U.S.—approximately doubled in 1973 compared to the average annual change during the seven preceding years. Davidson and Weil's estimates of restated income for the 60 companies they studied (1975a) related to 1973 income. How does a sharp change in the rate of inflation affect the VUA–CUA periodic earnings difference?

A breakdown of the periodic earnings difference that is relevant to this issue follows:

1. The gain or loss on net monetary position, $(MP)r_t$.
2. The restatement of cost of goods sold due to inflation during the inventory holding period—which, under FIFO, starts one turnover period prior to the accounting period in question and ends one turnover period before the end of the accounting period. Under the weighted average assumption the holding period is shorter, and under LIFO it is zero if the inventory level does not decrease. More generally, the holding periods of short-term, entry price, nonmonetary items are relevant here.
3. The restatement of depreciation and other amortization of OUI—which is dependent upon the inflation rate from the acquisition date of the oldest fixed asset through the current accounting period.
4. The roll-forward adjustment of revenues and expenses from midperiod to the end of the period, using the inflation percentage during the last half of the accounting period.

This review shows that only the inflation rate during the current accounting period is involved in the monetary gain or loss and the roll-forward adjustment, whereas the inflation rate for many periods is involved in the depreciation restatement. The restatement of cost of goods sold is affected largely by the inflation rate during the current period unless the inventory turnover is very slow.

Now suppose that a company has VUA earnings of $10 million

and CUA earnings under 3.5 percent inflation of $8.5 million, with the difference due to the factors listed in the first money column of EXHIBIT X-6. A sudden doubling of the rate of inflation in the next period, followed by continuation of the higher rate through a long enough period to permit replacement of all nonmonetary assets, say ten years, could result in numbers similar to those in the other columns of EXHIBIT X-6.

When the two factors that are influenced by the *current* rate of inflation have a *positive* effect on CUA earnings, a sudden increase in the inflation rate can easily increase CUA earnings relative to VUA earnings. Without a net monetary position, such an effect is extremely unlikely. For this reason, it appears that Davidson and Weil selected an unusual year for their study; the sharp jump in the inflation rate in 1973 contributed to the dispersion of earnings differences and raised the median CUA earnings, as 58 of their 60 companies were net debtors. Conditions favoring such relatively high and dispersed CUA earnings are not likely to recur frequently (although they did recur in 1974 and Davidson and Weil got similar results [1975c]). For this reason, results of 1973 and 1974 tests should not be accepted as representative; the 1975 and 1976 tests should yield more typical results.

Basu and Hanna have gathered data for 1971, a year that was more typical than the preceding years with respect to the inflation rate during the year. For a large sample of companies, they calculated a VUA rate of return on the common equity at 10.5 percent and a CUA rate of return of 6.7 percent, a difference of 3.8 percent compared to the 3.5 percent rate of inflation in 1971. Generally speaking, given a steady rate of inflation over several years preceding and including the reporting period, and assuming a company in a relatively steady physical state, the VUA–CUA difference in percentage return on residual equity should be only slightly below the inflation rate in the reporting period.

PROFITABILITY AND LENGTH OF REPORTING PERIOD

Profitability affects the periodic earnings difference through the roll-forward adjustment; it is not a factor in the lifetime earnings difference as originally recorded (at transaction dates). Thus, any

EXHIBIT X-6

EFFECTS ON EARNINGS DIFFERENCE OF DOUBLING THE RATE OF INFLATION

		Earnings Difference		
	Period t $r = 3.5\%$	Period t + 1 $r = 7\%$	Period t + 2 $r = 7\%$	Period t + 10 $r = 7\%$
Gain on debt	$+4.0	$+8.0	$+8.0	$+8.0
Restatement of cost of goods sold	−1.9	−3.5	−3.8	−3.8
Restatement of depreciation	−4.0	−4.3	−4.6	−8.0
Roll-forward effect	+0.4	+0.8	+0.8	+0.8
Total earning differences	$−1.5	$+1.0	$+0.4	$−3.0

variation in the excess of revenues over expenses affects the periodic VUA–CUA earnings difference by the rate of inflation from midperiod to period-end times the amount of the variation. If CUA earnings before being rolled forward are just under VUA earnings, the roll-forward adjustment could change the sign of the difference. Since the customary methodology calls for restating the old unit expenses (and revenues, if any) directly in end-of-period units, the separate roll-forward computation applies only to current unit revenues and expenses, the net of which normally is much larger than profit.

The length of the reporting period affects the periodic earnings difference through the r factor for the one-half-period roll-forward adjustment. As was pointed out early in this chapter, the selection of the date and associated "size of monetary unit" for stating the CUA profit is a key step in the determination of the amount of the VUA–CUA earnings difference. Once we recognize the potential for influencing the VUA–CUA comparison, and the absolute amounts of CUA earnings reported, by the purposeful choice of reporting periods, the question may arise whether quarterly and monthly income statements should be rolled forward to the year-end or added without restatement to obtain the annual income statement. The former solution puts all numbers that go into the annual income statement on a common basis and expresses them in the size of unit that is most familiar to those reading the statement after the end of the year.

GENERAL CONCLUSIONS

The preceding analyses suggest some general conclusions:

1. It is not feasible to estimate the difference between GAAP earnings and price-level restated earnings in a specific period for one company by a simple rule-of-thumb method.
2. The effects of price level restatements on periodic earnings vary widely across companies but are material in most instances.
3. The tests made in 1973 and 1974 are based on the least representative conditions in the last 25 years; the results of those tests should be used as a basis for policy decisions only with extreme caution and an understanding of the underlying influences.

4. If inflation rates run in the double-digit range for an extended period and then decline, and if GAAP rates of return continue in the 9–12 percent range, there is a possibility that the aggregate real income of the business sector could be negative while being reported as "normal" under VUA.

5. If earnings numbers based on a purchasing power unit are highly desirable for use by parties interested in the outcomes of investment activities, a systematic, uniform, and reasonably comprehensive method of computing such earnings is needed.

6. If a comprehensive system of current value accounting is adopted, as has been proposed in the U.K. (Sandilands Report, 1975), and in Australia (Accounting Standards Committee, 1976), the difference in any accounting period between VUA (unit-of-money) income including holding gains and CUA income including holding gains would equal the inflation rate times the average owners' equity in the period. This difference easily could exceed VUA income.

ADDITIONAL READING SUGGESTIONS

Basu, S. and J. R. Hanna, *Inflation Accounting: Alternatives, Implementation Issues and Some Empirical Evidence* (Society of Industrial Accountants of Canada, 1975).

Financial Accounting Standards Board, "An Analysis of Issues Related to *Conceptual Framework for Financial Accounting and Reporting: Elements of Financial Statements and Their Measurement*," *FASB Discussion Memorandum* (FASB, 2 December 1976), Appendix B.

STUDY QUESTIONS

1. Using a numerical example, explain how the lifetime earnings difference rule is applicable to fixed monetary items, revalued monetary items, revalued nonmonetary items and entry price nonmonetary items. Over a lifetime of two periods, would the VUA–CUA earnings difference be the same for these four types of items? If not, why not?

2. Explain how "deferred restatements" affect the timing of earnings differences.

3. What effects does leverage have on periodic and lifetime earnings differences? Explain.

4. Define TOR ratio. Explain why the TOR ratio does not affect the periodic earnings difference in a complete current value accounting system.

5. Under what circumstances is periodic CUA income most likely to exceed VUA income?

6. Why were the 1973 and 1974 comparisons of VUA earnings and CUA earnings unrepresentative?

7. Can you state a simple rule for estimating the VUA–CUA periodic earnings difference in a complete current value accounting system?

CHAPTER XI

ECONOMIC EVENTS AND FLOWS

In this chapter we turn away from the static concepts of stocks and their measurement in order to examine what might be called "accounting for economic dynamics." The term "economic event" is not used in any specialized sense here; economic events are simply those occurrences which have significant economic implications. Accounting, according to one definition, means identifying, classifying, measuring, and reporting the effects of economic events upon a specific economic unit (Staubus, 1961, p. 10). If this definition is accepted, it would appear that economic events deserve more attention than they have received in the preceding chapters. They get that attention in this chapter.

We use the term "flow" to mean a change in a stock—an increase or decrease in a net asset item. Neither continuity nor regularity is implied. Thus, in a department store, both sales of merchandise and the issuance of bonds involve flows. We noted early in chapter VI that flows are not measured directly in accounting; they are measured by comparing stocks at two different times. It follows that if stocks of cash flow potentials (assets and liabilities) are fundamental in accounting, they should be measured. We view the difference disclosed by successive measurements as a flow. Once we have solved the problems of measuring stocks, the issues involved in flow accounting are issues of classification and reporting. For example, which stock items should be the basis for flow statements? How should the flows be classified and organized for reporting? These types of issues involve the world of funds statements (chapter XII) and income statements (this chapter).

Both flow data and stock data can be of great use in predicting flows. Last period's flows are one good basis for predicting next period's flows. Alternatively, if stocks of cash flow potential are measured by relevant and reliable methods, they represent time-

317

adjusted (discounted) measures of future flows. One approach
to share investment decisions involves predicting dividends on
the basis of predictions of "distributable operating flows" (Revsine,
1973, pp. 33–35). If we accept the premise that a period's operating
flows are not distributable unless provision has been made for
replacing the resources that have been consumed in achieving
the gross inflows (an operating capacity concept of capital maintenance), then it would seem to follow that we would charge the
income statement with the replacement cost of those resources.
Replacement cost measurement of end-of-period stocks of resources held for use is only an incidental consequence of this
approach. Both flow information *and* stock data can be useful
in predicting future flows.

Some accounting teachers take a flow approach to the basic
mechanics of accounting (see Vatter, 1971). Starting with a series
of transactions that involve only cash and immediate revenues
and expenses, we can prepare a flow statement that is more
interesting than the balance sheet. Accruals and deferrals (recorded
primarily by end-of-period adjusting entries) are then tacked on
as exceptions to the basic idea that cash flows affect the income
statement. This "record-of-events" orientation plays down the role
of the balance sheet as a valuation statement and treats it primarily
as a post-closing list of balances which serves both as a check
on the accuracy of the work and as a means of carrying forward
items that apply to the next period's operations. If the history
of an enterprise were not chopped into artifical segments for
the sake of periodic reporting, the valuation of assets and liabilities
would not be of much concern. The accounting system would
then serve primarily as an operating control device, providing
information necessary for the clerks and operating managers to
carry on activities in an efficient manner. For example, there
would be no reason to allocate the cost of a plant asset between
depreciation expense of the period and remaining asset value.
Unfortunately, the desire for data on which to base decisions
prior to the cessation of enterprise operations leads to the seg-
mentation of history.[1]

---

[1]A role may still exist for venture accounting in lieu of periodic reporting.
The tremendous difficulties and dissatisfaction with the percentage-of-completion

CLASSIFICATION OF ECONOMIC EVENTS AND FLOWS

Economic events and flows were discussed at some length in *A Theory of Accounting to Investors* (1961, chapter 4); we will consider them only briefly here. Based on the residual equity point of view, all changes in net asset items can be divided into two classes: those changes favorable to residual equity holders and those unfavorable to residual equity holders. The former category includes increases in assets and decreases in liabilities; the latter includes the opposite effects. Thus, all changes in net asset items that are recorded by debits have a common feature: desirability from the residual equity holders' point of view (when the offsetting credit is ignored). Credit entries to net asset accounts record unfavorable movements. Noting that the literature of accounting did not include names for these categories, I dubbed them *receipts* and *costs*, respectively. Receipts in borrowing transactions (and some others) often are called *proceeds*.

The distinction between receipts and costs provides a means of classifying economic events; additional distinctions enable us to present a classification scheme that looks like this:

A. The distinction between events which involve transfers between the entity and its residual equity holders (residual equity transfers) and other (nontransfer) events. (Distinctions B through E are applied to nontransfers only.)

B. The distinction between transactions and intra-actions.

C. The distinction between one-sided events (involving a receipt or a cost) and two-sided events (involving both a receipt and a cost).

D. The distinction between a monetary receipt and a nonmonetary receipt, i.e., whether the debit is to a monetary net asset item or a nonmonetary net asset item.

E. The distinction between a monetary cost and a nonmonetary cost.

---

basis of accounting for long-term construction contracts suggest the possibility that no profit or loss should be computed on such contracts until they are essentially completed, at which date a separate contribution statement could be prepared for the project. Interim progress reports could be limited to schedule information, revisions of cost estimates, comparisons of costs to date with budgets, and descriptive comments on the difficulties and successes being encountered.

A transaction is an economic event in which something of measurable value is passed voluntarily from one party to another—and perhaps both ways—with both parties aware of the existence and participation of the other. An intra-action is an economic event that has a measurable effect upon the firm but does not involve the voluntary, explicit participation of two parties known to each other. The difference between transactions and intra-actions is significant because there typically is more objective documentary support for the former and, in the case of one-sided events, transactions tend to recur more regularly. The one-sided, two-sided distinction is important because the former always changes the residual equity while the latter often does not. Monetary items differ from nonmonetary items in that they typically are subject to measurement by forward-looking methods—future cash flow or discounted future cash flow—so are more closely related to the typical concern of readers of financial statements—the entity's future capacity to pay. Another important difference is that monetary items are affected differently by inflation.

The classification scheme based on these five dichotomies may be outlined as shown in EXHIBIT XI-1. A tabulation of the key features of the resulting 18 categories of events along with tentative labels for each event and its parts appears in EXHIBIT XI-2.

How can this analysis of economic events and flows help accountants provide useful information on flows? Does it distinguish several sets of flows that have differing significance to the user? Which sets of flows are most interesting? Relying on our future cash flow orientation, we might well say that flows affecting the entity's cash balance, or its liquidity, are of interest. An analysis of these flows for a recent period may give us a clue as to future flows, provided that we are able to make some distinction between recurring and nonrecurring flows. The reporting of liquid flows will be discussed at some length in the next chapter.

The other flows that are of great interest are those that change the residual equity. The significance of the residual equity to readers of financial statements is well known. To creditors and preferred stockholders it is a buffer, changes in which are of great concern. To the residual equity holders themselves it is the accountant's version of the amount of their interest in the entity. To managers who are working in the interests of residual equity

EXHIBIT XI-1

CLASSIFICATION OF ECONOMIC EVENTS

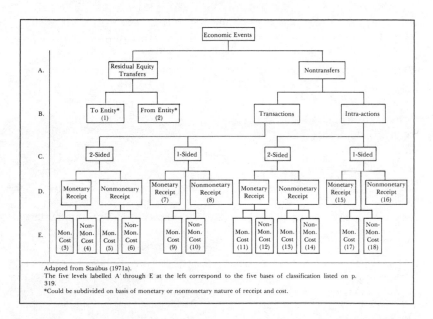

Adapted from Staübus (1971a).
The five levels labelled A through E at the left correspond to the five bases of classification listed on p. 319.
*Could be subdivided on basis of monetary or nonmonetary nature of receipt and cost.

holders, it is a focal point of their work. To income taxation authorities, changes in the residual equity are an object of taxation. To employees, suppliers, and customers, the amount of the residual equity and changes in it are measures of the entity's capacity to meet their wishes and demands. There appears to be no serious disagreement with the view that the residual equity is a, if not the, proper focal point of accounting for profit-seeking entities. Events that change the residual equity are indeed interesting events.[2]

Changes in the residual equity occur in several types of events. First, let's set aside residual equity transfers—investments by residual equity holders and distributions to them. The remaining changes may be classified in several ways. Some are "nonrecurring";

---

[2] See chapter 2 of *A Theory of Accounting to Investors* for more detailed support of the points in this paragraph.

I* or II†	Transaction or Intra-action	Number of Sides	Nature of: Receipt	Cost
(1) I	Transaction	1	Nonmonetary or monetary	—
(2) I	Transaction	1	—	Nonmonetary or monetary
(3) II	Transaction	2	Monetary	Monetary
(4) II	Transaction	2	Monetary	Nonmonetary
(5) II	Transaction	2	Nonmonetary	Monetary
(6) II	Transaction	2	Nonmonetary	Nonmonetary
(7) II	Transaction	1	Monetary	—
(8) II	Transaction	1	Nonmonetary	—
(9) II	Transaction	1	—	Monetary
(10) II	Transaction	1	—	Nonmonetary
(11) II	Intra-action	2	Monetary	Monetary
(12) II	Intra-action	2	Monetary	Nonmonetary
(13) II	Intra-action	2	Nonmonetary	Monetary
(14) II	Intra-action	2	Nonmonetary	Nonmonetary
(15) II	Intra-action	1	Monetary	—
(16) II	Intra-action	1	Nonmonetary	—
(17) II	Intra-action	1	—	Monetary
(18) II	Intra-action	1	—	Nonmonetary

Adapted from Staubus (1971a).

*I indicates transactions between the economic unit and its residual equity holders.
†II indicates events other than transactions between the economic unit and its residual equity holders.

XI-2
EVENTS FROM POINT OF VIEW OF RESIDUAL EQUITY HOLDERS

Change Residual Equity?	Recurring?	Type of:		
		Event	Receipt	Cost
Yes	No	Investment by residual equity holder	Investment by residual equity holder	—
Yes	?	Return to residual equity holder	—	Return to residual equity holder
No	Yes	Financial exchange	Financial receipt	Financial cost
Yes	Yes	Revenue-expense	Revenue	Expense
No	Yes	Purchase	Purchase receipt	Purchase cost
Sometimes	No	Real exchange	Exchange receipt	Exchange cost
Yes	Yes	Revenue	Revenue	—
Yes	Yes	Revenue	Revenue	—
Yes	Yes	Expense	—	Expense
Yes	Yes	Expense	—	Expense
Yes	No	Price level fluctuation	Price level receipt	Price level cost
Yes	Yes	Revenue-expense	Revenue	Expense
Yes	No	Demonetization	Demonet. receipt	Demonet. cost
Sometimes	Yes	Production activity	Production receipt	Production cost
Yes	No	Gain	Gain	—
Yes	No	Gain	Gain	—
Yes	No	Loss	—	Loss
Yes	No	Loss	—	Loss

others tend to recur. But this distinction is not clear-cut and must be used with caution—and with full disclosure. A more definite distinction is the one between changes occurring in transactions and changes occurring in intra-actions. I have suggested (in EXHIBIT XI-2) that the former changes are revenues and expenses and that the latter (with one exception) be labelled "gains and losses." We could also distinguish between (1) "operating" profits and losses recorded at a certain stage of the "operating cycle," and (2) revaluations of assets and liabilities due to changes in prices and price levels. The former require activity on the part of the entity and involve physical or legal conversions of net asset items. The latter are related to the passive holding of net asset positions. Holding gains and losses are recorded on the basis of measurements at replacement cost, current market value, net realizable value (NRV), or discounted future cash flows, but not on the basis of switches from one measurement method to another, except for the original departure from historical cost. Operating profits and losses involve measurements of the debit side of events independently of their cost (credit) sides.

Cost Accounting, Receipt Accounting, and Operating Cycles

Textbooks generally do not distinguish between cost accounting and receipt accounting. In cost accounting, an economic event is quantified by starting with the credit (cost) side of the entry. The debit side is then set equal to the credit side (to conform with the rule of double entry); no change in the residual equity is recognized. We can then say that the asset received or resource consumed is recorded *at* (the amount of) its cost. (Unfortunately, many textbooks still confuse assets recorded *at* their cost with the actual costs; for example, "Many assets are costs carried forward or unexpired costs.") Looking at any *account* in a cost accounting system, we see that the amounts of the credit entries are dependent upon the amounts previously debited to that account.

Receipt accounting is the opposite of cost accounting.[3] An economic event is quantified by reference to the debit (receipt)

---

[3] Much of the material in this subsection, including EXHIBIT XI-3, has been adapted from Staubus (1971a, chapter 7).

side first; the credit entry is then set equal to the debit entry. For example, when a collection of a receivable occurs, the amount of the cash inflow is first ascertained, then the credit to accounts receivable follows. Looking at the entries in a receipt-based *account*, we see that the amounts of debit entries are based on the prospective credits, even though the former may occur first.

Recognition of the cost and receipt approaches to entries and events gives us a basis for a more flexible view of flow accounting than that permitted by costing alone. A condensed T-account flow chart of the operating cycle of a manufacturing concern is a good basis for discussion. First, let us assume that the cycle achieves break-even results. The key events may be recorded as follows:

OPERATING CYCLE, COST ACCOUNTING, BREAK-EVEN RESULTS

Cash	Work in Process	Finished Goods	Accounts Receivable

In this oversimplified situation, every step in the cycle involves a receipt in an amount equal to the cost incurred. The numbering of the entries is based on the typical chronological order of the events. The direction of the arrow indicates that the amount of each entry is determined by the measurement of the credit side—an improbable approach to entries 3 and 4.

As soon as we relax the break-even assumption we encounter difficulties in completing the entries for the operating cycle in the limited system of accounts illustrated above. The recognition of a profit or a loss requires an inequality in an entry at some point in this system. The possibility of an inequality raises three questions: (1) At what point in the cycle will it be recognized? (2) What account is affected by the difference? (3) How do we measure the unequal amounts involved at the point of discontinuity? The question of when to recognize an inequality is usually answered by identifying a "critical event," upon the completion of which we are able to make an independent measurement of the new asset and feel that the essence of the earning process has occurred (Myers, 1954). This step is known as "recognition of revenue"; it is accompanied by recognition of associated expenses. The account that accepts the change in asset amount at the point of discontinuity is a residual equity account which might be called "retained earnings." (It is unnecessary here to use temporary subdivisions of retained earnings—revenue and expense accounts—to accumulate information about the sources of changes in it.) The inequality results from measuring the events in that portion of the cycle between the cash credit and the measurement gap on a cost basis and the events between the measurement gap and the cash debit on a receipt basis. EXHIBIT XI-3 illustrates all of the one-gap possibilities for a four-asset account system. (Cost-based entries are numbered; receipt-based entries are lettered.)

A review of the flow charts in EXHIBIT XI-3 may convince the reader that cost-based entries are the natural type. The chronological order of a series of cost-based entries is consistent with the order of measurement dependence; this permits the accountant to base each entry on numbers already appearing in the system. Materials and services are put into process before they are transferred to finished goods, from whence they "naturally" move on to accounts receivable and to cash. In each case, the accountant has historical data on which to base his entry. Not only are the entries easier to make but the technique is also easier to learn.

Receipt-based entries, on the other hand, involve some difficulties. Careful study of the series of receipt accounting entries in EXHIBIT XI-3 will reveal that the chronological order of entries may well be the reverse of the order of measurement dependence. In the fourth case, for example, we see that "finished goods" is debited with an amount based on a prospective cash receipt but that the entry is made, presumably, prior to the actual receipt. Subsequently, a receivable would be recorded, then the cash receipt. Receipt accounting requires predictions, and predicting events is much more difficult than chronicling them. But the use of predictions in receipt accounting is also its greatest merit. A reliable prediction of an event is much more valuable than a reliable chronicle of that event because the former provides a more *timely* basis for action.

Because receipt accounting often requires making debits to accounts on the basis of prospective credits, it is natural for

EXHIBIT XI-3
ALTERNATIVE T-ACCOUNT FLOW CHARTS OF THE OPERATING CYCLE IN A
MANUFACTURING FIRM

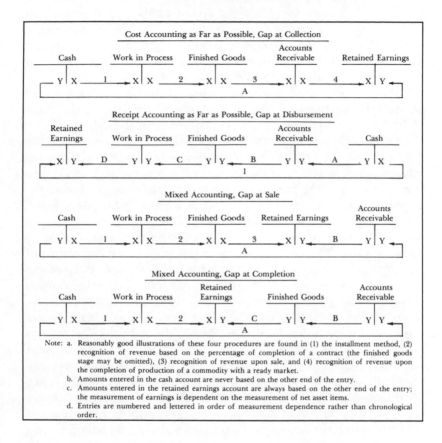

Note: a. Reasonably good illustrations of these four procedures are found in (1) the installment method, (2) recognition of revenue based on the percentage of completion of a contract (the finished goods stage may be omitted), (3) recognition of revenue upon sale, and (4) recognition of revenue upon the completion of production of a commodity with a ready market.

b. Amounts entered in the cash account are never based on the other end of the entry.

c. Amounts entered in the retained earnings account are always based on the other end of the entry; the measurement of earnings is dependent on the measurement of net asset items.

d. Entries are numbered and lettered in order of measurement dependence rather than chronological order.

accountants to view cost accounting as a more comfortable mode in which to work. Cost accounting entries—especially the simplest type in which there is only one debit and one credit—require a minimum of analysis and judgment; in many cases, no alternative amounts are obvious, so the accounting choices are easy to make. Consequently, the reliability of cost accounting measurements is often high. Unfortunately, the relevance of past-oriented cost accounting measurements to future decisions is often questioned.

In receipt-based accounting, on the other hand, reliability is likely to be the more critical criterion because that criterion may be only marginally, or submarginally, satisfied and thus may become a source of disagreement among accountants. The relevance of receipt-based accounting is less likely to be questioned because it is future-oriented. However, those accountants who are not concerned with the decision-usefulness objective can be expected to resist receipt-based accounting in favor of the more comfortable cost-based mode. Since conventional accounting includes a mixture of the two, the practical issue is one of preference and emphasis rather than of selecting one to the exclusion of the other.

The operating cycle portrayed in EXHIBIT XI-3 is unrealistically simple, of course. It does not show multiple inputs spread throughout the cycle. When additional inputs are considered, we can see that cost accounting has a *synthetic* aspect; the entries record the combining of resources. Receipt accounting, on the other hand, is more *analytic*; the prospective cash receipt is broken down into the part attributable to past inputs and the part attributable to future inputs. The latter is deducted to obtain the debit side of the entry. Historical cost, restated historical cost, and replacement cost are cost-based measurement methods, while NRV, discounted future cash flows, and future cash flows are receipt-based methods. The change from a cost-based measure to a receipt-based measure is significant because there is usually a discrepancy that affects the residual equity. (See the "gap chart" on p. 171.) The decision when to make this switch—to jump the gap—is critical in accounting. The choice depends largely upon the reliability of receipt-based measurements at the various stages of the operating cycle because the relevance criterion always favors a receipt-based measure. Unfortunately, the accountant's reliability standard often prevents him from using such a measure until contractual evidence of the receipt is at hand. That choice and the reporting of both the last outflow recognized on the cost side of the gap and the first inflow recorded on the receipt side of the gap have long been viewed as the heart of income accounting within the context of the cost-based system.

What sorts of classifications of flows do these insights suggest? The conventional scheme is to segregate outflows and inflows associated with the last critical event in the operating cycle. If the last critical event is so significant, perhaps assets could also be classified on that basis. Those assets committed to operations but which have not yet reached the last critical event could be distinguished from "post-critical-event" assets and cash. The former are "operating resources"; the latter are liquid assets. Liability classes could be matched with asset classes. Those liabilities, namely, deferred credits to revenue, which require the commitment of operating resources, would be distinguished from those calling for the relinquishment of liquid assets.

An alternative view, which typically would yield similar results, would focus on the measurement methods used. If asset and liability measurement is more basic to accounting than are definitions of revenue and expense, we could make the latter dependent on the former. Revenues and expenses could be reported when the measurement gap is jumped—when the accountant switches from a cost-based measurement to a receipt-based measurement. The two major possibilities are (a) the jump from replacement cost (or restated historical cost or historical cost) to a future cash flow method at the time of sale, and (b) the jump from one of these cost methods to NRV when production of readily marketable commodities is completed. Using such an approach, can we establish a simple and clear rule for the recognition of revenue? Our answer would appear to depend upon our ability to establish the rules for choices of measurement methods. If we cannot do that, we may have a more basic problem.

Simple Textbook Definitions of Revenue and Expense

Now let's review some types of definitions of revenue and expense. These terms are difficult to define for students in ways that are both technically sound and simple. Unfortunately, we often see definitions which are extremely vague. For example, "Revenue is the price of goods sold and services rendered during a given time period" (Meigs, Mosich, and Johnson, 1972, p. 66). The use of the term "price" as the key word in a definition of revenue appears to ignore the substance in favor of the form. A more substantive definition for students might be the following: *Revenue is the gross inflow of assets in exchange for products and services provided to other parties.* While this definition slides over the possibility that revenue may involve a decrease in a liability rather than an increase in an asset, and while it uses a vague term ("provided") as the main clue to the timing, it at least puts the emphasis on the inflow of assets.

Expense is more difficult to define because the definition must provide for the outflows that are not directly assignable to revenues as well as those that are. One possible definition is: *Expenses are costs of earning the revenues of the period, including those operating costs which are not assignable to the revenues of other periods.* While the term "costs" may be completely clear (economic sacrifices, recorded by credits to net asset items), "operating" and "not assignable" surely are not clear to many students. The likely result when students rely on sloppy definitions is that they learn how to identify revenues and expenses by remembering examples; the principles may prove elusive.

Financial and Operating Views of Revenue and Expense

To the financially oriented individual, revenue-expense transactions involve the release of a nonmonetary asset in exchange for a monetary asset. Revenues are the monetary inflows; expenses are the nonmonetary outflows. An alternative, and contrasting, view might be held by an operating executive, such as a production manager, who is concerned with the comparison of inputs and outputs in determining the efficiency of operations. To him, the outputs from any activity are the finished products that may, or may not, be measured on the basis of their selling prices. The inputs to be matched with the outputs are measured by the costs of resources used. To him, costs (and expenses) are associated with inputs, revenues with outputs. Revenue certainly could be, and has been, defined in terms of the entity's outputs, or products. [4] Combining the output-input emphasis with the view of revenues as inflows and expenses as outflows yields the following definitions: *Expense is the cost of using the resources employed in producing the products and services provided by the entity to others. Revenue is the receipt of monetary assets in exchange for the entity's products.* Note

---

[4] A survey of various types of definitions of revenue may be found in Staubus, (1956).

that the costs of using resources are not necessarily the same as the costs of acquiring them, because the sacrifice upon use would be measured by a market price at the time of use. In this view, revenue is measured by the value of outputs; expense is measured by the cost of producing outputs. The object of the business exercise is to maximize the difference between the two.

Operational Definitions of Revenue and Expense

When definitions of basic concepts are used to guide practitioners and students facing puzzling cases, any ambiguity in those definitions is a serious flaw. For that reason, heavy dependence on terms such as "products and services provided to other parties," "operating," and "in exchange for its products" should be avoided. There are too many cases in which it is difficult to determine *when* products and services are provided to other parties, which activities are *operating* activities and which are not, and which commodities or services are the *products* of the entity and which are not. Is credit a product of a manufacturer? Is a charitable contribution an operating activity? When are products provided to the client of a construction contractor? It was a desire to provide definite answers to the difficult cases that led me to offer these tentative definitions in chapter 4 of *A Theory of Accounting to Investors: Revenue* is a monetary receipt at a nonmonetary cost, or any receipt in a one-sided transaction. *Expense* is a nonmonetary cost of a monetary receipt, or any cost in a one-sided transaction. The hope was that the previous definitions of monetary, nonmonetary, transaction, one-sided, receipt, and cost would provide a basis for unequivocal answers. Unfortunately, there was still some room for dispute as to whether an asset was monetary or not, and the other definitions may not have been completely clear.

But the failure to eliminate all ambiguities was not the major problem with my tentative 1961 definitions. Certain clear-cut answers were troublesome. One such case was sales of plant assets and similar "nonrecurring" transactions involving flows that met the tentative definitions of revenues and expenses. I wished to include nonrecurring effects upon the residual equity in the gain and loss categories, and I believed that only the difference between the receipt and cost, rather than the gross flows, need be reported in such nonrecurring cases. This led me to suggest that an exception be made for such cases. Another problem case was that of deferred credits to revenues. If a customer paid for a service or product in advance of receiving it, the transaction appeared to meet the definition of a revenue-expense event; however, unreliability of independent measurements of the credit side of many such transactions seemed to justify excluding those measurements from the income statement and including the subsequent delivery of the product or service—which did not meet the definitions.

Still another problem—a more serious one—was the inclusion of the *sale* of standard, readily marketable commodities (such as wheat), rather than their *production*. From the point of view of relevance to the decisions of those appraising both management performance during a period and the success of the entity in achieving the objectives of owners, it would seem necessary to include the value of the output as revenue and the production costs as expenses, even if the product has not been sold by the end of the period. Surely the difference must be reported in the period of production if periodic reporting is to yield timely and relevant information. And if wheat production is the major operating activity of the entity, a gross monetary measure of accomplishment and the offsetting total costs should be reported. If both of these reporting objectives are met, is not revenue being recognized? (Sales of wheat could be reported as a funds flow event, with a gain or loss resulting from the change in price since the previous balance sheet date.)

In chapter 5 of *A Theory of Accounting to Investors*, I attempted to patch the above-mentioned flaws in the tentative definitions of revenue, expense, gain, and loss by adding exception clauses. Even so, I now believe that particular attempt to construct operational and informationally sound definitions of revenue and expense was only partially successful.

A Subordinate Approach to Revenue and Expense

If we agree that defining and measuring assets and liabilities are at the heart of accounting, perhaps we should try to define revenue and expense on the basis of measurement effects. Events in which the inflow is measured independently of the outflow, thus leaving an income gap, are an especially interesting category. Revenue is a measure of volume on the inflow side of the gap; expense is a measure of volume on the outflow side of the gap. If we accept the ideas that income is a net flow and revenues and expenses are gross flows, perhaps we will accept the following as attributes of one interesting flow concept:

1. a gross inflow;
2. occurring in an event that changes the residual equity, other than a residual equity transfer;
3. occurring in an event of a type that tends to recur frequently or regularly.

A flow meeting these criteria could be called revenue. Switch the direction of the flow and we have expense. Unquestionably, such definitions leave room for disagreement due to the lack of a clear distinction between recurring and nonrecurring events. But the issue is not such a serious one if we agree that the distinctions between revenues and gains and between expenses and losses are not to be used to justify the aggregation of items with substantially different significance to the financial statement reader; distinctions *within* each class can be critical. Differing probabilities or frequency of recurrence are critical to those attempting to predict the entity's cash flows; items differing in these respects must not be aggregated prior to presentation on the income statement. As long as this approach is observed, disagreements on the classification of items as revenues or gains and as expenses or losses are not likely to make a critical difference in their interpretation, so that the ambiguity inherent in the recurring-nonrecurring distinction may be tolerable.

We conclude this section with the following observations about flow concepts:

1. A revenue is a gross inflow in a recurring event that changes the residual equity.
2. An expense is a gross outflow in a recurring event that changes the residual equity.
3. A gain is the excess of an inflow over an outflow in a nonrecurring event that changes the residual equity.
4. A loss is the excess of an outflow over an inflow in a nonrecurring event that changes the residual equity.

5. Changes in market prices are gain or loss events, not revenue-expense events.
6. Residual equity transfers are excluded from the above categories.[5]

INCOME

Income has been a popular topic in the accounting literature of the twentieth century, as a glance at any volume of the *Accountant's Index*[6] will confirm. There is some doubt, however, whether the great investment that has been made in the concept has paid off for the profession and for users of financial statements. I am not an enthusiastic devotee of the income approach to accounting theory. The "comparative statics" approach yields better results, in my opinion. Nevertheless, the income-oriented literature includes some of the greatest contributions to the development of accounting theory. Let's look at a few of the milestones.

Features of the Income Literature

Several economists and economics-oriented accountants greatly illuminated the nature and measurement of income. One approach to income is usually attributed to Irving Fisher (1906) and was developed further by John Canning (1929) and Sidney Alexander (1950)—all economists—and by David Solomons (1962). Basically, they define assets as the present values of future returns, and income as the change in these present values, generally measured by the cash receipts of the period plus or minus the change in present values of future receipts.

The English economist J. R. Hicks (1946, p. 172) is credited with the most frequently quoted, common sense definition of

---

[5]This set of definitions seems to yield satisfactory results when applied to an entity producing a readily marketable commodity. Completion of production meets the definitions of revenue and expense if the finished product is carried at NRV. If any price change gain or loss occurring prior to the date of sale is recorded promptly, sale does not affect the residual equity so it is not a revenue and expense event.

[6](AICPA, quarterly, annually, or biennially.) Accounting students should be acquainted with this reference work.

income, which may be paraphrased as follows: Income is the
amount one can consume during a period and still be as well
off at the end of the period as he was at the beginning. The
intuitive appeal of Hicks's definition, together with the emphasis
it places on the determination of an ending position that is equal
to the initial wealth position, led to the development of a "capital
maintenance" approach to income. Jean Kerr (1956) and R. S.
Gynther (1974), both Australians, have contributed much to this
approach, including the explication of the capital maintenance
concepts discussed in chapter IX above.

Definitions of income for accounting use must have a scope
provision to indicate what is deductible. In other words, we must
select a well-defined interest group whose point of view is used
to distinguish the "bad" outflows (expenses) from the "good"
(distributions of income). Working from the narrow to the broader
interpretations, the term "net income" could be applied to (1)
what is left for the entity after providing for returns to all
contributors, including owners;[7] (2) what is left for the residual
equity interest (after preferred dividends, if any);[8] (3) what is
left for owners (including preferred shareholders);[9] (4) what is
left for long-term investors (including long-term creditors); (5)what
is left for all "capitalists"; or (6) what is left for capitalists and
the income taxing authority.[10] A still broader concept is (7) the
value-added measure of income: gross revenues less materials and
services purchased from other businesses, possibly including
depreciation.[11]

---

[7] This version of accounting income is comparable to the economist's profit,
in the sense of the remainder after providing for the returns necessary to attract
all resources used.

[8] The residual equity point of view was advocated in Staubus (1959 and 1961).

[9] This is the traditional "proprietary" view which is reflected in GAAP.

[10] The view that interest and income taxes are distributions of income rather
than expenses is associated with the writings of W. A. Paton, such as his *Accounting
Theory* (1922), and A. C. Littleton (1953), and their joint publication (1940).

[11] See Suojanen (1954), who suggests a value-added form of supplementary
statement. We may well question the usefulness of value-added as a measure
of the success of an entity from anyone's point of view, but it is certainly a reasonable
measure of the size of an entity from a social point of view. Hendricksen (1970,
chapter 5) includes a comprehensive discussion of all of these income concepts.

An additional set of issues is introduced by the desire to segment history and report income on a periodic basis. Like other accounting constructs, income is of interest to persons who want to predict something that is relevant to decisions that they face. If accountants are to produce an income number that is helpful, they should know what users want to predict. Much of the work of security analysts suggests that they would dearly love to *predict the entity's future income.* Thus, an income number is used to predict a future income number. If this objective is to be weighed heavily by accountants, it suggests the desirability of accounting methods that yield stable series of expenses and revenues. In fact, accountants have many opportunities to influence the reported periodic income so as to make it similar to last period's reported income. Is this helpful to users?

An alternative view is that income should be useful in *predicting the firm's future capacity to pay.* This view clearly is consistent both with the approach in this book and with the focus on income as a measure of distributable operating flows. In addition to requiring a choice of a capital maintenance concept, it also puts a great deal of emphasis on the distinction between recurring and nonrecurring income items. The difficulties encountered by the several American standards-setting bodies in this latter area have been manifested by a series of pronouncements on extraordinary charges and credits, prior period adjustments, and disclosure of unusual gains and losses.

An argument could be made that the most important decisions accountants can make in the process of preparing income statements (once all assets and liabilities have been measured) are those pertaining to the disaggregation of the net income number on the basis of flow sources that differ in predictive significance. Whether a component is called a revenue, a gain, or income— whether it is an expense, an operating cost, or a loss—is not as critical as is the presentation of sufficient clues to permit the analyst to predict the amounts of such flows in the future. To the analyst, a steady land rental of $X and a gain from an involuntary conversion of an asset of $X must not be aggregated before the income statement is prepared (and then reported as only one number), because he is likely to want to "capitalize" the rental revenue (attach a multiple to it) while the involuntary conversion may be viewed as a one-time change in wealth which deserves a multiple of only one in the estimation of the entity's value.

Furthermore, the recurring-nonrecurring distinction, or the operating-extraordinary items distinction, is not sufficient; there are all sorts of shadings that the analyst should be free to treat in his own way rather than depend on the management (and accountants) to judge. In this area, full disclosure is more than a motherhood concept. Segment reporting and line-item treatment of all flows that have any tendency to fluctuate in a pattern that differs from the pattern of primary revenues of the entity or segment provide the analyst with the raw material for predictions and judgments of value. Burying unique items by prestatement aggregation is a sign of a desire to conceal rather than a desire to inform. Disclosure is especially important in an accounting system that incorporates the types of measurements recommended in this book. Flow items such as holding gains and losses on assets, purchasing power gain on debt, revaluations of liabilities, and gains and losses on foreign currency holdings are examples of real changes in wealth that the analyst should be allowed to interpret as he chooses.

Income in the Present Work

As the reader will have noticed by now, I do not put as much stress on income in the basic decisions of accountants as many authors have in the past. My emphasis has been on the measurement of assets and liabilities. The following four paragraphs sum up the approach to income that follows from the previous chapters.

Many variations of the economic concepts of wealth and income are now in use. The most fundamental meaning of wealth is an entity's total stock of potential utility. The meaning most commonly accepted in finance is cash flow potential, which accountants label "assets" (if positive) or "liabilities" (if negative). Assets are a measurable subset of an entity's wealth. Liabilities are the interests of parties other than residual equity holders in the entity's wealth. The difference between total assets and total liabilities is a residual equity in the entity's assets. That difference is a common focal point attracting the attention of many persons interested in the economic affairs of the entity.

Income is a change in wealth. Once the wealth concept of interest has been delineated (in nature and scope), an income concept follows. In financial affairs, income is a change in assets (other than by contributions or withdrawals of investors) or, most commonly, assets net of some or all liabilities and perhaps the interests of preferred stockholders. The term "earnings" is often applied to the income on assets net of liabilities and the preferred share interest, that is, the income available to serve the residual equity holders.

The measurement of the change-in-net-assets concept of periodic income requires measurement of the cash flow potential of all net asset items at the beginning and end of the period. Cash flow potential need not be measured directly, but any surrogate attribute that is measured instead must have a demonstrable relationship to future cash flows. For the difference between the beginning and end-of-period measurements to be most significant to residual equity holders, it must be stated in a measuring unit with constant power to purchase the goods that are of concern to residual equity holders.

This chapter completes the development of the cash-flow-oriented theory of financial position and earnings. The following five statements summarize the linkage between investors' information needs and the concept of earnings based on changes in cash flow potential:

1. Investors want to predict cash flows to themselves, including those coming from the entity in which they invest.
2. The investee entity's future capacity to pay cash to investors is determined by its present cash balance and future cash flows.
3. Evidence of future cash flows to or from the entity is information relevant to investors' decisions.
4. Measurement of the future cash flow potential of assets and liabilities and changes in that cash flow potential requires use of a group of surrogate measures, but such measurements can be accomplished, with "useful accuracy," by accountants.
5. The periodic net change in the cash flow potential of net assets is the measure of earnings that is most relevant to investors' cash-flow-oriented decisions. A summary of the

several types of events affecting the entity's net cash flow potential—an earnings statement—can be useful to persons who want to predict the entity's future capacity to pay and changes therein.

ADDITIONAL READING SUGGESTIONS

General and Revenue

Bedford, Norton M., *Income Determination Theory: An Accounting Framework* (Addison-Wesley, 1965).

Financial Accounting Standards Board, "An Analysis of Issues Related to *Conceptual · Framework for Financial Accounting and Reporting: Elements of Financial Statements and Their Measurement, FASB Discussion Memorandum* (FASB, 2 December 1976), chapter 5 and Appendix A.

Hendriksen, Eldon S., *Accounting Theory*, rev. ed. (Richard D. Irwin, 1970), chapters 5, 6.

Myers, John H., "Critical Event and Recognition of Net Profit," *The Accounting Review* (October 1954), pp. 528–32.

Revsine, Lawrence, *Replacement Cost Accounting* (Prentice-Hall, 1973).

Staubus, George J., "Revenue and Revenue Accounts," *Accounting Research* (July 1956), pp. 284–94; rpt. in Sidney Davidson et al., eds., *An Income Approach to Accounting Theory* (Prentice-Hall, 1964), pp. 78–88.

————, *A Theory of Accounting to Investors* (University of California Press, 1961; rpt. Scholars Book Co., 1971), chapters 4, 5.

————, *Activity Costing and Input-Output Accounting* (Richard D. Irwin, 1971a), chapters 1, 7.

Nature of Income and Capital Maintenance

Alexander, Sidney S., rev. by David Solomons, "Income Measurement in a Dynamic Economy," in W. T. Baxter and Sidney Davidson, eds., *Studies in Accounting Theory* (Sweet & Maxwell, 1962), pp. 126–200.

Canning, John B., *The Economics of Accountancy* (Ronald Press, 1929), chapters 7, 8.

Fisher, Irving, *The Nature of Capital and Income* (Macmillan, 1906).

Gynther, Reg S., "Why Use General Purchasing Power?" *Accounting and Business Research* (Spring 1974), pp. 141–57.

Hicks, J. R., *Value and Capital*, 2d ed. (Clarendon Press, 1946).

Kerr, Jean St. G., "Three Concepts of Business Income," *The Australian Accountant* (April 1956), pp. 139–46; rpt. in Sidney Davidson et al., eds., *An Income Approach to Accounting Theory* (Prentice-Hall, 1964), pp. 40–48.

Points of View Towards Income (Scope)

Littleton, A. C., "Structure of Accounting Theory," *Monograph No. 5* (AAA, 1953).

Paton, W. A., *Accounting Theory* (Ronald Press, 1922).

——— and A. C. Littleton, "An Introduction to Corporate Accounting Standards," *Monograph No. 3* (AAA, 1940).

Staubus, George J., *A Theory of Accounting to Investors* (University of California Press, 1961; rpt. Scholars Book Co., 1971), chapter 2.

Suojanen, Waino W., "Accounting Theory and the Large Corporation," *The Accounting Review* (July 1954), pp. 391–98.

Vatter, William J., *The Fund Theory of Accounting and Its Implications for Financial Reports* (University of Chicago Press, 1947).

STUDY QUESTIONS

1. What would you deduct from total revenues to arrive at a measure of distributable operating flow?
2. What criticisms do you have of the scheme for classifying economic events discussed in this chapter and outlined in EXHIBIT XI-2?
3. Give one or two examples of each category of economic events listed in EXHIBIT XI-1.
4. Can you think of better terms than cost, receipt, cost accounting, and receipt accounting for the concepts to which these terms are applied in this chapter?
5. Does receipt accounting as illustrated in EXHIBIT XI-3 seem as natural to you as cost accounting? If not, why not? Assuming

they can both be executed with equally reliable results, which appears to yield the most useful data? Why?

6. Can you think of any exception to the assertion that revenue is recognized, per GAAP, at the occurrence of the last critical event in the operating cycle?

7. ". . . the basic nature of revenue is an outflow of services to customers . . ." (Bedford, 1965, p. 93). Define expense in such a way that the difference between revenue (as described above) and expense (as you define it here) yields some concept of income.

8. Analyze the following quotation and state what you think it means:
"This exchange of service gives rise to revenue and expense. Revenue is the money measure of the services the business transfers to its customers and expense is the money measure of the services exchanged with the customer in return for revenue" (Fess, 1961, p. 447).

9. Nine criteria for the evaluation of alternative accounting proposals were presented in chapter III. (a) On what criterion (or criteria) is the separation of recurring and nonrecurring changes in the residual equity desirable? (b) On what criterion (criteria) is the separation of holding gains and losses on assets and liabilities from "operating" effects desirable?

10. What would be the scope of an income concept consistent with a managerial point of view in (a) a family owned enterprise with a hired manager who has no ownership interest, and (b) the typical large corporation with thousands of shareholders and no concentrated ownership interest?

11. Define (a) revenue, (b) gain, and (c) income. Does revenue, gain, or income occur in the following events?
    (a) Sale of a plant asset for more than its book value.
    (b) Retirement of a liability for less than its book value.
    (c) Refund of federal income taxes for a prior year.
    (d) Production of gold.
    (e) Harvest of wheat.
    (f) Sale of wheat by a farmer.
    (g) Making contracts and delivering goods to be paid for in installments.

    (h) Partial construction of a supertanker under contract.

    (i)   Production of a $10,000 machine within one month under contract.

    (j)   Appreciation of an asset in proportion to the increase in the general price level.

    (k) Appreciation faster than the general price level increase.

    (l)   Receipt of an order and money for goods on hand to be delivered in the future.

    (m) Making of a contract to sell goods which are on hand.

    (n) Discovery of oil on company property.

    (o) Growth of trees on company's timber acreage.

12. Define expense and loss. Do the following events involve expense or loss according to your definitions?

    (a) Accrual of interest during construction period on mortgage bonds issued to finance construction of plant.

    (b) Above case, after completion (during operation).

    (c) Accrual of salary of president of corporation.

    (d) Estimated cost in lieu of insurance premiums (self-insurance).

    (e) Cost of sponsoring, for advertising, a major, one-time sports event.

    (f) Property taxes on land held for construction of plant to start in two years.

    (g) Dividends on cumulative, nonparticipating stock.

    (h) Depreciation on building, housing, manufacturing operations.

    (i)   Income tax not paid on income recognized on books and which will be taxed in the future.

    (j)   Transfer of saleable copper bars from work in process to finished goods.

    (k) Income tax (per tax law) on the period's income.

13. Is the distinction between recurring and nonrecurring events of great significance to users of financial statements? Should it be a factor in definitions of flow concepts?

14. Which of the definitions of revenue and expense suggested in this chapter do you like best? Why?

15. Criticize these two definitions of revenue, and present a third which you are willing to back. Explain the merits of the definition you favor.

"Revenue results from the sale of goods and the rendering of services and is measured by the charge made to customers, clients, or tenants for goods and services furnished to them. It also includes gains from the sale or exchange of assets (other than stock in trade), interest and dividends earned on investments, and other increases in the owners' equity except those arising from capital contributions and capital adjustments" (Committee on Terminology, 1955, p. 2).

"Revenue is an aggregate of all decreases in asset and cost factors attributable to the volume of business in question and the addition to equities (income) which arise out of the fact that the proceeds of the sale—assuming operation to be successful—exceed the expirations involved. In all those cases where the costs of revenue exceed the new asset values accruing from sales, the revenue figure evidently represents only the portion of the costs or expense equivalent to such new values" (Paton, 1949, p. 77).

16. Make a case for the view that accounting flows can be measured directly without first measuring stocks. Give examples.

17. It is possible that a company's earnings could equal the dividends it pays in each period of its life. Can you specify a set of accounting practices and financial policies that would, or could, lead to that equality?

CHAPTER XII

ALTERNATIVE FLOWS, LIQUIDITY, AND RISK

Revenues, expenses, and income were described in the preceding chapter as changes in the total of net assets, that is, flows in or out of the net asset pool. We also mentioned that flows in and out of a liquid segment of the net asset pool may be of considerable interest to users of accounting data. In this chapter, we review several asset flow concepts that are tied to several net asset pools with different boundaries. This analysis is intended to give a clearer view of the characteristics of different flow concepts. The distinction between accounting for wealth flows and accounting for liquidity flows should then also be clarified. This review leads us to examine the problem of accounting for liquidity which, in turn, leads us to the area of reporting risk-relevant data.

THE DEVELOPMENT OF RELEVANT FLOW STATEMENTS

The relationships between several asset flow concepts may be visualized if we think of how a businessman with no training in accounting might develop an accounting system.[1] His need to remain solvent and his acquaintance with the value of money are likely to lead him to maintain some kind of records of cash receipts and disbursements. Curiosity about his own affairs may suggest the separation of receipts and disbursements and some breakdowns of both. A statement similar to EXHIBIT XII-1 could be the culmination of the businessman's first efforts at accounting. After some experience with *cash receipts and disbursements state-*

---

[1] This section, including EXHIBITS XII-1 through XII-5, has been adapted from Staubus (1966).

EXHIBIT XII-1
HYPOTHETICAL COMPANY
CASH RECEIPTS AND DISBURSEMENTS
1976

Receipts:
Cash sales and collections from customers $11,600
Collections of interest, etc. 450
Investments by creditors and owners 2,000
Sales of unneeded plant and other facilities 500

Total cash receipts $14,550

Disbursements:
For merchandise $8,400
For selling and administrative cost 1,400
Interest 400
Income taxes 500
Capital expenditures for new plant facilities 2,300
Repayments to creditors 600
Dividends 350

Total cash disbursements $13,950

Net change in cash balance . . . . $ 600
Cash balance, January 1 500

Cash balance, December 31 . . . . $ 1,100

ments, the fledgling businessman may begin to see some relationships between cash movements other than their direction. As he, and perhaps his banker, attempt to foresee the results of operations, he may feel the need to distinguish between those cash transactions that tend to follow patterns, even though somewhat roughly, and those that show little tendency to recur. He may see that some categories of transactions keep happening over and over in sufficiently regular patterns that they can be used as indications of what is going to happen in the future. Such events may be distinguished, in the summary cash statement, from the nonrecurring cash transactions. Also, inflows and outflows of cash in financing transactions could be paired on the statement, as could receipts and disbursements in the sales and purchases of property

other than the stock-in-trade of the business, especially long-lived
items used in conducting the major activities of the organization.
Such pairings would help the reader to comprehend the impact
of financing activities and capital expenditures on the firm.
Consideration of these points could easily lead to a report similar
to EXHIBIT XII-2.

Working with *cash flow statements* may give the businessman ideas
for further improvements. If, for example, someone were to ask

EXHIBIT XII-2

HYPOTHETICAL COMPANY
CASH FLOW STATEMENT I
1976

Routine operations:
Inflows:

Cash sales and collections from customers . . .	$11,600	
Collections of interest, etc.	450	$12,050

Outflows:

Cash disbursements for merchandise	8,400	
Selling and administrative costs	1,400	
Interest paid	400	
Income taxes paid	500	10,700
Net recurring cash flow or "cash flow" . . .)		$ 1,350
Dividends paid		350
Net recurring cash flow retained		$ 1,000

Financing transactions:

Cash invested by creditors and owners	2,000	
Repayments to creditors	600	1,400

Capital expenditures, net of cash receipts from
dispositions of unneeded facilities ($500)

	(1,800)
Net change in cash balance	$ 600
Balance January 1	500
Balance December 31	$ 1,100

him how business was last month, he might find himself answering, "Not bad, according to our cash flow statement, but I'm not happy with the month's operations." "Why not?" "Well, I'm afraid our sales took a beating. Traffic in the store was light and goods piled up in the reserve stocks. This month's cash collections on account may be way down, but we won't know until we make up the cash flow statement at the end of the month." A few situations like this could give our potential accountant the idea that he could record both the inflows relating to sales and the outflows needed to produce the sales more promptly if he did not wait for the cash movements to occur.

The advantages of knowing more about what his customers owe him and what he owes suppliers could provide additional incentives to convert to an *accrual* basis of accounting. Sales, whether the sale price has been collected or not, would replace cash receipts; purchases of goods and services would be recognized as the major offsetting group of transactions. The budding accountant might not think of it this way, but he would be recognizing increases in net quick assets as favorable flows and decreases in net quick assets as unfavorable flows. EXHIBIT XII-3 reflects this *quick flow* approach to the reporting of asset flows.

Further experience with asset flow statements as representations of the firm's operations may disclose deficiencies in the quick flow statement. A few cases of substantial changes in inventories, which reflect poor matching of receipts of purchased goods with shipments of goods sold, may suggest the need for a change in the procedure for accounting for the cost of merchandise. Despite steady sales and steady prices, heavy purchasing could result in a negative net recurring quick flow in a short period, or slow purchasing could result in a bulge in the net recurring flow.

The alert manager-accountant might see that his flow statement would give a better indication of operating success if it included deductions from sales for the cost of those goods sold rather than those purchased. He might also recognize a similar, although less significant, improvement from spreading the costs of such things as insurance coverage evenly over the periods rather than deducting them when purchased. If his business operations involved frequent cases of collections from customers prior to the provisions of goods or services to those customers, he might feel

EXHIBIT XII-3

HYPOTHETICAL COMPANY

QUICK ASSET FLOW STATEMENT

1976

Routine operations:
Inflows:

Sales of merchandise and related services	$12,000	
Interest accrued on investments, etc.	400	$12,400

Outflows:

Purchases of merchandise	$ 8,700	
Routine purchases of supplies and services	1,600	
Interest cost accrued	400	
Income taxes for the year	600	11,300
Net recurring quick asset flow, or "quick flow"		$ 1,100
Dividends declared		300
Net recurring quick asset flow retained		$ 800

Financing transactions:

Long-term investments by creditors and owners . . .	$ 2,000	
Current maturities and premature retirements of debts · · · · · · · · · · · · · · · ·	600	1,400

Capital expenditures, net of receipts from sales of

unneeded facilities ($500)		(1,800)
Net change in net quick assets	$	400
Net quick asset balance January 1 (credit)		(100)
Net quick asset balance December 31	$	300

---

that he is not entitled to report the favorable flow until the related unfavorable flows can be matched with it; the deferral of credits to revenue might be appropriate. The merits of matching costs with revenues in these ways might have sufficient appeal to entice the recordkeeper to adopt the *deferral* technique of accounting for inventories of merchandise, short-term prepayments of routine operating costs, and precollections from customers. To defer the reporting of such transactions until some time after the cash movement, then, permits a more logical cause-and-effect matching on the *working flow statement* than on the previous flow statements. This is shown in EXHIBIT XII-4.

The adoption of the accrual and deferral techniques of accounting for short-lived assets has resulted in an asset flow statement that appears to have important advantages over the cash statements of EXHIBITS XII-1 and 2. However, the stockholders and other readers of these statements may feel that the net recurring working capital flow could be converted to a figure that would provide

EXHIBIT XII-4

HYPOTHETICAL COMPANY
WORKING CAPITAL FLOW STATEMENT
1976

Routine operations:		
Inflows:		
Sales of merchandise and related services	$12,000	
Interest accrued on investments, etc.	400	$12,400
Outflows:		
Cost of goods sold	$ 8,000	
Selling and administrative costs	1,600	
Interest cost accrued	400	
Income taxes for the year	600	10,600
Net recurring working capital flow or "working flow"		$ 1,800
Dividends declared		300
Net recurring working capital flow retained		$ 1,500
Financing transactions:		
Long-term investment by creditors and owners . .	$ 2,000	
Current maturities and premature retirements of debt.	600	1,400
Capital expenditures, net of receipts from sale of unneeded facilities ($500)		(1,800)
Net change in working capital		$ 1,100
Working capital balance January 1, ...		2,400
Working capital balance December 31		$ 3,500

a better indication of the management's success in serving the owners' objectives if it took into account the consumption of long-lived assets. The working flow statement shows the application of working capital to acquire plant assets, but it does not include those transactions in the computation of net recurring working capital flow, and it does not give any indication of whether the acquisitions were greater or less than the consumption of such properties by use or wastage during the reporting period. A measure of the consumption and loss of service potential embodied in long-lived assets would seem to be an appropriate deduction from revenues in the computation of a net recurring flow to be used as an indicator of the effects of routine operations on the owners' interests.

While this may seem to be a more difficult accounting task than the previous refinements that we assume have been adopted, the accountant may feel that he can improve upon the working flow statement if he simply deducts, from the revenues of each period during which a long-lived asset is expected to be used, a systematically computed portion of the acquisition cost of that asset. The accountant who has worked out such a refined system may also see the need for recognizing some costs that have not yet been paid for and do not require payment in the near future. Some types of pension plans and tax law provisions that permit postponement of the taxation of income are relevant examples. When such factors have been taken into consideration, a net asset flow statement, or earnings and owner's equity statement, reflecting greater use of the accrual and deferral techniques, may be prepared as in EXHIBIT XII-5.

The earnings and owners' equity statement is a great deal more *relevant* than was the original cash receipts and disbursements statement to the objective of telling the businessman, and others interested in his affairs, how successful he has been during the period at increasing his total wealth. He and the other interested observers may feel it is the best type of report that can be prepared for this purpose. However, a particularly curious and perceptive businessman might recognize that his business has some valuable features that are not included within the pale of net assets as defined for the purpose of preparing the earnings and owner's equity statement. He may feel that he has built relationships with

EXHIBIT XII-5
HYPOTHETICAL COMPANY
EARNINGS AND OWNER'S EQUITY STATEMENT
1976

Revenues:

Sales of merchandise and related services $12,000

Interest and miscellaneous earnings 400

Total revenues $12,400

Expenses:

Cost of goods sold . . . . $ 8,000

Selling expenses 1,000

Administrative expenses 1,400

Income taxes 700

Interest expenses 500

Total expenses 11,600

Net recurring earnings . . . . $ 800

Other changes in owner's equity:

Loss on sale of real property . . . . $ (400)

Gain on premature retirement of debt 300 (100)

Dividends declared . . . . (300)

Proceeds of stock issue 2,000

Net change in stockholders' equity . . . . $ 2,400

Stockholders' equity January 1 10,000

Stockholders' equity December 31 . . . . $12,400

customers, suppliers, bankers, and employees which add up to valuable goodwill. He may have invested substantial funds in research and development of new products that are very profitable. He may have paid for employee training that results in "human resources" of considerable value. Or he may have incurred substantial costs in developing accounting and operating systems that are still effective. Having made the decisions involved in the creation of these values, and having observed the contributions these intangibles have been making to his operations, he may feel that he can estimate their values periodically (on a cost or some other basis), and thereby include them in his balance sheet and include the changes in them in his flow statement. (Recognizing that such statements reflect his personal and subjective judgments, he may choose not to show them to his bankers or others—and we do not illustrate them here.) He has now reached the stage of accounting for his *wealth* and for the changes therein; the latter (excluding owner's equity transfers) are referred to as subjective earnings. (Economic capital and economic income—based on the discounting model—constitute still another possible set of concepts on which he might focus.)

In our stroll through the imaginary land of development of flow concepts in accounting, we have encountered five recurring net assets flow concepts which conceivably could be used as measures of operating success. This hypothesized order of development—from cash flow through quick flow and working flow to net recurring earnings and then to subjective earnings—reflects a search for a flow measure that is *relevant* to a major intermediate use of accounting data; appraising performance of activities and their management, which, in turn, is a major step towards many important decisions. The concepts may be summarized as follows:

1. *Cash flow* is the net change in cash plus marketable securities (broad cash) from recurring operations.
2. *Quick flow* is the net change in net short-term monetary assets (net quick assets) from recurring operations.
3. *Working flow*, or current flow, is the net change in working capital (net current assets) from recurring operations.
4. *Net recurring earnings*, or operating profit, is the term for the net change in net assets produced by recurring operations.
5. *Subjective earnings* is the term we have applied to the recurring change in net wealth (assets plus intangibles minus liabilities).

In the next section we apply another criterion—*reliability*.

DIFFERENCES IN FLOW MEASURES ON THE RELIABILITY CRITERION

Differences in the reliability of the several recurring net flow concepts arise from differences in the net asset items that are measured and in the measurement methods that are applied. In order that we may understand these differences, we should first make certain that we understand thoroughly the content of the flow concepts and the pools that are involved. EXHIBIT XII-6 is designed to illustrate the differences among the net recurring flow concepts in terms of the components of each. EXHIBIT XII-7 illustrates the five different net-asset-type pools that are associated with the five flow concepts. Each flow statement reflects changes in the net balance in a net asset (or net wealth) pool. The types of economic events that can affect the different pools are symbolized by the numbered multiple-pointed arrows. Type (1) events involve only accounts included in the "broad cash" pool. Events of types (2), (3), (4), and (5) involve an account within the pool penetrated by the right end of the arrow and an asset, wealth, or liability account outside that pool. The events in types (6) through (10) involve an account in the indicated pool and the residual equity. Examples of the ten categories of events follow:

1. Depositing cash in a bank; purchase or sale of money market instruments held as secondary cash reserves.
2. Collection of receivables; purchase of inventory or plant asset for cash.
3. Purchase of merchandise or plant asset for cash or on account; collection of rent in advance; sale of plant asset for cash or on account.
4. Capital expenditures; borrowing or repayment of long-term debt.
5. Expenditures on intangible investments.
6. Cash receipts that are current revenues, e.g., collection of interest; cash disbursements that are current expenses, e.g., officers' salaries; residual equity holders' investments and withdrawals.
7. Examples in (6); accrual of current revenues or expenses such as interest or property taxes.
8. Examples in (6) and (7); earning of revenue previously deferred and not involving delivery of assets; expiration of prepayments or use of supplies.
9. Examples in (6), (7) and (8); receipt of unrestricted gift of plant asset; depreciation expense.
10. Examples in (6) through (9); buildup of goodwill without specific cost; amortization of goodwill.

Now let's take a look at the reliability of the measurements

Exhibit XII-6
HYPOTHETICAL COMPANY
Asset Flow Statements
1976

	Earnings	*Working Flow*	*Quick Flow*	*Cash Flow*
Inflows:				
From customers				
Sales	$12,000	$12,000	$12,000	$11,600
Collections				
On investments				
Accrued	400	400	400	
Collected				450
Total inflows	$12,400	$12,400	$12,400	$12,050
Outflows:				
Merchandise:				
Cost of merchandise sold	$ 8,000	$ 8,000		

Purchases			$ 8,700	$ 8,400
Paid to suppliers				
Depreciation	600			
Pensions				
Funded	600	600	600	600
Additional	200			
Other operating costs	1,000	1,000	1,000	800
Interest				
Nominal	400	400	400	400
Amortization of discount and issue expense	100			
Income taxes				
Per returns	600	600	600	
Deferred	100			
Paid				500
Total outflows	$11,600	$10,600	$11,300	$10,700
Net recurring inflows	$ 800	$ 1,800	$ 1,100	$ 1,350

EXHIBIT XII-7

FIVE NET ASSET POOLS AND EVENTS AFFECTING EACH

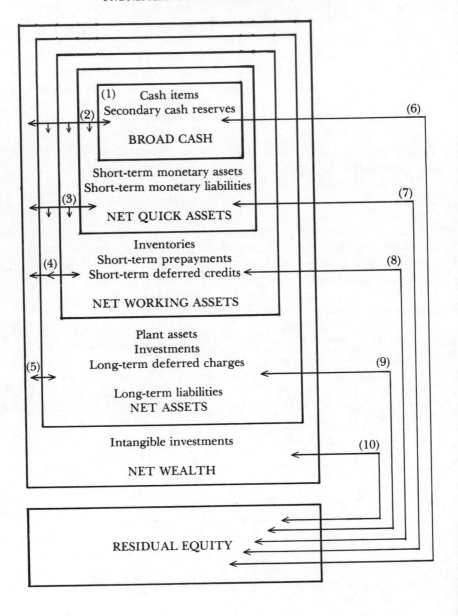

that are involved in accounting for the flows into and out of these five pools. Reporting *cash flows* requires measurement of cash items—and secondary cash reserves if we use the "broad cash" concept. The receivables, inventories, and plant assets on hand at the end of the period need not be measured in order to determine cash flows; if they are measured, the results do not affect the reported cash flows. Cash items generally are subject to measurement with the highest degree of confidence of any balance sheet item; secondary cash reserves, such as government securities, time deposits, and commercial paper, are also subject to measurement with a small margin of error because quotations are typically readily available. The *broad cash* pool, and changes in it, are subject to highly reliable measurement.

As we expand the net asset pool to include short-term receivables and payables we add some measurement problems. Gross receivables may need to be reduced, via a contra account, to provide for cash discounts, sales returns, or "allowances" on amounts billed; disputes sometimes arise in these areas. The risk of uncollectibility (other than due to disputes) must also be faced. In many situations, these complications are minor and the dispersion of a sample of measurements may not be very high; in other cases, as when Brunswick Corporation charged $111 million of uncollectibles against income in 1965, the error can be large. But typically, measurements of *net quick asset* flows are quite reliable, although not as reliable as measurements of broad cash.

The inclusion of inventories, short-term prepayments, and short-term deferred credits adds more substantial measurement problems, especially under historical cost measurements. The types of issues encountered in connection with inventories include the cost flow assumption, disposition of standard cost variances, inclusion of fringe acquisition costs, obsolescence, and lower-of-cost-and-market problems. The lack of uniformity and the arbitrary character of many of the solutions to these issues substantially weaken the reliability and comparability of the measurements of inventories and cost of sales on which *"working flows"* depend.

The next step in the expansion of the pool to be measured also brings us serious measurement problems. The cost inclusion, depreciation and amortization, valuation base, and equity method issues pertaining to noncurrent assets, along with the problems of accounting for deferred taxes and pensions, are formidable indeed, and the reduction in the reliability of the resulting flow measurements that are incorporated in *earnings* is substantial.

Finally, consider the problems of accounting for intangibles such as goodwill (whether "purchased" or not); human resources; assets resulting from research, development, and exploration efforts; and other intangible investments. Adding this set of measurement problems to those previously discussed lowers the reliability of the results so much that many accountants believe the profession would be unwise to expand its work in this area. (At present, the little accounting for intangible investments that is done is strictly superficial.) At best, we must recognize that independent readers of financial statements have a reasonable basis for doubting the usefulness of statements that include intangibles in an attempt to measure *net wealth*, even if the preparers do have faith in them. In fact, there is evidence that security analysts in America have, during the last fifteen years, toyed with the idea of going back another step—to the working flow concept described above. Their doubts about the traditional depreciation, amortization, deferred tax, and pension accounting practices of the accounting profession presumably have been a factor in this flirtation with working flow (usually called "cash flow" by American analysts). Unfortunately, the price of freedom from the most serious measurement errors of traditional accounting is a loss of relevance of the resulting flow measure to the appraisal of operating success. To accountants, this appears to be a classic case of throwing the baby out with the bath water, but to some concerned readers it is a case of ranking reliability of data over relevance—an order of priority with which cost-oriented accountants presumably are familiar.

The astute reader may have detected a paradox in the above discussion. It appears that as we develop net recurring flow concepts, starting with cash flow and "advancing" through quick flow, working flow, and recurring earnings, towards the subjective earnings concept, we are gaining relevance in the sense that the more advanced net recurring flow concepts are more relevant measures of the operating success of the enterprise. Subjective earnings are closer to what owners and owner-oriented observers would like to know as a basis for their various decisions. But is it not also true that "advancing" towards earnings and subjective earnings requires the accountant to utilize less relevant measurement methods? According to our analysis in chapter VII, measurements made on the basis of the face value of cash items, contractual evidence of future cash flows (discounted or not), and current market prices (exit or entry) yield more relevant data than measurements made at historical cost, restated historical cost, or the equity method. Under current, or likely near-future, accounting practices, cash items, secondary cash reserves, and short-term monetary assets and liabilities typically are measured by one of the more relevant methods, while the plant assets and intangible investments that must be measured in order to compute earnings or subjective earnings are likely to be measured by one of the less relevant techniques.[2] In other words, advancing to a more relevant net recurring flow concept requires use of less relevant measurement methods. How can we explain this? A subsequent paragraph offers one possible explanation.

Manipulation of Net Recurring Flow Measures

One aspect of the reliability of net recurring flow measures is the extent to which they are subject to manipulation by the management (including accountants) of the entity. Manipulation is a consequence of bias, the lack of which contributes to reliability (see chapter III). We will consider two types of manipulation: (1) operating manipulation, sometimes called "structuring the transaction," in the sense of choosing from among alternative types or timings of transactions with other entities in order to influence the operating results of the period; and (2) accounting manipulation, or choosing from among alternative accounting methods in order to influence the reported results.

---

[2] Or consider the alternative measurements related to cost of the products sold by the entity. Quick flow is charged with the purchases of goods which are measured by the amount of cash paid or accounts payable incurred, so the measurement method used is either face value of cash or future cash flow. Working flow, earnings, and subjective earnings, on the other hand, require measurement of the beginning and ending inventory—usually on a cost basis—in order to compute the cost of goods sold. It would not be much of an exaggeration to say that the cost of goods sold (under GAAP) reflects an irrelevant measurement of a relevant flow, while the inclusion of the purchases number in the computation of quick flow involves a relevant measurement of an irrelevant flow.

Operating manipulation. The *subjective earnings* measure may be influenced, in some entities, by choosing the period into which sales fall. Opportunities arise in some industries for speeding up or delaying the specific event that determines the record date of the sales transaction. Other opportunities may arise in relation to inventories. If the firm is on a specific identification basis of accounting for inventories and cost of goods sold, the choice of which unit to deliver, when more than one unit is on hand with different costs, can affect earnings. If the last-in, first-out cost flow assumption prevails, there may be an opportunity to choose between "dipping into basic LIFO stocks" or purchasing goods near the year-end to avoid such an effect. Most importantly, under the historical cost and historical receipt measurement methods, opportunities exist for achieving "instant earnings" or "instant losses" by liquidating undervalued or overvalued assets or liabilities (although many of these liquidations would not be included in the recurring flow measure). Most of these types of operating manipulations would affect earnings and working flow as well as subjective earnings.[3]

In addition to the above possibilities, *earnings* and *working flow* may be manipulated by timing discretionary expenditures on such items as maintenance (assuming it would affect the measurement of plant assets under the subjective earnings concept) and on "intangible investments" such as training, research, exploration, development, and improvements of accounting and operating systems. If expenditures on these intangibles are capitalized under the subjective earnings concept, manipulating their timing would not affect subjective earnings, but if they are charged to expense on a cash basis (as in computing GAAP earnings) their timing is crucial.

The *quick flow* measure of operating success is subject to influence by the above techniques plus by control of the timing of purchases near the end of a period (since purchases are not matched with sales). Periodic quick flow could be influenced very materially

---

[3]One could argue, contrary to the view just presented, that none of these opportunities for manipulation would be present if a subjective earnings concept were being implemented because that concept does not depend upon the objective manifestations of value changes that were mentioned in the examples given.

either by letting the inventory run down or by building it up near the end of the period. The advantage of controlling the timing of period-end sales is also much greater on the quick flow basis, because shifting the timing affects the quick flow by the entire selling price rather than by only the gross margin, as when costs are matched with inflows (in the more advanced flow measures). The *cash flow* concept gives managers the maximum operating control over the reported net recurring flow because it adds to the preceding opportunities the opportunity to control many cash disbursements, including payments to suppliers, plus, to some extent in many circumstances, a greater degree of control over inflows from cooperative customers. The general pattern revealed by this brief review is one of a minimal opportunity for operating manipulation of the subjective earnings flow measure, increasing opportunity as we move through the GAAP earnings, working flow, and quick flow measures to cash flow, which provides the greatest opportunity for operating manipulation.

Accounting manipulation. Here is another matter altogether: we encounter more opportunities for manipulation as we advance from cash flow to the "more relevant" measures of operating success. What choices of *cash flow* accounting methods are available? If we were to think hard enough we no doubt could come up with some type of borderline asset with respect to classification as a cash item or a secondary cash reserve, but the variations are likely to be minor. As we move to *quick flow*, we face a few more significant choices. The most obvious ones involve accounting for uncollectible receivables, but choices may also be available in the areas of cash discounts on sales and purchases, partial billing of work done, and accrual of property taxes.

The number of accounting choices available to a management bent on controlling the reported results increases substantially with the adoption of *working flow* as the key measure of success. Most such choices relate to inventory accounting because inventories are the major group of accounts that are added to the net asset pool that is the focus of attention. Choices may be available in writing down obsolete, slow-moving, or damaged merchandise; in selecting a cost flow assumption, in disposing of standard cost variances; in deciding on which fixed overhead costs to include in inventories; in applying the lower-of-cost-and-market method; and, in some industries, in choosing a basic measurement method.

Preparation of an *earnings* statement requires still more choices—those pertaining to plant assets, deferred taxation, and pension accounting figuring most prominently. The plant asset accounting choices include those involving capitalization of fringe acquisition costs, estimates of salvage valves and of service flow lives and patterns, and treatment of the investment credit. The *subjective earnings* flow measure involves most of the previously mentioned accounting choices plus those involving lives, service flow patterns, and unscheduled write-offs of intangible investments. The general trend clearly is toward more and more choices, estimates, and judgments as we switch to the more relevant measures of operating success, and each of these decision points provides an opportunity to control the reported results if the management is so inclined.

Conclusions Regarding Alternative Assets Flow Measures

The above discussion has been aimed at familiarizing the reader with five alternative possible net recurring asset flow measures, which have some potential value to users who want to predict the entity's liquidity and/or prospects for achieving owners' goals. We found variations among the measures with respect to (1) their relevance to the task of judging operating success, (2) the reliability of the measures as indicators of what they purport to represent, (3) their susceptibility to operating manipulation, and (4) their susceptibility to accounting manipulation. The general patterns of these variations are illustrated in EXHIBIT XII-8.

We left the reader to ponder the seeming paradox that less relevant measurement methods are used to obtain a more relevant measure of operating success. Consider this explanation: as we develop more relevant measures of success and utilize less relevant measurement methods we are not switching from a more relevant to a less relevant method of measuring any net asset item. The change consists of the substitution of a relatively irrelevant method for no measurement at all as we enlarge the net asset pool under examination by adding relevant items measured by relatively irrelevant methods. It is not unreasonable to think of the result

EXHIBIT XII-8
COMPARISON OF FIVE FLOW CONCEPTS ON FOUR DIMENSIONS

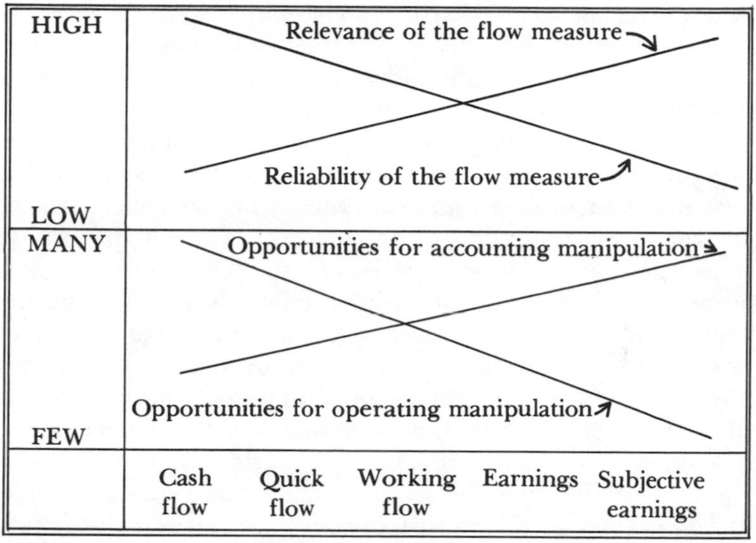

HIGH	Relevance of the flow measure
LOW	Reliability of the flow measure
MANY	Opportunities for accounting manipulation
FEW	Opportunities for operating manipulation
	Cash flow Quick flow Working flow Earnings Subjective earnings

as yielding a more relevant net asset flow measure.

One final observation may be of interest. It appears that the opportunities for accounting manipulation of earnings (and subjective earnings) could be reduced by tightening up on the alternatives and estimates permitted or required by GAAP, whereas there is no known remedy for the operating manipulation possibilities associated with the cash flow and quick flow measures. In other words, there is room for optimism about earnings accounting but not about cash flow accounting—as a measure of operating success. Cash flow accounting for the purpose of helping users judge the liquidity prospects of the entity is another matter which will be taken up in subsequent pages.

ACCOUNTING FOR LIQUIDITY

Many experienced businessmen argue that the two critical requirements for the continued successful operation of a business are maintenance of profitability and liquidity. This view is perfectly consistent with the emphasis we have placed on predicting the firm's capacity to pay and measuring the cash flow potential of assets and liabilities. Until this point in the book, however, we have concentrated very heavily on the total cash flow potential of the firm in the long run and have not attempted to segregate short-run cash flow potential. In this section we turn to the area of providing information relevant to the prediction of the firm's short-run liquidity. We believe that such predictions are relevant to the decisions of investors and others who are concerned with the firm's future capacity to pay, including the managers who are charged with the responsibility of maintaining the firm's solvency, keeping it in a position to take advantage of business opportunities that require cash, and planning its new financing. We also believe that some of the measurement and reporting techniques that are helpful in providing such information are within the pale of customary accounting methodology, and so we consider this topic appropriate for consideration here.

In view of the above observations, it seems strange that the official and sponsored literature of accounting gives so little explicit consideration to liquidity. For example, liquidity is not listed in the index to Grady's "Inventory" (1965). One might expect it to be discussed in the official positions on funds statements (or statements of changes in financial position), but a quick perusal of *APB Opinions No. 3* and *No. 19* and the Accounting Standards Steering Committee *Statement of Standard Accounting Practice No. 10* yields no information on the subject. There is, however, some academic literature on the specific subject of liquidity (Bierman, 1960; Sorter and Benston, 1960; Lemke, 1970) as well as some explicit attention to it in several articles dealing with funds statements, especially in that by Rosen and DeCoster (1969).

The literature on business failures could have developed the concept of liquidity, inasmuch as failure is generally viewed as synonomous with a failure to maintain liquidity, but a search of that literature proved fruitless. The fine empirical work that has been done in this area has not been accompanied by significant theoretical work.

This minimal explicit attention to liquidity contrasts sharply with the undercurrent of concern that is detectable in traditional accounting practices and literature. "Captions of assets and liabilities are to be arranged in the order of liquidity, as a general rule" (The Business Accounting Deliberation Council, Ministry of Finance, Japan, 1974, p. 8). "We think that the implicit ranking of goods by liquidity pervades accounting thought and practice" (Sterling and Flaherty, 1971, p. 455). The "realization principle" has had a great deal of influence on practice. It is usually interpreted as meaning that independent measurements of assets in the operating cycle are not made—that is, cost is not departed from—until cash or a claim to cash is received. In my opinion, much of the resistance to write-ups of assets has been based on the belief that profit should not be reported until it has appeared in the form of a liquid asset. Textbooks in financial accounting generally discuss the current ratio and the "acid-test," or liquidity ratio. It has often been said that concern with the credit-granting process was a dominant consideration in the choice of accounting practices in the late nineteenth century when the accounting profession was developing rapidly. And, of course, the credit-granting decision calls for a prediction of liquidity.

If liquidity is, and should be, of concern to managers, investors, and accountants, as we argue above, how can we account for it? Does the practice of giving it very little explicit attention serve satisfactorily? At present, accountants appear to be attempting to provide information about liquidity and changes in liquidity through the same financial statements that are used for reporting on wealth and income. But accounting for liquidity clearly takes a back seat.

We suggest that one of the major current debates in accounting—exit values versus other bases of valuation—reflects a difference in the role assigned to the basic accounting system with respect to reporting liquidity. Chambers certainly has presented an eloquent argument for the relevance of "the market selling price or realizable price of any or all goods held" (1966, p. 92) to the market decisions of actors. This idea is the basis for his definition of financial position: "Financial position may be defined as the capacity of an entity at a point of time for engaging in exchanges" (p. 81). "An asset is defined as any severable means in the possession of an entity" (p. 103). Service potential or cash flow potential through holding is not enough; the "means" must be subject to separation. Chambers prefers to measure all assets at their current realizable prices, whether they are held for sale or for use.

Sterling agrees on the importance of the selling prices of assets held: "They are necessary to define market alternatives, they express the investment required to hold assets and they are a component of a risk indicator. For all of these reasons, I conclude that the items on the balance sheet should be valued at their present selling prices" (1972, p. 208). Nothing is said about the use of financial statements in predicting the future cash flows from the firm to investors in the long run. Is it fair to say that those accounting theorists favoring the general use of exit values and those favoring future cash flows and surrogates therefore really differ in their relative emphasis on accounting for liquidity versus accounting for wealth? Looking at the accounting profession as a whole, one might be tempted to conclude that the subconscious effort to report on both liquidity and wealth in one set of statements is producing schizophrenia.

In chapter XI we suggested that the interests of investors and managers were focused strongly on cash and related items and on the residual equity—the upper left corner and lower right corner of the traditional American balance sheet. At this point we would like to pursue several questions pertaining to our concern with the upper left corner. First, what is the essence of the liquidity concept? How can it be measured? Does "proper" accounting for liquidity require both a liquidity-oriented stocks statements and a liquidity flow statement, or is only the latter needed? What form should liquidity statements take?

The Liquidity Concept

Definitions of liquidity are notably missing from the literature of accounting. We believe the essence of the liquidity concept is *short-term capacity to pay*. Liquidity is desirable in order that the entity be able to meet its obligations as they fall due and thereby avoid insolvency and possible bankruptcy. It is also desirable in order that a firm may be able to take advantage of business opportunities that may arise. Liquidity is necessary because of the *uncertainty* inherent in cash flow projections. Inaccurate projections, lack of profitability, and application of funds to the expansion of operating capacity are the basic causes of illiquidity.

Liquidity is based on liquid assets and any liabilities that are viewed as restrictions on those assets. The primary attribute of a liquid asset is *quickness of convertibility to cash*. Cash is, of course, the ultimate liquid asset. A secondary attribute, which we believe most businessmen expect of a liquid asset, is a *lack of adverse consequences to the entity from the conversion of the asset to cash*. The most likely adverse consequences are (a) impairment of operating capacity and (b) the sacrifice of existing wealth, that is, a loss.

If liquidity is to be an important secondary focal point of accounting, and if accountants are to measure and report on liquidity stocks and flows, the essence of the liquidity concept as stated above needs to be converted to an operational form. We have indicated that timing of convertibility is important. But timing differences are differences of degree, not principle. How can we set a cutoff point on the time continuum? Any definite cutoff point we set is bound to be more or less arbitrary. If, for example, we say that liquid assets must be convertible to cash within one year without adverse consequences, then we would be including in the liquid pool all those assets convertible within 365 days but none of those that take more than 366 days. In an intuitive sense, there may be as great a difference in the liquidity of two assets with due dates 300 and 360 days from now as between the latter asset and one due in 420 days. In other words, the dichotomous classification of assets as either liquid or illiquid tends to obscure the fact that there can be changes in liquidity from transactions affecting only items in the pool, and changes from transactions affecting only items out of the pool, as well as changes from transactions crossing the pool boundary. Perhaps this observation should lead us to avoid a liquid–illiquid basis of classification (as well as a current–noncurrent distinction). But before selecting that route, let's consider the possibility of making a feasible and useful distinction.

If we view degrees of liquidity as a continuum, can we identify any sharp slopes and plateaus as we move down from the most liquid to the least liquid assets? In a particular firm with a particular set of assets this would not be terribly difficult, but to identify such break points for application to all firms is difficult. Nevertheless, we will be so rash as to suggest that there are significant and identifiable distinctions between (a) cash items, (b) other assets that can be converted to cash within the period of time allowed for settling transactions on the securities exchanges (currently five working days in the United States), (c) other assets that are readily convertible within the period of the normal credit terms allowed customers of the firm, and (d) other less liquid assets. The classification of liabilities follows that of assets. On the assumption that dichotomous classification is appropriate, we believe that either the break between (b) and (c) or that between (c) and (d) would be the most useful to parties interested in appraising the liquidity position of a typical business firm. The practical difficulties involved in distinguishing between items falling into group (c) and those falling into group (d), together with the generally accepted definition of a liquid asset ("cash in banks and on hand . . . or a readily marketable investment" [Kohler, 1970, p. 265]), lead us to prefer the former cutoff point: *liquid assets are cash and those convertible into cash within a week without loss or impairment of operating capacity.* (An accumulated, unrealized loss on a security held would not be a loss on conversion.) Receivables should only be included if an entire class of claims fits this description on the basis of the normal credit terms, as in brokerage transactions not involving securities held on margin. While it could be argued that certain commodity stocks could be included in the description of liquid assets, we suggest that the issue be minimized by never permitting their inclusion.

Reporting on Liquidity

   Now we turn to the question of whether a separate set of statements is needed to report on liquidity. The previous discussion was based on the implicit assumption that flows of liquidity would be reported in a flow statement based on the same stocks measurements that are used in the wealth and profitability accounting system. This is the pattern followed in funds statements. Alternatively, a liquidity reporting system could include separate measurements of stocks of liquidity and changes in those stocks. A double-entry system could be developed to record measurements of all assets at NRV (net realizable value), liabilities at current liquidation value, and the difference as the residual equity (which may be negative in some going concerns). Changes in the residual equity would be flows of liquidity. A "contraction" of liquidity would be recorded when cash is committed to specialized resources such as intangible investments, specialized buildings, and specialized machinery; "expansions" of liquidity would be reflected in the accounts when the specialized resources were converted to marketable products, receivables, and cash. The typical short-term operating cycle would involve a contraction of liquidity at the beginning and expansions in the later stages. (Note that this discussion implies a broader definition of liquid assets than that given in the preceding paragraph.)

In the absence of significant experience with such a liquidity accounting system, we are inclined to speculate that its operating costs would be substantial. The major problem would be the obtaining of reliable estimates of the net realizable values of specialized plant assets and work in process; an independent appraiser may have to be engaged for such work. Reference to the nine criteria of chapter III lead us to the tentative conclusion that liquidity is best reported via a liquidity flow statement based on a liquid assets pool carved out of the wealth accounts, together with a liquid assets section of the comparative balance sheets. The ensuing discussion will reflect this conclusion.

EXHIBIT XII-9 is a liquidity flow statement based on the data used earlier in this chapter in the development of alternative asset flow statements. In this example, the liquid asset pool is identical with cash, as the company has no secondary cash reserves. Both the routine inflows and the routine outflows normally associated with working capital items (incidental liabilities, inventories, and prepayments) are included in the recurring section at the amounts shown on the income statement on the grounds that flows at different rates are inconsistent with the level of activities during the period and should, therefore, be considered nonrecurring. Thus, either an increase or a decrease in inventories is a nonrecurring item in a steady state firm, as is a change in receivables or payables. For this reason, the changes in short-term balances are included in the nonrecurring section of the statement. The amounts of the routine outflows related to the current level of operations should be computed at current prices without any impact of "inventory profits" or losses.

EXHIBIT XII-9
HYPOTHETICAL COMPANY
CASH FLOW STATEMENT II
1976

Routine operating activities

Inflows related to the level of revenues in the period		$12,400
Outflows for expenses requiring working capital currently:*		
Variable with volume of revenue or shipments	$ 8,600	
Nonvariable, committed cash expenses	1,000	
Nonvariable, discretionary cash expenses	400	
Cash expense contingent on earnings (income taxes)	600	(10,600)
Net cash flow from routine activities		$ 1,800
Dividends paid		(350)
Routine cash flow retained		$ 1,450

Nonrecurring activities

Adjustments of above cash flows due to changes in

short-term, noncash balances:

Increase in receivables	$ (350)	
Increase in inventories less increase in accounts payable	(400)	
Increase in incidental liabilities	300	(450)
Long-term investment transactions:		
Purchases of new plant assets (less dispositions for $500)		(1,800)
Financing activities:		
Issuance of common stock for cash	$ 2,000	
Current maturities and premature retirements of debt	(600)	1,400
Net change in cash and secondary cash reserves		$ 600
Balance of cash and secondary cash reserves, January 1		500
Balance of cash and secondary cash reserves, December 31		$ 1,100

*These outflows are calculated at prices prevailing in the current period for quantities required for the current level of sales; changes in inventory and liability balances are shown separately. Resources typically purchased more than a year in advance of usage (services of plant assets) are excluded from the recurring section. Expenses involving long-term liabilities (pensions, long-term leases, deferred taxes) are included in the recurring section on a cash basis.

Long-term items are treated differently. The cash payments on pensions and long-term lease liabilities are included as routine outflows, whereas the cash payments for plant assets are completely omitted from the routine section. The differential treatment is justified by the typically committed nature of the disbursements on pension and lease contracts, whereas cash outlays on plant assets have more of a discretionary character.

We suggest that an effort be made to classify the routine outlays in a way that has a chance of being helpful to a reader who is attempting to predict the liquidity effects of changes in the volume and profitability of operations. Contingent interest, royalties, rents, and taxes that would decline if earnings or volume declined can be set out separately. A note regarding the circumstances under which they would differ substantially may be helpful. If feasible, distinguishing between discretionary and committed outflows would also appear to be helpful. The variable–fixed distinction is aimed at permitting the reader to estimate the effects of volume changes on liquidity.

Concluding Comments on Liquidity

I recommend the substitution of a *liquidity flow statement* (or cash flow statement) for the funds statement or statement of changes in financial position. These latter statements have lacked a clear focus and have reflected a great deal of confusion with respect to objectives. The "all financial resources" concept of funds which has been advocated in some literature is essentially no concept of funds other than a balance sheet concept. The statement of changes in financial position provides for a rehash of the comparative balance sheet data but is tied to the income statement. The problem was recognized by Rosen and DeCoster (1969, p. 136) before *APB Opinion No. 19,* "Reporting Changes in Financial Position," appeared:

> Basically, the "funds" statement (in all its varieties) is being required to report all items of financial information and perspectives not disclosed by the income statement, balance sheet, and statement of retained earnings. This means that the "funds" statement must report changes in some definition of liquidity, reveal all important "inter-entity" transactions,

somehow reconcile the cash (or "near-cash") and accrual bases of accounting, be flexible, report different perspectives, and readily communicate with laymen. Surely accountants are asking one report to accomplish too much.

According to Spiller and Virgil (1974, p. 132), the situation has not improved since *Opinion No. 19* was issued:

> The purpose of the funds statement needs to be resolved. The funds statement should either report on flows into and out of some corpus of funds or serve to classify the different kinds of changes that occur in designated balance sheet categories or accounts. Strains of both purposes appear in Opinion No. 19, and the typical funds statement after Opinion No. 19 is a curious blend of practices serving both purposes.

We suggest that this confusion be eliminated by converting the funds statement to a statement aimed at reporting events changing a specific pool of liquid assets, including the financing and investment transactions which have such great effects on liquidity. There is no need to tie the liquidity flow statement to a wealth flow (income) statement; let's make them separate but equal. As a statement of changes in a liquid asset pool—a reconciliation of the beginning and ending balances of liquid assets just as the income and retained earnings statement reconciles retained earnings balances—the liquidity flow statement is tied to a specific section of the balance sheet. Not only should the balance sheet clearly show the liquid asset items and total in a separate section, but the chart of accounts should carefully distinguish between liquid assets and illiquid assets that are otherwise similar. Inasmuch as transactions involving financing and investments are generally understood to affect liquidity, any "bypassing" transactions, such as the issuance of securities for real property, should be "run through" the liquid asset pool on the report (with full disclosure of the nature of the transaction, of course).

Some of the interest in funds statements, as suggested in the first part of this chapter, has been associated with the thought that the net recurring funds flow from operations could be viewed as a "hard" income number, that is, a version of income pruned of the "soft," less reliable measurements of amortization and depreciation. We suggest that such a role not be assigned to the

liquidity flow statement. The value of being able to adjust some
income statement items to a "harder" basis is not denied, but
we suggest that the supplementary information required to do
so be provided in the income statement by (a) placing the hard
measurement and the soft part on separate lines, such as the
current and deferred portions of income taxes, (b) parenthetical
disclosures on the income statement, or (c) disclosure in accompanying notes.[4] (What about information required to convert
to a softer income statement, such as information for capitalizing
and amortizing research, development, and human resources
costs?) The inclusion of a genuine liquidity flow statement in the
set of customary financial statements should free accountants to
neglect liquidity on the income statements; they need not hesitate
to accrue, discount, and revalue freely in accordance with the
criteria of good accounting methods established in chapter III.
It follows that liquidity reporting reduces neither the importance
nor the difficulty of distinguishing those items of wealth (positive
or negative) that are includable on balance sheets from those that
are not.

Finally, we remind the reader that the criteria of chapter III
are fully applicable to decisions involving accounting for liquidity.
For example, we are seeking a version of liquidity which is most
relevant to the decisions of readers of financial statements—especially decisions which would be aided by some judgment of the
entity's near future capacity to pay. We want to define a pool
of net liquid assets which can be measured with a high degree
of *reliability*; that is, we want the reader to be able to depend
on the reported pool of liquidity as being genuine. The *comparability*
criterion is particularly critical in this area of accounting because
a classification made on the basis of degree rather than principle
is a fragile one; we can easily visualize similar items falling on

---

[4] Examples of areas in which "hard conversion" information might be disclosed
are amortization of exploration costs, income taxes, pension costs, and income
from affiliates reported on the equity method.

One could argue that the general inclusion of funds statements in annual reports
permitted the APB to choose softer accounting methods in some cases, e.g., the
equity method of accounting for common stock investments in unconsolidated
affiliates, tax allocation, and imputed interest.

different sides of the liquidity boundary in different periods or different entities, thus weakening the comparability of the liquidity reports. *Timeliness* of liquidity reporting may be more critical than in the case of profitability reporting because of its short-run orientation, so interim liquidity flow statements appear to be as valuable as annual statements. Meeting the *effects via other parties* criterion requires careful description and full disclosure of many transactions because investments in inventories, plant assets, intangibles, and other illiquid assets involve liquidity outflows, while sales of illiquid assets produce liquidity inflows; we must try to discourage readers from interpreting these flows as "bad" or "good" in connection with appraisals of management performance unless liquidity is a particularly important issue in the reporting period. Otherwise, managers may shun profitable investments and be too eager to sell existing assets in order to look good in the liquidity flow statement. Separation of recurring and nonrecurring flows is helpful in this regard. The *optimal quantity, cost,* and *intelligibility* criteria have their usual roles in decisions involving accounting for liquidity.

ACCOUNTING FOR RISK

We begin our discussion of risk accounting by referring back to the discussion in chapter IV of the need for financial information in making decisions. There we suggested that creditors, owners, managers, and others could use data relevant to predictions of the entity's capacity to pay. For the present purpose, these information needs may be divided into two segments: information for predicting the firm's capacity to make future payments that are fixed in amount by contracts, and information for predicting residual payouts. Decisions regarding granting credit, making loans, or investing in fixed income securities normally involve either an estimate of the probability of default or a quality rating which substitutes for such a quantitative estimate. The latter is exemplified by the credit ratings of agencies such as Dun and Bradstreet and the bond ratings of Standard & Poor's, Moody's, and Fitch Investors' Service. The literature of "trade credit" analysis includes quantitative models incorporating a variable for the probability of insolvency (Archer and D'Ambrosio, 1972, p. 344).

In general, the meaning of risk in connection with investments in fixed obligations is the chance of the obligor failing to pay on time in accordance with the contract. Such a failure almost always involves a loss (compared with the outcome if payment had been made on time), although the loss may range from a small loss of interest or administrative and legal costs to loss of the entire amount due plus administrative and legal costs.

Risk has a roughly analogous meaning in relation to residual securities such as common shares, convertible securities, participating preference shares, and ownership interests in unincorporated enterprises. Any reduction in the periodic return (dividend) or in the quoted price of the security is an event encompassed in the concept of risk in its traditional, popular meaning. Graham and Dodd incorporated the risk factor in their judgment of the appropriate multiplier to apply to estimated earnings. The AAA model included a specific "certainty equivalent factor" of less than one, which was to be used in conjunction with a risk-free discount rate in calculating the present value of future cash flows. (See chapter IV.)

In the late 1950s, the "two-parameter" model of portfolio choice was introduced. Prior to that time it was customary for economists to recognize that investors need to estimate the *return* to be realized on a security, but *risk* was only thought of as a modifying, unquantifiable consideration. The addition of risk as a second parameter to be estimated in judging the suitability of a security for a portfolio was a major step in the development of portfolio theory and has accounting implications which have been generally neglected. The variance of the distribution of returns is commonly accepted as a measure of risk. (The variance is computed as

$$\sigma^2(A) = \left[\sum_{t=1}^{n}(A_t - \bar{A})^2\right]\Big/ n$$

where A_t is the return—normally dividend or interest plus change in price—on security A in period t.) It is not intuitively obvious that variance is the best measure of risk, as it does not correspond to the traditional concern with "downside risk," or chance of a reduction in return from the present or "normal" level, and it incorporates the "quadratic loss function" popular among statisticians.

More recent portfolio theory recognizes a distinction between *systematic risk* (β), which reflects the volatility of a specific security (or a particular portfolio) in relation to movements in the market prices of some broad class of securities, and *individual security risk*, which is independent of general market movements. The former is due to factors that affect the prices of the whole class of securities included in the "market," while the latter is due to peculiar factors impinging on the individual firm. Individual security risk can be eliminated by diversification because the sources of the risk are unique to the firm. As a first approximation, one may hypothesize that greater individual security risk is not associated with greater returns; that is, the market does not compensate investors for bearing individual security risk because it need not be borne but can be avoided by diversification. But diversification is costly (due to higher percentage commissions on small trades, more analysis and record-keeping work), so there may be some value in predicting individual security risk. In addition, predictions of systematic risk in a security are needed if the investor wishes to select those securities which offer the combination of risk and return best suited to his circumstances and tastes.[5]

An alternative view is that risk analysis would seem to be made unnecessary by the combination of (a) a perfectly efficient market for common stocks and (b) the opportunity to choose an acceptable risk-return combination by investing in a representative sample of the market and either borrowing (to achieve a higher return and accompanying higher risk) or investing part of one's assets in a risk-free security (thereby reducing the risk and return). But it is generally recognized that the market cannot be efficient without the presence of nonbelievers (in market efficiency), so we must assume that there is a role for risk-relevant financial data in the making of common stock investment decisions. The need for such data in credit-granting and investment banking decisions is even more apparent. It appears that an estimate of the probability

---

[5] Some aspects of the theory of finance which are particularly relevant to accountants, including portfolio theory and the efficiency of capital markets, are neatly summarized in Lev (1974a, chapters 12–15).

of a significant decline in the company's liquidity is relevant to
both areas of risk analysis (credit and residual equity), so no
distinction need be made by the accountant.

Risk, Flows, and Stocks

Risk and uncertainty in business operations are related to the
timing and amounts of inflows and outflows of assets. If perfect
certainty characterized all business activities, the returns to investors
(in the broad sense) would also be certain—both because certainty
of other flows would permit the computation and scheduling of
the returns to investors and because the latter are included in
"all business activities." In the world as it exists, however, provision
must be made for uncertainty. One method of providing for
uncertainty is to carry a stock of an asset, such as cash or inventory,
to buffer temporarily unequal inflows and outflows. Thus, businessmen are willing to pay a premium in the form of costs of
holding stocks of goods in order to ensure against "stock-outs."
(Inventories are also carried in order to purchase in more economical lots and to provide merchandise for display to customers.)

A major risk that concerns investors in an enterprise is risk
of insolvency, that is, loss of liquidity. Avoiding insolvency requires
firms to carry a stock of cash, or "broad cash," to buffer the
unbalanced flows. A decline in profit is also a risk which concerns
the residual equity holder. To creditors, a decline in profit is
of concern primarily because it increases the probability of insolvency. The net worth of a company helps buffer creditors from
the effects of a period of negative profitability.

The amount of buffer stock (of goods or cash) that is needed
is entirely dependent upon the firm's ability to match its flows.
If the manager were able to predict demand for goods perfectly
and could purchase economically in any size lot, and if he could
depend on goods ordered arriving on schedule, he could match
his incoming orders and his shipments to customers in such a
way as to avoid the necessity of carrying an inventory. In some
cases, it is possible for a manager to control the outflow without
loss of sales, thus reducing the importance of predicting demand.
If not, absence of any of the conditions mentioned above provides
a reason for carrying an inventory. The most economical average

level of inventory to carry depends on the variability of the inflows and outflows; the wider the unpredictable fluctuations in the flows the larger the buffer required to absorb them. The exact shape of the curve relating minimum planned stock level to some measure of variability of flows (such as the variance of daily outflows) is a matter for students of inventory theory to consider.

In general, the same observations apply to cash. If variations in inflows cannot be offset on a daily basis by variations in outflows, maintenance of solvency requires holding a stock of cash. The cost of capital incurred to hold cash is the price paid to reduce the probability of insolvency. Since the probability of insolvency can never be reduced to zero, and since the incremental cost of reducing it another one percent presumably increases sharply as zero probability is approached, the probability of insolvency in any future accounting period tends to be materially greater than zero. In such circumstances, there is bound to be a demand for risk-relevant information.

Risk-Relevant Data in Accounting Reports

In line with the preceding discussion of the need for a stock of liquidity when flows are not balanced, it appears that the investor who is concerned with predicting either a potential loss of liquidity or a decline in earnings and net worth must focus attention on the inflow-outflow relationships, buffer stocks, and stock-flow relationships. We begin with *inflow-outflow relationships*.

The cash flow statement illustrated in EXHIBIT XII-9 was designed to provide information for predicting liquidity. It should be clear that the categories of routine outflows listed there cannot be used with perfect reliability; in fact, serious problems are likely to arise in their use in many enterprises. But to the extent that this classification scheme is feasible, the information it yields would appear to have some relevance to predictions of the liquidity effects of repeating the operations of the reporting period in the future and of changing the volume of revenue-producing activities. For example, we see that the net routine cash flow is running at about 15 percent of the gross routine flow, thus providing a substantial flow for management's use in replacement of long-term assets, paying dividends, expansion, or repaying debt. The variable margin (contribution margin) percentage is approximately 30 percent.

When this is divided into the net routine cash flow before contingent expenses ($2,400), we find that any reduction of sales volume up to around 65 percent ($8,000) would still yield a cash flow which would cover the other expenses. A still deeper decline in sales could be absorbed by temporarily foregoing the services classified as discretionary expenses. Similar calculations could be made in relation to the common dividend or the preferred dividend if one were being paid. These computations are easy when this type of statement is available. Preparing such a statement is not so easy.

This type of cash flow analysis must be viewed as essentially short-run oriented. In the long run, plant assets must be replaced if the firm is to continue its operations. The computation of income, or earnings, allows for the costs of all services consumed in the production of revenue, so it gives a clearer picture of the effects of continued operation under the conditions prevailing in the reporting period. The income statement, therefore, can be helpful in predicting long-run liquidity. Some of the relevant relationships include (1) net recurring income as a percentage of gross revenues, and (2) coverage of the common dividend, the preferred dividend, interest charges and, in some cases, interest and other fixed charges (although it is often difficult to achieve adequate comparability among companies due to variations in the nature and extent of leasing arrangements and other factors).

Stocks reported on the balance sheet represent the buffers between unbalanced flows. If a balance sheet is to provide the most helpful risk-relevant information, it should include classifications that permit the computation of a short-term monetary ratio (short-term monetary assets to short-term monetary liabilities), the current ratio, working capital, and the debt-equity ratio (or the coverage of net monetary liabilities by net nonmonetary assets for those analysts preferring this measure). More generally, the importance of the *timing of cash flows* suggests that an effort should be made to provide information about the times (maturities) as well as the present values of future cash flows appearing as assets and liabilities. The accountant should also be conscious of the reader's need to judge the *reliability* of the indicated timing and amounts, and to take that need into consideration when deciding on the classification and description of balance sheet items. The extent to which the future cash flows are dependent upon other parties and their financial capacity, legal obligation to perform, and satisfaction with the performance of the reporting entity affects the reliability of the indicated flows. Thus, the distinction between a receivable (claim to cash) and merchandise may be important enough to make the legal concept of a sale relevant. Also, the distinction beween incidental trade obligations and financing liabilities should not be obscured, as the analyst may want to offset the former against short-term monetary assets in computing the debt-equity ratio.

Relationships between buffer stocks and rates of flows are also relevant to predicting liquidity and the firm's ability to maintain its net worth. The financial statements should provide the information needed to compute the relationships between the balance of either "broad cash" or net short-term monetary assets and annual revenues, so that the reader may see how large a cash flow deficit could be absorbed by the stock of liquid, or nearly liquid, assets. For example, if annual revenues approximate $1 million and the balance of cash and secondary cash reserves is $150,000, a cash flow deficit of 15 percent of revenues could be borne for one year before the firm's liquidity was reduced to zero. Or, if there is a balance of net short-term monetary liabilities, the reader may want to state it in terms of the time required for it to be covered by net routine cash flow at the current rate of flow. The liquidity flow statement and balance sheet should provide the data needed for making these short-term liquidity tests.

The most popular measure of a company's ability to maintain the value of its owners' equity in the long run is the return on net worth. Financial statements normally provide the data needed for this calculation, although there are still too many cases of unclassified "reserves," which the reader must either include or exclude in owners' equity on the basis of inadequate information.

In addition to the above comments regarding the supplying of financial statement data pertaining to flows, stocks, and stock-flow relationships, we offer a few additional suggestions regarding financial data that might be useful in assessing risk.

1. The balance sheet should permit readers to rank claimants on the basis of their legal priority in bankruptcy, e.g., general creditors, subordinate creditors, shareholders with preferential claims, and residual shareholders.

2. Using the ideas of portfolio theory, accountants could visualize the operations and assets of a company as a portfolio in which diversification affects the variance of the total return. The financial statements and accompanying data could include a multi-column income statement showing the operating results of different segments of the business, or a graph showing the extent to which the sales of the different products fluctuate together or in different patterns over time. This permits the analyst to judge the extent to which risk is affected by covariability of the different segments.

3. The interest of the analyst in the variability over time of flows, such as dividends, income, sales, and net routine cash flow is obvious; the accountant should keep it in mind in applying the comparability criterion and in deciding upon various types of multiperiod presentations.

4. The accountant, like the reader of financial statements, should remember that the probability that the reporting entity will go into liquidation before the next reporting date is always greater than zero. Consideration of "downside risk" requires giving some thought to the low end of the distribution of possible future payoffs to investors. For this reason, even in cases of apparently healthy firms, there is some value in providing information about liquidation values. This means that the net realizable value, or other version of exit value, of assets that are not measured on such a basis for presentation in the primary balance sheet and in the computation of income could be useful information. Short-term assets that can be measured with acceptable reliability and cost at discounted future cash flows or at "completed-cycle NRV" presumably are stated at amounts not far from their liquidation values (assuming liquidation is pursued in a reasonably orderly manner); thus, no adjustment of such valuations would appear to be necessary. The measurement of plant assets at probable liquidation values appears to be quite feasible in a few cases but very difficult in most. We do not feel that the general measure-

ment of assets at liquidation values is worthwhile at this time.[6]

5. Accountants should disclose unusual exposures to uninsured risks of physical loss of assets, political risks, dependence on major contracts, concentration of sources of supply and markets, and exposure to the effects of inflation. The latter requires that the balance sheet permit the analyst to compute the monetary ratio (ratio of net monetary position to the residual equity). Creditors may want to compute the coverage of net monetary liabilities by net nonmonetary assets.[7]

Empirical Research on Accounting and Risk

Some empirical research has been done on the contemporaneous association between various accounting measures and the systematic risk (β) of common stocks. The first of these to receive much attention was Ball and Brown's 1969 study of the correlation of a measure of variability of earnings as reported in the financial statements and a measure of variability of the return to stockholders. Ball and Brown found statistically significant association, that is, that the stock prices of firms with greater variability of earnings fluctuated more widely. This suggests that reporting of earnings without excessive smoothing can help investors predict the risk associated with a stock.

Beaver, Kettler, and Scholes (1970) tested the association between seven accounting-based measures and the market β of 307 firms. The variables which were most clearly associated with β were (1) standard deviation of the earnings/price ratio of a stock over time, (2) dividend payout percentage (negative correlation), (3) accounting β (covariance of an individual stock's earnings/price ratios over time with that of the overall earnings/price ratio of the market as a whole), and (4) leverage (ratio of total senior securities to total assets). Gonedes (1973) found statistically signifi-

---

[6]Some interesting studies in this area have been made in recent years. See McKeown (1971) and Beidleman (1973).

[7]The SEC (1974) identifies some other possible circumstances which may require disclosure of risks.

cant association between changes in earnings from year to year and market β. Lev (1974b) found that the contribution margin percentage was positively correlated with market β while Lev and Kunitzky (1974) were able to detect association between measures of the stability of such series as sales, production, capital expenditures, earnings and dividends (as independent variables), and systematic security risk. To the extent that these empirical research results are accepted as valid, they have obvious implications for the reporting of risk-relevant accounting data.

Concluding Comments on Accounting for Risk

Investors and managers appear to be interested in predicting risks associated with an entity's activities and investments in the entity. Accounting for factors relevant to predictions of risk has not been developed nearly as far as accounting for variables relevant to predictions of returns. The association of risk with the firm's liquidity and its wealth suggests that the basic accounting system can be developed so as to provide significantly better risk-relevant data.

ADDITIONAL READING SUGGESTIONS

Lemke, Kenneth W., "The Evaluation of Liquidity: An Analytical Study," *Journal of Accounting Research* (Spring 1970), pp. 47–77.

Lev, Baruch, *Financial Statement Analysis: A New Approach* (Prentice-Hall, 1974a).

Rosen, L. S. and Don T. DeCoster, "'Funds' Statements: A Historical Perspective," *The Accounting Review* (January 1969), pp. 124–36.

Spiller, Earl A. and Robert L. Virgil, "Effectiveness of *APB Opinion No. 19* in Improving Funds Reporting," *Journal of Accounting Research* (Spring 1974), pp. 112–42.

STUDY QUESTIONS

1. Suggest some general and specific uses of information commonly reported in funds statements (statements of changes in financial position).

2. Which concept of funds is most useful for each of the uses that you named above?

3. Illustrate the form of funds statement that you believe would be most useful for external investors.

4. Suggest some advantages and disadvantages of starting with the gross inflow of funds as opposed to starting with net income in preparing a funds statement.

5. Several years ago, security analysts were giving a great deal of emphasis to funds flow from operations and were deemphasizing reported net income. What are the merits and weaknesses, from the point of view of investors, of funds flow from operations, based on a working capital concept of funds, as compared to earnings if they are seeking a primary measure of business success?

6. Which flow concept (earnings or some version of funds flow from operations) is most susceptible to manipulation? Which is least susceptible?

7. Compare three or four alternative net asset flow concepts on the basis of:
   (a) The reliability with which they can be measured;
   (b) Their relevance to a judgment of managerial performance in the interests of owners;
   (c) Opportunities for manipulation of the flow by management.

8. If you are preparing a funds statement based on the working capital concept and are starting with earnings before extraordinary charges, how would you show (if at all):
   (a) Capitalized interest on construction of plant assets?
   (b) Depreciation on factory equipment in a new plant that has been producing during the period, but whose products have not yet been put on the market?
   (c) Repurchase of the company's bonds outstanding at less than their book value?

9. Can depreciation accounting ever affect the amount of a firm's reported working capital? If so, how?

10. Criticize *APB Opinion No. 19* (or the U.K. *Statement of Standard Accounting Practice* on funds statements).

Chapter XII

11. Add some examples to the suggested opportunities for operating manipulation of the various net recurring flow measures discussed in this chapter. (Specialized industries may be a promising place to look.)

12. Add some examples to the opportunities for accounting manipulation suggested in this chapter.

13. Do you agree that accounting practices and the "official literature" of accounting give very little explicit attention to accounting for liquidity? What major exceptions to this generalization have you observed?

14. Is the recurring-nonrecurring basis of classification of liquidity flows (a) helpful, and (b) feasible?

15. If liquidity accounting is separated from accounting for wealth and profitability in the future, and if this separation leads to the evolution from our present earnings concept towards a more subjective concept, which assets and liabilities would you expect to be the prime candidates for inclusion in that evolution towards a more subjective earnings concept?

16. Build a case for either (a) the general operation of a double-entry liquidity accounting system, or (b) operation of such a system in a particular set of circumstances in which an entity could find itself.

17. Do you agree that exit value theory can be described as liquidity-oriented?

18. What changes in the cash flow statement illustrated in the chapter (EXHIBIT XII-9) would you suggest or consider?

19. Do you agree that the variance of the periodic return on a security is an appropriate ex post measure of risk? If not, can you suggest a more suitable measure?

20. Do you believe there is a relationship between individual security risk and returns on securities? What is your evidence or reasoning?

21. How could one argue that the disclosure of measurement methods used for various net asset items provides risk-relevant information?

22. Summarize the results of one or two empirical research studies pertaining to the relationship of accounting data to investment

risk (in addition to the studies mentioned in the chapter).

23. Describe and distinguish two general classes of techniques for "manipulating" the net recurring flow for a specific period.

24. Referring to EXHIBIT XII-8, explain each of the four lines, including its label and its slope.

CHAPTER XIII

ACCOUNTING DECISIONS: FINANCIAL ASSETS AND LIABILITIES

The APB invested great effort between 1968 and 1972 in an attempt to produce an "opinion" on accounting for marketable securities on a noncost basis.[1] These efforts failed, at least in the sense that no tangible product was forthcoming.[2] The disappointment was particularly deep among those who favored presentation of assets at current market values where feasible and thought it was more feasible to apply the current value approach to publicly traded securities than to any other category of assets. Why did these efforts "fail"?

Members of the APB during that period have indicated that the marketable securities opinion was killed by the unyielding opposition of the managements of firms in financial industries, particularly insurance companies, who were supported by the SEC.[3] The September 1971 draft opinion provided for valuation of equity securities at market values, with the change in value since the beginning of the period or date of purchase (whichever was later) appearing in the income statement as an unrealized gain or loss. If this principle were accepted for stocks, bonds would logically follow; then the issue would become more material to insurance companies, and banks would be involved as well. Officials of banks and insurance companies feared that swings in the market could

---

[1] The research underlying this chapter was supported by John F. Forbes & Company. The chapter is adapted from Staubus (1974).

[2] Perhaps the contribution that particular failure made to our understanding of the nature of the difficulties involved in obtaining agreement on accounting principles as well as to the creation of the FASB represents products more valuable than even a strong opinion.

[3] See Horngren (1974).

result in wide fluctuations in net income and even substantial impairment of the owners' equities in these thinly capitalized institutions. The consequent effects on the confidence of depositors, policy holders, and others could be disastrous, not only for the individual firms, but for the entire financial system and economy of the country. This specter, according to the general understanding, killed the marketable securities opinion.

The implications of this story are alarming to anyone who ranks shareholders' and creditors' rights to financial information alongside freedom of speech and freedom of the press in their importance to the preservation of a decentralized society. Was not our feared specter moaning that if accountants told depositors, policy holders and owners what the forces of the market have done to the values of the firm's assets these previously contented trustors would desert financial institutions in droves? Perhaps we should report only the historical costs so everyone can have a feeling of security.

How did this set with accountants? Were they unconcerned? Or were some of them bothered by nagging questions such as:

1. How can deception be adopted as a cornerstone of financial reporting?
2. How can older market values (historical costs) be more appropriate than recent values for such purposes as:
   - Judging the safety of one's deposits in a bank holding marketable securities?
   - Predicting the claim-paying ability of an insurance company holding marketable securities?
   - Making investment decisions pertaining to the stock of a firm holding marketable securities?
   - Judging the performance of the manager of a portfolio of marketable securities?

Questions along these lines must have plagued the members of the APB. Several of them have indicated privately that they were not at all happy with the outcome of their deliberations even though they agreed that no opinion was the least of the available evils. This chapter is based on a belief that the present state of financial reporting by firms in financial industries can be improved upon and that such improvement is a matter of some urgency from the point of view of all parties concerned with the health of our financial industries, especially their share-holders.

SELECTION OF THE ATTRIBUTE TO BE MEASURED IN PORTFOLIO ACCOUNTING

The criteria for evaluating alternative accounting proposals, set forth in chapter III, may be restated and reorganized to provide a slightly better fit for the issue at hand:

1. *Relevance* of the attribute to the decisions of users.
   a. Relevance of the asset amount to the cash-flow-oriented decisions of investors.
   b. Relevance of the changes in asset amounts (income effects) to the appraisal and comparison of the performance of managers of reporting entities.
2. *Reliability* of the measurements as representative of the phenomena they purport to represent.
3. *Comparability.* Like assets and events should be reported in a like manner; unlike items should be reported as being unlike.
4. *Effects via other parties.*
   a. Congruence. The financial statements should be useful indicators of management success in achieving owners' goals. They must not permit managers to look good without performing in owners' interests or to look bad while achieving owners' objectives because such appearances may distract managers from seeking owners' objectives.
   b. Macroeconomic consequences. The measurement and reporting of the chosen attribute should have "desirable" effects upon the economy from the standpoint of members of the society.
5. *Intelligibility* of the data presented.
6. *Timeliness* of reporting.
7. *Optimal quantity* of data presented, cost of producing the data, and cost of utilizing the data.

Once we have identified the criteria, our next step is to identify the alternative attributes that are under consideration. In the interest of expediency, let's eliminate face value and the equity method from consideration even though they could be serious contenders in some cases. Undiscounted future cash flows can also be eliminated. We pointed out in chapter VII that discounting future cash flows at the current market rate of discount yields the current market value of the security, so there is no need to recognize both of these attributes. Inasmuch as current market value is more generally available on a reliable basis, let's set aside discounted future cash flows. Replacement cost—current market value plus fringe acquisition costs—and net realizable value (NRV)—current market value less costs of selling—clearly are reasonable possibilities, but we shall eliminate them at this stage for reasons given in chapter VII. Restated historical cost could be recognized as a contender, and the choice of the measuring unit (nominal dollars or a purchasing power unit) will be discussed later in this chapter. The fundamental issue can be seen more clearly, however, if we reduce the number of alternatives to the two that have received the most attention in recent discussions: *historical cost* and *current market value.*[4]

Now let's look at the portfolio activities depicted in EXHIBIT XIII-1. Portfolios A, B, and C have the same values at the beginning of 1973. Each consists of one stock paying no dividend. The breaks in the lines indicate turnovers (a sale and reinvestment of the proceeds in a different security). The management of each portfolio changes at each year-end, at which point managerial performance

---

[4] A third possible method of accounting for securities, which has been advocated by a few people who are impressed by the tendency of managers to refuse to take unrealized losses on the historical cost basis, defers losses and gains that are taken "in order to switch the funds into other earning assets." The deferred loss or gain would be carried on the balance sheet and amortized to income over a future period such as five years or the remaining life of the asset sold. This method is not taken seriously for my purpose because it clearly ranks below historical cost on every criterion listed above except congruence. Its major fault is that it injects a completely irrelevant element into the balance sheets and income statements for the post-sale deferral periods. (Prior to sale, historical cost, with all of its weaknesses, would be used.) This method delays reporting value changes by carrying them as positive or negative balance sheet deferrals (which no investor would have any interest in considering as a part of the net assets of the firm). These deferrals contribute to a lack of comparability of balance sheet data (vis-à-vis firms with identical portfolios but different histories) as measures of investment value and of earnings numbers as measures of managerial performance and changes in economic resources.

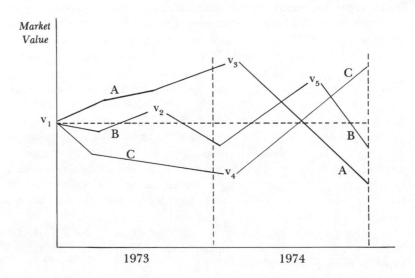

is to be evaluated. Manager A_{73} held a security while it rose steadily through the year; he had no sales so realized no gains or losses. His successor, A_{74}, "took" the accumulated profit and bought another security in which he invested $\$v_3$. The price of this stock fell while A_{74} hung on. B_{73} took a modest profit and reinvested the proceeds, $\$v_2$, in a security that fell to a value below $\$v_1$. His successor, B_{74}, took a profit at $\$v_5$ and reinvested in a loser. C_{73} ended the year with an unrealized loss, which his successor took in order to reinvest in a big gainer.

How would these events be reported under historical cost measurement of securities held and under current market value measurement? Under historical cost, portfolio B showed a realized profit in 1973; A and C would report break-even results (ignoring any operating expenses). In 1974, A would show a large profit, B a modest profit, and C a large loss. Under current value reporting with changes in market values reported on the income statement whether realized or not, the three portfolios would rank in A, B, C order according to profit in 1973 and in C, B, A order in 1974. The respective net worths of these portfolios, on the historical cost basis, would be the last $v level appearing to the left of the year-end line. On the current market value basis, the net worths are traced by the respective lines.

The next step is to evaluate each measurement method on the criteria set out above.

1. If you were buying or selling an interest in any of these portfolios at its book value, which measurement method do you think would be most *equitable*? Would you be willing to buy portfolio C at its historical cost at the end of 1973 or to sell portfolio A at its cost?

2. Which measurement method best reflects the *performance* of each manager? If you were manager A_{73} or C_{74}, how would you answer?

3. Which method produces the more *reliable* data? The answer to this question is not nearly so clear. It seems apparent that the historical cost of securities can be ranked higher on the reliability scale than the historical cost of most assets because there are far fewer judgments and calculations to be made. Fraud, clerical mistakes, and the cost flow choice seem to be the major sources of variation or error. On the other hand, market prices at the balance sheet date do not involve a cost flow assumption, and a set of rules can be prepared that will provide unambiguous determination of market value of those securities for which a market is regularly made.[5] Both historical cost and current market value are subject to manipulation by exerting enough buying or selling pressure on the market to move the price to a higher or lower level than it otherwise would be. Historical cost is clearly more susceptible to this weakness because the holder of the security unquestionably did exert buying pressure the day he bought it. Market prices at the balance sheet date would only be influenced upward if they were also costs.

---

[5] For some suggestions regarding such a set of rules, see Committee on Investment Companies (1973, pp. 33–38). One indication of the reliability of current market value reporting in investment companies is the absence of major scandals involving financial reporting by these companies.

Occasionally one hears a rash comment implying that historical costs are facts while current market prices are not. Such a statement reflects an unorthodox definition of "fact." Surely both current market values and historical costs (current market value the day the asset was purchased) deserve to be classified as empirical phenomena; I cannot insist that a transaction in which my firm allegedly took part really happened while all other transactions are fiction. Certainly accountants must stick to facts, but this is not a very helpful prescription; what we need is a set of criteria for selecting those facts that are relevant to the needs of financial statement readers.

Market prices involving the firm and other market prices are both available with adequate reliability; both sets of data are far more reliable than the vast majority of data that accountants report on financial statements. Whatever differences in reliability one can detect surely do not provide much basis for choosing between the valuation methods.

4. Which measurement method provides data that are more useful for comparison of the status and activities of the entities? Cost-based balance sheets say portfolios A and C were equal at the end of 1973. Cost-based income statements say A was much more profitable than C in 1974.

5. Which method of measuring managerial performance is more conducive to *management decisions in the owners' interest*? Under cost-based accounting, manager A_{73} would be sorely tempted to take his profit, while C_{74} would have needed exceptionally strong evidence to make him take the loss he inherited and give his stockholders the cash flow benefit of the immediate tax saving. It is easy to see how managers' decisions could be unduly influenced by cost-based reporting to stockholders.

6. Which measurement method can be expected to have the most desirable *macroeconomic consequences*? Assuming the analysis in chapter VII (and partially illustrated in EXHIBIT VII-3) is correct, current market values are more highly correlated with future cash flows produced by an asset than are older market values, including those paid by the entity. To the extent that users of a financial institution's balance sheet want to predict the entity's capacity to pay cash (on demand or when due), and if the degree to which an institution possesses such capacity

is called "safety," it follows that current market values provide the best basis for judging the safety of a financial institution's capital structure. Therefore, decisions of depositors, lenders, and regulatory authorities based on historical cost data will be suboptimal, on the average, and are likely to cause more resources to be entrusted to poorly managed and unsafe financial intermediaries than would be the case if current market values were used. Accordingly, financial intermediaries can be expected to serve society less satisfactorily if portfolio assets are reported at their costs. There is even a remote probability that the management and regulation of financial institutions on the basis of cost measurements could lead to a major financial and economic disaster. I conclude that the economic consequences of using old data are unlikely to be more desirable and could be much less desirable than the consequences of using up-to-date valuations.

7. Which method provides for the *quickest reporting* of changes in economic resources? Why should the owners of portfolios A and C have to wait so long to find out what's happening to their investments?

8. Which method is most costly? If only one set of data were to be produced, historical cost might be the less costly as the data would be recorded upon acquisition. But, in a more realistic setting, year-end market values are generally determined for such purposes as internal reporting and applying the lower-of-cost-or-market rule. Using current values for external reporting would not add much cost in these circumstances. A substantial cost saving would result from dispensing with the amortization of premiums and accretion of discount on bonds. The net difference in cost is not clear but is unlikely to be material.[6]

Current value reporting clearly has a wide margin of superiority on the first five criteria; historical cost may be slightly preferable

---

[6] In practice, we find that it is common to prepare the balance sheet and income statement on the basis of historical cost measurements of securities, then disclose their current market values in supplementary notes. Assuming a moderately perceptive (efficient) market, this reporting model would appear to achieve a satisfactory level of relevance but leaves something to be desired on the optimal quantity and cost-of-using criteria.

on the reliability criterion. Are there any other objections to current value reporting? The following points are brought up in this context.

1. *Market values should not be reported because a large holding could not be sold without depressing the market.* This point is an allegation of doubtful validity in a world of institutional investors searching for stocks in which a worthwhile position can be established without bidding up the price inordinately; it is also irrelevant to the argument. The case for current market values is not based on the assumption of liquidation of the portfolio; current market values are simply the most recent objective judgment of value. If reported amounts of assets are to be useful for making decisions, they must be as relevant to the future as they possibly can be because decisions pertain to future actions. If an accountant tells a reader of financial statements that he will tell him any one past market price he chooses, can you think of any circumstances in which the reader would select a price that is not the most recent one available? Liquidation values are not the objective; the most recent judgments of all of those investors (mostly full-time professionals) who are doing their very best to make a better judgment of securities values than their competitors result in market values that provide the best objective information about securities values that is obtainable. Historical cost represents a similar, but older, judgment and one that is not independent of the firm because the firm participated in its determination.

2. *Unrealized gains and losses may be reversed and never realized; a series of price reversals over a period of years could result in movements over the same price territory being reported more than once.* True, as long as a security is held, its price can be expected to fluctuate—whether it is reported at cost or at market. But, to expect reversal of a recent movement not only denies the random walk pattern of securities prices but assumes an alternating pattern for which there is, to my knowledge, no empirical evidence.[7] To wait until sale before reporting any change in

---

[7] For an inventory of the evidence accumulated through 1969 regarding the random walk price pattern, see Fama (1970). While it now appears that prices

values recalls the old venture accounting procedures when periodic reporting was not used. I cannot understand how accountants could elect to make all of the estimates involved in percentage-of-completion accounting for long-term contracts, rather than waiting for the completion of the. contract, while at the same time insisting that they must wait for the sale of a marketable security before recognizing that any change has occurred. The periodic reporting convention involves recognizing events that occur during the reporting period whether the venture has been wound down to a pure cash position or not. The profession gave up the cash basis of accounting for large businesses five hundred years ago.

3. *Current market values can be reported as supplementary information rather than as the primary data used in the computation of income.* The proper response to this argument seems to be: First, determine which type of data is most helpful to readers, then treat it as primary and report secondary data as supplementary information if desired.

4. *In an efficient market, current returns on securities are not indicative of managerial performance; an amateur can be expected to obtain results as good as any professional's.* While there is a good deal of evidence supporting this position with respect to a given segment of the whole securities market, such as common stocks or Treasury bonds (Fama, 1970), a money manager's job in a financial intermediary involves holding the right category of security, especially the right maturity, at the right time. If a portfolio manager is not held responsible for maximizing returns, then measurement of current returns is not required for the evaluation of managerial performance; the cost versus market argument thus becomes irrelevant for this purpose. Otherwise, current market values are needed, and generally used, for measuring portfolio performance.

5. *Reporting current market values and the related gains and losses*

---

on the New York Stock Exchange do not follow a perfect random walk, their patterns are so close to a random walk that it takes years of study and a great deal of computer time to detect the difference, and then it is limited to very small discrepancies. For valuation purposes, the random walk is certainly the safest general assumption.

could result in loss of confidence in a financial intermediary by its depositors, stockholders, and the general public. The result could be a "run" by depositors which could result in the liquidation of the institution. One answer to this is: Yes, it could, and that is precisely what should happen if the competitive system is to serve society properly. Poorly managed firms should be driven out of business. If the current financial condition of a bank causes its depositors to lose faith and switch their deposits to other banks, the system is working properly and financial information is playing its assigned role. Surely such depositor actions based on current objective information are preferable to actions based on rumors (perhaps exaggerated) about unreported losses. Furthermore, the deterrent to sloppy and high-risk management practices and the confidence engendered in the minds of depositors and stockholders by straightforward reporting of current market facts would appear to have favorable economic consequences.

I conclude that none of these arguments against reporting current values carries any significant weight. The fundamental objective of portfolio management in financial intermediaries is to hold the mix of assets that contributes the most to the return objective, subject to the risk constraint expressed in the portfolio policy. This requires giving a great deal of attention to predicting the course of interest rates and holding a maximum of short-term assets when interest rates are rising and a maximum of long-term assets when interest rates are falling. If the financial statements are to be helpful in evaluating the success of portfolio management, they must provide information relevant to the assessment of returns achieved during the period and the accompanying exposure to risk. If returns are not properly matched with the periods in which value changes take place, we cannot get a clear impression of success during that period. If our accounting practices give portfolio managers the choice of taking or delaying losses, of drawing on or holding in reserve unrealized gains, the opportunity to convert the unrecognized gains or losses to instant earnings or instant losses can easily affect managers' investment decisions and result in suboptimization in the form of lower gross investment returns and/or excessive transaction costs. These dysfunctional consequences can be avoided if gains and losses are not established by decisions to sell, as is true when assets are measured at current market values.

This seems to be an appropriate point to recall that investment companies, including open-end mutual funds, adhere strictly to the current market value basis of asset measurement even though the possible objections I have discussed above apply to them as much as they do to other holders of marketable securities. A major difference between the environment of open-end investment companies and those of other financial firms is that the book values (net asset values) of the former are used directly as the basis for pricing transactions in the firm's stock so investors will not accept any other valuations. Why should shareholders in other types of securities-holding firms not need the same type of information when they buy a share in the firm's portfolio?

COMPARABILITY, TAXATION, AND THE MEASURING UNIT

Now we present another example intended to help clarify several points. The valuation of three bond portfolios by three different methods is illustrated in EXHIBIT XIII-2. This example deals with a 5 percent, 35-year bond issued at par in 1964 and a 9 percent, 25-year bond issued at par in 1974. The 5 percent bond is assumed to have been trading on a 9 percent basis ($605) when the 9 percent bonds were issued in 1974. Perusal of the cost column reminds us that (1) two bonds identical except for cost may be shown on a balance sheet at widely different amounts (Portfolio D); (2) two very different bonds (9 percent and 5 percent, Portfolio D) may be reported at like values; (3) portfolios identical, except for their cost (D and E), may be reported at different values; and (4) substantially different portfolios (D and F, which differ in annual cash return by $40) are listed at the same values. None of these points applies to the market valuation column. Cost valuation, then, fails miserably on the comparability criterion: like assets are not reported at like values, and different assets are reported as if they were alike.

Now let's look at another comparability issue. Should a difference in tax bases be recognized in the valuation of assets? Portfolio D includes two 5 percent bonds with equal market values but

EXHIBIT XIII-2

COMPARABILITY AMONG THREE BOND PORTFOLIOS

	At Cost	At Market	At Tax-Adjusted Market*
Portfolio D			
1 TT&A 9% bond, due 1999, acquired in 1974	$1,000	$1,000	$1,000
1 TT&A 5% bond, due 1999, acquired in 1964	1,000	605	723
1 TT&A 5% bond, due 1999, acquired in 1974	605	605	605
Total	$2,605	$2,210	$2,328
Portfolio E			
1 TT&A 9% bond, due 1999, acquired in 1974	$1,000	$1,000	$1,000
2 TT&A 5% bonds, due 1999, acquired in 1974	1,210	1,210	1,210
Total	$2,210	$2,210	$2,210
Portfolio F			
2 TT&A 9% bonds, due 1999, acquired in 1974	$2,000	$2,000	$2,000
1 TT&A 5% bond, due 1999, acquired in 1974	605	605	605
Total	$2,605	$2,605	$2,605

*With a 30% tax rate.

different costs to be deducted in the computation of taxable income when the bonds are sold (whenever that may be); hence, D will yield different after-tax proceeds to the owner. Which is worth more, a 5 percent TT&A bond with a basis of $1,000 or a similar bond with a basis of $605? As of the balance sheet date, either bond could have been sold for approximately $605 but the sale of the high-basis bond would also yield a cash benefit equal to the incremental tax rate in the period of sale times the $395 loss; the balance sheet representations of the two bonds should reflect such a difference. Looking at the income statement, if the high-basis bond is written down to $605 in period one when A is the portfolio manager and is sold for $605 in period two when B is the manager, A is charged with too large a loss, and B gets unwarranted credit for a quick profit (in the form of a reduction in income tax expense). In fact, B may be tempted to sell the security just to improve his reported income even if it would be wise to hold it on its investment merits. The generally accepted principle of comprehensive tax allocation requires recognition of this tax aspect, although it is customary to treat it as a separate balance sheet item rather than as an adjustment of the related asset value.

The tax-adjusted market column in EXHIBIT XIII-2 reflects the difference in basis between the two 5 percent bonds held in Portfolio D; all other bonds in that example have bases and costs equal to their market values. The standard computation of tax-adjusted market values is:

$$M_{ta} = M + (B - M)T$$

where M is the market quotation, B is the basis for computation of taxable gain or loss, and T is the aggregate incremental tax rate (state and federal) for the type of income in question (ordinary or long-term capital gain). [8]

There is one other problem that needs attention—the effect of *changes in the size of the measuring unit* (the dollar) on the comparison of measurements that is involved in the computation of gain or loss. I assume we all agree that, if we paid $1,000 for something a year ago and sell it for $1,040 today while a general price level index has risen by 5 percent, the $40 difference between the two measurements would not represent income in any meaningful sense—except that it would be taxed. Allowing

---

[8] Capital gain rates probably should be applied to capital asset securities acquired within the last six months.

for inflation in the computation of income is particularly important in long-term investment operations; the inflation adjustment can completely wipe out the nominal investment income. To report current nominal interest returns as real income is a major error. The same inflation that bloats nominal interest rates also erodes the purchasing power of the investment base; to show the favorable effect of inflation on the former while ignoring its unfavorable effect on the latter does not meet my standards of informative reporting. The restatement procedure illustrated in chapter IX surely is appropriate in this case.

Now let's return to the bond portfolios. EXHIBIT XIII-3 illustrates the calculation of income and ending values for Portfolio D of EXHIBIT XIII-2. Additional assumptions are: a 5 percent increase in the shareholder-consumer price index, 12/31/75 market quotations as shown, 30 percent (capital gain) tax rate, bonds held through the year, and a 50 percent tax on ordinary income. If the bonds are sold during the year, all calculations would be similar, subject to variations in the price level change, interest earned (and related tax), and whatever selling price was substituted for the ending market quotation. Note that bonds are treated as a monetary asset, so that a purchasing power loss is calculated first and the revaluation to current value is based on the restated beginning value. Alternatively, one could merge the purchasing power loss and the revaluation into one income item, as we would do in the case of stocks owned or other nonmonetary assets.

One weakness in these calculations is that the tax adjustment portion of the asset value is not discounted for the period between the balance sheet date and the tax payment date because the latter date is unknown. If one believes that losses are likely to be taken quickly (perhaps in portfolio "roll-over" operations), discount would not appear to be material; in fact, unrealized losses at year-end would not be substantial. This, however, depends upon the taxpayer's ability to utilize such losses as deductions—a serious limitation on capital assets held by corporations. Gains, on the other hand, may remain unrealized for years and the owner may avoid paying the tax; for an asset with no, or a distant, maturity date, one could make a case for a discounted tax liability approaching zero. These thoughts suggest the apparently unconservative

EXHIBIT XIII-3

PORTFOLIO VALUATION AND INCOME MEASUREMENT

(HYPOTHETICAL PORTFOLIO D, 1975)

	TT&A 9%		TT&A 5%		TT&A 5%		Total	
	B/S data	I/S data	B/S data	I/S data	B/S data	I/S data	B/S data	I/S data
Tax basis	$1,000		$1,000		$605		$2,605	
12/31/74 valuation:								
Per market quotation	1,000		605		605		2,210	
Per market, tax adjusted	1,000		723		605		2,328	
Restated in 1975 $	1,050		759		635		2,444	
Purchasing power loss[a]	50	$(50)	36	$(36)	30	$(30)	116	$(116)
Change in quotation[b]	40	40	45	45	45	45	130	130
1975 quotation—sale or 12/31	1,040		650		650		2,340	
30% tax on change in quotation[c]	(12)	(12)	(13)	(13)	(13)	(13)	(38)	(38)
Net proceeds or 12/75 valuation[d]	1,028		755[d]		637		2,420	
Nominal interest (for year)[e]		90		50		50		190
50% tax on nominal interest[f]		(45)		(25)		(25)		(95)
Net income		$23		$21		$27		$71

[a] Recorded by Dr. to Purchasing Power Loss; Cr. to Owners' Equity (restatement).
[b] Dr. to Investment Account; Cr. to Income from Bond Market Fluctuations.
[c] Dr. to Tax Expense; Cr. to Investment Account.
[d] $M + (B - M)T$
[e] Customary entry.
[f] Dr. Tax Expense; Cr. Tax payable.

approach of adjusting fully for the prospective tax saving associated
with unrealized losses, while ignoring the tax liability pertaining
to unrealized gains. Is this acceptable? In the case of assets with
maturity dates, an alternative would be to assume that the tax
on gains will be paid at maturity and to discount it accordingly.
For the present, I assume full recognition without discount.

It is important to group the five different income effects shown
in EXHIBIT XIII-3 for any analysis of the results of portfolio
operations. For example, neither the change in quotation nor
the nominal interest tells us much about the success of portfolio
activities until we take into account the purchasing power loss.
Taxation is also critical now that it is common for investors to
pay income taxes in periods of real losses. In my opinion, accountants should make a sincere effort to calculate the "real return"
on investments, including the five elements shown in EXHIBIT
XIII-3. The principles applied to bonds in this illustration apply
to stocks and loans as well.

VALUATION OF UNQUOTED ASSETS

At this point it seems safe to assume that the merits of current
value accounting for portfolio assets, from the point of view of
users of financial statements issued by financial intermediaries,
are clearly recognized. The next step is to work out procedures
for applying the concept to assets for which market prices are
not regularly quoted. This is desirable for two reasons: (1) Changes
in market interest rates affect the values of such assets in the
same ways that they affect quoted bond values, and readers of
financial statements have the same need for current values of
unquoted assets as they have in the case of quoted securities.
(2) Unquoted securities and loans are practical (though imperfect)
substitutes for quoted securities in portfolios; failure to apply
current value accounting uniformly across portfolio segments
weakens the intercompany comparability of value and return
information as well as the additivity of these data in one set of
financial statements. While failure to obtain current values for
minor segments of the portfolio, or for segments with only minor
discrepancies between conventional valuations and current values,
would not invalidate the financial statements, it does seem clear

that 100 percent application of current value accounting procedures to the portfolio of "earning assets" should be our objective. Accordingly, we must attempt to extend the concept of current value accounting to unquoted securities and to loans, especially long-term loans.

The market value of a monetary asset is the sum of the future cash flows promised by the asset, discounted at the current market rate of interest for that type of asset. Thus, prices for bonds may be quoted as a percent of par or as a yield rate and buyers and sellers can understand each other and execute transactions on either basis. The issues of securities that are traded on organized securities markets involve many identical units known as shares of stock or as bonds or notes. A quotation per share or per $100 of par value, when the issue is identified, permits a meeting of the minds of traders. In other markets, such as for mortgages and treasury bills, it is common to express prices in terms of interest (or discount) rates. If a current market yield rate can be established, it can be applied to the asset's future cash flow provisions to calculate the market value of the asset. Market values and future cash flows discounted at the current market interest rate for the particular asset are basically the same. Our concern, in the remainder of this section, will be with market interest rates.

Market interest rates for some classes of assets are quoted directly by participants in the market. The best known examples are the prime rate, commercial paper rates (for several maturity and risk categories), certificates of deposit (for various maturities), and treasury bills. Commercial paper is rated by Standard & Poor's, Moody's, and Dun and Bradstreet; quotations are available by rating. Any of these assets held in a portfolio may be discounted at the current yield rate to obtain the asset amount. In some of these cases, a spread or range is quoted. In such cases, the average of the high and low rates may be used.

One special, and major, category of assets that are easily valued consists of loans made on a floating rate basis, that is, with a provision that the effective interest rate will vary as the lender's current lending rate for that category of loans varies. Thus, banks make many large loans at the prime rate, or at prime plus a specified percentage premium, with the provision that the effective rate will vary as the bank's prime rate varies. Such loans always have a current value of par, providing there has been no clear change in the borrower's credit rating. The large issues of floating rate notes that appeared on the market in the summer of 1974 do not fall into this category because the interest rate is fixed for some future period of time, commonly two years at date of issue and for six month intervals thereafter. However, most such notes are listed on the New York Stock Exchange bond market, so specific price quotations are available for them.

Now we must face the difficult cases—the unique assets for which neither a market price nor a clearly applicable current interest rate can be found. A basic procedure for valuing these assets follows: (1) Calculate the effective rate inherent in the original contract. (2) Determine the difference between the original effective rate and a related, publicly quoted base rate such as the prime rate. (3) At the time of revaluing the asset, discount at the currently quoted base rate plus or minus the original yield differential. For example, if a loan is made at prime plus 1.5 percent, revalue it at the current prime rate plus 1.5 percent. Over long periods during which factors determining interest rate differentials vary considerably, the difference used in valuing an asset may need to be recomputed according to some more specific formula.

The calculation of the yield rate inherent in the original contract typically is a straightforward "internal rate of return" calculation. It requires knowledge of the timing and amounts of all cash flows (in either direction) related to the loan or investment. Loan fees and "points" (discounts) are offset against the nominal loan. Loans with no fixed maturity are not generally a problem because they usually carry a floating rate which permits their valuation at par. Long-term mortgage loans are usually fully paid before maturity, if their terms do not permit assumption of the liability by a new owner, because properties usually change hands. Experience with such loans provides a basis for estimating a premature "balloon payment" date for use in the rate-of-return calculation. A common compounding period (perhaps quarterly or semi-annually) should be selected and either a 360- or 365-day year used uniformly.

The base rate chosen for comparison should depend on the type of loan. Bankers commonly price commercial loans in relation to the prime rate so it is a natural base rate for such loans. A widely quoted mortgage loan rate is the yield on Federal National

Mortgage Association weekly auctions of FHA-insured residential mortgage commitments. The FHA insurance removes the quality factor from consideration and the secondary market does not involve fees and points. The assumption as to the average payoff date is a variable that does remain, but it is fairly stable in a representative sample of loans. In the tax-exempt securities area, indexes such as Bond Buyer's and Standard & Poor's are available. Corporate bond yield indexes abound; Standard & Poor's publishes twelve, representing different categories and grades of bonds, on a weekly basis. While no index of consumer loan rates has been encountered, construction and maintenance of such an index by an independent agency such as the FDIC or Department of Commerce would appear to be easy; all that is needed is a demand for it.

The rate differential approach to pricing financial assets, as described above, occasionally can produce prices which experienced judges would consider unreasonable because of changes in rate-determining factors since the asset was acquired. The most common of these are (1) change in the remaining life of the instrument, (2) change in the capital gain component of the yield as the price drops to a discount, (3) change in perceived risk, and (4) change in the impact of a call feature as the difference between the current price and the call price changes and as the time remaining before the bond or note is callable diminishes.

Fortunately, the major bond houses, such as Salomon Brothers and Merrill Lynch, offer bond portfolio pricing services to which the portfolio manager and the auditor can turn for valuations. If, for example, a portfolio includes $2 million of a corporate private placement or $10,000 of a local school district issue, a professional pricing service will estimate its market value. The auditor may wish to split the portfolio list among two or three such agencies, perhaps with some overlap, in order to reduce the risk of poor valuations. We should keep in mind that the magnitude of this problem is not great, as banks concentrate most of their bond holdings in U.S. and agency issues, state and municipal issues for which ratings and indexes are available, publicly traded corporate bonds, and privately placed issues of major corporations which have other outstanding rated and publicly traded issues which can serve as a base point for pricing the untraded issues.

And we should not forget that Standard & Poor's Corporation quotes approximately 7,000 corporate issues in its monthly *Bond Guide*. Term loans can be priced in the same manner as privately placed bonds.

The need to adjust the asset values discussed in this section for taxation of differences between prices as computed at current yield rates and tax bases is the same as it is for other assets. Restatements of earlier measurements to recognize changes in the size of the measuring unit are also needed. To provide for such a measurement process, the record for each portfolio asset should include date of acquisition, original yield, identification of the base rate to which the asset's pricing is related, and the original yield differential (between the base rate and the specific original yield on this asset). Small loans may be packaged by category and month of origin and handled on a group basis.

ACCOUNTING FOR LOAN LOSSES

Banks and finance companies use the allowance method of accounting for loan losses. Prior to 1975 the total "Reserve for Loan Losses" on a typical bank balance sheet originated from three sources: (1) an amount that had been charged to expense and was comparable to the allowance for uncollectibles in other enterprises, (2) an amount that had been charged to undivided profits or retained earnings and was viewed as a contingency reserve, and (3) an amount that had been charged to income tax expense representing deferred taxation of the sum of (2) and (3). This loose practice began to change after the SEC's chief accountant (Burton, 1974) urged that the reserve be broken down and the parts shifted to their normal positions according to GAAP: contra asset, deferred tax liability, and retained earnings.

The question to be considered at this point is: Why should an allowance for uncollectibles be deducted from assets that are valued at the contractual amounts of future cash claims less unearned interest, that is, at discounted future cash flows? As I understand the banking business, interest rates are set at levels that are explicitly intended to cover the risk of uncollectibility. Thus, the prime rate is higher than what is considered to be a risk-free rate and loans made at prime plus a specified percentage provide for a higher probability of loss. Morgage loan interest rates, too, are intended to exceed the risk-free rate by enough to cover administrative costs and a loss factor. If loans were valued at future amounts required by contract less a risk-free interest rate, unearned interest would be deducted but no provision for loss would be recognized. If, however, future contractual amounts were reduced by a rate of interest which included the probability of loss that the loan officer felt was appropriate, an allowance for uncollectibles would seem to have been deducted. To deduct another allowance would be double counting.

Now consider the timing of loan loss deductions on the income statement. If the accountant made a special provision for uncollectibles as soon as a new loan were made, the charge to income would appear before any interest was earned and the contra asset account would reduce the net asset amount below the amount of cash advanced to the borrower. A loss would be recorded when the loan was made. This violates the basic accounting principle that neither a loss nor gain occurs when an earning asset is acquired; it is valued at acquisition cost.

In practice, the allowance method of accounting for loan losses is sometimes used as a smoothing device. In years of high income and low losses, the allowance is built up by charges to expense in excess of the amount of charge-offs; when large losses occur, the allowance bears the abnormal amount so that reported income will not be hit so hard. This permitted banks which were clobbered by bankruptcies of major borrowers in the period 1969–1972 to report income as if nothing of significance had happened; banks which were hit hard were able to report just as favorable earnings as banks which had no large losses. Remember that, with respect to income accounting, it is all a question of timing. Does it make sense to report that a recession year in which several of a bank's major borrowers default on their loans is as good a year for the bank as a year that is prosperous for all? Do losses really occur evenly over good and bad years (for the economy)? Or is it more reasonable to admit that a firm that has heavy exposure to the risk of adverse business conditions has some bad years and some good ones? Perhaps the accountant should let his write-offs of bad loans reduce income when he writes them off as uncollectible and let the investor do his own smoothing if he is so inclined. [9]

But let's extend the analysis a bit further. If the risk premium incorporated in a nominal interest rate is designed to cover the probability of loss from failure of the debtor to pay, should it be added to the asset amount over time just as interest is? If a one-year, $1,000 loan is made at 10 percent including 1 percent as a risk premium, and if no interim interest payments are made, it is reasonable to view the 9 percent as accruing evenly over time, but the risk premium could be treated differently. There is a tendency for bad loans not to be recognized as such until they fall due. If this is typical, then the probability of future debtor failure remains essentially unchanged over the term of the loan. The hour before payment is due, the loan that required a 1 percent risk premium is still worth only 99 percent of its maturity value. EXHIBIT XIII-4 illustrates this view.

Since the above practice calls for building up the allowance for loss on a particular loan by crediting the risk premium to the allowance account gradually as interest accrues, one-half the allowance of the average (middle-aged) loan would already be recorded, and the other half should be matched off against the nominal interest earnings during the remainder of the loan's life. If the allowance for loan losses is maintained at approximately the level indicated by this calculation, the risk premium will not be added to the net asset valuation and the latter will tend to follow the pattern of line AC in EXHIBIT XIII-4. Journal entries recording the above analysis follow:

> Dr. Interest receivable   (at 10%)
>   Cr. Interest earned   (at 9%)
>   Cr. Allowance for loan losses   (at 1%)
>   To record the accural of interest at the
>   nominal rate, the recognition of revenue
>   at the risk-free rate, and the setting aside
>   of the risk premium as a contra receivable.

---

[9] The direct write-off method is acceptable to the Federal Reserve Board of Governors according to Regulation F.

EXHIBIT XIII-4

LOAN VALUE PATTERN

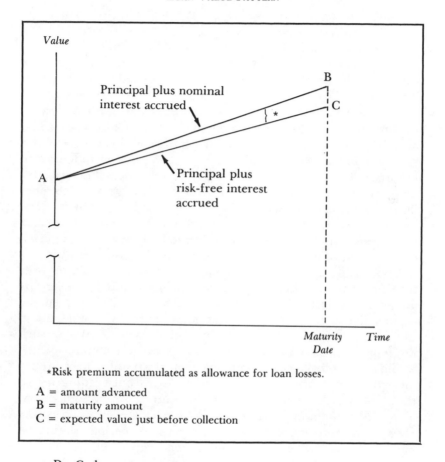

*Risk premium accumulated as allowance for loan losses.

A = amount advanced
B = maturity amount
C = expected value just before collection

Dr. Cash   (Mty. Val.)
    Cr. Note receivable   (Principal)
    Cr. Interest receivable   (Nom. Int.)
        To record the collection of the maturity
        amount at the maturity date, assuming all
        interest had been accrued beforehand.
Dr. Allowance for loan losses   (Mty. Val.)
    Cr. Note receivable   (Principal)
    Cr. Interest receivable   (Nom. Int.)

To record the write-off of an uncollectible
note.

Note that this scheme results in the matching of loan losses
with the interest revenues. Any error in the estimation of the
risk premium (and probability of loss) would call for an adjustment
of the allowance for loan losses in the period of maturity. For
example, if a group of 100 similar loans were made in one month,
if a 1 percent risk premium had been built into the interest rate,
and if that risk premium had been accumulated in the allowance
for loan losses as interest accrued, then the latter account could
absorb the write-off of one loan. If, however, there were either
no losses or more than one bad loan, the error would have to
be offset in the period of maturity, thereby signalling a better
or worse outcome than had been foreseen. The income statement
impact of the error would be "news" for consideration by readers.

Unfortunately, it is not likely to be convenient to keep track
of the experience with each monthly batch of loans, or even each
quarterly or annual batch, so the error in the risk premium will
not be readily determinable. If all risk premiums accruing over
time are credited to the allowance for loan losses, and if all write-offs
are made against this allowance, the discrepancies between the
estimated risk premiums and the actual losses will build up in
the allowance account. Over a period of several years, such
discrepancies could well accumulate to a sizeable amount, which
would leave the balance unacceptable from the standpoint of proper
measurement of the asset amount, the loans outstanding net of
the allowance. A periodic check on the contra account is necessary.
The proper amount would seem to be calculated as follows: the
ratio of losses to maturing amounts in recent periods should be
halved and multiplied times the aggregate loan balance on the
books. This calculation should be made for each differentiable
class of loans. The one-half factor is appropriate because some
of the loans on the books are nearing maturity, some have just
been made, and the average is likely to be halfway through its
life.

LIABILITIES

In conventional accounting practice, as reflected in *APB Opinion
No. 21,* monetary liabilities are carried at the amounts of future

cash payments promised less interest not yet accrued, that is, at future cash flows discounted at the original yield rate. This practice provides a pool of instant earnings when interest rates go up and the market value of the outstanding debt declines. It is particularly convenient for any manager who is inclined to use all available defects in accounting principles to manage reported earnings, because the pool of instant earnings created by the overvaluation of liabilities typically is at its largest when the asset undervaluation pool is likely to be small or nonexistent. When interest rates rise, the values of monetary assets decline, leaving little scope for quick profits, but the market value of the firm's debt also declines, thereby creating a beautiful pool of instant earnings. Similarly, when interest rates decline, the market value of outstanding debt rises so as to eliminate the pool of instant earnings and perhaps create a pool of instant losses, but the accompanying rise in asset values is likely to provide quick profit opportunities on that side of the balance sheet. This is a most convenient situation for managers who are dedicated to reporting earnings in a preconceived pattern, regardless of the success of their operations.

Examples of the achievement of instant earnings by the retirement or refunding of debt abound; McGraw-Hill, McCulloch Oil, United Brands, and Western Union come to mind. (I do not claim that these debt retirements were motivated by the desire for instant earnings.) A *Wall Street Journal* report on the McCulloch Oil case is instructive:

> McCulloch Oil: This resources company seemed headed for a bleak operating year through the first nine months of 1973, when it reported a net loss of nearly $7.5 million, equivalent to 45 cents a share on its 16.6 million shares. Sale of oil and gas leases and related properties at a loss of $8.2 million in September accounted for the red ink.
>
> To balance the losses, the company said in September it would make holders of its 5% convertible subordinated debentures a swap offer. The new issue was a similar debenture, except that interest was set at 10½% and each $1,000 of principal amount on the older issue was exchangeable for $550 of the new.
>
> The result for McCulloch's Income statement was to give the company a gain of nearly $9.4 million that could be taken

directly into earnings, and McCulloch reported earnings of
15 cents a share for the year. It also said that net would
have been eight cents a share if it hadn't had either the $8.2
million loss on the sale or the gain from the debenture swap.
By swapping the debentures the company averted a losing
year.[10]

The decisions pertaining to the financing of enterprise activities
(financial management) have a significant impact on the firm's
success in achieving owners' objectives. As in other segments of
management responsibilities, it is reasonable to expect that both
owners and managers are interested in managerial performance
on a periodic basis. This requires that we take stock of our position
at the beginning and end of the period. If the periodic performance
of financial management is to be reflected in financial statements,
the consequences of such decisions as the lengths of maturities
of loans and the timing of long-term financing, as well as capital
structure decisions, should be measured as promptly as possible.
A hypothetical case that I have used as a class exercise for several
years follows:

> Once upon a time male twins were born to a famous merchan-
> dising magnate. As they reached manhood their father refused
> to take them into the business because they quarreled inces-
> santly. So I. Magnate and J. Magnate each, independently,
> decided to start their own businesses. The similarity of their
> backgrounds resulted in their making similar decisions in
> forming and operating their businesses except that I. Magnate
> selected "Shorty" Financio as his financial vice president while
> J. hired "Slim" Financio. Shorty talked I. into a major one-year
> bank loan at 6 percent because he thought interest rates would
> fall, while Slim convinced J. that the issuance of 20-year bonds
> at 6 percent was the way to go because interest rates were
> going to rise.
>
> Lo and behold! Interest rates rose and Shorty issued 8 percent,
> 19-year bonds at the end of the year to replace his 6 percent
> bank loan.
>
> *Query 1:* Which financial manager was most successful in year

---

[10] Elia (1974, p. 23). Reprinted with permission of *The Wall Street Journal,* ©
Dow Jones & Company, Inc. (1974). All rights reserved.

one? How should this be reflected in the financial
statements just before Shorty's refinancing?

Query 2: Immediately after Shorty's refinancing, is there a
difference in the obligations of the two companies?
If so, how should it be reflected in the balance sheet?

Students were expected to say that Slim's 6 percent bonds should
be written down to an 8 percent basis at the end of year one
with the gain reflecting Slim's superior financial management *in
year one.* The two 19-year bonds—Slim's 6 percent and Shorty's
8 percent bonds—must be shown at different values on the balance
sheets.

On a more general level, we might ask these questions pertaining
to liability accounting:

1. Would you as a buyer of real estate be willing to pay the
same price for a property with a 10 percent mortgage
(to be assumed) as you would for a similar property with
a 7 percent mortgage? If not as an independent investor,
would you when buying shares of a corporation investing
in real estate (or other assets)? Why should two such widely
different situations be reported identically on balance
sheets?

2. Do managers who use short-term financing in years of
rising interest rates and long-term financing in years of
falling interest rates achieve their shareholders' goals in
those periods as well as managers who follow the opposite
financing pattern? How long should we wait for the differences between those decisions to show up on the income
statement?

3. Are you willing to rely on an income figure that includes
the amount of instant earnings that management has chosen
to realize in the period by retiring or refunding overvalued
debt?

I suspect that your answers will indicate that you, as a shareholder,
would prefer to use balance sheets and income statements based
on current value accounting for liabilities.

If you still are not convinced, consider the costing aspect of
liabilities. A financial intermediary acquires funds from its suppliers
and sells them to its customers. If it acquires funds under a
long-term contract at a fixed price and sells then at a later date

after current market buying and selling prices have risen, it is difficult to avoid reporting a profit under conventional accounting practices. In merchandising and manufacturing, this is known as an "inventory profit"; it is generally conceded that such profits need to be isolated in order to judge the success of the firm's operations in any period. For the purpose of judging managerial performance and for making sales (lending) decisions, the current (opportunity) cost of the resources consumed appears to be more relevant than their original acquisition cost. If we could save 11 percent by retiring debt, it does not make much sense to lend at 10 percent just because the funds were acquired on a long-term contract years ago at 6 percent. Historical costing of capital funds can give a very misleading indication of the success of current operations; while not exactly instant earnings, this effect might well be called "living off an inheritance." A legatee gets no such break under current costing. The distinction between the cost of acquiring funds and the cost of using funds is recognized just as it is for any other resource under current value accounting.

The tax aspect of revalued debt is comparable to that of revalued assets. If the liability is written down and a gain recorded, the amount should be reduced by the tax effect, leaving the debt at tax-adjusted market value. While the unfamiliarity of this application of comprehensive tax allocation may require that you think it through for yourself and express it in your own style, I am convinced that once you have done so you will see that it involves the same principle: the difference between the tax basis and accounting valuation of an asset or liability is an additional valuation factor.

The price level adjustment of the previous measurement of a liability is also comparable to the asset case. The restatement of the beginning amount (assuming inflation) would be a debit to the owners' equity as a restatement and a credit to a purchasing power gain account. If there were a change in the market value of the liability, it would be another income effect (subject to the tax adjustment). EXHIBIT XIII-5 illustrates the common factors involved in the revaluation of a long-term liability and the computation of the income effects. It is especially important to note that the real after-tax cost of debt funds for any reporting period cannot be computed without considering the price level

EXHIBIT XIII-5

LIABILITY MEASUREMENT AND RELATED INCOME EFFECTS WITH CURRENT
VALUE ACCOUNTING, RECOGNITION OF A CHANGE IN THE MEASURING
UNIT, AND TAX ALLOCATION*

	Liability	Income Effect Dr (Cr)
Valuation, 12/31/74	$1,000	
Restated in 1975 dollars	1,050	
Purchasing power gain	(50)	$(50)
Decline in quoted value	(70)	(70)
Market quotation, 12/31/75	930	
Tax on change in quotation, 50%	35	35
Valuation, 12/31/75	965	
Nominal interest expense		80
Tax on nominal interest, 50%		(40)
NET INCOME EFFECT		$(45)

*The debt consists of a $1,000 long-term bond bearing an 8%
coupon, selling at par on 12/31/74, and at 93 on 12/31/75 with
a 5% increase in the price index in 1975; incremental income tax
rates total 50%.

gain in conjunction with the nominal interest and its tax effect.
This exhibit may give us some insight into the bases for the
popularity of debt financing and the incentive to carry it too
far.

FINANCIAL REPORTING BY BANKS

Commercial banks have traditionally neglected financial reporting to shareholders. Considering the nature of the banking business, I suspect that an accountant or businessman who is unfamiliar
with bank financial statement practices would be surprised to learn
that, until about 1968, most banks omitted loan losses and gains
and losses on sales of securities from the computation of net income.
While these particular transgressions have ceased, a number of

questionable practices remain. They include measurement of irrelevant attributes, misclassifications, and insufficient disclosures.

Measurement of irrelevant attributes

—Use of historical values instead of current values of assets and liabilities in the computation of income and balance sheet aggregates.

—Use of loan reserves to smooth income and understate stockholders' equity.

Misclassifications

—"Capital notes" representing legal obligations to creditors in forms that would be called long-term debt in other corporations. Prior to 1975, such notes often were excluded from liabilities and shown as a separate category between liabilities and stockholders' equity, or even included, along with stockholders' equity, under the caption "capital." Starting in 1975, banks filing with the SEC have corrected this misclassification, but other banks may still be subject to criticism.

—"Unearned interest" on loans written on a discount basis, often included in assets and also reported as a liability. It is not a liability by the standards used in other industries and reporting an interest-earning asset at its maturity value is not in accordance with GAAP or other standards. Unearned interest and discount should be deducted from loans. This practice, like the one discussed above, has been corrected by SEC-controlled banking companies.

—Segregation of security gains and losses and computation of an income figure before deducting or adding the net after-tax effect of security transactions. A common practice is to compute a figure labeled "Income before income taxes and security gains and losses," then deduct income taxes to obtain "Income before security gains and losses," then deduct (or add) the net-of-tax security losses (or gains) to obtain net income. Note that most securities held by banks are not classified as capital assets so no special tax treatment applies. Gains and losses on their sale would not appear to be extraordinary in any sense: *APB Opinion No. 9* made this clear in 1966, and *APB Opinion No. 30* made it much stronger. Securities gains and losses should be closely associated with interest earned on loans in the income statement because both vary, in opposite directions, with inflation. As inflation bloats nominal interest rates it erodes securities values; to show the one effect as operating and the other as extraordinary is a type of poor matching.

Insufficient disclosures

—Required reserves. The portion of "Cash and due from banks" that is required as reserves deposited with the Federal Reserve Bank should be disclosed in order to give a clearer indication of the cash available for routine banking purposes.

—Interbank deposits not involved in routine business. Further breakdowns of "Due from banks" and "Deposits" are needed to disclose such items as investments in certificates of deposits of other banks and outstanding certificates of deposits held by other banks. As an example, some explanation is needed as to why the Chase Manhattan Bank had over $8 billion cash and due from banks out of total assets of $30.4 billion in 1972. How much of this money was available for regular depositors and borrowers, and how much of it was involved in interbank window dressing? The Crocker Bank does set out "Time deposits with the other banks" separately, and Wells Fargo shows "Time deposits with foreign banks." More information is needed along these lines.

—Other assets and other liabilities. Some banks show very large amounts described only as "other assets" or "other liabilities." One large West Coast bank showed other assets amounting to nearly 95 percent of its stockholders' equity and other liabilities in excess of its stockholders' equity. Surely such secrecy would not be condoned by auditors or stockholders in any other industry.

—Loan commitments. The total amount of loan commitments that borrowers have not yet drawn down but that could be demanded immediately after the balance sheet date is relevant to an appraisal of a bank's liquidity but is not usually disclosed.

—Other income and other operating expenses. All of the bank financial statements I examined showed "Other income" in excess of 50 percent of net income, and the "Other operating expense" item varied from 65 percent to 190 percent of net income. The nature of the items concealed in these categories can only be guessed.

—Maturity schedules on loans and investments. Some banks

give a moderate amount of information about the maturities
of their investment securities but others give no information.
In general, maturity information on loans is not provided.
Such data are needed by an analyst who is concerned with
a bank's liquidity.
—Subclassification of deposits. Insufficient information is
provided to permit the serious analyst to judge the risk
of deposit runoffs. Breakdowns among categories that vary
substantially in stability are needed. One atypical category
is deposits from other banks.
—Segment reporting. Bank holding companies, as well as
commercial banks themselves, are engaged in a variety of
lines of business. Nonbank activities should be segregated,
and banking operations should be divided on a governmental jurisdiction basis (at least into domestic and foreign).

The most significant of these criticisms are those pertaining
to measurements of financial statement items. The arguments for
current value accounting and charging loan losses to expense on
a direct write-off basis were presented in earlier sections of this
chapter. Now we must consider their impact on the financial
statements of commercial banks.

Banks operate in financial markets. The impacts of fluctuations
in those markets cannot be avoided; they can only be obscured.
The return is not available without the risk. Fluctuations in financial
markets are not only a critical factor in bank values and earnings;
they are a focal point for bank management. Acquiring funds
at favorable times and at favorable rates and investing those funds
on favorable terms is the essence of bank management. Decisions
as to the types and maturities of assets and liabilities to hold
and owe must be made daily. Sometimes the decisions are good
ones; sometimes they are not. Some managements make better
decisions than others. If a financial reporting system is to reveal,
instead of conceal, the successes and failures of bank management
on a periodic basis, beginning and ending valuations of the assets
and liabilities are essential. We understand, of course, that bank
managers do not like an uncontrollable, objective evaluation of
their activities any more than anyone else does, but those who
play the game must recognize that not everyone can be a winner.
And outsiders have more than a spectator's interest in the results
of the bank management game.

It is an inescapable fact that the values of many bank assets decline as interest rates rise and vice versa; financial statements must be rated as deceptive if they conceal phenomena as critical as these. Bank liabilities also decline as interest rates rise. Those liabilities that will require cash disbursements at predictable times can be discounted at current interest rates. The loss on assets is partially offset by a gain on liabilities as interest rates rise; declines in interest rates have opposite effects. These inevitable consequences of exposure to money rate risk should not be obscured; they are inherent in the nature of banking.

Revaluation of earning assets and of liabilities with predictable outflow dates typically leaves a net revaluation loss when interest rates rise and a net revaluation gain when interest rates fall. Are these net effects true indicators of the effects of interest rate changes on the interests of bank stockholders? Does a rise in interest rates make bank stockholders worse off? The answer to this question is not at all clear. The market agrees with the accounting procedure advocated above: the values of bank stockholders' equities do vary inversely with interest rates. Bank stock prices plunged when soaring interest rates knocked down bank asset values in 1969–1970 and in 1973–1974. In fact, Standard & Poor's New York City bank stocks average hit its low in the same week that its index of yield rates on long-term government securities peaked in each of the last three cycles—1966, 1970, and 1974. Investors apparently do take current yield rates into account in judging the values of assets, liabilities, and stock equities.

On the other hand, we also know that reported earnings of banks rise sharply as the interest rates they charge rise, and they continue to pay zero interest on demand deposits and the low and relatively stable passbook rate on large amounts of savings deposits. Sharply rising interest costs on large certificates of deposit and on "borrowed funds" only partially offset this effect. The basis for this earnings increase (and the possible accompanying increase in the value of a bank) is the cheap sources of funds: demand and passbook deposits. To a banker, these are almost pure gold (when lending rates are high). They are a valuable resource which is omitted from the balance sheet resources. Is there a way to put them on the balance sheet—other than as liabilities at face value?

The earning power value of a bank's deposits can be computed.

Assume that the demand and passbook deposits can be held constant in perpetuity by incurring service and advertising costs at the current level. The total annual cost of such deposits may then be calculated as a percentage of face value; for demand deposits it is only the related operating expenses. Savings deposit costs include the interest paid and operating expenses. According to the *Functional Cost Analysis* (1976) data of the Federal Reserve System, the cost of servicing demand deposits in 1975 averaged 3.011 percent in large banks. Passbook savings deposits cost 1.300 percent for operating expenses plus 4.644 percent interest, or a total of 5.944 percent. These cost percentages can be subtracted from portfolio yield percentages (net of portfolio expenses and adjusted for reserve requirements) to obtain a margin on the employment of deposit funds. Suppose this is 2 percent for the period just ended. One could then ask: What is a perpetuity of $.02 worth when capitalized at the "required rate of return"? If the required return is 20 percent before taxes, each dollar of deposits would be worth $.10. In other words, under these conditions, the deposits the bank has on its books would have an asset value equal to 10 percent of the deposit balances. A spread and asset value of this magnitude would nearly double the stockholders' equity in the typical commercial bank. Needless to say, if the spread narrowed to zero, this deposit value would be wiped out.

Does this type of analysis reflect the value of deposits to a commercial bank? I would argue that in a rough way it does. But the assumption that the current yield-cost spread will continue in perpetuity is a serious weakness. Generally speaking, competition and restructuring of industry tends to force unusual profits to revert to a more normal range. The development of money market instrument mutual funds (and shifts of deposits to high cost certificates of deposit) illustrates this tendency. Consequently, I consider the calculation of the asset value of deposits to be insufficiently reliable to put on balance sheets. However, it would seem appropriate to include, in the audited material, a note on percentage interest costs and earnings (including loan fees) in a consistent format that would permit the analyst to note the changes in spread. This could help the analyst make his own appraisal of the earning power value of a bank's deposits in order to round out the bank's current valuation picture.

It appears, then, that it is feasible for banks to value all of their assets except "bank premises and equipment,"[11] as well as their fixed maturity liabilities at current values. Nonmonetary assets can be carried and depreciated on a restated historical cost basis. Unfortunately, our inability to revalue deposits may cause some readers to reject the current value technique for application to those broad categories of assets and liabilities that are easily revalued. Intrastatement comparability certainly is a virtue, other things remaining equal. But is it wise to sacrifice the relevance of the current value information that can be presented just for the sake of comparability? My own preference is for maximizing the portion of the balance sheet that is stated in current values even though we must continue with the familiar mixture of bases of valuation that we presently use in nearly all industries, that is, showing cash, short-term receivables and payables and some inventories at current values and most nonmonetary assets at older (historical) values. Putting it another way, we cannot avoid mixed balance sheets, so we might as well maximize the portion that is stated at current values. We must remember that accountants cannot determine the value of the firm; they can only report those partial values which are helpful to a reader who is attempting to judge the value of the firm. The estimation of the intangible value of deposits, like the valuation of many intangibles, will have to be left to the judgment of the reader.

While the bank financial statements available to me do not provide enough information to permit me to test the effects of the valuation reforms proposed in this chapter, it is likely that, under current economic conditions, the write-downs of assets would exceed the write-downs of fixed maturity liabilities plus the reduction in the loan loss reserve (all net of tax). The result would be a decrease in stockholders' equity. This tells us that cumulative income would have been lower on a current value basis. It is also apparent that net income will fluctuate more widely when

---

[11] Nonmonetary assets can be valued and depreciated on a restated historical cost basis. Further reform in this area—adoption of replacement cost measurements—can reasonably be given a much lower priority than establishment of current value accounting for monetary items.

actual loan losses and unrealized gains and losses on revalued assets and liabilities are included in income. This instability of reported income is a natural consequence of operations in financial markets; to obscure it is to mislead the public. While bankers have expressed concern about the effects of unstable reported earnings on their images as solid financial institutions, accountants surely put themselves in an unbecoming position if they agree to conceal the effects of market fluctuations on bank assets and liabilities. A much more healthy approach would be to tell the story of fluctuating values and to add a great deal of additional information which will help the depositor, borrower, and stock-holder appraise the liquidity and stability of the institution. This means providing information on past and future flows. Some suggestions follow:

1. Publish a graph of monthly cash flow data for the last three years, including operating cash flow, loan collections (principal), and net deposit flows each month. EXHIBIT XIII-6 is illustrative. This type of report can convey a great deal of evidence of seasonal patterns and cyclical changes in the bank's cash flows.

2. A statement of flows of investable funds may be preferable to the mechanical type of "Statement of Changes in Financial Position" that is now presented. The statements now appearing in annual reports usually represent the difference column of comparative balance sheets, with the debit differences shown as applications and the credit differences as sources—except for the listing of net income, "add backs," and dividends (see EXHIBIT XIII-7).

   a. Change the title to "Flows of Investable Funds."

   b. Avoid listing depreciation and other additions to net income by showing cash revenues in excess of cash expenses on one line.

   c. Use flow (action) terminology instead of balance sheet
   · line captions.

   d. Organize the items on the basis of the normal direction of flow in an expanding bank: inflows through liability and capital accounts and outflows to asset accounts. Stick to this pattern, showing negative amounts when necessary.

   e. Include a three-year or four-year cumulative statement

EXHIBIT XIII-6

NTH NATIONAL BANK: MONTHLY FLOW DATA, 1971–1973

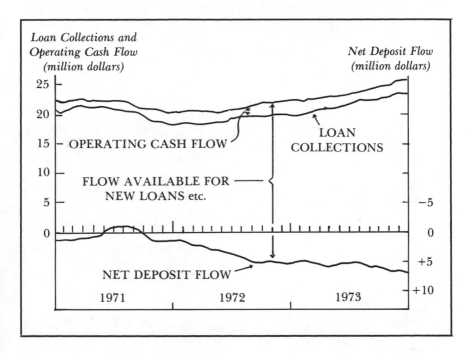

along with the most recent year's data, and perhaps those of the previous year, in order to show the flows over a representative cycle of business conditions.

3. Emphasize multi-year income statement data.
   a. Perhaps a three-year or four-year income statement should be included with percentage data to give a picture of "normal" relationships.
   b. Audited notes explaining accounting methods and the unevenness inherent in them could also include multi-year averages for such items as loan losses, portfolio revaluations, and liability revaluations.
4. Accountants should attempt to develop methods for reporting evidence of future cash flows by future periods. While bank balance sheet data consist mostly of future cash flow data, they are not scheduled by periods and most are shown at discounted amounts rather than future

EXHIBIT XIII-7

NTH NATIONAL BANK FLOWS OF INVESTABLE FUNDS 1973 AND 1971–1973

(in millions)

	1973		1971–1973	
Sources of Investable Funds				
Depositors (net):				
Demand	$ x		$ x	
Savings	x		x	
Time	x	$ x	x	$ x
Long-term financing		x		x
Other borrowings		(x)		x
Miscellaneous sources		x		x
Provided by operations (revenues less funds expenses)	x		x	
Less cash dividends paid	x	x	x	x
TOTAL FUNDS AVAILABLE FOR INVESTMENT		$xx		$xx
Investment of Available Funds				
Invested in loans (net)		$ x		$ x
Invested in securities (net)		x		x
Invested in bank premises and equipment (net of sales)		x		x
Miscellaneous uses		x		x
Added to cash and due from other banks		x		x
TOTAL USES OF INVESTABLE FUNDS		$xx		$xx

amounts. The bond maturity schedule that some banks present is a good, but limited, example of the information that is needed. It could be expanded to include many categories of loans and it could be broken down by shorter periods. The objectives are: (a) to show the expected inflow available to meet the needs of depositors and borrowers; and (b) to provide evidence of interest rate risk. This latter objective requires that maturity information be given about the liability side as well and that the amounts of "rate sensitive" assets and "rate sensitive" liabilities be disclosed.

5. More timing information can be given in the balance sheet, especially if a fairly comprehensive asset and liability maturity schedule is not provided.

Expanded reporting along these lines would provide the serious reader of the financial statements with enough information so that he would not be misled by fluctuations in the reported loan losses and in asset and liability revaluations reported in the income statement. It is possible, of course, that this total reporting package would result in occasional cases of loss of confidence in a bank; we cannot guarantee that it won't as long as banks are exposed to substantial risks and some are poorly managed. But it would appear preferable that such cases be based on full disclosure of the facts rather than on doubts fostered by deceptive reporting. As an accountant, I would not want to encourage unsafe banking practices by using accounting methods that cover up the risks that are being taken. Should not people dealing with banks have a right to know how the bank is being managed? Needless to say, not all bank managers can be expected to agree with this view, except superficially.

Bank Financial Reporting can be improved in several ways:

1. Recognize changes in the size of the monetary measuring unit by revising all beginning-of-period (or later acquisition date) values by the percentage change in a consumer price index. This would be a comprehensive application of price level accounting to all balance sheet accounts (and to depreciation).
2. Revalue investments and loans to tax-adjusted current values; include the changes from price-level restated beginning values as clearly disclosed components of net income.

(The tax adjustment amounts may not be large under depressed conditions because of the incentive to take tax-saving losses when current values affect the financial statements anyway.)

3. Revalue fixed maturity liabilities to current values and include the changes from price-level restated beginning values as clearly disclosed income statement items.
4. Revise the accounting for loan losses to reduce the smoothing effect and to measure loans at their discounted expected payoffs.
5. Improve the disclosure in the nine areas listed at the beginning of this section.
6. Improve and expand the information provided about past income and cash flows and provide more evidence of future cash flows.

CONCLUDING COMMENTS

In this chapter we have examined the valuation of the major categories of assets and liabilities that appear on the balance sheets of firms in the financial sector. The income effects follow from these valuations. The opportunities for reform of the accounting practices of commercial banks—a major industry in the financial sector—were given special attention. The valuation procedures advocated for these firms also apply, in general, to savings banks, savings and loan associations, insurance companies, and finance companies. The valuation of "nonearning" assets, such as "bank premises and equipment," has been touched on only in passing; it seems likely that people who find the proposals in this chapter acceptable for earning assets would prefer to revalue or at least restate the costs of physical plant assets.

The analysis of measurement aspects of accounting for portfolio assets and liabilities has resulted in the development of a revised reporting format as well. We saw that the association of purchasing power gains and losses with interest expenses and earnings is absolutely necessary if the reader is to perceive the economic cost of borrowing and the economic income from lending money. The reporting practices I am suggesting require the division of monetary items into three groups as follows:

i. Debt (both short- and long-term) representing explicit

borrowing. A full picture of the cost of debt capital must include the nominal interest cost net of tax, the purchasing power gain on outstanding debt, and the revaluation of debt net of the related tax effects.

ii. Monetary investments and loans that are treated as earning an interest return. The income effects of this group of assets include the nominal interest earned net of tax, the purchasing power loss associated with inflation, and the revaluation from the market quotation at the beginning of the period to the market quotation at the end of the period.

iii. Net incidental monetary items and cash. This group includes non-interest-bearing receivables and payables that exist primarily for convenience in executing transactions or to facilitate the sale of the entity's products. The purchasing power gain or loss associated with the average net balance of this group of items should be disclosed.

Proposals for drastic change in accounting are commonly faulted for their complexity and lack of objectivity. But consider: Which of the procedures that we have advocated is more complex than customary product cost accounting, than pension cost accounting, than dollar-value LIFO, or than calculation of life insurance policy reserves in accordance with the 1972 audit guide? Which features of our proposals involve less objectivity than estimating future uncollectibles, than estimating future lives and salvage values of plant assets, than estimating the lives and payoff patterns of goodwill and research and development outlays (which many CPAs prefer over the more objective alternative), or than estimating the rate of return on investment portfolios over the life of a new block of insurance policies (which is called for by the audit guide)? Anyone who considers these present practices acceptable cannot validly question the objectivity or complexity of the accounting proposals for financial industries presented here.

One other point deserves mention. Current value accounting for securities is widely accepted and commonly practiced. Current market values are used as the primary amounts that go into the computation of net worth in the following partial listing of cases:

1. Open end mutual funds.
   a. Stock funds

    b. Bond funds
    c. Short-term money market instrument funds.
    d. Mixed funds.
  2. Closed end investment companies.
  3. Brokerage firms.
  4. Securities trading departments of banks.
  5. Common trust funds operated by banks.
  6. Common stocks held by life insurance companies, in annual reports.
  7. Common and preferred stocks and bonds held by life insurance companies, for regulatory reports.
  8. University endowment funds and private foundations, e.g., Ford Foundation.

Note that in most of these applications financial statements are relied upon heavily as a basis for decisions such as buying and selling shares in the entity, judging and controlling the solvency of the firm (brokers and insurance companies), or appraising the performance of managers (securities trading departments). As a profession, accountants have had a great deal of experience with current value reporting of financial assets and should find that further applications pose no great problem.

In the face of overwhelming evidence of the need for current value information, it would seem that the accounting profession would want to get on with the development of techniques for implementing current value accounting for all portfolio-type assets and liabilities. Some accountants will argue, of course, that the evidence is not clear, that my tests of relevance are oversimplified, that investors should not expect the net worth number reported in the balance sheet to be a sound basis for pricing the company's shares. Fair enough! The financial statements must not be accepted as the last word. But what is the public to think of a profession that claims to be concerned with the measurement of wealth and changes therein but insists that its major products should not be used for making decisions that logically are based on the amounts of the reporting entity's wealth and changes in it, and that refuses to take steps to make those products more useful? I find it hard to believe that such cynical disregard for the public interest is consistent with the long-run health of the accounting, or any other, profession.

Common unit accounting's time has come! Current value accounting is ready for application to portfolio assets and liabilities. How much longer will preparers of financial statements resist these reforms?

ADDITIONAL READING SUGGESTION

Storey, Reed K. and Maurice Moonitz, "Market Value Methods for Intercorporate Investments in Stock," *Accounting Research Monograph No. 2* (AICPA, 1976).

STUDY QUESTIONS

1. Why might managers of firms in financial industries prefer that their financial statements be based on historical cost and historical receipt measurements rather than on current values?
2. Give examples of portfolio accounting situations that pose serious reliability problems.
3. What adverse macroeconomic consequences could result from financial institutions using historical entry value (cost or receipt) measurements? From using current value measurements?
4. Give examples of situations in which historical entry value measurements could lead to a lack of congruence of managers' goals and stockholders' goals.
5. Argue for and against the major alternative solutions to the tax allocation controversy in relation to portfolio assets.
6. Referring to EXHIBITS XIII-3 and XIII-5, state the circumstances under which you would advocate the close association and disclosure on the income statement of the five income effects identified in each of those exhibits.
7. Using a copy of the latest annual report of a prominent bank in your community, identify those criticisms of bank accounting that are listed in this chapter that apply to your bank's current statements.
8. Prepare a statement showing the "flows of investable funds" for a bank of your choice.
9. Is the shareholders' equity in a commercial bank changed when a new depositor opens an account with a substantial

balance? If so, how can the change be measured with acceptable reliability?

10. How would you advocate handling the loan loss accounting problem in a commercial bank? Why?

11. On the basis of the published financial statements of a financial institution familiar to you, plus data from other sources, prepare rough comparative balance sheets and an income statement on a current value basis.

12. Here is an excerpt from the 1971 *Annual Report* of International Telephone and Telegraph Corporation, the parent of Hartford Fire Insurance Company:

"Realized Investment Gains:

Hartford invests in common and preferred stocks to produce earnings from a combination of dividends and appreciation. The Corporation feels that shareholders are entitled to participate currently in the earnings generated by appreciation. However, present accounting rules require the sale of securities in order to record these earnings. Hartford, therefore, sells securities to realize investment gains each year which are equivalent to the appropriate historical rate of return on its portfolio of stocks." (p. 19)

(a) In your own words, describe Hartford's practices regarding realization of appreciation and accounting for it.

(b) Comment on this practice giving special attention to the information content of the "realized investment gains" line on the income statement.

13. This question relates to *FASB Statement No. 15* on accounting for troubled restructurings of debt:

(a) On what criteria does that standard rate high? Low?

(b) What changes would you recommend in that standard? On what criteria would your revised standard rate higher than the FASB Standard? On what criteria does your standard rate lower?

14. Mr. E. M. de Windt, Chairman, Eaton Corporation, recently expressed concern about changes in accounting standards and the direction the FASB and other bodies engaged in setting accounting standards were headed. Some excerpts from Mr. de Windt's address to the Milwaukee Chapter of the Financial

Executives Institute (October 12, 1976) follow:

(a) "The overtones of current value accounting threaten the insurance industry and state, municipal, and school bonding programs by lessening the attractiveness of long-term obligations and literally forcing unsound financial decisions." Can you provide examples that will support or refute this contention?

(b) "It's a definite 'no-no,' according to FASB #5, to put something aside for a rainy day. I once thought that reserving for contingencies was a matter of prudent management judgment based on experience and knowledge." Explain and comment.

(c) "Rules on translating foreign currency can transform a solid and profitable international operation into a big loser in dollars. Yet, that's been the effect of FASB #8." Explain and comment.

(d) "It is difficult to believe that the value of a 15-year foreign obligation could easily be revalued some 59 times before it has any real impact on the business. FASB #8 tells us to do it anyway; thus, our P & L statement is adjusted each time there is any fluctuation between the dollar and the Swiss Franc—from bitter experience let me assure you there have been more than a few in recent months." Give arguments for and against the feature of *FASB Statement No. 8* to which Mr. de Windt alludes.

(e) "I find it difficult to believe that accounting standards, rather than good business judgment, should be the governing fact in arriving at sound business decisions." Explain how accounting standards can affect decisions within the reporting companies.

CHAPTER XIV

ACCOUNTING DECISIONS: PLANT ASSETS

Most securities and monetary assets and liabilities can be measured by highly relevant methods—discounting future cash flows at a current market rate of interest, or one of the current market price methods—as we saw in the preceding chapter. Current (entry or exit) market prices are available for many commodity stocks— raw materials and supplies, finished products, merchandise held for sale. Plant assets, on the other hand, pose a much greater challenge to the accountant who wants to apply highly relevant measurement methods because current market quotations for equivalent assets are often not available due to either (a) uniqueness in design, location, or other physical features, or (b) cessation of production of the model in question combined with a thin market for used units in comparable circumstances. This is the setting in which we launch a search for plant asset measurement techniques consistent with the general measurement pattern discussed in previous chapters.

To begin with, we might note a widely quoted definition of depreciation accounting published by an authoritative source (AICPA Committee on Terminology, 1953, p. 25):

> Depreciation accounting is a system of accounting which aims to distribute the cost or other basic value of tangible capital assets, less salvage (if any), over the estimated useful life of the unit . . . in a systematic and rational manner. It is a process of allocation, not of valuation. Depreciation for the year is the portion of the total charge under such a system that is allocated to the year.

We quote this definition in order to indicate precisely the type of approach to depreciation accounting that we do *not* want to take. If depreciation accounting is not intended to yield a remaining asset amount that is a usefully accurate estimate of the asset's cash flow potential (or other version of value), why should that asset amount appear on a statement of financial position? If the depreciation number deducted on the income statement is not a measurement of the sacrifice of cash flow potential during the period, why should it be deducted from inflows of cash flow potential (revenues) in calculating a net change in the enterprise's cash flow potential (income)? We emphatically reject the "systematic and rational allocation" approach to depreciation and plant asset accounting.

If assets represent cash flow potentials, as we argued in chapter V, and if expenses and operating costs are diminutions in net cash flow potential, it follows that plant asset accounting must be aimed at measuring the cash flow potential of plant assets. Depreciation, according to this approach, is a reduction in cash flow potential other than due to price changes (although this distinction cannot always be made satisfactorily). Plant asset accounting, in other words, is a process of valuation. Just as in the case of any other net asset item, we are seeking surrogates for discounted future cash flows—typically current market values or surrogates for them.

THE VALUATION OF PLANT ASSETS ON A COST BASIS

We begin by reaffirming our willingness to accept prices in an active market as surrogates for discounted future cash flows. In particular, if a *perfect market*[1] for our asset existed, we would happily accept both the current market price as the asset amount

---

[1] We are adapting Fama and Miller's (1972, p. 21) perfect capital market to the market for plant assets. In the following definition of a perfect capital market, substitute "plant assets" for "securities":

1. All traders have equal and costless access to information about the ruling prices and all other relevant properties of the securities traded.
2. Buyers and sellers, or issuers, of securities take the prices of securities as given; that is, they do, and can justifiably, act as if their activities in the market had no detectable effect on the ruling prices.
3. There are no brokerage fees, transfer taxes, or other transaction costs incurred when securities are bought, sold, or issued.

to report on the balance sheet and the change in price as the
measure of depreciation (in the absence of both general price
level movements and changes in the "reproduction cost new" of
the asset in question). Imagine, for example, a used machinery
market with as many buyers and sellers of a particular category
and condition of machine, and with transaction costs as low, as
in the U.S. Treasury Bond market or in the market for General
Motors common stock. Prices in such a market would be rated
high on all criteria, especially attribute relevance and reliability.
In the absence of such a market, however, we have two major
alternative approaches: (1) accept a price quotation from a less
satisfactory market, if one is available, or (2) estimate the price
that would be quoted in a perfect market if one existed. We
turn first to the latter approach.

Estimating Market Prices of Used Assets

How does a perfect market behave and what does it accomplish?
We can visualize many buyers, each attempting to acquire a good
for the lowest possible price—preferably for less than the good's
utility to him and never for a sum of money which would produce
greater utility if spent on something else. We also visualize many
sellers who are equally determined to obtain the highest possible
price and to avoid selling the good for less than it is worth to
them. One consequence of this behavior is the equating of equilibrium market price with both the cost of production of the good
(if it is reproducible) and its contribution to either individual utility
(of a consumer good) or estimated marginal revenue product (of
a producer's good). The marginal revenue product of a plant
asset may be calculated by familiar present value techniques. The
investment analysis ("capital budgeting") problem is to determine
the present value of the marginal revenue product of a proposed
asset, although it often is computed on a cost saving basis, in
which case the output-level decision remains to be made by separate,
perhaps more subjective means. When the asset purchase decision
is formulated as a cost-saving problem, the typical objective is
to acquire a particular type of service at the minimum unit cost.
The required information may be organized somewhat as follows:

$$c_A = \frac{\sum\limits_{t=1}^{n} C'_{t,A}\,(1 + r)^{-t+1}}{\sum\limits_{t=1}^{n} S_{t,A}\,(1 + r)^{-t}} \qquad c_B = \frac{\sum\limits_{t=1}^{n} C'_{t,B}\,(1 + r)^{-t+1}}{\sum\limits_{t=1}^{n} S_{t,B}\,(1 + r)^{-t}} \qquad [1]$$

The average cost, c, per unit of service obtained via either alternative A or B is calculated by discounting all periodic costs, C', from acquisition date through retirement in period n at the cost-of-capital rate, r, and dividing by the discounted units (not by value) of services which the alternative will provide. Discounting the services is necessary because their timing makes a difference and because the costs are stated as of the acquisition date. Cost of capital is excluded from C'. We assume that costs are incurred at beginnings of periods and services are received at period-ends.

The choice of service source is made on the basis of minimum average unit cost, either c_A or c_B. If the patterns and quantities of service flows offered by the two (or more) available sources are equal, the choice may be made on the basis of aggregate costs; the denominator calculation and division are unnecessary. Otherwise, the model calls for estimates of the times and amounts of service flows. If the service flow is estimated to be steady over time it may be stated as one unit of service each calendar period. Then the cost of a unit of service is computed by dividing the present value of all costs by the present value of an annuity of one per period (as in the familiar annuity method of depreciation).

Equations of type [1] may be converted to a contemporaneous, full cost form (without discounting the periodic costs and the periodic service units and including the cost of capital on the net asset value in each periodic C) as follows:

$$c = \frac{\sum\limits_{t=1}^{n} C_t}{\sum\limits_{t=1}^{n} S_t} \qquad [2]$$

A salvage value (undiscounted) is most conveniently treated as a negative cost in period n. The cost, c, per unit of service may be thought of as full-cost depreciation.[2] That equations [1] and [2] yield the same unit cost, c, is shown in the Appendix (p. 455).

The comparison of c_A and c_B by many buyers of the service tends to result in their equalization—or one of them drops out as a viable alternative. In particular, if A is a new asset and B is a used asset of the same model, an active and efficient market will tend to equalize c_A and c_B. More generally, when a particular type of service is available from two different sources, a perfect market will adjust the prices of the two sources for (1) differences in the timing and amounts of service flow potential possessed by each source and (2) differences in the timing and amounts of other outlays (other than for purchase of the source) required to obtain the services, so as to make c_A equal to c_B in equation [1] above.

Now, assuming that the perfect market has established a price, c, for a unit of a particular type of service, and that all pure profit has been eliminated so that the cost and value of an asset are equal at acquisition date, we can write:

$$C_1 = V_1 = \sum_{t=1}^{n} S_t c(1 + r)^{-t} - \sum_{t=2}^{n} C_t' (1 + r)^{-t+1} \qquad [3]$$

where the last term excludes both initial acquisition price and subsequent cost of capital.

At the beginning of any period, i, during the life of the asset, its value can be expressed either in terms of (1) accumulated costs less service received (inputs to date less outputs to date), (2) replacement cost of future service flows less future costs including cost of capital (future outputs less future inputs), or (3) the present value of future services less the present value of future costs excluding cost of capital.

$$V_i = \sum_{t=1}^{i-1} C_t - \sum_{t=1}^{i-1} S_t c = \sum_{t=i}^{n} S_t c - \sum_{t=i}^{n} C_t$$

---

[2] A depreciation method that includes the cost of financing a plant asset in depreciation cost has been dubbed "cost-of-capital depreciation" (Staubus, 1968).

$$= \sum_{t=i}^{n} S_t c(1 + r)^{-t+i-1} - \sum_{t=i}^{n} C'_t (1 + r)^{-t+i} \qquad [4]$$

EXHIBIT XIV-1, designed to illustrate the input-output view of

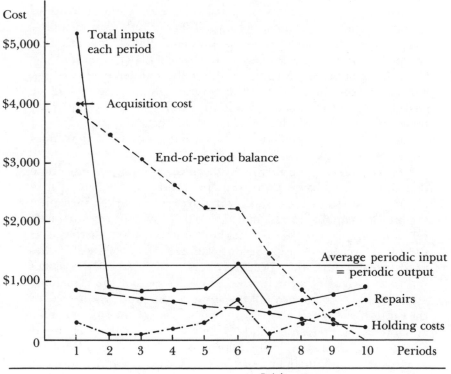

EXHIBIT XIV-1

MACHINE ACCOUNT INPUTS, OUTPUTS, AND BALANCES BY PERIODS

	Period										
	1	*2*	*3*	*4*	*5*	*6*	*7*	*8*	*9*	*10*	*Average*
Acquisition	4,000	0	0	0	0	0	0	0	0	0	400
Holding cost	860	796	719	648	581	582	462	358	274	213	549
Repairs	300	100	100	200	300	700	100	300	500	700	330
Total inputs (drs.). . .	5,160	896	819	848	881	1,282	562	658	774	913	1,279
Outputs (crs.)	1,279	1,279	1,279	1,279	1,279	1,279	1,279	1,279	1,279	1,279	1,279
Balance (ending). . . .	3,881	3,498	3,038	2,607	2,209	2,212	1,495	874	369	3	

Reproduced with the permission of the publisher from Staubus (1971a).

plant asset accounting (Staubus, 1971a, pp. 55–70), includes a set of numbers which can be used to exemplify these relationships. (Assume that "holding costs" are limited to the cost of capital and that repair costs are incurred at the beginning of each period.) EXHIBIT XIV-2 is set up to show how this set of numbers fits into equation [4].

Now let's take a look at this model in a real world light. We have suggested a technique for estimating the net present value of a plant asset so as to simulate the valuation that would be reached by a perfect market. It calls for estimating all costs of using the asset over its life as well as all service outflows, including any salvage value, in order to compute the unit "depreciation charge," or outflow of service from the asset, per equation [2]. Once the asset has been acquired, all repair, maintenance, holding, and other costs of obtaining the services of the asset would be charged to the asset account, while the outflow of service (quantity times unit cost) would be credited to the account, as called for in the first part of equation [4]. What defects or limitations does this approach have in practice?

First, considering the attribute relevance criterion, we must note that this is a cost-based measurement technique. While cost may equal discounted future cash flow in the perfect market, we cannot expect such equality in real markets. The quality of the surrogate relationship will vary across markets and the assets involved as the pure profit "gap" varies. Secondly, the reliability of the estimates used in computing the "predetermined unit cost" of the asset's service, which affects the depreciation charge and the remaining asset balance, is bound to fall far short of the ideal. In particular, the estimates of repair and maintenance costs, of the cost of capital and other holding costs, and of the service outflow, all made at the acquisition date, cannot be expected to be very accurate as measured by subsequent outcomes. However, the product cost accounting notion that standard unit costs may be preferable to actual unit costs for uses such as pricing and inventory valuation may be relevant here. The idea is that future costs, not past costs, are relevant to decisions and carefully developed standard costs may be the better bases for predicting future costs. Transferring this idea to plant asset costs, one might place a moderate amount of confidence in the estimates that provided the basis for the

EXHIBIT XIV-2

MACHINE VALUATION, BEGINNING OF PERIOD FIVE

$$V_5 = \sum_{t=1}^{4} C_t - \sum_{t=1}^{4} S_t c = \sum_{t=5}^{10} S_t c - \sum_{t=5}^{10} C_t = \sum_{t=5}^{10} S_t c (1+r)^{-t+i-1} - \sum_{t=5}^{10} C_t' (1+r)^{-t+i}$$

Period	Inputs To Date	Outputs To Date	Future Services	Future Costs	Present Value of Future Services*	Present Value of Future Costs (ex. COC)†
1	$5,160	$1,279				
2	896	1,279				
3	819	1,279				
4	848	1,279				
5			$1,279	$ 881	$1,066	$300
6			1,279	1,282	888	583
7			1,279	562	741	69
8			1,279	658	616	174
9			1,279	774	514	241
10			1,279	913	428	281
Rounding			3		2	
Totals	$7,723 –	5,116 =	7,677 –	5,070 =	4,255 –	1,648
Value	2,607	2,607	2,607	2,607	2,607	

*$1,279 discounted at 20% to beginning of period 5.

†Beginning-of-period repair costs discounted to beginning of period 5 at 20%.

acquisition decision, even in the face of subsequent variances between estimates and actual. Careful revisions of the estimates and the related unit depreciation charge and asset valuation, like revisions of standards, may also provide some relief from unreliable ex ante calculations.

A third problem with this approach to plant asset accounting is its rating on the cost-of-production criterion. The effort required to make the initial estimates and to revise them as actual data are accumulated probably is substantially greater than that involved in the application of traditional formulae. While some accountants may argue that the initial estimates are required for the acquisition decision and that follow-up estimates are needed for retention-replacement decisions regardless of how refined an accounting method is selected, we probably should recognize that many of these decisions are so easy to make (with no close alternatives) that they require no careful calculations. The cost of the additional calculations required in applying this approach surely is a strike against it.

Appraisals of the above-described valuation approach to plant asset accounting on the basis of the attribute relevance, reliability, cost, and other criteria are almost certain to stimulate the accountant to search for an alternative method. How frequently he will find a superior method is somewhat less certain. One approach to seeking an alternative is to concentrate on reducing the cost with a minimal loss of relevance and reliability. The following *complementary method* may achieve such results in many cases:

1. Simplify the computation of the unit service cost by omitting estimates of periodic postacquisition costs (including the cost of capital) and periodic service flows. Continue to estimate the total service flow and the salvage value (if material).

2. Capitalize, in the plant asset account, only the acquisition cost. Account for post-acquisition costs, including cost of capital, on a cash basis.

3. Determine the depreciation charge, and the credit to the plant asset account, as follows:
   a. Estimate the pattern of the service flow, i.e., the shape of the service flow line when graphed over time.
   b. Estimate the level and a simple pattern for (i) the cost

of financing the asset and other holding costs, and (ii) repairs, maintenance, and other costs of obtaining the asset's services.

c. Select a simple depreciation pattern (formula) which complements the costs in *b* so as to yield a total cost pattern similar to the service flow pattern in *a*.

Let's look at some examples. If the service flow pattern is constant, if the cost of capital and other holding costs are material and decreasing over time, and if the repair and maintenance costs are material and increasing so as to roughly offset the decrease in the holding costs, select the straight-line calendar method of depreciation (see EXHIBIT XIV-3 a). If the repair costs are too small or too flat to offset the decreasing cost of capital, an increasing charge method of depreciation (such as the annuity method net of the cost of capital) may be appropriate (see EXHIBIT XIV-3 b). If, on the other hand, increasing repair and maintenance costs more than offset decreasing holding costs, a decreasing charge pattern of depreciation (such as the constant-percentage-of-dimin-ishing-balance method or the sum-of-the-years-digits method) might be elected (see EXHIBIT XIV-3 c). And, of course, the accountant need not limit himself to a linear view of the world. We believe that in the stable prices case, it is proper to describe the results of a conscientious application of this complementary method of depreciation and plant asset valuation as estimates of the replacement cost of both the services received and the remaining stock of services. The quality of these estimates as surrogates for cash flow potential can be expected to vary widely, of course.

Several other comments may be made regarding the use of cost-based depreciation and plant asset valuation so as to simulate market valuation.

1. We must not forget that the cost-of-capital rate should be net of any inflation premium unless we are building an inflation rate into the service flow (and depreciation) pattern—a technique not recommended here because it requires predictions of market prices. The real cost of debt financing, as discussed in chapter XIII, must be computed net of the price level gain on debt, and the real cost of equity financing need not cover inflation because the

EXHIBIT XIV-3
COMPLEMENTARY DEPRECIATION PATTERNS

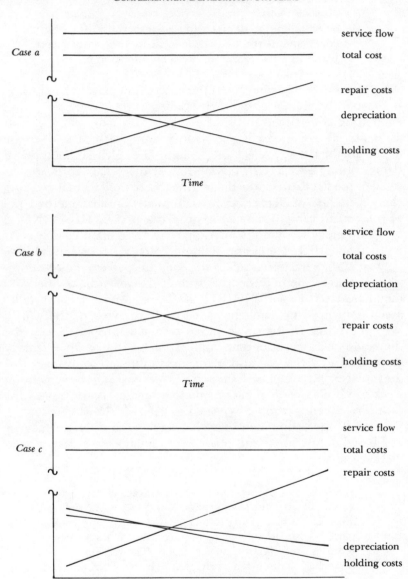

owners' equity in nonmonetary assets tends to maintain its value during inflation.

2. Variations in the rate of service flow over time call for corresponding variations in the total cost pattern; a complementary depreciation pattern may be selected in this case too.

3. If a units-of-production depreciation method is considered appropriate (because the value of the asset declines in proportion to use rather than with time), this approach is somewhat more complicated. Some post-acquisition costs (e.g., repairs) may follow the service flow pattern, while others (taxes, insurance, and cost of capital) may follow the value pattern. Under such circumstances, the reliability of the differential (complementary cost) pattern may not be acceptable.

4. The measurement of plant assets should take into consideration their tax bases as discussed in chapter VI (pp. 154–55). A plan for incorporating tax deduction payoffs into the cost-based, cost-of-capital valuation scheme of this chapter may be outlined.

   a. Divide an asset's service potential into two parts:
      (i) Tax-saving service.
      (ii) Primary services.

   b. Amortize the two parts separately, determining the factors as follows:
      (i) Tax-saving service:
         (a) Base valuation—present value (at cost-of-capital rate) of tax savings through depreciation and salvage value deduction as specified in (i) (b), (c), and (d) below.
         (b) Salvage value—per tax requirements.
         (c) Life—as chosen for tax return.
         (d) Pattern—as chosen for tax return.
         (e) Amortize by present value (annuity, cost-of-capital) method.
      (ii) Primary services:
         (a) Base valuation—gross base less base of (i).
         (b) Salvage value—gross salvage less salvage of (i).
         (c) Life—per best estimate.
         (d) Pattern—per best estimate.
         (e) Amortize per (a) to (d).

Any revaluation incorporated in the gross book value base

and in the base valuation for primary services should be on an after-tax basis. For example, if the asset is revalued to a current market price $100 greater than its book value and the tax rate is 48 percent, the gross base should be increased by $52. Alternatively, a $100 write-up in the gross base could be offset by a $48 tax adjustment contra account.

5. No one interested in the market simulation approach should have any illusions about its potential role in a calculation of the value of the firm as a whole. We have no basis for expecting the sum of asset amounts computed by this approach to equal the value of the firm, not just because of "inaccuracies" in the application of the technique, but because it is a version of the incremental approach to valuation that we discussed in chapter VII. When each asset is measured by the addition it appears to make to the value of the firm, the sum of such measurements cannot be expected to equal the value of the firm. This, of course, is true of all measurement methods used in accounting.

THE CHANGING PRICES CASE: REVALUATION OF GROSS INPUTS

In the preceding section, we described a general approach to plant asset valuation based on the assumption that the price for a given bundle of physical service potential was stable. Now let's consider the changing prices case.

The model in equation [4] includes the costs of all inputs involved in obtaining the services of the asset. If the market price of any one of these inputs should change between the date of the original estimates used in computing the unit cost of services and the valuation date, such a change should be taken into consideration in applying this model so as to simulate a current market price. Two changes are necessary. To the extent that the particular input is a factor in the periodic cost numbers that constitute the numerator of equation [2], the unit cost of plant asset services can be recalculated and the credits to the plant asset account for services yielded to date can be revised. To the extent that the price of a particular input already charged to the plant asset account has changed, a revision on the debit side is in order. This type of revaluation could relate to any input: acquisition price, repair costs, cost of capital, taxes, and so on, if it is being charged to the plant asset account.

If, on the other hand, a simplified, less costly version of this approach is being applied so that all post-acquisition costs bypass the plant asset account, the only basis for a revaluation of the asset would be a change in the market price of the asset in the form in which it was originally purchased. This measurement method may be called "depreciated replacement cost new." Replacement cost new may be measured in any of the following ways:

1. *Direct pricing* by obtaining a quotation from a supplier. This approach frequently can be applied to vehicles, machinery, and equipment.
2. *Indexing,* that is, multiplying the original historical cost by the factor that reflects the relationship between the current reading of an index of prices for the specific class of goods that includes the asset being measured and the level of that index at the date the asset was acquired.
3. *Unit pricing,* that is, obtaining a quotation on a unit of capacity basis. For example, if buildings like the one being measured now cost approximately $32 per square foot and our building has 100,000 square feet, its replacement cost is $3,200,000. This method can be applied to facilities such as piping, wiring, paving, and fencing.
4. *Functional costing,* in which an estimate is made of the cost of an asset that will perform the same function as the asset, or group of assets, in question even though it looks very different. For example, if the function of a mimeograph machine could be performed by a xerographic device, a quotation for the latter may be accepted as the replacement cost of the former, subject to adjustments for differences in operating costs.

If common unit (general purchasing power) accounting is being applied in conjunction with "depreciated replacement cost new" in a complete common unit, current value accounting system (as described in chapter IX), the difference between the specific, nominal *revaluation* of the asset and its *restatement* would appear as a holding gain or loss.

THE CHANGING PRICES CASE: REVALUATION OF USED ASSETS

In the preceding sections we have discussed the use of prices of specific inputs and estimates of quantities of inputs and outputs to simulate a perfect market price for a used asset. Now we turn to a much different approach: obtaining current market quotations for used assets—presumably in far-from-perfect markets. We may consider the possibility of using either "replacement cost used" or "as-is net realizable value (NRV)." In the context of a used equipment market, these represent retail price and wholesale price, respectively, that is, the price at which a dealer would sell and the price at which he would buy. The tendency of active and well-informed markets to price used assets so as to equate the cost per unit of service from a used asset with that from a new asset should be kept in mind.

The relevance of replacement cost and *as-is* NRV was discussed in chapter VII. We concluded that replacement cost was the closer surrogate for discounted future cash flows in active and well-informed markets because of the relationships expressed in the "gap chart" of EXHIBIT VII-2. As-is NRV was only considered highly relevant in cases of assets which were likely to be sold in approximately their existing condition. This means that assets held for use might reasonably be recorded initially at their acquisition prices, then periodically revalued to replacement cost used as long as they are considered up-to-date. As they reach the stage of semi-obsolescence, when they would not be replaced in kind if destroyed by accident even though they may still be in use, a switch to as-is NRV seems to be appropriate on the relevance criterion. The weakest feature of this approach, aside from the lack of used asset quotations in wholesale and retail markets, is the problem of deciding when to switch from the higher to the lower quotation—a time when a material percentage decline in value would be recorded in most cases because the retail-wholesale price spread for plant assets typically is large in percentage terms. The monetary amount involved, however, may not be so large as the asset approaches retirement.[3]

---

[3] In the present context, three stages may be recognized in the life of a plant asset between its acquisition and its retirement:

The relationships between replacement cost used (dealer selling price), as-is NRV (dealer buying price), and depreciated replacement cost new as computed by the market simulation approach discussed earlier in this chapter and summarized in equation [4] is illustrated in EXHIBIT XIV-4.[4] The market simulation method of asset measurement starts with the acquisition cost, which may be revalued to replacement cost new, and aims at reaching the salvage value at the retirement date. The spread between replacement cost used and as-is NRV is traversed gradually over the course of the asset's life, if the estimates are accurate. It follows that the market simulation approach conceptually is free of the gap problem that is encountered in applying the used market value approach, namely, the loss that must be taken at whatever date is chosen for making the leap from replacement cost used to as-is NRV. Some accountants, including Chambers, would prefer to make that leap at the acquisition date. Others would wait until retirement; a third possibility is to attempt to identify the date of the technological improvement that makes the asset semi-obsolete, if that does occur, and record the loss at that date. One clue to semi-obsolescence is the manufacturer's discontinuance of the old model.

The model of asset values illustrated in EXHIBIT XIV-4 may raise questions regarding the spreads between the three values. The difference between replacement cost used and NRV may be attributed to transaction costs, dealers' costs, and transportation, removal, and installation costs. Explanations for a buyer's willingness to pay a replacement cost used that exceeds simulated market value include desire to avoid the risk involved in buying

---

1. An up-to-date asset—one that, if it were to be replaced, would be replaced with the same model or design. Typically, in the machinery and equipment field, an up-to-date asset is of a model that the manufacturer is still producing.
2. A semi-obsolete asset, which is not up-to-date because a more economical model is available or a better way of performing its function has been found. This asset is still worth using because the cost of using it, excluding depreciation, is less than the total operating cost of its challenger, including depreciation.
3. An obsolete asset, which compares unfavorably in the cost test mentioned in the preceding sentence. This asset cannot be used economically on a regular basis, although it might be retained as a standby unit.
[4] Cf. Baxter (1971, p. 35).

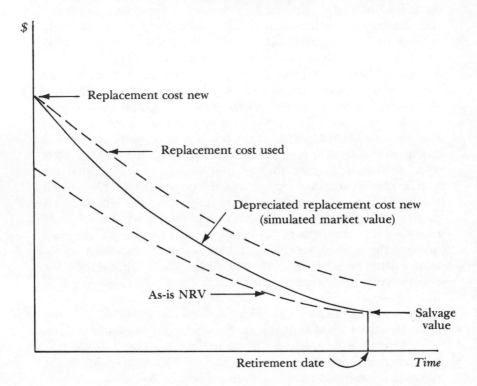

the more expensive and longer-lived new asset as well as difficulties encountered by small businesses in financing a new asset (which could be interpreted as a higher than average cost-of-capital rate). The most obvious reason for an owner selling a used asset for less than its simulated market value is that changes in his operations make the asset no longer useful to him.

Returning to the used market price approach to asset measurement, depreciation appears to be the difference between market quotations at two successive dates. But we should consider the possibility of distinguishing between a change in market price due to the aging, wearing out, or obsolescence of the asset and a change in price due to changes in economic conditions affecting the price of such assets. The former may be called depreciation and the latter a holding gain or loss. The advantage of such a distinction is that it permits the reader of financial statements to judge the firm's success in routine operations separately from the impact of price changes on it. Unfortunately, the necessary price quotations often are unavailable. The preferred procedure for measuring the holding gain or loss would appear to involve a comparison of (a) the beginning-of-period price of the particular asset held and (b) the end-of-period price for an asset that is comparable in model, age, and condition to the one that was held at the beginning of the period. For example, if at the beginning of the period we held a four-year old S & W 3A turret lathe, its price should be compared with an end-of-year quotation for a four-year-old S & W 3A turret lathe, not the price of a five-year-old lathe. Such comparable quotations would be available only if the specified model had stayed in production long enough to provide a supply of both four- and five-year-old assets to the market. A second comparison of a four-year-old, end-of-period price with the price of a five-year-old asset would yield the depreciation number. This version of current value accounting may be integrated with common unit accounting in the same manner as was described at the end of the preceding section.

Revaluations of used assets appear to depend heavily upon active markets from which to obtain quotations. However, we should mention the regression technique, pioneered by McKeown (1971) and Beidleman (1973), for estimating used asset prices in thin markets. In the simplest case, asset age is the single independent variable used to estimate market price via least squares linear regression. If an acceptable sample of market quotations for assets of the same model at different ages can be obtained, a regression equation can be estimated and then used to estimate the price for an asset of the same model at an age not represented in the sample. In fact, the estimated (regression line) price may even be considered preferable to an actual price quotation that has been reported (for a different unit) because out-of-line actual prices may be influenced by erratic factors which could not be expected to influence the price that is relevant to the specific circumstances of the asset now being measured. Unfortunately, this method is relatively costly. Beidleman also tested multiple regression versions, incorporating variables such as level of output in the industry and interest rates, but his evidence suggests that any improvement in results is not likely to be worth the cost.

CONCLUDING COMMENTS

In chapter IV we argued that the major users of financial statements want financial statements that will help them predict the firm's capacity to pay cash to investors (creditors and owners). A balance sheet which provides evidence of cash flow potential and an income statement which provides information about the economic events that changed the firm's net cash flow potential during the reporting period might reasonably be expected to provide information which is useful in making cash-flow-oriented decisions. Traditional depreciation accounting, as described in AICPA literature and as observed in practice, does not, in general, appear to be *aimed* at providing evidence of cash flow potential or changes therein, so it cannot be *expected* to provide such information. Accordingly, we suggest that traditional depreciation accounting be abandoned.

We suggest the adoption of plant asset accounting methods that yield asset amounts and operating cost numbers that have some demonstrable economic relationship to current values of assets in an existing market or to values that would be reflected in an active and well-informed market for the asset if such a market did exist. I freely concede that the latter (market simulation) approach yields measurements that are not as relevant, reliable, or economical as I would like; whether they can be of positive net value in a majority of cases in which current market quotations are missing is a question which I would prefer to postpone answering until the accounting profession accumulates some relevant experience. I do recommend that the profession give the market simulation approach a chance.

ADDITIONAL READING SUGGESTIONS

Baxter, W. T., "Depreciating Assets: The Forward-Looking Approach to Value," *Abacus* (December 1970), pp. 120–31.

———, *Depreciation* (Sweet & Maxwell, 1971).

―――― and N. H. Carrier, "Depreciation, Replacement Price, and Cost of Capital," *Journal of Accounting Research* (Autumn 1971), pp. 189–214.

Hendricksen, Eldon S., *Accounting Theory*, rev. ed. (Richard D. Irwin, 1970), chapters 12, 13.

Johnson, Orace, "Two General Concepts of Depreciation," *Journal of Accounting Research* (Spring 1968), pp. 29–37.

McKeown, James C., "Comparative Application of Market and Cost Based Accounting Models," *Journal of Accounting Research* (Spring 1973), pp. 62–99.

Staubus, George J., "Statistical Evidence of the Value of Depreciation Accounting," *Abacus* (August 1967), pp. 3–22.

――――, "Plant Financing, Accounting, and Divisional Targetry," *California Management Review* (Summer 1968), pp. 81–94.

Thomas, Arthur L., "The Allocation Problem in Financial Accounting Theory," *Studies in Accounting Research, No. 3* (AAA, 1969).

――――, The Allocation Problem: Part Two," *Studies in Accounting Research, No. 9* (AAA, 1974).

Wright, F. K., "Towards a General Theory of Depreciation," *Journal of Accounting Research* (Spring 1964), pp. 80–90.

Young, T. N. and C. G. Peirson, "Depreciation—Future Services Basis," *The Accounting Review* (April 1967), pp. 338–41.

STUDY QUESTIONS

1. Russ Corbin owns some rugged acreage including the peak of Roundtop Mountain, which is on the edge of a substantial metropolitan area. At a cost of $40,000 he has erected a steel tower on which radio transmitter antennae may be placed. He leases space on the tower to several firms which operate citizens' band radio communication systems. Upon completion of the tower, he signed leases for all available space at rentals totalling $4,400 per year, payable annually at the end of each year. These leases run for 25 years, at which time the tower is expected to fall down. It requires no maintenance. Corbin's cost of capital is 10%.

(a) If Corbin records depreciation on the tower on the straight-line calendar method, what will the book value of the asset be at the end of 13 years?

(b) If at the end of 13 years the market rate of return on investments of this type is 10%, what would you estimate to be the fair market value of this tower at that date?

(c) If Corbin records cost-of-capital depreciation as described in this chapter, what will the book value of the asset be at the end of 13 years?

(d) Compare your answers to (a), (b), and (c). Is correspondence between book value and market value a reasonable objective of plant asset accounting?

2. How, if at all, should ex ante computations of the unit cost of plant asset services anticipated from a proposed investment differ from ex post costing of plant asset services?

3. Using the set of criteria outlined in chapter III, compare (a) typical plant asset–depreciation accounting in current practice, (b) the valuation approach described in equation [4] in this chapter, and (c) valuation at current exit market price (as-is NRV).

4. "Usefully accurate and nonarbitrary estimates of depreciation and remaining value of assets owned can be made under the same conditions as those under which usefully accurate and nonarbitrary ex ante estimates of net present value of prospective assets can be made." Comment.

5. "One problem with cost-of-capital depreciation is that it is not clear to what investment base the cost-of-capital rate should be applied. Is the amount of the investment at any post-acquisition date the amount of unrecovered cost or the NRV of the asset?" How does the cost-based valuation approach to plant asset accounting solve this, assuming constancy of replacement cost new?

6. A machine was purchased for $10,000. Data pertaining to the tax-saving services it offers are: life, 3 years; salvage value, $1,000; sum-of-years-digits pattern; tax rate, 50%; cost of capital, 10%. Data pertaining to its primary services are: life, 4 years; salvage value, $0; straight-line pattern; cost of capital omitted.

Prepare a depreciation schedule for this machine.

Appendix

We want to show that the unit cost of plant asset services calculated on an ex post basis per (2) equals the unit cost calculated on an ex ante basis per (1), that is, that

[2]
$$\frac{\sum\limits_{t=1}^{n} C_t}{\sum\limits_{t=1}^{n} S_t} = c = \frac{\sum\limits_{t=1}^{n} C'_t (1 + r)^{-t+1}}{\sum\limits_{t=1}^{n} S_t (1 + r)^{-t}}$$
[1]

where $C' + k = C$. The aggregate cost of financing the asset during a period is designated k. Let us examine the two-period case in which $k_1 = C'_1 r$ and $k_2 = (C'_1 + k_1 - S_1 c + C'_2)r$. Dividing (2) by c,

$$1 = \frac{\sum\limits_{t=1}^{n} C_t}{\sum\limits_{t=1}^{n} S_t c} \quad \text{so} \quad \sum\limits_{t=1}^{n} C_t = \sum\limits_{t=1}^{n} S_t c$$

Expanding: $\quad C'_1 + k_1 + C'_2 + k_2 = S_1 c + S_2 c$

Substituting for k:

$$C'_1 + C'_1 r + C'_2 + (C'_1 + k_1 - S_1 c + C'_2)r = S_1 c + S_2 c$$

Rearranging: $\quad C'_1 (1 + r)^2 + C'_2(1 + r) - S_1 cr = S_1 c + S_2 c$

Add $S_1 cr$: $\qquad\qquad\qquad\qquad\qquad\qquad S_1 cr = S_1 cr$

$$\overline{C'_1(1 + r)^2 + C'_2(1 + r) = S_1 c(1 + r) + S_2 c}$$

Multiply by

$(1 + r)^{-2}$: $\quad C'_1 + C'_2(1 + r)^{-1} = S_1 c (1 + r)^{-1} + S_2 c (1 + r)^{-2}$

Condensing: $\quad \sum\limits_{t=1}^{2} C'_t (1 + r)^{-t+1} = \sum\limits_{t=1}^{2} S_t c (1 + r)^{-t}$

Dividing:
$$\frac{\sum_{t=1}^{2} C_t' (1 + r)^{-t+1}}{\sum_{t=1}^{2} S_t (1 + r)^{-t}} = c$$

CHAPTER XV
SOME CLOSING THOUGHTS

The fourteen chapters preceding this one are intended to provide an approach to accounting issues that can help an accountant make choices pertaining to financial reporting. This approach will not work perfectly for any of us. It does not eliminate judgment, and does not assure that a choice made on the basis of the framework presented here can be proved to be the one and only correct choice. I think of accounting as a science—a branch of economics, one of the social sciences—but, like economics, it is a relatively soft science. Nevertheless, a premise of this book is that accounting decisions can be based on harder evidence than they often have been in the past. While we should never think of accounting as a field in which it is typically possible, even with the benefit of hindsight, to say whether or not the best alternative was chosen, we can make some systematic effort to make accounting decisions that help us to achieve our objectives.

Chapters II through XIV are intended to constitute a related series of thoughts—to represent a systematic effort, perhaps. The present chapter, on the other hand, includes several mini essays that break away from the book as a unit. They are meant to provoke you into thinking about the importance, first, of accounting principles to the field of accounting, and, secondly, of the field of accounting to our society. I assume that people who read this book are deeply enough interested in the future of the accounting profession, in the broad sense, to stop occasionally to think about where it is going. Whether or not you agree with the decidedly unsystematic and definitely unscientific musings in the following paragraphs is not important, but I do hope they stimulate some serious thinking on your part.

The Old Accounting and the New

Readers may wish to contrast the old accounting and the new by thinking about some of the key ideas associated with each. A brief review of some traditional literature discloses several dominant concepts and assumptions.

Conservatism. Sterling (1967) has shown that the doctrine of conservatism is the most basic of all concepts underlying the old accounting. Although defenders of this doctrine occasionally have tried to support it by suggesting that it can serve as a rough counterweight to the natural optimistic tendency of investors and businessmen, it seems obvious that any service to investors favored the buyer and hurt the seller of securities. No justification for this was ever provided, to my knowledge. On the other hand, it is easy to see how conservative reporting could help protect the management and auditors against the risk of lawsuits by unsuccessful investors and could protect the management against having to report poor results by building up "secret reserves" that could be called on when needed. This emphasis on the needs of managers and auditors over those of investors was typical of the old accounting.

Objectivity. Both the old and the new accounting recognize objectivity in accounting work as desirable. The major difference is that it is one of several criteria to be taken into consideration in making accounting choices within the new framework whereas it was often used unevenly in the old accounting as the major basis for supporting a practice that was preferred for some other reason, often conservatism, but was ignored when it did not serve the purpose at hand. For example, the estimation of uncollectibles and of depreciable lives and salvage values and the use of current market values when they were lower than historical cost indicate that objectivity was not used in an even-handed way.

Diversity in Accounting Among Independent Entities. Grady included diversity in his "Inventory" (1965) as descriptive of the accounting practices of the time. Differences in circumstances were not alleged to be the basis for this diversity; rather, the right of management to "choose the accounting practices and methods of application most suitable to the needs and purposes of the entity and which, in the judgment of management, will most fairly present the financial position and results of operations" (p. 34) was thought to be the basis for diversity of practices. This preference for diversity over comparability, which was omitted from Grady's list, was consistent with the traditional emphasis on the needs of management and accountants over those of external users of financial reports.

Consistency Over Time. Modern accountants do not, of course, object to emphasis on consistency. In fact, we may prefer to give it more attention than it gets in the old accounting, where it gave way to conservatism in the lower-of-cost-and-market rule. It has also been called on as a defense against proposed changes in accounting principles. Why was consistency not included in a broad version of comparability as was discussed in chapter III of the present work?

The Going Concern (Continuity) Assumption. Advocates of historical cost measurement have often supported it over current exit market values on the assumption of the going concern. The modern trend is towards replacing this concept with the assumption that exchange transactions are break-even events unless the new net asset item is either measured on the basis of independent evidence or is written off as unmeasurable. The break-even assumption as a "measurement method of last resort" appears to be more consistent with the decision-usefulness objective than the assumption that the entity will not go out of existence in the foreseeable future.

The Stable Measuring Unit Assumption. To avoid the necessity of adopting common unit accounting, some accountants have fallen back on the assumption that the measuring unit was stable. Most accountants now recognize it as irreconcilable with their experience but have, by means that we discussed near the end of chapter IX, avoided the obvious implications of its unreality. The pervasive distortions introduced into most financial statements by ignoring changes in the significance of the measuring unit must not be allowed to continue if the accounting profession is to lay any claim to serving society as best it can.

The Business Entity Concept. Two versions of the entity concept have been emphasized in the literature: the entity as a scope concept associated with any one set of financial statements, and the entity point of view in measuring income and net assets. The former is neither terribly critical nor objectionable. As Vatter (1947, p. 3) wrote, "To define the area of attention in terms of an enterprise merely restricts the *scope* of a set of books or a series of reports; the way in which materials are dealt with within them is quite another matter." The entity *point of view* is too closely allied with the point of view used to defend diversity in accounting among independent entities to be acceptable to those who favor the decision-usefulness objective.

In contrast to the above ideas, and some others that were mentioned less frequently in the old literature, the new accounting offers, at the most fundamental level, the decision-usefulness objective; then adds a layer of criteria for use in evaluating accounting proposals (attribute relevance, reliability, comparability, effects via other parties, intelligibility, timeliness, cost, and so on); makes an effort to ascertain what types of financial information are relevant to the decisions of financial statement users; then tries to select measurement methods and reporting techniques that best meet the entire set of criteria. The contrast is striking.

We may also emphasize the contrast by calling attention to what the old accounting failed to accomplish. First and most importantly, it did not even attempt to provide information for investment decisions, to serve present or prospective investors, or to treat them equally. "The purpose for which annual accounts are normally prepared is not to enable individual shareholders to take investment decisions" (Council, 1965, p. 2). Not only did the old accounting neglect to establish investor service as an explicit objective, but it insisted on reporting old measurements in preference to up-to-date measurements and relied on concepts like those listed above that were not oriented towards investor service. It follows that the old accounting made no effort to report the current values of assets or liabilities, or the difference between their totals.

Another task the old accounting never attempted was to measure the cost of using resources or the cost of performing activities. If it had been concerned with these matters it would have had to focus on the sacrifices of service potential made at the time the resources were used, an approach that was foreign to the old accounting's orientation. Similarly, the performance of an entity or its managers during a specific accounting period was neglected, although lip service was paid to these concepts. But how conscientious could the old accounting have been and still have failed to insist on measuring the entity's resources at the beginning and end of the reporting period? It seems more descriptive to say that the only period for which any attempt was made to measure performance was the life of the enterprise, and the assumption that the measuring unit was stable defeated that attempt.

That the old accounting failed to accomplish these tasks is sufficient cause for us to give it a dishonorable discharge. That it denied interest in such goals must be a shocking indictment in the minds of students of the new accounting.

ACADEMIC ACCOUNTANTS' INFLUENCE ON PRACTICE

The relationship between accounting theory, the academic community as a major incubator of accounting theory, and the American Accounting Association, on the one hand, and the world of accounting practice on the other is a topic that may be of interest to those concerned with how accounting decisions are made. If so, some recently published observations may be thought relevant (Staubus, 1975a, pp. 163–64):

> First, let us take a look at our accomplishments in the field of establishment of accounting principles and standards. The Association has, through its executive committee and concepts and standards committees, issued five broad statements starting with the tentative one in 1936 and continuing through 1941, 1948, 1957, and the 1966 *Statement of Basic Accounting Theory*. Have these statements had any impact on the practice of accounting? Have those preparing and auditing and using financial statements paid any attention? If you can answer these questions affirmatively, you have a more lively imagination than I have. Nor have the individual efforts of academic authors had much effect, with a few notable exceptions. I think Professor Paton, the elder, could be said to have had some influence which is detectable within his lifetime, but only because he has been blessed with good health. We all know that his *Accounting Theory* (Paton, 1922) was published

in the early twenties and we also know that the constant interest rate method of amortization of premium and discount on bonds payable and the treatment of discount as a contra liability, both of which he recommended in 1922, were not considered the generally accepted methods until *APB Opinion No. 21* in 1971. While that may give you youngsters cause for hope, it can also raise the question as to whether you can trust anyone over thirty to put much effort into the development of accounting thought. We may never see the payoff. In fact, I have often thought that publishing a book on accounting theory is a little like dropping a rose petal down the Grand Canyon and waiting for the echo. I don't recommend it if you are short on patience. While the pen may be mightier than the sword, I suspect that those who want to have some impact had better recognize that in union there is strength. For this reason, I recommend that you band together with your colleagues to respond to FASB and CASB exposure drafts. To date, the AAA as an organization has had about as much effect on the establishment of accounting principles as that little boy depicted in fountain statuary would have on a forest fire.

If those remarks are accepted as a reasonably accurate description of the influence normative theorists have had on the development of accepted accounting principles, how can that influence be explained? Why has such a cleavage developed between practitioners and theorists? Perhaps practitioners have not felt a need for the types of changes that theorists have proposed. If so, is it due to the insensitivity of practitioners to the public's needs? Or to the vivid imaginations of theorists who see unmet needs that do not exist? Perhaps there is enough blame for all to share. The "I'm all right, Jack" attitude of practitioners matched by the "I'm not interested in accounting practice" attitude of theorists can easily prevent any serious communication between the two groups. As a member of the academic community, I am convinced that our lack of effort to teach "the best accounting we know" and to solve the associated implementation problems is part of the explanation for our lack of influence. When we publish our research results in the most academic journals and speak at academic conferences and workshops we are communicating only with ourselves. Is that the limit of our aspirations?

One result of the exciting work of the past decade in areas such as information economics, information theory, and cognitive processing is that hundreds of young academics are now attempting to emulate the new generation of intellectual giants in these fields. Ambition and faith in one's own capacities are personal qualities I would not want to denigrate, but before we encourage a young scholar to concentrate on the most "far-out" frontiers that few are capable of grasping, we should consider a couple of relevant factors. One is his or her probability of success. Another is the values, both to the individual and to the field of accounting, of devoting more attention to making accessible to students and practitioners some of the nearby "generally accepted accounting theory" that has survived years of examination in academic circles but has not been proven, or even tested, in practice. The development of innovative teaching materials and implementation techniques as well as communication with the profession and businessmen should be recognized as worthy activities and proper bases for promotion of accounting teachers.

THE ACCOUNTING PROFESSION'S SERVICE TO SOCIETY

Serious "students" of accounting theory have a right, if not a duty, to think about the importance of accounting principles choices to their societies. What is the significance of the accounting principles game? When one looks beyond the relatively close circle consisting of accountants themselves, managers who are appraising subordinates and in turn being appraised by their superiors, and investors who willingly take risks and usually win or lose only from or to each other—besides this relatively unimportant group of "money grubbers," who cares?

One type of response, perhaps not an answer, is that the set just described is a rather large and influential group of people in advanced, decentralized, industrial societies. Those people form a big part of the "establishment," and their decisions and influence have a substantial impact on their fellow-citizens. Given the general structure of our society and the objectives accepted by the majority of citizens, the decisions made by managers in both the public and private sectors and by those controlling capital have an undeniable significance to all of us. The extent to which those

decisions rest on a foundation of financial information may not
be so clear; it may depend, in part, on the quality of that
information. But surely accountants would not appear unduly
immodest if they said that accounting principles do play more
than a bit part in the drama of western civilization.

In fact, if we were to warm up to the drama theme and argue
the case for accounting's importance to "our way of life," without
concerning ourselves with the objectivity or completeness of our
analysis, we might even be able to cast accounting in a leading
role—whether as hero or villian is for you to decide. Picture a
major decentralized (that is, relatively democratic) country that
is having economic problems, including inflation, unemployment,
environmental degradation, and lack of confidence in the economy,
the government and in other groups in the economy. The farmers
feel undercompensated for the work they do; investors see their
returns falling short of their expectations; workers think everyone
is getting rich except them; businessmen wonder how much longer
they can stay in business under the prevailing conditions. One
obvious question bearing on the intergroup relationships in such
circumstances is just how clearly people perceive the relative
economic returns to the various parties. Accounting, including
macro-accounting, surely has a role in the state of the economic
information that circulates, or fails to circulate within society.

Now consider two more roles, that of capital in advanced
economies and that of individuals who make decisions to save
and invest. Individuals no doubt save and invest for various
combinations of reasons, but I have heard no one argue that
prospective returns have no influence on those decisions. To the
extent that past returns are one basis for predicting returns,
information on investment performance is a basis for investment
decisions. It follows that inaccurate information on investment
performance may mislead investment decision makers. Decisions
based on misleading information are unlikely to yield the intended
results.

Accounting practices have the potential to provide misleading
information about the returns on capital investments, both returns
on investments in the assets appearing on company balance sheets
and returns to security holders and lenders. We might raise
questions such as the following:

1. Is the profitability of those activities making use of substantial amounts of capital being reported accurately?
2. Is entity profitability being reported accurately?
3. Are the returns on security investments being reported accurately?

Some readers will immediately question the meaning of "accuracy" in this context. One answer is that profits and returns are being reported accurately if they represent what they purport to represent, or if the measurement techniques that are used are understood by the receiver of the data, or if his perception of the data corresponds with the perception of one who fully understands the techniques that are used. In this sense, one might argue that full disclosure of the accounting principles employed results in accurate reporting to the sophisticated reader who is knowledgeable about accounting and takes the trouble to trace through the implications of the accounting methods that were said to have been used. But how many members of the society are included in the group just described? Many observers who are in a good position to judge this matter feel that this group includes a small minority of professional securities analysts, only a moderate percentage of professional accountants, a very small minority of business managers, and practically no politicians or union leaders.

Now consider the implications of the above-described state of affairs in the context of the traditional political process, a process of making decisions regarding price controls, taxation, regulation, and government operation of basic economic activities. How likely are these decisions to yield the intended results if the data produced by accountants are misleading? Putting it another way, we should not expect good decisions if the basic economic data produced by accountants do not mean what the decision makers, broadly including all voters but especially elected officials, think they mean.

This raises the question of how the public interprets the words "profit," "income," and related terms that are so critically involved in many public policy issues. If, as Hicks (1946) suggests, the most generally understood meaning of income is the amount a person could spend during a period and still be as well off as he was at the beginning of the period, accountants might well face up to the question of whether they should adapt their concepts to those of the public or try to convince the public to accept fixed accounting concepts. Which set of ideas is the easier to change? For that matter, which set of concepts is the more serviceable? If income and profits taxes are viewed as permanent features of our societies, and if the public intends to use an income tax to take a slice of the "better-offness" of taxable entities without touching their capital, the effectiveness with which an income measure that does *not* reflect "better-offness" can be used to achieve the taxing objective is certainly questionable—given that few of those who are influential in formulating public policy, especially tax laws, understand the intricacies of accounting practices.

Sanders, Hatfield, and Moore (1938) may have come closer to the mark than they were given credit for when they wrote (p.1): "Making effective and effectively maintaining as near as may be the distinction between the capital and income of a particular enterprise are the ultimate objectives which determine the activities of accountants and the functions of accounting." If accountants were able to effectively maintain that distinction they would deserve much credit for contributing to public-policy types of decisions. They would certainly be making real progress towards providing data on which individual investors could make decisions and on which managers and investors could appraise the performance of entities, parts of entities, and managers. But if the profession makes no serious effort to achieve these objectives, how much credit does it deserve?

I respectfully suggest that the accounting profession give more thought to its responsibilities to society.

APPENDIX I-i

ROBERT R. STERLING

ACCOUNTING POWER

Accountants were not much more than specialized craftsmen, i.e., book-keepers, when an almost overwhelming responsibility was rather suddenly thrust upon them. They switched from bookkeeper to independent auditor. As auditors they were required to make public what had been previously jealously guarded private information. They were asked to make independent judgments about the affairs of persons who had previously directed their activities. They were asked to provide information via a device that had previously been used to misinform or conceal. They were required to have integrity when deceit was not uncommon.

As an independent auditor, the accountant needed a strong defense against the always optimistic, sometimes dishonest, financiers and entre-preneurs. Unfortunately, he was not given this defense. Instead, he was placed in the precarious position of being the employee of the person he was obliged to keep honest. In the absence of a cohesive theory, in the absence of police power, in the presence of ignorance and apathy of the community, his only defense was precedent and persuasion. Precedent soon became rule and the rigid application of rules was his primary weapon. It is much easier and more diplomatic to accuse someone of breaking a rule than to accuse him of telling a lie.

INDEPENDENCE

I originally expressed the above thoughts about ten years ago.[1] At that time they raised the hackles of a great many people. My critics

Robert R. Sterling is Dean of the Jesse H. Jones Graduate School of Administration at Rice University.

From a lecture given at Oklahoma State University, 6 March 1972; first published in *The Oklahoma CPA* (July 1972), pp. 28–41, 44; and excerpted in *The Journal of Accountancy* (January 1973), pp. 61–67. Reprinted by permission of the Oklahoma Society of CPAs.

[1] See Robert R. Sterling, *Theory of the Measurement of Enterprise Income* (University Press of Kansas: Lawrence, 1970), pp. 255–56.

said that I was casting doubt upon the independence of auditors and that independence is the keystone of the profession. By casting doubt upon the keystone, I was, according to my critics, casting doubt upon the professional status of accountants. My critics stated that the independence of accountants was beyond question and that my criticism was, therefore, irresponsible. The only result that could come from such criticism, they said, would be detrimental to the profession.

Accountants have defined independence to be a state of mind. Then, within the community of accountants, we have reassured ourselves that our minds are independent and that, therefore, there is no problem. However, my reading of *The Wall Street Journal, The New York Times, Business Week, Forbes,* etc., has convinced me that although we have persuaded ourselves, we have not persuaded the rest of the world.

Consider the most famous accountant in English literature—Bob Cratchit. As Scrooge's bookkeeper, there is no question about the lack of independence of Bob Cratchit. Scrooge was the boss, he had all the power and Bob Cratchit did as he was told. I expect that if Scrooge had directed Cratchit to record some cash receipts as debits and others as credits, Cratchit would have complied without a murmur. You will recall that *A Christmas Carol* was published in 1843 and that, although Dickens probably exercised literary license, his depiction of Cratchit in a subservient role is an accurate one. Now compare the date of the publication of *A Christmas Carol*—1843—to the date of the rise of auditing in England. Sir Harold Howitt[2] tells us that the professional public practice of accounting in England changed from being concerned primarily with bookkeeping to a preoccupation with auditing in about the middle of the nineteenth century. Given this information, we can write a sequel to *A Christmas Carol.* It was on Christmas Eve of 1843 when Cratchit was Scrooge's bookkeeper. It is now Christmas Eve of 1850 and Cratchit has switched from bookkeeper to "independent" and "professional" public accountant. Cratchit has completed his examination and approaches Scrooge.

Cratchit: Good day to you, Mr. Scrooge.

Scrooge: Bah! Humbug!

Cratchit: I notice here that you have been capitalizing development costs. I believe that those should be expensed.

Scrooge: Bah! Humbug!

Cratchit: I note that your parent company has been lending money to affiliates and that these affiliates have been in turn lending money

---

[2] Sir Harold Howitt, ed., *The History of the Institute of Chartered Accountants in England and Wales 1870–1965* (London: Heinemann, 1966), p. 4.

to you. Unless you are willing to guarantee the loans, it seems clear that the affiliates cannot repay their loans to the parent company. In those circumstances, I don't think we could show these receivables as assets.

Scrooge: Bah! Humbug!

Cratchit: I have here a number of other adjustments on my worksheet. Consider adjustment number three.

Scrooge: Bah! Humbug!

Cratchit: Consider adjustment number four.

Scrooge: Bah! Humbug!

Later that night . . .

Cratchit: Consider adjustment number n.

Scrooge: Bah! Humbug!

At some point Cratchit will have to consider the options open to him. Those options are clear. Cratchit can:

1. Swallow his convictions and give Scrooge a clean opinion,
2. Refuse to express an opinion, or
3. Resign.

Usually, the refusal to express an opinion is equivalent to resignation. You will have to tune in next week to find out which course of action Cratchit selected. In the meantime, however, you might consider the following factors: Cratchit has four mouths to feed at home and his wife is pregnant. His son, Tiny Tim, is a cripple and is in desperate need of an operation. Will Cratchit swallow his convictions and grant a clean certificate or will he stand on principle? Will he let his economic straits and his love for his family affect his professional judgment?

Conflict of Interests—1850

Now, you and I know what Cratchit will decide. We know that independence is a state of mind and that Cratchit is mentally independent. Even though cynical sociologists would cite this as a classic case of conflict of interests, we know that Cratchit is an accountant and, therefore, he cannot feel any such conflicts. On this basis, Cratchit will decide to deny an opinion to Scrooge.

Let me now give you a preview of next week's episode. After Cratchit has decided to disclaim an opinion, but before Cratchit has told Scrooge of his decision, Cratchit learns that Joe Softnose, CPA, has been invited to make a presentation to Scrooge. Softnose has never denied a clean opinion to a client. Cratchit is now faced with the following problem: if Cratchit denies Scrooge a clean opinion, Softnose will issue him a clean opinion. The net result of Cratchit's standing on principle will be that Scrooge will get the opinion and Softnose will get the engagement.

Again, you and I know what Cratchit will decide. The literature keeps telling us that independence is a state of mind and that Cratchit is mentally independent. Therefore, it is clear that Cratchit will decide that virtue is its own reward. The fact that Scrooge will get an opinion anyway does not affect his judgment. Thus, Cratchit is fired, Softnose gets the engagement, Scrooge gets the clean opinion and Cratchit gets a feeling of virtue.

All fairy tales must have a happy ending. This is no exception. The textbooks tell us that Cratchit's reputation will be built by this incident and that, although he loses this engagement, he will get many bigger and better engagements in the future. However, since I am the author of this particular fairy tale, my happy ending is different. As Cratchit is walking home, dejected, and wondering what he is going to tell his wife and Tiny Tim, the Great Bookkeeper in the Sky swoops down and crossfoots all of Cratchit's working papers and inducts him into the accounting hall of fame.

Research Topics

Of course, my critics will immediately point out that the above is a fairy tale and that, although this may have been true in 1850, it is not true in 1970. In order to meet this anticipated criticism, I would like to share with you a letter that I recently received. Prior to discussing that letter, however, let me give some background.

Lanny Chasteen recently published a piece[3] in which he demonstrated that the revered notion of "differences in circumstances" as a justification for using different accounting techniques is pure hokum. That is, as you know, when we accountants discuss the existence of alternative accounting techniques, we have argued that like events ought to be accounted for in the same way and that unlike events ought to be accounted for in different ways. Thus, the existence of differing circumstances calls for the existence of different accounting techniques. Now Lanny went out and proved that this is hokum. He examined a bunch of different firms that used different accounting techniques and tried to correlate them with the differing circumstances in those firms. He found that there was no correlation. I think that is a very significant piece of research. Rich Flaherty recently took a look at the role of liquidity in exchange valuation.[4] I thought Rich's paper was excellent. (My evaluation of Rich's

---

[3] Lanny G. Chasteen, "An Empirical Study of Differences in Economic Circumstances as a Justification for Alternative Inventory Pricing Methods," *Accounting Review* (July 1971), pp. 504–08.

[4] Robert R. Sterling and Richard E. Flaherty, "The Role of Liquidity in Exchange Valuation," *Accounting Review* (July 1971), pp. 441–56.

paper—the fact that I think that it is excellent—is based upon an *independent* judgment of mine. That is, whenever I made the evaluation of Rich's paper, I was mentally independent and, therefore, I was completely unaffected by the fact that I was a coauthor of that paper.)

The point that I wish to contrast here is that although I think such subjects as differing circumstances and liquidity are interesting and significant, my practitioner friends have a different idea. Many of them chide me about my research interests. They say that the issues that I research are of the wrong kind. There is a gulf between academics and practitioners because practitioners believe that academics should research an entirely different type of problem than that which we actually study. This difference has come to light in regard to the colloquies that have been held at the University of Kansas. Practitioners have attended these colloquies and the reaction of several of them has been that the papers presented were addressed to the wrong kinds of issues. This has resulted in some lengthy correspondence between me and several practitioners. I have attempted to find out what kinds of issues practitioners think that we academics ought to investigate. There has been a general theme followed by a number of these letters. This theme is most succinctly summed up in a letter from a particularly thoughtful practitioner.

Conflict of Interests—1972

In his letter he describes a company "that is diversifying and quite obviously is interested in making a name for itself as well as showing continued growth and continued earnings." He describes the chief executive as "a volatile individual whose chemistry has frequently reacted adversely to our representatives." This chief executive "had published preliminary operating results and in effect had established an earnings amount that put pressure on the company accountants . . . to seek to attain the operating results which he had forecast."

In short, the auditor is faced with a very ambitious, perhaps dishonest, Scrooge who is trying to build his fame and fortune.

The letter from the practitioner continues: "As we approached the wind-up of this engagement we found ourselves confronted with three very significant problems, namely:

"1. In starting up new businesses the company has sought to defer development costs. . . .

"2. A significant number of audit adjustments which the company should make were developed during the course of the work, but the . . . [chief executive] was very adamant about considering recording these adjustments.

"3. Substantial advances had been made to certain affiliated companies which were owned by the chief executive. These companies had in turn made rather substantial advances to the chief executive for his personal use. These companies were also in a development stage and consequently did not have the financial substance to repay the advances to the lending company unless the chief executive who had financial substance would guarantee the amounts."

These are the *kinds* of issues that my practitioner friends would like us academics to consider. All right, let us consider them. It seems clear to me that the development costs should not have been capitalized. Everyone that I have talked to agrees with me on this issue. The practitioner also agreed that the development costs should not have been capitalized as is indicated by the fact that he thought that this was a problem. The practitioner also managed to convince the chief executive that these development costs should be expensed and the entries were in fact reversed.

That would seem to settle the case. Unfortunately, it did not. The result of expensing the development costs was that the company showed a net loss instead of a net income. Now the chief executive argued that this net loss ought to be capitalized as a start-up cost. As you know, this is sometimes done in accounting. The practitioner notes this in his letter. He states: "In seeking to find a solution to these problems, illustrations in actual practice were found where companies in the development stage had deferred start-up costs including initial operating losses until such time as the businesses became profitable. . . ." Insofar as I am concerned there is even less justification for capitalizing these losses than there was for capitalizing the development costs. The whole thing appears to me to be a sham.

The chief executive of this firm is saying, in effect: "I have lost money this year, but I expect to make money next year and now what I want to do is to defer my loss of this year so that I can show a gain for both years." . . . It seems to me that the theoretical issue is clear cut: the loss should not be capitalized.

The particular adjustments mentioned in (2) were not described by the practitioner so there is no way for us to consider the theoretical issues there. In regard to (3) the issue is cut and dried. The chief executive is causing the parent company to loan money to affiliates and these affiliates in turn are advancing money to the chief executive for his personal use. This situation borders on fraud. Neglecting the fraudulent aspects, we can just look at the notes themselves. As my practitioner friend states delicately, "These affiliates do not have the financial substance to repay the notes." In plain English, these notes are worthless. What does one do with worthless notes? Obviously, one writes them off. Then, what is the problem? What is the theoretical issue involved here that this practitioner wants us to examine?

The answer seems to be that, despite the fact that his letter was written this year instead of in 1850, this practitioner faces the same problem that Bob Cratchit faced. I noted above what Cratchit's options were. I am now ready to confess that I stole that statement of options from another practitioner—namely, Leonard Spacek. Spacek writes, ". . . which courses are open to the public accountant in certifying the statements, assuming the difference is material? He can (1) swallow his convictions, or (2) he can qualify his opinion on the basis of his own convictions or (3) he can resign. Usually the latter two courses are one and the same."[5]

Competition

In the same way that Cratchit had to consider the possibility of Joe Softnose taking over the account, this practitioner must consider the same problem. Although we accountants keep reassuring each other that there is no competition among accounting firms and that particularly there is no competition regarding standards, I present for your consideration an excerpt from *The Wall Street Journal*:

"Companies of course, can change CPAs for a variety of reasons and sometimes changes can be frequent. In 1958, the accounting firm of Arthur Andersen & Co. handled the accounts of Alaska Juneau Gold Mining Co. and . . . included many qualifications in its certification of the annual report. The next year the company had a new auditor, Arthur Young & Co. . . . Arthur Young handled Alaska Juneau until 1961, when it listed at length two major qualifications in its certification of the annual report. The next year the company . . . changed again, this time to Haskins & Sells. That firm saw no need for qualifications in the 1962 report."[6]

If you like, you can continue to believe that practicing accountants are supermen and do not consider such things whenever they make their decisions. However, I am afraid, since I am a mere mortal, that if I were to make such decisions, I would consider my competition. If I knew that I was going to lose an engagement by qualifying a report and that my competition would not qualify the report so that the net result would be that the company gets an unqualified opinion and my competition gets the fee, I must confess that I would weigh that fact whenever I made my decision.

---

[5] Leonard Spacek, "The Need for an Accounting Court," *Accounting Review* (July 1958), p. 371.

[6] *Wall Street Journal*, November 15, 1966, p. 1.

THE PROBLEM

A prerequisite to the solution of a problem is the recognition of the existence of that problem. My purpose in going through the previous discussion is to try to demonstrate that a problem exists. Most of the literature that I read is in the nature of a fairy tale. In this literature we continue to reassure ourselves that no problem exists. Although we believe these fairy tales, it appears that nonaccountants do not believe them. There is, in fact, a problem and the reason this problem has existed for over one hundred years is that we have failed to recognize or admit that it is a problem.

Specifically, the problem is that the accountant has been given a responsibility without concomitant authority. His responsibility far outweighs his authority. Let us consider the responsibility and authority in turn.

Responsibility

I expect that there will be little disagreement in regard to the overwhelming responsibility of the accountant. The dean of the Harvard Law School [Erwin N. Griswold] has compared the accountant to a judge in these words: "In performing this [audit] function, the accountant acts in a very real sense *judicially*. He must decide questions, and he must be wholly free to decide questions against his client's interest if his investigation and judgment lead him to that conclusion."[7] If anything, Griswold has understated the case. The judicial system has divided responsibilities. Codified laws are provided by legislatures, the jury decides questions of fact, and the judge decides questions of law and equity. All of these functions are rolled into one in the accounting case. The auditor must first decide on questions of fact such as the number of units of inventory and the costing of those units. Analogous to deciding on questions of law, the accountant must decide which principles are applicable or acceptable. Analogous to questions of equity, the accountant must present the information so that it is fair to all segments of society. It has also been traditional for theory to come from practice and, thus, the practitioner has the burden of developing the theory—he does not have a legally constituted legislature to help him draft authoritative principles. Finally, the accountant realizes that his is the ultimate decision; he has no system of appellate courts to correct his errors. Worse, when

---

[7] Erwin N. Griswold, "The Tax Practice Problem I," JofA, Dec. 55, p. 31, emphasis added.

a lower court judge errs, he is simply reversed by an appellate court. The lower court judge is not held liable for his errors. By contrast, when the court finds that an accountant has erred, the accountant has been held liable for those errors.

Authority

In the history of law Maine tells us: "Whenever in the records of very ancient societies, . . . we come upon a personage resembling him who we call the King, he is almost always associated with the administration of justice. . . ."[8] Maine goes on to tell us that judge and king are almost synonymous in the many early societies. The authority of a king is unquestioned, and judges have either been kings or representatives of kings and, therefore, the authority of a judge from the earliest time has been equivalent to that of a king. The authority of judges in today's society is equivalent to the authority of the state. When necessary, judges can call upon the police or even the militia to enforce their rulings.

Compare the authority of accountants. Their main weapon is precedent and persuasion. Wise writes that senior partners of accounting firms ". . . devote most of their time to what might be called 'diplomacy'—e.g., persuading clients that furniture cannot be written off in two years. . . ."[9] Evidence that diplomacy or persuasion is their primary weapon also comes from the language that practitioners use. They often speak of the difficulty of "selling a troublesome adjustment." That is, when the auditor finds an error in the books or a misapplied principle that requires an adjustment, he must sell the management on the idea of making the adjustment. Can you imagine a judge in a criminal case being required to sell the defendant on the idea of going to jail? Can you imagine a judge in a civil case being required to persuade the loser to pay off? Judicial opinions end with the words, "So ordered," and there is a vast difference between ordering someone to do something and persuading him to do it.

Persuasion or diplomacy is not the accountant's ultimate weapon. Whenever things really get rough he can pull out his heavy guns. If a client refuses to go along with what the accountant has decided, the accountant can resign. His ultimate weapon is resignation and, hence, silence. That is, note that despite the fact that we have in recent years instituted the possibility of an adverse opinion, when things get really

---

[8] Sir Henry Maine, *Early Law and Custom*, 1886, Ch. 6, p. 160.
[9] T. A. Wise, "Part I: The Auditors Have Arrived," *Fortune* (November 1960), p. 157.

bad the accountant does not issue an adverse opinion. Instead, he resigns from the engagement. The result of a resignation from an engagement is that the accountant does not issue any opinion at all—i.e., he is silent. Now, again, compare this to a judge. Can you imagine a judge, failing to persuade the defendant to go to jail, resigning?

Whenever we examine the situation in this light, and recognize the precarious position that the practitioner has been put in, I hope you will join with me in admiration of the practitioner. There are two ways of looking at the state of accounting: logically and sociologically. When I logically examine the structure of accounting theory, I am depressed by how bad things are. By contrast, when I sociologically examine the structure of the accounting profession, particularly the balance of responsibility and authority, I am impressed by how well the practitioner has done. Whenever we consider the accountant's overwhelming responsibility and his almost complete lack of authority, I applaud the practitioner for the number of times that he does stand on principle. I do not condemn him for those occasions when he rationalizes his way to issuing a clean certificate.

The Profession's Response

There is some evidence that the profession has recognized the imbalance of responsibility and authority. I have not been able to find any direct evidence of this recognition in a search of the literature. Instead, the evidence is indirect. If we put someone in a position in which his responsibility outweighs his authority, we could expect him to try to move toward a proper balance. There are two ways of trying to move toward a proper balance: (1) increase the authority or (2) decrease the responsibility. Many of the things that the profession has tried to do in recent years can be interpreted as the second course of action, i.e., a decrease of responsibility.

As a minor example, consider the substitution of the word "examination" for the word "verification" in the auditing literature. Statement on Auditing Procedure No. 33 says that we ought to substitute "examination" for "verification," [10] and since examination is obviously a weaker term, this could be interpreted as an attempt to lessen the responsibility of the auditor. As another example, consider the change in the wording of the opinion. It used to be that the opinion stated that financial statements presented a "true and correct view of the financial condition of the

---

[10] Committee on Auditing Procedure, AICPA, "Auditing Standards and Procedures," Statement on Auditing Procedure No. 33 (AICPA, 1963), p. 94.

company." We have now substituted the weaker statement that the statements are presented in accordance with generally accepted accounting principles. Legal scholars have noted the attempt to avoid responsibility for the truth of the statements by changing these words and have openly questioned whether or not the courts will allow it. The accepted dictum that the statements belong to management and are the responsibility of management is another bit of indirect evidence that accountants have been trying to lessen their responsibility by placing the responsibility upon management. Whether it is management or the public accountant that is ultimately responsible for the financial statements has been questioned in the legal literature, as well as in the accounting literature.[11] Finally, Alexander, an economist, states the proposition directly:

"Another very powerful factor operating on the development of accounting methods has been the attempt to reduce the accountant's responsibility for the human judgments which must be made in passing from a consideration of the accounts to the conduct of business affairs. This attempted avoidance of responsibility has led accountants to. . . ."[12]

These examples are included in an attempt to demonstrate that accountants have recognized the imbalance of responsibility and authority, not to criticize the profession. It seems to me that if a person is put in a position where his responsibility outweighs his authority, it is quite legitimate for him to try to reduce that responsibility. However, it is also clear that the courts are not going to allow us to take this course of action. The decisions that have been handed down in recent years have had the effect of assigning more responsibility to the accountants. No case that I am aware of has lessened the accountant's responsibility. Two recent cases—*Continental Vending* [*U.S.* v. *Simon*] and *Pacific Acceptance* [*Pacific Acceptance Corporation Ltd.* v. *Forsythe and Others*]—have added significantly to the accountant's responsibilities. As I read these cases, the courts are telling us that we can no longer defend ourselves on the basis of accepted accounting theory and practice. Instead, we must assure ourselves that the statements are true, correct and understandable by nonaccountants.

If this interpretation is valid, it seems clear that there is only one other course of action open to us. Since we cannot lessen the responsibility and since the responsibility outweighs the authority, we must increase the accountant's authority.

---

[11] See, e.g., Herbert E. Miller, "Audited Statements—Are They Really Management's?" JofA, Oct. 64, pp. 43–46.

[12] Sidney S. Alexander, "Income Measurement in a Dynamic Economy," *Five Monographs on Business Income* (New York: Study Group on Business Income of the American Institute of Accountants [now the AICPA], July 1, 1950), p. 2.

Interpreting the History of Accounting

Many people have wondered why it is so difficult to agree upon a set of accounting principles. They cannot understand why we cannot reform accounting in the sense of establishing a fairly clear-cut theory or set of principles. Moonitz has examined this question in a very important, but unfortunately neglected, article by the name, "Why Is It So Difficult to Agree Upon a Set of Accounting Principles?" [13] A logical examination of this question will fail to yield an answer. However, a sociological examination—an examination of the power structure—will yield an answer.

Consider the following bit of history. At the turn of this century several famous names in accounting were writing texts and monographs. On several fundamental issues Hatfield, Dickinson, Montgomery, Esquerré and others were in agreement at least in regard to the essentials. These people wrote at the turn of the century. Moving up to the 1930's, we can examine the writings of several other famous names in accounting, such as Canning, Gilman, Sweeney and MacNeal. Concentrating on MacNeal, we find him arguing the same points that Dickinson, Esquerré, Montgomery and Hatfield had argued. Since then, there have been a number of other people who have made similar points. Despite this list of illuminaries, we find that the situation in regard to accounting principles in 1972 is much the same as it was in 1902.

Several principles, such as "diversity among entities" will not stand up to logical scrutiny and there is plenty of evidence that the application of this principle has led people astray. The continued general acceptance of these false principles cannot be explained on the grounds of logic. However, if we view the situation as a power struggle between the accountant and management, the explanation seems obvious.

Moonitz hits the nail on the head when, in this context, he notes that "management as a class has sought to consolidate its power." [14] He views the problem as a power struggle between management and accountants. Managements want such things as diversity and flexibility, and accountants want to tell it like it is. Given the relative power of the two groups, you could predict who won. As Grady says, diversity is a fact of life. [15] He might have said that the reason why diversity is a fact of life is that management wants to apply diverse accounting principles and

---

[13] Maurice Moonitz, "Why Is It So Difficult to Agree Upon a Set of Accounting Principles?" *The Australian Accountant* (Nov. 1968), pp. 621–31.

[14] *Ibid.*, p. 629.

[15] Paul Grady, "Inventory of Generally Accepted Accounting Principles for Business Enterprises," *Accounting Research Study No. 7* (AICPA, 1965), p. 33.

management has more power than the accountant has.

In short, the lack of progress in agreement upon accounting principles and the lack of ability to institute accounting reforms cannot be explained on the grounds of logic. However, whenever we look at the progress of accounting in the context of a power struggle, the explanation is obvious. The accountant could not reform a deficient theory because the dominant institution opposed that reform.

The corollary of this is that management and accountants have opposing interests. We keep kidding ourselves to the effect that we and management are on the same side. This is a myth. Management wants to win; it wants to show increased earnings; it wants to have a good report card. The objective of the public accountant is, or ought to be, to tell it like it is. Given these opposing interests, it seems clear to me that we ought to get management out of the business of establishing accounting principles, especially when the main principle that they want to establish is one of diversity or flexibility. As noted above, the accountant must act judicially. When one acts judicially, one is judging an event rather than being a participant in that event.

Managerial accountants and public accountants are adversaries in the same way that the opposing lawyers in a trial are adversaries. We have already seen from Chasteen's investigation [16] that managerial accountants do not select their accounting techniques on the basis of differing circumstances. Since we know that they do not select them upon that basis, we might ask the question, Upon what basis do they select them? If you think that they select accounting techniques on the basis of which one presents most fairly or accurately, you have a more lively imagination than I.

I don't have empirical evidence in support of my hypothesis, as did Chasteen and Cadenhead, but I do have several personal experiences and a rather telling quotation. We all know about the recent debacle in regard to the Penn Central. The vice president and controller was a man by the name of William S. Cook who, on October 5, 1967, wrote a "personal and confidential" memo to David C. Bevan, the chief financial officer of Penn Central. The subject of this memo was another accountant, Charles S. Hill, who was manager of general accounting. The memo recommended that Hill's salary be raised by $2,000. As justification for this raise, Cook said: "His imaginative accounting is adding millions of dollars annually to our reported income." [17] This memo does not refer

---

[16] Chasteen, *op. cit.*; see also Gary M. Cadenhead, " 'Differences in Circumstances': Fact or Fantasy?" *Abacus* (September 1970), pp. 71–80.

[17] Peter Binzen and Joseph Paughen, *The Wreck of the Penn Central* (Boston: Little, Brown and Company, 1971), p. 244.

to the imaginative production, or imaginative marketing, that contributed millions to Penn Central's income. Instead, it refers to the imaginative accounting that contributed millions to the income of Penn Central. Further, note that this memo was from one accountant to another referring to a third accountant. These other accountants not only approved of these practices, they encouraged it by giving this man a raise. As long as managements, including managerial accountants, have the flexibility to do this sort of thing and as long as we permit them to do it, I expect that they will continue to use accounting to show what it is that they want to show.

SUMMARY AND CONCLUSION

The major problem facing public accounting today is its lack of power. First, in comparing the power or authority to the responsibility, we find that the responsibility far outweighs the authority. The public accountant must act judicially but he has not been given the power to enforce his rulings. His ultimate weapon is resignation and silence, which puts him in a conflict-of-interest position. No other profession that I know of is put in a position where it must make economic sacrifices in order to enforce the judgments for which it is responsible. The authority is lessened further by the existence of competition among accounting firms. Resignation from an engagement might be an effective means of enforcement if it were not for the fact that other firms may take the engagement and issue an opinion.

Second, in comparing the power of the public accountant to that of management, we find that management's power far outweighs the accountant's. This imbalance is not undesirable per se. When one considers the fact that accountants must judge managements, however, it is not only undesirable, it is intolerable. It would wreck the legal system if litigants were able to hire and fire judges. It would be equally damaging to the legal system if litigants were able to select from diverse or flexible laws as they saw fit. The same is true in regard to accounting: if accountants are to judge managements, then we must deny managements the power to hire and fire accountants and the power to select from diverse accounting principles as they see fit.

Thus, my practitioner friends were right. I have been researching the wrong kinds of problems. The major problem facing accounting is institutional, not theoretical. Of course, there are defects in the theory of accounting, but these defects cannot be corrected by logic and evidence alone. A prerequisite to theoretical reform is obtaining the power to institute those reforms.

When viewed in this way, we can explain several things in the history of accounting that were previously unexplainable. The lack of progress in establishing principles is due to the relative lack of power, not to inherently unresolvable theoretical problems. Moonitz makes a strong case for this point of view by comparing progress in establishing auditing standards to establishing accounting principles. I suspect that there are many other anomalies in the history of accounting that could be explained in the same way. Another example is the profession's attempt to reduce its responsibility. It seems to me that this attempt is evidence of a tacit recognition of the imbalance of authority and responsibility. The attempt to reduce responsibility was an attempt to bring about a balance. However, the courts have not allowed us to use this means of obtaining a balance; instead, they have thrust more responsibility upon us.

Since the problem is a lack of power and since the reduction of responsibility is not available to use, the conclusion is inescapable: the power of the accountant must be increased.

The question that remains is how to increase the power. It seems to me that there are two major alternatives: (1) by law, i.e., seek power from the government, or (2) by organization, i.e., solidify the profession.

The former alternative doesn't seem to be compatible with the profession's views. Quite the contrary, we often scare ourselves by holding up the specter of "government intervention." One of the common themes in the literature is the threat that if we don't reform, the government will intervene. This threat assumes that all government intervention is bad per se. I believe that assumption to be erroneous and offer the judiciary as a counter example. The judiciary has not been ruined by government intervention. Indeed, it is difficult to imagine the judiciary functioning in the absence of government intervention. Of course, I am referring to the government intervention that resulted in the power of the judiciary to enforce its rulings. On most occasions when we speak of government intervention in accounting, we seem to be thinking of the government's writing a rule book of individual detailed practices. That need not be the form of government intervention. The government could grant power to the CPA to enforce his decisions without specifying the particular decision. This is the way that a judge operates. The government doesn't tell the judge what decisions to make. Instead, it sets him free from conflicts and competition and then gives him the power to enforce his decisions. It is possible for the government to do the same for the CPA.

The second alternative requires that CPAs give up part of their individual independence in order to obtain professional independence. By solidarity they could give the power to their organization, say, the AICPA. The AICPA would then police its ranks and sanction its members. Note that other organizations do this. If a teamster crosses a picket line, two things happen: first he is called a "scab" and second he gets his head busted. A CPA who competes by the flexibility of his accounting principles needs to be called a "bookkeeper" and be sanctioned in some fashion. If you find it unflattering to be compared to the Teamsters Union, perhaps we should compare ourselves to the strongest labor union in the world, namely, the American Medical Association. A surgeon, for example, is subjected to postoperative reviews and, if those reviews reveal too many errors in the application of medical principles, then that surgeon is called a "butcher" and is barred from practicing. If we are going to strengthen public accounting, we need a postaudit review and, if that review reveals too much flexibility in accounting principles, then we need to bar that firm or CPA from future audit engagements.

Which of these alternatives is preferable is an open question. The purpose of this paper has been to attempt to establish the existence of a problem. Once we recognize the existence of the problem, then collectively we can set about deciding on the best course of action for its solution.

APPENDIX I-ii

ROBERT R. STERLING

IN DEFENCE OF ACCOUNTING IN THE UNITED STATES*

In 'Financial Information and the Securities Market' (*Abacus* Vol I, No. 1) Professor Chambers presented some figures which reflected unfavourably on U.S. accounting relative to U.K. accounting. Specifically, he asserted that there are 124,416 different ways of getting cost in the U.K. but only 9,100 different ways in the U.S. No direct comparisons were made but the figures are there for all to see and the clear implication is that U.K. accounting is richer in variety than that of the U.S. That is a slander of U.S. accounting and cannot be left unchallenged. This note will demonstrate that the figures are wrong and that the opposite is true: U.S. accounting is much richer than that of the U.K.

Two separate types of errors may be identified in Mr. Chambers's figures: (1) logical fallacies[1] and (2) inadequate research.

LOGICAL FALLACIES

Chambers listed the possibilities of valuing only inventory in the U.S. but he listed commodity stocks, fixed assets (three classes) and security

---

*The author would like to thank Mr. Duns Scotus for reading this manuscript. Unfortunately, under some theories at least, that is impossible.

Reprinted from Abacus (December 1966), pp. 180–83, by permission.

[1] A recent article showed that logical consistency is a symptom of an illness called valuitis. It is well known that Chambers has been suffering from valuitis for a long time. This fallacy is evidence of the absence of the symptom and therefore we may hope that he is recovering his health. However, I do not wish to draw that conclusion since it might be logically valid and therefore it would indicate that I am ill. For the same reason, I do not wish to conclude that a valid conclusion of mine would indicate that I was ill because that might be valid and therefore it would indicate that I was ill. Thus, I must conclude a contradiction but then the conclusion that I must conclude a contradiction might be valid. This is a question I intend to research further at a later time.

investments (three classes) for the U.K. Obviously, a larger number of classes will yield a larger number of combinations, other things being equal. Thus, the comparison is grossly unfair because the U.K. figure was calculated from a larger number of classes.

Second, he erred in calculating the number of different costs to be derived from inventory methods. He is talking about a manufacturing operation in which there are four different classes of inventory: materials, supplies, work-in-process and finished goods. Even a modest firm will have several different kinds of materials, etc. Any one of the ten methods may be used for each inventory and the order of using them is important. For example, Lifo for finished goods and Fifo for materials will produce a cost different from Fifo for finished goods and Lifo for materials.

Thus, under the conservative assumption that there are only ten inventories in a given firm, the number of different costs is 10! not 10. This yields 3,628,000 different costs from a consideration of different *rules for inventory alone*. If we now take account of the other factors listed by Chambers we have 10! × 7 × 13 × 3 × 3 = 2,971,332,000. The U.K. figure of 124,416 pales in comparison.

INADEQUATE RESEARCH[2]

Evidently in getting the '10 rules' for inventory valuation, Chambers took a cursory look at the *Accountants' Handbook*. Had he bothered to look further he would have found that this is a highly abstract list and that each category contains a rich variety of methods. Neuner[3] for example, lists five different kinds of Lifo:

  1. Lifo — perpetual
  2. Lifo — periodic

---

[2] The results of the following are part of a two-stage study on accounting which is forthcoming. First, I am preparing a complete inventory of accounting practices. The second stage will be to weave together the practices into a coherent body of principles. In this way, the principles can be inductively derived out of the facts of accounting action in practice without relying on assumptions and premises except where assumptions are necessary because the data are not perceptible facts.

The study will take a little longer than originally planned because I have not yet finished with Lifo inventories. So far, I have observed 1984 different methods of Lifo. It is too early to draw distinctions or perceive objectives or sense relevance but I can tentatively report a corroboration of the A.I.C.P.A. definition of assets. All accounts with a debit balance after the books are closed except those that are contra liabilities are *in fact assets*. The reader is cautioned that this corroboration pertains only to Lifo inventories in only 1984 cases.

[3] John W. Neuner, *Cost Accounting Principles and Practice*, 6th ed, p. 136ff.

Increases in inventory under 2. may be valued at

3. earliest purchase price
4. latest purchase price
5. average purchase price.

Later he lists six areas 'on which there is no uniform practice'. Freight-in is one category for which there are three different methods, for example. Each of these six categories has at least three different methods.

Next, there is a list of four categories of 'Debatable inventory costs' and each of these four has at least three different methods. There are others but I will conclude with the 3 × 3 cost-or-market rule which Chambers mentions. Thus, there are 5 × (3×6) × (3×4) × (3×3) = 9,720 different costs for *Lifo alone.*

We could go through each of the ten methods with similar results. However, one case is sufficient to demonstrate the inadequate research upon which Chambers bases his figures. In the U.S. we have more different methods for Lifo alone than he gives us credit for in total!

These calculations have dealt only with actual costs. There are 9,720 different *actual costs* under the Lifo method. In the U.S. there is a regrettable trend toward recording standard costs in the accounts. 'Standards' are useful for comparison purposes but they are *fictitious* and therefore they should not be entered in the accounts. [4] The accounts must be records of events that have actually occurred, not what might have occurred or what will occur. There is, of course, no objection to putting standard costs in a footnote.

The inclusion of standard costs would strengthen our case against Chambers since there are different times for isolating the variance, different methods of calculation and different methods of disposition. Thus, standards would extend the richness of U.S. accounting but this would be an unfair tactic since they are not actual costs.

---

[4] In addition to being fictitious, standards are based solely on someone's projections and are not actual facts of economic experience. I can see no reason why anyone would want to put standards in the accounts when 9,720 different objective Lifo costs are available. Variance analysis is helpful to management but managerial desires should not be confused with sound financial accounting. Moreover, accountants have completely overlooked a fertile source of variance. We could calculate the difference between the costs of the particular method in use and the costs of the alternative methods. Thus, for Lifo we could calculate 9,719 variances and then we could extend the analysis to Fifo, averages and so forth. In this way we could generate an almost infinite number of variances without ever referring to standards. Such variances would be completely *objective* since they are differences in *actual* costs.

Of course, the *actual* actual costs can be obtained only by the method
of specific identification.[5] This is the only way to measure the actual
income but unfortunately it is sometimes impossible to use. This method
would also have strengthened the richness case. Observe that if we have
a large number of items in an inventory at different actual costs, there
are almost an infinite number of combinations and hence almost an
infinite number of actual actual costs and actual incomes. I did not use
this method in making the calculations for this note because it would
have required an estimate of the bias introduced by the shipping clerk
or an assumption of randomness and I wanted my figures to be objective
and verifiable.

But, I digress. Theoretical issues are not pertinent here. The important
point is that I have shown that U.S. accounting is much richer than
Chambers has given us credit for and, using the figure of 124,416, it
is richer than U.K. accounting. The actual facts demand an immediate
retraction and apology.

October 1966

RETRACTION AND APOLOGY

I grant Mr. Sterling's point, and apologize to all who may have been
misled or misrepresented by my conservatism. We have it on the highest
authorities that conservatism is virtuous, and gives a fair representation.
Perhaps it is not, and does not. I have since raised the estimate ('A
Matter of Principle', *The Accounting Review*, July 1966) but even then
in the same wantonly cursory manner. My apologies on that score too.

R. J. CHAMBERS

---

[5] Specific identification avoids the subjectivity of assuming a flow and accounts
for the *real* flow of the goods. Many people have noted this and the fact that
accounting for the real flow prevents management from manipulating their profits
by assuming an unrealistic flow. It is true that some managers might instruct
their shipping clerks to ship the goods on a highest-in-first-out basis in order
to reduce taxes. This is not a valid objection to the method because if the goods
were shipped in this order, then this would be the real flow (hence the actual
costs and actual income) but it does present an auditing problem. The auditor
must insist that the goods be indelibly marked with their actual costs. Some managers
may object to the added expense of this procedure and they are often too obtuse
to understand the subtleties of actual costs and income. The auditor can then
explain that the expenses incurred in marking the goods will further reduce
the income and thus further reduce taxes in accord with the original goal. This
can also be applied to the managers who ship their goods on a lowest-in-first-out
basis in order to increase their income. The expense of marking the goods is
a small price to pay for the increase in actual income.

APPENDIX II-i

STUDY GROUP ON THE OBJECTIVES OF FINANCIAL
STATEMENTS

A SUMMARY OF OBJECTIVES OF
FINANCIAL STATEMENTS

The basic objective of financial statements is to provide information useful for making economic decisions. . . .

An objective of financial statements is to serve primarily those users who have limited authority, ability, or resources to obtain information and who rely on financial statements as their principal source of information about an enterprise's economic activities. . . .

An objective of financial statements is to provide information useful to investors and creditors for predicting, comparing, and evaluating potential cash flows to them in terms of amount, timing, and related uncertainty. . . .

An objective of financial statements is to provide users with information for predicting, comparing, and evaluating enterprise earning power. . . .

An objective of financial statements is to supply information useful in judging management's ability to utilize enterprise resources effectively in achieving the primary enterprise goal. . . .

An objective of financial statements is to provide factual and interpretive information about transactions and other events which is useful for predicting, comparing, and evaluating enterprise earning power. Basic underlying assumptions with respect to matters subject to interpretation, evaluation, prediction, or estimation should be disclosed. . . .

Excerpted from *Objectives of Financial Statements* (AICPA, 1973), pp. 61–66, by permission of the American Institute of Certified Public Accountants. Copyright 1973 by the American Institute of Certified Public Accountants, Inc.

An objective is to provide a statement of financial position useful for predicting, comparing, and evaluating enterprise earning power. This statement should provide information concerning enterprise transactions and other events that are part of incomplete earnings cycles. Current values should also be reported when they differ significantly from historical cost. Assets and liabilities should be grouped or segregated by the relative uncertainty of the amount and timing of prospective realization or liquidation. . . .

An objective is to provide a statement of periodic earnings useful for predicting, comparing, and evaluating enterprise earning power. The net result of completed earnings cycles and enterprise activities resulting in recognizable progress toward completion of incomplete cycles should be reported. Changes in the values reflected in successive statements of financial position should also be reported, but separately, since they differ in terms of their certainty of realization. . . .

An objective is to provide a statement of financial activities useful for predicting, comparing, and evaluating enterprise earning power. This statement should report mainly on factual aspects of enterprise transactions having or expected to have significant cash consequences. This statement should report data that require minimal judgment and interpretation by the preparer. . . .

An objective of financial statements is to provide information useful for the predictive process. Financial forecasts should be provided when they will enhance the reliability of users' predictions. . . .

An objective of financial statements for governmental and not-for-profit organizations is to provide information useful for evaluating the effectiveness of the management of resources in achieving the organization's goals. Performance measures should be quantified in terms of identified goals. . . .

An objective of financial statements is to report on those activities of the enterprise affecting society which can be determined and described or measured and which are important to the role of the enterprise in its social environment. . . .

APPENDIX II-ii

Derek Boothman et al.

Accounting Standards Steering Committee Summary of *The Corporate Report*

Section One

8.1 Our basic approach has been that corporate reports should seek to satisfy, as far as possible, the information needs of users. We believe there is an implicit responsibility to report incumbent on every economic entity whose size or format renders it significant. This responsibility arises from the custodial role played in the community by economic entities. Although we believe this principle of public accountability to be applicable to every type of entity we have not attempted to consider in detail non-commercial public sector reporting. We recommend further study in this area.

8.2 We define users as those having a reasonable right to information concerning the reporting entity arising from the public accountability of the entity. We have assembled a list of user groups which we identify as the equity investor group, the loan creditor group, the employee group, the analyst-adviser group, the business contact group, the government and the public. Although corporate reports should seek to satisfy as far as possible the information needs of these user groups it is impractical to suggest all needs of all users could be entirely met by such general-purpose reports.

Reprinted from *The Corporate Report* (Accounting Standards Steering Committee, 1975), pp. 77–79, by permission.

Section Two

8.3 Having reviewed the rights and needs of user groups we conclude that corporate reports may be able to contribute to user information needs in:

(a)   Evaluating the performance of the entity.

(b)   Assessing the effectiveness of the entity in achieving objectives established previously by its management, its members or owners or by society. This includes but is by no means limited to, compliance with stewardship obligations.

(c)   Evaluating managerial performance, efficiency and objectives, including employment, investment and profit distribution plans.

(d)   Ascertaining the experience and background of company directors and officials including details of other directorships or official positions.

(e)   Assessing the economic stability and vulnerability of the reporting entity.

(f)   Assessing the liquidity of the entity, its present or future requirements for additional fixed and working capital, and its ability to raise long and short term finance.

(g)   Assessing the capacity of the entity to make future reallocations of its resources, for either economic or social purposes or for both.

(h)   Estimating the future prospects of the entity, including its capacity to pay dividends, remuneration and other cash outflows and predicting future levels of investment, production and employment.

(i)   Assessing the performance, position and prospects of individual establishments and companies within a group.

(j)   Evaluating the economic function and performance of the entity in relation to society and the national interest and the social costs and benefits attributable to the entity.

(k)   Attesting to compliance with taxation regulations, company law, contractual and other legal obligations and requirements (particularly when independently verified).

(l)   Ascertaining the nature of the entity's business and products.

(m)   Making economic comparisons, either for the given entity over a period of time or with other entities.

(n)   Estimating the value of users' own or other users' present or prospective interests in or claims on the entity.

(o)   Ascertaining the ownership and control of the entity.

Section Three

8.4 In our view **the fundamental objective of corporate reports is to communicate economic measurements of and information about the resources and performance of the reporting entity useful to those having reasonable rights to such information.** To fulfil this objective we conclude that corporate reports should be relevant, understandable, reliable, complete, objective, timely and comparable.

8.5 This fundamental objective will apply to all corporate reports, whoever the reporting entity and whatever the reason for publication. However, the degree of disclosure appropriate in each particular case will be limited by practical considerations of cost and confidentiality and by the need to arrive at a balance which will imbue corporate reports with the desired characteristics outlined above and the need to serve, as far as possible, the general interests of all users.

Section Four

8.6 In reviewing the relevance of the conventional view of the aim of published financial reports to current conditions and attitudes we note the trend towards the acceptance by business enterprises of multiple responsibilities and conclude that distributable profit is no longer the sole or premier indicator of performance in the corporate reports of such entities. We recognise the trend in new and proposed legislation towards the recognition of the rights to information of a growing number of groups including employees and the public. We suggest there is a need for additional indicators of performance in the corporate reports of all entities.

APPENDIX II-iii

FINANCIAL ACCOUNTING STANDARDS BOARD

OBJECTIVES OF FINANCIAL STATEMENTS OF BUSINESS ENTERPRISES

Financial statements of business enterprises should provide information, within the limits of financial accounting, that is useful to present and potential investors and creditors in making rational investment and credit decisions. Financial statements should be comprehensible to investors and creditors who have a reasonable understanding of business and economic activities and financial accounting and who are willing to spend the time and effort needed to study financial statements.

Members of numerous groups make economic decisions based on their relationships to and knowledge about business enterprises and thus have a potential interest in the information provided by financial statements. Among the potential users of financial statement information are owners, lenders, suppliers, potential investors and creditors, employees, management (including directors), financial analysts and advisors, brokers, underwriters, stock exchanges, lawyers, taxing authorities, regulatory authorities, financial press and reporting agencies, labor unions, trade associations, and customers. Many of those groups are interested in essentially the same kinds of financial information. General purpose financial statements are based on the presumption that many users of financial statements have common information needs. Although investors and creditors may need essentially the same kinds of financial information as several other groups of potential users, there are reasons to focus the objectives of financial statements on the financial information needs of investors and creditors.

First, investors and creditors and their advisors are among those who use general purpose financial statements as a principal source of financial

---

Reprinted from *Tentative Conclusions on Objectives of Financial Statements* (FASB, 2 December 1976), pp. 3–6, by permission.

information about individual business enterprises. Some of those who use financial information in various kinds of economic decisions need specialized or detailed information and can usually obtain it. For example, management needs many kinds of specialized and detailed information to decide day-to-day matters and establish policies. But management also controls the accounting of the enterprise, and much of the accounting effort may be managerial accounting designed to help management plan and control operations. Similarly, the information needed to measure taxable income to determine tax payments according to tax law and regulations and the information needed to set rates for public utilities are both specialized information needs not usually satisfied by general purpose financial statements. But both taxing authorities and rate-making bodies have statutory authority to require the specific information they need to fulfill their functions. Many governmental regulatory bodies not concerned with taxation or rate-making also have a statutory authority to require specific information. Although not all investors and creditors need to rely on general purpose financial statements for financial information—for example, a bank or insurance company negotiating with an enterprise for a large loan or private placement of securities can often obtain desired information about the enterprise by making the information a condition for completing the transaction—most do not have access to financial information except through financial statements. To identify investors' and creditors' needs as the focal point of financial statement information greatly narrows the range of economic decisions and varied needs for specialized information that general purpose financial statements must try to satisfy, thereby increasing the possibility that the statements can reasonably satisfy the narrower range of needs.

Second, investors' and creditors' needs for financial information and the ways that they and their advisors use it are better understood than those of other groups who may rely on general purpose financial statements or information obtained from them. Little or no information is available on how customers, employees, and similar groups use information from financial statements or other sources. Despite numerous gaps that exist in the knowledge of investors' and creditors' information needs and the fact that no study has been able to identify precisely how financial statement information affects investors' and creditors' decisions and securities' prices, the essential characteristics of investment and credit decisions have been described in detail, are reasonably well understood, and have been incorporated in various investment decision models. Further, many investment and credit decisions result in transactions in markets for which detailed data are available, permitting study and analysis of the investment decision process and testing of hypotheses about it.

Financial statements are but one source of information about business enterprises. Financial statement information is a particular kind of information that is necessarily limited by the nature of financial accounting and by certain constraints on the financial accounting process (paragraph 6). Investors, creditors, and others are therefore expected to use financial statement information in conjunction with other information about a business enterprise, the industries in which it operates, the securities markets, and the economy as a whole.

Individual investors and creditors have varying degrees of understanding of the business and economic environment, business activities, securities markets, and related matters. Their understanding of financial statements and the extent to which they use and rely on financial statement information may also vary greatly. However, an attempt to provide different financial statements for different perceived levels of investor and creditor competence would require assessments concerning those differences that could not be supported except arbitrarily. Relevant information should not be excluded from financial statements merely because it may be difficult for someone to understand or because some investors or creditors choose not to use it.

Financial statements of business enterprises should provide information that helps investors and creditors assess the prospects of receiving cash from dividends or interest and from the proceeds from the sale, redemption, or maturity of securities or loans. Those prospects are affected (1) by an enterprise's ability to obtain enough cash through its earning and financing activities to meet its obligations when due and its other cash operating needs, to reinvest in earning resources and activities, and to pay cash dividends and interest and (2) by perceptions of investors and creditors generally about that ability, which affect market prices of the enterprise's securities relative to those of other enterprises. Thus, financial accounting and financial statements should provide information that helps investors and creditors assess the enterprise's prospects of obtaining net cash inflows through its earning and financing activities.

Investment and credit decisions normally involve choices between present cash (price of a security that can be bought or sold or amount of a loan) and rights to expected future cash receipts from dividends or interest and proceeds. Investors and creditors need information to help them form rational expectations about those future cash receipts and assess the risk that the amounts or timing of the receipts may differ from expectations. Business enterprises, like investors and creditors, invest cash to earn more cash, and they receive cash as a result of the transactions and other events that affect their economic resources and obligations to transfer resources to other entities. Since an enterprise's ability to bring in cash affects both its ability to pay dividends and interest and the market prices of its securities, expected cash flows to investors and creditors are related to expected cash flows to the enterprise in which they have invested or to which they have loaned funds. Expected cash flows to investors and creditors from sale of securities are also affected by other factors that affect market prices.

Financial statements of a business enterprise should provide information about the economic resources of an enterprise, which are sources of prospective cash inflows to the enterprise; its obligations to transfer economic resources to others, which are causes of prospective cash outflows from the enterprise; and its earnings, which are the financial results of its operations and other events and conditions that affect the enterprise. Since that information is useful to investors and creditors in assessing an enterprise's ability to pay cash dividends and interest and to settle obligations when they mature, it should be the focus of financial accounting and financial statements.

Investors and creditors often use information about the past to help in assessing the prospects of an enterprise. Although investment and credit decisions reflect investors' and creditors' expectations about future enterprise performance, those expectations are commonly based at least partly on evaluations of past enterprise performance, including evaluation of how management has discharged its responsibility to stockholders for its use of enterprise resources entrusted to it, and evaluation of the enterprise's present economic resources and obligations.*

Financial accounting cannot directly measure the value of a business enterprise—the present value of its expected net cash receipts—because of the uncertainty of expected cash receipts and payments, particularly those expected far in the future. Nor can accounting statements that show only cash receipts and payments during a short period, such as a year, adequately indicate whether or not an enterprise's performance is successful. Enterprise earnings (net income or net profit) measured by accrual accounting, which recognizes the financial effects of transactions and other events when they occur rather than only when cash is received or paid, are usually considered a better indicator of an enterprise's present and continuing ability to bring in the cash it needs to acquire resources, produce salable output, pay for goods and services it uses, meet its other obligations, and pay cash dividends to stockholders than is information about current cash receipts and payments. Financial statements reflecting

---

*Investors and creditors ordinarily invest in or lend to enterprises that they expect to continue in operation. Information about the past is usually less useful in assessing prospects for the enterprise's future if it is in liquidation or is expected to enter liquidation. Then, emphasis shifts from operating or earning activities to liquidation values of the enterprise's resources and the obligations that must be met. The objectives of financial statements do not change if an enterprise shifts from expected operation to expected liquidation, but the kind of information, including measures of elements of financial statements, that is relevant may change.

accrual accounting are composed of individual elements that represent the enterprise's economic resources, its obligations to transfer resources to other entities, inputs to and outputs from its earning activities, and the financial results of other events and circumstances. In recognizing likely cash effects of transactions and events as well as actual cash receipts and payments, accrual accounting emphasizes the incidence of the transactions or events having cash consequences rather than the cash receipts or payments themselves. That emphasis recognizes that the earning activities of an enterprise during a period, as well as other events that affect periodic earnings, often do not coordinate with the cash receipts and payments of the period.

Although periodic financial measures of enterprise performance provided by accrual accounting may tend to fluctuate less than measures of net cash receipts for the same accounting periods, the purpose of accrual accounting is to measure and report changes in resources and obligations and to relate sacrifices and benefits—efforts and results—to accounting periods rather than to reduce fluctuations in reported results by averaging the results of several periods. To apply the concepts and techniques of financial analysis and to base their expectations about an enterprise's future performance on a "more representative" result, investors or creditors may average or normalize the performance of several periods or otherwise adjust the measures of enterprise performance reported in financial statements.

Financial statements of business enterprises should provide explanatory information about particular aspects of an enterprise's operations and other events and circumstances affecting it if that information is necessary to an understanding of the past financial results and financial position of the enterprise. The usefulness of financial statement information as an aid to investors and creditors in forming expectations about a business enterprise is usually enhanced by management's explanations of the information. Management has knowledge of enterprise affairs to an extent that investors, creditors, and other "outsiders" can never attain and can often increase the usefulness of financial statement information by explaining certain transactions, other events, and circumstances that affect the enterprise and their financial impact on it. In addition, financial statement information often depends on, or is affected by, management's estimates and judgment. Investors and creditors are aided in evaluating information affected by estimates and judgment by explanations of underlying assumptions or methods used, including disclosure of significant uncertainty about assumptions or estimates.

APPENDIX III-i

JAMES C. MCKEOWN

ACCURACY AND VERIFIABILITY

Ijiri and Jaedicke have defined a measure they call reliability.[1] Unfortunately, this measure requires that the decision-maker's predictive function be known. This means that the measure of reliability depends upon the decision-maker. For this study (and probably other purposes), it is more useful to define a measure of accuracy which is independent of the decision-maker and his predictive function.[2]

Thus, accuracy, A, is defined by

$$(1) \qquad A^{-2} = \frac{1}{n} \sum_{i=1}^{n} (x_i - T)^2$$

where the x_i are a set of n measurements of the same attribute of a particular item or entity. T is the true measure of the attribute.

The concept of accuracy can also be related to the accountant's concept of objectivity. Because objectivity is a state of mind (freedom from bias), it cannot be measured directly. This does not present a problem since the average accountant considers a measurement to be objective if many different accountants, measuring the same attribute, would give the same

---

Reprinted from Appendix to "An Empirical Test of a Model Proposed by Chambers," *The Accounting Review* (January 1971), pp. 28–29, by permission.

James C. McKeown is Professor of Accounting at the University of Illinois.

[1] Yuji Ijiri and Robert K. Jaedicke, "Reliability and Objectivity of Accounting Measurements," THE ACCOUNTING REVIEW (July 1966), pp. 474–83.

[2] The reliability measure combines two factors, verifiability and accuracy of predictive function. If the predictive function chosen is poor, the set of measurements is automatically very low in reliability regardless of the susceptibility to measurement of the attribute being measured and the precision of the methods used. Since this study is concerned with the susceptibility to measurement of certain attributes of a firm and the precision of the methods which can be employed to measure these attributes, the reliability measure must be rejected.

or similar measures as their result. The concept might more properly be called verifiability and could be defined as:

(2)
$$V^{-2} = \frac{1}{n} \sum_{i=1}^{n} (x_i - \bar{x})^2$$

where: the x_i are a set of n measurements of the same attribute of a particular item or entity

$$\bar{x} = \frac{1}{n} \sum_{i=1}^{n} x_i = \text{the mean of the measurements.}$$

or

$$V = \sqrt{\frac{n}{\sum_{i=1}^{n} (x_i - \bar{x})^2}} = \frac{1}{\sigma}$$

σ = the standard deviation of the x_i, from (1)

$$A^{-2} = \frac{1}{n} \sum_{i=1}^{n} (x_i - T)^2$$

$$A^{-2} = \frac{1}{n} \sum_{i=1}^{n} [(x_i - \bar{x}) + (\bar{x} - T)]^2$$

$$A^{-2} = \frac{1}{n} \sum_{i=1}^{n} [(x_i - \bar{x})^2 + 2(x_i - \bar{x})$$
$$\cdot (\bar{x} - T) + (\bar{x} - T)^2]$$

(3)
$$A^{-2} = \frac{1}{n} \sum_{i=1}^{n} (x_i - \bar{x})^2$$
$$+ \frac{2}{n} \sum_{i=1}^{n} (x_i - \bar{x})(\bar{x} - T)$$
$$+ \frac{1}{n} \sum_{i=1}^{n} (\bar{x} - T)^2$$

but

$$\sum_{i=1}^{n} (x_i - \bar{x}) = 0$$

and $\bar{x} - T$ is constant over all i so

$$\frac{1}{n} \sum_{i=1}^{n} (\bar{x} - T)^2 = (\bar{x} - T)^2$$

Therefore (3) becomes

(4) $$A^{-2} = \frac{1}{n} \sum_{i=1}^{n} (x_i - \bar{x})^2 + (\bar{x} - T)^2$$

substituting from (2)

$$A^{-2} = V^{-2} + (\bar{x} - T)^2 \quad \text{or,}$$

(5) $$A^{-2} = V^{-2} + B^2$$

where

(6) $$B = \bar{x} - T = \text{bias}$$

Since $B^2 \geqq 0$,

$$A^{-2} \geqq V^{-2} \quad \text{or}$$

$$\frac{1}{A^2} \geqq \frac{1}{V^2}$$

inverting

$$A^2 \leqq V^2$$

taking positive square root

(7) $$A \leqq V$$

Therefore the measure of accuracy, A, is less than or equal to the verifiability, V, of the same set of measurements. The condition for equality of (7) is that B (from (6)) = 0. This would be the case where the mean of the measurements was equal to the true measure of the attribute, i.e., where bias is zero. Otherwise $A < V$.

GROUPS OF ITEMS

The measure of accuracy A, of the sum of a group of n items which were independently measured will be defined by

$$(8) \qquad A_s^{-1} = \sqrt{\sum_{i=1}^{n} A_i^{-2}}$$

Similarly for the verifiability of such a sum

$$(9) \qquad V_s^{-1} = \sqrt{\sum_{i=1}^{n} V_i^{-2}}$$

from (7) $A_i \leqq V_i$ for each i, $i = 1, 2, ..., n$,
Since each element in the sum in (8) is less than or equal to each element of the sum in (9),

$$(10) \qquad A_s \leqq V_s$$

The condition for equality in (10) is that $\sum_{i=1}^{n} B_i = 0$, or that the mean of the measures for each item in the group must be exactly equal to the true measure of that item. If this seemingly rather improbable condition does not exist, the more likely relationship is $A_s < V_s$.

Prem Prakash and Alfred Rappaport

The Feedback Effects of Accounting

When accounting first emerged as an independent profession about a century ago, it acknowledged only one obligation: to tell the proprietors of an enterprise how it was performing. A generation ago, it enlarged its scope to provide information for investor decisions, thus contributing to the orderly functioning of the securities markets. It is now time for the profession to enlarge its responsibilities once again—by recognizing that accounting policy has an impact on the economy as a whole and not just on the company being audited.

Consider one example of the way accounting rules feed back into the economy. Antitrust lawyers argue that permissive accounting standards contributed substantially to the great merger boom of the 1960s, which materially changed the industrial organization of the U.S. But now that the rules have been tightened, American firms complain that they are at a disadvantage because they must set up a goodwill account representing the excess of purchase price over asset value of the acquired company. This account has to be amortized in their income statements, putting a drag on earnings. Merger-minded foreign companies, on the other hand, are permitted to dispose of goodwill as a one-shot charge against stockholders' equity.

External reports. No matter what accounting practice a company follows, its financial reports constitute a description of its operations, and much of what the economy "knows" about the company is based upon the

---

Reprinted from *Business Week* (12 January 1976), p. 12, by permission.

Prem Prakash is Associate Professor of Accounting and Information Systems at Northwestern University.

Alfred Rappaport is Professor of Accounting and Information Systems at Northwestern University.

information produced by its accounting system and disclosed in its external reports. Moreover, business statistics generated from external reports of all firms constitute a description of the economy. This description becomes a major part of what an economy "knows" about its own functioning.

External reports and business statistics are used—or misused—selectively by the investors for whom they were intended and by others—labor, consumers, competitors—who piggyback upon the published information. What completes the circle and keeps the process feeding upon itself is that the response of these outsiders affects the firm's operations both directly and by shaping the economic environment.

The feedback can take several forms. Financial analysts may change their opinion of the company's prospects. Labor may increase its wage demands. Government regulators may intervene to require something and forbid something else. And the economic policies of the nation—in areas such as price control, investment incentives, and tariffs—may be tailored to conditions indicated by the business statistics.

The feedback effects are anticipated—and, at times, conjured up when they do not exist—by company management. These anticipations can lead to important policy changes within the company. For example, the price-level accounting proposed by the Financial Accounting Standards Board, the principal policymaking body for the profession, would favor the reported earnings of higher-leveraged corporations compared to the ones with less leverage whenever the rise in the deflator index exceeds the after-tax interest rate. If this proposal is adopted, it will give corporations a strong incentive to increase debt in proportion to equity and thus report higher earnings per share.

Congressional intervention. Though one may plead for "economic reality" in accounting, every accounting description is nonetheless a description of some facet of economic reality. No accounting choice, therefore, is neutral. Each involves potential redistribution of wealth. In this sense, the accounting choice involves a social choice.

This poses a serious challenge for the profession and for the FASB. If the FASB continues to ignore the macroeconomic consequences of accounting policy, then, undoubtedly, there will be increased pressure for Congress to intervene in accounting decisions. For in the last analysis, the responsibility for mediating conflicting values in our society rests with Congress.

We suggest that the FASB should enlarge the scope of its concern and that it create a full-fledged research division responsible for conducting inquiry into the potential macroeconomic consequences of alternative accounting methods under consideration. This research staff would draw up a brief to accompany each exposure draft, summarizing the technical considerations and the economic consequences involved in each alternative. The exposure draft itself should contain the FASB's recommendations and a statement of the reasons for making the social choice these recommendations entail.

Such an explicit statement of choice would force critics of the proposal to put their arguments into sharp focus. At the same time, it would give them an opportunity to point out any consequences not considered by the FASB, any errors in the board's assessment of the economic effects, and any questions of fairness to particular groups that may be involved.

Many accountants will react to this idea with horror—protesting that the concern of accounting is with measurements at the company level and not with consequences that follow from such measurements. But the fact remains that accounting policy is a much broader issue. The profession's microeconomic frame of reference, with its focus on information for investor decisions, may have been adequate in the past, but its limitations are beginning to show. If the accounting profession is to remain a major force in shaping financial reporting practices in an increasingly complex society, it must recognize that such practices involve not just adding up figures but making social choices as well.

APPENDIX III-iii

GEORGE J. STAUBUS

EXAMPLES OF ALLEGED POTENTIAL ECONOMIC CONSEQUENCES OF ACCOUNTING STANDARDS

FASB Statement No. 2, "Accounting for Research and Development Costs":

1. Immediate expensing of R & D costs, which in many cases would result in lower reported earnings, lower stockholders' equity, and a higher debt-equity ratio, would have an adverse impact on the markets for the securities of research-intensive companies. The resulting higher cost of capital would lead to underinvestment in research-intensive industries.
2. Immediate expensing of R & D costs would bias managers against investments in R & D (in comparison with capitalizable investments).
3. Capitalizing R & D would bias managers in favor of R & D expenditures (in comparison with other expenditures).

FASB Statement No. 5, "Accounting for Contingencies":

1. Elimination of catastrophe loss reserves would encourage property and casualty insurance companies to purchase uneconomical reinsurance to smooth their reported expenses.
2. The reinsurance in (a) is likely to be placed abroad (for example, through Lloyds of London), thereby adversely affecting the U.S. balance of payments.
3. Catastrophe loss reserve accounting, by spreading the impact of catastrophe loss claims over several accounting periods, would encourage insurance companies to take excessive risks.
4. Outlawing self-insurance reserves would encourage managers to buy uneconomical insurance to smooth their reported expenses.

Previously unpublished.

504

5. Permitting self-insurance reserve accounting would encourage managers to take excessive risks.

FASB Statement No. 7, "Accounting and Reporting by Development Stage Enterprises":

1. Expensing pre-operating costs would handicap development stage companies in raising capital, especially venture equity capital, because it would require the reporting of losses and a deficit.

FASB Statement No. 8, "Accounting for the Translation of Foreign Currency Transactions and Foreign Currency Financial Statements":

1. Inclusion of foreign currency gains and losses in operating profit would cause fluctuations in reported earnings which would (rightfully or wrongfully) give the impression of greater risk and thereby lead to lower prices for a multinational's securities.
2. Inclusion of foreign currency gains and losses in operating profit would encourage multinational companies to engage in uneconomical hedging transactions to avoid fluctuations in reported earnings.

FASB Statement No. 12, "Accounting for Certain Marketable Securities":

1. Failure to reflect declines in market values of securities in the financial statements would result in overconfidence in, overinvestment in, and overextension of investments by the financial institutions holding securities that had declined in price.
2. Reporting declines in market values of securities in the financial statements would cause a loss of depositors' and shareholders' confidence in a financial institution and result in a reallocation of capital.
3. Requiring that declines in market values of securities be reported as losses would cause investor companies to switch their investment funds from marketable equity securities to other categories of investments.

FASB Agenda Project, "Accounting by Debtors and Creditors When Debt is Restructured":

1. Creditors' failure to record as losses various events associated with the restructuring of lending relationships can result in overconfidence in, overinvestment in, and overextension of loans and investments by the financial intermediaries involved as creditors.
2. Recording losses would reduce the net worth of lending institutions and thereby reduce their lending capacity due to regulatory agencies' limitations tied to capital structure standards based on "book values." This type of limitation could act as a damper on economic expansion and/or as a deterrent to unsafe banking practices.

3. If an FASB standard were to require the recording of losses on restructurings, lenders would thereafter shy away from more risky loans in categories such as:
   (a) Inner city projects.
   (b) Municipalities.
   (c) Foreign loans.
   (d) Real estate loans.
   Such increases in lenders' "risk aversion" could have favorable or unfavorable consequences for the U.S. economy.
4. Reporting losses on troubled loans would cause depositors and shareholders to lose confidence in a financial intermediary.
   (a) This loss of confidence would have the desirable effect of shifting resources away from poorly managed firms thereby contributing to the proper functioning of the competitive economic system.
   (b) A general loss of confidence in the banking system could have disastrous consequences for the U.S. economy.

APPENDIX IV-i

ROBERT R. STERLING

DECISION ORIENTED FINANCIAL ACCOUNTING

I. INTRODUCTION

The purpose of this paper is to consider the various measures (valuation methods) of wealth and income that have been proposed in the recent literature. A prerequisite to the consideration of that issue is the development of criteria by which the various measures are to be judged. I will review some of the major conflicts that have arisen about the criteria, state my reasons for selecting an overriding criterion and then attempt to show how that criterion can be applied.

II. CONFLICTING OBJECTIVES

There are conflicting viewpoints about the objective of accounting reports. This conflict is rather difficult to detect. One must look closely for it. Almost all the literature on accounting states that accounting reports must be 'useful' or that accounting is a 'utilitarian art'. It seems that we all agree that the objective of accounting is to provide useful information. However, we discover conflicts when we examine the remainder of the 'basic concepts' of accounting. Consider the requirement that accounting data be objective and verifiable. It is possible for a measure to be useful even though it is not objective and verifiable. Thus, a conflict arises: Should we accountants provide useful data even if it is not objective, or should we provide objective data even if it is not useful?

There are many other conflicts. The particular terms that are used depend upon the author that one is reading. In regard to income, many

---

Reprinted from *Accounting and Business Research* (Summer 1972), pp. 198–208, by permission of the Institute of Chartered Accountants in England and Wales.

authors begin their discussion with a remark about the need for providing useful information, but then they switch their attention to the realisation convention. It is possible that realised income is not the most useful measure of income. Thus, there is a conflict between realisation and usefulness. Other authors speak of the need to be conservative, and since it is possible for the most useful measure to be liberal, there is a conflict between conservatism and usefulness. Other authors note that a particular measure would violate the going concern assumption and reject the measure on those grounds without regard to the usefulness of that measure. And so forth for most of the other concepts of accounting. Each one of them may be set off against the notion of usefulness and be seen to be in conflict with it at some point.

Given the conflicts, we must decide which of the concepts is to be the overriding criterion. If we simply pay lip service to the notion of usefulness by allowing it to be constrained by all of these other concepts, then we are in fact denying the criterion of usefulness. Of course, if we can have our measures meet all of these requirements, then we are in the happy position of having no conflicts. The unfortunate fact is that they often are conflicting and we must decide which is the overriding criterion.

I think the overriding criterion should be usefulness. The other concepts are important but they are secondary. If, in order to make a decision, someone needs a measure of a particular property, then a rough guess at the magnitude of that property is useful. Of course, a precise, objective measure of that property is *more* useful, but the converse does not hold. If one does not need to know the magnitude of a particular property, then a measure of that property is useless no matter how precise and objective it may be.

Thus, I view accounting as a measurement-communication activity with the objective of providing useful information. Once we have discovered which properties are useful, then we must devise methods of measuring those properties. Hopefully, we can devise measurement methods which fulfil the requirements of objectivity, verifiability, etc. However, these requirements are secondary. They are desirable, but usefulness is indispensable. Therefore, providing useful information must be the primary objective of accounting.

III. Conflicting Definitions of Usefulness

Problems arise whenever we attempt to define the concept of usefulness. Like other hortatory concepts (e.g. truth, justice, fairness) everyone is in favour of usefulness in the abstract. All of us agree with Spacek's postulate of fairness. Who could speak out in favour of being unfair?

The difficulty is in defining fairness. In the same way, the difficulty with 'usefulness' is in making its meaning precise enough to be applicable to a concrete situation. In an attempt to be more precise, I have in previous works[1] replaced 'usefulness' with 'relevance'.

The dictionary defines 'relevant' as 'bearing upon or relating to the matter in hand'. This is what I mean by 'relevant information', except that I substitute 'decision model' for 'matter in hand'. In the same way that one cannot determine what is relevant to the matter in hand without being aware of the matter in hand, I cannot determine what is relevant information without being aware of the decision model. One of the characteristics of a well defined decision model is that it will specify the measurement (or estimation) of certain properties. This allows my definition of relevance to be simple and straightforward:

> If a property is specified by a decision model, then a measure
> of that property is relevant (to that decision model). If a
> property is not specified by a decision model, then a measure
> of that property is irrelevant (to that decision model).

One conflict that has arisen is concerned with that definition. Several people have argued that we should focus on decision *makers* instead of decision *models*. They say that if decision makers want to know the measure of a particular property, then that property is relevant or useful. Some of them have run tests designed to determine whether or not people (decision makers) use certain kinds of accounting data. When they found a certain kind of data being *used,* they concluded that this data was *useful.* They argue that we should supply the decision makers with the kind of data that they want and that this is the end of the question of relevance.

At first glance this view is rather appealing. In the same way that we give the voter and consumer a free choice, so the argument goes, we should give the decision maker a free choice. Thus, the argument is stated in terms of democracy or consumer sovereignty, and it is difficult for anyone to be against democracy. At the risk of making you think that I am a dictator, let me briefly outline my reasons for being opposed to this view.

(1) In the present system, the decision maker can either use the accounting reports that we give him or make his decision in the absence of that information. His choice is to use or not use our data. There

---

[1] Robert R. Sterling, *Theory of the Measurement of Enterprise Income* (The University Press of Kansas, 1970), pp. 50, 132, 354, *et passim* and 'On Theory Construction and Verification', *The Accounting Review,* July 1970, p. 454.

is no third alternative.[2] If we were to adopt my suggestions for changing the kind of data to be included in accounting reports, the decision maker would have the same choice. Therefore, the adoption of my suggestions would be equally as 'democratic' as the present system. The only difference would be in the kind of data being reported.

(2) Decision makers are a diverse lot. They make their decisions on a wide variety of different bases. We have all heard about people who trade the market on the basis of astrological signs or arthritic pain. 'Technical analysts' on Wall Street trade the market on the basis of the 'flags', 'heads and shoulders' and 'double bottoms' they see in their charts. Given this diversity, it is an economic, if not a physical, impossibility for us to supply *all* the information that *all* decision makers want. Therefore, we must select and in the process of selection, we will fail to satisfy the wants of some decision makers. What we are arguing about then is the *basis* for selection.[3]

(3) The basis for selection that I prefer is to supply information for rational decision models. The modifier 'rational' is defined to mean those decision models that are most likely to allow decision makers to achieve their goals. Since I don't believe that astrology allows people to achieve their stated goals, I am not interested in supplying them with an astrology report even though they use that kind of information in trading the market. For the same reason, I am not interested in supplying decision makers with some of the kinds of data now being included in accounting reports even though they use that data.

The above is only a rough sketch of the conflict. I have gone into some other aspects of the problem elsewhere.[4] Although there are a

---

[2] This is the basis for a technical criticism of the tests that have been run to see if decision makers use accounting data. Most experiments require a 'control' of some kind. The tests would have more force if the decision makers were offered a choice between using accounting data and using some kind of control data. To put it another way, suppose we ran a test in which decision makers could choose either (1) zero information or (2) x information. I suspect that the decision makers would choose x information. A more powerful test would be to offer them the choice between x and y information.

[3] Section II was, in effect, an argument about the basis for selection. That is, it was an argument against excluding data on grounds of objectivity, realisation, etc. Thus, accountants are *now* being selective in the kind of data that they report. Indeed, they must be selective since no information system can report everything. The pertinent grounds for argument then must be the basis for selection and it is impertinent—the commission of the fallacy of alleging a non-existent difference—to argue on the grounds that one information system is selective (dictatorial) and another is not.

[4] Sterling, *Enterprise Income*, pp. 54–61.

good many scattered remarks in opposition to this view, insofar as I know, there is only one article devoted exclusively to the problem.[5] As I have said before,[6] I believe that the proponents of the decision maker view have overlooked the distinction between pragmatic and semantic information. Pragmatic information is defined by the receivers' reaction to the report. For example, if I yelled 'Fire' and all of you ran to the exits, my report would be said to contain pragmatic informational content. Semantic informational content is concerned with the connection of reports to objects and events. For example, if there were a fire, my report would be said to contain semantic informational content. If there were no fire, it is semantic misinformation, or in plain English, a lie. Note that the two kinds of information are separable and that one kind does not imply anything about the other. Of course, we accountants know this from harsh experience. Everybody agrees that decision makers used the McKesson-Robbins financial statements and therefore there was pragmatic informational content. The problem was the absence of the inventory and therefore the presence of semantic misinformation.

Although many of my critics agree in principle with the decision model approach, they throw up their hands in despair at the prospect of trying to apply it. There are a great many different kinds of decision models, e.g. EOQ, PERT, Linear Programming, Capital Budgeting, etc. Such decision models are applicable to only certain kinds of decisions, e.g. inventory ordering, scheduling, allocations, investments, etc. In addition, there are a great many choice criteria that are used in reaching decisions, e.g. minimax, maximin, Hurwicz, least regret, etc. Thus, we have a great variety of decision models applicable to a variety of decision situations with a variety of proposed criteria. It appears to be impossible to set up a general information system or to design a set of general purpose financial statements which would meet the requirements of all these models. An even more difficult problem arises whenever we encounter decision situations for which there is no well defined decision model.[7]

The trick is to generalise—to try to capture the elements that are common to all decisions. Although such a generalisation, like all other generalisations, leaves out many important details, it allows us to get a handle on the problem. Let me attempt such a generalisation. All decision models require information about:

---

[5] A. Rashad Abdel-khalik, 'User Preference Ordering Value: A Model', *The Accounting Review*, July 1971, pp. 457–71.

[6] Sterling, 'Theory Construction', p. 453.

[7] See Robert R. Sterling, 'A Statement of Basic Accounting Theory: A Review Article', *Journal of Accounting Research*, Spring 1967, p. 107.

1. Alternatives = $A = \{a_1, a_2, ..., a_n\}$
2. Consequences = $C = \{c_1, c_2, ..., c_n\}$
3. Preferences = P = a function for ordering consequences.

Alternatives (or possible courses of action) must be presently feasible. There is no point in choosing a course of action that is not feasible. One may plan what he will do if and when an alternative becomes feasible or he may ruminate about past alternatives, but the choice is always restricted to the alternatives that are feasible at the time of the decision—the present. The alternatives must be competing in the sense that the selection of one obviates the selection of the other, and hopefully, the list would completely specify all alternatives. If alternatives are not competing, then no decision is required. One need not choose between x and y if one can select both x and y. If the list is not complete, then one may not know about the existence of a preferred alternative. Thus, a decision maker is faced with a set of alternatives, the elements of which are mutually exclusive and exhaustive. The decision maker may contemplate a broad range of possible courses of action but he must select from 'alternatives'— those courses of action that are available to the decision makers at the moment of choice.

Consequences (or outcomes or payoffs) of the alternatives lie in the future. They must be predicted. The consequences may be stated in terms of certain uncontrollable events, and then probabilities assigned to the uncontrollable events. For example, one can predict that if a_1 is selected the consequence will be c_i^1 if event x_1 occurs, c_i^2 if event x_2 occurs, etc. By assigning probabilities to events, x_1, x_2, ... and aggregating c_i^1, c_i^2, ... one can speak of 'the' consequence, c_1, associated with a_1.

Preferences are personal. Even though different decision makers are faced with the same alternatives and they predict the same consequences, they may make different decisions. This may come about from different assignments of probabilities or different choice criteria of different utility functions or simply the inexplicable choice of the decision maker. I include such things under the category of 'preferences' and in the present state of the art they are 'matters of taste' that are personal to the decision maker. Given the one to one correspondence of alternatives and consequences, the preference for a given consequence uniquely determines the alternative to be selected.

A summary of the decision process is shown in Figure 1.

Decision models are abstractions which are separate and apart from decision makers. For example, the EOQ model is an idea which can be thought about separately from the persons who hold or use that idea. It is the decision *model* that requires information about alternatives, consequences and preferences. The decision maker can be thought of

FIGURE 1
THE DECISION PROCESS

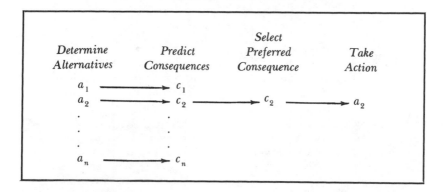

as a supplier of information to the decision model. Consider Figure 2.

The accounting system is also a supplier of information, but it is not necessary for it to supply all of the information required by the model. In non-feedback situations, such as providing financial statements to investors, it is impossible for the accounting system to provide information about the preferences of the decision makers. Since the decision makers already know their preferences, the point may seem to be unimportant. However, there are many accountants who have become bogged down in their efforts to design an information system because they were unable to specify the decision maker's utility function or because there were several different decision makers with different utility functions. If we view the decision maker as the supplier of this kind of information to the decision model, then this problem is by-passed, if not solved. The accounting system could then concentrate on supplying information which would aid in defining alternatives and predicting consequences.

In summary, an accounting system should be designed to provide relevant information to rational decision models. The accounting system cannot supply all the information desired by all decision makers and therefore, we must decide to exclude some kinds of information and to include other kinds. Restricting the decision models to rational ones permits the exclusion of a raft of data based upon the whims of decision makers. It permits us to concentrate on those models that have been demonstrated to be effective in achieving the decision makers' goals. Information specified by decision models may be classified as alternatives, consequences and preferences. Excluding information about preferences, on the grounds that the decision makers already possess this information,

Appendix IV-i

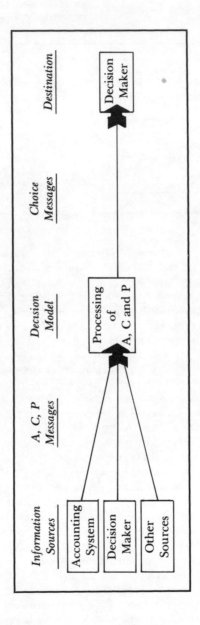

FIGURE 2
INFORMATION SYSTEM

permits us to concentrate on supplying information concerning the definition of feasible alternatives and the prediction of consequences.

IV. Conflicting Valuation Methods

Although we sometimes attempt to separate the question of how to value assets from the question of how to measure income, the two are, in fact, inextricably entwined. This is indicated by the fact that we often say that our financial statements 'articulate'. It is even clearer whenever we consider the basic accounting equation.

$$(1) \qquad\qquad\qquad A = L + P$$

Almost every elementary accounting textbook has a problem which is concerned with the determination of income by utilising this equation. They assign a time index (t_i) and state the proprietorship as a residual.

$$(2) \qquad\qquad\qquad A(t_i) - L(t_i) = P(t_i)$$

Then the income (neglecting investment and disinvestment) for the period t_i to t_{i+1} is given by (3).

$$(3) \qquad\qquad\qquad P(t_{i+1}) - P(t_1) = Y$$

It is obvious that if the assets take on different values, then the income for the period will take on different values. For example, a switch from straight-line to accelerated depreciation or from FIFO to LIFO will affect both the reported asset values and the reported income. The same is true if we state the assets at their historical cost as opposed to, say, current market value. Thus, when one talks about different methods of valuation, and the conflicts between them, then one is also at the same time talking about conflicts in income measurement.

There are four major valuation methods that have been proposed in the literature:

(1) historical cost (HC),
(2) replacement cost (RC),
(3) exit values (EV), and
(4) discounted cash flows (DCF).

Some people have argued that price-level adjusted historical costs should be listed as a fifth valuation method. However, one could adjust each of the above methods for changes in price-levels and thereby add a total of four more methods. I am in favour of price-level adjustments, but I think that the selection of a valuation method is a separate problem. We must first select the valuation method(s) and *then* we can consider the necessary adjustment for price-level changes. Therefore, I will neglect the problems of price-level adjustments in this paper and concentrate on specific price changes.

The incomes that result from applying these valuation methods have been called

(1) realised income,
(2) business income,
(3) realisable income, and
(4) economic income.

All of these names are somewhat inaccurate. Some economists would say that 'realisable income' is 'economic income' and therefore, they would object to the names that we have used. 'Historical cost' is somewhat inaccurate in that there are many assets on the balance sheet that are not valued at cost, e.g. cash and accounts receivable. 'Realised income' is somewhat inaccurate as, for example, when the percentage of completion method of revenue realisation is used. In addition, these methods sometimes borrow from one another. For example, HC sometimes uses DCF in accounting for bonds or notes. In the same way, some of the authors who propose, say, EV will occasionally revert to either RC or HC. Thus, none of the methods are pure. Finally, there are different procedures within each of the methods. Just as income may be calculated by using either LIFO or FIFO, and both of them referred to as 'realised income', there are different procedures within the other methods. I will not attempt to discuss all of these exceptions and differences; instead, I will concentrate on describing the major differences among the methods.

All four valuation methods use a price of some kind as the basis for valuing, but each method endorses a different price. The endorsed prices differ by their temporal location and by the market in which they are found. Both HC and RC use the prices found in the purchasing market. They differ only in the temporal location of those prices. A past (time of purchase) price is used in HC while a present (time of statement preparation) price is used in RC. Thus, except for the temporal location of the prices, RC is identical to HC. EV, by contrast, focuses on the present (time of statement preparation) prices in the selling market. EV is similar, but not identical, to the 'net realisable values' used in HC in applying the lower of cost or market rule to inventories.

DCF uses both purchase and selling prices, but it focuses on the future—the prices that will be in effect at the time of future exchanges. DCF is similar to the 'present value method' of accounting for bonds used in HC. In DCF the cash receipts from the future sale of the products and the cash expenditures for the future purchase of the factors of production are predicted and then discounted to get 'present value' or 'present worth'. Hereafter, I will substitute 'discounted value' for 'present worth' to avoid confusion.

These differences are summarised in the following matrix.

Time \ Market	Past (*Purchase*)	Present (*Statement Preparation*)	Future (*Exchange*)
Purchasing	HC	RC	DCF
Selling		EV	DCF

The differences in income may also be described in general terms. The revenues (asset inflows from sales) would be the same for all four methods, but the amount charged to expense would differ considerably. We all know how the allocations are made in HC. RC uses the same allocation techniques, but it costs out the quantities at their current purchase prices. The argument is that we should match current costs with current revenues and thus the line of reasoning is the same as that of many LIFO proponents. However, unlike LIFO, RC also uses current purchase prices on the balance sheet which results in including 'holding gains' (also called 'cost savings') in income. EV looks to the market to determine the expenses. Initially, the expense is the difference between the purchase price and the exit value at the date of statement preparation. Subsequently, it is the difference in the exit values at two statement preparation dates. Both HC and RC are *allocations* (amortisations) of a purchase price on the basis of use or sale or passage of time. EV attempts to avoid the allocation problem by going to the market to determine how much the asset could be sold for. The decrease (increase) in the amount it could be sold for is the amount of the cost (gain) of using or holding that asset.

DCF recognises a gain at purchase equal to the difference between the discounted value of the products produced by the acquired asset and the face value of the cash sacrificed. The amount of the subsequent income is simply the interest earned (the interest rate times the discounted value) in exactly the same way that interest income is the yield rate times the discounted value of bonds receivable in HC. Adjustments are required in DCF whenever events are different from those predicted. These adjustments present problems similar to those encountered in HC when, say, the actual life of an asset is different from its predicted life.

There are many arguments in favour of and in opposition to all of these valuation methods. However, the proponents of the various schools rely most heavily on the usefulness or relevance criterion. Each school claims that its particular valuation method would be more useful than the others. For this reason, and also because I believe that usefulness should be the overriding criterion, I will ignore the other criteria and try to select the appropriate valuation method by applying the criterion of relevance.

V. APPLICATION OF THE RELEVANCE CRITERION TO MARKET DECISIONS

Although there are a good many decisions that do not involve a market exchange, in a market economy such as ours probably a majority of decisions are concerned with whether or not to make an exchange in the market. The market operates with prices, and since the conflicting valuation methods differ mainly in their endorsement of certain prices, a general consideration of prices and market decisions is pertinent to the conflict.

Market Alternatives

The market alternatives that are available to any person or any firm depend upon two factors:

(1) The funds that are currently available to invest in the contemplated project.

(2) The magnitude of the investment required to engage in the contemplated project.

Specifically, the funds available for a given project must be greater than or equal to the investment required for that project. Otherwise, that project is not a feasible market alternative.

Although this point is obvious, I wanted to make it explicit in order to demonstrate that 'profitability' is *not* the first nor the sole criterion for selecting projects. There are many projects which I think would be very profitable, but I cannot undertake them because my available funds are less than the required investment. For example, I would like to purchase General Motors, but since my available funds are less than the purchase price this is not a feasible alternative for me.

Market Consequences

The market consequences of undertaking a given project are the future cash flows that result from that project. There may be non-market consequences which the decision maker should consider (e.g. one may be sent to jail for engaging in an illegal project or one may get satisfaction from beating the competition), but I will concentrate on the market consequences. Since these cash flows lie in the future, they must be predicted.

Preferences

The decision maker is faced with an array of future cash flow magnitudes. He must select one of those magnitudes by applying his personal preference function. He may do this by converting the money magnitudes to utility magnitudes, assigning subjective probabilities to the flows under varying conditions, and utilising one of the various choice criteria. Such information is to be supplied to the decision model by the decision maker because it is a matter of personal preference.

In addition, the discount rate should be supplied by the decision maker because each decision maker is likely to have different needs for liquidity and different views on the time value of money. That is, people are likely to have different 'reservation rates' and these rates are likely to be different from the cost of capital rate of the firm. For this reason, I will distinguish 'future cash flows' (FCF) and 'discounted cash flows' (DCF) henceforth.

After appropriate adjustment for risk, I would select the project with the largest cash flows. That is, I am a maximiser. However, that is a personal preference and there may be some who have different preferences. The above discussion does *not* depend upon the assumption of profit or wealth maximisation for its validity. If one wants to minimise he can be a more efficient minimiser by following this general outline for decisions.[8]

---

[8] This point should be underscored because several people have criticised my previous works for assuming profit maximisation or postulating an economic man. In the above classification scheme, the goal of the decision maker is included in the category of preferences. A maximiser's preferences will cause him to select a consequence different from the one selected by a minimiser. A satisficer will cease searching for additional alternatives whenever he has found a satisfactory consequence. Regardless of the goal, an accounting system which provided information about alternatives and consequences would aid the decision maker in achieving that goal. Of course, decision models are not usually designed to minimise, but that is simply an indication that few people are minimisers and that most minimisation problems are trivial. For example, a linear programming model could be used to search for the lowest profit-highest cost solution by simply altering the objective function, but a minimiser could more easily achieve his goal by considering the consequences of selling his product at a negative price or by burning his plant.

The main point about preferences is that, as before, they are to be supplied to the decision model by the decision maker. Therefore, in the following discussion I will concentrate on supplying information about alternatives and consequences.

Price Interpretation

The market alternatives and consequences have been defined and the preferences have been left to the decision makers. It is now necessary to give these alternatives and consequences a price interpretation. Recall that the market alternatives depend upon the available funds and the required investment. In turn, the available funds depend upon:

(1) The present selling prices of all assets held, including the 'selling price' of cash.
(2) The ability to borrow.
(3) The ability to raise equity capital.

I will consider (2) and (3) *infra*. In regard to (1), note that the present selling prices are the only prices relevant to defining the available funds. Past prices are irrelevant, because they are no longer obtainable and future prices will be relevant to defining future alternatives, but they are irrelevant to defining the current alternatives. Purchase prices are obviously irrelevant if one is trying to determine how much cash he can get if he sells.

The required investment is given by:

(1) The present purchase prices of assets *not* held.
(2) The present selling prices of assets held.

Obviously, if one is contemplating the purchase of an asset, then the present purchase price of that asset is relevant to the determination of whether or not the alternative is feasible. The investment required for maintaining the status quo, however, is given by the selling prices of the assets held. Since the individual or firm already holds the assets necessary to maintain the status quo, then there is no need to contemplate their purchase. Instead, the (implicit) required investment is the amount of cash that one could get if one sold those assets. That is, the decision not to disinvest is structurally identical to the decision to invest, and therefore, the required investment for continuing the status quo is the amount of cash that was not received by not disinvesting.

The future cash flows require a prediction of the future selling prices of the outputs of the project as well as the quantities that will be sold. The future selling prices of the inputs are also relevant. That is, the salvage values of productive assets at the termination or abandonment of a project are future cash inflows and are, therefore, relevant. If a project requires future replacement of productive assets or the purchase of the factors of production, then the future purchasing prices of the inputs are also relevant.

The decision requires the comparison of the future cash flows of each project. Other things equal, the decision maker can make his selection by scanning the array of future cash flows and applying his preference function. However, in this case other things are seldom equal. Usually, the required investments are not of equal magnitude. If the projects have unequal required investments, it is not possible to make a rational decision by considering only their future cash flows. One project may have large cash flows but an even larger required investment. A common method of overcoming this difficulty is to calculate the rate of return on the required investment and then compare the rates of return. Note that this method is a comparison of the required investment to the future cash flows, i.e. rate of return is the time adjusted quotient of the future cash flows and required investment. In general, whenever required investments are not equal one needs to compare the required investment to the future cash flows.

The above is simply a generalisation of the capital budgeting model, absent an explicit consideration of discounting. The capital budgeting model specifies the prediction of future cash inflows and outflows, and then the time adjusted net flows of the various projects are compared to one another or to the required investment. Since the capital budgeting model is usually applied to new projects, we tend to forget that it is also applicable to existing projects. Sometimes our predictions are wrong and sometimes we change our predictions after initiating a project. For this reason, existing projects should be re-evaluated periodically. In this re-evaluation, the decision model specifies a comparison of the *updated* prediction of cash flows to the *present* required investment. That required investment is given by the selling prices of assets held. Obviously, if one wishes to maximise, he should discontinue a project and sell the assets if the future cash flows are less than the sum of the selling prices. Just as in the case of a new project, a maximiser should not commit the required investment if it is greater than the predicted cash flows. In the case of an existing project, the required investment is the sum of the present selling prices of the assets.

In summary, a rational market decision model specifies the following prices:

(1) The present selling prices of all assets held because
    (*a*) when compared to (2), they define the feasible market alternatives, and

(*b*) they completely define the investment required to maintain the status quo.

(2) The present purchase prices of all assets not held because

(*a*) when compared to (1), they define the feasible market alternatives, and

(*b*) they completely define the investment required for new projects.

(3) The future purchase and selling prices associated with a given alternative because when compared to the required investment [(1*b*) or (2*b*)], they permit a rational decision.

Creditor and Investor Market Decision Models

The above analysis is general. In addition to managerial decision models it is also applicable to creditor and investor decision models. Each creditor and investor must determine the feasible alternatives by comparing the available funds to the required investments. The available funds are defined, as before, by the selling prices of the assets held (by the creditor-investor) and the ability to borrow or raise equity capital. That is, investors borrow and creditors issue equity shares, and therefore, the funds available to them are determined in exactly the same way as outlined above. The required investment for new projects is the amount of the loan application or the present purchase price of the stock. For existing projects, the required investment is the present selling price of the debt or equity instrument.

The creditor-investor decision model also calls for a comparison of the required investment to the future cash flows. In this case, the future 'selling prices' of the 'output' is the interest or dividends. The 'salvage value' is the maturity or liquidation value of the instrument. Since the project may be abandoned or aborted prior to the maturation of the debt or liquidation of the firm, the salvage value may be a future selling price of the instrument.

In short, the investor-creditor decision model specifies exactly the same prices as those given above. However, these prices refer to assets held *by the creditor-investor* and to the various prices *of the debt-equity instrument*. Strictly speaking, this is *all* that the creditor-investor needs to know. That is, after an investor has narrowed the stocks down to those that are feasible alternatives, the only thing he needs to know is their purchase prices and their future selling prices (including dividends) *in the stock market*. He can then compare and make his choice(s).

If the creditor-investor can predict these future prices without regard to the operations of the individual or firm to whom he is lending-investing, then we need go no further with this analysis. Many investors do not look beyond the securities market when they make such predictions. They act as if the price fluctuations in the stock market were completely independent of the economic fluctuations of the firms that issue the stock. If this is true, then the stock market is simply a lottery with no underlying economic meaning, and we accountants should quit wasting our time and paper by issuing financial statements. Instead, we should draw the income numbers out of a hat and thereby determine who has won and lost. However, I, personally, am not interested in the stock market qua lottery. I believe that stock prices (as well as dividends, interest and ability to repay loans) do in fact depend upon the economic conditions of the firms. Moreover, I believe that stock prices *ought* to depend upon the economic conditions of the firms and that if we accountants supplied better information about the firms, the stock prices would conform more closely to those conditions. In short, I believe that a well designed investor-creditor decision model should specify information about the states and operations of the firms. I am not trying to dictate to investors. If they want to trade the market by 'reading the tape', then that is their business. If they can be successful on that basis, then more power to them. However, I believe that information about the firms should be available to investors, whether they use it or not. For all these reasons, I will concentrate upon the information specified by a rational creditor-investor decision model and assume that other information about the market will be supplied from non-accounting sources.

Future cash flows of the firm. The ability of a firm to service a debt, pay dividends or simply to survive depend upon its future cash flows. Thus, the future cash flows of a debt-equity instrument depend upon the future cash flows of the firm. It follows that the future cash flows of the firm are relevant to the creditor-investor.[9] The creditor-investor may make his own predictions of the flows or be supplied those predictions by someone else. The predictor may assign probabilities to the completion of the project and the abandonment of the project and predict the cash flows under both conditions. Many other refinements of this kind could be listed. The only point that I want to make is that the future cash flows of the firm are relevant to the investor-creditor, because the future flows of debt-equity instruments depend upon them.

I would urge that the prediction of the future cash flows used by the creditor-investor be independent of the prediction made by the management. This is not to impugn the honesty of managements, but rather to note that managements are likely to be optimistic about their own projects. If they were not, they would not have proposed them. Thus, an independent prediction is called for. This means that, as a

---

[9] Again, there are many other factors that are relevant, such as the 'character' of debtors and the 'resilience' and 'ingenuity' of management. However, I will focus on the more immediate market factors.

minimum, the creditor-investor needs to know *which* projects are planned by management. Then, the creditor-investor (or his agent) can independently assess the probability of success and independently predict the future purchase and selling prices of the project, as well as applying his personal discount rate.

Selling prices of firm assets. Whenever someone lends, invests or purchases, he is acquiring some value that exists now as well as some values that are predicted to exist in the near and distant future. The presently existing values can vary from zero to 100 per cent of the purchase price. For example, if I 'purchase' a ten dollar bill with two fives, then the presently existing value of the ten is 100 percent of the purchase price. Moreover, the ten will not increase in value in the future. On the other hand, if I grubstake a miner in return for a share of his find, then the presently existing value is zero—*all* of the value that I have purchased lies in the future. That future value may be much greater than $10, or it may be zero. Obviously, grubstaking a miner is much riskier than purchasing a ten dollar bill. This risk relationship of the presently existing value to the purchase price is true in general. The smaller the presently existing value in relation to the purchase price, other things equal, the higher the risk.

This means that the present selling prices of the assets held (and the selling prices that will exist immediately after purchase) are relevant to the decision. Perhaps the point in regard to an investor can be made clear by considering mutual funds. Suppose you have the option to purchase one share of either the L or the N fund for $100. Now the managers of both funds would promise you the moon if the SEC would let them get by with it. Therefore, you ought to make an independent prediction of the future 'performance' of both funds. Suppose you predict that the selling prices x years from now will be $140 and $120 for the shares of the L and N funds, respectively. Without further analysis, you can make your selection. If you are a maximiser, you will select the L fund. However, let me add two facts and then see if you agree that these facts should be specified by a well-designed decision model.

The L fund is a load fund and the amount of the load is $90. The N fund is a no-load fund. That is, the per share exit value[10] is $10 for the L fund and $100 for the N fund. Therefore, the value of the assets held by L must increase by 1,300 per cent to reach the predicted price while the increase required by N is only 20 per cent. Almost all of the value of L lies in the future while most of the value of N exists presently. Other things equal, L is a much riskier investment.

---

[10] The sum of the present selling prices of the assets held by the fund less the liabilities divided by the number of shares outstanding.

As many people have correctly pointed out, one should go ahead and buy a load fund if one thinks that it will out-perform a no-load fund by more than the amount of the load. However, the amount of the load is relevant to a well-designed decision model. This amount is determinable if the present selling prices of the assets held are disclosed.

There is also a 'load' or 'premium' on the price of the stock of industrial firms. The price of some stock is several hundred times its per share exit value. In such cases the purchased value lies almost wholly in the future. Other things equal, the greater the portion of the value that lies in the future the higher the risk. That is, if the firm does not perform in accordance with expectations the price of the stock is likely to drop drastically. By contrast, some stocks sell at a 'discount'—the price of the stock is less than its per share exit value. Closed-end funds, for example, often sell at a discount. The future price and dividends of discounted stock still depend upon the future cash flows of the firm, but, other things equal, it is much less risky. The value presently exists and therefore even if the firm liquidated immediately the investor would not lose. Indeed, he would profit.

Therefore, I conclude that the magnitude of the discount or premium is relevant to a well-designed decision model. That accountants know this is evidenced by their lower of cost or market rule. Although formally applicable only to inventories, it is also applied to a great many other assets. For example, I know of a case where the auditors insisted upon writing the value of land down to 'fair market value', even though they knew that this write-down would be likely to result in the liquidation of the firm. The land had been purchased at a price which reflected the expectation of mineral deposits which had failed to materialise. The auditors evidently thought that the 'fair market value' (exit value?) of this land was relevant to investors and creditors.

The problem is that this is a one-way rule. I know of another case where the stock of a retail chain is selling at about $10 per share. Based on its poor earnings, this is a reasonable price. That is, if it continues in the future as in the past, its future cash flows will be meagre and its reported income even less. However, this firm owns the land upon which its stores are built and the per share exit value of the land alone is conservatively estimated to be $40 per share. This land is carried on the balance sheet at its ancient historical cost of about 20¢ per share. I believe that the exit value of that land is equally as relevant in this case as in the above case.[11] If the *Gerstle* v. *Gemble* case[12] is taken as

---

[11] The only reason why I don't buy all the stock and liquidate the firm is that I lack the required investment of $10.00 per share for over two million shares.

[12] *Gerstle* v *Gamble-Skogmo*, 298 Federal Supplement 66 (1969).

evidence, it appears that the SEC also believes that exit values are relevant to investors.

Although these cases are extreme, they illustrate the fact that the price of stock ought to depend upon the presently existing exit values of the firm as well as depending upon the future cash flows of the firm.

I have spoken only of investors above because creditors have long recognised the relevance of the selling prices of assets. They are usually willing to loan only at a discount. That is, if a particular asset is pledged, they are willing to loan only a fraction of that asset's selling price. If they are general creditors, they are willing to loan only a fraction of the conservative (lower of cost or market) value of the total assets. Of course, creditors also look to the future cash flows of firms, if for no other reason than that they would prefer to avoid the expense of foreclosure. However, the selling prices are also relevant to them and they explicitly recognise the risk relationship when they speak of the amount of the discount or the amount of the net worth as providing a 'cushion of safety'.

VI. IMPLICATIONS FOR WEALTH AND INCOME MEASUREMENT

If the above analysis is correct and complete, then the implications are fairly straightforward. We noticed that

(a) Present selling prices (EV) of assets held by the firm,
(b) Present purchase prices (RC) of assets not held, and
(c) Future cash flows (FCF) of the firm

are relevant to well-designed market decision models of managers, investors and creditors.

Conspicuous by their absence from this list are past purchase prices (HC). I do not find them specified by any market decision model, and therefore, I conclude that they are irrelevant. This is a conclusion that I have held for many years and one that I have spoken about and written about many times. On one occasion, I challenged all readers to demonstrate just one case where historical costs were relevant to economic decisions. [13] It has now been five years since that challenge was made, and no one has published a direct reply. Since then, several people have argued for historical cost on the grounds of objectivity, feasibility, etc. This is the reason why I said in Section II that there were conflicting views on the objectives of accounting. Other people have argued for historical costs because managers, creditors and investors do, in fact, use the financial

---

[13] Sterling, *ASOBAT Review*, p. III.

statements that we give them. However, the fact that they use HC does not indicate that they would use HC if other information were supplied or that they ought to use them, in the sense that other information may be more likely to allow them to achieve their goals. This is the reason why I discussed the conflict between decision makers and decision models in Section III. If we really mean it when we say that accounting data should be useful or relevant, then we should demonstrate the relevance of HC or the superiority of HC to other valuation methods, and if we cannot do that, then we should abandon HC as a valuation method.

I exclude present purchase prices (RC) for a different reason. Present purchase prices of the assets *not* held are relevant to market decisions models. The source of information about these prices is the market itself, and they are already being supplied to management by the purchasing department. Financial statements report on assets held, and since present purchase prices are not relevant to assets held, they should not be used as a basis for the valuation of assets on financial statements. [14]

Every decision requires a prediction of the future consequences of various alternatives. For this reason, if I thought it were possible, I would urge that accountants report future cash flows. Knowledge of the future is always the most valuable kind of information. The reason it is so valuable is that it is so scarce. We have no way of knowing what the future holds, and there are many conflicting views about it. The existence of these conflicting views of the future partially makes the market operate. Except for specialisation and liquidity requirements, there would be no market if buyers held the same view of the future as sellers. This is most obvious in the commodity markets, where there is a long for every short. The speculators hold diametrically opposed views of the future—the

---

[14] Future purchase prices of planned replacements and additions are also relevant since they are a component of FCF. Many people argue that income should be calculated on the basis of RC because it is a good predictor of FCF. This may or may not be true. It is an empirical question that cannot be settled here. It is important to note, however, that the claim of this argument is not that RC are relevant per se but rather that RC are good predictors of FCF. Note that this is my interpretation of the argument. It is usually stated that RC income is superior to other income concepts because it is a better predictor of future *RC income.* Using this reasoning, one could argue that straight-line depreciation is the superior depreciation concept because it is a perfect predictor of future straight-line depreciation. Obviously, this is not what the RC proponents mean. I think they mean that business income is the superior concept because it is a good predictor of a relevant property (FCF), not that it is superior because it is a good predictor of itself.

long (buyer) expects a price increase and the short (seller) expects a price decrease. One of them must be wrong. The same thing happens in varying degrees in other markets. Thus, differing predictions of the future are an inherent part of the operation of a market.

It is this difficulty which causes me to reject the notion that accountants ought to report FCF. First, we cannot report FCF, we can only report predictions of FCF. If we were perfect predictors, we would destroy the market, i.e. prices would be set equal to the discounted value of the future cash flows and, except for liquidity requirements and specialisation, no exchange would occur. For example, if we all had access to future issues of the *Wall Street Journal,* the price of every stock would be bid so as to equal the discounted value of the known future prices and dividends. [15]

Of course, we really needn't worry about destroying the market because it is not very likely that we will be perfect predictors. That is, accountants are, in the present state of the art, about as prone to err in predicting FCF as are decision makers. Thus, we have the choice of (1) not predicting or (2) presenting erroneous predictions. Erroneous predictions are not relevant to decision models. Indeed, they are likely to be harmful and, given the attitude of the courts about accountants' legal liability, this harm is likely to redound to accountants. For these reasons, I don't think that accountants should at this time report their predictions of FCF. [16] Since DCF is simply FCF discounted by a rate and since different

---

[15] *Supra* I said that the reason that knowledge of the future is so valuable is that it is so scarce. Note that in this case, it would not be valuable because it is not scarce. That is, the price of exclusive access to future issues of the *Wall Street Journal* would be extremely high. However, when everyone has equal access, the price would probably be about the same as the price of today's issue.

[16] This leaves the predictions of FCF up to the decision makers. This presents no problem insofar as managements are concerned. A major part of managements' function is to try to peer into the future in order to select the preferred consequence. The problem is that the managements' decisions, based upon *their* predictions, affect the well being of the creditor-investor. Unless the creditor-investor is willing to rely solely upon the managements' predictions, he must make independent predictions. In order for the creditor-investor to make an independent prediction, he must know, at least in broad outline, the managements' plans. The budget is the most likely source of information about managerial plans. The creditor-investor can peruse this budget and then make (or have his agent make) a prediction of the future cash flows that will result. Therefore, I would urge that we include a partially audited management budget in our reports because it provides the basis for an independent prediction of the future cash flows.

Thus, I am not opposed to expanding the accounting function so that it includes information about expected futures. On the contrary, I think that we should rates are appropriate for different decision makers, it follows *a fortiori* that DCF is not an acceptable method of measuring income and wealth.

We noted that selling prices (EV) were relevant to all three market decision models. They are necessary to define market alternatives, they express the investment required to hold assets and they are a component of a risk indicator. For all of these reasons, I conclude that the items on the balance sheet should be valued at their present selling prices. Since income is defined as the difference between wealth (net worth) at two points in time, it follows that the income statement would be an explanation of the changes in the exit values on two successive balance sheets.

---

provide all the relevant information that we can. However, I don't think that erroneous predictions are relevant. (This includes those erroneous predictions which are disguised as 'past' cost allocations in HC. Recall those costs capitalised because of the 'future benefits' expected from the Edsel, Cleopatra, TFX, supersonic transports, etc.) If we get to the point where our ability to predict is better than that of the decision makers, then I will argue that we ought to report our predictions. In the meantime, I think the best we can do is to supply information to decision makers which will aid them in making their predictions.

APPENDIX IV-ii

AAA COMMITTEE ON EXTERNAL REPORTING

AN EVALUATION OF EXTERNAL REPORTING PRACTICES

The charge of this committee is: "To survey present external accounting practices, to assess their merits in the light of the standards for accounting information suggested in the *AAA Statement of Basic Accounting Theory*[1] and to suggest changes to bring practice into line with the standards."

Accounting is defined by ASOBAT as ". . . the process of identifying, measuring, and communicating economic information to permit informed judgments and decisions by users of the information." Adhering to this emphasis on the needs of the users of external financial reports, we decided to limit our study to the needs of equity investors and creditors of corporations. Our general philosophy has been to search for a logical process of selecting information and methods of communicating this information to permit informed judgments and decisions by investors and creditors and to search for a logical process of evaluating these and currently existing procedures in light of the ASOBAT standards.

While our selection procedure is hopefully adequate to serve as a basis for evaluating existing external accounting practices and for searching for better alternatives, we have applied our suggested procedures only to some of the areas of present external accounting practices and we have evaluated only partially our suggestions for alternative methods of reporting to bring practice into line with the ASOBAT standards. A much more exhaustive study would be required to assess the merits of all current practice and to examine thoroughly many alternative methods

---

Reprinted from A Report of the 1966–68 Committee on External Reporting, *The Accounting Review* (Supplement 1969), pp. 79–88, by permission of The American Accounting Association.

[1] American Accounting Association, *A Statement of Basic Accounting Theory* (1966). Hereafter referred to as ASOBAT.

of financial reporting. Therefore, while we recognize the basic limitations of this study, we hope that by presenting our findings others will be encouraged to continue research in this area.

I. GENERAL APPROACH

By choice and by necessity our general method is based on normative concepts. We start with normative investor's and creditor's valuation models and a normative dividend prediction model. These models are necessarily based upon observations regarding economic and social behavior of investors and creditors in the valuation process and of managers and directors in the dividend process and supported by the writings of researchers in the areas of economics and finance. Our procedure is, therefore, subject (as any normative model) to refutation or change as more is known about the actual goals of the decision makers and how the decisions are actually made. This is not meant to imply, however, that the models should eventually be descriptively derived. Decision makers may continue to utilize what appears to be irrelevant or misleading information. Such information should be brought into the models only when and if further research finds it to be, in fact, relevant in the decision process to meet the real or apparent goals of the decision makers. Note that we are not interested so much in how investors and creditors use accounting information in their decision processes as we are in what information they should be using to meet their goals.

In the evaluation process, we rely heavily on a flow chart analysis with sequential decision points. The objective of this evaluation process is to explain the logic of our recommendations regarding the disclosure of that information and the presentation of those statements which permit the investors and creditors to make informed judgments and decisions. It is not the responsibility of the accountant to make predictions or decisions for the investors and creditors, although the extent to which expectations should supplement accounting reports (through the use of budget data for example) is subject to evaluation in light of the standards. The conceptual process of moving from the valuation models to the selection of accounting concepts and procedures is outlined in the following steps:

1. Select normative investor's and creditor's valuation models.

2. Select a model for the prediction of dividends and other distributions to stockholders and creditors.

3. List object and activity inputs (potentially relevant identifications of items and events) and their related attributes and measurement concepts.

4. Evaluate each of the attributes of each object or activity input for relevancy (its ability to permit a prediction of a variable or relationship in the models).

5. List potentially acceptable measurement procedures.

6. Assess each procedure for each attribute in light of the standards of quantifiability, verifiability, and freedom from bias.

7. Select the attributes and measurement procedures that should be included in financial reports.

These steps are discussed in greater detail in Sections II, III, and IV. In Section V, we apply our evaluation procedures to current accounting practices and in Section VI, we suggest alternative information and methods of presentation that appear to meet the standards better than current practice.

II. A Normative Investment Valuation Model

In accordance with our general approach as outlined in the preceding section, our first step in the evaluation of external accounting practices was the development of a normative investor's valuation model. This model had to include the variables and interrelationships which should be considered by an investor. In order to limit the scope of our analysis, the following valuation model relates primarily to long-term investors in equity and fixed income securities, i.e., investors who intend to retain their positions for relatively long periods. This does not necessarily imply that the model is of no value to the short-term investor. However, short-term investors are generally more interested in changes in security prices than in cash distributions by the firm; and short-term fluctuations in security prices are frequently more closely related to external factors in the economy than to expectations regarding the individual firm. This condition makes accounting data of less assistance to short-term investors than to those interested in taking a long-term position in corporate securities.

The Basic Investment Valuation Model

We view the investment decision as one of choice among available alternatives. The model we are using is designed to reduce the alternatives to the lowest common denominator, the utility-adjusted present value of the gain or loss from holding a security to time period "n". This analysis of alternative investments permits the investor to select a portfolio which is most favorable to him and which comes closest to meeting his goals and objectives.

The model which we use in our analysis is an adaptation of the model described by Robicheck and Myers in *Optimal Financing Decisions*.[2] Modifications have been made to make it more relevant for our specific problem. The basic model is as follows:

(1)
$$V_{ok} = \left(\sum_{i=1}^{n_k} \frac{(\alpha_{ik})(CF_{ik})(m_{ik})}{\prod_{j=1}^{i} [1 + \beta_j (m_{jk})]} \right) - I_o$$

where:

V_{ok} = the net subjective value of the gain or loss to be obtained by an investor (k) for a specific investment at time period (o).

n_k = the discrete time period used by the investor.

CF_{ik} = the expected value of before tax cash distributions to the investor in year (i) including the final liquidation. Each investor (k) may have a different expected value in each time period.

α_{ik} = a "certainty equivalent" factor which adjusts the expected cash flows to a value such that a given investor is indifferent between CF_{ik} and a cash flow which is certain to be paid. This factor is determined by each investor's utility preference for risk.

$m_{ik}(m_{jk})$ = one minus the expected marginal tax rate for each cash flow for each investor (k) and for each time period (i) or (j).

β_j = the before tax opportunity rate for a riskless investment. The rate may change over time (j).

I_o = the transaction price at the time of decision.

We state in this basic model that an investor's calculation of the present value of his gain from making an investment is determined by his evaluation of the utility adjusted present value of the expected cash flows from the investment less the outlays necessary to obtain the securities. His calculation of the present value of the expected cash is determined by computing the expected value of each year's gross cash receipts, adjusted for his utility preference or aversion for risk and for his income tax effect. This product is then discounted by the investor's tax adjusted

---

[2]Alexander A. Robicheck, and Stewart C. Myers, *Optimal Financing Decisions*, (Englewood Cliffs, N.J.: Prentice-Hall Inc., 1965), Chapters V and VI.

rate of return for a riskless investment. The utility adjustment for risk $(\propto_{ik})$ is based upon the investor's personal evaluation of the expected cash flow distributions in each time period. Conceptually, any distribution of expected cash flows can be adjusted to a "certainty equivalent" by the factor $\propto_{ik}$. This certainty equivalent represents the value for which an investor is indifferent between the estimated distribution of cash flows and a cash flow which is certain to be paid. If the investor is risk averting, $\propto_{ik}$ will take on values between 0 and 1. If the investor is a speculator, $\propto_{ik}$ may be greater than 1.

The value of $\propto_{ik}$ is a function of:

1. The form and dispersion of the subjective probability distributions of the expected cash flows.

2. The attractiveness of the probability distribution to the investor.

We have not included in the valuation model any personal utility considerations other than for the investor's preference or aversion for risks evaluated on the basis of the distribution of expected cash flows. There are, of course, many other types of considerations which may alter the investor's actual investment decision. For example, he may wish to avoid some investments entirely for ethical reasons or because of personal biases. On the other hand, he may have a favorable disposition toward holding certain securities because of a personal relationship with the firm (such as being an employee) or because of a personal relationship with family or friends who own significant amounts of stock or other securities. These personal utility factors must be included in the investor's decision rule which governs a specific investment action.

The Creditor's Valuation Model

The basic investment valuation model can be made more specific by separately identifying a creditor's and stockholder's valuation model. For a creditor, the amount of the cash flow (CF_i) and the time horizon (n) in the above general model are usually specified by contract. But, because the tax rates for ordinary income (interest received in this case) and capital gains are different, the cash flows (CF_i) are separated into two parts—the contractual interest receipt (R_i) and the amount to be received at maturity (MV_n). However, unless the investment is riskless there is some probability of the cash flow being less than that specified in the contract. Therefore, expected values (R_{ik}) and (MV_{nk}) are used even though they will usually be very close to the contractual interest return and the contractual amount to be received at maturity. Since I_o is the transaction price at the date of decision, the main subjective variables for the investor in contractual obligations are the expected before tax opportunity rates of return (β_j), the subjective adjustment for the risk ($\propto_{ik}$) of nonpayment of the interest or maturity value and the estimated marginal tax rates. The investment model for contractual obligations can be expressed mathematically as follows:

$$(2) \qquad V_{ok} = \left(\sum_{i=1}^{n} \frac{(\propto_{ik})(R_{ik})(m_{ik})}{\displaystyle\prod_{j=1}^{i} [1 + \beta_j (m_{jk})]} \right)$$

$$+ \left(\frac{(MV_{nk} - CG_{nk})(\propto_{nk})}{\displaystyle\prod_{j=1}^{n} [1 + \beta_j (m_{jk})]} \right) - I_o$$

Where:

R_{ik} = the expected value of the interest to be received in year i.

MV_{nk} = the expected value to be collected at maturity, the end of year (n).

CG_{nk} = the expected capital gains tax to be paid by investor (k) when the securities are sold in period (n).

The main objective of external accounting reports in the presentation of information to creditors is to aid the creditor in his subjective evaluation of the expected values and their probability distributions and possibly in his evaluation of probable opportunity rates of return, although the latter would be indirect.

The Stockholder's Valuation Model

The expected cash receipts for the stockholder are made up of two basic components—the expected dividend stream for the period the stock is to be held and the net sale price of the stock at the end of the holding period.

The expected dividend stream (including any partial liquidating dividends) adjusted for the marginal income tax rate and the certainty equivalent factor is discounted to the date of decision by the tax adjusted opportunity rates for a riskless investment. The expected market price at the expected date of sale less transaction costs adjusted for the marginal capital gains tax and the risk preference factor, is discounted by the same tax adjusted opportunity rates of interest. The present value of the gain from making an investment in a stock is, therefore, the sum of the discounted adjusted expected dividend stream and the discounted adjusted expected cash receipt from the sale of the security less the transaction price of the stock at the time of decision. This model can be expressed mathematically as follows:

$$(3) \qquad V_{ok} = \left(\sum_{i=1}^{n} \frac{(\alpha_{ik})(D_{ik})(m_{ik})}{\prod_{j=1}^{i} [1 + \beta_j(m_{jk})]} \right)$$

$$+ \left(\frac{(I_{nk} - CG_{nk})(\alpha_{nk})}{\prod_{j=1}^{n} [1 + \beta_j(m_{jk})]} \right) - I_o$$

where:

V_{ok} = the net subjective present value of the gain which can be obtained by an investor (k) at time period (o) from buying one share at the market price I_o.

D_{ik} = the expected value of cash flows (dividends per share) during each period (i).

I_{nk} = the expected transaction price of the stock at period (n) as projected by investor (k), less commission and other direct outlays.[3]

We can conclude that the relevant functions which must be estimated by a stockholder using our normative model in making his investment decision are as follows:

1. The estimated cash flows per share to the stockholders for each time period during the life of the firm (D_{ik}). These estimates should include subjective probability distributions as well as expected values.

2. The expected marginal tax rate on dividends applicable to the investor for each year the stock is expected to be held. This rate must take into

---

[3]Note that by introducing the investor's expectation of what the market's assessment of future factor values will be, I_{nk} can be expressed notationally as the discounted values of these future expectations.

$$(4) \qquad I_{nk} = \sum_{i=n_k+1}^{\infty} \frac{(D_{ir})(m_{ir})}{\prod_{j=1}^{i-n_k} [1 + \beta_j(m_{jr})]}$$

where:

r = an investor's expectation of the market's assessment of future factor values, including any from liquidation payments.

consideration all other taxable income of the investor.

3. The expected capital gains tax to be paid when the stock is sold (CG_{nk}).

4. The quantification of the certainty equivalent factor ($\propto_{ik}$) which is based upon the individual investor's utility preference for risk.

5. The before tax opportunity rate of interest for a riskless investment for each year until the period of expected sale of the stock (β_j).

Summary

We have found it impossible to evaluate current practice in light of the standards without first defining a user and his informational needs; therefore, we have presented in this section a version of a valuation model which describes the basic needs of investors. In the following section, we will analyze in greater detail the information needed by equity investors by means of description, in functional form only, of a model for the prediction of asset distributions to common stockholders.

III. The Dividend Prediction Model

Of the five data needs cited in the preceding section as being essential in the stock investor's valuation model, we are of the opinion that reports to external parties can be expected to provide the greatest assistance in the estimation of D_{ik} (dividends per share).

If D_{ik} is the expected cash to be received by the holder of each share of stock in period (i), then we can say:

$$D_{ik} = \frac{CDS_{ik}}{N_{ik}}$$

where:

CDS_{ik} = the total cash to be distributed to all common stockholders in period (i) as predicted by investor (k).

N_{ik} = the number of shares of common stock estimated by investor (k) to be outstanding at the time of distribution in period (i).

Cash Distribution to Common Stockholders (CDS_{ik})

We view the dividend decision of the firm as part of a complex decision making process concerned with the allocation of a scarce resource, cash. The decision with respect to the amount of cash to be distributed (CDS_{ik}) to the owners can be made only after making many other interrelated

decisions with respect to cash sources and uses. The following factors
are among those which must be considered: (1) net cash flows from
operations (CFO_{ik}); (2) net cash flows from routine events excluded from
the concept of operations (CNR_{ik}); (3) net cash flows from changes in
the level of investment by outsiders (CI_{ik}); (4) net cash flows from changes
in the investment in assets including all working capital and plant facilities
(CIA_{ik}); (5) cash distributions made to investors with priority claims against
the assets of the firm (CPC_{ik}); (6) net cash flows from random events,
a distribution of which may or may not be predicted (CRE_{ik}); (7) attitudes
toward accumulation of stocks of resources to meet precautionary and
liquidity needs (STK_{ik}); and (8) philosophy with regard to the necessity
or desirability of regular periodic disbursements to common stockholders
(DP_{ik}) (i.e. is the dividend viewed as the residual balance of cash after
other needs have been met or is the dividend viewed as a disbursement
which must be made before other discretionary outlays are made?).

We do not view our assignment as requiring the development of a
formal dividend decision model, for no generic model can be relevant
to all firms; however, we are of the opinion that at least the functional
relationship between dividends and other cash flows should be expressed
in order to visualize more clearly the data which are relevant to the
equity investor in his attempt to evaluate the alternatives available to
him. The investor is interested in predicting the cash to be distributed
to stockholders (CDS_{ik}) for each time period indefinitely into the future.
If he knows the variables and their relationships which are important
in making the decision with respect to CDS_{ik} in a time period, then
his prediction of the desired cash distribution (CDS_{ik}) can be improved
through his prediction of the variables. The predicted variables can then
be processed through the prediction model to get an estimate of CDS_{ik}.
If we know the variables that are functionally related to the dividend
decision, then we can set forth information requirements which are relevant
to the prediction of the important variables.

The following expression sets forth the relevant variables in the dividend
decision without specifying the relationship of the variables to each other
or the decision:

$$CDS_{ik} = f(CFO_{ik,}\ CNR_{ik,}\ CI_{ik,}\ CIA_{ik},$$

$$CPC_{ik},\ CRE_{ik},\ STK_{ik},\ DP_{ik})$$

These several variables are discussed sequentially in the following
paragraphs.

Net Cash Flows From Operations (CFO_{ik}).

The prediction of net cash flows from operations (CFO_{ik}) can, of course, be based upon a direct extrapolation from historical reports of actual cash flows from operations. This extrapolated approach is limited in several respects. A more useful approach requires that the investor consider the expected behavior of the several components of cash flows from operations. There are at least these components:

1. Cash derived from sale of products or services
2. Cash required for the purchase or manufacture of the products or services being sold
3. Cash required for promotion and sale of products and services
4. Cash required for the general administration of the firm
5. Cash required to maintain the facilities in a productive state
6. Cash required to satisfy tax obligations to federal, state, and local governments

In order to be able to make a prediction of these flows, the investor needs information about the environment in which the firm exists. He must have some idea about the demand for the products and the price structure which is likely to prevail. He must be able to assess the nature of the competition and the effect of competitive decisions of other firms in the industry. He must be able to evaluate the conditions in the markets supplying the firm with labor, materials and capital. He will find it extremely helpful to know the stock of various resources held at the beginning of the period. For example, in order to predict the cash required for the purchase of merchandise, the change in the stock of goods from the beginning to end of the period under consideration is important information. The change in the stock of receivables is also crucial in the prediction of cash flows from customers.

The knowledge required about the firm itself must include such factors as information about the stock of productive resources, cost structure determined by the mix required of the various inputs for a reasonable period, and innovative capabilities of the management team. Some of this knowledge can be obtained from reports of several past periods which provide information about the firm under conditions which are reasonably well known and understood. Prediction is thus based upon a knowledge of the relationships which have existed and the results obtained under certain particular circumstances.

In addition to the knowledge about the results of activities with a given stock of productive resources, if the investor is to predict cash flows from operations for any reasonable period into the future, he must have information about plans for expansion or changes in the stock of productive resources and major changes in the operations of the firm. In brief he needs capital budget plans for as far in the future as they can be obtained—this is probably the best and only way for the investor to determine the direction the management expects the firm to take.

The most relevant form of financial reporting is that which (1) reports budgets for the forthcoming period or periods and (2) reports actual results in a form consistent with that of the budget together with a detailed comparison of the plan and the actual results for the past period. The deviations from the plan should be explained in detail to aid the investor in: (1) his forecasts for future periods and (2) his appraisal of management and its ability to foresee and take advantage of the opportunities open to it.

Some of the important variables in the prediction of CFO_{ik} are:

1. The demand for and price of output factors.
2. The requirements and price of input factors.
3. The cost structure in terms of variable and fixed components required for prediction of levels of input factors.
4. The productive capacity in terms of units of output per time period.
5. The requirements for tax payments.

Nonoperating Cash Flows (CNR_{ik})

The prediction of net cash flows from events excluded from the concept of operations (CNR_{ik}) depends to a large degree on the repetitive nature of the events. These flows are derived from activities of the firm considered ancillary to its main function; for example, they include interest received from investments in marketable securities or rent received from space leased to outsiders (assuming the firm is not in the business of leasing space), cash derived from sale of assets not held for resale, and cash outflows such as political and charitable contributions.

The prediction of the cash receipts from marketable securities is, of course, dependent on the stock of securities held, changes expected in the stock and environmental changes which affect the interest rates. Cash received from rentals is dependent on the stock of space which the firm holds that is excess to its own needs and the rental price it can charge. Conditions, of course, may change making the cash flow fluctuate as the space available for rental by the firm increases or decreases and as the supply and demand for alternative space available to the lessee increases or decreases. Cash derived from sale of assets not held for resale depends on the need for these assets, the rate at which such assets become obsolete in terms of product produced or technological progress in development. The predictability of this flow may not be subject to accurate prediction if such sales do not follow regular patterns. Thus we see once again that the predictability of cash flows depends on the supply or stock of resources and commitments and changes in the stock and the environment.

Cash Flows from Changes in the Level of Investment by Stockholders and Creditors (CI_{ik})

The net cash flows resulting from changes in the level of investment by current and potential stockholders and creditors is determined by at least two main variables—the anticipated change in the total assets required to be held by the firm to carry out its plans and the net cash expected to become available to the firm from internal sources. While the fund requirements to meet expected changes in total assets can be obtained from expectations regarding capital expenditures and working capital changes (CIA_{ik}), it can also be estimated by looking at the stock of assets held by the firm at the beginning of the period and the stock which the firm desires to hold at the end of the period. The internal sources of funds depend upon the following variables: (1) net cash flows from operations (CFO_{ik}); (2) net cash flows from events excluded from the concept of operations (CNR_{ik}); (3) net cash flows expected to result from random events (CRE_{ik}); (4) cash distributions made to investors with priority claims against the assets of the firm (CPC_{ik}); and (5) management's philosophy relating to the payment of cash dividends to common stockholders (DP_{ik}).

Cash Flows Arising From Investment in Assets (CIA_{ik})

The net cash flows from changes in the investment in assets (CIA_{ik}) including working capital items and plant facilities can be predicted only if one has knowledge of the current cost of replacing assets or acquiring additional assets. The change reflects replacement policy and expansion policy. The capital budget is a starting place for the prediction of cash outflows for the purchase of plant assets. Historical perspective combined with predicted operating levels may be the best starting point for the prediction of changes in working capital items.

Cash Flows for Priority Claims (CPC_{ik})

The cash distributions made to investors with priority claims against the assets of the firm (CPC_{ik}) are functionally related to the terms of the contracts specifying the priority claims. These include interest payments, repayment of principal provisions, sinking fund provisions and asset maintenance provisions.

Cash Flows from Random Events (CRE_{ik})

In a large firm, the total cash flows estimated to result from random events (CRE_{ik}) are generated by stochastic processes and as a result the cash flows resulting from such events may be predictable within acceptable limits. In smaller firms, the cash flows resulting from such random events may be highly unpredictable particularly for specific years in the future. Examples of such random events would be unexpected windfalls or casualties.

Management's Attitudes Regarding Stocks of Resources (STK_{ik})

Management's attitudes toward holding precautionary and liquidity resource balances in excess of those required to maintain the expected level of operations (STK_{ik}) are functionally related to the risks and uncertainties which management perceives in the future operations of the firm. The uncertainties are not necessarily related to unfavorable events. Management may hold resource balances to enable the firm to take advantage of opportunities which may appear unexpectedly. There is, of course, the negative aspect or cost of holding resources in order to meet emergencies.

Cash Dividend Policy (DP_{ik})

Management's philosophy relating to the payment of cash dividends to stockholders (DP_{ik}) may be embodied in a formal statement or it may be an informal policy which is substantiated by actions of past periods. The dividend policy may, of course, be in terms of a minimum annual dividend, a percentage of some annual measure of success such as reported income or cash flow from operations, a residual policy related to the stock of cash, or indeed no policy at all with each dividend declaration being the result of an ad hoc decision.

Comment

These variables and relationships are not necessarily all inclusive; but they are important factors in the prediction of the cash to be distributed to the common stockholders in a given period. It should be clear that this aspect of the creditor's model (the prediction of cash distributed to creditor investors) is much simpler than the stock investor's model because the prediction of cash distribution to creditors is much more closely related to the contractual provisions of the debt instruments.

Number of Shares of Stock (N_{ik})

The estimation of the total cash to be distributed by the firm to all common stockholders (CDS_{ik}) is an important determinant of dividends per share (D_{ik}), but it is not sufficient. The investor is interested in the cash to be distributed per share of common stock. For this reason the investor is also interested in predicting the number of shares of stock which will be outstanding in period (i). As we have already observed, the prediction of CDS_{ik} is related to the net cash flows from investors (CI_{ik}) which involves decisions on the part of the firm as to the securities which it will issue to the investment community.

The number of common shares which will be outstanding in period (i) is a function of expansion opportunities, management's philosophy with regard to raising new capital, existing and future convertible preference securities and the rate of actual conversion, the public's attitude toward various instruments of ownership, cash available for discretionary uses after payment of cash dividends, the distribution of common shares as stock dividends and/or splits, the acquisition of treasury shares, and the use of stock options as a means of management compensation.

Conclusions

With the relationships discussed here, the common stock investor (k) has a basis for predicting the dividends which will be paid to each holder of a share of common stock in period (i). The data that should be included in financial statements of the firm are those which will be most helpful to the investor in his efforts to predict the total cash to be distributed to common stockholders (CDS_{ik}) and the number of common shares outstanding (N_{ik}). We are of the opinion that these statements should include some historical data to permit the investor to identify important variables and relationships which have existed and the forces which have been at work in changing previous patterns. Through this knowledge the investor can begin to forecast what quantities he should assign to variables in the future. The investor's forecasting efforts may also be appreciably enhanced by the inclusion of management's short run and long run budgets in the financial report insofar as they meet the ASOBAT standards.

APPENDIX IV-iii

HAROLD BIERMAN, JR.

THE IMPLICATIONS TO ACCOUNTING OF EFFICIENT MARKETS AND THE CAPITAL ASSET PRICING MODEL

Statements made by two committee reports of the American Accounting Association as well as implications of recent accounting research—if correct or if assumed to be correct and are followed—have significant impact on accounting theory and practice.[1] I will argue that several of the conclusions are either ambiguous or in serious error and that the relationship of accounting and financial theory research should be reinspected. Currently good financial (investment) theory research is being applied to accounting theory in ways that are not appropriate. Positions are being overstated.

Specifically:

(a) It has not been shown that the efficient market hypothesis reduces the importance of improving conventional financial accounting.

Reprinted from *The Accounting Review* (July 1974), pp. 557–62, by permission of the American Accounting Association.

Harold Bierman, Jr. is Nicholas H. Noyes Professor of Business Administration at Cornell University.

The arguments presented in this paper were refined in discussions with Seymour Smidt and Peter Dukes. Tom Hofstedt offered several helpful editorial suggestions. This assistance is greatly appreciated.

[1] See Supplement to Vol. XLVII, 1972, of *The Accounting Review*, "Report of the Committee on Research Methodology in Accounting," pp. 407–36 and "Report of the Committee on Corporate Financial Reporting," pp. 525–33. The former report was written solely by William H. Beaver and was not passed on by other members of the Committee. It was published as a Committee Report.

(b) It is wrong to imply that the systematic risk coefficient (β) is all the information needed by an investor. Individual security reporting errors affecting the perceptions of unsystematic risk are of concern to the imperfectly diversified investor and thus are of concern to a majority of investors.

(c) The relationship between accounting data and security price behavior cannot generally be used as the primary basis to choose among alternative methods of recording and presenting the financial affairs of a corporation.

I am not saying that the theory of finance cannot have important inputs into accounting theory and practice. For example, Beaver has properly argued the use of market prices in valuation of readily marketable securities held for investment, citing the efficient market hypothesis.[2] Also, the efficient market hypothesis has significant implications on how and when financial information is to be disseminated by corporations.

EFFICIENT MARKETS AND ACCOUNTING

We will initially assume that capital markets are efficient and "prices always 'fully reflect' available information."[3] This is the "semi-strong" form of the efficient market hypothesis.[4]

Let us consider the following statement made by the Committee on Corporate Financial Reporting: ". . . recent evidence suggests that in an efficient market, securities fully reflect available information in an instantaneous and unbiased fashion. If this is indeed so, then the individual investor should not be the focus of investing reporting efforts."[5]

It is not clear what type of information would replace reports focusing on the needs of individual investors. In addition, the need for a change is far from obvious. Even with the efficient market assumption it does not follow that the needs of the individual investor should not be the

---

[2] W. H. Beaver, "Reporting Rules for Marketable Equity Securities," *The Journal of Accountancy* (October 1972), pp. 57–61. For a different and even stronger justification for this position see G. J. Stigler, *The Theory of Price* (Macmillan, 1966), pp. 96–7.

[3] E. F. Fama, "Efficient Capital Markets: A Review of Theory and Empirical Work," *Journal of Finance* (May 1970), p. 383. For an evaluation of a wide range of efficient market literature see D. Downes and T. R. Dyckman, "A Critical Look at the Efficient Market Empirical Research Literature as It Relates to Accounting Information," *The Accounting Review* (April 1973).

[4] The "strong" form makes the assumption that the market also has access to so-called inside information.

[5] Committee on Corporate Financial Reporting, p. 525.

focus of investing reporting efforts. Individual investors make the market efficient. For example, Fama states: "Similarly . . . the market may be efficient if 'sufficient numbers' of investors have ready access to available information. And disagreement among investors about the implications of given information does not in itself imply market inefficiency unless there are investors who can consistently make better evaluations of available information than are implicit in market prices."[6]

Intrinsic value analysis is essential to the maintenance of an efficient market. If a large number of experts and nonexperts are performing financial analysis based on the accounting data presented, then the market is likely to be reasonably efficient. The buying and selling activities of these analysts had to make the market efficient.

An individual lacking special information or insights should be willing to rely on the market's judgment and dispense with intensive analysis, if he accepts the efficient market hypothesis. But even if the market is generally efficient, this does not guarantee that all stocks will be appropriately priced at all times since the accounting information supplied is not always reliable. Even with an efficient market, the market clearing price set with generally available information may differ from an equilibrium value that would have been set if the market had better information.

To say the market is efficient hides a great deal of information about what is actually going on in the market. At any moment in time the introduction of "news" is being evaluated by a large number of investors. As the market adjusts to the news one group of investors will sell based on the news and one group will buy. If the news is ambiguous or misleading, one or the other of the groups may be harmed.

Assume financial reporting for a firm is deficient in some sense, and that only a small percentage of the market's investors (e.g., expert accountants or insiders) know that the reported information is not reliable and is in fact greatly different from measures that would be intuitively appealing to analysts if they had the measures. In this situation, even if the market is efficient, and even if it were to reflect available information, individual investors will be harmed if they act differently than they would have acted if they had possessed the alternative information.[7]

---

[6] Fama, p. 388. Gonedes also implies the use of financial analysis. See N. J. Gonedes, "Efficient Capital Markets and External Accounting," *The Accounting Review* (January 1972), p. 16

[7] This sentence implies that the strong form of the efficient markets hypothesis is not true. See Fama p. 383 and pp. 409–16 for evidence that this assumption is valid.

It is possible that the expected value of financial analysis net of costs is zero or negative some time period after information is generally available, but this does not lead to a conclusion that the accounting information decision is meaningless. If the prices of all securities reflected their intrinsic value, it would be because of the type of information and analysis that the accountant supplied. If enough investors abandoned financial analysis the market could well cease to be efficient, and if accountants ceased to improve financial accounting the gap between intrinsic stock value and market price could well increase.

Another argument for improving accounting is that resources are expended to produce and evaluate the information necessary to make markets socially desirable as well as efficient. If financial accounting can produce this information at lower cost than alternative methods, then it is wasteful not to have good financial accounting reports.

THE CAPITAL ASSET PRICING MODEL AND ACCOUNTING

Portfolio theory tells us that it is possible to select combinations of securities that have better return-risk characteristics than can be obtained by investing in a few individual securities. The capital asset pricing model brings the market into the analysis so that we can make statements about how that market trades off return for risk. Taken together, portfolio theory and the capital asset pricing model are powerful tools for both descriptive and normative analysis for many areas of finance and investments.

If all or nearly all investors were perfectly diversified, then only the systematic risk of a firm would be relevant to an investor (risks peculiar to the firm are diversified away). The only relevant risk would be the correlation of the specific firm with the market (the Greek letter β, beta, is often used to refer to the relationship of the firm and the market). There is no question that accounting should aim at supplying the necessary information for estimating a firm's β. But it is wrong to imply that an estimate of the systematic risk coefficient (β) is all the information needed by an investor.

Application of the capital asset pricing model to accounting ignores the fact that a very large number of investors are not perfectly diversified. In fact the largest number of investors have a very small degree of diversification. The New York Stock Exchange 1965 *Census of Shareowners* indicates that the average American shareowner owns three to four different stock issues. The 1970 census indicated that 19 million shareowners held portfolios worth less than $10,000. There is no way, including mutual funds, for such investors to be diversified in such a manner that the unsystematic risk of one component of the portfolio is not important.[8]

The 1970 Census of Amex Shareowners confirms the above statistics. The average Amex shareowner owned a total of 6.6 stock issues and 8 out of 10 owned fewer than 10 issues and one in a thousand owned 100 or more issues.[9]

Beaver uses the capital asset pricing model to go much further than the suggestion that a firm's β is a useful measure. Consider the following statement by Beaver: "More importantly, the portfolio model emphasizes that the relevant level of concern to the decision maker is the portfolio level, not the individual security level. . . . Hence, the decision maker clearly would be unwilling to pay anything for any data that only would permit him to reduce the variance of the individualistic factor . . . suppose it was empirically demonstrated that the existing reporting rules led to prediction errors in the return distributions of several individual securities. Such evidence is insufficient to indict current reporting methods."[10]

Beaver relies on the investor's diversification to eliminate the importance of the errors. But while the capital asset pricing model is a logical model of the securities market, the application of the conclusions to an individual investor's portfolio requires that the investor only have a very small percentage of his portfolio in any one security. If all individual investors are not perfectly diversified, then the reporting method for individuals and of individual securities is important. Errors, even where they are independent of each other, are not always diversified away.[11] The failure

---

[8] The Fund of Funds has cured the temptation to cite a mutual fund as a means of obtaining perfect diversification. There are risks associated with any single mutual fund that are not a function of the number of securities it holds.

[9] Evans has shown that a portfolio with equal dollar amounts invested in 10 securities will on the average have 7% more standard deviation than an investment in the market. Since the 7% is itself an average, this does not prove the lack of importance of unsystematic risk with small portfolios. See J. L. Evans, "Diversification and the Reduction of Dispersion: An Empirical Analysis," Doctoral dissertation, Graduate School of Business Administration, University of Washington, 1968.

[10] Beaver, *The Accounting Review* (1972), pp. 422–3.

[11] The assumption that the individualistic component of risk is not relevant requires that investors are perfectly diversified. If the situation is one where material amounts (from the point of view of the investor's wealth) are invested in individual securities, then the individualistic component is relevant to those investors. I do not mean to question the argument stressing the importance of β, but rather I am objecting to arguments that suggest that other information might not be relevant to investors.

of investors to diversify perfectly may be rational. The reasons could be a preference for positive skewness or the presence of transaction and information costs.

The Relationship of Security Prices and Financial Information

The relationship of accounting data and security price behavior cannot generally be used as the basis of choosing among alternative methods of accounting.[12] Beaver takes a different position and states: ". . . it is inconceivable that optimal information systems for investors can be selected without a knowledge of security behavior."[13] The difference between Beaver's position and mine might be classified as being semantic since I would agree that information that could predict stock prices is valuable to investors and should be supplied. However, not all such information should be classified as accounting and affect the accounting reports of corporations.

Let us consider three different approaches to arriving at a financial accounting system:

(a) Pay some attention to the needs of investors but tend to invoke *ad hoc* rules such as adhering to original cost in the face of new information, use of LIFO inventory, etc. This description is meant more or less to describe current practices.

(b) Use normative models of investor behavior to determine what information would be needed by a rational investor.

(c) Use empirical data to determine what information system can predict security prices.

I would reject (a) because of lack of usefulness and (c) because of reasons to follow, and would prefer (b).

Accounting should have limits as to its function. An investor makes

---

[12] There are exceptions where one might want to consider the effect of an accounting practice on security prices in choosing the practice. For example, departures from good accounting practice because of cost of reporting may be justified based on materiality, which is another way of saying the stock price is not significantly affected.

[13] Beaver, p. 409. Beaver is not alone in this position; see Nicholas J. Gonedes, "Efficient Capital Markets and External Accounting," *The Accounting Review*, (January 1972), pp. 11–21. For example (pp. 11–21): "The major argument of this paper is quite simple (though, I hope, not simple-minded); observation of the market reaction of recipients of accounting outputs should govern evaluations of the actual information content of accounting numbers produced via a given set of procedures and the informational content of accounting numbers produced via an alternative set of accounting procedures."

his decision about the desirability of a stock based on the historical record of the firm, its risk characteristics and his risk preferences, and forecasts of the financial future of the firm, of its stock price, and of the economy. All these factors are combined to form a value for the stock which is then compared to the stock price and to alternative investments. The accounting information is only a small part of the evaluation process.

One can use security prices to tell whether the market is using other information than the reported accounting data, or which of several current accounting practices are being used by the market. But, there is no way that inspection of market prices can identify accounting measures that best measure financial affairs (inspection can reveal that the market is not using the current measures). It should not be argued that since observations of security prices can be used to determine which one of several accounting measures (methods) of income is being used, this measure (method) is superior to all other measures. Interestingly, while we can never be certain of what income measure the market is using, we can be sure of the market's measure of net asset value (assets minus liabilities). It is the stock price. The accountant currently measures net assets using a set of theories and conventions. Alternatively one could use the market price of the common stock to measure the net asset value of a firm. Should the accountant use the market value of the firm's stock as the basis of recording the firm's assets? This would not be desirable since the market is looking to accounting for information that it can use to value the stock.

Rather than information about "security price behavior" the accountant needs to know how rational investors should be making decisions, and to supply the relevant financial information. If investors are using astrology, or sunspots, the accountant does not have the responsibility for supplying this information. However, if a theoretically correct capital asset pricing model indicates that the covariance of the company's return with the market return is relevant, then the accountant should at a minimum supply reliable information about the nature of the firm's business and, ideally, supply an estimate of the firm's β measure. Also, investors who are not perfectly diversified will need information about the firm beyond the estimate of β. It should be remembered that in the presence of transaction costs it may be rational for an investor to be less than perfectly diversified.

CONCLUSIONS

While stock prices are likely to be based on good financial information (some of which, hopefully, can be supplied by accounting), we should not use accounting procedures because they happen to be correlated with stock prices.

Accounting procedures leading to financial reports to be used by investors should be based on good accounting theory. The objective of the accounting is to measure economic events, not to predict stock prices. If the accounting is good and if the market is efficient, it would be surprising if the accounting reports did not normally serve as useful predictors of value. But it is important to get the direction of the causal relationship correct. Stock prices are determined by accounting reports; the accounting theories and practices should not be dictated by stock prices. For example, assume we know that an action by management will depress conventionally measured earnings and will depress the stock price. We do not want the decrease in stock price to be accepted as evidence that the accounting was correct.

There is no question that a better understanding is needed about the relationship between accounting data and security price behavior if only to highlight the fact that accounting information should be taken seriously. This does not imply that the choice among accounting alternatives will be decided by this type of research. The capital asset pricing model cannot be used as a justification for assuming that individual security return errors that are random or independent in nature are not of concern because they can be diversified away. Unsystematic risk is of great concern to the nondiversified investor.

If a proposed accounting procedure is theoretically superior to what is done in practice and if price observations indicate that the market is using it, then this can be used to support the contention that the superior practice should be used. Failure to use the superior practice will force the market to incur costs to obtain or adjust the accounting data and these costs could be avoided. Inspection of how stock prices react to information cannot help the accountant identify the best measure of income or financial position. At most the information that investors are modifying the information presented should cause the accountant to review the appropriateness of the information he is presenting, and to check its theoretical soundness.

The efficient markets hypothesis is extremely important to financial and investment analysis and strategy; it is much less relevant to the content of financial reports (it does affect the accounting for investments in common stock). With less than strong-form efficient markets and with the likelihood of a significant percentage of the market being fooled by faulty accounting practices, there is still a place for intrinsic value analysis. However, we can agree that once information is published the investor who discovers it later than the other investors will probably benefit less, if at all (the price will tend to adjust to the information).

Most importantly, if the accounting information has helped move the price of the stock to a level that more appropriately reflects the firm's intrinsic value, it has served an important economic function.

Efforts to coordinate accounting and financial research are to be commended. It would seem that an appropriate message of the efficient market research is that the corporation and the accountant have an obligation to make good information available at the same moment in time to as wide a range of audience as possible. The type of information and method of dissemination both require study, because they greatly affect investors.

APPENDIX IV-iv

WILLIAM H. BEAVER

IMPLICATIONS OF SECURITY PRICE RESEARCH FOR ACCOUNTING: A REPLY TO BIERMAN

The purpose of these remarks is to comment upon some issues raised in a recent article by Professor Bierman.[1] The Bierman article took issue with some statements that appeared in Section II of the *Report of the Committee on Research Methodology in Accounting* (hereafter referred to as Section II).[2] Since I was the author of that section, the responsibility is mine, if anyone's, to respond. I decided to reply because Bierman's remarks in several respects represent common misinterpretations and it seems appropriate to air them now. Moreover, a discussion of them will serve to highlight what I feel are some major areas for further research.

GENERAL NATURE OF THE INVESTOR SETTING

The individual investor's demand for information is a derived demand, reflecting his underlying investment decision. Stated in most general terms, the investor faces a multiperiod, investment-consumption choice problem, where investment is viewed as a decision to exchange current (certain)

Reprinted from *The Accounting Review* (July 1974), pp. 563–571, by permission of the American Accounting Association.

William H. Beaver is Professor of Accounting at Stanford University.

[1] H. Bierman, "The Implications of Efficient Markets and the Capital Asset Pricing Model to Accounting," *The Accounting Review* (July 1974).

[2] "The Behavior of Security Prices and Its Implications for Accounting Research (Methods)," *Committee Reports, Supplement to The Accounting Review* (1972), pp. 407–437.

consumption for future (uncertain) consumption claims. Uncertainty is commonly characterized by partitioning the future into a set of mutually exclusive states, on which the investor assesses a probability distribution. Different portfolios of securities offer alternative packages of future, state-dependent consumption claims. The investor's objective is to choose an optimal portfolio from among the available alternatives. Commonly, this selection process is characterized as the maximization of a preference function whose arguments are current consumption and future, state-dependent consumption claims. The opportunity set is circumscribed by the individual's wealth, and hence the optimization occurs subject to a wealth constraint.[3]

The role of information in this context is to alter the investor's probability assessments that future states will occur. If the investor were viewed in isolation, the information decision would be a relatively straightforward one. The value and cost of generating information would be assessed in terms of his preference function for consumption.[4] However, the investor cannot be viewed in isolation because he constitutes only one agent in a securities market. Most corporate reporting issues concerning financial statement preparation have implications for the exchange sector, as well as the productive sector of the economy. It is impossible to incorporate the impact of information for exchange purposes in our environment without explicitly introducing a securities market.

In a market setting, the role of information in altering investors' probability beliefs will manifest itself in two respects: (1) in exchanges of securities reflecting the desire of individuals to hold different portfolios[5] and (2) in a change in the prices of securities, which will affect the opportunity set available to the investor.[6] If this general view is simplified

---

[3] For a development of this model at a primitive level, see K. Arrow and F. Hahn, *General Competitive Analysis* (Holden-Day, 1971) and G. Debreu, *Theory of Value* (Wiley, 1959). A more simplified treatment of the model appears in J. Hirshleifer, *Investment, Interest and Capital* (Prentice-Hall, 1970). For an application of the model to an accounting context, see J. Demski, "Choice Among Financial Accounting Alternatives," *The Accounting Review* (April 1974), among others. I am indebted to Joel Demski for his comments on an earlier version of this paper.

[4] G. Feltham and J. Demski. "The Use of Models in Information Evaluation," *The Accounting Review* (October 1970), pp. 623–40.

[5] In general, information can also affect the amount of total current consumption versus total investment, as well as the way the investment is allocated among securities.

[6] Note that the security price change is neither necessary nor sufficient for information to have value. For example, consider inside information and price changes but no securities exchanged.

Beaver

555

to a "one-period," two-parameter setting, the role of information is to alter individuals' assessments of the expected value of the end-of-period proceeds and of the risk associated with each security. These individual assessments are aggregated to form the market's assessments of the expected return, risk, and price of each security. Whereas, in general, little can be said regarding the nature of the aggregation process, Lintner has examined the problem under restricted forms of the probability assessments and preference functions.[7] His model provides considerable conceptual insight into how information might affect individual behavior and security prices. The model admits to heterogeneous expectations and specifies how individuals' probability assessments are aggregated to form the market's assessment of the value (i.e., price) of the security. The model further specifies how heterogeneous expectations would affect the portfolio holdings of individual investors.

In this context, the concept of beta—the systematic risk of a security—is an ex ante concept formed at the individual level. Under heterogeneous expectations, those assessments will differ among individuals with the market's assessment of beta reflecting some aggregation over the individual investors who comprise the market. One important issue for accounting is what exogenous data (e.g., financial statement data) will alter investors' assessments of beta and in what way. As I shall indicate shortly, this concept of beta differs considerably from the view held by Bierman.

MULTIPERSON CONSIDERATIONS

Once one admits to the distributive effects of accounting information, it is readily apparent that the relevant group of individuals to consider in any information decision is much broader than "users," since nonusers may be as dramatically affected by information. For example, this is readily apparent in the generation of "inside information" where the insiders are the users of the information who exchange securities with nonusers. However, it has much broader implications, extending to a market where information is publicly available, but only a subset of "experts" is literally involved in the process of interpreting the implications of the data for security price.

Moreover, in general those affected by the information decision will not unanimously prefer the same information alternative because the

---

[7] J. Lintner, "The Aggregation of Investor's Diverse Judgments and Preferences in Purely Competitive Security Markets," *Journal of Financial and Quantitative Analysis* (September 1969), pp. 347–400. Note, however, the Lintner model is a "static" model and does not explicitly introduce information.

information cost, security price, and other distributive effects will fall upon individuals differently. In fact, under heterogeneous expectations, there will not even be an agreement in general as to what the consequences will be, let alone agreement on how important each individual's welfare is.[8] Furthermore, a problem arises in attempting to make comparisons or trade-offs among the welfare of different individuals.

Arrow's Impossibility Theorem ensures that any complete and transitive ordering of information alternatives at the social level will violate one or more of his conditions.[9] However, this does not preclude that under certain special conditions a principle such as Pareto-optimality may resolve a particular issue.[10] In fact, I have argued elsewhere that many of the popular accounting controversies, which have expended much of the resources of the APB and others, approximate those conditions and might have been resolved by invoking such a principle.[11] However, in general we cannot hope all controversies will be resolved so fortuitously. In fact, it may merely suggest that accounting has been focusing its attention on the wrong (i.e., trivially resolvable) sorts of issues and that it should direct itself to more substantive ones, such as choice among differing levels of disclosure.

---

[8] In fact, under heterogeneous expectations, individuals' beliefs may be mutually inconsistent. For example, both "long" and "short" investors may be willing to pay for the revelation of the "true" state, under the belief its revelation will benefit them, even though such beliefs are mutually incompatible. Hirshleifer cites the example of a horse-race. See J. Hirshleifer, "The Private and Social Value of Information and the Reward to Inventive Activity," *American Economic Review* (September 1971).

[9] K. Arrow, *Social Choice and Individual Values* (Wiley, 1963). These conditions constitute intuitively appealing criteria which seem plausible to impose on any method of social ranking. These conditions are: (a) universal domain, (b) responsiveness, (c) independence of irrelevant alternatives, (d) nondictatorship, and (e) nonimposition. By violating assumption (a), a form of unanimity can be attained. Two examples are perfect and complete markets and teams. See R. Wilson, "The Theory of Syndicates," *Econometrica* (January 1968), and R. Wilson and S. Ekern, "On the Theory of Firm in an Economy with Incomplete Markets" (Working Paper No. 19R, The Institute for Mathematical Studies in the Social Sciences), March 1973. However, the Wilson-Ekern result does not extend, in general, to information; see S. Ekern, "On the Theory of the Firm in Incomplete Markets" (unpublished doctoral thesis, Stnaford, 1973).

[10] Essentially, the Pareto-optimality criterion was invoked in W. Beaver and R. Dukes, "Interperiod Tax Allocation, Earnings Expectations, and the Behavior of Security Prices," *The Accounting Review* (April, 1972), 320–32.

[11] W. Beaver, "What Should be the Objectives of the FASB?" *Journal of Accountancy*, (August 1973), pp. 49–56.

This is the context in which I will address Bierman's remarks. Although the framework exposes the difficulty of evaluating normatively the consequences of various information alternatives, it does indicate that the security price effects of information are an important aspect of the consequences of information alternatives and, hence, it provides a rationale for the literature discussed in Section II.

BIERMAN'S ANALYSIS

Bierman offers three major propositions:

(a) It has not been shown that the efficient market hypothesis reduces the importance of improving conventional financial accounting.

(b) It is wrong to imply that the systematic risk coefficient (β) is all the information needed by an investor.[12] Individual security reporting errors affecting perceptions of unsystematic risk are of concern to the imperfectly diversified investor, and thus are of concern to a majority of investors.

(c) The relationship between accounting data and security price behavior cannot generally be used as the primary basis to choose among alternative methods of recording and presenting the financial affairs of a corporation.

The first issue is a "straw man." None of my previous work, including Section II, has ever stated or implied that improvement of financial accounting was vitiated by market efficiency of the semi-strong form (i.e., with respect to published data). In fact, elsewhere I have explicitly taken the position that there were issues of substance with respect to financial reporting.[13]

However, the point is that the nature of the problem may be substantially different from what it has traditionally been viewed to be. For example, what does Bierman mean by such terms as *improving financial accounting,* or *deficient financial reporting?* Much of his discussion would seem to imply the existence of a "true earnings" or an "intrinsic value" of a security. Those terms have no clear meaning in a world of uncertainty, where they must be viewed as ex ante concepts dependent on investors' probability assessments, which in turn are conditional upon the information available. In general, these assessments will differ across individuals, even when holding the information constant. For the market as a whole, the

---

[12] Bierman's statement on β is misleading. Beta is not information at all. As indicated earlier, it is ex ante concept reflecting an investor's probabilistic assessment of the systematic risk of a security. This confusion will become evident later when Bierman discusses how accounting information decisions ought to be determined.

[13] W. Beaver, pp. 54–56.

assessment of intrinsic value (i.e., price) represents some aggregation across individuals' beliefs. I can understand that different information may result in different assessment of price. However, I do not understand in what sense one information set produces a *better* assessment of price (with the possible exception of some special cases). Such statements imply clairvoyance or the existence of *true* values for the firm. I have considerable difficulty with either interpretation.[14]

However, I can understand substantive issues concerned with alternative levels of disclosure. As I interpret the efficient market hypothesis, it implies a shift in emphasis away from the determination of "true" earnings toward considerations of disclosure, where the market interprets the implications of the events for the price of the security.

If the premise of some form of inefficiency of the strong form (i.e., with respect to nonpublished data) is tentatively accepted, disclosure issues are potentially substantive, although some empirically observed special cases may admit to trivial solution.[15] As expressed by Bierman and by myself, undisclosed data provide one social "cost" in the sense that those who have access to such data reap speculative profits at the expense of the rest of the investors. To the extent that no real resources are expended and the effect is purely distributive, and the relative desirability of different levels of disclosure is unclear since we may be comparing two points in a set of Pareto-optimal solutions. When real resources are being expended, the justification for disclosure is also unclear when (1) the policy of greater disclosure induces a cost incidence different from that of lesser disclosure (even when greater disclosure may induce lesser total cost) or (2) disclosure "confiscates" the speculative returns without any compensatory relief. There may be a number of disclosure policies that are contained in the set of Pareto-optimal solutions.[16] In any event, a major area for future research is the determination of the costs and security price effects of various levels of financial disclosure. It is premature, and potentially incorrect, to conclude that more disclosure is preferable to less. One aspect of such research is the examination of market efficiency with respect to nonpublished data. Currently we know virtually nothing about the extent to which nonpublished data are reflected in security prices.

---

[14]Correspondence from Bierman indicates that he does in fact believe in true values with respect to earnings, intrinsic value, and beta.

[15]W. Beaver, pp. 54–56.

[16]Optimal disclosure is also addressed in an unpublished paper by M. Jensen and R. Watts, "A Normative and Positive Theory of Accounting," (Rochester, 1973).

With respect to the importance of unsystematic risk, the excerpts chosen by Bierman omit the context in which those statements were made. For example, consider the following *complete* citation (pages 422–3):

> This is an extremely important implication for accounting, because all of accounting's concern about errors in accounting data has stressed only the *individual security* level, with no consideration of the portfolio context. For example, suppose it was empirically demonstrated that the existing reporting rules led to prediction errors in the return distributions of several individual securities. Such evidence is insufficient to indict current reporting methods. The reason is that investors may be able to diversify out of the errors in securities, and hence, it is in the nature of an individualistic or avoidable risk.
>
> Errors, independent in nature (i.e., uncorrelated with market factors), can be effectively diversified away and are not of major concern. Only systematic errors, which still persist at the portfolio level, are detrimental to optimal predictions and decisions. This implication substantially alters the entire context within which accounting has traditionally viewed errors in accounting data and issues of information alternative.

In other words, the thrust of the remarks was to suggest that accounting view information issues at the portfolio level rather than the individual security level. As long as the investor holds more than one security, the unsystematic risk of the portfolio is less than the average unsystematic risk of the securities. In the case of complete diversification, unsystematic risk may be trivially close to zero, and virtually nothing will be paid for its reduction even at the individual investor level. The passages cited above were not originally intended to be interpreted as a general call for the ignoring of unsystematic risk in information policy decisions. As I now reread those passages, I still feel those passages carry no such implication. To move to such a level of inference would require a consideration of the issue at the social level, and hence would require moving from the level of the individual investor (i.e., single-person portfolio theory) to that of the entire market (i.e. a model of capital asset pricing).[17] Hence, although such an issue was not raised in my

---

[17]As will become apparent shortly, this movement from the individual to the social level is the source of major disagreement between Bierman and myself. Bierman's analysis is based on private incentives to reduce unsystematic risk. I view this to be an inappropriate level of analysis.

earlier work, I will discuss some aspects of the issue that has been raised by Bierman's comments. In this respect, Bierman's position is not convincing for several reasons.

First, he raises an empirical question as to whether individual investors in fact diversify out of unsystematic risk. His evidence in support of such a position is inconclusive. The average number of securities held by investors gives no information regarding how well diversified they may be. Such statistics do not consider how much of individuals' total amount of capital assets (including human capital) is represented by direct holdings of common stocks. For example, there was no evidence offered on the proportion of holdings in the form of mutual funds or pension funds. In this regard, Bierman asserts:

> There is no way, including mutual funds, for such investors to be diversified in such a manner that the unsystematic risk of one component of the portfolio is not important.
>
> There are risks associated with any single mutual fund that are not a function of the number of securities it holds.

I am curious as to what evidence Bierman has for making such extraordinary statements. He cites none, and I know of none. In fact, the evidence of which I am aware would suggest precisely the opposite conclusion.[18]

Morever, even if we accept this evidence as conclusive, such evidence should be disregarded if one accepts Bierman's own criterion. Bierman invokes the criterion "of how rational investors should be making decisions." The two-parameter portfolio theory represents one such model of investor behavior at the individual level, although by no means the only one.

Bierman rejects this model as a basis for information policy making. However, he does so based primarily upon empirical evidence that purports to show that investors do not follow this model. It could be argued, if one adopts the Bierman criterion, that such empirical evidence is irrelevant, since that constitutes no evidence as to how they "should" be acting. For example, investors may be less than perfectly diversified because they hold "erroneous" beliefs that they can "beat the market" using published accounting data in some intrinsic value approach. If this were the case, then, as I interpreted Bierman's criterion, they *should*

---

[18] William F. Sharpe," Mutual Fund Performance," *Journal of Business* (January, 1966), pp. 119–38; and Michael C. Jensen, "Risk, the Pricing of Capital Assets, and the Evaluation of Investment Portfolios," *Journal of Business* (April 1969), pp. 167–247.

be fully diversified and the empirical evidence on this matter is beside the point.[19]

Moreover, to say that a given model is deficient implies that there is a "better" model. No such model is provided by Bierman, although he may implicitly have one in mind. Hence, it is difficult to assess his criticism of the two-parameter portfolio model without comparing it with some other available alternative. Bierman does suggest at various times that, if the model were appended to include preference for skewness and transactions cost, nontrivial nondiversification would be normatively dictated. Again I wonder where is the support for such statements. They are far from intuitive. For example, it is unclear to me what cost mechanisms would suggest that a diversified portfolio is more costly to hold than a single security. For example, consider the alternative of closed-end investment companies or no-load mutual funds.

With respect to the issue of preference for skewness, several aspects are ignored by Bierman. Preference for skewness is not a sufficient condition to provide any alteration in the original formulation of the two-parameter portfolio model. For example, the common assumption introduced when deriving the model is that security returns are jointly normal. Under such an assumption, the implications of the two-parameter model follow regardless of the form of the risk aversion preference function of the investor. In particular, preferences that are a function of higher moments than the first two become "irrelevant" in a world of jointly normal security returns. Fama indicates that return distribution empirically is approximately normal, and, more importantly, Fama concludes that the return distributions are well approximated by symmetry.[20] Recent empirical work by Krause and Litzenberger calls into question Fama's finding.[21] They derive a three-parameter (skewness is the third parameter) capital asset pricing model and test it empirically. They conclude it does somewhat better in explaining ex post security returns than does the two-parameter model. The three-parameter capital asset pricing model asserts that expected return is not only a function of

---

[19] However, his criterion is essentially dictatorial in nature and hence violates Arrow's axioms of nondictatorship or nonimposition. Bierman is clearly making a nontrivial ethical judgment here, one which, at the present time, I (and some of my friends) would be unwilling to support. For example, also see J. Demski, *op. cit.* Such paternalism is particularly objectionable in light of the evidence supporting market efficiency in the semi-strong form.

[20] Eugene Fama, "The Behavior of Stock-Market Prices," *Journal of Business* (January 1965), pp. 34–105.

[21] A. Kraus and R. Litzenberger, "Skewness Preference and the Valuation of Risk Assets," *Journal of Finance* (forthcoming).

systematic risk but also of systematic skewness. However, the model does not compensate investors for unsystematic risk, which is the variable of concern to Bierman. Hence, even if we accept the Kraus-Litzenberger form of the capital asset pricing model as the more valid (which is premature), it still falls considerably short of supporting Bierman's position on unsystematic risk.

Bierman's motivation for introducing preference for skewness was to provide a theoretical basis for positing nondiversification as optimal behavior by individual investors. However, the justification could have been introduced much more simply by merely assuming heterogeneous expectations among investors. The Lintner model indicates that, under heterogeneous expectations, investors will in effect take speculative positions (i.e., disproportional holdings) in those securities which they perceive to be mispriced.[22] However, the point is that nondiversification at the individual investor level is not sufficient to warrant a consideration of unsystematic risk when making information policy decisions.

It is important to distinguish between the private value of information (which considers one investor in isolation) and the social value of information (which considers all investors in the market).[23] While an individual investor may be willing to pay to reduce his unsystematic risk, this in no way implies that society as a whole would be willing to expend real resources in the same manner.[24] In particular, note that neither the two- nor three-parameter form of the capital asset pricing model compensates investors for incurring unsystematic risk. To the extent society as a whole is capable of diversifying out of unsystematic risk, it is not going to compensate individual investors for unsystematic risk, regardless of how nondiversified an individual investor may choose to be. Incorporating unsystematic risk in information policy decisions may be tantamount to recommending that accounting expend society's real resources in attempting to reduce a factor (unsystematic risk) for which the securities market is not compensating the investor.

The real issue then is: Is the capital asset pricing model valid or does the market in fact compensate investors for unsystematic risk? Work

---

[22]J. Lintner, "The Aggregation of . . . "

[23]The discrepancy between the private and social value of information has been well documented. In addition to Section II, see J. Hirshleifer, "The Private and Social Value . . .," E. Fama and A Laffer, "Information and Capital Markets," *Journal of Business* (July 1971), and J. Demski, "The Choice Among. . . . "

[24]A similar disparity between private incentives and the social value has been raised regarding the production of unsystematic risk, see E. Fama, "Production Under Uncertainty," *Bell Journal of Economics and Management Sciences,* (Autumn, 1972), 509–30, and R. Wilson and S. Ekern, "On the Theory of . . . "

by Douglas and by Lintner suggest the ex post risk premiums may be a function of unsystematic risk. However, subsequent work by Miller and Scholes and by Fama and Macbeth cast serious doubts on the validity of these findings.[25] At present, the issue is, at best, an unresolved one empirically. At the conceptual level, a theoretical capital asset pricing model which compensates investors for unsystematic risk has not been derived.

With respect to the third issue, Bierman incorrectly infers that I contend association tests can *generally* be used to rank alternative accounting methods for policy purposes. In fact, elsewhere I have explicitly taken the opposite position.[26] A careful reading of the sentence of mine he cites takes no such position.[27] The sentence states that research on the relationship between security prices and accounting data constitutes, in my opinion, knowledge that a policy maker should have before him when making an accounting information decision. It is essential to distinguish between statements that certain evidence should be provided and statements that some association metric (such as a correlation coefficient or an API) can be generally used to obtain a social preference for alternative information systems. In simplest terms, although evidence cannot indicate what choice to make, it can provide information on the potential consequences of various choices. Had Bierman cited other parts of the section, the distinction would have been clear. For example, I indicated (page 426) the general nature of the problem of selecting alternative information systems in a multi-person setting, specifically emphasizing the problems of making interpersonal preference comparisons. Moreover, on page 428, when I discuss the use of association tests as policy making metrics, I consistently use the term, *simplified preference ordering*, where I explicitly indicated why I considered it to be a simplification of the underlying choice problem facing policy making bodies. In fact, I state (page 428) that "The ultimate issue is the extent to which this simplified preference ordering is consistent with the ordering obtained

[25] G. Douglas, "Risk in the Equity Markets; Empirical Appraisal of Market Efficiency," *Yale Economic Essays* IX (Spring 1969) pp. 3–45; Lintner's work is described in Douglas; M. Miller and M. Scholes, "Rates of Return in Relation to Risk: A re-examination of some Recent Findings," *Studies in the Theory of Capital Markets* (Praeger, 1972), pp. 47–8; E. Fama and J. Macbeth, "Risk, Return, and Equilibrium; Empirical Tests," *Journal of Political Economy* (1973), 607–35.

[26] W. Beaver, "What Should be the Objectives. . . ."

[27] The Sentence (page 409) reads: "Given the importance of security prices upon the wealth and overall level of well being of investors, it is inconceivable that optimal information systems for investors can be selected without a knowledge of security price behavior."

under a complete analysis." May and Sundem have touched upon some aspects of problems where information costs are introduced. Multiperson aspects of the problem are discussed in detail by Demski.[28]

As indicated at the outset, the role of information is to alter investors' assessments of the probability distributions of security returns over various states. Evidence on security prices provides knowledge regarding what (accounting) data affect investor expectations about the return distributions such that security prices are altered. As such, it provides evidence to the policy maker on what consequences may be expected from alternative information systems.

Instead, Bierman contends that: "Rather than information about 'security price behavior' the accountant needs to know how rational investors should be making decisions, and to supply the relevant financial information." Bierman argues two sentences later that ideally the accountant should supply beta itself. Beta is not an item of information. It is an ex ante concept involving individual probabilistic assessments. To assert that the accountant should supply these probabilistic assessments would require a level of measurement that would be costly (if not impossible) to attain, given the current state of measurement techniques.[29]

Moreover, Bierman acts as if inspection of the decision model will automatically reveal what exogenous data are "relevant" to assessing parameters such as systematic risk. I contend that the decision model itself will not provide such insight. Instead, what is needed is theory and evidence regarding what (financial statement) data affect assessments of the parameters such as systematic risk. This is precisely a role security price research performs.[30]

Concluding Remarks

Originally I placed a constraint upon myself that this reply would not exceed the length of Bierman's comments. It is a constraint that

---

[28] R. May and G. Sundem, "Cost of Information and Security Prices: Market Association Tests for Accounting Policy Decisions," *The Accounting Review* (January 1973), pp. 80–94. J. Demski, "Choice Among. . . . "

[29] For a discussion of some aspects of the measurement issues involved here, see D. Krantz, R. Luce, P. Suppes, A. Tversky, *Foundation of Measurement* (Academic Press, Vol. 1, 1970). Of course, beta estimates based on ex post security returns can be computed. However, given the nature of the data (i.e., publicly available) and the measurement issues involved, it is unclear whether any comparative advantage exists in incorporating such measurements as part of corporate reporting.

[30] With respect to the issue of systematic risk, see William Beaver, Paul Kettler, and Myron Scholes, "The Association Between Market Determined and Accounting Determined Risk Measures," *The Accounting Review* (October 1970), pp. 654–82.

I have already exceeded, and so I will close with the following remarks which hopefully will place my comments in perspective.

The purpose of my earlier work was primarily informative—i.e., to make accounting aware of a literature in finance that I feel has important implications for accounting. In doing so, I took the current state of the art as a given. Obviously, as the literature extends itself, my earlier statements may have to be modified in light of the subsequent developments. For example, if I were to write the statements now, I might also call for research on the relationship between financial statement variables and systematic skewness. However, the point of the earlier paper was to motivate the accounting profession to incorporate a class of literature into their thinking and research. I hope these comments will serve to clarify why I feel such incorporation is valuable and to further direct attention to this area.

APPENDIX V-i

MAURICE MOONITZ

CHARACTERISTICS OF A LIABILITY

The following four characteristics will serve as a starter to establish an accounting definition of liabilities:

1. A liability involves a future outlay of money, or an equivalent acceptable to the recipient.

2. A liability is the result of a transaction of the past, not of the future. "Transaction" is used here in its primary sense of an event involving at least two accounting entities—an "external transaction."

    "Transactions" encompass the following types of financial events: (a) The receipt of money from someone outside the enterprise; (b) the payment of money to someone outside the enterprise; (c) the acquisition of goods or services—materials, supplies, power, services of human beings of all types and grades, equipment, land, mineral deposits, leaseholds, etc.; (d) sales of goods or services of all types; (e) lending and borrowing of money on a short- or long-term basis; (f) the imposition and collection of taxes.

    Accruals of all sorts are omitted from this list; so are the amortization of costs, as well as all "internal transactions" such as the transfer of work in process to finished goods. These accruals, amortizations, and transfers, however, are all consequences of the transactions listed above, and hence fit into the picture neatly as arising from past events. What does not fit in so neatly are events that have not yet occurred, e.g., next month's payroll, next year's purchase of fixed assets, next quarter's

Reprinted from "The Changing Concepts of Liabilities," *The Journal of Accountancy* (May 1960), p. 44, by permission of the American Institute of Certified Public Accountants. Copyright 1960 by the American Institute of Certified Public Accountants, Inc. Only a portion of the original article is reprinted here.

Maurice Moonitz is Professor of Accounting at the University of California at Berkeley.

borrowings against a bond issue, etc. Therefore, none of these future events will qualify as a liability under this second characteristic.

3. The amount of the liability must be the subject of calculation or of close estimation. This condition is true generally of all accounting entries and is not restricted to liabilities. Accounting Research Bulletin No. 47, issued in September, 1956, presents excellent material in this connection. After some introductory remarks, the committee states in paragraph 4 that "because of these factors, the total cost of the pensions that will be paid ultimately to the present participants in a plan cannot be determined precisely in advance, but, by the use of actuarial techniques, reasonably accurate estimates can be made. There are other business costs for which it is necessary to make periodic provisions in the accounts based upon assumptions and estimates. The committee believes that the uncertainties relating to the determination of pension costs are not so pronounced as to preclude similar treatment."

   And in paragraph 5: "In the view of many, the accrual of costs under a pension plan should not necessarily be dependent on the funding arrangements provided for in the plan or governed by a strict legal interpretation of the obligations under the plan." In other words, let the pension costs be a function of the operating factors to which they relate. Use of the legal definition of debt, however, is relied on in one recommendation of the committee (paragraph 7): " . . . for the present, the committee believes that, as a minimum, the accounts and financial statements should reflect accruals which equal the present worth, actuarially calculated, of pension commitments to employees to the extent that pension rights have vested in the employees, reduced, in the case of the balance sheet, by any accumulated trusteed funds or annuity contracts purchased."

4. Double-entry is taken for granted. If, for example, we do wish to consider the presence and influence of *future* purchases of depreciable assets, for any reason, we should consider the obligation to pay for the blamed things.

APPENDIX VI-i

FINANCIAL ACCOUNTING STANDARDS BOARD

UNIT OF MEASUREMENT AND ATTRIBUTE TO BE MEASURED

Accounting measures of the elements of financial statements require selection of the attribute of those elements that is to be measured and selection of the unit of measure to be used in measuring that attribute. This Chapter calls attention to two possible units of measurement (units of money and units of general purchasing power), but its primary purpose is to set forth five attributes that are candidates for measurement in financial statements.

Presently, financial accounting measurements in the United States and in most other countries are made in units of money. As a result of the marked decline in the general purchasing power of units of money that has been experienced in recent years, however, the use of units of general purchasing power for financial accounting measures has been receiving widespread consideration.

At the same time, various proposals have emerged that call for accounting measures of attributes that are different from those measured and presented in financial statements currently. Five attributes that either have been used or proposed for measuring and presenting various classes of assets and liabilities or have been proposed for measuring all classes of assets and liabilities are: (1) historical cost/historical proceeds, (2) current cost/current proceeds, (3) current exit value in orderly liquidation (current market value), (4) expected exit value in due course of business (net realizable value), and (5) present value of expected cash flows.

Those five attributes differ with respect to (a) whether they focus on the past, present, or future; (b) whether they relate to the acquisition

Reprinted from chapter 8 of "An Analysis of Issues Related to *Conceptual Framework for Financial Accounting and Reporting: Elements of Financial Statements and Their Measurements*," *FASB Discussion Memorandum* (FASB, 2 December 1976), pp. 189–90, by permission of the FASB.

of assets and incurrence of liabilities (entry values) or the disposition of assets and elimination of liabilities (exit values); and (c) whether they are based on actual, expected, or hypothetical events.

The initial measure of each of the five attributes may be provided by the historical exchange price and therefore initially may be identical, but subsequent measures during the period the asset or liability is held by the enterprise may differ significantly.

The historical cost of an asset is the amount of cash (or its equivalent) paid to acquire it.

The current cost of an asset is the amount of cash or other consideration that would be required currently to obtain the same asset. Proponents differ about the meaning of "the same asset" (some mean current cost of replacement in kind and some mean current cost of replacement of equivalent productive capacity) and about the disposition of holding gains and losses (some include holding gains and losses in earnings and some accumulate holding gains and losses as a separate component of capital).

The current exit value of an asset is the amount of cash that could be obtained currently by selling it under conditions of orderly liquidation.

The expected exit value of an asset is the amount of cash (or its equivalent) into which that asset is expected to be converted in due course of business less direct costs expected to be incurred in converting it to cash.

The present value of an asset is the net amount of the discounted cash inflows and discounted cash outflows pertaining to that asset. Several different rates of discount might be selected to measure present value.

Each attribute of assets has a counterpart pertaining to liabilities.

THE ROUSE COMPANY

ITEMS FROM THE 1976 ANNUAL REPORT

**Consolidated Cost Basis
and Current Value
Basis Balance Sheets**

May 31, 1976 and 1975
(in thousands)

Assets	—1976—		1975
	Current Value Basis (note 1)	Cost Basis	Cost Basis
Property and deferred costs of projects (notes 3 and 9):			
Operating properties:			
Current value	$372,105		
Cost		$314,205	$297,766
Less accumulated depreciation and amortization		54,230	50,542
		259,975	247,224
Construction and development in progress	60,075	60,075	60,226
Pre-construction costs, net . . .	7,761	7,761	7,723
Other furniture, fixtures and equipment, net	4,459	3,734	4,105
Net property and deferred costs of projects	444,400	331,545	319,278

Reprinted from The Rouse Company 1976 *Annual Report,* by permission of The Rouse Company.

Mortgage banking (notes 4 and 9):

Notes receivable.	15,760	15,742	8,730
Accounts receivable.	674	674	855
	16,434	16,416	9,585

Investment operations (notes 5 and 9):

Notes receivable.	15,190	15,190	20,827
Real estate owned.	9,755	9,755	12,219
Accounts receivable.	203	203	708
	25,148	25,148	33,754
Less reserve for possible loan losses.	3,950	3,950	2,405
	21,198	21,198	31,349

Net investment in Rouse-Wates (note 6).	3,364	3,364	1,650
Due from HRD (note 7)	692	692	755
Other assets and deferred charges, primarily prepaid expenses and deposits	7,364	7,364	7,078
Accounts and notes receivable (note 8).	10,058	10,058	9,163
Cash and temporary investments	3,805	3,805	6,007
Total assets	$507,315	$394,442	$384,865

Liabilities, Deferred Credits and Shareholders' Equity	—1976—		1975
	Current Value Basis (note 1)	Cost Basis	Cost Basis
Debt (note 9):			
Debt not carrying a parent company guarantee of repayment:			
Debt of operating properties	$208,962	$208,962	$236,627
Debt of properties under development	17,484	17,484	4,229
Debt of parent company and debt carrying a parent company guarantee of repayment:			

Debt of operating properties	44,265	44,265	18,984
Debt of properties under development	23,888	23,888	23,827
Term loan credit notes payable:			
Parent company	18,250	18,250	25,400
Investment operations . .	13,800	13,800	19,481
Senior subordinated notes payable	12,096	12,096	13,432
Other debt	4,097	4,097	4,798
Notes payable—Mortgage banking	15,522	15,522	8,640
Accounts payable and accrued expenses	15,877	15,877	17,486
Commitments and contingencies (notes 4, 6, 13, 14 and 16)			
Deferred credits:			
Deferred gains on sale-leasebacks of property (note 2) . . .	2,243	2,243	2,275
Deferral associated with sales of interests in retail centers (note 11)	1,936	1,936	1,939
Shareholders' equity:			
Capital stock (note 12):			
$6 Cumulative Preferred stock of $100 par value per share			
Authorized 25,000 shares; issued 24,991 shares . .	2,499	2,499	2,499
Common stock of 1¢ par value per share. Authorized 20,000,000 shares; issued 14,077,524 shares in 1976 and 13,991,524 shares in 1975	141	141	140
Total capital stock	2,640	2,640	2,639
Additional paid-in capital . . .	20,171	20,171	20,103
Deficit	(6,491)	(6,491)	(14,697)
Revaluation equity (note 1 (c))	112,873		
	129,193	16,320	8,045

Less common stock held in trea- sury, 1,164,940 shares at cost.	298	298	298
Total shareholders' equity . . .	128,895	16,022	7,747
Total liabilities, deferred credits and shareholders' equity . . .	$507,315	$394,442	$384,865

NOTES TO CONSOLIDATED
FINANCIAL STATEMENTS

May 31, 1976 and 1975

---

(1) Current value presentation

(a) Development of current value reporting

The management of The Rouse Company has consistently stated that the current value of its operating properties, its major asset, far exceeds the net book value of these assets as reflected in the financial statements prepared in accordance with generally accepted accounting principles. In a special report contained in the 1975 Annual Report to Shareholders, we described the process of creating a high quality operating property and the process by which its value is increased over time through professional merchandising and management. In the company's last several annual reports, management has supported its position by reporting an estimate of the value of the company's operating properties. Again, because generally accepted accounting principles do not allow us to report these values in the cost basis (historical cost) financial statements, we reported such values in the letter to shareholders. This was done because we believe that reporting the current value of assets is an integral and important part of reporting the actual economics of the company's financial position—the economics which, in fact, are the basis for developing, financing, operating and selling the operating property assets of investment builders.

Over the past year the company has developed a current value financial reporting format which places the current value of all of our resources in the context of a full statement of financial position. Our presentation takes a step beyond the Securities and Exchange Commission's recent requirement for certain companies to disclose replacement cost information in notes to the cost basis financial statements. It is our intention to make this current value reporting a continuing part of our formal financial statements on an annual basis.

In addition to their normal involvement, our auditors, Peat, Marwick, Mitchell & Co., engaged the services of James D. Landauer Associates, Inc. (Landauer), real estate consultants, who reviewed and analyzed our estimates of the value of our operating properties. Our estimates of value were based on an evaluation of the history and future of each operating property and included for each retail center:

• complete five-year market study covering basic demographic and market volume projections plus competitive alignment and market share expectations;

• tenant-by-tenant analyses of lease terms, sales performance and rent projections for the next five years; and

• analyses of projections of operating expenses over the next five years (including those portions passed on to tenants under lease agreements) plus financing costs—principal, interest and lender participations.

Landauer rendered an opinion to our auditors stating their concurrence with our estimates of these values. Landauer's opinion is contained on page 26. Our auditors' opinion respecting the consolidated current value basis balance sheet is contained in their report on page 25.

The company's financial position on a current value basis is reported on pages 20 and 21 as a supplementary column alongside our cost basis balance sheet. The current value and net book value is shown for each asset category, and the $112,873,000 aggregate increment of current value over net book value has been reflected in shareholders' equity as "revaluation equity." We believe this consolidated current value balance sheet more realistically reflects the economics of the company's cumulative operations and financial position.

The consolidated current value basis balance sheet recognizes the value of the company's assets based on the presumption that such assets will be retained and utilized by the company for a significant period of time. This current value basis balance sheet does not necessarily represent the liquidation value of assets or of the company. The most significant difference in value (comparing the current value of assets against the cost basis net book values) is in our operating properties. The values of these particular properties approximate the current investment which investors would make to purchase 100% of the company's interest in their present and future cash flow streams. We believe that the investment value of a property's cash flow stream is the most appropriate measurement of the current value of the asset and therefore, of its net replacement cost. These values also represent the economic value of the company's income-producing resources—value which is utilized by the company as a source of capital. In the context of a two-year program to improve the company's liquidity and general financial condition, approximately $29,000,000 of equity value in operating properties has been received in cash through sales of partial interests in seven operating properties and the refinancing of three others.

(b) Bases of valuation

The bases of management's estimates of current values are as follows:
- The current value of the company's operating property assets has been defined as each property's equity value, (i.e., the value of its future net cash flow after paying both interest and principal on the debt specifically related to the property) plus the outstanding balance of related debt. Net cash flow represents the operating revenues less all operating expenses, current taxes and ground rents, debt principal, interest and participations to lessors, lenders and equity partners. The estimate of each property's equity value was based on criteria currently utilized by investors in income-producing real estate. The valuations recognized the considerable differences between properties in terms of quality, age, outlook and risk. Landauer, independent real estate consultants, reviewed, analyzed and concurred with our $113,820,000 appraised value of the company's equity interest in operating properties. Concurrence, as used by Landauer, is defined as a variation of less than 10% from the probable value that might be estimated by Landauer in a full and complete appraisal. Landauer did not review our valuation of fringe land contiguous to operating properties—land not being utilized in the operations of such properties or as security for project mortgages. The company's estimate of the gross value of this fringe land (approximately 150 acres) is $7,073,000.
- Construction and development in progress and pre-construction costs are carried at the same values as in the cost basis financial statements— values which represent the lower of cost or net realizable value. While the company believes that the properties under construction (some of which will open in the next several months) have value in excess of stated cost, management has taken the more conservative position in not adjusting the cost basis by any value increment.
- Other furniture, fixtures and equipment is valued at its current replacement cost which was determined by reference to recent prices of similar assets and estimates of the current cost to duplicate similar assets. The gross replacement cost of furniture, fixtures and equipment is $5,856,-000, which reflects an increase of $941,000 over the cost basis. The related accumulated depreciation and amortization was $1,397,000 after an increase of $216,000 to reflect that portion of the increase in current

replacement cost of the assets which would have been charged to operations through May 31, 1976.

• Mortgage banking notes receivable represent mortgage notes held for sale to long-term investors usually under pre-arranged take-out commitments from such investors. The mortgages are purchased from developers at a price which may be different from the price at which the company will ultimately resell such mortgages. Those notes for which sale commitments have been pre-arranged are carried at the commitment price. The remainder of the notes are carried at their market value. This value exceeds the cost basis by $18,000 at May 31,1976.

• The following resources are carried on the current value balance sheet at the lower of cost or net realizable value—the same stated value as on the cost basis balance sheet:

—Mortgage banking accounts receivable (net of doubtful receivable reserves);

—accounts of the Investment operations, including notes and accounts receivable and real estate owned (net of loan loss reserves);

—the company's net investment in Rouse-Wates (net of liquidation reserves);

—amounts due from HRD;

—other assets and deferred charges;

—accounts and notes receivable (net of doubtful receivable reserves); and

—cash and temporary investments.

The stated values of these accounts represent their current value as the underlying assets will be realized in the relatively near-term.

• All liability accounts are carried at the same stated value as in the cost basis balance sheet. Long-term debt relating to our operating properties is carried at the same amount as in the cost basis statement because the difference between the current value and cost basis of such debt, if any, is an integral part of the revaluation equity attributable to operating properties. A significant portion of the debt which is not specifically related to our operating properties carries interest rates which fluctuate with the prime interest rate. Therefore, the outstanding balance of this debt represents its current value. This is also the case with the notes payable—Mortgage banking.

The application of the foregoing methods for estimating current value represents the best judgment of management based upon its current evaluation of the economy and money markets today and in the future. These kinds of judgments regarding the economy and money markets are not subject to precise quantification or verification, and may change from time to time as economic and market factors, and management's evaluation of them, change.

(c) Revaluation equity

The aggregate difference between the current value basis and cost basis net book value of the company's assets is carried as revaluation equity in the shareholders' equity section of the consolidated current value basis balance sheet. The components of this revaluation equity at May 31, 1976 are as follows:

Operating properties:	
Value of equity interests	$113,820,000
Outstanding balance of debt related to equity interests, excluding $2,015,000 of debt related to fringe land	251,212,000
	365,032,000
Value of fringe land	7,073,000
Total asset value	372,105,000
Depreciated cost of operating properties . .	259,975,000
Revaluation equity in operating properties	112,130,000
Mortgage banking notes receivable	18,000
Other furniture, fixtures and equipment, net of accumulated depreciation and amortization	725,000
Total revaluation equity	$112,873,000

No income tax charge has been imputed against the revaluation equity as the differences between the current value and cost basis net book value of our properties and the changes in these increments over the lives of such properties will not enter into the determination of taxable income until such differences are realized over the long-term through future operations or sales. Although realization of current values through future operations or sales will ultimately enter into the determination of taxable income, management has no current intention to sell additional operating properties and, therefore, such realization is expected to occur over an extended period of time. Consequently, the payment of Federal income taxes, based on the company's anticipated business activities and existing Federal income tax laws, will be made over an extended, indefinite future time period, Accordingly, the current value of the future obligation for Federal income taxes is indeterminable at this time.

Presently, our current value reporting model does not include a statement of operating results and / or annual changes in value. One reason for this is that comparable values as of the beginning of fiscal year 1976 are not available. While the company, in previous years, had provided a conservative estimate of the values of its operating properties, these estimates did not undergo the rigorous process, including external professional review and analysis, which the May 31, 1976 valuations have undergone. In addition, we have not defined what we believe to be the most appropriate information or format for reporting periodic operating results and value changes. This reporting will be developed as we, along with others in our industry, define the appropriate information and presentations.

(d) Replacement cost of assets

On March 23, 1976, the Securities and Exchange Commission (SEC) issued Accounting Series Release No. 190 requiring disclosure of certain replacement cost data. The SEC's requirements, as described in Accounting Series Release No. 190, "were designed to enable investors to obtain more relevant information about the current economics of a business enterprise in an inflationary economy than that provided solely by financial statements prepared on the basis of historical cost." Assets of the company subject to the SEC's disclosure requirements include operating properties and furniture, fixtures and equipment. The current value of furniture, fixtures and equipment in the consolidated current value balance sheet represents the replacement cost of such assets. While management's valuation of operating properties is based on the current value of cash flow rather than the cost to reconstruct such properties, management believes that this current value is the most appropriate measure of the cost of replacing the cash flow stream generated by income-producing properties held as long-term assets. If the current values of these resources were ratably charged to operations in the same manner as is used in the company's cost basis financial statements, the depreciation and amortization charged to 1976 operating results would total approximately $10,100,000, the majority of which relates to operating properties. Because the value of these properties, as reflected in the current value balance sheet, represents the current value of such properties at May 31, 1976, depreciation and amortization related to operating properties would have no effect on the net asset values of properties or on shareholders' equity as reflected in the consolidated current value balance sheet.

APPENDIX VIII-i

ROBERT R. STERLING

A CASE OF VALUATION AND LEARNED COGNITIVE DISSONANCE

In "A Case of Valuation,"[1] Howard W. Wright presented an array of different values of the Nickel Smelting Company and drew the following conclusions:

> In summary, at least eight different values, ranging from zero to $15 million, were involved. These different values may make it easier to understand why many accountants consistently adhere to recorded cost, with all its weaknesses, and to verifiable, objective evidence.

The eight different values referred to were:

1. Reproduction cost less depreciation. $11,921,233
2. Number 1 less 10% for risk factors 10,730,000
3. Fair market value 9,440,000
4. Company's appraisal presented to tax
   commission 11,723,593
5. Negotiated tax appraisal 15,113,240
6. Unamortized cost on Company's books . . . . -0-
7. Unamortized cost by IRS guidelines 11,500,000
8. Formula-computed purchase price 1,700,000

My examination of these figures leads me to the opposite conclusion. Note that the figures in 1 through 5 are appraisals. Wright excluded from his conclusions the appraisals by the State Tax Commission and the amount the plant was insured for. I think this is proper but I would go further. Figures (4) and (5) are a haggle over the amount of taxes

---

Reprinted from *The Accounting Review* (April 1967), pp. 376–77, by permission of the American Accounting Association.

[1] Howard W. Wright, "A Case of Valuation," *The Accounting Review*, July 1966, pp. 559–60.

Appendix VIII-i

to be paid and have little if anything to do with the value of the plant. If this is granted, then there are three appraisals to be considered. They range from $9.4 to $11.9 million and the $2.5 million deviation is unfortunate and sufficient cause for concern. Inclusion of figure (5) increases the deviation to $5.7 million and is worse.

Compare these to the possibilities for recorded cost. The Company used an amortization method that resulted in a zero book value. If it had used IRS guidelines it would have $11.5 million book value, and if it purchases the plant as agreed it will have $1.7 million book value. The deviation of $11.5 million is about five times as large or twice as large as the appraisal deviations. In fact, by any variation measure that one chooses, the recorded cost figures come out a poor second.

Second, there is the concern over the number of different appraisals with the implication, I presume, that there is a single cost figured. Mr. Drebin states it directly: "If ten skilled appraisers are called . . . it is likely that they will provide ten different estimates. Accountants would rather rely upon a single cost figure. . . ."[2] Everyone would agree with the "ten different appraisals" proposition but the "single cost" proposition is rather odd in view of the commonplace complaints about different depreciation methods, different life estimates, and different salvage estimates. Certainly in the case of Nickel Smelting there is no single cost.

We all know that initial construction costs ($21.0 million) are subject to various methods of allocation (e.g., overhead) which are subject to various methods of accumulation (e.g., depreciation of equipment included in overhead) which are subject to various methods of cost collection (e.g., amount capitalized and attached to the equipment), and so forth until we get back to the cash expended or a fair market value at some past time or some other value. Thus, the initial cost is subject to (perhaps wide) variation. Then the additions and replacements ($1.8 million) are subject to variations of the same kind. After all of this we are ready to apply different life estimates, etc. and depreciate "the" cost by various methods.

Finally, there is the objective and verifiable notion. This is even more puzzling. The accountant takes a set of figures (dollars expended,

---

[2]Allan R. Drebin, "Accounting for Proprietary Research," *The Accounting Review,* July 1966, p. 419. Mr. Drebin is arguing that market values provide more realistic and more important information and says "Accountants are generally reluctant to utilize market values because subjective estimates are usually required . . .," and then continues with the different appraisals-single cost propositions. He may be reporting an argument that he doesn't support.

allocations of previous dollars expended, years of life, salvage value) which he freely admits are subjective, arranges them in an equation, and then calculates a figure (depreciation, book value) that he considers to be objective. Exactly how one can get objectivity by manipulating subjectivity is not clear to me. The auditor then "verifies" this figure. This must mean that he verifies the physical existence of the object and checks the arithmetical accuracy of the figure.

In summary, I find:

(1) A wider variation in the recorded costs than in appraisal values.

(2) Equally as many recorded costs as appraisal values.

(3) Equally as much subjectivity in recorded costs as in appraisal values.

That is, all the arguments against appraisal values can be applied to recorded costs with at least equal force. Accountants seem to be aware of this situation when they lament the lack of uniformity and the subjective estimates in recorded costs. Yet when appraisal values (or other alternatives) are suggested they reject them *because* they are subjective and diverge. They often imply and sometimes state that costs are objective and univocal. They almost always argue that costs are more objective and subject to less variation than appraisals.

Sometimes this is called cognitive dissonance. In accounting I think it is learned; I think we *teach* cognitive dissonance. The typical text devotes a chapter to "theory" in which cost is characterized as objective, verifiable, and univocal. Alternative values are dismissed as subjective, conjectures, and divergent. The remainder of the text considers the assets seriatim and laboriously explains the different methods, comments on subjective estimates, and gives examples of variations in costs. The advanced students have assimilated this compartmentalization so well that they can parrot the pejoratives on a theory question and practice them on a problem question without ever making a connection. It takes about a semester of graduate work to unlearn them. Perhaps we shouldn't teach it in the first place.

APPENDIX IX-i

NATIONAL COUNCIL OF THE INSTITUTE OF
CHARTERED ACCOUNTANTS IN AUSTRALIA AND
GENERAL COUNCIL OF THE AUSTRALIAN SOCIETY
OF ACCOUNTANTS

CURRENT COST ACCOUNTING

INTRODUCTION

1.01 The purpose of this Statement is to introduce "Current Cost Accounting" (CCA) as the accounting system to be followed in the preparation of financial statements.

1.02 Financial statements under CCA will include a statement of change in shareholders' (or proprietors') equity. This statement is intended to explain the movement in such equity between the beginning and end of an accounting period by reference to movements in the accounts which, together, make up the equity.

1.03 In broad terms, the operational features of CCA are summarised as follows:

(a) The result for any one period of accounting is determined by matching the revenue for the period with the current cost of producing that revenue. To this end, the cost of goods sold is calculated (or adjusted) to reflect the current cost of goods when consumed. Similarly, depreciation charges are calculated (or adjusted) to reflect the current cost of the service potential of depreciable assets consumed or expired in the period. No adjustment is normally required in respect of any other costs brought to account as expenses for the period because such

Reprinted from "Current Cost Accounting," *Statement of Provisional Accounting Standards,* DPS 1.1/309.1 (Institute of Chartered Accountants in Australia and Australian Society of Accountants, October 1976), pp. 2–6, by permission of the Australian Accounting Research Foundation.

582

costs are already expressed in terms of the current prices of the goods or services to which they relate.

(b) In the balance sheet, the resources of the entity are stated, where applicable, on the basis of their current costs at balance date.

1.04 The accounting standards set forth in this Statement apply to all accounting entities irrespective of the form in which they are legally constituted, and of the business activities in which they are engaged. Any reference in this Statement to "shareholders" should be construed as encompassing proprietors in any form of entity.

1.05 The application of this Statement sets aside existing accounting standards to the extent that they are in conflict with this Statement and, in particular, where they require or presuppose the use of historical costs for any purpose for which this Statement requires the use of current costs.

DEFINITIONS

2.01 For the purposes of this Statement the following definitions are adopted and should be interpreted by reference to Statement DPS 1.2/309.2, "The Basis of Current Cost Accounting."

(a) **"Service potential,"** in relation to an asset, means its utility to the entity, based on the total service expected to be derived by the entity from use (including exchange) of the asset

(b) **"Current cost,"** in relation to an asset, means its cost measured by reference to the lowest cost at which the service potential of that asset, when first acquired, could currently be obtained by the entity in the normal course of business.

(c) **"Written-down current cost,"** in relation to a depreciable asset, means its current cost less accumulated depreciation calculated on the basis of such cost to reflect the already consumed or expired service potential of the asset.

(Note: Any subsequent reference to "current cost," in relation to a depreciable asset, should be read as a reference also to "written-down current cost" unless a contrary intention is evident in the context in which the expression is used).

(d) **"Recoverable amount,"** in relation to an asset, means such portion of its current cost as can be expected to be recovered by the entity through charges against revenue as the asset is consumed and/or through its sale.

(e) **"Net realisable value,"** in relation to assets other than inventories, means the net amount expected to be recovered by the entity on disposal of an asset in the normal course of business.

In relation to inventories, "net realisable value" means the estimated proceeds of sale less, where applicable, all further costs to the stage of completion and less all costs to be directly incurred in marketing, selling and distribution to customers.

(f) **"Carrying amount,"** in relation to an asset, means the amount at which the asset is recorded in the books of account at a particular date. In application to a depreciable asset, "carrying amount" means the net amount after deducting accumulated depreciation.

(g) **"Goods,"** in the context of the expression "cost of goods sold," includes

    (i) any property (including rights and entitlements) acquired for sale in the normal course of business, and

    (ii) services rendered where these are accounted for in the first instance as inventory.

(h) **"Monetary assets"** means cash, and claims to cash the amounts of which are fixed in terms of numbers of dollars regardless of any subsequent changes in prices.

PROVISIONAL ACCOUNTING STANDARDS

Preparation of Financial Statements

3.01 **The financial statements of an entity should be prepared on the Current Cost Accounting (CCA) basis as set out in this Statement.**

3.02 **CCA should be implemented by entries in the accounting records.**

3.03 **For the purposes of a CCA balance sheet, the basis of measuring monetary assets should be the amounts at which they were initially brought to account, subject to the constraint that no such asset should be carried at an amount greater than is expected to be recovered when it is converted to cash.**

3.04 **For the purposes of a CCA balance sheet, the bases of measuring non-monetary assets should be as follows—**

    (a) the current cost (or written-down current cost, as applicable) at balance date, provided it can be expected that such cost will be recovered through charges against revenue, as each asset is consumed and/or through its sale;

    (b) the recoverable amount at balance date, where it cannot be expected that the current cost (or written-down current cost) will be recovered in full.

3.05 **The current cost of land (other than land acquired for resale) should be ascertained, both for balance sheet purposes and for** determining any gain or loss on disposal of the land, by reference to the open market value of the land. Where there are improvements on the land, the value of the land should be determined having regard to the existing use of the land.

3.06 When a non-monetary asset is restated in terms of current cost—whether at balance date, time of sale, or any other time—the credit or debit corresponding to the adjustment to the asset account (or, in the case of a depreciable asset, to the asset account and the related accumulated depreciation account) should be to an account styled "current cost adjustment account."

3.07 When a non-monetary asset is written down to recoverable amount, such write-down should be from the current cost of that asset at the time of write-down. The amount of the write-down should be brought to account in the profit and loss account.

3.08 Where a non-monetary asset is carried at recoverable amount, this amount should be reassessed at least annually. Any consequent adjustment to the asset account should be reflected in the profit and loss account. However, no credit to profit and loss account should exceed the amount of the original write-down (pursuant to paragraph 3.07). Any credit in excess of that write-down should be to current cost adjustment account.

3.09 For the purposes of a CCA balance sheet, liabilities should be stated at the amounts expected to be paid.

3.10 In order to determine operating profit, cost of goods sold and depreciation charges for the period should be calculated, as closely as practicable, as follows:

(a) Cost of goods sold—at current cost of the goods at the time of sale, except where the goods had previously been written down to recoverable amount (net realisable value), in which case cost of goods sold should be that amount.

(b) Depreciation charges—on the average-for-the-period current cost, or, where applicable, on the recoverable amount at the beginning of the period, of the depreciable assets held.

3.11 When assets other than inventories are sold or scrapped, the difference between the proceeds from the sale or scrapping and the carrying amount of the assets at the date of sale or scrapping should be brought to account in the profit and loss account and not as an adjustment to the current cost adjustment account.

3.12 For the purpose of determining current cost, reference to specific market prices or, alternatively, to expert valuations should be made at intervals of no more than three years. In the intervening years, current cost may be ascertained by use of suitable indices.

Presentation of Financial Statements

4.01 Financial statements under CCA should comprise a profit and loss statement, a balance sheet, and a statement of change in shareholders' equity.

4.02 The statement of change in shareholders' equity should disclose separately all significant movements during the period in capital, current cost adjustment account, and retained earnings. Disclosure of such movements in the current cost adjustment account as relate to assets should distinguish between the respective classes of assets (as shown in the balance sheet).

4.03 The current cost adjustment account should be shown in the CCA balance sheet as a separate item of shareholders' equity.

4.04 The CCA balance sheet should disclose separately—
(a) depreciable assets stated at written-down current cost showing separately their gross current cost and the related depreciation; and
(b) depreciable assets stated at recoverable amount.

4.05 The CCA profit and loss statement should disclose separately—
(a) where depreciable assets are restated from their written-down current cost to recoverable amount, the amount of the write-down;
(b) where the recoverable amount of a depreciable asset is reassessed, the amount of any adjustment consequent upon such reassessment.

4.06 The comparative amounts in CCA financial statements should be the amounts shown for the corresponding items in the financial statements of the immediately preceding period, without any restatement for subsequent price changes.

Transitional Provisions

5.01 All non-monetary assets at the beginning of the period for which financial statements are first prepared on a CCA basis should be restated at current cost or, where applicable, recoverable amount, as at the beginning of that period. The resulting net adjustment to asset accounts should be credited or debited to the current cost adjustment account.

5.02 The financial statements prepared on a CCA basis in respect of the first accounting year commencing on or after July 1, 1977 should be presented as a supplement to financial statements prepared on an historical cost basis. With the exception of the balance sheet, these supplementary financial statements need not show comparative amounts for the immediately preceding period.

5.03 In respect of all subsequent accounting periods, financial statements prepared on a CCA basis should be the principal financial statements of the entity for the purposes of external reporting and should include comparative amounts of a CCA basis.

NATIONAL COUNCIL OF THE INSTITUTE OF
CHARTERED ACCOUNTANTS IN AUSTRALIA AND
GENERAL COUNCIL OF THE AUSTRALIAN SOCIETY
OF ACCOUNTANTS

FROM "THE BASIS OF CURRENT COST ACCOUNTING"

INTRODUCTION

10.01 The purpose of this Statement is to discuss the conceptual framework of "Current Cost Accounting" (CCA) and to explain its implementation. The accounting standards for CCA are set out in Statement of Provisional Accounting Standards "Current Cost Accounting," DPS 1.1/309.1.

10.02 Information presented in financial statements may be misleading unless recognition is given in those statements to the impact which changing prices have on the operations and affairs of the reporting entity. The entity is affected by changes in the prices of the specific goods or services currently needed for its operations. It may be argued that the entity is also affected by changes in the general price level or, expressed conversely, changes in the purchasing power of money (inflation or deflation). Neither of these aspects is systematically recognised in financial statements prepared on an historical cost basis.

10.03 Any system of accounting followed in the preparation of financial statements is essentially a system of financial measurement. The

---

Reprinted from "The Basis of Current Cost Accounting," *Explanatory Statement*, DPS 1.2/309.2 (Institute of Chartered Accountants in Australia and Australian Society of Accountants, October 1976), pp. 2–10, by permission of the Accounting Standards Committee.

objective of CCA is to ensure that, having regard to changes in specific prices, the results and resources of an entity, as reported in its financial statements, are so measured as to reflect the realities of its operations and thus are relevant and of maximum use to the users of such information.

10.06 The term "current cost accounting" emphasises that the accounting system explained in this Statement does not depart from the accepted transaction approach to the determination of periodic results, except that, as a broad generalisation, current costs are substituted for historical costs in measuring the cost of goods or asset services consumed in a period. Similarly, in the balance sheet, current costs are substituted for historical costs as the principal basis for stating the non-monetary assets of the entity.

10.07 CCA will introduce into financial statements a greater degree of subjectivity than hitherto present. Much of the data required for the implementation of CCA will depend on estimates and subjective judgments. However, this greater subjectivity will be more than compensated for by the benefits of increased realism and hence relevance of the information presented in financial statements.

DEFINITIONS

11.01 For the purpose of this Statement the following definitions are adopted:
   (a) **"Operating capability"** means the ability of the entity, at a given time, to provide goods and/or services in accordance with its then-existing resources.

DISCUSSION

The Conceptual Framework of CCA

(i) The unit of account
12.01 The unit of account can be either the unit of money or a unit of general purchasing power. In CCA, the unit of account is the unit of money.

(ii) The underlying concepts of profit, capital, and capital maintenance
12.02 In general terms, the profit of an entity for a period may be defined as the amount which the entity could distribute in respect of the period and still have as much capital at the end of the period as it had at the beginning. This definition implies that

profit can only emerge after capital has been maintained intact. Different concepts of what is meant by "capital" in this context give rise to different concepts of profit.

12.03 For the purposes of CCA, capital is to be understood as the operating capability provided by the resources (assets) of the entity. Profit, therefore, is considered to be the total gain, arising during a period, which could be distributed in full whilst still maintaining capital, in the sense of the operating capability, at the level which existed at the beginning of the period.

12.04 Operating capability is rarely, if ever, capable of exact quantification. Maintaining operating capability, therefore, is to be seen as a broad objective rather than a test to be carried out by comparing two mathematically calculable amounts.

12.05 The concepts of profit, capital, and capital maintenance underlying CCA place prime emphasis on the whole entity as an organisational unit of economic activity. This approach will improve financial reporting and protect shareholders* interests.

12.06 The CCA profit and capital maintenance concepts imply an assumption that the reporting entity may be expected to continue its activities into the future. To continue these activities on the same scale, the entity needs to remain in command of resources which, in the aggregate, will support activities on that scale.

12.07 In times of rising prices the costs of the resources on which operating capability depends will increase. Maintenance of such resources, therefore, will require increased funds. These funds might not be available if dividend distribution by the entity were based on a profit determined without recognition of the rising costs of assets consumed in operations. CCA, by substituting current cost for historical cost in the calculation of cost of goods sold and as the basis for calculating depreciation charges, brings to account changes in specific prices as they affect the entity. In so doing, it yields a profit consistent with the aim of maintenance of an entity's operating capability, and thereby precludes inadvertent erosion of the entity's resources.

12.08 The possible implications, on management action, of the concept of maintaining operating capability are sometimes misunderstood. In no way does the concept imply or commit to a replacement of used-up assets with like assets, or to preservation of a "status quo" of operational goals; the entity, being dynamic, may extend,

---

*"shareholders" should be construed as encompassing proprietors in any form of entity.

contract, or change its activities in whichever way desired.

12.09 The CCA profit will not necessarily be equal to the increase in an entity's net assets between the beginning and end of the period for which the profit is measured. Other factors may contribute to the increase. An example is increments in shareholders' equity resulting from restatement of the current cost of assets the service potential of which has yet to be consumed in earning revenue. It follows that the CCA profit concept cannot be described as "all inclusive" where this is intended to mean the total increment in net assets.

(iii) The basis for measuring assets and liabilities

12.10 The basis for asset measurement, to be compatible with the objective of a particular accounting system, needs to be consistent with the profit, capital, and capital maintenance concepts underlying that system.

12.11 Asset measurement is a controverisal issue. Besides historical cost (and historical cost adjusted for changes in the general purchasing power of money), the following bases have been proposed for such measurement:

—current market buying prices;

—current market selling prices;

—present value, that is, the sum of the discounted future net receipts expected to be generated by the use of an asset.

12.12 At times, each of these bases has been suggested as the sole measurement basis, and there have also been suggestions for combining several of these bases as alternatives within a single measurement system. The following discussion is concerned merely with the measurement bases appropriate to CCA.

12.13 For a CCA balance sheet to constitute a link between two successive CCA profit and loss statements, the basis for measuring assets in that balance sheet must be consistent with the basis of charging, in the profit and loss statements, for assets consumed in operations. Current cost thus becomes the principal basis, under CCA, for stating non-monetary assets in the balance sheet.

12.14 However, it is a valid principle under CCA, as it was under historical cost accounting, that no asset should be carried in the balance sheet at an amount greater than is expected to be recovered as the asset is consumed in operations and/or when the asset is sold. Consequently, as soon as it becomes apparent that the recoverable amount of an asset is less than its current cost, that recoverable amount becomes the appropriate measure of the asset in a CCA balance sheet.

12.15 In relation to assets held for sale, the recoverable amount is their net realisable value.

12.16 When determining the recoverable amount of assets held for continuing use in the operations of the entity, it is necessary to distinguish between depreciable assets (both physical and non-physical) and non-depreciable assets.

12.17 For depreciable assets held for continuing use, it would ordinarily be presumed that their current cost is progressively recovered through depreciation charges against revenue from operations. However, particular circumstances may indicate that the revenues from continued use of an asset, or a group of assets, will not be sufficient to cover depreciation on the basis of current cost, in addition to all other expenses incurred in earning the revenues. In this case, the recoverable amount would be the amount of depreciation which would be covered by revenues after allowing for related expenses.

12.18 For non-depreciable assets held for continuing use, the recoverable amount would be their net realisable value.

12.19 In summary, the bases for measuring non-monetary assets for the purposes of a CCA balance sheet may be stated as follows:
  (a) Current cost is the proper measure provided it can be expected that such cost will be recovered through charges as the asset is consumed and/or through its sale.
  (b) The recoverable amount is the appropriate measure where it cannot be expected that current cost will be recovered in full.

12.20 For monetary assets, the amount at which they were initially brought to account will be relevant at balance date and thus be the proper measurement basis for balance sheet purposes, subject to the constraint that they must not be carried in the balance sheet at an amount greater than is expected to be recovered when the assets are converted to cash.

12.21 Similarly, the amount at which liabilities were initially brought to account will usually be relevant at balance date and thus be the proper measurement basis for balance sheet purposes. An adjustment may be necessary to recognise a change in the amount expected to be paid, for example, in foreign borrowings.

  (iv) Purchasing power gains and losses on monetary items

12.22 Changes in the general level of prices (inflation or deflation), with corresponding changes in the general purchasing power of money, can be said to have consequences relative to holdings of monetary assets or liabilities. It has been argued that, if monetary assets are held during a time of rising prices, a loss is suffered in terms of purchasing power, measured by the difference between the purchasing power which these assets commanded when acquired and their current purchasing power; conversely, that a gain in terms of purchasing power arises when liabilities exist during a time of rising prices. The opposite applies in a time of falling prices. These losses and gains are not recognised in financial statements where the unit of account is the unit of money, unless specific steps are taken to do so.

12.23 Opinions differ considerably as to the justification or otherwise of bringing to account purchasing power gains or losses on monetary items. Broadly, three viewpoints can be distinguished:
—those who advocate that such gains or losses should be completely ignored;
—those who advocate that all such gains or losses should be brought to account;
—those who advocate that such gains or losses should be brought to account only to the extent that they relate to monetary assets and liabilities which form part of the working capital of the entity.

12.24 The question arises as to whether, and if so to what extent, CCA needs to take cognisance of such purchasing power gains or losses, for the purpose of profit determination. It could be argued that the capital and capital maintenance concepts underlying CCA would require recognition of purchasing power gains and losses in respect of monetary items included in the entity's working capital pool. This matter requires considerable further research, including adequate field testing, before any decision can be made as to the most appropriate accounting treatment.

12.25 In the meantime, CCA, as set out in Statement DPS 1.1/309.1 does not give recognition to purchasing power gains or losses on monetary assets and liabilities. To bring to account such gains or losses, a modification to the system would be needed.

(v) Restatements of non-monetary assets: holding gains and losses?

12.26 Increments resulting from a restatement of non-monetary assets in recognition of increases in their current cost are sometimes referred to as "holding gains." Conversely, decrements resulting from such a restatement when current costs are falling are similarly referred to as "holding losses."

12.27 The notion of regarding such items as gains or losses is incompatible with the underlying profit and capital maintenance concepts of CCA.

12.28 If the current cost of non-monetary assets supporting the operations of an entity has increased, the capital requirement of the entity, in money terms, will also have increased by an equal amount. To include an increment arising from a restatement of non-monetary assets in determing CCA profit would result in running down the entity's operating capability if such profit were distributed in full.

12.29 On the other hand, if the current cost of non-monetary assets supporting the operations of the entity has decreased, this will merely mean that a smaller amount of capital, in money terms, will be required to sustain operations at the same level. To bring to account a decrement arising from a restatement of non-monetary assets, as a loss in determining CCA profit, could result in a retention of funds which would effectively represent additional operating capability.

(vi) The meaning of service potential

12.30 The concept of service potential has general applications to all assets. It basically means the utility of an asset to the entity. The utility of individual assets to an entity will depend on their function in the operations of the entity. Considerations in the following paragraphs will be limited to the two classes of assets which are of paramount importance in the application of CCA as set out in Statement DPS 1.1/309.1: inventories and fixed assets.

12.31 The utility of inventories to an entity is the manufacturing, servicing, or merchandising capability, as the case may be, which they represent. Each individual line or item comprised in the total inventory can be said to have its own particular utility, depending on its ability to satisfy a particular need connected with the operations of the entity. This ability will be determined by many different factors, including potential use, quality, and price.

12.32 All inventories have one characteristic in common. The service potential of each physical unit of inventory is realised in a single transaction in which the unit is consumed. This could be an internal transaction as, for example, the consumption of raw materials, components or factory supplies in the course of manufacturing operations; or it could be an external transaction, such as the sale of a unit of finished product by a manufacturer, or the sale of a unit of merchandise by a trader.

12.33 For the manufacturing, servicing or merchandising capability represented by inventories to continue to be available, the service potential of inventory units consumed in internal or external transactions must be restored by the acquisition of inventory units of equivalent service potential. Replacing the service potential of inventories does not, of necessity, imply replacing like with like.

12.34 Depreciable assets such as buildings, plant and equipment differ

from inventories in that their service potential is consumed or expires progressively over an extended period. The service potential of such assets is dependent on three factors:
—the nature of the service to be derived by the entity from use of the asset;
—the physical characteristics of the asset (which include its capacity);
—the period over which the asset is expected to be used (referred to in this Statement as the useful life of the asset).
Thus, two assets may provide the same type of service but may differ in their capacity to yield such service; they would be said to have each a different service potential. The service potential of freehold land is normally dependent only on the first two factors, as its useful life is generally unlimited.

12.35 The service potential of a depreciable asset must be replaced eventually if it is intended to maintain the operating capability provided by the asset. As in the case of inventories, this in no way implies that the existing asset is to be replaced with an identical asset. In fact, in most cases, the extent of technological change over the useful life of the existing asset will be such as to render replacement with an identical asset improbable.

APPENDIX IX-iii

ACCOUNTING STANDARDS COMMITTEE, INFLATION ACCOUNTING STEERING GROUP

CURRENT COST ACCOUNTING

INTRODUCTION BY THE INFLATION ACCOUNTING STEERING GROUP

1 The continuing and high rate of inflation in the United Kingdom has reduced the usefulness of accounts prepared on the historical cost basis to management, investors, employees and others to such an extent that it is necessary to make a major change in accounting practice. Historical cost accounts have always suffered from the failure to show the impact of changing price levels, but in recent years the rate of inflation has made it essential to remedy this defect. The nature of the necessary change has been debated within the accounting profession for many years and a number of solutions have been put forward. However, the recommendations in the Sandilands Committee's report for the introduction of a system of current cost accounting (CCA) were broadly accepted by the Government and the Consultative Committee of Accountancy Bodies last year, and this Exposure Draft is based on these recommendations.

2 Management needs up-to-date information on costs and values for the proper running of the business. The system of current cost accounting described in the Exposure Draft will help to provide such information in the management accounts of companies and in their published annual accounts. If more realistic information is to be available to management than is provided by historical cost accounts, the change to current cost accounting needs to be made at the basic management accounting level. It would not be adequate merely to provide once-a-year adjustments

---

Reprinted from "Current Cost Accounting," *Exposure Draft 18* (Accounting Standards Committee, 30 November 1976), pp. x–xiv, 1–3, 16, by permission of the Accounting Standards Committee.

in the annual accounts to a basically historical cost system.

3 As long as industry uses historical costs for management accounts, it may unknowingly undercost with dangerous consequences for the business. It is essential that industry uses immediately for its estimates of cost:

(a) depreciation calculated on the value to the business of plant and machinery—in most cases this will be replacement cost;

(b) the estimated cost at the date of sale of materials consumed.

These CCA conventions should be used as soon as possible in compiling all management control figures including monthly profit and loss accounts. It is appreciated that because of the effects of market forces and of the Price Commission, industry may not be able to reflect fully its current costs in the prices it obtains.

4 The introduction of CCA will lead to five major improvements by comparison with the present historical cost system:

(a) depreciation will be calculated on the value to the business of the assets concerned and not on their historical cost and will thus give a more realistic measure of the cost of resources used;

(b) cost of sales will be calculated in most cases on the cost of replacing the goods sold and not on their original cost;

(c) there will be a new statement in the annual account—the appropriation account—in which there will be brought together the current cost profit, the revaluation surpluses, the amount which the directors consider should be retained within the business having regard to their assessment of its needs, and dividends;

(d) the balance sheet will show current values for most assets and will no longer show their historical cost;

(e) the statement of the change in the equity interest after allowing for the change in the value of money will clearly show how the company has performed in relation to the rate of inflation and will also show its losses or gains from the holding of monetary items.

5 CCA will provide management, and the users of published accounts, with more realistic information on costs, profits, the value of assets, and the return on capital and on assets. CCA also provides a distinction between the profit earned from the operations of the business and the money gains resulting from changes in the price of a company's assets.

6 This more realistic information should enable a clearer picture to be obtained of the relative performance of:

(a) managers and products within a company;

(b) different companies; and

(c) different industries
and should help to lead to better decisions being taken in such areas
as pricing, cost reduction, levels of remuneration, resource allocation
between and within companies, dividends, gearing and borrowing levels.

7 The essence of the CCA system is simple: the charge against income
in arriving at profit for stocks consumed and fixed assets used is based
on current replacement costs and not on out-of-date and irrelevant
historical costs. Similarly, the balance sheet shows up-to-date values in
place of historical costs.

8 If it is as simple as that, it may be asked, why is the Exposure Draft
so long? The answer is that it was decided that it would be more helpful
to companies to deal with as many of the known problems of implementing
CCA as possible. It should be appreciated, however, that relatively few
companies are likely to meet all of the problems in any one year. Much
of the Exposure Draft is concerned with putting flesh on the simple
system just described.

9 The Steering Group, however, is conscious that there are a number
of areas where it has been able to put forward only an interim solution
which will almost certainly require modification in the light of experience.
The Steering Group believes that it is more important to produce, as
a matter of urgency, a reasonably comprehensive Exposure Draft containing interim solutions in some areas rather than to delay the whole of
the Exposure Draft until a final solution is found for all problems. The
interim solutions include the treatment of the effects of inflation on
the owners' capital and on monetary items, and retentions to maintain
the substance of the business. Part of the problem is a lack of consensus
on what is the substance of the business (is it the physical assets, or
all the assets, or the long-term capital, or the owners' capital, etc?) and
whether it should be maintained in money or real terms. It is considered,
however, that the suggested treatment, (namely a statement of the change
in the equity interest after allowing for the change in the value of money,
and a voluntary transfer to or from the revaluation reserve in an
appropriation account) forms a basis for further development when a
greater degree of consensus becomes evident. The Steering Group also
proposes to give further consideration to its interim proposals in the
areas of liabilities other than deferred tax, goodwill, and other intangible
assets.

10 Whilst the need to find solutions to the problems of accounting for
rapidly changing prices is urgent, the Steering Group was conscious of
the burden that changing to a new system might put on companies (running
the new system, once installed, may not be materially more difficult than

the old) and has, therefore, decided to phase its introduction. There was a choice between phasing by item in the accounts or by size of company. The Steering Group chose the latter because the former had two major disadvantages:

(a) the most important adjustments which would require to be phased in first (depreciation and cost of sales) probably involved the greatest part of the work;

(b) the resulting accounts would have been produced on a mixture of conventions which could hardly be described as true or fair.

11 Another possibility would be to introduce CCA by means of a supplementary statement. This was rejected because such statements would cause confusion as to which figures were considered to be the right ones.

12 It should be noted that no starting date has been set for the mandatory use of CCA by small companies. It is intended to develop an appropriate method of CCA for such companies in the light of the experience gained during the first years' operations of CCA by other companies.

13 It has been necessary in producing this Exposure Draft to balance three requirements:

(a) the need for more useful information;

(b) the need to minimise the extra work required to produce the information;

(c) the need to minimise the opportunity for misleading manipulation of the figures.

The Steering Group believes that it has got the balance about right, and this view is supported by initial reactions from the companies which have appraised the Steering Group's proposals, but it would particularly welcome comments on this point.

14 It has been argued that CCA will increase the degree of subjectivity in annual accounts. If this is so, then this is part of the price that has to be paid to make accounts more relevant in a period of rapidly changing costs. It will be appreciated that historical cost accounting also contains a degree of subjectivity, particularly in the area of depreciation. Moreover, the amount of subjectivity in CCA should not be exaggerated. With the possible exception of the transfers to or from revaluation reserves, the figures in the accounts will normally be backed by evidence on which both management and the auditors can base their judgement. The Steering Group has maintained close liaison with the Auditing Practices Committee throughout the production of the Exposure Draft and has endeavoured to meet as many as possible of the points raised by that Committee; nevertheless, audit difficulties under CCA will be greater than under historical cost accounting, and the Auditing Practices Committee proposes to issue a booklet early in the new year setting out some of the principal problem areas and recommending ways in which they should be approached.

15 Many major industrial countries are developing inflation accounting systems. The United Kingdom is amongst the leaders in this field but is developing systems which will not be unique or incompatible. The importance of comparability is recognised and it is hoped that further development of CCA will take place in close consultation amongst interested countries, the EEC and the International Accounting Standards Committee.

16 The Steering Group is well aware of the importance companies attach to acceptance of CCA by the Inland Revenue and the Price Commission, and is holding discussions with the former and will be with the latter when appropriate. It is also conscious of the need to simplify record keeping, so it is discussing with the appropriate authorities requirements for the retention of historical cost records within the EEC. The legal implications of the introduction of CCA are being discussed with the relevant bodies.

17 The Steering Group has already modified its proposals in the light of comments and will do so again, if necessary, after studying the comments received during the exposure period when preparing proposals for a Statement of Standard Accounting Practice for consideration by the ASC.

18 It is appreciated that some organisations and companies in certain industries may need to modify the application of this Standard in order to give a true and fair view. The statement of the change in the equity interest after allowing for the change in the value of money, for instance, presents problems for nationalised industries arising from their special capital structure. There may be different problems in other industries. The Steering Group will give full consideration to reasoned proposals for modification from the relevant trade associations and similar bodies, or from the nationalised industries themselves.

19 The Steering Group wishes to thank all those who have helped it in its work and, in particular, the "field test" companies and representative bodies which have commented on earlier versions of the proposals in this Exposure Draft.

PART 1 PROPOSED STANDARD ACCOUNTING PRACTICE

Several words and phrases used in this part have been given a special meaning. They are defined in Part 2.

Scope of this Standard

1 It is the intention that this Standard should apply in due course to all financial accounts intended to give a true and fair view of the financial position and profit or loss but, in order to spread the workload on those concerned in its introduction, it has been decided to divide the introduction into four phases:

(a) Phase 1 will apply to:
   (i) companies listed by The Stock Exchange;
   (ii) limited companies not within category (i), nationalised industries and public trading entities which disclose in their audited accounts for the previous period either:
      (A) a turnover in excess of £10 million; or
      (B) total assets in excess of £10 million.

Phase 1 will *not* apply to companies which have more than 50 percent of their assets outside the United Kingdom of Great Britain & Northern Ireland and the Republic of Ireland, and which would have difficulty in producing accounts within the Phase 1 time scale. Such companies will be in Phase 2 or 3, depending on their size.

(b) Phase 2 will apply to all limited companies, nationalised industries and public trading entities not included in Phase 1, provided that they disclose in their audited accounts for the previous period either:
   (i) a turnover in exesss of £1 million; or
   (ii) total assets in excess of £1 million.

(c) Phase 3 will apply to all other financial accounts intended to give a true and fair view of the financial position and profit or loss not included in Phases 1 or 2, provided that they disclose in their audited accounts for the previous period either:
   (i) a turnover in excess of £100,000; or
   (ii) total assets in excess of £100,000.

Phase 3 will, therefore, include all non-trading public entities, trade unions, employers' associations, friendly societies and building societies, provided that they are above the minimum size specified above.

(d) Phase 4 will apply to all other financial accounts intended to give a true and fair view of the financial position and profit or loss not included in Phases 1, 2 or 3.

2 For companies producing group accounts, the size criteria in paragraph 1 should apply to the group (see also paragraphs 80 et seq.).

3 An appropriate method of current cost accounting for companies with an annual turnover and assets below £100,000 (i.e., companies in Phase 4) is under consideration by the Inflation Accounting Steering Group. The method will be devised in the light of further experience.

Dates from Which Effective

4 The accounting practices set out in this Standard should be adopted as soon as possible and regarded as standard in respect of financial statements relating to accounting periods beginning:
  (a) for organisations included in Phase 1, on or after 1 July 1978;
  (b) for organisations included in Phase 2, on or after 1 January 1979;
  (c) for organisations included in Phase 3, on or after 1 January 1980.

5 No commencing date for Phase 4 has yet been set. Ample advance notice of the starting date will be given.

Content of Accounts

6 Annual accounts prepared and presented on the bases set out in this Standard should contain a profit and loss account, an appropriation account and a balance sheet. Except for wholly-owned subsidiaries, there should be included in the notes to the accounts a statement of the change in shareholders' net equity interest after allowing for the change in the value of money. Accounts of enterprises within the scope of SSAP 10 will also include a statement of source and application of funds.

Profit and Loss Account

7 The profit and loss account should show (inter alia)
  (a) the operating profit or loss for the year;
  (b) interest payable less receivable;
  (c) the current cost profit or loss before taxation;
  (d) taxation;
  (e) the current cost profit or loss before extraordinary items;
  (f) extraordinary items; and
  (g) the current cost profit or loss for the year.
The operating profit or loss is arrived at after charging depreciation and the cost of sales on the basis of the current value to the business of the physical assets consumed during the year.

Statement Showing Effect of Change in the Value of Money

76 The accounts should include a statement, by way of note, setting out prominently the gain or loss for the period of account in the shareholders' net equity interest after allowance has been made for the change in the value of money during the period. In the case of a holding company the note should relate to the group accounts only.

77 The statement should show:

(a) the net equity interest as shown in the balance sheet at the beginning of the period, plus any amount brought into the accounts in respect of new equity capital introduced during the period, plus, or minus, the amount of the allowance needed to compensate these amounts for the change in the value of money during the period;

(b) the net equity interest at the end of the period before provision for dividends on the equity capital;

(c) the net gain or loss in the net equity interest during the period, being the difference between the amounts referred to in (a) and (b);

(d) the dividends on the equity capital for the year.

78 An analysis of the gain or loss on holding monetary assets and liabilities during the period should also be provided, showing separately the figures for:

(a) long-term liabilities;

(b) bank overdrafts;

(c) non-equity share capital.

79 The allowance for the change in the value of money should be made by applying a general price index as follows:

(a) for companies registered in the United Kingdom; the general index of retail prices;

(b) for companies registered in the Republic of Ireland; the official consumer price index.

The name of the relevant index, the figures of the index at the beginning and end of the period, and the base date of the index, should be stated.

APPENDIX IX-iv

ACCOUNTING PRINCIPLES AND PRACTICES COMMITTEE
THE SOCIETY OF INDUSTRIAL ACCOUNTANTS OF CANADA

SUMMARY OF POSITION

It is our view that if only two alternatives were available, mixed-dollar and GPL restated historical cost, the latter would be preferable. But this is not the case. The considerable timing errors that can result from using either of these historical cost models make it imperative that steps be taken in the direction of current value accounting if changing prices as they effect particular firms *and* inflation rates are to be adequately reflected by accountants in external financial statements. We, therefore, would like to recommend an immediate move by the CICA and FASB in the direction of experimenting with different forms of current value accounting, preferably GPL restated and thus, *not* incorporate into the Handbook any recommendation on the use of GPL historical cost statements.

Although a GPL restated current output price approach is conceptually preferable on the basis of exclusion of measuring and timing errors, a number of pragmatic considerations—such as data availability, objectivity constraints, cost factors and the ability of financial statement users to understand the data presented—should all impact on any decision to change or supplement our present historical cost income measurement model. In the first place, it may be unreasonable to suggest an immediate change from historical cost based data, that are familiar to financial statement users, because of education training and work experience.

Reprinted from S. Basu and J. R. Hanna, *Inflation Accounting: Alternatives, Implementation Issues And Some Empirical Evidence* (Society of Industrial Accountants of Canada, 1975), pp. v–vi, by permission of the Society of Industrial Accountants of Canada.

Therefore experimentation with the provision of *supplementary* GPL restated current value data should be encouraged until experience gained is sufficient to permit a decision as to whether to proceed with the promulgation of detailed rules for current value accounting (analogous to those now in existence for historical cost accounting). Retention of the conventional model for purposes of preparing the basic financial statements—at least during a transitional period—should reduce concern as to the dangers of excessive subjectivity and/or the possibility of manipulation of current value amounts and promote a willingness to experiment with different techniques for the determination of such values.

At the present time, it seems clear that a requirement to disclose in financial statements, even on a supplementary basis, either all current output price or all current input price data would be inappropriate. It is unlikely that such current value output or input numbers are available in a practical sense for all statement items. Initially, at least, we believe that it will be necessary to use a *combination* of input and output prices in preparing current data. While items such as marketable securities and finished goods inventories can be valued most appropriately at current output prices, other items, such as raw materials, may be more appropriately valued at current input prices to obtain an acceptable degree of objectivity.

Another consideration that may have merit, at least as a transitional measure, concerns the proposal that current values be reflected in the balance sheet but that they be included in income only when realized. A somewhat similar proposal would disclose realized and unrealized income separately in the income statement.

In summary, we therefore prefer a "multi-option" GPL restated current value approach with a separation of realized and unrealized income as the preferred form of supplementary financial statement data at this time.

APPENDIX IX-v

SECURITIES AND EXCHANGE COMMISSION

FROM ACCOUNTING SERIES RELEASE NO. 190

NOTICE OF ADOPTION OF AMENDMENTS TO REGULATION S-X
REQUIRING DISCLOSURE OF CERTAIN REPLACEMENT COST DATA

Rule 3–17. Current Replacement Cost Information. (New rule)

Statement of Objectives

The purpose of this rule is to provide information to investors which will assist them in obtaining an understanding of the current costs of operating the business which cannot be obtained from historical cost financial statements taken alone. Such information will necessarily include subjective estimates and it may be supplemented by additional disclosures to assist investors in understanding the meaning of the data in particular company situations. A secondary purpose is to provide information which will enable investors to determine the current cost of inventories and productive capacity as a measure of the current economic investment in these assets existing at the balance sheet date.

Exemption. This rule shall not apply to any person where the total of inventories and gross property, plant and equipment (i.e., before deducting accumulated depreciation, depletion and amortization) as shown in the consolidated balance sheet at the beginning of the most recently completed fiscal year is less than $100 million or where the total of inventories and gross property, plant and equipment is less than 10 percent of the total assets of the person as shown in the consolidated balance sheet at the beginning of the most recently completed fiscal year.

Reprinted from *Accounting Series Release No. 190* (SEC, 23 March 1976) by permission of the Securities and Exchange Commission.

The information set forth below shall be shown in a note to the financial statements or as part of a separate section of the financial statements following the notes. The note or the separate section may be designated "unaudited."

(a) The current replacement cost of inventories at each fiscal year end for which a balance sheet is required shall be stated. If current replacement cost exceeds net realizable value at that date, that fact shall be stated and the amount of the excess disclosed.

(b) For the two most recent fiscal years, state the approximate amount which cost of sales would have been if it had been calculated by estimating the current replacement cost of goods and services sold at the times when the sales were made.

(c) State the estimated current cost of replacing (new) the productive capacity together with the current depreciated replacement cost of the productive capacity on hand at the end of each fiscal year for which a balance sheet is required. For purposes of this rule, assets held under financing leases as defined in Rule 3-16(q) shall be included in productive capacity. In the case of any major business segments which the company does not intend to maintain beyond the economic lives of existing assets, the disclosures set forth in Rules 3–17(c) and (d) are not required provided full disclosure of the facts, amounts and circumstances is made.

(d) For the two most recent fiscal years, state the approximate amount of depreciation, depletion and amortization which would have been recorded if it were estimated on the basis of average current replacement cost of productive capacity. For purposes of this calculation, economic lives and salvage values currently used in calculating historical cost depreciation, depletion or amortization shall generally be used. For assets being depreciated, depleted or amortized on a time expired basis, the straight-line method shall be used in making this calculation, For assets depreciated, depleted or amortized on any other basis (such as use), that basis shall be used for this calculation.

(e) Describe the methods used in determining the amounts disclosed in items (a) through (d) above. Describe what consideration, if any, was given in responding to items (a) and (b) to the related effects on direct labor costs, repairs and maintenance, utility and other indirect costs as a result of the assumed replacement of productive capacity. Where the economic lives or salvage values currently used in historical cost financial statements are not used in (d) above, an explanation of other bases used and the reasons therefor shall be disclosed. If depreciation, depletion or amortization expense is a component of inventory costs or cost of sales, indicate that fact and cross-reference the answer for this item in item (b) in order to avoid potential duplication in the use of these data. (f) Furnish any additional information—such as the historical customary relationships between cost changes and changes in selling prices, the difficulty and related costs (such as those related to environmental regulations) which might be experienced in replacing productive capacity—of which management is aware and which it believes is necessary to prevent the above information from being misleading.

* * * * *

This amendment to Regulation S-X is adopted pursuant to Sections 6, 7, 8, 10 and 19(a) of the Securities Act of 1933; Sections 12, 13, 15(d) and 23(a) of the Securities Exchange Act of 1934, and Sections 5(b), 14 and 20(a) of the Public Utility Holding Company Act of 1935.

Rule 3-17 of Regulation S-X is effective for financial statements for fiscal years ending on or after December 25, 1976, except that the rule shall be initially applicable to the mineral resource assets of registrants engaged in the extractive industries and to registrants' assets located outside the North American continent and the countries of the European Economic Community in financial statements for fiscal years ending on or after December 25, 1977, provided that the historical cost and a description of any such assets excluded from the supplemental replacement cost data are disclosed.

By the Commission.

George A. Fitzsimmons
Secretary

APPENDIX XI-i

JOHN H. MYERS

THE CRITICAL EVENT AND RECOGNITION OF NET PROFIT

The matching of cost and revenue has grown during the past fifteen or twenty years into a cardinal principle of accounting. We have learned to postpone or accelerate either cost or revenue, as the case might require, in order to get all the elements of a single transaction into the same period. In spite of such problems as price level fluctuations and requirements of governmental regulatory bodies, we have made considerable headway in sharpening the determination of net income. However, in this effort to sharpen the determination of net income we have given very little attention to the timing of income recognition. We have relied on a variety of rules for specific situations, not on an over-all principle. In this paper I review both the economic concept of net income and the accounting procedure in a number of specific business situations, and then suggest a principle which is compatible with economic theory and at the same time coordinates most current accounting practice. I hope this discussion will provoke further thought on the subject leading to the ultimate refinement and acceptance of a principle which is both (1) as clear and uniform in its applicability as that of matching cost and revenue and (2) sound from an economics standpoint.

Economic theorists since the days of Adam Smith have spoken of land, labor, and capital as the three factors of production. Compensation to these factors has been known as rent, wages, and interest. Under a perfectly functioning system, these three factors receive all the income. Any residual that remains in an actual case is due to the imperfections of the system in the individual case at the particular moment of time. Later economists

Reprinted from *The Accounting Review* (October 1959), pp. 528–32, by permission of the American Accounting Association.

John H. Myers is Professor of Accounting at the University of Indiana.

acknowledged a fourth factor of production: entrepreneurship. Its compensation is known as profit. Profit is the reward for bearing risk—the risk of enterprise, the risk of venturing in business, the risk of owning something in hope of selling it later. This profit may be positive or negative depending upon the entrepreneur's decisions as to the directions in which to risk his capital, his labor, and his land. This profit is very close to what the accountant calls profit.[1]

Let us assume for accounting purposes that profit is the same as the profit of the economist, a reward for having taken the risks of enterprise. This being the case, profit is earned by the operating cycle, the round trip from one balance sheet position back to that position, whether the starting point be cash or inventory or any other factor. Even in a simple merchandising business several steps occur: buying, selling, collecting. The question arises as to when during that cycle any profit should be recognized. Should the profit be recognized when a specific point on the cycle is reached, or should it be spread over that cycle in some manner? If it should be recognized at a point, what is that point? If it should be spread, what criterion should be used? In order to set some limits on this article, I have assumed that profit should be recognized at a single moment of time. This article will be devoted, therefore, to a consideration of the moment of time at which to recognize the profit. Perhaps after considering carefully the implications of the assumption we shall be in a better position to consider the question we have by-passed.

If profit is to be recognized at a moment of time, we must select that moment. The economist gives a clue in the function of entrepreneurship as the function of directing a business, bearing the pain of the risks, and reaping the rewards of astute decisions. This suggests that profit is earned at the moment of making the most critical decision or of performing the most difficult task in the cycle of a complete transaction. Just what event this is may not be easy to distinguish in many cases. Although in most types of business we recognize profit at

---

[1] The accountant's profit includes, in addition to the economist's reward for bearing the risks of enterprise, "interest" on the owner's investment and, in some cases, "wages" to the owner of an unincorporated enterprise. However, these two variations do not negate the basic relationship between the profit of the accountant and of the economist. The wage element may be omitted for it is pertinent only in the unincorporated business, and even in such businesses there is a growing tendency to include a fair wage to the owner among the expenses. Interest is seldom if ever set out separately but in profitable corporations it may well be a minor part of the profit.

the moment inventory is converted into accounts receivable, such timing is far from universal.[2]

Let us examine a number of different types of businesses (1) to determine what is done and the apparent theory behind such action and (2) to test the applicability of the critical function theory in that business. In so testing the theory, we must remember that it must not fall merely because the critical function is difficult to determine. A proposed accounting theory must provide the basic objective and leave room for developing means of implementing that theory. Objectivity is one of the desiderata of any means of achieving a goal, but it in itself must not be allowed to be the goal.

Merchandising is one of the most common businesses. The merchant generally performs three steps: (1) wise buying, (2) effective selling, and (3) efficient collecting. If "wise," "effective," and "efficient" permit, there is a profit. We recognize the profit at the time the second step, selling, is performed. Two reasons commonly are given for recognizing profit at this time: (1) an asset has been transferred for a valid claim (transfer); (2) the merchant's opinion as to value is not needed (objectivity). To claim that any profit was realized at the time of purchase would be contrary to our past heritage, but to defer profit until cash has been collected is not uncommon. Major reasons for deferring profit realization until receipt of cash are the risk of collecting in full and the possibility of incurring additional expense. Bad debt and collection expenses are common, but most businesses feel that they can set up adequate reserves for the estimated expense. Thus, it sounds as if the real principle behind current practice were certainty, but that cannot be so for we do prepare income statements in spite of such major uncertainties as unaudited income tax returns and renegotiable contracts.

The principle of the critical event seems to fit the situation of the merchant very well. Where collection is a critical problem (and I doubt if there are many cases where it is), profit may be taken up at collection time. For most businesses, most of us would agree that selling is the critical event and that profit should be recognized at that time. In rare cases buying might be critical, as where an extremely good price is paid for some rapid-turnover, staple item.

A manufacturer's business is much like that of a merchant except that

---

[2]One clue to the most difficult or crucial task in the operating cycle may be the function of the business from which the president was selected. Was he in sales, manufacturing, collection or something else? A background in sales would tend to confirm most present accounting practice.

an extra step is added, converting the purchased raw materials into salable units. This gives an extra point at which profit might be recognized, i.e. time of efficient manufacture. In general we do not use this time because of uncertainty as to eventual sale price. However, in the case of gold refining where the market is assured, profit is recognized at the time of manufacture. The same reasoning as in the case of the merchant seems to apply; again it is the certainty principle. The critical event principle also is pertinent. Selling is very important in most cases; in gold mining it is a mere clerical detail, for the market and the price are assured by the government.

However, in contracting and manufacturing goods to order, especially if the manufacturing time will extend over several fiscal periods, the situation is quite different. In many cases there is no assurance the goods can be made at the contracted price. Therefore, profit is recognized when it becomes certain, when the goods have been made. The critical event theory, if applied to this situation, might be construed to come to the same answer as the certainty theory. In many cases it probably will. However, there may well be cases when profit should be recognized at sale date before the goods are manufactured. If a manufacturer regularly makes standard items for stock, it does not seem right to defer profit recognition beyond sale date merely because the item is temporarily out of stock. Somewhere between these two extremes there will be a twilight zone in which determination of the critical event will be difficult, but knowing that such an event is the determining factor would clarify thinking considerably.

Some people argue that profit can be recognized only when a transaction has been completed, when both purchase and sale have taken place. They argue that both of these elements are necessary and that the sequence of the two is immaterial. This almost assumes that the normal position is to have nothing but cash and that any other position is one of risk. A merchant would consider himself on dangerous ground, assuming he plans to stay in business, if he did not have a stock of merchandise. Anyone who has maintained a heavy cash position in the last decade or so has been assuming a position in which risk (of price level change) has been high. Consider an individual who has accumulated more funds than needed for current living and for an emergency cushion. The normal position for him is to have an investment in stocks or bonds. When he is out of the market, he is assuming substantial risk until he reinvests. There is a real question if he is to measure profit from purchase to sale of a security or to measure from the time he gets out of the market until he again assumes his normal position with respect to the market. Point of view seems all important. What is the critical function in making a profit? This question may be a most useful over-all guide.

Profit is recognized by magazine publishers in the period when the magazines are distributed. In most cases sale occurs and cash is received at the time the subscription is booked. Manufacturing costs are incurred shortly before distribution date. Advertising revenue as well as sale price are considered earned at the time of publication. There is serious question if this routine is correct even using the theory of certainty typically followed by manufacturers. Long in advance of publication date, the sales of magazines (by subscription) and of advertising are known. Printing costs are usually incurred under long-term contracts, so no element of uncertainty appears here. The only other element is the editorial one. Since most or all of the editorial staff will be paid fixed salaries, no uncertainty exists here. If the certainty thoery is to be used, profit should be recognized at the time the subscription is sold. Among the currently used theories, only the completed contract theory explains the present practice.

Under the critical function theory we must determine whether sales of magazines, sales of advertising, or production of the magazines is the critical function. Without good advertising contracts, the firm cannot prosper. Since advertising rates are based on circulation, sales of magazines seems all important. However, unless the editorial work pleases the subscriber, he soon will fail to renew his subscription. The readers' response will be felt much more quickly in newsstand sales. Choice as to which of these functions is the critical one may well not be unanimous. If it is agreed that editorial work is critical and that editorial work culminates in publication, then the current practice is appropriate.

Lending agencies (banks, small loan companies, etc.) generally recognize profit over the period a loan is outstanding. When the note is discounted at the inception of the loan, the banker has, in a sense, collected the fee in advance. The fact that this fee is called interest might lead the unwary to assume that it should be spread over the period, because the payment is based on time. However, closer inspection shows that the theory behind the lending agency's recognition of gross income over the period of the loan is that many expenses (particularly interest paid on money loaned out and collection and bookkeeping expenses) are spread fairly evenly over the loan period. If expenses of setting up the loan are also spread over the collection period or are minor, the matching of revenue and expenses is well done. The resulting net income is spread over the loan period. In a sense the situation is somewhat comparable to the contractor and magazine publisher in that the customer has been "sold" at the beginning and only rendering of service is left to be performed. Profit is taken up as each piece of the service contract is completed. However, a fundamental difference exists, the manufacturer and banker have different responsibilities after "sale." The manufacturer or publisher must incur many costs to complete the service to the buyers. The banker's

role is much more passive; he has only to wait for payments in the
normal order of business.

The current practice of recognizing income during the period the
loan is outstanding does not seem to agree with the critical function
idea. The only things happening while the loan is outstanding are (1)
the money borrowed to lend is incurring interest charges and (2) the
economic situation is changing, especially as regards the borrower and
his ability to pay. If the loan requires periodic payments there is an
additional bookkeeping function. Perhaps in individual cases the critical
function is the decision to loan or not to loan. If that is so, profit probably
is earned at that time even though collection and exact determination
of the amount might be delayed quite some time. This delay is, I am
sure, one of the reasons profit is measured over the life of a loan. The
service-rendered concept might be another reason for accruing profit
over the life of a loan, but my experience is that the borrower receives
the greatest service at the time he gets the money. Many merchants
selling on the installment plan recognize all profit at time of sale of
the merchandise and set up adequate reserves for loss. Their situation
is only slightly different from that of a lending agency. The goods are
sold and the loan is made in a single transaction. In the merchant's
case, more rests upon this event than does in the case of merely making
a loan. Nevertheless, a satisfactory or unsatisfactory lending policy, it
seems to me, is the one thing that makes loans profitable or unprofitable.

A company owning and renting real estate presents an interesting case.
Typically, rents are taken into income in the period to which the rent
applies. Expenses are recognized as incurred. A major function of such
a firm is providing various building services through payment of taxes,
insurance, and the costs of maintenance, heat, and elevator operation.
Rental of small dwelling units on a month-to-month basis is very different
from rental of large areas for manufacturing or office use. Not only
may more service be required for commerical purposes, but also the
term of the lease will probably be considerably longer so that the tenant
may feel justified in making many improvements to suit his operations.
Even though the lease term may be short, there will be a strong presumption
to renew because of the large expenses of moving. Under these circumstances, is profit really earned merely by serving the present tenants?
When a major tenant occupying a whole floor or two is secured or lost,
it would seem a renting firm would have real cause for a feeling of
profitability or loss thereof. I would suspect the agent securing a long-term
tenant would be well paid in recognition of his great service to the real
estate company. The critical function theory would seem to demand that
all profit for the term of the lease be recognized at this time. Practical
difficulties of determining the ultimate profit from such a contract are

large. The basic cause of the problem is the custom of determining profit at least annually. Although this custom is the root of the whole problem discussed in this paper, the problem is larger here because of the length of term of the contract. The practical difficulties of applying the theory in this case must not be the cause of rejecting the theory. If the critical function theory should be correct theoretically, then we must strive to find a way to apply it to the practical situation.

The theory of the critical event as the moment at which to recognize profit or loss on a transaction seems very useful. In the types of business which we have considered, it rather closely matches current practice and gives insight into the true nature of the business. It is a theory based on a fundamental economic process rather than upon such frequently used rationalizations as convenience, conservatism, certainty, tax timing, and legal passage of title. This theory may, at first, seem a radical departure from current practice. Upon further thought it does not seem so different. Perhaps this critical event theory will be rejected in favor of another, but the present status of relying upon many different theories of when to match revenue and expense cannot long stand in a profession. We need to give special attention to the development of a single theory for the timing of profit recognition.

APPENDIX XI-ii

Dan Dorfman

HEARD ON THE STREET

The effort to cool inflation and the lack of progress in Vietnam are the most frequently cited reasons for the current market battering.

But one analyst, Thorton L. O'Glove, who handles securities of financial concerns for Blair & Co., offers what he regards as another significant negative factor—the "deteriorating quality of per-share earnings," at a growing number of companies.

In fact, Mr. O'Glove contends that the practice of numerous concerns of "inflating earnings through various accounting "gimmicks"—rather than judging profit on the basis of a higher level of business activity—could lead to widespread reassessment of the price-earnings multiples of many companies.

It's his contention that such a development is rapidly taking shape and he thinks that various groups of securities, as well as individual stocks, have declined even more than anticipated in the current bear market as a result of this reassessment. He cites, in particular, a number of concerns in such fields as computer leasing, insurance holding companies and the conglomerate field. Mr. O'Glove also believes that a number of land development companies are "highly vulnerable" because of what he terms "liberal accounting practices."

Asserting that "no analyst worth his salt can any longer afford to accept per-share earnings estimates at face value," particularly in what he characterizes the "current treacherous market," Mr. O'Glove urges investors to confine their purchases to "true earnings," not profit that is "exaggerated through liberal bookkeeping methods."

Here, in brief, are some of his key guidelines:

—Isolate capital gains transactions from operating income.

—Determine whether investment tax credits are being amortized or flowed through in reporting earnings. If the latter is the case, Mr. O'Glove

Reprinted from "Heard on the Street," *The Wall Street Journal* (15 July 1969), p. 35, by permission of Dow Jones & Co., Incorporated.

says, "earnings are being inflated because the entire credit in a given year is offset against taxes."

—Be alert to "excessive" deferrals of research and development expenditures—described by Mr. O'Glove as a "rising trend." He says such an accounting procedure can result in future earnings being severely penalized by the amounts deferred.

—Try to determine whether a particular company has paid excessive amounts for acquisitions. Mr. O'Glove concedes this is a difficult thing to do, but he thinks an insight may be obtained by examining prospectuses for the amount of good will (the difference between book value and the cost of the acquisition) that may have been "hidden" via pooling-of-interests accounting.

—Look for changes in inventory evaluation that would "considerably boost profit" during an inflationary environment, Mr. O'Glove says.

—Be aware of instalment sales accounting, which permits a company to include its entire profit on a particular transaction—even though the payment may be made over a period longer than 12 months.

—Determine a company's true reporting policy concerning credit delinquencies in relation to outstanding receivables. Some companies, Mr. O'Glove contends, "will hide their delinquencies for an extended period of time."

The effect of utilization of alternative accounting principles—and their ultimate impact on earnings—is reflected in an illustration of two hypothetical companies engaged in the same line of business, possessing the same revenue, costs, assets and liabilities and with an identical amount of common shares outstanding. Company B, utilizing liberal accounting procedures, is able to increase its earnings 45% higher than Company A ($2.41 to $1.66) by what Mr. O'Glove says are the following techniques:

Company B includes its net equity in a 40%-owned joint venture in the amount of $400,000. It doesn't provide for U.S. income taxes on its unremitted foreign subsidiary earnings, which would be in the amount of $250,000. Company A does so provide. Company B flows through its investment tax credit, while Company A amortizes the credit.

Thus Company B is able to offset its income taxes by $500,000 more than Company A, which also doesn't include its equity in a 40% joint venture and provides for U.S. taxes on its unremitted foreign earnings in the amount of $250,000. Company B doesn't have to include a $525,000 tax-loss carry-forward as an extraordinary credit as it isn't material in relation to total net income. Company A, on the other hand, treats the same credit as an extraordinary credit.

APPENDIX XI-iii

SANFORD L. JACOBS

HEARD ON THE STREET

Western Union Corp. has lots of boosters among analysts. But one perennial bear has issued a new report in which he contends that the company's image is tarnished by accounting practices that artificially inflate earnings.

Robert K. Golden, a technology specialist at Edwards & Hanly, says, "My greatest concern with Western Union is its facade—few people are aware of how little operations contribute to earnings." Indeed, he says he figures that only about 45 cents of the $2.50 to $2.75 a share net income he expects the company to post for 1972 was from operations; the balance, over $2 a share, results from "bookkeeping devices," he avers.

His report to institutional clients zeroes in on four nonoperating items that boost Western Union's reported earnings: capitalization of interest costs (thereby avoiding a deduction from income of the entire expense in one year); capitalization of pension costs and severance pay costs, and the flow-through to net income of income-tax credits.

During an interview, Mr. Golden also criticized the company's reporting as net income a gain from acquiring its own long-term debt below par. "That's not operating income," he says. "Most companies would show the acquisition of debt below par as extraordinary income, not put it in operating income," he adds.

The 47-year-old analyst has been bearish on Western Union for some time. His reports, however, don't seem to have much effect on the stock, perhaps because some prestigious research houses are bullish on the company. However, Mr. Golden, who is also well respected in the financial community tracks the company, meticulously analyzing its monthly reports to the Federal Communications Commission and talking with accounting

Reprinted from "Heard on the Street," *The Wall Street Journal* (24 January 1973), p. 39, by permission of Dow Jones & Co., Incorporated.

experts to verify his conclusions about bookkeeping practices.

"It's trying to figure out what nonoperating items will be used to increase earnings that makes forecasting Western Union so difficult," the analyst says. He adds that the computer companies he follows don't give him "anywhere near the trouble" in forecasting earnings that Western Union does.

His current estimate for 1973 per-share net is more in line with other analysts. He forecasts per-share earnings of $2.80 to $3.15 this year, but only 30 cents to 40 cents a share will come from operations, he says. He figures a hefty "$2.50 to $2.75 a share" will result from "deferred expenses and tax credits." He declares that "when expense deferrals reach the level they have, it's a farce."

In addition, Mr. Golden asserts that Western Union's $1.40 annual dividend hasn't been covered by operating income, except for one year, since 1968.

"They've been paying the dividend out of depreciation," except for 1969, he says. Mr. Golden also figures that cash flow from operations (excluding depreciation) has been negative in the past four years except for 1969. "Looking at the poor cash flow, I wonder why they continue to pay the dividend," he declares. Answering his own question he adds: "Stopping it would, of course, wreak havoc with the price of the stock." Yesterday, the issue closed on the New York Stock Exchange at $38.75, off 62½ cents. It has traded as high as $69.50 a share and as low as $37.75 in the past year.

In response to Mr. Golden's criticisms, a Western Union spokesman said: "The important thing about earnings is that they are comparable. With the exception of severance costs this year, we've calculated earnings the same way every year." He added that the telegraph company, Western Union's 90%-owned and principal subsidiary, is regulated by the Federal Communications Commission and uses "normal utility accounting."

Russell W. McFall, Western Union's chairman, who came to the company from Litton Industries Inc. in 1965, issued a statement in response to the Edwards & Hanly report. "It is obviously true that Western Union, in recent years, has had major problems to overcome while pursuing major opportunities," Mr. McFall said.

"Other analysts, however, who have more balanced perspective, recognize not only the magnitude of the company's task, but the significant progress that has been made," Mr. McFall declared.

Among such analysts is Otis Bradley, known on the Street as an optimist. An analyst at Spencer Trask & Co., Mr. Bradley still sees good things ahead for Western Union, though some problems in the near term.

In a brief report bearing the same date as Mr. Golden's, Mr. Bradley says the company's results for the last quarter of 1972 were disappointing and will be for the first quarter this year. He looks for improvement in this year's second half. He adds that the company "still maintains as exciting a potential over the next year or two, corporate-wise, as we had expected earlier and that eventually the stock will reflect this." But, right now, he says "near-term performance will be difficult."

Generally, Western Union's prospects for growth have been based on its closing several hundred telegraph offices, thereby reducing labor costs; automating message-switching facilities, eliminating more labor, and building teleprinter-exchange revenue and Mailgram business as the telegram business drops off. The company has eliminated most of the offices it planned to close, and computer switching of messages is nearly systemwide. However, the drop in telegram revenue fell more than some analysts expected in the past few months.

The telegraph company, however, recently asked the FCC to let it raise rates for teleprinter-exchange services, TWX and Telex, to add some $12 million a year to revenue. Mr. Golden figures the boost could add 50 cents a share to 1973 net, depending on when the rise goes into effect.

APPENDIX XII-i

ARLENE HERSHMAN

HOW TO FIGURE WHO'S GOING BANKRUPT

"Who's next?" has become a common question in corporate circles. And the answers have included such big names as Mammoth Mart, Interstate Stores, Bowmar Instruments, Hartfield-Zody's, Bohack, Potter Instrument and Daylin.

Those are just a few of the more than 10,000 U.S. companies that filed petitions of bankruptcy last year—often with little or no warning—seeking protection from their creditors. Worse yet, Wall Street and business alike fear that stepped-up inflation, profit declines and periods of expensive money ahead will precipitate an even greater wave of business bankruptcies. This year, the number of bankrupties is expected to rise 25%.

In other words, not since the 1930s have investors been more in need of help in predicting corporate failure. And at least some help is at hand in the form of new mathematical forecasting methods designed to red-flag potential bankruptcies. Wall Street analysts, banks, insurance companies and auditors are all experimenting with one or more of these formulas. "We are using two forecasting methods in our analysis program," reports James Loebbecke, partner and director of audit research for Touche, Ross, the Big Eight accounting firm. "We believe there is no downside risk in singling out companies possibly headed for trouble," Loebbecke explains, "and the advantages of catching just one situation we might otherwise have missed are incalculable."

Utilizing very nuts-and-bolts methods of measuring performance, mathematical forecasting can signal changes in corporations' financial status

Reprinted from *Dun's Review* (October 1975), pp. 63–65, 107–8, by permission of *Dun's Review*.

Arlene Hershman is a Senior Editor of *Dun's Review*.

621

that trained analysts might miss. As a result, they are proving useful not only in predicting failures, but in keeping track of ups and downs in solvent companies as well. "We use mathematical forecasting for more than just sorting out good apples and bad apples," says Ralph Verni, director of investment research at Equitable Life Assurance Society. "We also use them in determining how good the good apples are."

The two most popular mathematical forecasting methods currently being explored:

• The "Z-score," or bankruptcy, rating. Developed by Associate Professor Edward I. Altman of the Graduate School of Business of New York University, the Z-score is designed to forecast failure in the short term; that is, up to two years. There are two formulas: one for manufacturing companies, which uses five ratios of management ability and financial strength to arrive at a Z-score; the other for railroads, which uses seven ratios. Companies with a Z-score lower than 1.81, Altman's study indicates, have a high probability of failure within two years. Any company with a Z-score higher than 3, on the other hand, has a low probability of bankruptcy. In an exclusive study done for *Dun's Review,* the table on page 65 shows the fourteen weakest and fourteen strongest U.S. manufacturing companies according to the Z-score.

• The gambler's ruin prediction of bankruptcy. This formula is designed to forecast failure for both manufacturing and retailing companies up to five years ahead. Advanced by management consultant Jarrod Wilcox of The Boston Consulting Group when he was an assistant professor at MIT's Sloan School of Business, this method computes the probability of bankruptcy based on a corporation's estimated "liquidation" value and the rate of change in this "liquidation" value.

Depending on the company's ability to generate funds for paying dividends and making capital expenditures in the past, and to hold onto or increase its financial resources, the formula produces a percentage result—similar to a weather forecast probability percentage—estimating the company's chances of staying afloat if its present management policies and the nature of its business stay the same. As any blackjack gambler will understand, the underlying principle is that the odds are against a player with a small pile of chips in a high-stakes game because he may be out of the game before he can win.

How well do these formulas actually work in predicting corporate failure? Examining the financial statements of companies that had already gone bankrupt, Altman's formula forecast failure up to two years ahead in better than eight out of ten cases. Also testing against companies that had already gone bankrupt, Wilcox' formula predicted bankruptcy in 76% of the cases five years beforehand and increased its rate of success to 96% of the cases one year prior to bankruptcy filing.

These formulas, it is important to remember, depend on data from companies' own financial statements to compute their probabilities. So the formulas may not be able to predict bankruptcy in cases where the financial statements incorporate gross misstatements. "I completely failed in predicting failure on Westec," Wilcox admits, "because the numbers were misstated."

Despite this obvious handicap, analysts interviewed by *Dun's Review* claim that their own applications of the formulas have confirmed the academic results in predicting bankruptcy. In reviewing all the mathematical forecasting formulas, Baruch Lev, visiting assistant professor at the University of Chicago, concluded in his book *Financial Statement Analysis: A New Approach* that these techniques "are capable of providing an early warning at least two to three years before bankruptcy."

FIGURING THE Z-SCORE

It is not difficult for an investor to work out the formulas in order to judge how the companies in his stock and bond portfolio are faring. To compute the Z-score, for example, the investor has only to copy out about a dozen numbers from a company's financial statement in its last annual report. The formula is: Z-score equals the sum of the current assets less the current liabilities, divided by total assets times 1.2; plus the retained earnings divided by total assets times 1.4; plus pretax income and interest charges divided by total assets times 3.3; plus market value of common stock and preferred stock at liquidating value divided by all debt times 0.6; plus sales divided by the total assets times 1.

It may sound complicated, but one Wall Street railroad analyst says he can pick out the numbers needed for the seven ratios in the railroad formula and run them on a hand calculator in only ten minutes. "What's amazing," says Equitable Life's Verni, "is to get these dramatic results with this seemingly modest effort."

Beyond the mathematical calculations, the investor can also learn much about a company by examining its performance and estimating its relative financial strength according to the principles involved in the formulas. What is its management efficiency, its financial position—and how are these changing over a number of years? "The Z-score," says Verni, "is not the end. It is only the beginning of the analysis."

In the Z-score formula, the most important factor in a company's performance is its management efficiency. And the prime indicator of this efficiency is the company's return on assets before taxes and interest charges. In his original study of bankrupt companies, Altman tested more than 22 ratios used by business and financial analysts to determine which ratios in which combination worked in predicting bankruptcy. He found that this single ratio of management efficiency worked most consistently, so its importance or weight is many times greater than any of the others.

As the table on page 65 shows, there are dramatic differences in return on assets among companies, ranging from negative numbers to returns of 30% and better. Also significant, but not shown in the table, is the trend of a company's performance from year to year. Financially troubled retailer W. T. Grant, for example, has shown a decline in return on assets each year since 1970, and the return turned negative this year. More surprisingly, Polaroid, one of the strongest companies, has seen its rate of return drop 72% since 1970. "When a company's rate of return starts dropping," says analyst Thornton O'glove, publisher of the *Quality of Earnings Report,* "it is a sure sign that the company is having trouble. Even if it is not always trouble in the sense of bankruptcy, it is a tremendously valuable early-warning indicator."

In Altman's study, the financial indicators that failed companies typically score low on are the ones reflecting a company's ability to generate money either internally or externally. Can it find the cash to pay its bills? Can it borrow more or sell bonds or equity?

The three indicators that signal trouble here are: inadequate working capital (current assets minus current liabilities as a percentage of assets); debt greater than the market value of the company's stock; and low or negative retained earnings in relation to assets (which indicates a company's profitability over a number of years as well as the strength of its balance sheet).

Telex Corp., for example, though recently profitable, is hampered in its operations by a negative net worth. The computer peripheral maker may be headed for a cash bind resulting from its court contest with IBM. "If the Appeals Court ruling releasing IBM from any damages while reaffirming the $18.5-million assessment against Telex is upheld by the Supreme Court," a Value Line analyst observes, "this would undermine the company's already weak financial position." He warns: "Investors . . . must be prepared to take a total loss on their investment."

Altman's work also tends to disprove the value of some of the accepted corporate performance tests as bankruptcy predictors. For example, the most common test of corporate viability is the current ratio; that is, the difference between current assets and liabilities, which is supposed to show a company's ability to pay the bills. In his study of past corporate bankruptcies, however, Altman found the current ratio to be an undependable test for failure and possibly downright deceptive. In fact, the ratio often goes up before a company goes bankrupt because the company sells fixed assets to improve its cash position; while the sale may help the company generate the cash to deal with its problems in the short run, its overall earning power is diminishing fast. "Cash is too easy to manipulate and therefore can be misleading," says Altman.

Another misleading indicator when it comes to predicting failure is the widely used management efficiency test: the ratio of sales to assets. While this ratio is a good scorecard of management's ability to meet competition and hold onto its market share in normal times, Altman's study indicates that its actions can be confusing in bankruptcy-prone situations. Imminently bankrupt companies can show a surprisingly high ratio of sales to assets—almost, but not quite, as high as a healthy company of similar size and type. The explanation, Altman believes, is simply that some declining companies may be losing assets faster than sales as inventory write-downs and bad-debt write-offs reduce the asset side of the balance sheet.

THE "LIQUIDATION" VALUE

In addition to forecasting potential for failure, the gambler's ruin prediction formula tests a corporation's capability of generating cash for plant expansion and dividends. It can signal possible dividend cuts or changes in market value of outstanding long-term bonds.

To figure it, the investor first calculates a company's "liquidation" value: by subtracting all current liabilities and long-term debt from its assets (valuing cash and marketable securities at market; valuing inventories, accounts receivable and prepaid expenses at 70% of the balance-sheet figure; and valuing other assets at 50% the balance-sheet figure). Then the investor figures how much the "liquidation" value changed from the previous year by subtracting from earnings, after special items, all dividends and 50% of the year's capital expenditures and depreciation; then subtracting 30% of the increase in inventories and accounts receivables since last year.

According to the formula, clothing maker Botany Industries could have liquidated and realized cash five years before it filed bankruptcy papers in 1972. But one year later its "liquidation" value had dropped to zero. And in 1969 further reverses had brought the "liquidation" value down to a negative number. Considerably weakened Botany might still have come through in a good year; unfortunately, 1970 was one of the worst for almost every company. "When a company's 'liquidation' value drops to negative," says consultant Jarrod Wilcox, "it needs to see a big upswing immediately to pull through at all."

These formulas are bound to be more reliable as predictors of danger than they are of calling actual bankruptcy because many companies these days are kept alive by artificial means. Government aid (in the form

THE BAD AND THE BEAUTIFUL

One of the major mathematical forecasting formulas, the Z-score devised by Associate Professor Edward I. Altman of New York University's Graduate School of Business, rates companies for a high or low probability of failure. The ratings—or Z-scores—are based on five performance ratios of management efficiency and financial strength. According to Altman's study, these five ratios taken together are the best single indicator of potential corporate bankruptcy. Z-scores lower than 1.81 indicate a high probability of failure, while Z-scores higher than 3 indicate a low probability of failure.

In a special study prepared for *Dun's Review* by Investors Management Sciences, a Denver-based corporate data service, the Z-scores of some 1,200 publicly held industrial companies were computed. Listed below are the fourteen weakest and fourteen strongest manufacturing companies on the list, along with the individual ratios that make up the Z-score. The individual weighted ratios, in the order shown, indicate: working capital adequacy; cumulative profitability; management efficiency in using corporate assets productively; market strength and capacity to raise additional capital; and sales efficiency.

It is important to remember that ratios are not absolute numbers, and analysts use them only in comparisons between strong and weak companies, preferably in the same industry. In the altman formula, note that weak companies often appear to perform almost as well as strong companies in their sales efficiency as measured by the ratio of sales to assets; therefore, relatively good performance in this ratio can be a confusing ratio when used alone.

THE WORST PERFORMERS

Company	Z-score	Working Capital as a % of Assets × 1.2	Retained Earnings as a % of Assets × 1.4	Pretax Income + Interest as a % of Assets × 3.3	*Market Value of Common + Preferred at Liquidating as a % of Debt × 0.6	Sales Divided by Assets × 1
Memorex	0.74	0.23	-0.69	0.14	0.15	0.92
Mohawk Data Sciences (4/75)	0.91	0.34	-0.20	-0.06	0.03	0.80
Electronic Associates	0.94	0.57	-1.15	0.27	0.13	1.12
Todd Shipyards (3/75)	1.03	0.30	-0.03	-1.12	0.10	1.79
Puerto Rican Cement	1.06	0.04	0.17	0.07	0.08	0.69
ICN Pharmaceuticals (11/74)	1.34	0.17	0.10	-0.21	0.08	1.21
Duplan (9/74)	1.37	0.42	0.02	-0.32	0.02	1.23
Sanders Associates (7/74)	1.56	0.53	-0.27	-0.47	0.09	1.68
Cooper Laboratories (10/74)	1.61	0.27	0.06	0.17	0.38	0.72
Amcord	1.69	0.10	0.28	0.26	0.23	0.81
Condec (7/74)	1.69	0.25	0.13	0.20	0.09	1.04
Schaefer, F. & M.	1.71	0.13	0.08	0.17	0.03	1.31
Arvin Industries	1.77	0.13	0.19	0.23	0.16	1.06
Telex (3/75)	1.78	0.26	-0.27	0.44	0.21	1.12

THE BEST PERFORMERS

Company	Z-score	Working Capital as a % of Assets × 1.2	Retained Earnings as a % of Assets × 1.4	Pretax Income + Interest as a % of Assets × 3.3	*Market Value of Common + Preferred at Liquidating as a % of Debt × 0.6	Sales Divided by Assets × 1
Taylor Wine (6/74)	304.09	0.62	0.85	0.79	300.87	0.97
American Home Products	169.10	0.54	0.75	1.17	164.99	1.65
Starrett, L.S. (6/74)	125.08	0.72	0.82	0.79	121.58	1.17
Schering Plough	88.39	0.52	0.94	1.00	84.86	1.07
Marion Laboratories (6/75)	78.80	0.56	0.82	1.32	74.81	1.29
Bandag	58.83	0.62	0.71	1.19	54.89	1.43
Eastman Kodak	52.06	0.40	0.82	0.82	49.05	0.97
Nalco Chemical	47.88	0.38	0.91	0.87	44.24	1.48
Polaroid	42.38	0.64	0.88	0.20	39.68	0.98
Merck	38.08	0.35	0.78	0.96	34.92	1.07
Betz Laboratories	37.98	0.41	0.64	0.81	34.63	1.50
Northwestern Steel & Wire (7/74)	37.65	0.54	0.79	0.88	34.15	1.28
Johnson & Johnson	36.60	0.45	0.80	0.68	33.29	1.38
Data General (9/74)	36.32	0.56	0.44	0.89	33.27	1.17

Figures used in compiling table are for fiscal year ending 12/74 except where otherwise indicated. *As of year-end 1974.

of direct grants or life-supporting contracts), for example, keeps many companies afloat during tough years.

Todd Shipyards, for example, experienced a financial crisis in 1974 when profit losses amounted to $43 million on sales of only $146 million. As a result, working capital almost ran out. But Uncle Sam stepped in: Todd got a bank loan to replenish its diminishing working capital that is 90% guaranteed by the federal government.

Or take Puerto Rican Cement, which manufactures more than 80% of the cement used in Puerto Rico. The company was forced by poor earnings to skip its dividend this year; however, the Puerto Rican government recently wrote an agreement with the company allowing it to raise prices enough to earn a 12% return on its capital after taxes.

The banks are also helping companies that otherwise might be forced up against the wall—by holding onto their loans beyond their due dates. The lenders are obviously more patient than they were in 1970, when Penn Central was forced over the edge lacking a paltry $100 million.

Today, much smaller companies are carrying awesome debts at their bankers' pleasure. Southern-California-based ICN Pharmaceuticals, for example, with sales of roughly $180 million, had more than $20 million in bank debt due last year. This whopping payment, however, was postponed when its bankers agreed to extend the maturities of almost $30 million in loans. Value Line analysts note that ICN's finances "are weak" after two years of profit losses. "Indeed, ICN is largely dependent on its banks," the analysts conclude.

Despite these caveats, however, mathematical forecasting is obviously a step forward in evaluating corporate performance. For the investor, the first step is to get a grip on the corporation's current status—a job that these new methods are designed to do. Then he can figure out what the future holds.

APPENDIX XIII-i

PAPER MONEY

The first few lines of General Host's 1974 income statement sing a mournful song: Pretax income from continuing operations was *down* 25%, to $4 million. Ah, but General Host's bottom line hums a different tune: Net income for 1974 was *up*—up 300%!—to a record $9.17 per share.

How do you produce higher profits out of lower profits? It's one of the marvels of modern bookkeeping. In this case a nice little gimmick called "gains on extinguishment of debt."

"Extinguishment" is a cute term. It doesn't mean that General Host paid off its debt at less than 100 cents on a dollar and thereby earned a substantial discount. What General Host did was shuffle some pieces of paper and produce a paper profit of nearly $17 million—turning a poor year into a triumphant one. The old paper was "extinguished." New paper was substituted in its place.

It worked like this: Outstanding was $33.9 million in convertible debentures due in 1988, paying 5% interest—total annual interest, about $1.7 million. Management offered to swap for it $20.3 million new convertible debentures, paying 11% total interest, about $2.2 million. At the same time, the company reduced the conversion price from $27 per common share to $16. The bondholders took the offer. Why not? The holders' current income was enhanced by about 32% and conversion terms were improved.

Thus, even though Host's interest expense was increased from $1.7 million to $2.2 million, its books were improved by the wiping out of nearly $13.6 million in debt. And the "profit" came through in 1974, despite the fact that the debt wasn't due.

That is a lot easier way to make money than selling meat and tourism.

For some peculiar reason, the Financial Accounting Standards Board has put its imprimatur on this exercise in funny finance, calling these gains "extraordinary" income—whatever that means. But as Harvard Business School Professor John Shank puts it: "The board didn't raise the basic issue, which is whether this is income at all and in what period."

Reprinted by permission of FORBES Magazine from the July 1, 1975 issue.

Boil it down and what you get is this: The company reports a "profit" but incurs a huge increase in interest liability against a very-far-in-the-future reduction in capital liability. Concedes William McHugh, a partner in Coopers & Lybrand: "They've effectively taken a profit this year and will pay it back over the life of the new bonds, through increased charges to future income." Is this what the accounting board calls clearer and more straightforward accounting?

"We're on the horns of a dilemma here," agrees Frank T. Weston, partner of Arthur Young & Co. Weston believes that the only solution to the dilemma is adoption of current value accounting, under which changes in the market value of debt would be recognized as they occur. On the other hand, Philip Defliese, managing partner of Coopers & Lybrand, dissented from the accounting board's ruling in this matter, wanting to see the "profit" amortized over the life of the bonds so that the price paid for the gain would be increased interest in subsequent periods. But he was overruled.

General Host is quick to point out that it didn't invent the gimmick. The ruling is that of the FASB. Nor is General Host the only company to take advantage of this murky provision. Grumman did too last year. Gulf & Western got 19% of its reported profits in 1973 that way. Western Union Corp. played the game. In Eli Black's time, United Brands was big on "extinguishment."

Why shouldn't companies be made to amortize the gain, the way Defliese suggested? It seems a mockery to have profit statements—which most investors think reflect the company's health—embellished with "profits" from paper shuffling.

HYPOED INCOME: SOME COMPANIES RETIRE, OTHERS SWAP DEBT.

Company	Type of Extinguishment	Gain (millions)	Pretax Income (millions)	Gain as % of Income	Recent Stock Price	P/E Ratio
Allen Group	Exchange	$ 1.4	$ 5.7	25%	7⅝	9
GAF	Retirement	5.5	56.0	10	10⅝	5
General Host	Exchange	16.9*	20.8	81	7¼	1
Grumman	Exchange	9.3†	49.8	19	17½	6
McCulloch Oil	Exchange	0.8	5.1	16	5⅜	22
Pacific Gas & Elec	Retirement	20.0**	293.5	7	20¼	7
Pan East Pipe	Retirement	4.2** ††	103.8	4	29¼	6
Trans World Air	Retirement	2.7**	(22.8)	—	7⅜	—
UAL	Retirement	20.6	224.0	9	18⅜	6

*Includes $751,000 debt retirement. †No income tax paid on gain. **Gain result of sinking fund requirement. ††Gain is being amortized, under Federal Power Commission accounting change Jan. 1, 1974.

APPENDIX XIV-i

W. T. BAXTER

VALUATION THEORY

DEPRECIATION COST AS A FUNCTION OF VALUE DECLINE

If depreciation is a matter of fall in an asset's value over time, then the primary step in measuring it must be to establish the successive value figures. When these figures have been found, the depreciation costs emerge as a by-product.

This is another way of suggesting that accounting must not try to measure cost *in vacuo*, leaving asset value as an unimportant and possibly meaningless residual. The tail should not wag the dog: the value is the thing that matters, and the cost is the residual. If the accountant declines to treat his asset figures as part of a valuation process, then he divorces his values and costs from the reality that he is striving to measure, and reduces them to empty abstractions.

THE MANY DEFINITIONS OF DEPRECIATION

However, the value of an asset at any time can usually be found in one or other of several ways, according to the valuer's choice of valuation concept. There are many such concepts; and they view assets in very different manners, and produce very different value figures.

Thus the choice of value concept must affect in turn the measurement of depreciation. One might indeed say that each value concept gives rise to its attendant depreciation concept. Accordingly, a full definition of depreciation can hardly be given without some reference to the chosen

---

Reprinted from *Depreciation* (Sweet & Maxwell, 1971), pp. 28–32, by permission of Sweet and Maxwell.

W. T. Taxter is Professor of Accounting at the London School of Economics.

value concept. This explains in part why Chapter 1 did not attempt to list the many possible definitions.[1]

It follows that anyone who tries to explain depreciation should, as one of his earliest steps, put all his cards on the table and state clearly how his explanation fits in with value theory. The rest of the chapter is accordingly devoted to this matter. However, a study of depreciation can scarcely be the right place for a full-dress discussion on value theories. It does enough, surely, if it sketches the various concepts, and makes clear which one of them it will use as its framework, and why; it may also help to test the logic and usefulness of the chosen concept.

CONCEPTS OF WEALTH AND GROWTH OF WEALTH

"Value" means many different things. Most of them are concerned with expectations of benefits. Such expectations are elusive and personal. Thus household goods yield satisfactions that vary from one owner to another; if the goods are durable, the satisfaction will come in doses that may stretch over a long time and be hard to predict. Business assets at first sight may seem simpler, because of the assumption that their values can be quantified by reference to cash flow. But the link between today's assets and the next decade's cash flow is roundabout and unsure; it too must be subjective, since it depends on personal expectations of quantities, probabilities, and discount rates of cost-of-capital. Even the basic assumption—that the firm's objective is to maximize the present value of the cash flow—is plainly not always the whole truth, and must be looked on only as a helpful simplification.

Whole Firm

Where the value of the firm as a whole is the issue, there are perhaps two main concepts, each of which can be split into various sub-concepts; and, if one regards income as the growth in this value between two dates, there is a corresponding array of income concepts.

One concept is "forward-looking", and equates the firm's value with the present value of the firm's net receipts (found by discounting the

---

[1] Further, there are definitions that go beyond money values, *e.g.* impaired serviceableness in a purely physical sense. For a broader list of definitions, see J. C. Bonbright, *The Valuation of Property*, McGraw-Hill, New York, 1937, reprinted in 1965 by the Michie Company, Charlottesville, Virginia; Louis Goldberg, *Concepts of Depreciation*, Law Book Company of Australasia, Sydney, 1960; and Eugene L. Grant and Paul T. Norton, *Depreciation*, Ronald Press, New York, 1949.

expected future cash flow of the firm as a whole). Plainly this concept
is subjective, and its value figures must often be highly debatable. It
is the concept that anyone buying or selling a firm or shares will usually
employ, at least at the back of his mind, to find a suitable price. It
pays heed to the state of individual assets in an indirect way only, and
so can be largely ignored in a study of depreciation.

The second concept is more down-to-earth. It finds the firm's wealth
by summing values of all the separate assets (for example, in a balance
sheet). Its sub-concepts differ from one another in using somewhat
different ways of valuing the assets.

Separate Assets

The sub-concepts fall into two groups—historical and non-historical.
The former values assets at their historical cost (less, where appropriate,
depreciation based on historical cost). The latter feels free to change
an asset's value whenever circumstances warrant such change. Notably
it may change the value in step with current market prices.

When an accountant lists and adds separate asset values, as in a balance
sheet, his ideal should presumably be to choose the kind of values that
will give most information to the managers, investors, etc., who will use
the figures. A sensible aim may well be to try to depict the "size" of
the firm's resources in such a way that performance can be judged by
the ratio of earnings to assets. To be sure, "size" on this asset-plus-asset
basis is something far less meaningful than "size" as the value of a whole
firm (*i.e.* the present value of the entire cash flow, without much regard
to separate assets). But it meets a need, and the refinement of its figures
seems a worthwhile task.

Changing Price Levels

Whatever the concept or sub-concept adopted, an embarrassing further
trouble arises (because of price change) when one tries to compare wealth
at different dates. One must then choose between some three possible
interpretations of one's favourite sub-concept—that is, in effect split it
up further into three sub-sub-concepts.

This complication will, however, be left till Chapters 11 and 12. The
intervening chapters will in the main assume prices to be constant.

MARKET VALUES AND DEPRECIATION

For the purpose of this study, current market prices provide the main
forms of non-historical values.

Types of Market Value

When he uses market prices, a valuer must choose between *buying* prices (replacement cost) and *selling* prices (for merchandise, often the "net realizable value" of sale to ordinary customers; for fixed assets, often the prices of the second-hand or junk markets).

The gap between buying and selling prices may in theory be slight, but can in the real world be considerable. With merchandise, sale price (*e.g.* in the retail market) will tend to be higher than buying price (*e.g.* in the wholesale market). With depreciating assets, sale price is likely to be the lower (particularly where an asset is *specific* to the needs of the one firm, so that other firms have little or no use for it); indeed, sale price may well fall to the derisory figure for junk. Such low figures tend to be uninformative unless the machine, etc., is in fact to be sold soon. This is a strong argument for valuing it, for most accounting purposes, at replacement cost rather than sale price.

SELECTION FROM ALTERNATIVE FIGURES

It sometimes is helpful for a valuer to rely on not one but several figures, selecting one or another for each asset according to circumstances. The conventional "lower of cost or market" rule for valuing current assets may not be sound in logic, but it provides a familiar example of the technique.

Later pages will suggest that the most satisfactory value is a selective one that I call *deprival value*. This recognizes that replacement cost normally fills the bill, but on occasion is inadequate: it therefore uses the lower of replacement cost and certain other figures.

TESTS FOR MEASURES OF VALUE AND DEPRECIATION

The next problem is that of how to test the many values, to find out which is best for depreciation estimates.

Where most techniques of physical measurement are concerned, presumably an expert can with fair confidence assess the rival methods well enough for practical purposes, and pick the best. The choice between value methods, on the other hand, bristles with difficulties, alike at the technical and more fundamental levels.

Thus it is crying for the moon to ask for solid, unassailable figures of value. The valuer cannot even say that any one concept is in all senses better than the others. Probably all that he can do is to ask, first, which concept gives the best answers to the practical questions of life; and, second, which provides figures with least trouble, cost and doubt. Here truth is usefulness.

If this argument is right, one must approach depreciation in a pessimistic mood. No clear tests of correctness are likely to emerge. One can do no more than ask what are the problems that depreciation measurements help to solve, and therefore which of the measurements looks like being most useful. (And possibly the measurements most helpful for answering one set of questions may be less good for another set.)

Values for depreciating assets may be used to help with problems of "size" (see p. 29) and return on investment; they may in particular help analysts who are studying the efficiency with which assets are employed by a department, a company, an industry and so on. Figures for depreciation cost are used in calculating income, and so help indirectly with problems of consumption, reward-sharing (and one may include tax here) and future investment; more directly, they may throw light on working methods (*e.g.* depreciation may be part of the costs that show the efficiency or otherwise of a given method or manager). At least if their avoidable and fixed parts can be unravelled, the figures may help with pricing; I do not want to defend the "full cost" system of pricing (mainly because it is so insensitive to demand), but plainly a manager ought to know the avoidable costs of products, jobs, etc., when deciding on price.

MARKET VALUE AND THE TESTS

In general, the values that help best with these problems are those of the current market. Market values are familiar, and alert to change; and often they can be verified more objectively than their critics suggest. More important, decision budgets (on the use of assets) must normally work with market values, because a decision to use up an asset often forces the firm to go into the market for a replacement.

The argument seems to hold well for depreciating assets. If a depreciation method is to be helpful, it must show economic reality in live and current terms—and in particular how much of the firm's wealth is consumed in a period and how much remains at the end. The wealth in question is the asset's stock of potential services. The method must try to appraise them in a sensitive way. But this is precisely what is done by the market for worn assets. So a plausible starting point is that a good depreciation method should simulate what goes on in the minds of buyers and sellers of worn assets. These people presumably make some estimate of how many units of input (time or use, according to the kind of asset) an asset can still give; and then they try to assess what the units are worth, having regard to prices of alternatives and to the pattern of pending repair outlays, etc. A good method should reflect much the same considerations.

DEPRECIATION METHODS AS A SUBSTITUTE FOR THE MARKET

Buy why, if market values are the key to asset values, does not the accountant find depreciation by direct reference to market quotations for assets of different ages, and abandon his formulae? Various answers suggest themselves. Most firms link value with historical rather than current price. Second-hand markets tend to be small and scrubby, so that quotations may be hard to find and harder to trust. Many assets are built specially for the one firm, and therefore worn replicas do not exist. An owner usually regards his own worn assets as different from, and better than replicas in the market, because he knows their history, condition and foibles. Finally, where he would if deprived of a used asset replace it by a new rather than another used one, second-hand prices are somewhat irrelevant.

For such reasons, adequate values for depreciating assets often cannot be got from the real market. Therefore, if he is impressed by the merits of market values, the accountant must try to make his own appraisals in ways that mirror the market's forces. A depreciation formula can be a helpful ally. The task of his formula is to create a synthetic market for each asset. In other words, the success of a depreciation method depends on how well it finds out what the price would be if a suitable market did in fact exist.

APPENDIX XIV-ii

Arthur L. Thomas

The FASB and the Allocation Fallacy

Off to an impressively active start, the Financial Accounting Standards Board has already wrestled with a broad range of accounting issues. Topics on its active agenda or on which it has issued Standards include

1 Accounting for leases.
2 Accounting for research and development costs.
3 Contingencies and future losses.
4 Gains and losses from extinguishment of debt.
5 Interest costs and capitalization.
6 Accounting for pensions.
7 Segment reporting.
8 Business combinations.
9 Interim financial statements.
10 Reporting by development stage entities.
11 Reporting in units of general purchasing power.
12 Translation of foreign currency transactions and financial statements.
13 The recommendations of the Trueblood Report.[1]

All these topics involve some kind of *allocation*, which is the assignment of a total to one or more locations or categories. A thesaurus gives "division," "partition," "slicing," "splitting" and "apportionment" as synonyms of "allocation." Accounting's allocations include assignment of a

---

Reprinted from *The Journal of Accountancy* (November 1975), pp. 65–68, by permission of the American Institute of Certified Public Accountants. Copyright © 1975 by the American Institute of Certified Public Accountants, Inc.

Arthur L. Thomas is Whittington Professor of Accounting at Rice University.

[1] "Objectives of Financial Statements," Report of the Study Group on the Objectives of Financial Statements, Robert M. Trueblood, chairman (New York: AICPA, October 1973).

lease's costs to the individual years of its life, assignment of R&D costs to the single year of their expenditure and assignment of long term investment interest to successive annual revenues. All the FASB topics listed above fall into one of the following two classes of allocations, with items 7 through 9 falling into both:

1 The first nine topics require deciding when to recognize revenues, expenses, gains or losses—that is, deciding to what periods they should be assigned. For example, the FASB may eventually specify how to allocate pension costs to successive annual pension expenses.

2 The last seven topics involve ways of preparing financial statements composed mainly of allocated data. For example, this is implicit throughout the Trueblood Report and explicit in its position statement and income statement recommendations.

In fact, almost all of our revenue recognition and matching efforts require allocation.

THE ALLOCATION PROBLEM

The foregoing is background to a problem that we accountants acknowledge, but whose severity we usually misjudge. To use a term from formal logic, recent research indicates that, unfortunately, our allocations must almost always be *incorrigible*—that is to say, they can neither be refuted nor verified.[2] Incorrigibility will be a central concept in this discussion, and it is well to give a few examples even if doing so may initially seem to be a detour.

Let's suppose that someone claims that beings live among us who look and act exactly like humans, but who actually are aliens, seeded on this planet by flying saucers. We ask: do they come equipped with authentic looking birth certificates? Yes. Would tests of their internal structure, chromosomes or the like expose them? No. Could psychiatrists unmask them? No. The horrible thing is that they have such good counterfeit memories that even the aliens themselves don't know their real nature— you may be one yourself.

Such claims are incorrigible, for no experiment could prove either that such aliens exist or that they don't. Here are some other incorrigible claims:

☐ Charles Dickens may not have been a greater author than Shakespeare, but he was more of a person.

☐ Our bourbon is mellower.

---

[2] Arthur L. Thomas, Studies in Accounting Research No. 9, *The Allocation Problem: Part Two* (American Accounting Association, 1974), hereafter SAR 9.

☐ The official state flower of Unicornia is the marsh mallow.
☐ Even if the colonists had lost their war of independence, by now America would be independent of Britain.
☐ Since I've lost weight, I've become more spiritual.

Now, if our allocations are incorrigible, practicing accountants should be deeply concerned. We attest that financial statements present fairly the positions of companies and the results of their operations. But if both our revenue recognition and matching are founded upon allocations that we can neither refute nor verify, *we have no way of knowing whether these attestations are true.*

Are they incorrigible? I'll begin with matching and for brevity will disregard extraordinary items (and other nonoperating gains and losses), lower-of-cost-or-market writedowns and the like. Our matchings assign costs of a firm's nonmonetary inputs (inventories, labor, other services, depreciable assets, etc.) to the expenses of one or more accounting periods, temporarily reporting as assets costs assigned to future periods. We're all familiar with the theory behind these matching assignments; each input's purchase price should be allocated to successive periods in proportion to the contribution it makes to each period's revenues. Academics and most practitioners also know that an equivalent matching theory can be developed around contributions to net cash inflows.

The allocation problem has several dimensions, some of which are subtle. But one is easily described: to match costs with revenues, we must know what the contributions of the firm's individual inputs *are.* Unfortunately, as I'll illustrate below, there's no way that we can know this.

Seeing why this is so requires introducing a final concept, *interaction.* Inputs to a process interact whenever they generate an output different from the total of what they would yield separately. For instance, labor and equipment interact whenever people and machines working together produce more goods than the total of what people could make with their bare hands and machines could make untended. As this example suggests, interaction is extremely common. Almost all of a firm's inputs interact with each other—their failure to do so would ordinarily signal their uselessness.

Surprising as it may seem, it can be proved that whenever inputs interact, calculations of how much total revenue or cash flow has been contributed by any individual input are as meaningless as, say, calculations of the proportion of a worker's services due to any one internal organ: heart, liver or lungs. Thus, despite all textbooks and American Institute of CPAs or FASB releases to the contrary—despite what you've been trained to believe—our attempts to match costs with revenues must almost always fail. The next section tries to demonstrate this.

A Simple Example

A complete demonstration, meeting all possible counterarguments, is very lengthy.[3] But a simple example reveals the kernel of the matter. What follows is offered in the same spirit as Robert Sterling's recent illustration in these pages that only price-level-adjusted current-value financial statements are fully relevant and interpretable:

"A highly simplified case will be considered in this article. The advantages of simplified cases are that they are easily understood by both the reader and the author and they are more easily solved. If we cannot solve the simplified cases, then we can be fairly certain that we also cannot solve the complex cases. Thus, if a particular approach fails to provide a solution for simplified cases, then we can avoid wasting effort by trying that approach on complex cases."[4]

However, instead of Sterling's cash, securities, bread and milk trading economy, I'll describe a production process for bread alone and confine the discussion to strictly physical measures (to avoid complications introduced by monetary valuations).[5] If individual contributions are necessarily incorrigible even in the following example, it's hard to imagine how they could be otherwise in the vastly more complex processes by which business enterprises generate their products, services, revenues and cash flows.

A prospector manufactures sourdough bread by a three-stage process:
1 He makes leaven by mixing flour, sugar and water in a crock, then keeps it in a warm place for about a week (until it bubbles).
2 He makes bread by transferring all but a cup of leaven to a large pot, where he mixes it with soda and additional flour, sugar and water, kneads it slightly and then lets it rise. He digs a shallow pit, fills it with coals from his camp fire, covers the pot, places it in the pit, buries it in hot coals and keeps it there until the bread is baked.
3 He replenishes the leaven (for the next baking) by adding enough flour and water to restore the crock to its original level.

Water, airborne yeasts and wood are free goods here. We accountants would be concerned with the following inputs to this process: flour, sugar, soda, labor, the crock, the pot and a shovel. Finally, part of the flour

---

[3] See SAR 9, chapters 1–6, for the attempt.
[4] Robert R. Sterling, "Relevant Financial Reporting in an Age of Price Changes," JofA, Feb. 75, p. 42.
[5] As a technical point, I've also simplified by discussing only incremental contributions of inputs. See SAR 9, especially pp. 32–40, 47–48 and 141–44, for the parallel problems that arise for their marginal contributions.

and sugar leaven for one loaf becomes included in the leaven for the next. The output of each baking is one loaf of bread.

Although its manufacture is simple, the moment we try to calculate the contributions of any individual input to this output we face a dilemma. Each input (except, perhaps, the soda and the shovel) is essential. Therefore, we could plausibly assign all of the output to any individual input. For example, we could assign all of the output to the flour, reasoning that were flour withheld from the process there would be no bread. Yet we could equally well assign all of the output to the pot, since without it the loaf would have been incinerated.

Having assigned all output to any one input, we've implicitly assigned zero to each other input. But if either all or zero is appropriate for each input, any intermediate allocation will be equally appropriate—say, half the loaf to the flour and a sixth each to the pot, labor and the crock.

I'm unable to prove which of the infinitely many possible ways of allocating the loaf is correct. Therefore, I can't specify the individual contributions of the inputs; instead, all I'm entitled to say is that they generate the loaf jointly. Research shows that other writers on economics and accounting—even efficient-markets investigators—are equally unable to solve this problem. Perhaps the reader can. But until someone does, any contributions calculated for these inputs must be incorrigible:

1 One can't verify them, because any other calculation is just as good.
2 One can't refute them, because their calculation is just as good as any other.

Therefore, any attempts at matching based on these contributions (say, depreciation of the pot or calculation of a value for the ending leaven inventory) will also be incorrigible. But the sourdough process is so much simpler than the productive processes of business enterprises, that *matching must necessarily be incorrigible for them, too*—unless, again, the reader can show how complications ease the calculations. To generalize, when a company tries to match costs with revenues there's no way either to refute or to verify the results. Instead, all possible ways of matching will be just as good—or bad—as each other.

If it's any consolation, I don't like this conclusion either, and have spent years trying to disprove it. Nor should you accept it without further inquiry. But I urge you at least to suspend disbelief in it (and in what follows) until you've read the detailed research, cited earlier, that backs it up.

And please notice that the difficulty here isn't one of being unable to allocate—there might be some way of getting around that problem. Instead, we're drowned in possible allocations, with no defensible way to choose among them. To be sure, since we must prepare reports, we eventually do pick one set of figures or another. Long before completing our training, we became accustomed to do this with few (if any) pangs. First, we narrow the possibilities by looking to generally accepted accounting principles and then select one of the survivors according to industry custom, apparent advantage to the company, apparent appropriateness of the method to the firm's circumstances or some other plausible rationale. But how can the incorrigible results be useful to decision makers?

Unless you (or someone) can suggest ways in which calculations that can neither be verified nor refuted assist decisions,[6] our allocations of the costs of depreciable assets, inventories, labor and other inputs are irrelevant to investor needs. Indeed, although it's painful to say this, they are mere rituals—solemn nonsense—and our beliefs in them are fallacies. This should trouble all of us, because practitioners spend much time conducting such rituals, and theorists much time elaborating on such fallacies.[7]

The Accounting Principles Board was well aware of this, but, underrating its severity, was satisfied to claim that exact measurements are seldom possible and that allocation often requires informed judgment.[8] With all due respect, acknowledging that few allocations are exact is like replying, "Few animals are ever completely healthy," in response to the statement, "Sir, your cow is dead."

Finally, since what's true of individual inputs also holds for groups of inputs, I'm forced to conclude that our revenue recognition practices are rituals, too. For revenue recognition allocates the firm's *lifetime* output to the groups of inputs that constitute its resources during the individual years of its life. Once again, the details of this appear in SAR 9.

THE FASB'S RESPONSIBILITY

What, then, of the FASB? We've seen it worry, or propose to worry, about which allocations are most appropriate for various accounting situations. The FASB should stop doing this. Instead, whenever possible, it should *eliminate* allocations. Such incorrigible figures don't do readers of our reports any real good, and they
1 Cost money.
2 Strain relations between auditors and clients (when they disagree about

---

[6]Assistance that goes beyond the unsatisfactory, short run utilities is described on pp. 8–9, 40–46, 65–70, and 163–74 of SAR 9.

[7]For examples of the latter, see SAR 9, pp. 94–110, 116–19 and 128–55.

[8]For examples, see APB Statement No. 4, pp. 11, 13–15, 21–22, 46–48 and 102.

which incorrigible figures to report).

3 Cause much of the nonuniformity problem that plagues us (since allocations are incorrigible, naturally GAAP conflict—there's no way to settle which rules are right).

4 Thereby confuse individual readers, thus violating what the Trueblood Report designates as the basic objective of financial statements.

5 Generally breed distrust in our profession.

When their elimination isn't possible, the FASB should keep allocations unsophisiticated (if we must be incorrigible, at least let's be simple), choose allocation rules on expedient, political grounds (ceasing to worry about theory) and be candid about what it's doing. In particular, the FASB should actively

1 Try to convert conventional reporting practices to allocation-free ones. There are two main allocation-free alternatives to conventional accounting: current value reporting and the type of funds statement reporting that defines "funds" as net quick assets.[9] Certainly, Sterling is correct that merely adjusting allocated historical costs for changes in purchasing power serves little purpose: adjusted ritual remains ritual. The same is true of foreign currency translations.

2 Meanwhile, avoid launching any new incorrigible allocations in such areas as interim and segment reports, leases, contingencies, interest and pensions. And eliminate the more flagrantly incorrigible allocations that we now commit. A prime example of the latter (despite its being one of the APB's greatest political triumphs) is tax deferral: we take the difference between an incorrigible book allocation and an incorrigible tax allocation and allocate it, incorrigibly.

In conclusion, I would emphasize that none of these remarks are intended to disparage accounting practitioners. As SAR 9 points out (p. 157), practitioners have honestly believed that allocations are appropriate and have struggled to cope with them, while we academics saddled practitioners with a matching theory that requires such assignments, then failed to provide defensible ways for their calculation. But the hard fact remains that so long as we continue to certify that incorrigible allocations present fairly a firm's financial position and the results of its operations, we're making claims that we just can't back up. Professional responsibility urges that we, and the FASB, cease to tolerate this.

Author's note: I'm grateful to Paul Rosenfield for his comments on an earlier draft of this article.

---

[9] See SAR 9, chapter 7.

BIBLIOGRAPHY

Abdel-khalik, A. Rashad, "User Preference Ordering Value: A Model," *The Accounting Review* (July 1971), pp. 457–71.

Accountants' Index (AICPA, quarterly, annually, or biennially).

Accounting Standards Committee, "Current Cost Accounting," *Statement of Provisional Accounting Standards* (Institute of Chartered Accountants in Australia and Australian Society of Accountants, October 1976).

Accounting Standards Steering Committee, "Accounting for Changes in the Purchasing Power of Money," *Provisional Statement of Standard Accounting Practice, No. 1* (The Institute of Chartered Accountants in England and Wales, 1974).

————, "Statements of Source and Application of Funds," *Statement of Standard Accounting Practice No. 10* (The Institute of Chartered Accountants in England and Wales, 1975).

Alexander, Sidney, "Income Measurement in a Dynamic Economy," *Five Monographs on Business Income* (Study Group on Business Income of the American Institute of Accountants, 1950), pp. 1–95.

————, revised by David Solomons in W. T. Baxter and Sidney Davidson, eds., *Studies in Accounting Theory* (Sweet & Maxwell, 1962), pp. 126–200.

American Accounting Association, *Accounting and Reporting Standards for Corporate Financial Statements and Preceding Statements and Supplements* (AAA, 1957). Consists of:

    (1) Executive Committee, "Alternative Statement of Accounting Principles Underlying Corporate Financial Statements" (1936);

    (2) Executive Committee, "Accounting Principles Underlying Corporate Financial Statements" (1941);

    (3) Executive Committee, "Accounting Concepts and Standards Underlying Corporate Financial Statements" (1948);

    (4) Committee on Concepts and Standards Underlying Corporate Financial Statements, Supplementary Statements Nos. 1–8. (1950–55);

    (5) Committee on Accounting Concepts and Standards, "Accounting and Reporting Standards for Corporate Financial Statements—1957 Revision" (1957).

————, Committee on Concepts and Standards—Internal Planning and

Control, "Report of the Committee on Concepts and Standards—Internal Planning and Control," *The Accounting Review* (Supplement 1974), pp. 79–96.

———, Committee on External Reporting, "An Evaluation of External Reporting Practices," *The Accounting Review* (Supplement 1969), pp. 79–123.

———, Committee to Prepare a Statement of Basic Accounting Theory, *A Statement of Basic Accounting Theory* (AAA, 1966).

American Electric Power Company, *Annual Report* (1962).

American Institute of Certified Public Accountants, *AICPA Professional Standards, Volume 3: Accounting, Current Text* (Commerce Clearing House, 1975).

American Institute of Certified Public Accountants, Accounting Principles Board, "The Statement of Source and Application of Funds," *APB Opinion No. 3* (AICPA, 1963).

———, "Reporting of Leases in Financial Statements of Lessee," *APB Opinion No. 5* (AICPA, 1964).

———, "Accounting for Leases in Financial Statements of Lessors," *APB Opinion No. 7* (AICPA, 1966).

———, "Accounting for the Cost of Pension Plans," *APB Opinion No. 8* (AICPA, 1966).

———, "Reporting the Results of Operations," *APB Opinion No. 9* (AICPA, 1966).

———, "Omnibus Opinion—1967," *APB Opinion No. 12* (AICPA, 1967).

———, "Business Combinations," *APB Opinion No. 16* (AICPA, 1970).

———, "The Equity Method of Accounting for Investments in Common Stock," *APB Opinion No. 18* (AICPA, 1971).

———, "Reporting Changes in Financial Position," *APB Opinion No. 19* (AICPA, 1971).

———, "Interest on Receivables and Payables," *APB Opinion No. 21* (AICPA, 1971).

———, "Accounting for Lease Transactions by Manufacturer or Dealer Lessors," *APB Opinion No. 27* (AICPA, 1972).

———, "Reporting the Results of Operations—," *APB Opinion No. 30* (AICPA, 1973).

———, "Financial Statements Restated for General Price-Level Changes," *Statement of the Accounting Principles Board, No. 3* (AICPA, 1969).

———, "Basic Concepts and Accounting Principles Underlying Financial Statements of Business Enterprises," *Statement of the Accounting Principles Board, No. 4* (AICPA, 1970).

American Institute of Certified Public Accountants, Accounting Research Division, "Reporting the Financial Effects of Price-Level Changes," *Accounting Research Study No. 6* (AICPA, 1963).

American Institute of Certified Public Accountants, Committee on Accounting Procedure, "Inventory Pricing," *Accounting Research Bulletin No. 29* (AICPA, 1947).

————, "Restatement and Revision of Accounting Research Bulletins," *Accounting Research Bulletin No. 43* (AICPA, 1953).

American Institute of Certified Public Accountants, Committee on Investment Companies, *Audits of Investment Companies* (AICPA, 1973).

American Institute of Certified Public Accountants, Committee on Terminology, "Review and Resume," *Accounting Terminology Bulletins, No. 1* (AICPA, 1953).

————, "Proceeds, Revenue, Income, Profit, and Earnings," *Accounting Terminology Bulletin No. 2* (AICPA, 1955).

American Institute of Certified Public Accountants, Study Group on the Objectives of Financial Statements, *Objectives of Financial Statements* (AICPA, 1973).

American Telephone and Telegraph Company, *Annual Report* (1975).

Archer, Stephen H., "The Structure of Management Decision Theory," *Academy of Management Journal* (December 1964), pp. 269–87; rpt. in Alfred Rappaport, ed., *Information for Decision Making* (Prentice-Hall, 1970), pp. 3–19.

———— and Charles A. D'Ambrosio, *Business Finance: Theory and Management,* 2d. ed. (Macmillan, 1972).

Arthur Andersen & Company, *Objectives of Financial Statements for Business Enterprises* (Arthur Andersen & Co., 1972).

Arrow, Kenneth J., *Social Choice and Individual Values,* 2d. ed. (John Wiley & Sons, 1963).

Ball, Ray and Philip Brown, "Portfolio Theory and Accounting," *Journal of Accounting Research* (Autumn 1969), pp. 300–23.

Barton, A. D., "Expectations and Achievements in Income Theory," *The Accounting Review* (October 1974), pp. 664–81.

Basu, S. and J. R. Hanna, *Inflation Accounting: Alternatives, Implementation Issues and Some Empirical Evidence* (Society of Industrial Accountants of Canada, 1975).

Baxter, W. T., *Depreciation* (Sweet & Maxwell, 1971).

Beaver, William H., "Financial Ratios as Predictors of Failure," *Empirical Research in Accounting: Selected Studies, 1966* (Supplement to *Journal of Accounting Research,* vol. 4), pp. 71–111.

————, "The Behavior of Security Prices and Its Implications for Accounting Research (Methods)" in "Report of the Committee on Research Methodology in Accounting," *The Accounting Review* (Supplement 1972), pp. 407–37.

———— and Joel S. Demski, "The Nature of Financial Accounting Objectives: A Summary and Synthesis," *Studies on Financial Accounting Objectives: 1974* (Supplement to *Journal of Accounting Research*, vol. 12), pp. 170–87.

————, John W. Kennelly, and William M. Voss, "Predictive Ability as a Criterion for the Evaluation of Accounting Data," *The Accounting Review* (October 1968), pp. 675–83.

————, Paul Kettler, and Myron Scholes, "The Association Between Market Determined and Accounting Determined Risk Measures," *The Accounting Review* (October 1970), pp. 654–82.

Bedford, Norton, *Income Determination Theory* (Addison-Wesley, 1965).

Beidleman, Carl R., "Valuation of Used Capital Assets," *Studies in Accounting Research, No. 7* (AAA, 1973).

Bevis, Herman W., *Corporate Financial Reporting in a Competitive Economy* (Macmillan, 1965).

Bierman, Harold, "Measuring Financial Liquidity," *The Accounting Review* (October 1960), pp. 628–32.

Blackwell, David H. and M. A. Girshick, *Theory of Games and Statistical Decisions* (John Wiley & Sons, 1954).

Board of Governors, Federal Reserve System, *Functional Cost Analysis* (1972).

————, *Functional Cost Analysis: 1975 Average Banks* (1976).

"Boothe Computer Says It Will Have Write-Down of $35 Million for 1972," *Wall Street Journal*, 27 March 1973, p. 7.

Boothman, Derek, et al., *The Corporate Report* (Accounting Standards Steering Committee, 1975).

Briloff, Abraham J., "$200 Million Question," *Barron's*, 18 December 1972, pp. 5, 12–16.

Burton, John C., Chief Accountant, SEC, Letter dated 23 May 1974, addressed to Mr. Forrest J. Prettyman, Counsel, Association of Registered Bank Holding Companies.

The Business Accounting Deliberation Council, Ministry of Finance, Japan, *Financial Accounting Standards for Business Enterprises*. Translated by Committee on International Relations, Japanese Institute of Certified Public Accountants (30 August 1974).

Butterworth, John, "Accounting Systems and Management Decision: An Analysis of the Role of Information in the Management Decision

Process," Ph.D. dissertation, University of California, Berkeley, 1967.

Canning, John B., *The Economics of Accountancy* (Ronald Press, 1929).

Carsberg, Bryan, John Arnold, and Anthony Hope, "Predictive Value: A Criterion for Choice of Accounting Method" in W. T. Baxter and S. Davidson, eds., *Studies in Accounting Theory*, 3rd ed. (London: Institute of Chartered Accountants in England and Wales, 1977).

Carsberg, Bryan, Anthony Hope, and R. W. Scapens, "The Objectives of Published Accounting Reports," *Accounting and Business Research* (Summer 1974), pp. 162–73.

Chambers, Raymond J., "Blueprint for a Theory of Accounting," *Accounting Research* (January 1955), pp. 17–25; rpt. in Raymond J. Chambers, *Accounting, Finance and Management* (Arthur Andersen & Co., 1969), pp. 347–55.

———, "Measurement in Accounting," *Journal of Accounting Research* (Spring 1965), pp. 32–62.

———, *Accounting, Evaluation and Economic Behavior* (Prentice-Hall, 1966; rpt. Scholars Book Co., 1974).

Christiana Securities Company, *Annual Report* (1957 through 1972).

Churchman, C. West, "The Systems Approach to Measurement in Business Firms" in Robert R. Sterling and William F. Bentz, eds., *Accounting in Perspective* (South-Western Publishing Co., 1971), pp. 51–57.

Cochrane, James L. and Milan Zeleny, eds., *Multiple Criteria Decision Making* (University of South Carolina Press, 1973).

Council of the Institute of Chartered Accountants in England and Wales, *Member's Handbook*, Statement N15 (1952).

Cutler, R. S. and G. A. Westwick, "The Impact of Inflation Accounting on the Stock Market," *Accountancy* (March 1973), pp. 15–24.

Cyert, Richard M. and Yuji Ijiri, "A Framework for Developing the Objectives of Financial Statements" in Joe J. Cramer and George Sorter, eds., *Objectives of Financial Statements: Selected Papers* (AICPA, 1974), pp. 30–35.

Davidson, Sidney, Samy Sidky, and Roman L. Weil, "Dow Jones and Standard & Poor's Utilities Income for 1974 on Conventional and (Estimated) GPLA Bases," unpublished, 1976.

Davidson, Sidney and Roman Weil, "Inflation Accounting," *Financial Analysts Journal* (January–February 1975a), pp. 27–31, 70–84.

———, "Inflation Accounting: Public Utilities," *Financial Analysts Journal* (May–June 1975b), pp. 30–34, 62.

———, "Impact of Inflation Accounting on 1974 Earnings," *Financial Analysts Journal* (September–October 1975c), pp. 42–54.

Dearden, John, "Problem in Decentralized Financial Control," *Harvard*

Business Review (May–June 1961), pp. 72–80.

Defliese, Philip, *Should Accountants Capitalize Leases?* (Coopers & Lybrand, 1973).

Demski, Joel S., *Information Analysis* (Addison-Wesley, 1972).

—— and Gerald A. Feltham, *Cost Determination: A Conceptual Approach* (Iowa State University Press, 1976).

Devine, Carl Thomas, *Essays in Accounting Theory,* vol. III (1971).

de Windt, E. M., "The New Rules on Financial Reporting—'Who's on First—What's on Second?'," *Financial Executive* (December 1976), pp. 18–23.

Elia, J., "Heard on the Street," *Wall Street Journal,* 29 August 1974, p. 23.

Fama, Eugene F., "Efficient Capital Markets: A Review of Theory and Empirical Work," *Journal of Finance* (May 1970), pp. 383–417.

—— and Harvey Babiak, "Dividend Policy: An Empirical Analysis," *Journal of the American Statistical Assoication* (December 1968), pp. 1132–61.

Fama, Eugene F. and Merton H. Miller, *The Theory of Finance* (Holt, Rinehart and Winston, 1972).

Feltham, Gerald A., "A Theoretical Framework for Evaluating Changes in Accounting Information for Managerial Decisions," Ph.D. dissertation, University of California, Berkeley, 1967.

——, "Information Evaluation," *Studies in Accounting Research, No. 5* (AAA, 1972).

Fess, Philip E., "The Theory of Manufacturing Costs," *The Accounting Review* (July 1961), pp. 446–53.

Financial Accounting Standards Board, "Accounting for Research and Development Costs," *Statement of Financial Accounting Standards No. 2* (FASB, 1974).

——, "Financial Reporting in Units of General Purchasing Power," Exposure Draft of Proposed Statement of Financial Accounting Standards, 31 December 1974.

——, "Reporting Gains and Losses from Extinguishment of Debt," *Statement of Financial Accounting Standards No. 4* (FASB, 1975).

——, "Accounting for Contingencies," *Statement of Financial Accounting Standards No. 5* (FASB, 1975).

——, "Accounting for the Translation of Foreign Currency Transactions and Foreign Currency Financial Statements," *Statement of Financial Accounting Standards No. 8* (FASB, 1975).

——, "Accounting for Certain Marketable Securities," *Statement of*

Financial Accounting Standards No. 12 (FASB, 1975).

Financial Executives Institute Committee on Corporate Reporting, "FEI Views Purpose of Financial Statements," *FEI Bulletin* (March 1972), pp. 1–2.

Fisher, Irving, *The Nature of Capital and Income* (Macmillan, 1906).

Foster, George J., "Mining Inventories in a Current Price Accounting System," *Abacus* (December 1969), pp. 99–118.

Gonedes, N. J., "Evidence on the Information Content of Accounting Numbers: Accounting-based and Market-based Estimates of Systematic Risk," *Journal of Financial and Quantitative Analysis* (June 1973), pp. 407–43.

Gordon, Myron, J., *The Investment, Financing, and Valuation of the Corporation* (Richard D. Irwin, 1962).

Grady, Paul, "Inventory of Generally Accepted Accounting Principles for Business Enterprises," *Accounting Research Study No. 7* (AICPA, 1965).

Graham, Benjamin, David L. Dodd, and Sidney Cottle, with the collaboration of Charles Tatham, *Security Analysis: Principles and Technique,* 4th ed. (McGraw-Hill, 1962).

"The Green Boom for Forest Products," *Business Week,* 25 May 1974, pp. 90–93, 96.

Green, Paul E. and Yoram Wind, *Multiattribute Decisions in Marketing: A Measurement Approach* (Dryden Press, 1973).

Greenball, Melvin N., Letter to the author dated 6 October 1972.

————, "The Predictive-Ability Criterion: Its Relevance in Evaluating Accounting Data," *Abacus* (June 1971), pp. 1–7.

Gregory, Robert H. and Richard L. Van Horn, *Automatic Data-Processing Systems* (Wadsworth Publishing Co., 1960).

Gynther, Reg S., "Why Use General Purchasing Power?" *Accounting and Business Research* (Spring 1974), pp. 141–57.

Hendriksen, Eldon S., *Accounting Theory,* rev. ed. (Richard D. Irwin, 1970).

Hicks, J. R., *Value and Capital,* 2d. ed. (Clarendon Press, 1946).

Higgins, W. Rodgers, "Valuation of Readily Marketable Inventories," *Journal of Accountancy* (July 1964), pp. 25–32.

Horngren, Charles T., "The Marketing of Accounting Standards," *Journal of Accountancy* (October 1973), pp. 61–66; rpt. in Robert R. Sterling ed., *Institutional Issues in Public Accounting* (Scholars Book Co., 1974) pp. 291–303.

Ibbotson, Roger G. and Rex A. Sinquefield, "Stocks, Bonds, Bills, an

Inflation: Year-by-Year Historical Returns (1926–1974)," *Journal of Business* (January 1976), pp. 11–47.

Ijiri, Yuji, *The Foundations of Accounting Measurement* (Prentice-Hall, 1967).

———, "Theory of Accounting Measurement," *Studies in Accounting Research, No. 10* (AAA, 1975).

———, "The Price-Level Restatement and Its Dual Interpretation," *The Accounting Review* (April 1976), pp. 227–43.

———and Robert K. Jaedicke, "Reliability and Objectivity of Accounting Measurements," *The Accounting Review* (July 1966), pp. 474–83.

International Accounting Standards Committee, "Valuation and Presentation of Inventories in the Context of the Historical Cost System," *International Accounting Standard IAS 2* (International Accounting Standards Committee, 1975).

International Telephone and Telegraph Corporation, *Annual Report* (1971).

Kaplan, Robert S. and Richard Roll, "Investor Evaluation of Accounting Information: Some Empirical Evidence," *Journal of Business* (April 1972), pp. 225–57.

Kelly Blue Book (S. H. [Buster] Kelly and Robert S. Kelly, bimonthly).

Kenley, W. John and George J. Staubus, *Objectives and Concepts of Financial Statements* (Australian Accountancy Research Foundation, 1972).

Kerr, Jean St. G., "Three Concepts of Business Income," *The Australian Accountant* (April 1956), pp. 139–46; rpt. in Sidney Davidson et al., eds., *An Income Approach to Accounting Theory* (Prentice-Hall, 1964), pp. 40–48.

Kohler, Eric L., *A Dictionary for Accountants*, 4th ed. (Prentice-Hall, 1970).

Kristol, Irving, "The Credibility of Corporations," *Wall Street Journal*, 17 January 1974, p. 12.

Leasco Data Processing Corporation, *Annual Report* (1970).

Lemke, Kenneth W., "Asset Valuation and Income Theory," *The Accounting Review* (January 1966), pp. 32–41.

———, "The Evaluation of Liquidity: An Analytical Study," *Journal of Accounting Research* (Spring 1970), pp. 47–77.

Lev, Baruch, *Financial Statement Analysis: A New Approach* (Prentice-Hall, 1974a).

———, "On the Association between Operating Leverage and Risk," *Journal of Financial and Quantitative Analysis* (September 1974b), pp. 627–41.

——— and Sergius Kunitzky, "On the Association between Smoothing

Measures and the Risk of Common Stocks," *The Accounting Review* (April 1974), pp. 259–70.

Littleton, A. C., "Structure of Accounting Theory," *Monograph No. 5* (AAA, 1953).

McDonald, Daniel L., "Feasibility Criteria for Accounting Measures," *The Accounting Review* (October 1967), pp. 662–79.

McGraw-Hill, Inc., *Annual Report* (1973).

McKeown, James C., "An Empirical Test of a Model Proposed by Chambers," *The Accounting Review* (January 1971), pp. 12–29.

Marschak, Jacob and Roy Radner, *Economic Theory of Teams* (Yale University Press, 1972).

Mason, Perry, " 'Cash Flow' Analysis and the Funds Statement," *Accounting Research Study No. 2* (AICPA, 1961).

May, George O., *Financial Accounting* (Macmillan, 1943).

Mechanical Engineering Economic Development Committee, *Inflation and Company Accounts in Mechanical Engineering* (National Economic Development Office, 1973).

Meigs, Walter B., A. N. Mosich, and Charles E. Johnson, *Accounting: The Basis for Business Decisions*, 3rd ed. (McGraw-Hill, 1972).

Mock, Theodore J., "The Evaluation of Alternative Information Structures," Ph.D. dissertation, University of California, Berkeley, 1969.

Moody's Bond Survey (Moody's Investors Service, Inc., monthly).

Moonitz, Maurice, "The Changing Concept of Liabilities," *The Journal of Accountancy* (May 1960), pp. 41–46.

————, "The Basic Postulates of Accounting," *Accounting Research Study No. 1* (AICPA, 1961).

Myers, John H., "The Critical Event and Recognition of Net Profit," *The Accounting Review* (October 1959), pp. 528–32.

National Lead Company, *Annual Report* (1973).

Owens-Illinois, Inc., *Annual Report* (1972).

Parker, R. H., *Management Accounting: An Historical Perspective* (Macmillan, 1969).

Paton, William A., *Accounting Theory* (Ronald Press, 1922).

————, *Essentials of Accounting*, rev. ed. (Macmillan, 1949).

———— and A. C. Littleton, "An Introduction to Corporate Accounting Standards," *Monograph No. 3* (AAA, 1940).

Peloubet, Maurice, "Is Value an Accounting Concept?" *Journal of Accountancy* (March 1935), pp. 201–09.

Pennsylvania New York Central Transportation Company, *Annual Report* (1967).

Penn Central Company, *Annual Report* (1968, 1969, 1970).

Petersen, Russell James, "Interindustry Estimation of General Price-Level Impact on Financial Information," *The Accounting Review* (January 1973), pp. 34–43.

Price Guide for Used Computers (Time Brokers, Inc., quarterly).

Revsine, Lawrence, *Replacement Cost Accounting* (Prentice-Hall, 1973).

——— and Jerry J. Weygandt, "Accounting for Inflation: The Controversy," *Journal of Accountancy* (October 1974), pp. 72–78.

Rice, C. D., H. C. Ford, R. J. Williams, and G. W. Silverman, *The Businessman's View of the Purposes of Financial Reporting* (Financial Executives Research Foundation, 1973).

Rosen, L. S., *Current Value Accounting and Price-Level Restatements* (The Canadian Institute of Chartered Accountants, 1972).

——— and Don T. DeCoster, " 'Funds' Statements: A Historical Perspective," *The Accounting Review* (January 1969), pp. 124–36.

Rosenfield, Paul, "Accounting for Inflation—A Field Test," *Journal of Accountancy* (June 1969), pp. 45–50.

Ross, Howard, *The Elusive Art of Accounting* (Ronald Press, 1966).

Sanders, Thomas H., Henry Rand Hatfield, and Underhill Moore, *A Statement of Accounting Principles* (American Institute of Accountants, 1938).

Sandilands, F. E. P., Chairman, Inflation Accounting Committee, *Inflation Accounting: Report of the Inflation Accounting Committee*, Cmnd. 6225 (Her Majesty's Stationery Office, 1975).

Saunders, Donald H. and Paul G. Busby, "Accounting for Inflation: To Be, or Not to Be?" *Public Utilities Fortnightly* (29 January 1976), pp. 15–21.

Securities and Exchange Commission, "Disclosure of Unusual Risks and Uncertainties in Financial Reporting," *Accounting Series Release No. 166* (23 December 1974).

Security Owner's Bond Guide (Standard & Poor's Corporation, monthly).

Security Owner's Stock Guide (Standard & Poor's Corporation, monthly).

Skinner, R. M., *Accounting Principles: A Canadian Viewpoint* (The Canadian Institute of Chartered Accountants, 1972).

Smith, James E. and Nora P. Smith, "Readability: A Measure of the Performance of the Communication Function of Financial Reporting," *The Accounting Review* (July 1971), pp. 552–61.

Snavely, Howard J., "Accounting Information Criteria," *The Accounting Review* (April 1967), pp. 223–32.

Sorter, George H. and George Benston, "Appraising the Defensive Position of a Firm: The Interval Measure," *The Accounting Review* (October 1960), pp. 633–40.

Spiller, Earl A. and Robert L. Virgil, "Effectiveness of APB Opinion No. 19 in Improving Funds Reporting," *Journal of Accounting Research* (Spring 1974), pp. 112–42.

Sprague, Charles E., *The Philosophy of Accounts* (Ronald Press, 1908).

Sprouse, Robert T. and Maurice Moonitz, "A Tentative Set of Broad Accounting Principles for Business Enterprises," *Accounting Research Study No. 3* (AICPA, 1962).

Standard & Poor's Earnings and Ratings Bond Guide (Standard & Poor's Corporation, monthly).

Staubus, George J., "Payments for the Use of Capital and the Matching Process," *The Accounting Review* (January 1952), pp. 104–13.

———, "An Accounting Concept of Revenue," Ph.D. dissertation, School of Business, University of Chicago, 1954.

———, "Revenue and Revenue Accounts," *Accounting Research* (July 1956), pp. 284–94; rpt. in Sidney Davidson et al., eds., *An Income Approach to Accounting Theory* (Prentice-Hall, 1964), pp. 78–88.

———, "The Residual Equity Point of View in Accounting," *The Accounting Review* (January 1959), pp. 3–13.

———, *A Theory of Accounting to Investors* (University of California Press, 1961; rpt. Scholars Book Co., 1971).

———, "Alternative Asset Flow Concepts," *The Accounting Review* (July 1966), pp. 397–412.

———, "Statistical Evidence of the Value of Depreciation Accounting," *Abacus* (August 1967a), pp. 3–22.

———, "Current Cash Equivalent for Assets: A Dissent," *The Accounting Review* (October 1967b), pp. 650–61.

———, "Plant Financing, Accounting, and Divisional Targetry," *California Management Review* (Summer 1968), pp. 81–94.

———, *Activity Costing and Input-Output Accounting* (Richard D. Irwin, 1971a).

———, "The Relevance of Evidence of Cash Flows" in Robert R. Sterling, ed., *Asset Valuation and Income Determination* (Scholars Book Co., 1971b), pp. 42–69.

———, "Current Value Accounting in Financial Industries," *Publications of the Professional Accounting Program* (Graduate School of Business Administration, University of California, Berkeley, 1974).

———, "The Responsibility of Accounting Teachers," *The Accounting Review* (January 1975a), pp. 160–70.

————, "Price-level Accounting: Some Unfinished Business," *Accounting and Business Research* (Winter 1975b), pp. 42–47.

————, "The Effects of Price-Level Restatements on Earnings," *The Accounting Review* (July 1976a), pp. 574–89.

————, "The Multiple-Criteria Approach to Making Accounting Decisions," *Accounting and Business Research* (Autumn 1976b), pp. 276–88.

Sterling, Robert R., "Conservatism: The Fundamental Principle of Valuation in Traditional Accounting," *Abacus* (December 1967), pp. 109–32.

————, "The Going Concern: An Examination," *The Accounting Review* (July 1968), pp. 481–502.

————, *Theory of the Measurement of Enterprise Income* (University Press of Kansas, 1971).

————, "Decision Oriented Financial Accounting," *Accounting and Business Research* (Summer 1972), pp. 198–208.

————, "Accounting Power," *Journal of Accountancy* (January 1973), pp. 61–67; excerpted from *The Oklahoma CPA* (July 1972), pp. 28–41, 44.

————, "Relevant Financial Reporting in an Age of Price Changes," *Journal of Accountancy* (February 1975), pp. 42–51.

———— and Richard E. Flaherty, "The Role of Liquidity in Exchange Valuation," *The Accounting Review* (July 1971), pp. 441–56.

Stone, Marvin, " 'Tis the Age of Aquarius—Even for Accounting" in Robert R. Sterling, ed., *Asset Valuation and Income Determination* (Scholars Book Co., 1971), pp. 145–52.

Storrs, Thomas I., Chairman of the Board, NCNB Corporation, Letter dated 16 April 1976.

Study Group at the University of Illinois, *A Statement of Basic Accounting Postulates and Principles* (University of Illinois, Center for International Education and Research in Accounting, 1964).

Sunder, Shyam, "Relationships Between Accounting Changes and Stock Prices: Problems of Measurement and Some Empirical Evidence," *Empirical Research in Accounting: Selected Studies, 1973* (Supplement to *Journal of Accounting Research*, vol. 11), pp. 1–45.

Suojanen, Waino W., "Accounting Theory and the Large Corporation," *The Accounting Review* (July 1954), pp. 391–98.

Thomas, Arthur L., "The Allocation Problem in Financial Accounting Theory," *Studies in Accounting Research, No. 3* (AAA, 1969).

"USLife Vows to Sell All Common Stocks if Ledger Rule Changes," *Wall Street Journal* (12 November 1971), p. 5.

The Value Line Investment Survey (Arnold Berhnard & Co., semimonthly).

Vatter, William J., *The Fund Theory of Accounting and Its Implications for Financial Reports* (University of Chicago Press, 1947).

———, *Managerial Accounting* (Prentice-Hall, 1950).

———, *Accounting Measurements for Financial Reports* (Richard D. Irwin, 1971).

von Bohm-Bawerk, Eugene, *The Positive Theory of Capital.* Translated by William Smart (G. E. Stechert and Co., 1891).

von Neumann, John and Oskar Morgenstern, *Theory of Games and Economic Behavior* (Princeton University Press, 1944).

Wald, Abraham, *Statistical Decision Functions* (John Wiley & Sons, 1950).

Webster's Third New International Dictionary of the English Language (G. & C. Merriam Co., 1961).

Weise, Robert F., "Investing for True Values," *Barron's* (8 September 1930), p. 5.

Williams, John Burr, *The Theory of Investment Value* (Harvard University Press, 1938).

INDEX

659